A MANUAL OF
THE HISTORY OF DOGMAS

VOLUME II

THE DEVELOPMENT OF DOGMAS DURING
THE MIDDLE AGES AND AFTER,
869-1907

BY

REV. BERNARD J. OTTEN, S. J.

PROFESSOR OF DOGMATIC THEOLOGY AND THE HISTORY OF DOGMAS
IN
ST. LOUIS UNIVERSITY

B. HERDER BOOK CO.
17 SOUTH BROADWAY, ST. LOUIS, MO.
AND
68 GREAT RUSSELL ST., LONDON, W. C.
1918

IMPRIMI POTEST

Sti. Ludovici, die 10 Maii, 1918

A. J. Burrowes, S. J.,

Praep. Prov.

NIHIL OBSTAT

Sti. Ludovici, die 31 Julii, 1918

F. G. Holweck,

Censor Librorum.

IMPRIMATUR

Sti. Ludovici, die 31 Julii, 1918

✠*Joannes J. Glennon,*

Archiepiscopus,

Sti. Ludovici.

FOREWORD

The first volume of this *Manual* traced the history of dogmatic development from the beginning of the second century
to the end of the ninth; the second follows that development
up to the present time. However, the greater part of these
pages is devoted to the study of mediæval theology. The author deemed this course proper because the great Scholastics
of the Middle Ages prepared the way for the important work
accomplished by the Council of Trent, and thereby materially
contributed to the full development of a large number of
dogmas. Post-Tridentine theology has received rather scant
attention — too scant, perhaps, in view of the intense activity displayed by its many eminent representatives. But,
considering the purpose of the present work, that was un-
avoidable. For the *Manual* is primarily intended as a text-
book, and as such it should not be too bulky. Hence, as it
was impossible to attempt anything like a thorough review of
the theology of both periods — for they cover a thousand
years — it appeared preferable to accord a merely summary
treatment to the less important of the two, and then give to
the other all the attention which its valuable contribution to
the history of dogmas seemed to demand.

Eastertide, 1918.

BIBLIOGRAPHY

Aside from the works of theologians whose teaching is reviewed in these pages, the following is a partial list of books consulted in the composition of the present volume. Those marked * are by non-Catholic authors. Works specially adapted for supplementary reading are referred to in a footnote at the beginning of each chapter.

Bach, J., Die Dogmengeschichte des Mittelalters vom christologischen Standpunkte, oder die Mittelalterliche Christologie, in drei Theilen, Wien, 1874, 1875.

Bachelet, Le, L'Immaculée Conception, Paris, 1903.

Baudrillart, L'Eglise catholique, la Renaissance, le Protestantisme, 6th ed., Paris, 1905.

Bellamy, J., La Théologie Catholique au XIX Sièle, Paris, 1904.

Capéran, L., Le Probleme du Salut des Infidèles. Essai Historique, Paris, 1912.

Catholic Encyclopedia, New York, 1907 foll.

Denifle, H., Luther und Luthertum, 3 vols., Mainz, 1904.

―― Die Entstehung der Universitaeten des Mittelalters bis 1400, 2 vols., Berlin, 1885.

Denifle-Chatelain, Chartularium Univ. Parisiensis. Paris, 1889-91.

Denifle-Ehrle, Archiv fuer Litteratur- und Kirchengeschichte des Mittelalters, 6 vols., Freiburg im Breisgau, 1885-1892.

Denzinger-Bannwart, Enchiridion Symbolorum, Definitionum et Declarationum de Rebus Fidei et Morum, 11th ed., Freiburg im Breisgau, 1911.

Dictionnaire Apologétique de la Foi, Paris, 1911 foll.

Dictionnaire de Théologie Catholique, Paris, 1909 foll.

Doellinger, I., Die Reformation, ihre innere Entwicklung und ihre Wirkungen, 3 vols., Ratisbon, 1846-48.

* Dorner, A., Grundriss der Dogmengeschichte, Berlin, 1899.

Du Plessis D'Argentré, Collectio judiciorum de novis erroribus qui ab initio XII s. usque ad a. 1713 . . . proscripti sunt, Paris, 1755 foll.

Dummermuth, A. M., S. Thomas et doctrina praemotionis physicae, Paris, 1886.

Ehrhard-Kirsch, Forschungen zur Christlichen Literatur- und Dogmengeschichte, vols. V–XI, Mainz, Paderborn.

* Fisher, G. P., History of Christian Doctrine, New York, 1911.

Frins, V., Scti. Thomae A. doctrina de cooperatione Dei cum omni natura creata praesertim libera, Paris, 1893.

Funk, F. X., A Manual of Church History, 2 vols. Authorized
    Translation from the 5th German Edition by Luigi Cappadelta,
    St. Louis, 1910.
* Gairdner, J., Lollardy and the Reformation in England, 4 vols.
    London, 1908.
Ghellink, J., Mouvement Théologique du XIIe Siècle, Paris, 1915.
Gietl, R. P., Die Sentenzen Rolands, Freiburg, 1891.
Goetzmann, W., Das Eucharistische Opfer nach der Lehre der ael-
    teren Scholastik. Eine dogmengeschichtliche Studie, Freiburg
    im Breisgau, 1901.
Grabmann, M., Die Geschichte der Scholastischen Methode, 2 vols.
    Freiburg im Breisgau, 1909, 1911.
Granderath, G., Constitutiones dogmaticae s. oecum. Concilii Vati-
    cani explicatae, Freiburg, 1892.
Granderath-Kirsch, Geschichte des Vatikanischen Konzils, von seiner
    ersten Ankuendigung bis zu seiner Vertagung, nach den authen-
    tischen Dokumenten, 6 vols. Freiburg, 1903, 1906.
Grisar, H., Luther, 6 vols. Authorized Translation by E. M. La-
    mond, St. Louis, 1913.
* Harnack, A., Lehrbuch der Dogmengeschichte, vierte neu durchar-
    beitete und vermehrte Auflage, 3 vols. Tuebingen, 1909, 1910.
Hefele, C. J., A History of the Councils of the Church, 7 vols. Sec-
    ond German Edition, 1879 foll. Only the first three volumes
    have been translated into English.
Hergenroether, J., Handbuch der allgemeinen Kirchengeschichte, 3
    vols. Vierte Auflage, neu bearbeitet von Dr. J. P. Kirsch. Frei-
    burg, 1902.
Klee, H., Lehrbuch der Dogmengeschichte, 2 vols. Mainz, 1887 foll.
* Loofs, F., Leitfaden zum Studium der Dogmengeschichte. Halle,
    1901.
Mansi, J. D., Sacrorum Conciliorum Nova et Amplissima Collectio, 63
    vols. Paris, 1854 foll.
McCormick, P. J., History of Education. Washington, D. C., 1915.
Mignon, A., Hugues de Saint-Victor et les origines de la Scolastique,
    2 vols. Paris, 1896.
Minges, P., Der Gottesbegriff des Duns Scotus, Wien, 1907.
—— Die Gnadenlehre des Duns Scotus, Muenster, 1906.
Moehler, A., Symbolism: an Exposition of Doctrinal Differences be-
    tween Catholics and Protestants. Translated by J. B. Robert-
    son, New York, 1844.
Pastor, L., History of the Popes from the Close of the Middle Ages,
    5 vols. Translated by F. I. Antrobus, London, 1891 foll.
Pesch, C., Theologische Zeitfragen; Glaube, Dogmen und geschicht-
    liche Tatsachen. Freiburg im Breisgau, 1908.
Pourrat, P., Theology of the Sacraments. Authorized Translation
    from the Third French Edition. St. Louis, 1910.
Rapin, R., Histoire de Jansénisme. Paris, 1861.

* Rashdall, H., The Universities of Europe in the Middle Ages, 2 vols. Oxford, 1905.
* Realencyklopaedie fuer Protestantische Theologie und Kirche, 22 vols. Leipzig, 1896–1909.
Renz, F. S., Die Geschichte des Messopfer-Begriffs, oder der alte Glaube und die neuen Theorien ueber das Wesen des Unblutigen Opfers, 2 vols. Freising, 1901.
Riviere, J., The Doctrine of the Atonement, 2 vols. Authorized Translation by Luigi Cappadelta. St. Louis, 1909.
Salembier, L., The Great Schism of the West. Authorized Translation by M. D., New York, 1907.
Schill, A., Die Constitution *Unigenitus*. Freiburg, 1876.
* Schaff, P., Creeds of Christendom, 3 vols. New York, 1877.
Schwane, J., Histoire des Dogmes, 6 vols. French Translation from the Second German Edition by A. Degert and P. Belet. Paris, 1903–4.
Schneemann, G., Controversiarum de divinae gratiae liberique arbitrii concordia initia et progressus. Freiburg im Breisgau, 1881.
Swoboda, H., Das Concil von Trient. Wien, 1913
Taylor, H. O., The Mediæval Mind, 2 vols. London, 1914.
Toner, P. J., Dissertatio Historico-Theologica de Lapsu et Peccato Originali. Dublin, 1904.
Turmel, J., Histoire de la Théologie Positive, 2 vols. Paris, 1904–6.
Vacandard, E., Histoire de Saint Bernard, Paris, 1895.
Werner, K.. Der heil. Thomas von Aquino. Ratisbon, 1858.
—— Joh. Duns Scotus. Wien, 1881
—— Franz Suarez und die Scholastik der letzten Jahrhunderte. Ratisbon, 1861.
Wetzer und Welte, Kirchenlexikon, 2nd ed. Freiburg im Breisgau, 1882 foll.
Wulf, De, History of Mediæval Philosophy. Translated by P. Coffey. London, 1909.

TABLE OF CONTENTS

ix

CHAPTER X

CHAPTER XI

CHAPTER XII

CHAPTER XIII

CHAPTER XIV

CONTENTS

CONTENTS

CHAPTER XX

CHAPTER XXI

CHAPTER XXII

CHAPTER XXIII

CONTENTS

xv

A MANUAL OF THE HISTORY OF DOGMAS

INTRODUCTION

RISE, DEVELOPMENT, AND DECLINE OF SCHOLASTICISM [1]

In the study of doctrinal development during the Middle Ages, and also in modern times, no account need be taken of the Eastern Church. For after the schism caused by Michael Cerularius, patriarch of Constantinople (1053–1059), the East contributed nothing to the development of doctrine. Cut off by its own suicidal act from the source of ecclesiastical life, it became absolutely sterile. Its theology is to-day where it was left by John Damascene in the eighth century, except that along some lines it has actually fallen into error. Hence, while investigating this second period of dogmatic development, the student can give his undivided attention to the theology of the West.

In western lands, moreover, the learned world shifted its center of intellectual activity from the Latin to the Germanic nations. After the seventh century it was chiefly the British Isles, France, Germany, Northern Italy, and Visigothic Spain, that supplied the men who preserved what was still left of the old learning and prepared the way for the gradual development of the new. Venerable Bede, Aldhelm, and Al-

---

[1] Cfr. Grabmann, Geschichte der Scholastischen Methode, I, II; Ghellink, Le Mouvement Theologique du XIIᵉ Siecle; Denifle and Ehrle, Archiev fuer Litteratur-und Kirchengeschichte des Mittelalters; De Wulf, Scholasticism Old and New; *Rashdall, Universities of Europe in the Middle Ages; De Wulf, History of Medieval Philosophy; *Taylor, The Medieval Mind; Denifle, Die Entstehung der Universitaeten des Mittelalters bis 1400.

I

cuin in England, Paulinus of Aquileia, Haymo and Rabanus Maurus of Fulda, Walafried Strabo of Reichenau, Servatus Lupus of Ferrieries, Druthmar, Paschasius Radbertus and Ratramnus of Corbie, Hincmar of Rheims, Prudentius of Troyes, and Aeneas of Paris, were some of the writers and theologians who bridged over the dark chasm that intervened between the Patristic past and the Scholastic future. None of them displayed much originality and independence of thought, but they were all industrious workers and did good service in preparing the way for the greater men that were to follow.

During the Patristic period, embracing, roughly speaking, the first seven centuries of the Christian era, there was not only a gradual and more or less continuous fixation of dogmas, but also a constant growth of theological knowledge, touching nearly every point of revealed truth. Even such doctrines as were not directly connected with what had been explicitly defined, or what had been embodied in the various symbols of faith, were in many instances placed beyond all reasonable doubt by the consensus of approved teachers and the universal acceptance of the faithful. The *Ecclesia docens* and the *Ecclesia discens* ever worked hand in hand to push forward the process of doctrinal development. Consequently, aside from defined truths, there was at the close of the Patristic age a large body of doctrines that were a matter of common belief, although strictly speaking they did not yet form a part of the Catholic faith. Many of them received their full development, and were incorporated into the faith, during the following centuries.

We shall witness the same harmonious coöperation of these two agencies during the Scholastic period. In one sense, however, the *Ecclesia discens,* precisely as represented by theologians of recognized authority, stands out with far greater prominence than at any previous time. Since the beginning of the Middle Ages comparatively few great heresies, attacking fundamental doctrines of the faith, called for conciliar or even for papal definitions of revealed truths; while the intensely speculative spirit of Scholasticism was ever active in deducing new theological conclusions and in bringing out into clearer light the full contents of revelation. In this, great assistance was derived from the application of philosophical methods to the exposition of Christian doctrine, with the result that the *depositum fidei* and the contents of Christianized philosophy were brought into closest contact.

However, it must not be imagined that there was anything like an abrupt break between the two periods of doctrinal development just indicated. The transition from the one to the other was very gradual, extending over a space of fully three hundred years. Still less was there anything like a doctrinal change as Patristic theology passed into that of the Scholastic period. Scholastic theology is the legitimate offspring of Patristic teaching, having essentially the same contents although it differs somewhat in method and form. Both admit Augustine's " Intellige, ut credas," and its converse, " Crede, ut intelligas "; but each in its own way. The representatives of the Patristic age used reason but emphasized authority, while their successors of the Scholastic period used authority but emphasized reason.

SCHOLASTICISM

This term is used to designate both a pedagogical method and a doctrinal system, and as such it is applied to theology as well as to philosophy. In the present connection it need be considered only in reference to theology. Scholastic theology is distinguished from Patristic theology on the one hand, and from positive theology on the other. Its distinctive feature is speculative investigation of the data of revelation, chiefly by the aid of philosophical methods. In reference to this particular characteristic the Schoolmen themselves distinguish between *theologia speculativa seu scholastica* and *theologia positiva*. The latter gathers and coördinates the data of revelation, the former philosophizes about these data and deduces theological conclusions. However, it was not a barren speculation that interested the Schoolmen; they were ever intent on giving to their investigations a practical turn.

They speculated much, but primarily to enable the faithful to lead a fuller Christian life.

Historically the term Scholasticism, as now employed, probably dates back to the seventh century. By that time it seems to have become customary to call the head of any Christian institution of learning *magister scholae, capiscola,* or *scholasticus.* Furthermore, as it was then generally incumbent on the head of the school to teach dialectics, the usage gradually crept in to designate any branch of studies in which dialectics were used, whether its subject-matter was philosophy or theology, Scholastic studies, that is, studies which came primarily under the direction of the *scholasticus.* Hence Scholastic theology really means, as was stated above, a system of theological teaching in which the dialectic method prevails. It is moreover, though to a limited extent, the union of philosophy and theology in contents as well as in method.

Historical Development

It is customary to distinguish three different stages in the gradual development and decline of the Scholastic system, although there are no hard and fast lines of demarcation. From the tenth to the thirteenth century the system was and remained more or less in a state of preparation. During the thirteenth century it reached its full development and greatest perfection. From the beginning of the fourteenth century up to the end of the fifteenth it fell into a condition of decline, and finally lost much of its ancient prestige. A brief outline of this historical aspect of Scholasticism may here be given, as it will enable us to follow more intelligently the development of doctrine in its relation to the labors of the Schoolmen.

A — Preparatory Stage

The early Middle Ages received from the Patristic period a fairly complete body of formulated doctrines, built up on the basis of divine authority. The principle enunciated by Pope Hormisdas, " The first condition of attaining salvation is to safeguard the rule of right faith and not to deviate from the teaching of the Fathers " [2] found universal acceptance. Hence the main effort of the earliest Schoolmen was to preserve what had been delivered to them by their forbears in the faith. As Rabanus Maurus expressed it : " It is above all things necessary to have the right and immaculate faith, and to know by heart the symbol drawn up by the holy Fathers, in accordance with the rule laid down by the teaching of the Apostles." [3]

From this dominating tendency of harking back to the Patristic past, both as regarded the contents of the faith and its outward expression, resulted in course of time the *Libri Sententiarum,* in which the teachings of different Fathers were collated and grouped under certain general heads of doctrine and more or less extensively commented upon by the author or compiler. Thus originated the Sentences of William of Champeaux, of Anselm of Laon, of Robert Pulleyn, the *Sic-et-non* of Abelard, and a little later the *Summa Sententiarum* of the Lombard. For their material these authors depended chiefly on the *Florilegia,* or *Catenae,* of Patristic excerpts, compiled in the preceding centuries. The works of Augustine, of Pseudo-Denis, of Gregory the Great, and of John Damascene, were in most instances the direct sources whence these excerpts had been taken; but through them, and therefore indirectly, the works of many other Fathers were also laid under contribution.

Up to the eleventh century Scholastic activities were almost exclusively directed by traditionalism, but thereafter a new tendency began to manifest itself. Men were no longer satisfied with repeating and systematizing traditional teaching, although the contents of this teaching were even then universally regarded as sacrosanct. They began to emphasize the rational side of revealed doctrines, to search for philosophical proofs, which, though in the very nature of things incapable of demonstrating the mysteries of Christian revelation, would at least be helpful towards showing their congruity and reasonableness to the inquiring mind. It was from these first

[2] Epist. 7, 9.　　　　　　　　[3] De Ecclesiastica Disciplina, 3.

attempts at placing the faith, so far as might be, on a rational basis that Scholasticism in the strict sense of the term was born.

ANSELM AND ABELARD

The two men who contributed most to the development of Scholasticism in its earlier stages, though along different lines of thought and method, were Anselm of Canterbury (+1109) and Abelard of Pallet (+1142). Both were true Scholastics in the sense that they brought reason to bear upon the data of revelation, but in their methods and viewpoints they stood worlds apart. They may be regarded as the founders of two different schools of theological thought, which existed and worked side by side during the Scholastic period. The one was inclined to mysticism and found its best representative in Bonaventure; the other emphasized intellectualism and reached its highest perfection in Aquinas.

In Anselm's case the following points are decisive in determining his position and his influence upon Scholastic speculation. 1°. He is to all intents and purposes an extreme realist. Universals are to him not a mere *flatus vocis,* nor mere mental concepts; they exist *ante rem* as objective realities, not indeed in the physical order of things, but in the mind of God.[4] Hence in his theological speculations he does not deal with forms only, but with things. From this results the elaboration of concepts in conformity with the reality which they express, the form being subordinated to the contents. 2°. A close follower of Augustine, he emphasizes the predominance of the will, both in God's government of the world and in man's correspondence with God's intentions. God's ruling will is supreme in the world, and man's free will is his noblest faculty. 3°. He admits that reason has its legitimate field of inquiry in matters theological, nevertheless in the study of revealed truths faith should precede reason.[5] The " Credo ut intelligam " comes first, and then the " Intelligo ut credam "[6] 4°. Furthermore, this *in-*

---

[4] Monol. 26–27.
[5] Cur Deus Homo? 1, 1–2.
[6] Proslog. 1.

telligere or understanding is not precisely the result of dialectic speculation, but rather of contemplation, of intuition.
The mental process consists in experiencing rather than in reasoning. Hence Anselm is a Christian mystic, not a Christian
rationalist.

In Abelard the entire viewpoint is different. 1°. Compared to Anselm, he is an anti-realist. Universals do not
exist *ante rem,* nor merely *post rem,* but rather *in re.* They
have no existence apart from the individual.[7] Their universality is conferred by the mind, which forms an abstract concept of what is common to the different individuals of the
same species or genus. Hence he may be classed among the
moderate realists, although his views on the subject of universals are rather undeveloped. 2°. He conceives the object
of theological science to consist in the application of his *Sic-et-
non method* to tradition and revelation, in as much as dialectical reasoning must show that apparently contradictory propositions in the writings of the Fathers and in Holy Scripture
are in real agreement. 3°. He has no desire of doing away
with authority, but he wishes to make it amenable to reason.[8]
The part of reason, however, is not to demonstrate the truths
of revelation, but rather to show that they are conformable to
the requirements of the human intellect.[9] 4°. He regards it
as a fundamental principle that the writings of the Fathers
do not compel belief, but leave the reader's freedom of judging for himself intact. Holy Scripture alone is of itself infallible.[10] Hence the two chief sources of arguments are the
Bible and reason. 5°. Intellectual processes in the domain
of theology do not consist in contemplating and experiencing,
but in analyzing concepts, in distinguishing propositions, and
in deducing conclusions by dialectical methods. He is, therefore, not a Christian mystic, but a Christian rationalist.

It is thus in the writings of these two men that we find the
sketchy beginnings of the whole Scholastic system. Both endeavor to combine authority and reason, but each in his own
way. Anselm is wholly intent upon appropriating the con-

[7] Sum. Dial. 204.   [9] Ibid. 2, 2.
[8] Introduct. ad Theol. 2, 3.   [10] Sic et Non, Prolog.

tents of revelation, and then meditating on them for the purpose of showing forth their striking harmony with all the requirements of the human intellect; yet he is prepared at any moment to cling to revelation even where reason fails. Abelard criticizes received forms, weighs authorities, distinguishes what appears identical in meaning, combines what seems contradictory in expression, and thus gives full scope to the vast resources of keen dialectics. Anselm is speculative, Abelard is critical; Anselm deals exclusively with realities, Abelard operates chiefly with concepts. Both give reason its due; but while Anselm's reverence for tradition keeps him always within the lines of orthodoxy, Abelard's critical propensity brings him at times into conflict with the teachings of faith. Anselm Christianizes Plato and works in the spirit of Augustine; Abelard takes over the technique of Aristotle and discusses theological problems from the standpoint of a jurist.

FURTHER DEVELOPMENT

Whilst Anselm's views and methods commended themselves especially to mystic contemplation, Abelard's mode of procedure was admirably adapted to school purposes. It stimulated the speculative trend of the age, and in a short while found wide acceptance. At the same time, however, violent attacks were made on its rationalizing tendencies, which were regarded by many as inseparable from the new system of thought. Bernard of Clairveaux, William of St. Thierry, John of Salisbury, Walter of St. Victor, and the brothers Geroch and Arno of Reichersberg fought strenuously to counteract Abelard's influence in the schools. But when Peter Lombard (+1164) issued his *Summa Sententiarum*, Abelard's method, if not his views, gained the day. Peter had been a disciple of Abelard, but he was more conservative than his master, and in writing his great work he carefully eliminated all rationalistic elements, in so far as they tended to subordinate authority to reason. He did not escape condemnation on the part of such men as Walter of St. Victor,

but the intellectual world of the day decided in his favor, and
so he became for all times the *Magister Sententiarum.*

With the *Summa Sententiarum* of the Lombard the first
period of Scholasticism may be said to have formally opened.
Up to that date matters were still in a state of transition.
Even this great work appears somewhat sketchy as compared
with the *Summae* that originated in the following century,
but it marked a decided advance along the lines traced out
by Abelard. It soon became the favorite text-book of the
schools, and remained so till the end of the sixteenth century,
when it yielded its place to the *Summa* of St. Thomas.
Nearly all the great Scholastics wrote commentaries on its
text, of which more than three hundred are still extant. The
following is a brief sketch of its contents and the method of
discussion adopted by the author.

Adhering rather closely to the general outline of systematic
theology as found in the *De Doctrina Christiana* of St. Augustine,[11] Peter divided his subject matter into *res* and *signa*
— realities and signs.[12]   The *res* are subdivided into realities
that are the object of fruition, and realities that are intended
for use. The former are contained in the triune God as the
summa res, the latter comprise the world and all created
things. By signs are understood those religious observances,
ceremonies, and rites, which symbolize something beyond their
own constituent elements. They are of two kinds: Those
which only symbolize that of which they are signs, and those
which actually confer what they symbolize. To the former
class belonged the sacraments of the Old Law, the latter class
is made up of the sacraments of the New Law. This division
is, however, only imperfectly carried through in the body of
the work, especially as regards the *signa;* hence St. Thomas
points out that the real principle of divisions underlying the
Sentences is God as *principium* and *finis* — God as the source
whence all creatures come, and God as the end to which all
creatures must return.[13]

[11] Op. cit. I, 2.
[12] Sent. I, d. I, c. I–2.

[13] In Sent. I, d. 2: Divisio Textus.

The body of the work is divided into four books. The first contains the teaching of the Church on the Blessed Trinity. The principal points discussed are: The existence of the mystery (d. 2–34), the generation of the Son (d. 4–91), the procession of the Holy Spirit (d. 10–18), the equality and circuminsession of the three divine persons (d. 19–21). Then follows a discussion on Trinitarian terminology (d. 22–26, 30), personal properties (d. 27–29, 33), and appropriations (d. 31–32, 34). The remainder of the first book treats of the attributes of God in reference to the world: omniscience, omnipresence, providence, predestination (d. 35–41). omnipotence (d. 42–44), and finally the will of God (45–48).

The second book treats of creation. The first part is devoted to a discussion of the Church's teaching on the angels (d. 1–11): their nature and endowments (d. 3–4), probation and fall (d. 5–7), evil spirits and good angels in their relation to the world (d. 8, 9–11). Then the creation of the material world is considered, the hexaemeron (d. 12–15), creation of man (d. 16–20). This is followed by treatises on the fall of our first parents (d. 21–23), on grace and free will (d. 24–29), on original sin (d. 30–44).

The third book has for subject-matter the Incarnation, infused virtues, and the gifts of the Holy Spirit. The points considered in reference to the Incarnation are: The mystery and its causes (d. 1–5), the properties of the God-Man (d. 6–16), the work of redemption (d. 17–22). The second part discusses the theological virtues (d. 23–32), the cardinal virtues (d. 33), the gifts of the Holy Ghost (d. 34–35), the relation of the virtues (d. 36), and the law of the Old and New Covenant (d. 37–40).

The fourth book contains the theology of the sacraments (d. 1–42), and eschatology (d. 43–50).

The exposition runs on freely, without much attention to the *Videtur quod,* the *Videtur quod non,* and the strictly syllogistic forms of argumentation found in the works of later Scholastics. However, instead of simply citing a series of texts for and against a given point of doctrine, as Abelard had done in his *Sic-et-Non,* Peter usually interweaves with his authorities his own speculations, though not to the same extent as the authors who wrote about a century later.

Among the Lombard's immediate successors must be mentioned Peter of Poitiers (+1205), who left a *Summa* divided into five books: Alanus of Lille, whose *Apologia Christiana, De Arte seu Articulis Fidei,* and *Regulae Theologicae* bear witness to his dialectical skill as well as to his theological learning; William of Auxerre (+1230), author of the *Summa Aurea,* in four books, in which a strictly logical method is followed; William of Auvergne (+1248), also called Parisiensis, whose treatises *De Fide, De Trinitate, De Causis, Cur Deus Homo, De Anima, De Sacramentis,* form the greatest achievement in Scholasticism prior to the *Summae* of Alexander Halensis and Thomas Aquinas.

Side by side with the Lombard and his disciples worked the representatives of mysticism, which had found a home in the Abbey of St. Victor at Paris. The best known writers of this school, commonly called the Victorines, are Hugh (+1141), Richard (+1173), and Walter (+c. 1190). To the "Credo ut intelligam" and the "Intelligo ut credam," they added a third principle, "Amo ut intelligam." They all strongly emphasized the insufficiency of reason for the proper study of things divine, but it is especially in the works of Walter that opposition to speculative learning is carried to great length. For him dialectics are simply "the devil's art." In a work commonly cited under the title *In Quatuor Labyrinthos Franciae* he denounces Abelard, Peter Lombard, Peter of Poitiers, and Gilbert de la Porrée as heretics because they had treated with "Scholastic levity" the mysteries of the Trinity and the Incarnation. However, the opposition of the Victorines to dialectical reasoning had no effect in checking the rapid development of the Scholastic method.

B — THE GOLDEN AGE OF SCHOLASTICISM

A powerful impulse to the further development of Scholasticism was derived from the contact of the West with eastern learning during the Crusades. For although the East no longer played a part in the development of doctrine, it was nevertheless the storehouse of earlier Patristic lore. Besides, it was there that the philosophy of Aristotle had been preserved from utter oblivion. The first Scholastics were familiar only with the *Categories* and the *De Interpretatione* — the *Dialectica Vetus* — of the Stagirite. Then in the first half of the twelfth century the whole *Organon* — the *Dialectica Nova* — was made available for school purposes in its translation by John of Venice. But it was not until a century later that all of Aristotle's works, Physics, Metaphysics, and Ethics, became known to the Christian scholars of the West. And yet it was upon the knowledge of these works that the progress of Scholasticism largely depended.

Unfortunately, it was an adulterated Aristotelian philosophy that was thus introduced into western lands. After the sixth century, when Justinian banished the Athenian philosophers, Aristotelianism had found a home in Syria, and there, in the course of time, the philosophers of Islam corrupted the original text to suit their own religious views. Neoplatonic pantheism, the unity of the active intellect, the denial of personal immortality, the principle that what is true in philosophy may be false in theology, were some of the many Mahometan errors interwoven with the teaching of the Stagirite. And it was this corrupted Aristotle that was then introduced into the schools of Christian Europe.

Hence it was that the Church took at first an antagonistic stand in reference to Aristotelian philosophy, and more especially to its use in theological speculations. In 1210, a provincial synod of Paris ruled: *Nec libri Aristotelis de naturali philosophia, nec commenta* (Averroes) *legantur Parisiis publice vel secreto, et hoc sub poena excommunicationis inhibemus.*[14] The prohibition was renewed in 1215 by the legate Robert: *Non legantur libri Aristotelis de Metaphysica et de naturali philosophia, nec Summae de eisdem.*[15] In 1231, Pope Gregory IX modified this ruling by adding: *Quousque examinati fuerint et ab omni errorum suspicione purgati.*[16]

[14] Chartul. Univ. Paris. I, 70.   [16] Ibid. I, 138.
[15] Ibid. I, 79.

With this proviso, the faculty of arts of the University of Paris, 1255, placed the writings of Aristotle on the list of books that must be read by the students. Finally, when about this time the Dominican William of Moerbeke, at the request of Thomas Aquinas, translated the works of Aristotle anew from the original text, all opposition on the part of the Church was withdrawn. It was then that Aristotle became to the Scholastics simply *the Philosopher*.

The second period of Scholasticism is coincident with the rise and first spread of the mendicant orders whose teaching members soon became its most distinguished representatives. There was also a gradual shifting of the centers of Scholastic activities. During the first period some of the principal seats of learning had been Tours, Rheims, Laon, Auxerre, and Chartres, in France; Fulda and Reichenau in Germany; Utrecht, Liege, Tournai, and St. Laurent, in the Low Countries. In the second period most of these lost their importance, chiefly owing to the rapid growth of the University of Paris. This latter drew nearly all the most famous teachers, and consequently vast numbers of students, to its schools. Next to Paris, Oxford, Cologne, Naples, and Bologna became famous during the golden age of Scholasticism.

A word may be said here about the methods of teaching that became more or less universal after the beginning of the thirteenth century. There were two principal forms, lectures and disputations. The lecture usually consisted in a running commentary on some text which the *magister* took as a basis of his instruction. In theology the first text was the Bible, which was studied from the literal standpoint, little or no attention being given to the scientific exegesis of the text. Then came the Sentences of the Lombard, which were analyzed, explained, and developed. This was followed by a thorough study and scientific exposition of the Sacred Scriptures. It was usually after having spent some years in working out and delivering this last form of lectures that the magister would gather together the ripe fruit of his many studies in a *Summa,* or a systematic presentation of the whole of theology.

The disputations were of two kinds: the *disputationes ordinariae,* which turned about the subject-matter of the lectures, and formed a part of the ordinary curriculum; and the *disputationes generales de quolibet,* which usually occurred twice a year, at Easter and Christmas. In these latter the topics discussed were exceedingly varied; masters, students, and any of the auditors being free to propose questions. To the difficulties thus proposed, either the presiding master, or a bachelor in theology under his guidance, would then and there give a detailed solution. Then, on some subsequent day, the master himself would give his *determinatio,* that is, sum up and arrange in their proper order the various questions and difficulties dealt with, and at the end give definite and final replies. It was chiefly from these *determinationes,* or closing exercises of the disputations, that the numerous *quodlibeta* of the Schoolmen originated.[17] This accounts for the many trifling and irrelevant questions discussed in their pages.

The first great master of the second period of Scholasticism, who may in fact be said to have inaugurated it, was Alexander of Hales (Halensis), *Doctor Irrefragabilis.* He was an Englishman, born at Hales in Northumbria. At first he taught as a secular priest at the University of Paris, but in 1225 he entered the Franciscan order. Although up to that time no religious had ever taught at the University, he was nevertheless allowed to retain his chair and continued teaching until his death in 1245. He was as much revered for his piety as he was respected on account of his learning.

Besides many exegetical writings, Alexander composed a *Summa Theologica,* most probably at the suggestion of Pope Innocent IV. In depth of thought and sublimity of ideas it

[17] The *modus procedendi* in the theological schools of the time is thus outlined by Peter of Capua, who wrote in the thirteenth century: "Modus autem tractandi quaestiones theologicas secundum Magistrum talis est. Primo jacietur fundamentum auctoritatum, secundo erigentur parietes argumentorum et quaestionum, tertio supponetur tectum solutionum et rationum, ut quod in domo Dei auctoritas quasi certum proponit, argumentatio sive quaestio discutiat, solutio sive ratio elucidet et clarum reddat." Cfr. Grabmann, Die Geschichte der Scholastischen Methode, II. 532.

may almost be compared with the corresponding work of St. Thomas, but in precision of reasoning and finish of expression it falls short of that masterpiece of the Schools. It was the first real theological *Summa* ever written, and, in respect of voluminousness, also the greatest. Still largely Platonic in speculation, but at the same time Aristotelian in method, it forms an easy transition from the theology of the twelfth to that of the thirteenth century. It is the original type of what afterwards became known as Franciscan theology.

Like the Sentences of the Lombard, the *Summa* of Alexander is divided into four parts, each of which is subdivided into *quaestiones,* these into *membra,* and the *membra* into *articuli.* The first part contains seventy-four *quaestiones,* treating of God, His existence, His attributes, and the Trinity. The second, comprising one hundred and eighty-nine *quaestiones,* investigates the subject of creation, of angels and men, and of sin. The third, in eighty-three *quaestiones,* has for its subject-matter the Incarnation, the person of Christ, the redemption, and grace. The fourth, numbering one hundred and fourteen *quaestiones,* sets forth the author's teaching on the sacraments. These several divisions embrace the whole of theology, both dogmatic and moral. The treatment, though not quite as formal, is practically the same as that followed later on by St. Thomas, being more or less a development of the *Sic-et-non* method of Abelard. Usually the article begins with a *Videtur quod non,* followed by a number of *Items.* Then comes the *Sed contra,* in its turn followed by the *Resolutio,* or *Corpus,* and lastly the *Ad primum, Ad secundum,* etc.

The work of Alexander was continued by St. Bonaventure (1221–1274), who, though probably not a pupil of the Doctor Irrefragabilis, was nevertheless thoroughly imbued with his spirit. Besides his large Commentary on the Sentences and another one on Holy Scripture, he composed a compendious *Summa,* entitled *Breviloquium Theologicae Veritatis,* which is considered the best presentation of the theology of those times. His *Itinerarium Mentis ad Deum* and his many mystical writings are also held in great repute, while in his

Centiloquium he has presented the world with a new and original *Summa Sententiarum.* Bonaventure and Alexander have been officially proclaimed by the Franciscans as the two great doctors of their order.

Towards the middle of the thirteenth century a powerful impulse was given to the further development of Franciscan theology by Robert Grosseteste ($+$1253), chancellor of the University of Oxford and later on bishop of Lincoln. Though not a Franciscan himself, he was a devoted friend and influential protector of the order. In his teaching and writings he usually followed the lead of Alexander of Hales. The best known of his works are his *Commentarius in Mysticam Theologiam S. Dionysii* and his *Dicta Theologica.* The latter contains discussions on one hundred and forty-seven different theological topics. He also wrote a *Summa,* but it is extant only in manuscript.

Another light at Oxford was Richard Middleton (Mediavilla), an English Franciscan ($+$1300), who wrote an excellent *Commentary on the Sentences,* and also a volume of *Quodlibeta.* Of all the Franciscan theologians, he approaches most closely to the method, viewpoint, and perspicuity of St. Thomas, although he attacked the latter on several points of doctrine.

Closely allied with the Franciscan school, though not exactly a follower of it, was Henry of Ghent (Gandavensis), at first a secular priest and later on a member of the Servite order ($+$1293). He was a pupil of Albertus Magnus, but an independent genius and at ·times somewhat erratic. Freer in method and form than St. Thomas, he was almost his equal in depth of thought and wealth of ideas. The best known of his works is his folio volume of *Quodlibeta,* but his genius appears to better advantage in his *Summa;* of this, however, only the first part is complete.

The Dominican school of theology properly begins with Albertus Magnus (1193–1280). He was, however, more of a philosopher and scientist than a theologian, and his chief merit consists in having popularized the philosophy of Aristotle. In theological knowledge, systematic treatment, and clearness of exposition, he falls short of Alexander of Hales, and is in the same respects far surpassed by his pupil Thomas Aquinas. He began his dogmatic writings between 1240 and 1250, with a complete commentary on all the works of the Pseudo-Areopagite and on the Sentences of Peter Lombard. In his old age he composed a *Summa,* of which, however, only the first and second parts were completed. In this he supplements to some extent the *Summa* of St. Thomas. Earlier in life he wrote a *Summa de Creaturis,* which corresponds to the *Summa contra Gentiles* of St. Thomas. Besides these works, he also wrote a commentary on the four Gospels and nearly all the Prophets, and numerous homiletic and ascetic treatises.

Scholasticism reached its highest perfection in Thomas Aquinas, a pupil of Albertus Magnus (1225–1274). In accurate knowledge of Scripture and tradition, in depth of thought, wealth of ideas, clearness of expression, and orderliness of treatment he is facile princeps. He ranges over the whole field of philosophy and theology, apologetics and exegesis, and proves himself a master in every subject he treats. His principle works are the following:

1°. His *Commentum in Quatuor Libros Sententiarum.* This he wrote during his first years of teaching, and on many points of doctrine advanced in it he later changed his mind. Yet the clear explanation of the text and the organically arranged exposition of particular doctrines already reveal the mind of a master.

2°. The *Quaestiones Disputatae,* a collection of extensive monographs on the more important topics of theology and philosophy. There are in all sixty-three *quaestiones,* divided into four hundred *articuli.* In many respects they constitute his best work and contain the key to a right understanding of his *Summa Theologica.* They are all gathered under the general titles *De Potentia, De Malo, De Spiritualibus Creaturis, De Virtutibus, De Veritate.* In reference to their contents they might perhaps be better divided into the treatises *De Ente et Potentia, De Veritate et Cognitione, De Bono et Appetitu,* and thus they would form a complete system of ontology, epistemology, and ethics. The treatment is both philosophical and theological, according to the demands of the subject-matter. God, the Trinity, creation, the Incarnation, free will, grace, virtues, and sin are some of the chief theological subjects discussed.

3°. *Summa contra Gentiles.* This is in contents mainly a philosophical work, written against the errors of the day; but the topics treated have in one way or another a bearing upon theology, and some of them are strictly theological. It has been said that in no other human work is there such a wealth of ideas compressed into so small a compass. It is divided into four parts. The first two treat of the essence and existence of God and of creatures; the third discusses the tendency of creatures towards God and their union with Him; the fourth takes in theological subjects in one way or another connected with this tendency and union, as the Trinity, original sin, the Incarnation, the sacraments, and the resurrection of the dead. In this last part the arguments are chiefly drawn from Holy Scripture. The treatment is not dialectic, as is that of the *Summa Theologica,* but thetic. An excellent commentary on this monumental work was written towards the end of the fifteenth century by the Dominican Franciscus of Ferrara, usually cited as Ferrariensis.

4°. The principal work of St. Thomas, at least for theological purposes, is his *Summa Theologica.* It was composed towards the end of his life, for the purpose, as he states in the prologue, of putting into the hands of theological students a compendious presentation of the whole of Christian theology. However, like most other *Summae,* it was never completed, death putting an end to his labors whilst he was engaged on the third part. It ends abruptly in the middle of the treatise on the sacrament of penance. This *Summa* is divided into three parts. The first part corresponds to our treatises *De Deo Uno et Trino* and *De Deo Creante et Elevante;* the second, which is subdivided into *Prima et Secunda Secundae,* treats of the tendency of rational creatures towards God, thus roughly corresponding to our treatises *De Gratia* and *De Virtutibus,* but it is at once dogmatic and moral; the third part has for its subject-matter the Incarnation, the person of Christ, and the means of grace, containing therefore the same matter as our treatises *De Verbo Incarnato* and *De Sacramentis.*

In treatment the *Summa Theologica* is strictly dialectic. Each part is divided into *quaestiones,* and each *quaestio* into *articuli.* The *articulus* invariably begins with a statement of the chief difficulties against the doctrine to be proved, embodied either in a *Videtur quod non* or a *Videtur quod.* Then comes the argument for the doctrine under discussion, introduced by the phrase *Sed contra.* This is followed by the corpus, the *Dicendum quod,* or exposition of the doctrine in question. Lastly, the difficulties proposed in the beginning of the *articulus* are answered in due order, *Ad primum, Ad secundum,* etc. As an organic whole, the *Summa* may be gathered up in this one phrase: *Ex Deo per Christum in Deum,* thus making God the beginning and end of all things.

5°. Besides these various works, St. Thomas began also a *Compendium Theologiae,* in which, following the footsteps of St. Augustine, he intended to explain the contents of revelation in reference to the three theological virtues, faith, hope, and charity; but only the first part is complete. The *Expositio Symboli Apostolorum* and the *Expositio Primae Decretalis* (Caput Firmiter, IV Lateranensis) are also valuable productions of his busy pen. To these must be added his *Commentarii in Sacram Scripturam,* his *Quaestiones Quodlibetales Duodecim,* and some minor works.

While St. Thomas stood thus head and shoulders above his contemporaries, several of his doctrines, especially that of the unity of the substantial form in man, aroused violent opposition on the part of his confreres in the order of St. Dominic, even as other points of doctrine brought him into conflict with the followers of the Franciscan school. Of his Dominican opponents the most prominent were Roland of Cremona, Richard Fitzacre, and Robert Kilwardby. Owing to the influence of the latter, who was archbishop of Canterbury, the University of Oxford carried its opposition to Thomism so far as to censure as dangerous the denial of the *rationes seminales* and the doctrine of the unity of the substantial form in man. This occurred in 1277, three years after the saint's death; but the following year the general chapter of the order put a stop to the opposition in its own ranks, by decreeing severe penalties against those brethren " qui in scandalum ordinis detraxerunt scriptis venerabilis Patris Fratris Thomæ de Aquino."

But this authoritative coercion did not affect the Franciscans, who made common cause with the discontented Dominicans. Chief among them were William de la Mare, author of the *Correptorium Fratris Thomae;* Richard of Middleton, who was appointed to the Franciscan chair at Paris in 1281; John Peckham, who, after teaching at Paris, was chosen to succeed Kilwardby in the see of Canterbury; and Peter John Olivi, who in 1283 was condemned on account of his unorthodox teaching on religious poverty.[18]

This opposition, however, was as shortlived as it was violent. The number and influence of the defenders of St. Thomas grew steadily as time went on. First among these were Ulrich of Strasburg, a disciple of Albertus Magnus; Bernard of Hotun, bishop of Dublin; William Mackelfield, who taught at Oxford; the Augustinian Aegidius Romanus, *Doctor Fundatissimus;* Peter of Auvergne, and Godfrey of Fontaines; all of whom wrote towards the end of the thirteenth or during the first part of the fourteenth century.

[18] The state of mind which gave rise to this opposition on the part of the Franciscans appears from the words of Peckham: " Quod philosophorum studia minime reprobamus, quatenus mysteriis theologicis famulantur, sed profanas vocum novitates, quae contra philosophicam veritatem sunt in Sanctorum injuriam citra viginti annos in altitudines theologicas introductae, abjectis et vilipensis Sanctorum assertionibus evidenter. Quae sit ergo solidior et sanior doctrina, vel filiorum Beati Francisci, sanctae scilicet memoriae fratris Alexandri et fratris Bonaventurae et consimilium, qui in suis tractatibus ab omni calumnia alieni sanctis et philosophis innituntur, vel illa novella quasi tota contraria, quae quidquid docet Augustinus de regulis aeternis, de luce incommutabili, de potentia animae, de rationibus seminalibus inditis materiae et consimilibus innumeris, destruit pro viribus et enervat, pugnas verborum inferens toti mundo." It was the opposition of the old Platonizing theology to the new Aristotelian method and world-aspect.

After that the opposition practically ceased, although outside the Dominican order the different theological schools continued to defend their own views.

With St. Thomas Scholasticism reached the height of its development, and in less than a half a century after his death it began to decline. At the very beginning of this decline, though still belonging to the golden age of Scholasticism, appeared Duns Scotus (1266–1308), the *Doctor Subtilis*. He was a disciple of William Ware, the successor of de la Mare both in his chair of theology and in his opposition to Thomism. That Scotus was an intellectual giant, who boldly tackled even the most abstruse problems, is universally conceded; but at the same time he is not rarely accused of having used his extraordinary talents in tearing down rather than in building up. His was an analytical mind, and as a natural consequence he found much to criticize in the works of his predecessors and contemporaries. As a general rule, however, his criticism was objective, resulting from the keenness of his intellectual perceptions and not from an innate tendency to find fault. Unlike the great masters who preceded him, he wrote no commentary on Holy Scripture, and as a result the positive basis of his teaching is at times lacking in broadness and in depth. He was a man of intense piety, and also of most sincere orthodoxy, although he came occasionally very near the danger line in the logical trend of his reasoning.

The principal work of Scotus is his *Commentary on the Sentences (Opus Oxoniense)*, written whilst he was teaching at Oxford. This is completed by the *Reportata Parisiensia,* in part compiled from the notes taken down by his pupils at Paris. He also published a number of *Quaestiones Quodlibetales,* and some *Opuscula,* treating of metaphysical topics. His reasoning is always clear, but is not as direct as that found in the works of St. Thomas. Besides, his profuse critical remarks make the study of his writings somewhat of a task. Owing perhaps to his critical attitude, he failed to work out a well-connected theological system, although he covered practically the whole field of theology. He is the founder of the Neo-Franciscan or Scotistic school of theology, which occupies an honorable position in the theological world. In substance, however, this school does not differ very much from that founded by Alexander of Hales and developed by St. Bonaventure.

C — DECLINE OF SCHOLASTICISM

After the death of Scotus, in 1308, the decline of Scholasticism was very rapid. Men wholly devoid of his intellectual powers, and in many instances sadly lacking in orthodox instincts, tried to imitate him in criticizing the theology of the past, with the inevitable result that they wasted their time and energy in the discussion of meaningless subtleties, and thus drew down the contempt of the world upon Scholasticism itself. It was not a question of the times having outgrown the system, as is frequently maintained; but of the system being too big for the times. The strong faith, the profound sense of the supernatural, and the prayerful intellectuality of the Middle Ages were on the wane, and deprived of these the fertile fields of Scholasticism were doomed to be changed into a barren waste. Empty sounds were made to function as ideas, very much as made-money is substituted for gold at times of national distress. An outward show of learning was maintained, but its substance had vanished.

It was in this condition of intellectual destitution and religious atrophy that nominalism, or terminism, as others prefer to call it, began to flourish in the schools. This was a modified form of the nominalism of ancient Greece, which had sporadically cropped out in various quarters during the Middle Ages. In the second half of the fourteenth century, and still more so in the fifteenth, it threatened to drive moderate realism entirely from the field. Its first influential representative was William Ockam (+1347), for whom the way had already been prepared by Durandus of St. Pourçain (+1332). Strictly speaking he was a conceptualist rather than a nominalist, in as much as he defined the universal as "an intention of the mind," but to all intents and purposes this is a distinction without a difference. Like a thorough-going nominalist, he maintained that propositions, not things, are the object of all scientific knowledge, and consequently also of theology. *Scientia quaelibet, sive sit realis sive rationalis, est tantum de propositionibus tanquam de illis quae sciuntur, quod solae propositiones sciuntur.*[19] And again: *Omne enim universale est intentio animae, vel aliquod signum voluntarie institutum tale. . . . Universale non est aliquid extra animam; et certum est quod non sit nihil; ergo est aliquid in anima, . . . non objective tamen, . . . ergo subjective et per consequens est qualitas mentis.*[20]

The inevitable result of thus operating with merely subjective concepts, and equivalently with empty sounds, soon showed itself in an unwarranted distrust of the mind's reasoning powers in the attainment of truth. Such religious truths as the existence, unity, and infinity of God, the immediate creation of the universe by the Deity, the immortality of the soul, and many others, which the great teachers of the thirteenth century had proved by arguments drawn from natural principles, were held to be undemonstrable and therefore entirely relegated to the sphere of faith. On the other hand, the rôle of dialectics was unduly emphasized, and in course of time developed into mere logic-chopping. Along with this, new words and terms were constantly introduced, and before long the language of the schools became a jumble of outrageous barbarisms.

Ockam's work was continued by men like Gregory of Rimini, Robert Holcot, John Buridan, and Peter d'Ailly. Of these it was especially John Buridan who contributed powerfully to the success of terminism. As rector of the University of Paris, he wielded a wide influence, and during a quarter of a century he defended Ockam's teaching with great skill and boldness. After his time Ockamism spread very rapidly. Even Gabriel Biel (+1495), a man of great talent and sometimes called "the Last of the Scholastics," had nothing better to offer his pupils than a *Collectorium ex Occamo.* Outside the terminist school there were indeed a few earnest

[19] In I Sent. d. 2, q. 4, o.   [20] Quod. lib. V, 12, 13.

and learned men who strove to preserve the glorious traditions of the thirteenth century, but they were not of sufficient influence to meet with permanent success.

This condition of things continued till the Council of Trent, when men like de Vittoria, de Soto, Salmeron, Toletus, and many others ushered in a second spring of Scholasticism. The revival was very rapid, and by the end of the sixteenth century theological learning had reached a state of perfection that was almost unprecedented. It was the classical age of Neo-Scholasticism, followed by the age of the " Epigones," in both of which the great masters of the thirteen century seemed to have come back to life. Of this, however, it will be better to give a brief outline later on in its own proper place.

D — SOURCES OF ARGUMENTS

The work of the Fathers consisted primarily in proposing the faith as they found it contained in Holy Scripture and tradition, while the efforts of the Scholastics were largely directed towards placing this faith on a rational basis. Hence the writings of the Fathers are above all else practical, whereas those of the Scholastics are chiefly speculative. The latter no less than the former accepted St. Augustine's " Crede, ut intelligas," but they placed a greater emphasis upon his " Intellige, ut credas." During this period, therefore, our study of the development of dogmas must to a considerable extent be occupied with reviewing the arguments by which the great masters established the various doctrines of the Christian faith.

These arguments were drawn chiefly from three different sources : natural reason, tradition, and Holy Scripture. Those drawn from natural reason were used for a threefold purpose : First, to prove the existence of God and of revelation, or to establish the *praeambula fidei,* without a clear apprehension of which supernatural faith would be impossible; secondly, to demonstrate those points of faith that could be deduced from natural principles, as, for instance, the immortality of the soul; thirdly, to confirm supernatural truths that had been proved by arguments taken from revelation. In this latter instance they were not advanced as conclusive proofs, but simply as *rationes congruentiae,* that is, as arguments which were put forward to show a certain degree of conformity between the revealed truths in question and the demands of right reason.

Referring to the first purpose which these arguments from reason were meant to subserve, St. Thomas states: " It is evident that faith flows from two sources: First, from God, by reason of an interior enlightenment upon which the assent of the intellect is made to rest; secondly, from the manner in which revealed truths are presented to the mind as objects to be believed. This presentation is related to the knowledge of faith in a manner similar to that in which sense perceptions are related to the cognition of first principles." [21] It is not, strictly speaking, the foundation of faith, but a prerequisite condition.

Tradition, as a source of theological arguments, was regarded by the Scholastics under a twofold aspect: First, as identified with the *vivum magisterium Ecclesiae* — the teaching authority of the Church herself, as exercised in each succeeding age through her legitimate representatives, that is, either the Pope alone or the bishops in union with the Pope. Taken in this sense, tradition was universally held to speak with an infallible voice, so that the truths thus borne witness to could not be rejected without an error in faith. In the second place, tradition was not rarely understood as synonymous with the teaching of the Saints or of the Fathers, either as presenting the views of individual Patristic writers or as embodying what was more or less commonly held by them as a class. Thus considered, the authority of tradition was again accepted as final, provided it could be shown that the consent of the Fathers regarding a point of faith or morals was practically unanimous. In other cases it was indeed commonly regarded with profound respect, but not as necessarily precluding deviation from the view in question. Thus it sometimes happened that the Scholastics set aside the opinions of individual Patristic writers, yet in so doing they always proceeded cautiously and with evident reluctance.

[21] In Boeth. de Trin. op. 63, q. 3, a. 1 ad 4^m.

The third source of theological arguments, or Holy Scripture as interpreted by the Church, was looked upon by the Scholastics as having the very highest authority. And the reason is that the Sacred Writings were accepted by all of them as God's word, which was held to carry with it the full authority of His essential truthfulness. "The author of Holy Scripture," says St. Thomas, "is God, and the human writer acts merely as His instrument. For other branches of learning are the fruit of human genius, but what is contained in Holy Scripture is the result of divine inspiration." [22] And this teaching of the Angelic Doctor agrees in substance with the views commonly held in the schools of the Middle Ages. Nearly all the Scholastics admitted a fourfold sense in the interpretation of Holy Scripture — the literal, the allegorical, the moral, and the anagogical; but it was from the literal sense only that they drew their dogmatic arguments. [23]

The respective values of the arguments derived from the three sources mentioned in the preceding paragraphs — natural reason, tradition, and Holy Scripture — are thus indicated by St. Thomas: "Sacred doctrine is especially based upon arguments from authority, in as much as its principles are obtained by revelation: . . . but it has also recourse to human reason, not, indeed, to prove faith (for thereby the merit of faith would come to an end), but to make clear other things that are put forward in this doctrine. Since grace does not destroy nature, but perfects it, natural reason should minister to faith as the natural bent of the will ministers to charity. . . . Consequently, sacred doctrine makes use also of the authority of philosophers in those questions in which they were able to know the truth by natural reason. . . . Nevertheless, sacred doctrine has recourse to these authorities only as extrinsic and probable arguments; but appositely uses the authority of the canonical Scriptures as an incontrovertible proof, and the authority of the Doctors of the Church as one that may properly be used, yet merely as probable. For our faith rests upon

[22] Sum. Theol. I, q. 1, a. 10; Quodl. 7, a, 16; Proem. Comment. in Psalmos.

[23] Cfr. Thomas, Quodl. 7, a. 14, 15; Halens. Sum. I, q. 1, m. 4, a. 4; Albert. Magn. In Sent. I, d. 1, a. 5.

the revelation made to the Apostles and Prophets, who wrote the canonical books, and not on the revelations (if any such there are) made to other Doctors." [24]

The need there is of supernatural revelation, in order to bring about the salvation of men, is thus explained by the same author: " It was necessary for man's salvation that there should be a knowledge revealed by God, besides philosophical science built up by human reason. Firstly, indeed, because man is ordained to God, as to an end that surpasses the grasp of his reason. . . . But the end must first be known by men who are to direct their thoughts and actions to its attainment. Hence it was necessary for the salvation of man that certain truths, which exceed human reason, should be made known to him by divine revelation. Moreover, even as regards those truths about God which human reason could have discovered, there was need of their being taught by the revelation of God; because otherwise they would be known only by a few, and that after a long time, and with the admixture of many errors: whereas man's whole salvation, which is in God, depends upon the knowledge of these truths. Therefore, in order that the salvation of men might be brought about more fitly and more surely, it was necessary that they should be taught certain truths by divine revelation." [25]

[24] Sum. Theol. I, q. 1, a. 8.   [25] *Ibid*. I, q. 1, a. 1.

CHAPTER I

THE EXISTENCE OF GOD: GOD'S ESSENCE

In tracing up the doctrinal development that took place during the Middle Ages, it appears advisable to arrange the various topics of dogmatic interest in the same order that is commonly observed in modern textbooks of theology. For thereby is secured that continuity of thought with which modern students are most familiar. This requires, indeed, some rearrangement of the subject-matter as treated by the Schoolmen, but only to a limited extent; because most modern authors retain the order of treatment established by the theologians of the Middle Ages. Furthermore, it is hardly necessary to remark, as the point is sufficiently obvious, that in the study of mediæval theology the writings of the most representative Scholastics call for special consideration, and that the works of less important writers need be studied in so far only as they contain points of special interest to the history of dogmas

A — THE EXISTENCE OF GOD

In all the great *Summae,* whatever be the date of their composition, one of the first questions turns about the existence of God. The old arguments made use of by the Apologists of the second century, and incidentally also by many of the later Fathers, were overhauled and scientifically examined. The arguments from design, from the different degrees of perfection, from the contingency of all finite beings, and from the obvious necessity of a *Causa Prima,* were all investigated and retained. Besides these, however, others also were excogitated, as may be seen by referring, for instance, to the *Summa* of Alexander of Hales.[1]

[1] Op. cit. q. 2, m. 3.

An entirely new argument to prove the existence of God, commonly called the *ontological argument*, was devised by St. Anselm. He derived it from the idea of a being than which none can be more perfect. This idea, he contended, is found in the mind of every man who uses his reason, and from its very presence there we may legitimately infer the objective existence of such a being. For if it did not actually exist outside of the thinking mind, we should have a contradiction in terms. Because, on the one hand, our idea represents the being in question as perfect in every respect, so that nothing can be added to its perfection; yet on the other hand, if it had no existence outside of our minds, it could obviously be more perfect. Hence the necessary inference seems to be that it has objective existence. And if so, then God exists: because a being than which none can be more perfect is the infinitely perfect God.[2]

Soon after its appearance the argument was attacked by Gaunilo, a monk of Marmoutiers. As Anselm in formulating it had alluded to the fool (*insipiens*) who, according to the Psalmist, "hath said in his heart: There is no God," Gaunilo entitled his critique, *Liber pro Insipiente*. His refutation of Anselm's reasoning is divided into two parts. First he calls in question the author's assumption that the idea of a most perfect being is found in the mind of every man who uses his reason. That is something that can be asserted, but nevertheless lacks convincing proof.[3] Then he points out that from the mere presence of an idea in the mind one is not entitled to infer the existence of a corresponding object. Thus if one has an idea of a most beautiful island, as situated somewhere in the broad ocean, is that any reason why the island should really exist? And so with the idea of a being than which none can be more perfect.[4]

Anselm replied to this criticism in a *Liber Apologeticus contra Gaunilonem*, in which he first thanks his adversary for his criticism and then proceeds to defend his own position.

Most of the subsequent Scholastics refer to Anselm's *onto-*

---

[2] Proslogium, c. 2; cfr. cc. 1, 3.   [3] Op. cit. c. 2.   [4] Ibid. c. 6.

logical argument, but there is little agreement in their views concerning its value. Alexander of Hales[5] and St. Bonaventure[6] seem inclined to accept it as conclusive, while St. Thomas rejects it on the ground that it implies an unwarranted transition from the ideal order of things to the real.[7] Scotus makes it his own, and endeavors to give it greater strength.[8] Some centuries later it was brought out in a different form by Decartes and Leibnitz.

It was chiefly St. Thomas who cast the traditional proofs for the existence of God in their present form. And in this, as in many other matters that have a philosophical bearing, he drew largely on Aristotle. By way of forestalling an obvious objection, suggested by the incomprehensibility of the divine nature, he first points out that in order to prove God's existence we need not have a perfect knowledge of His essence. Objectively the two are indeed identical, but their relation to the human mind is not the same. Hence whilst God's essence can be known to us here on earth only imperfectly, the same is not necessarily true of His existence. For if we cannot strictly demonstrate, by the use of an essential and convertible middle term, that God exists, we can at least prove it by a *reductio ad absurdum,* in as much as the supposition that there is no God necessarily leads to an absurd conclusion. It is, therefore, a *demonstratio quia,* not *propter quid.*

Having thus cleared the way, he advances five proofs for the existence of God, which are calculated to satisfy every reasonable mind. A brief outline of them may be indicated as follows.

The first proof is taken from motion. It is evident to our senses that some things are moved, that is, they pass from a state of potentiality to a state of actuality. Now nothing can be thus moved, except by something already in the state of actuality. Thus wood, which is potentially hot, is made actually hot by its contact with fire, which is actually hot.

---

[5] Sum. Theol. I, q. 3, m. 3.
[6] In Sent. I, d. 3, q. 2.

[7] Sum. Theol. I, q. 2, a. 2; Contr. Gent. I, 3, 9.
[8] In Libr. I Sent. d. 2, q. 2.

And so in every similar instance. This implies either a *processus in infinitum* of beings that move and are moved, or the existence of a being that moves and is not moved — a *Primum Movens non mobile*. The former supposition is obviously repugnant to reason; hence the latter must be admitted. But this First Mover, this *Primum Movens non mobile,* every one understands to be God.

The second proof is drawn from the nature of efficient causation, as observed in the world around us. Every efficient cause produces an effect different from itself. There is no cause that is self-productive, and the very concept of such a cause implies an evident contradiction. Hence we must admit either an infinite series of subordinated causes, each one of which has been produced by a preceding one, or an unproduced, self-existing First Cause. The former supposition is evidently absurd. For if in efficient causes it is possible to go on to infinity, there will be no first efficient cause, neither will there be an ultimate effect, nor any intermediate efficient causes; all of which is plainly false. Therefore it is necessary to put forward a First Efficient Cause, unproduced and self-existent, to which every one gives the name of God.

The third proof follows from the contingency of all mundane things. Whatever there is in the world is of such a nature that it can exist or not exist, as is quite obvious from the observed fact of generation and corruption. Hence follows the possibility that at some time there was nothing in existence. And this being so, there would be nothing in existence now, except on the supposition that beyond this contingent world there is a being the existence of which is necessary. This necessity of existence, moreover, cannot come from without, since that would lead to an infinite series of subordinate causes. Therefore we cannot but postulate the existence of some being having of itself its own necessity, and not receiving it from another, but rather causing in others their necessity. This all men speak of as God.

The fourth proof is based upon the different degrees of perfection in the various beings of which this world is made up. Some are more and some are less good, true, noble, and the like. But "more" and "less" are predicated of different things according as they resemble and share in the perfections of an absolute standard. For what is more complete in any genus is the cause of all in that genus. Therefore there must also be something which is to all beings the cause of their being, goodness, and every other perfection; and this we call God.

The fifth proof is taken from the governance of the world; for we see that things which lack intelligence, such as natural bodies, act for some purpose, which fact is evident from their acting always, or nearly always, in the same way, so as to obtain the best results. Hence it is plain that not fortuitously, but designedly, do they achieve their purpose. Yet whatever lacks intelligence cannot achieve a purpose unless it be directed by some being endowed with intelligence and knowledge; as the arrow is shot to its mark by the archer. Therefore some intelligent being exists by whom all natural things are ordained towards a definite purpose; and this being we call God.[9]

Duns Scotus reproduces these various proofs with some modifications, pointing out as a final conclusion that the existence of the world, both when considered in itself as a whole and when viewed in the manifold relations of its several parts, can be satisfactorily explained only by postulating the existence of a being that is at once the efficient and exemplary first cause, and also the final cause, of all else. And this threefold cause is God.[10]

The force of these different arguments was first called in question by Ockam, and after him by theologians of the Nominalist school in general. Human reason, Ockam contends, is impotent to prove either the existence of God or His infinite perfection.[11] Both of these truths must be accepted from revelation as contained in Holy Scripture and proposed by the Church.[12]

[9] Sum. Theol. I, q. 2, aa. 2, 3.; cfr. Contr. Gent. I, 11, 12.
[10] In Sent. I, d. 2, 10 sqq.
[11] Quodlib. VII, 17–21; II, 1.
[12] Ibid. III, 1, 3.

In this contention the Nominalists placed themselves in open opposition both to the teaching of Holy Scripture [13] and to the unanimous consent of the Fathers.[14]   They, moreover, prepared the way for the traditionalism and skepticism of later ages, which received their final condemnation in the Vatican Council.[15]

Leaving aside these vagaries of a decadent Scholasticism, it may be said that with regard to the existence of God, and the source of our knowledge concerning it, all the great teachers of the Scholastic period were in perfect agreement on the following points:

1°. We can arrive at a certain knowledge of God's existence without any supernatural revelation. As Albertus Magnus expresses it, "the fact that God exists is not exclusively an article of the faith, but is presupposed to every article." [16]   True, God has revealed His own existence, and in so far we know it from a supernatural source; but antecedent to this knowledge of faith, we have of it a natural knowledge, which properly belongs to the *praeambula fidei*.[17]

2°. We acquire this natural knowledge of God indirectly, that is, from a consideration of the world around us.   The proposition, " God exists," is indeed self-evident *quoad se*, in as much as God is His own existence; but it is not self-evident *quoad nos,* since we do not have a perfect knowledge of God's essence.[18]   Hence the existence of God cannot be demonstrated *a priori,* from the very concept of His being; but it must be proved *a posteriori,* that is, from the effects of which He alone can be the cause.[19]

3°. The immediate intuition of God's essence lies beyond the unaided powers of all finite nature.   Hence even the writers of the mystic school of theological thought, of which the Victorines and St. Bonaventure are the best representatives, are careful to note that the divine illumination of which

[13] Wisdom, 13, 1–9; Rom. 1, 18–20.

[14] Cfr. vol. I, pp. 70, 71; Ibid. 256 sqq.

[15] Sess. III, de Revel. can. 1.

[16] Sum. Theol. tr. 3, q. 17.

[17] St. Thom. Sum. Theol. I, q. 2, a. 2 ad 1.

[18] St. Thom. Sum. Theol. I, q. 2, a. 2.

[19] Ibid.

they frequently speak does not terminate at a facial vision of God. " That refulgence of light," says St. Bonaventure, " by the aid of which God is seen face to face, does not belong to nature, but is a gift of divine condescension and grace." [20] And in another place, when speaking of the angels, he affirms that the intuitive vision of God is beyond their natural powers. " And this," he says, " is evident, because such a knowledge of God constitutes the first reward, in the possession of which the created mind rests as in its perfect beatitude. But this reward no one can obtain except by the help of a gratuitous gift of God." [21] Hence, when some fifty years later, the Beguines and Beghards asserted that " the soul has no need of being elevated by the light of glory — *lumine gloriae* — in respect of the vision and blessed fruition of God," the Council of Vienne, through the mouth of Clement V, condemned their teaching as heretical.[22]

4°. The knowledge of God and His existence is in no true sense innate. Most of the Scholastics, as also the Fathers before them, express themselves at times as if our knowledge of God were inborn. Thus St. Thomas states: " To know in a general and indefinite way that God exists is implanted in us by nature, in as much as God is man's beatitude." [23] But thereby they did not mean to assert a real inborn knowledge of God. Hence St. Thomas, in his commentary on the *De Trinitate* of Boethius, clearly states: " Our knowledge of God is said to be inborn in as much as through our innate principles (of cognition) we can easily arrive at the knowledge of God's existence." [24] What is inborn is not the idea of God, but the rational faculty by the right use of which we can readily discover God in His creatures. And St. Bonaventure explains: " If any men of authority be found to say that God can be seen and beheld in the present life, they are not to be understood as teaching that He is seen in His essence, but that He is known by some interior

[20] In Sent. II, d. 3, p. 2, a. 2, q. 2.
[21] Ibid.
[22] Mansi, 25, 410A.

[23] Sum. Theol. I, q. 2, a. 2 ad 1.
[24] In Boeth. De Trin. q. 1, a. 3, ad 6.

effect produced by Him." [25]   Later Ontologists appealed to both of these writers as fathering their peculiar views, but without just cause.

B — God's Essence

The various arguments made use of to demonstrate the existence of God, as outlined in the preceding section, point to Him as the efficient, final, and exemplary cause of the world. This necessarily implies that He contains in Himself all the perfections found in finite beings, possible as well as actual, since in the physical order of things there can be no perfection in any given effect which is not in some way precontained in its cause. Hence some Scholastic theologians, among whom is Duns Scotus,[26] infer from these same arguments that God is infinitely perfect; whilst others, as St. Thomas,[27] derive the infinite perfection of God from the established fact that He is being itself. But on the fact that God is infinitely perfect, all are agreed; and this fact immediately gives rise to two questions: First, what is God's essence? Second, what is the relation of the divine perfections as referred to one another and to the Godhead?

The first question admits of two different answers, according as we consider God's essence as a physical or a metaphysical entity. Considered as a physical entity, the essence of every being, and therefore also of God, is simply the sum total of perfections which constitute the being in question, aside from its accidents and relations. This is called the physical essence, about which, as referred to God, there is no difference of views among theologians. Considered as a metaphysical entity, the essence of a being is that particular perfection which is expressed in its essential definition. It is conceived as the ontological principle from which all essential properties or attributes emanate. As applied to God, and in our human way of considering the matter, it is that

[25] In Sent. II, d. 23, a. 2, q. 3.
[26] In Sent. I, d. 2, n. 20, 25, 30; cfr. Quodl. q. 7, n. 31.
[27] Sum. Theol. III, q. 4, a. 2.

divine perfection which is logically not derived from any other, and from which all others are conceived to flow as from their primary source. Theologians call it the *metaphysical* essence of God. It is with this that we are here concerned.

Patristic writers usually contented themselves with stating that " God is being itself — not being in the abstract, but in its very fullness; nor being in the passive sense, but as the source and fountainhead of all activity." [28]   They did not, as a rule, enter into the particular aspects of the question of God's being. Thus St. Chrysostom says: " That God is without beginning and unbegotten and eternal, I know; but the manner of it all I do not know. For neither can it be shown by arguments, how He is a substance which received being neither from itself nor from another." [29]   They pointed out with considerable clearness that the divine nature is necessarily unproduced, that God has the reason for His being within Himself, but beyond that they did not venture.[30]

Nor did the earliest Scholastics go much deeper into the subject, as it is here considered. Thus St. Anselm conceives God as a being than which none can be more perfect; [31] and after pointing out that God does not depend for His being on any cause outside of Himself, he states that the divine substance is through itself and of itself, and that God's essence is identical with His existence.[32] But he does not attempt to define what God's essence is. Nor is St. Bernard much more explicit. He answers the question, *Quid est Deus? What is God?* by saying: " Nothing occurs to the mind that is more to the point than *He Who Is*. Goodness, greatness, blessedness, wisdom, are all contained in the one word, *He Is*.[33] Hugh of St. Victor merely repeats the statement of St. Augustine that God does not produce Himself; [34] and the same is true of Peter Lombard.[35]

[28] Cfr. vol. I, p. 256 sqq.
[29] Hom. I, de Incompreh. Dei Natura, n. 3; MG, 48, 704.
[30] Cfr. August. De Trin. I, c. 1, n. 1; ML, 42, 820; Jerome, In Eph. 3, 14; ML, 26, 489.
[31] Proslog. c. 2.
[32] Monol. c. 6.
[33] De Consid. V, c. 6, n. 13.
[34] Sent. I, tr. 1, c. 11.
[35] Sent. I, d. 3, n. 23; d. 5, n. 1, 2.

Even the later commentators of the Lombard do not treat the question with that minute attention to details which we are accustomed to look for in the works of more recent theologians. They all show that God has the reason for His being within Himself, that He is infinitely perfect, absolutely simple, immutable, eternal; but they do not determine scientifically which of these perfections must be considered as the metaphysical essence of God. This is, to some extent, also true of St. Thomas, although he leaves us in no doubt concerning his own views on the matter.

Arguing from the established fact that " God is the first efficient cause," he concludes that " it is impossible that in God His existence should differ from His essence." [36] Furthermore, as God is an *actus purus,* without all potentiality, " it follows that in Him essence does not differ from existence. Therefore His essence is His existence." Now " God is His own essence; if therefore He is not His own existence, He will not be the First Being — which is absurd. Therefore God is His own existence, and not merely His own essence." [37] Moreover, " God's existence includes in itself life and wisdom," and all other perfection, " because nothing of the perfection of being can be wanting to Him who is the Self-subsisting Being." [38]

That he regards the perfection of self-subsistence as the most radical of all, he brings out more clearly when he speaks of the Divine Names. Putting the question, " whether this name, *He Who Is,* is the most proper name of God," he answers that it must be so considered for three reasons. The first of these reasons is taken from the signification of the term. " It does not signify form, but simply existence itself. Hence since the existence of God is His essence itself, which can be said of no other, it is clear that among other names this one specially denominates God, for everything is denominated by its form." [39] The second reason is derived from the universality of the term. " By any other name some mode of substance is determined, whereas this name,

---

[36] Sum. Theol. I, q. 3, a. 4.
[37] Ibid.

[38] Ibid. ad 3.
[39] Ibid. q. 13, a. 11.

He Who Is, determines no mode of being, but is indeterminate to all; and therefore it names the infinite ocean of substance itself." [40]   The third is drawn " from its consignification, for it signifies present existence; and this above all properly applies to God, whose existence does not know past or future." [41]

Hence, although St. Thomas, when speaking about the divine intellect and will, says that they are God's essence,[42] and elsewhere makes the general statement that whatever God has He is,[43] it is sufficiently evident from the above citations that he regards self-subsistence, the *esse a se,* as that which ultimately distinguishes God from every other being and which must be conceived as the ontological principle of all other divine perfections.   Hence, according to St. Thomas, self-subsistence, or *aseity,* to use the term now commonly employed in this connection, is the metaphysical essence of God.

Duns Scotus took a different view.   He looked upon *infinity* as the most perfect and most simple notion we have of God, " because it is neither an attribute nor a modification of him of whom it is predicated." [44]   It is at once essential, distinctive, and underived.[45]   No other concept of the Godhead can be compared to it in this respect — not even that of aseity.[46]   This infinity he calls fundamental or radical, in contradistinction to formal infinity as predicated of every other divine attribute; " for each of them has its own formal perfection derived from the infinity of the essence as its root and foundation." [47]   Hence this radical infinity — *infinitas radicalis* — is that fundamental attribute of the Godhead in virtue of which God necessarily possesses all other perfections, and in this sense it is conceived by Scotus and his followers as the metaphysical essence of God.

An entirely different view was taken by Ockam, Biel, and the Nominalist school generally.   As they denied the objective value of universal concepts, they held that all divine

40 Sum. Theol. I, q. 13, a. 11.
41 Ibid.
42 Ibid. q. 14, a. 4; q. 19, a. 1.
43 Ibid. q. 3, a. 3.
44 In IV Sent. I, d. 3, q. 2, n. 17.

45 Miscel. q. 5, n. 25.
46 Ibid. n. 26, 27.
47 In IV Sent. IV, d. 13, q. 1, n. 31; cfr. Quodl. q. 5.

names have the same signification, and consequently that all attributes of the Godhead equally designate the fullness of divine being. Hence they made no distinction between the physical and metaphysical essence of God. They described God's essence simply as the *cumulus omnium perfectionum,* the sum total of all His perfections. From this sum total, however, they excluded, as was evidently required by the teaching of the Church, the divine relations and hypostases.

＊　　＊　　＊　　＊　　＊

Closely connected with the question of God's essence, as treated by the Scholastics of the Middle Ages, are the considerations of His simplicity, spirituality, unicity, and infinite perfection. A few words concerning these will here be in place.

1. *Simplicity.* — That there can be no real distinction in the essence of the Godhead, and consequently no physical composition, was clearly taught by the writers of the Patristic period. St. Gregory the Great neatly summarized their teaching in this one sentence: " Whatever God has, that He is; in Him it is not one thing to be and another to have." [48] This view was taken over by the early Scholastics, St. Anselm,[49] Richard of St. Victor,[50] Peter Lombard,[51] Alanus of Lille,[52] and also by St. Bernard.[53] At the same time, however, owing to the dissentient teaching of Gilbert of Porrée, the matter became the subject of a theological discussion, which was finally settled by an ecclesiastical definition.

Gilbert's views on the point in question may be thus summarized. In all things one must distinguish between what is common to the class and proper to the individual. Substance is the highest genus of all corporeal and spiritual beings. It is taken in a two-fold sense: as that which is, *quod est subsistens,* and as that by reason of which it is, *quo est subsistens.* The latter is identical with nature, and this is ultimately the substantial form.[54]

---

[48] Moral. XVI, c. 43 ; PL. 75, 1147.
[49] Monol. c. 16; Proslog. c. 22.
[50] De Trin. I, c. 13.
[51] Sent. I, d. 8, c. 3.

[52] Ars Fidei, I, 8.
[53] De Consid. V, c. 7.
[54] Gaufredi Ep. ad Albinum Card.

These two concepts of substances — *quod est subsistens* and *quo est subsistens* — apply also to God. The divine nature, or *deitas,* is distinct from the Self-subsisting Being, or *Deus.* Nature is the substantial form in God, through which God is God, even as man is man through his humanity. Hence such forms of speech as the Godhead is God, wisdom is God, goodness is God, and also such as God is wisdom, goodness, truth, are theologically incorrect.

Gilbert was at the time bishop of Poitiers, and exception was first taken to his views when he expressed them in one of his sermons. His arch-deacon, Arnaldus " *qui non ridet,*" pointed out to him that his teaching was untenable. When that had no effect, appeal was made to Pope Eugene III, who during the Eastertide of 1146 was staying in Paris. The Pope submitted the matter to a council, which he convened at Paris during the following year, and over which he himself presided. But as Gilbert denied that he had ever taught the errors laid to his charge, Abbot Gottschalk, a Premonstratensian, was appointed to examine his writings and then report to the council which was shortly to be held at Rheims.[55]

Gottschalk performed the task assigned to him, but as he was unable to discuss the matter properly before the assembled bishops, that part was entrusted to St. Bernard. The latter marked four errors as opposed to the common teaching. They are: 1. The divine substance or nature is not God. 2. The three persons are not one God, one substance. 3. The persons are three by reason of three unities (*unitatibus*), and are different on account of three properties, which are not the same as the persons themselves; but they are three eternal differences, both in respect of themselves and of the divine substance. 4. The divine nature did not become incarnate, nor did it assume the human nature.[56]

These points were thoroughly discussed at the Council, which was held in 1148. As the cardinals present were in favor of Gilbert, it was feared that the Pope would be prevailed upon to abstain from giving a decision in the matter.

[55] Ibid.   [56] Mansi, 21, 712.

Hence the French prelates chose a committee of four, which was sent to the Pope with the following confession of faith: 1. We believe that the simple nature of the Godhead is God, nor can it in any Catholic sense be denied that the divinity is God and God the divinity. 2. When we speak of the three persons, Father and Son and Holy Ghost, we confess that the three persons themselves are one God, one divine substance. 3. We believe that only God the Father and the Son and the Holy Ghost are eternal and that there is no property in God which is eternal and not God. 4. We believe that the Godhead itself, or the divine substance or nature, has become incarnate, but in the Son.[57]

When the Pope had read this confession of faith, he answered the deputation that the articles contained therein were in conformity with the teaching of the Catholic Church. Then he added that although some of the cardinals were in favor of the person of Gilbert, they nevertheless all rejected his teaching. Thereupon, in a plenary session of the Council, Gilbert voluntarily retracted his teaching as formulated in the four articles, which were then publicly condemned by the Pope.[58]

This is the account given by Gaudefredus, Abbot of Clairveaux, while Otto of Freising states that the Pope contended himself with ruling, "*ne aliqua ratio in theologia inter naturam et personam divideret, neve Deus divina essentia diceretur ex sensu ablativi tantum sed etiam nominativi.*"[59] Nearly seventy years later (1215), the Fourth Lateran touched this same point when it defined the Blessed Trinity as "one absolutely simple essence, substance, or nature." [60]

The absolute simplicity of God's essence having thus been defined by the Church, the great theologians of the thirteenth century, Alexander of Hales,[61] St. Bonaventure,[62] Albertus Magnus,[63] and St. Thomas,[64] set forth in detail how this

[57] Mansi, 21, 712.
[58] Gaufredi, loc. cit.
[59] Gest. Frid. I, 5:.
[60] Mansi, 22, 982 sqq
[61] Sum. Theol. I, q. 5, m. 1, 2, 3.

[62] In IV Sent. I, d. 8, p. 2, q. 1.
[63] Sum. Theol. I, tr. 4, q. 20, m. 1–4.
[64] Sum. Theol. I, q. 2, a. 3–8.

simplicity is to be understood. They point out that the very concept of the divine essence excludes all composition, physical, metaphysical, and logical. As God is an *actus purus,* reasons St. Thomas, there is in the Godhead no composition of matter and form, of potency and act, of essence and existence, of nature and personality, of substance and accident, of genus and species, of general and particular; for all these kinds of composition presuppose corresponding potencies, and every potency is necessarily excluded from the *Esse Purum.* Hence God is His own essence, and whatever He has, that He is. And hence also, there can be no strict definition of God.[65]

Yet this absolute simplicity of God is not such that our concepts of His perfections, as in some way distinct, are without objective value. A merely mental distinction, *distinctio rationis,* does not seem sufficient, nor can the distinction which we make between them be based solely on God's relation to the world of creatures. For God is good, and wise, and all-powerful, independently of creation. Moreover, as St. Thomas argues,[66] in Holy Scripture God reveals these different perfections, and surely He does not reveal mere names. Hence that which corresponds to our concepts is more than a mere mental relation; it must in some way have a foundation in God's being. What is this foundation?

St. Thomas reduces it to God's absolute perfection — *plena et omnimoda perfectio* — which no single concept of ours can ever adequately express. He reasons thus: " Those things which in creatures are diverse, are one in God on account of His absolute simplicity. Thus therefore it must be said, that in God is wisdom, goodness and the like, each one of which is the divine essence itself, and in this way all are one *in re.* Then because each one of them is in God after its truest significance, and because the nature of wisdom is not the nature of goodness, when formally considered as such, it follows that they are diverse, not only as viewed by the reasoning mind, but on the part of the object — *ex parte rei.* . . . And thus it is obvious that the plurality of those names

---

[65] Ibid.   [66] Quaest. Disp. c. i, a. 6; cfr. c. 7.

is not derived from our intellect alone, when it forms diverse concepts of God, . . . but also from the being of God Himself, in so far, namely, as there is something in God corresponding to all these concepts, that is, His full and absolute perfection; whence it comes about that every one of the names signifying these concepts is truly and properly predicated of God: not, however, in such a way that any diversity or multiplicity is, by reason of these attributes, affirmed in the object, which is God." [67]

Hence, according to St. Thomas, that which corresponds to our different concepts of God's perfections is more than a pure relation; it is something objective, something virtually distinct for each particular concept. This virtual distinction, however, reduces ultimately to God's infinite perfection and the limitation of our finite minds.

Henry of Ghent, a disciple of Albertus Magnus, comes practically to the same conclusion, though his method of reasoning it out is different. He admits, however, a threefold plurality in God — plurality of ideas, plurality of attributes, and a trinity of persons.[68] This peculiar view, at least as regards the divine intellect and will, was later on defended by Dionysius the Carthusian.[69]

Duns Scotus was not satisfied with these explanations. He regarded them as placing between the divine attributes a merely mental distinction, a *distinctio rationis ratiocinantis,* derived from God's relation to the created world. After arguing against them at great length, he states his own view as follows: "I maintain that between the essential perfections there is not merely a mental distinction, that is, of different ways of conceiving the same formal object; for such a distinction there is between the person who has wisdom and wisdom itself, and obviously a greater distinction between wisdom and truth: nor is there only a distinction of the formal objects as they are in the intellect, because, as was shown before, such a distinction is never found in intuitive cognition unless it is also in the object intuitively known. . . . Hence

[67] In Sent. I, d. 2, q. 1, a. 2, 3;   [68] Quodl. 5.
cfr. De Poten. q. 7, a. 6.   [69] In Sent. I, d. 2, q. 2.

there is a third distinction, which precedes the intellect in every way; and it is this, that wisdom is in the object objectively, and goodness is in the object objectively. But wisdom in the object is formally not goodness in the object. And this statement is thus proved, because if infinite wisdom were formally infinite goodness, then wisdom in general would also formally be goodness in general; for infinity does not destroy the formal nature of that to which it is added. . . ."

"Hence there is a certain formal non-identity of wisdom and goodness, in so far as their definitions would be distinct, if they could be defined; but a definition does not indicate that alone which has its origin from the intellect, but also the nature of the object (*quidditatem rei*), and hence there is objectively no formal identity. I, therefore, understand the matter thus: The intellect, combining the ideas of the proposition, wisdom is not goodness formally considered, does not by its own act cause the truth of the combination, but finds the extremes, on account of whose combination its judgment is true, in the object. . . . Thus I concede that by way of identity truth is goodness objectively, but formally truth is not goodness.[70]

This "third distinction," which Scotus holds to lie midway between a real and a purely mental distinction, is usually called *distinctio formalis*, because it is based upon certain supposed *formalitates* in the absolutely simple essence of God. What these *formalitates* really are, neither Scotus nor his followers have ever made clear. That they are not distinct realities is conceded by all, and necessarily so; for the absolute simplicity of God, as taught by the Church, requires that whatever perfection is in the Godhead is God Himself. And yet if they are not distinct realities, they would seem to be neither more nor less than the *plena et omnimoda perfectio* of which St. Thomas speaks. Hence it is that, although the *distinctio formalis* of Scotus has never been condemned, nearly all subsequent theologians teach the virtual distinction formulated by St. Thomas — a mental distinction which is based

[70] In IV Sent. I, d. 8, q. 4.

upon God's infinite perfection, as containing *via eminentiae* all the perfection of our distinct concepts.

However, this virtual distinction was rejected by the Nominalists of the school of Ockam, as sinning by excess. According to them, all the names and attributes of God are synonymous *per se,* and offer no basis for a distinction except in their relation to the world of creatures. Hence whatever distinctions we make between God's essence and His attributes, or between His attributes referred to one another, can in the very nature of things be only logical, a purely mental distinction without a foundation in God's being. This exaggerated view of God's simplicity has not been explicitly condemned by the Church, but it is universally regarded as false and dangerous to the faith.

2. *Spirituality.*— This term is usually taken to imply three distinct concepts: immateriality, superiority to matter, and intellectuality. All three concepts are brought out by the Scholastics in connection with God's essence. Thus St. Anselm writes: " No nobler essence is known than that of spirit or body; and of these the spirit is nobler than the body: hence it is to be held that the divine essence is a spirit, and not a body." [71] The same view is taken by Hugh of St. Victor,[72] St. Bernard, Alanus of Lille,[73] Peter Lombard,[74] and all his commentators. The only exception, leaving aside Scotus Erigena, were some theologians of the pantheistic school of Chartres, especially Amalry of Bène and David of Dinant. Of these two St. Thomas relates that the former held God to be " the formal constituent principle of all things," whilst the latter " most absurdly taught that God was primary matter." [75] The spirituality of God, which was always treated as a matter of faith by theologians, was first explicitly defined by the Vatican Council, to offset the vagaries of modern errors.[76]

3. *Unicity.*— The unity of God, as opposed to plurality, was usually considered by the early Scholastics in connection

[71] Monol. c. 27.
[72] Didascal. VII, c. 19.
[73] Theol. Reg. 7.

[74] Sent. I, d. 35, 45.
[75] Sum. Theol. I, q. 3, a. 8.
[76] Sess. 3, c. 1.

with the mystery of the Blessed Trinity. They pointed out,
as the Fathers had done before them, that, although the three
divine persons are really distinct, yet there is only one God.
Hence in that connection they took unity in the sense of
unicity. On this point there never was any difference of
opinion; nor could there be among Catholics, since the unicity
of God had been recognized from the beginning as a fundamental dogma of the faith.

Some, moreover, like St. Anselm,[77] Hugh of St. Victor,[78]
and Peter Lombard,[79] proved this doctrine by philosophical
arguments. Nearly all of them based their reasoning upon
the obvious necessity of one sole First Cause. The same
line of reasoning was followed by St. Thomas in his *Commentary on the Sentences,*[80] but in his *Summa Theologica* he
derives the unicity of God from the attribute of infinity.[81]
This latter method was also adopted by Duns Scotus.[82]

4. *Infinity.*— St. Anselm puts forward the idea of God's
infinity in his ontological argument for the existence of God,
which, as was pointed out above,[83] is derived from the concept of a being than which none can be more perfect. But
in another place he bases the infinite perfection of God upon
His sovereign goodness, which necessarily implies plenitude
of being.[84] St. Thomas takes self-subsistence as the basis of
his argument. He reasons in this way. From a being whose
very essence is self-subsistence all potentiality is necessarily
excluded, hence it "must contain within itself the whole perfection of being." [85] A being is called infinite because it is
not finite — its perfection is without limit; and this is necessarily implied in self-subsistence. Consequently, "it is clear
that God is infinite and perfect." [86] The same conclusion is
also deduced from the notion of first cause; [87] for the very
idea of first cause implies all possible perfections and that
without any limitation in their concept. This latter argument

[77] Monol. cc. 3, 4.
[78] Didascal. VII, c. 19; cfr. De
Sacr. I, p. 3, c. 12.
[79] Sent. I, d. 2; II, d. 1.
[80] In Sent. II, d. 1.
[81] Sum. Theol. I, q. 11, a. 3, 4.

[82] In IV Sent. I, d. 10, 13, q. 5.
[83] P. XX.
[84] Monol. c. 15.
[85] Sum. Theol. I, q. 7.
[86] Ibid.
[87] Ibid.

is also used by Scotus,[88] who deduces God's infinity directly from the proofs advanced for His existence. That God is infinite in every line of perfection, and therefore infinite in the strict sense of the term, is one of the doctrines explicitly defined by the Vatican Council.[89]

[88] Quodl. q. 7, n. 31.   [89] Sess. 3, c. 1.

CHAPTER II

THE ATTRIBUTES OF GOD

By the attributes of God are understood essential perfections of the divine nature, which, in our human way of thinking, are conceived as emanating from God's metaphysical essence. Objectively, essence and attributes are indeed identical in the Godhead, so that it is perfectly true to say, God is wisdom, God is goodness, God is justice; but, as was pointed out in the preceding chapter, we necessarily place a virtual distinction between them, and thus rightly consider God's indivisible essence under many distinct aspects. These distinct aspects, based upon the plenitude of divine perfections, we call attributes.

Bearing in mind God's infinitude and our mental limitations, it is obvious from the very nature of the case that these attributes are exceedingly numerous. All the distinct perfections which we observe in the created world, and others which might acquire existence in any possible world, must necessarily be found in the Godhead. Not formally as created perfections, but as self-subsistent actuality, whence all created perfections are derived.

This immediately gives rise to the question, how are we to conceive these perfections to exist in the Godhead? Our concepts of them are derived from the consideration of creatures; can we predicate them of God as thus derived, or must they first be rectified in accordance with the requirements of the divine nature?

In answering this question, it is customary to divide created perfections into two classes. In the first class are gathered together all such as imply no imperfection in their concepts, and are therefore called simple perfections. In the other class all those are placed whose concepts do imply certain

49

imperfections, and these are termed mixed perfections. To the former belong such as wisdom, justice, and mercy; to the latter, rationality, animality, and in general all those that are in some way connected with matter. Simple perfections are said to be formally in God, in as much as they are predicated of Him in their own proper sense. Mixed perfections are attributed to God only *eminenter,* that is, whatever actuality they possess is in God, but in a different and higher sense. In either case, as attributed to God, these perfections must be conceived as infinite.

A further distinction must be made between these perfections in their relation to the divine essence. Some of them, as simplicity, unicity, spirituality, and infinitude, are attributes only in a wider sense of the term; because they belong to God's essence as such and cannot be conceived as emanating therefrom. Others are of a transcendental nature, in as much as their formal concept lies beyond all the categories of being. They are oneness, truth, and goodness. The former class has already been considered in connection with the divine essence; of the latter nothing further need be said than that their existence has always been a matter of faith.

Besides these there are the divine attributes strictly so called, which are conceived by us as superadded to God's essence, or as perfections emanating from the divine essence as their ontological principle. They are usually divided into negative and positive attributes. The former deny in God certain imperfections contained in their concepts as derived from creatures. Thus in regard to time and place God is said to be eternal, immutable, immense. They are also called incommunicable, as they can in no true sense be communicated to creatures. The other class comprises all simple perfections, which may be referred either to God's intellect, will, or power. They are communicable, in as much as they may be imitated in created beings.

Of the negative attributes little need be said in the present connection, since they do not readily lend themselves to doctrinal development. God's *eternity* is clearly taught in the Athanasian Symbol, and was correctly defined by Boethius as

" the whole and simultaneous possession of interminable life." [1] It is not merely duration without beginning and without end, but also without succession. It is the everlasting and unchangeable present, excluding from its concept both past and future. Hence the Scholastics usually derived this divine attribute from God's immutability.[2]

The *immutability* or unchangeableness of God necessarily follows from the fact that He is an *actus purus,* pure actuality, and also from the other fact that He is infinitely perfect. St. Thomas assigns both of these reasons,[3] while Scotus insists more upon the latter.[4] The early Scholastics observed a slightly different order of deduction. Thus St. Anselm derives God's immutability by way of corollary from the attributes of simplicity, eternity, and omnipresence;[5] whereas Hugh of St. Victor[6] and St. Bernard[7] deduce it directly from the simplicity of the divine essence. Peter Lombard bases his arguments for its existence exclusively upon Holy Scripture and the writings of the Fathers.[8]

God's *immensity* may be viewed under a twofold aspect: First, absolutely as it is in itself; and in this sense it excludes all spatial relations. By reason of His immensity God is above all space, as by reason of His eternity He is above all time. Secondly, immensity may be taken in a relative sense, as *omnipresence,* in as much as God is intimately present to all His creatures, and thus without change and extension fills all space. Under the former aspect God's immensity was admitted by all Scholastics, while under the latter it was at various times made a matter of discussion.

Thus Honorius of Autun answered the query, " where does God dwell?" by saying: " Although He is everywhere by His power, still by His substance He is only in the intellectual heaven," that is, in the place where He is seen face to face by the blessed.[9] A similar view was held by Theodoric of

---

[1] De Cons. Phil. V, 6; ML. 63, 858.
[2] Cfr. Thomas, Sum. Theol. I, q. 10, a. 1; Scot. Quodl. q. 6, n. 13–15; De Rerum Princ. q. 22, n. 5.
[3] Sum. Theol. I, q. 9, a. 1, 2.
[4] In IV Sent. I, d. 8, q. 5.
[5] Monol. c. 25.
[6] De Sacr. I, p. 3, c. 13.
[7] In Cant. Serm. 80, n. 5.
[8] Sent. I, d. 8, n. 2.
[9] Elucid. 3.

Chartres [10] although he is quite frequently accused of having taught pantheism. Scotus accepted the traditional teaching of the Church, that God is everywhere present by His essence, but he denied the force of the argument commonly advanced to establish this truth.[11] The same position was taken by the Nominalists.[12]

Others, however, as St. Anselm,[13] Hugh of St. Victor,[14] Walter de Mortagne,[15] Richard of St. Victor,[16] and Peter Lombard,[17] not only admitted the doctrine as contained in the teaching of the Church, but also assigned reasons for their belief. The statement of the Lombard, *quod Deus incommutabiliter semper in se existens, praesentialiter, potentialiter, essentialiter est in omni natura sive essentia sine sui definitione, et in omni loco sine circumscriptione, et in omni tempore sine mutabilitate,* was more fully developed by nearly all subsequent Scholastics. St. Thomas thus concludes his reasoning on the subject: " Therefore, God is in all things by His power, in as much as all things are subject to His power; He is in all things by His presence, in as much as all things are bare and open to His eyes; He is in all things by His essence, in as much as He is the cause of existence to all things." [18] And again: " Indeed, by the very fact that He gives existence to everything in every place, He fills every place." [19]

Of the positive attributes we can here consider only God's knowledge, His omnipotence, and the freedom of His will. The following is a brief summary of the most important points on the subject as treated by the Scholastics.

1. *Divine Knowledge.*— As God is self-subsistent being and the first cause of creatures, it necessarily follows that intellect and understanding must be predicated of Him as essential attributes. And as He is absolutely simple, it also follows that He is His own intellect and His own understanding. On these points there never was any difference of

---

[10] Cfr. d'Achery, Spicil. III, p. 522.
[11] Report. I, d. 37, q. 1.
[12] Cfr. Biel, Collect. I, d. 38.
[13] De Fide Trin. c. 4.
[14] Didasc. VII, c. 19.
[15] Cfr. d'Archery, op. cit.
[16] De Trin. II, 22.
[17] Sent. I, d. 37.
[18] Sum. Theol. I, q. 8, a. 3.
[19] Ibid. a. 2.

opinion, either among the Fathers or the Scholastics. " That
which is knowledge in God," says St. Augustine, " the same is
wisdom, and that which is wisdom, the same is (His) essence or substance." [20]   Peter Lombard repeats this statement in the terse sentence: " God's knowledge, of course,
is His essence." [21]

Assuming the fact of divine knowledge as sufficiently obvious, most of the Scholastics limited their investigation to
its nature and object. How does God know, and what does
God know?

In answer to the first question — how does God know? —
all state, either explicitly or implicitly, that divine cognition
is an absolutely simple act, in which intelligible species, intellect, and essence are all identified. St. Thomas puts his
reasoning in this form: " Since God has nothing of potentiality, but is pure act, the intellect and its object in Him are
altogether the same; . . . nor does the intelligible species differ from the substance of the divine intellect." [22]   And " thus
it follows that in God the intellect, and the object understood,
and the intelligible species, and His understanding act are entirely one and the same." [23]   In substance this is the view of
all Scholastics, except that Scotus introduces here his *distinctio formalis.*[24]

Furthermore, the one medium of divine cognition is God's
essence itself, in the sense that no object apart from God
has a determining influence on His intellect. " As existence
follows on form,' writes St. Thomas, " so in like manner to
understand follows on the intelligible idea. In God there is
no form apart from His existence. Hence, as His essence
itself is also His intelligible species, it necessarily follows that
His act of understanding itself must be His essence and His
existence." [25]   Scotus puts this same teaching in a slightly
different form, when he says: " Assuming that there is a
passive intellect in God, which needs a form or *quasi* form
for its operation, this form may be said to be His own es-

[20] De Trin. XV, c. 13.
[21] Sent. I, d. 36, n. 1.
[22] Sum. Theol. I, q. 14, a. 2.

[23] Ibid. q. 14, a. 4.
[24] Report. I, d. 35, q. 1.
[25] Sum. Theol. I, q. 14, a. 4.

sence as such, which in its absolute perfection is the medium of knowing, not only itself, but also everything else that is in any way knowable." [26]

The object of divine cognition — what God knows — is two-fold: First, His own being, or Himself as one in nature and three in person; secondly, things apart from Himself, whether at some time actually existing or merely possible.

Regarding the first, God's knowledge of Himself, there never was any difference of opinion. St. Thomas only formu-lates the common teaching on this point, when he writes that in God "the intelligible idea itself is the divine intellect itself, and thus He understands Himself by Himself." [27] And this understanding of Himself is comprehensive, or as infinitely perfect as is the divine essence. For "the power of God's own knowledge is as great as His actual existence; because from the fact that He is actuality separated from all matter and potentiality, He is knowable in a corresponding de-gree. It is manifest that He knows Himself as much as He is knowable; and for that reason He perfectly comprehends Himself." [28]

Things outside God, in the sense that they are not identi-fied with His being, are of two kinds: First, beings which at some time or other have actual existence; secondly, beings which always remain in the state of mere possibility. The latter are subdivided into three classes: purely possibles; fu-turibles whose futurition is conditioned by the action of nec-essary causes; and futuribles whose futurition depends on the self-determination of free agents. Concerning divine cognition of these various classes of beings, different views were held by different theologians. Only a brief outline of the more important of them can here be given.

(a) Regarding the mere fact that God knows all things, whether actual or possible, there never was any disagree-ment among the Schoolmen; but, as St. Thomas points out, according to some "God knows other things (than Himself) only in general, that is, only as beings." [29] Against these he

---

[26] In Sent. I, d. 35, q. 1.
[27] Sum. Theol. I, q. 14, a. 2.
[28] Ibid. a. 3.
[29] Ibid. a. 6.

argues, that "as God's essence contains all the perfections contained in the essence of any other being, and far more, He can know in Himself all of them with proper knowledge." The same position had already been taken by Peter Lombard, who reasons that God's knowledge is necessarily eternal, essential, unchangeable, extending itself not only to the things that are or shall be, but also to such as are possible indeed yet are never realized.[30]   St. Bonaventure expresses his view in similar terms; for answering the question whether God's knowledge can be increased or diminished, he says: "The knowledge of God is unchangeable as is His essence, and He always knows all things by one and the same act.[31] The contrary view he regards as heretical.

(b) All are agreed that God's knowledge of finite beings, in so far as they are considered in the state of possibility, is necessarily included in His comprehensive knowledge of His own essence; whether, as in the view of St. Thomas,[32] the possibles as such are conceived to be by supposition prior to divine cognition, or, as in the opinion of Scotus,[33] they are held to be formally constituted in the state of possibility by the act of divine knowledge. This cognition theologians usually call the knowledge of simple intelligence, to distinguish it from the knowledge of vision, which has for its object all finite beings in so far as they are at one time or another actually existing.

(c) As no finite beings exist from all eternity, and as God's knowledge of them is necessarily eternal, they are in one sense all known to God under the aspect of futurition; hence the question arises, what precise relation do future things bear to God's knowledge? Is God's knowledge of them the cause of their future existence, or is their future existence the cause of God's knowledge? Or is there a third way of conceiving the matter?

In answering the first question, the Scholastics distinguish between God's knowledge taken in an exclusive sense, simply as knowledge, and God's knowledge conceived as directive of

[30] Sent. I, d. 39, n. 5.
[31] In Sent. I, d. 39, 1, 4.
[32] Sum. Theol. I, q. 15, a. 2.
[33] Report. I, d. 35.

the divine will, or as knowledge of approbation. Taken in the former sense, divine cognition, as all are agreed, is purely speculative, and as such it cannot be regarded as the cause of anything; in the latter sense it is practical, and may be denominated the cause of things, but only on account of its connection with the will.[34] It is in this sense that St. Thomas writes: "It is manifest that God causes things by His intellect, since His existence is His intelligence; and hence His knowledge must be the cause of things, in so far as His will is joined to it. Therefore, the knowledge of God as the cause of things is commonly called the knowledge of approbation."[35]

In this connection the Scholastics also note that God's foreknowledge of future events does not interfere with the free action of secondary causes. What God foreknows will come to pass, but as determined by the finite causes that bring it about. Thus God foreknew from all eternity the fall of Peter, and His foreknowledge of the event was infallible; hence as the object of God's eternal prevision the fall was inevitable, yet Peter fell by freely consenting to a temptation which he then and there might have resisted. And the ultimate explanation is that God foreknows all things as they are in themselves and in their relation to their proximate causes — the necessary as necessary, and the contingent as contingent.[36]

The second question, whether future things are the cause of God's knowledge, is by all Scholastics answered in the negative. They usually touch this point in explaining an apparent difficulty drawn from a text of Origen, namely: "A thing will not happen because God knows it as future; but because it is future, hence it is that it is known by God before it exists." Peter Lombard[37] and Alexander of Hales[38] call future events a *causa sine qua non* of divine cognition, in the sense of mere concomitance. The fact of

[34] Lomb. Sent. I, d. 38, n. 5; Halens. Sum. I, q. 33, m. 2; Bonavent. In Sent. I, d. 38, 1.
[35] Sum. I, q. 14, a. 8.
[36] Halens. op. cit. q. 23, m. 6.
[37] Sent. I, d. 38, 4.
[38] Sum. I, q. 23, m. 2.

its future occurrence is in a manner the reason why an event is foreknown, but it does not cause God's foreknowledge. Practically the same explanation is given by St. Bonaventure.[39] St. Thomas interprets Origen in this way: "When we say that God foreknows some things because they are in the future, this must be understood according to the cause of consequence; and not according to the cause of existence. If things are in the future, it follows that God knows them; but nevertheless the futurity of things is not the cause of God's knowledge."[40] Scotus agrees with this explanation, in as much as he holds that things apart from God are objects of divine cognition only *terminative*.[41]

(d) It was stated above that the sole medium of divine cognition is God's essence; and from what is said in the preceding paragraph it necessarily follows that God's essence is also its sole primary object. That essence is the archetype of all that is or can be, and as a *species intelligibilis* it exhibits to the divine intellect all that is knowable. In this sense St. Thomas states: "God sees Himself in Himself, because He sees Himself by His essence; and He sees other things not in themselves, but in Himself; in as much as His essence contains the similitude of other things besides Himself."[42] And the same view is expressed by Scotus, when he says that God sees all things *mediante essentia sua infinita*.[43] This is, however, not merely a knowledge of the divine essence as imitable *ad extra,* but also of the things themselves. St. Thomas, after giving a rather lengthy illustration drawn from human cognition, arrives at this conclusion: "We must say therefore that God does not only know that things are in Himself; but by the fact that they are in Him, He knows them in their own nature and all the more perfectly, the more perfectly each one is in Him."[44]

Here, however, a distinction is to be made between God's knowledge of necessary things and of things that are contingent. Necessary things are infallibly known by Him either

---

[39] In Sent. I, d. 38, 1.
[40] Sum. Theol. I, q. 14, a. 8 ad 1m.
[41] Report. I, d. 36, q. 1, n. 5-7.

[42] Sum. Theol. I, q. 14, a. 5.
[43] Loc. cit.
[44] Sum. Theol. q. 14, a. 6, ad 1m.

because they flow from His essence, or because they are determined by a decree of His will; and so a knowledge of them in their causes is sufficient. But the same does not hold true of contingent things. For as St. Thomas points out: " Whoever knows a contingent effect in its cause only, has merely a conjectural knowledge of it "; but divine knowledge is not conjectural — it is infallible. Hence, " God knows all contingent things not only in their causes, but also as each one is actually in itself." [45]

In this connection the difficult question suggests itself, how does God know these contingent things in themselves? St. Thomas answers: " Although contingent things become actual successively, nevertheless God knows contingent things not successively, as they are in themselves, as we do; but He knows them all at once; because His knowledge is measured by eternity, as is also His existence; for eternity existing all at once comprises all time. Hence all temporal things are present to God from eternity, not only in such wise that He has the ideas of all things before Him, as some say; but because His glance is carried from eternity over all things, as they are in their presentiality. Consequently, it is manifest that contingent things are infallibly known by God, in as much as they are subject to the divine sight in their presentiality; still they are really future contingent things in relation to their own proximate causes." [46]

Substantially the same answer is given by St. Bonaventure, who says that all things are present to God, not according to the truth of their existence, but in reference to perfect cognition; and the reason of this intimate presentiality is that God's eternity comprises in the indivisible *now* all succession of time.[47]

However, this presentiality by itself does not seem to solve the difficulty, since it must always be held that the divine essence is the primary object of cognition. For how can that essence represent a future event that flows from a free cause? In other words, what is the ultimate reason of the eternal

[45] Ibid. a. 13.   [46] Ibid.   [47] In Sent. I, d. 35, dub. 6.

presentiality of contingent events to the divine intellect? No explicit answer is given by any of these writers, but they all seem to fall back upon some kind of divine causality in reference to the events in question. Thus St. Thomas says that " God knows all things apart from Himself in so far as He is their cause ";[48] and St. Bonaventure holds that the divine will, fully known, is a sufficient reason for His knowledge of all other things.[49] Similar statements are found in the works of Albertus Magnus[50] and Alexander of Hales.[51] Of course, this causality may be conceived as identical with the divine *concursus,* necessarily postulated for every finite action; but modern writers are not agreed in their interpretation of the old Scholastic teaching on this point.

The position of Scotus in this respect is not altogether clear. He is not satisfied with the explanation given by St. Thomas and St. Bonaventure, but postulates for the divine cognition of future contingent events a decree of futurition. The divine essence, he maintains, represents all things, in so far as they are future, in virtue of a determination of the divine will.[52] Some Scotists, like Mastrius,[53] interpret this decree of futurition to be merely concomitant, but others look upon it as antecedent to the action of the finite cause. And this, it seems, Scotus really had in mind; for he says: " It may be assumed that the divine intellect represents simple ideas, the combination of which is contingent in its actual existence; or that it represents a combination of ideas, which is still indifferent with regard to its actuality: and then the will, selecting one part or combination of ideas for actuation at a given point of time, makes the event definitely true." [54] God has indeed a certain knowledge of contingent events antecedently to His decree of futurition, but that is only a phase of His knowledge of purely possible events. Contingent events are known as future solely in virtue of a determination

---

[48] Cont. Gent. I, c. 49, 65; Sum. Theol. I, q. 14, a. 11.
[49] Op. cit. d. 35, q. 2, a. 2 ad 4m.
[50] Sum. I, tr. 15, q. 60, m. 4.
[51] Sum. I, q. 23, m. 3, a. 4.

[52] In Sent. I, d. 39, q. unic. n. 23; d. 41, q. unic. n. 10; Report. d. 40, q. unica.
[53] Disp. Theol. I, d. 3, q. 3, a. 8.
[54] In Sent. I, d. 39, n. 23.

of the divine will, although that determination does not interfere with the free action of the finite agent.

This looks very much like the teaching of the later Thomists, yet it is different from it in one very essential point. Scotus, as appears from the whole trend of his philosophical teaching, was decidedly opposed to the *praemotio physica* which is inextricably bound up with the *decreta voluntatis Dei* of the Thomists. Hence the decree of futurition, as understood by Scotus, would seem to be limited to the *concursus,* although his words cited above imply more.

The Nominalists, who in regard to many other points develop the views of Scotus, regard divine cognition of future contingent events as an inscrutable mystery. Hence they content themselves with pointing to the infinite perfection of God's intellect, which in some way must be able to know all things, whether actual or purely possible.[55]

Finally, it may be added that although the Scholastics speak of God's knowledge as extending to all contingent future events, they do not explicitly consider the question of divine cognition in reference to conditionally free actions of the future. Consequently, they divide God's knowledge into knowledge of vision and knowledge of simple intelligence, without saying anything about the *scientia media* which played such an important part in later theological discussions. Still, they state or imply all the principles upon which that knowledge is founded.

2. *The Divine Will.*— As the divine intellect and cognition, so are also, according to the teaching of the Scholastics, the divine will and volition identified with God's essence. Similarly, as God's essence is the primary object of divine cognition, so is that same essence also the primary object of divine volition. Lastly, as God knows things apart from Himself, so does He also will things apart from Himself. Still, His knowledge is more extensive than His volition; for while He knows evil, He cannot will evil — that is, in the moral order.

The attributes reducible to the divine will, which here call

[55] Cfr. Gregory of Rimini, In Sent. I, d. 39, q. 2, a. 2.

for special consideration, are omnipotence and freedom. For it was chiefly in regard to these that there was some difference of opinion among the early Schoolmen.

(a) *Omnipotence.*—Like all others of these attributes, omnipotence is predicated of God in reference to His actions *ad extra.* His own interior life does not, properly speaking, come within the sphere of His power. He exists necessarily, in the sense that He is self-subsistence; and by His very essence He is one in nature and three in person. Hence it is only in regard to things apart from Himself that His power can be exerted in the strict sense of the term. And in this sense His power is co-extensive with His practical knowledge; so that whatever He knows to be operable by an infinitely perfect being, the same He has power to execute both in the physical and moral order of things. Now, in the physical order everything is operable that does not imply a contradiction in terms; and in the moral order, everything that is not opposed to God's sanctity. In respect of all this, therefore, God is called omnipotent.

God's omnipotence, as thus understood, was first called in question by Abelard, according to whom God can do only what He at some time or other actually does; because God can do only what it becomes Him to do, and whatever it becomes Him to do He does not fail to do.[56] Abelard was strongly attacked by William of Saint Thierry,[57] St. Bernard,[58] Robert Pulleyn,[59] and Hugh of St. Victor.[60] His error was condemned by the Council of Sens, held in 1140. In his *Second Apology* he retracted his statements and subscribed to the proposition: "I believe that God cannot do anything that is not in harmony with Himself, but that He could have done many other things than those which He has done."

Omnipotence, as is obvious, may be viewed under a twofold aspect: First, absolutely, as it is in itself, without refer-

[56] Introd. ad Theol. III, c. 5; cfr. Theol. Christ. 5.
[57] Disp. adv. Abelard. c. 6; ML. 180, 266.
[58] Ep. 190, 5.
[59] Sent. I, n. 16.
[60] De Sacr. I. p. 2, c. 22; Sent. tr. I, c. 14; Didasc. VII, c. 2.

ence to any decree of the divine will; and so viewed it is called *potentia absoluta*. Secondly, relatively, in reference to certain divine decrees, by which it is restricted in its operation; and in this sense it is termed *potentia ordinata* or *ordinaria*. By His *potentia absoluta* God could have decreed to establish a different order of things from that which He did establish; but having once decreed to establish this particular order, His *potentia ordinata* is limited in its operation by the scope of His decree.

This distinction is taken account of by all the early Scholastics, but they do not all make the same application of it in their reasoning on God's operations *ad extra*. Thus St. Thomas emphasizes God's wisdom as a directive norm of His power,[61] while Scotus admits no other norm than the divine nature itself.[62] In the theological system of St. Thomas, as is well known, it is the intellect that holds the primacy among attributes and faculties; whereas in the theology of Scotus this primacy is assigned to the will. The reasoning of St. Thomas, that in command and execution intellect and wisdom must ever be regarded as a directive norm, Scotus tries to refute by saying: "The divine will, which is the first rule of all that is operable and of all actions, and the action of the divine will whence the first rule is derived, constitute the first rectitude. . . . But whatever does not include a contradiction is absolutely not repugnant to the divine will, and therefore whatever God does or effects is by that very fact right and just." [63] Hence Scotus places a much greater emphasis upon the *potentia absoluta* than does St. Thomas, though not to such an extent as to make God's actions arbitrary. For they must always be in harmony with the sanctity of the divine nature.

This view of Scotus in reference to the *potentia absoluta* was taken over by the Nominalists and carried to its last extreme. Not only could the historical facts of God's world-plan have been different, as all Scholastics admitted, but the

---

[61] Sum. Theol. I, q. 22, a. 3; ibid. q. 19, a. 4.

[62] In Sent. IV, d. 49; Report. I, d. 10; Quodl. q. 16.

[63] Report. IV, d. 46, q. 4.

same must be said of what belongs to ethics and morality. Thus Ockam writes: *Odium Dei, furari, adulterari, . . . quantum ad esse absolute in illis actibus, . . . etiam meritorie possent fieri a viatore, si caderent sub praecepto divino, sicut nunc de facto eorum opposita cadunt sub praecepto divino.*[64] This teaching is only one short step removed from the blasphemous utterance of Calvin, that " God not only foreknew the fall of the first man and the ruin of his descendants, but ordained the same by an act of His sovereign will." [65]

(b) *Freedom of the Divine Will.*— The common teaching of the early Scholastics in reference to the freedom of God's will is thus formulated by St. Thomas: " The divine will has a necessary relation to the divine goodness, since that is its proper object. Hence God wills His own goodness necessarily, even as we will our own happiness necessarily." . . . But " since the goodness of God is perfect and can exist without other things, in as much as no perfection can accrue to Him from them, it follows that His willing things apart from Himself is not absolutely necessary. Yet it can be necessary by supposition; for supposing that He wills a thing, then He is unable not to will it, as His will is not mutable." [66] Hence God's will is not free in reference to its primary object, which is His own goodness; but it is free in respect of its secondary object, which includes all creatures in so far as they are expressions of His goodness in their being and actions.[67] This freedom, of course, does not suppose passive indifference on the part of God; nor does it extend to what is morally evil, except by way of permission.[68]

Scotus conceives the freedom of God's will in a somewhat different way. He distinguishes in God an essential and a contingent liberty. The former consists in the power of self-determination and of dominion;[69] the latter is a volitional indifference, not in respect of divine volition itself, but with regard to its objects or effects.[70] In view of this distinction

---

[64] In Sent. II, q. 19, litt. O.
[65] Instit. III, c. 21, n. 7.
[66] Sum. Theol. I, q. 19, a. 3.
[67] Cfr. Bonavent. In Sent. II, d. 25, p. 2, q. 1, 2, 3; d. 45, a. 2, q. 1.

[68] Thomas. op. cit. q. 19, a. 5, 9; Bonavent. op. cit. d. 45, a. 3, q. 1, 2.
[69] Report. I, d. 10; Quodl. q. 16.
[70] In Sent. I, d. 39, n. 21, 22.

he holds that God wills or loves freely, not only His creatures, but also His own nature and purely possible entities. With this difference, however, that His love of Himself proceeds from His essential liberty only, whilst His inefficacious complacency in purely possible entities, and His efficacious complacency in His creatures — past, present, and future — proceed both from His essential and contingent liberty. God's essential liberty is perfectly compatible with the necessity of willing and loving Himself, though this necessity excludes the liberty of contingence or contradiction.[71] In some respects, this view is a development of the teaching of St. Bonaventure on the freedom of immutability as predicated of the divine will.[72]

The will of God in reference to creatures and their actions, is usually divided by the Scholastics into the will of good pleasure or complacency and the will of expression — *voluntas beneplaciti et voluntas signi*.[73] The former is the divine will taken in its proper sense; the latter is attributed to God by way of metaphor and comprises the various outward manifestations of the divine will. These manifestations are commonly summed up as prohibition, precept, counsel, operation, and permission. Thus St. Thomas, after explaining how these " five expressions of will are rightly assigned to the divine will," concludes: " Or it may be said that permission and operation refer to present time, permission being with respect to evil, operation with regard to good. Whilst as to future time, prohibition is in respect to evil, precept to good that is necessary, and counsel to good that is of supererogation.[74]

God's will of good pleasure or complacency was also distinguished by these writers into antecedent and consequent — *voluntas antecedens et voluntas consequens*.[75] Antecedent and consequent, in this connection, is a denomination that is taken, not from the will itself, but from the different condi-

---

[71] Quodl. q. 16; In Sent. III, d. 32, n. 2, 5.
[72] In Sent. I, d. 8, p. 1, a. 2, q. 1, 2.
[73] Halens. Sum. I, q. 36, m. 1; Thomas, In Sent. I, q. 1, a. 4; Sum.

I, q. 19, a. 11; Albert. Sum. I, tr. 20, q. 80.
[74] Sum. I, q. 19, a. 12.
[75] Halens. op. cit. I, q. 36; Thomas, Sum. I, q. 19, a. 6 ad 1m.

tions of the object of divine volition. This distinction was already frequently made use of by Patristic writers, in their efforts to uphold and explain the universality of God's salvific will. Thus St. John Damascene writes: " Antecedently God wills all men to be saved; for, as He is good, He did not create us for punishment, but that we might share in His goodness. However, as He is just, He wills that sinners be punished. The first will, therefore, is called antecedent and of good pleasure, and this proceeds from Himself; but the second is called consequent and permissive, and this is conditioned by our own action." [76] The Scholastics made a similar application of this distinction when treating the question of predestination and reprobation, as will be set forth in another chapter.

The nature of God and His attributes, which forms the subject-matter of this and the preceding chapter, is thus defined by the Fourth Lateran Council, held in 1215: " We firmly believe and sincerely confess that there is one sole true God, eternal, immense and immutable, incomprehensible, omnipotent and ineffable, . . . one essence, substance, or nature, altogether simple." [77]

[76] De Fide Orth. II, c. 29; ML. 94, 970.
[77] Mansi, 22, 982; DB. n. 428.

CHAPTER III

PREDESTINATION

PREDESTINARIAN CONTROVERSY: TEACHING OF THE SCHOLASTICS

As predestination consists in a divine decree which ordains the direction of rational creatures to their appointed end, theologians usually investigate this difficult question in connection with their treatises on the intellect and will of God. It is not the most logical order that could be adopted, for thus the fact of creation and elevation must be presupposed; but as it will serve our present purpose sufficiently well, there appears no need of rearranging what has the sanction of long usage. Hence in this chapter we shall give a brief review of both the historical and theological aspect of the chief points involved in the question of predestination.

A — PREDESTINARIAN CONTROVERSY

Predestination became a matter of controversy as early as the fifth century, owing to certain statements of St. Augustine which were interpreted as implying that God predestined some men to eternal punishment by refusing to give them sufficient grace for the working out of their salvation.[1] The Semi-Pelagians of Southern Gaul took up these statements and endeavored to show that they were out of harmony with the accepted universality of God's salvific will. At the same time a certain Lucidus, a priest of the diocese of Riez, openly taught that God predestined some men to hell as He predestined others to heaven, and that neither the one class nor the other could do aught to shape their eternal destiny. His

---

[1] Cfr. vol. I, p. 379 sqq.

teaching was condemned by the Council of Arles, held in 473. The teaching of St. Augustine remained meanwhile somewhat uncertain, but his friend St. Prosper gave the following interpretation of it in regard to the reprobate: " Of their own will they went out; of their own will they fell, and because their fall was foreknown, they were not predestined (to eternal life) ; they would however be predestined if they were to return and persevere in holiness. Hence God's predestination is for many the cause of perseverance, but for no one the cause of falling away." [2]

The controversy was revived towards the middle of the ninth century by Gottschalk, the son of a Saxon nobleman. While still a child he had been received as an oblate in a monastery at Fulda, and when arrived at man's estate he was refused permission to return to the life of a secular. Somewhat later he was transferred to a monastery at Orbais, in the diocese of Soissons. There, brooding over his uncongenial life, he sought consolation in the study of St. Augustine's teaching on predestination. The result of his studies is embodied in these three propositions: First, God predestines some men to eternal damnation in the same way that He predestines others to eternal life. Second, God's salvific will extends only to those who are saved. Third, Christ did not die for all men, but only for the predestined.

The first of these three points, which implicitly contains the other two, is clearly set forth in his *Chartula Professionis,* drawn up in 848.[3] However, in his *Confessio Prolixior,* composed in the following year, occurs the sentence: " I confess that Thou hast foreknown all future things, whether good or evil, but that Thou hast predestined only what is good." [4] Hence he certainly did not hold that God had predestined the reprobate to commit sin.

[2] Resp. ad Cap. Gall. 12.

[3] The profession reads: "Ego Gotteschalcus credo et confiteor . . . quod gemina est praedestinatio, sive electorum ad requiem, sive reproborum ad mortem. Quia sicut Deus incommutabilis ante mundi constitutionem omnes electos suos incommutabiliter per gratuitam gratiam suam praedestinavit ad vitam aeternam, similiter omnino omnes reprobos, qui in die judicii damnabuntur propter ipsorum mala merita, idem ipse incommutabilis

Protestants usually contend that Gottschalk's view on reprobation was solidly based upon the writings of the Fathers. Thus St. Fulgentius, they point out, uses the expression *predestinatio sive praeparatio ad poenam;*[5] and St. Isidore of Seville speaks of a twofold predestination, that is, a predestination of the elect to eternal life and of the reprobate to everlasting death.[6] Again, St. Augustine, they contend, suggests quite definitely that Christ died only for the elect.[7] However, aside from a certain similarity of the terms employed, the contention has no value. Thus St. Augustine states very clearly: *Pro omnibus passus est Christus,* for all men did Christ suffer.[8]

In itself, of course, the twofold predestination — *gemina praedestinatio* — may be understood in an orthodox sense, in as much as God not only predestines the elect to eternal life, but also predestines the reprobate to everlasting death by way of punishment for their sins. It is not here that the difficulty lies. For so long as He gives sufficient grace to all, and only decrees eternal punishment for those who culpably fail to coöperate with the grace that is given them, there is nothing arbitrary or unjust in His action. Predestination of the reprobate to the torments of hell becomes unintelligible only when it is taken independently of their evil deeds; or, as modern theologians express it, when it is held to be *ante praevisa demerita.* And this appears to have been the view of Gottschalk. For he says that God predestines the reprobate in precisely the same way as the elect — *similiter omnino* —; and the elect, according to him, are predestined *ante praevisa merita.*

At all events, this was the interpretation put upon his teaching by Hincmar, archbishop of Rheims, under whose presidency the Council of Quiercy, held in 853, condemned the views advanced and defended by Gottschalk. And the same

Deus per justum judicium suum incommutabiliter praedestinavit ad mortem merito sempiternam" (ML. 125, 89 sqq.).
[4] Ibid. 121, 349 D.

[5] De Verit. Praedest. 3, 5, 8; ML. 65, 656.
[6] Sent. 2, 6, 1; ML. 83, 606.
[7] In Ps. 64, 2.
[8] Serm. 304, 3.

position was taken by Rabanus Maurus of Mayence,[9] Amala-rius of Metz,[10] and Scotus Erigena.[11] Gottschalk himself was sentenced to lifelong imprisonment in the monastery of Hautvilliers, where after twenty years of futile efforts to re-gain his liberty he died apparently unrepentant.

Hincmar's views on the subject of predestination, which were adopted by the Council of Quiercy,[12] involve the follow-ing points: Through the sin of Adam the whole human race was lost, yet God desired all to be saved. Hence (a), in ac-cordance with His foreknowledge, He chose from this mass of perdition — massa perditionis — those whom through His grace He predestined to life; while He foreknew that the rest, whom by the judgment of His justice He left in the same mass of perdition, would perish forever. Yet He did not predestine them to perish; but because of His justice He de-creed for them eternal punishment. (b) The freedom of the will in regard to supernatural actions, which had been lost through sin, was restored by Christ; consequently, assisted by grace, we all have the power to do good, but when deserted by grace, we are capable only of doing evil. (c) God has the sincere will to save all men. (d) Christ died for all without exception.[13]

Meanwhile many other bishops and theologians had been drawn into the discussion, and not a few of them defended Gottschalk's thesis on the twofold predestination. The most eminent among these latter were Ratramnus of Corbie,[14] Servatus Lupus of Ferrieres,[15] Prudentius of Troyes,[16] Remigius of Lyons,[17] and Magister Florus.[18] It must be noted, however, that the point at issue had been considerably modified as compared with the statement of Gottschalk that God predestined the elect and the reprobate in precisely the same way. The discussion now turned about the propriety of terms rather than about the doctrine itself. For both parties admitted that God decreed eternal punishment for the

[9] ML. 112, 1530 sqq.
[10] ML. 121, 1054.
[11] ML. 122, 347 sqq.
[12] Mansi, 14, 920 D sqq.
[13] Mansi, 14, 920 D sqq.

[14] ML. 121, 13 sqq.
[15] Ibid. 119, 606 sqq.
[16] Ibid. 115, 971 sqq.
[17] Ibid. 121, 985 sqq.
[18] Ibid. 119, 95 sqq.

reprobate only in view of their evil deeds; but while Ratramnus and his side affirmed that this decree must be called predestination, Hincmar and his followers contended that the term as used in this connection was inappropriate. Hence, while the one side defended the *gemina praedestinatio,* the other rejected it as inadmissible.[19] The former appealed, among others, to the authority of St. Augustine.[20]

In 855, the party opposed to Hincmar held a synod at Valence, and severely criticized the decisions given at Quiercy. These decisions are said to be inept, useless, harmful, and opposed to the truth. Emphasis is placed upon the fact that God foreknows the future actions of men, that He foresees how the good will coöperate with His grace and be saved, and how the wicked will follow their own evil counsels and be lost.[21] But by this divine foreknowledge, it is pointed out, the free will of man is in no wise interfered with. Hence, if the wicked are lost, it is not because they were unable to lead virtuous lives, but because they freely persevered in evildoing.[22]

With regard to the redemption by Christ, the Synod es-

[19] Retramnus sets forth his views in the following terms: "Sicut enim novit (Deus) opera singulorum, id est, electorum et reproborum, sic quoque nec numerum eorum ignorat. Quapropter is qui singulorum actus intuetur, qui finem aspicit universorum, qui novit quid singulis retribuat, jam apud se praedestinatum habet, quid ex eis sit acturus, et qui in fine gloria regni donentur vel qui poenarum supplicio feriantur" (De Praedest. 8; Mansi, 121, 13).

[20] Thus Ratramnus: "Hac sententia ostendit venerabilis Augustinus malos propter iniquitatem superbiae damnationi praedestinatos, non ad peccatum, quoniam peccatum, non est a Deo. Neque enim auctor mali est Deus, poenae vero redditio ex Deo est" (Ibid.).

[21] The decision of the Council reads as follows: "Fidenter fatemur praedestinationem electorum ad vitam, et praedestinationem impiorum ad mortem: in electione tamen salvandorum misericordiam Dei praecedere meritum bonum: in damnatione autem periturorum meritum malum praecedere justum Dei judicium. Praedestinatione autem Deum tantum statuisse, quae ipse vel gratuita misericordia vel justo judicio facturus erat" (DB. 322).

[22] The Council states its view in these terms: "Verum aliquos ad malum praedestinatos esse divina potestate, videlicet ut quasi alius esse non possint, non solum non credimus, sed etiam si sunt, qui tantum mali credere velint, cum omni detestatione, sicut Arausicana synodus, illis anathema dicimus" (Ibid. 322).

tablishes the following three points: First, Christ did not die for those who were already condemned to eternal punishment at the time of His passion. Second, all those who are at any time baptized and incorporated into the Church, were truly redeemed and obtained the forgiveness of their sins. Third, some of these latter may fall away and be eternally lost, while others are saved by reason of their free coöperation with the grace of God.[23]

At the suggestion of Charles the Bald, Hincmar next explained his position in the treatise *De Praedestinatione,* which is now lost; and three years later in a similar work entitled, *Posterior Dissertatio de Praedestinatione,*[24] in which he defends his view as formulated at the Council of Quiercy. Thereupon, the matter was again discussed at the National Synod of Savannierres, but without definite results. Finally the Synod of Toucy, in 860, commissioned Hincmar to compose a synodal letter, which was to be directed to all the faithful of France, so as to counteract the religious disturbances that had been occasioned by the discussions of the last few years. In this letter the *Capitula of Quiercy* were approved, and thus Hincmar's party carried the day. It was inevitable that, in spite of local opposition, this result should finally be reached; because Hincmar's view coincided with the traditional teaching of the Church.

Thereafter the term *gemina praedestinatio* was set aside, and in its stead were used *praedestinatio* and *reprobatio* as referred respectively to the elect and the reprobate. Thereby all confusion of ideas was avoided, and so peace was restored to the theological world. Incidentally it may be noted here, although the matter did not form a part of the discussion at the time, that most of the men engaged in the controversy regarded predestination to eternal life as absolute, that is, *ante praevisa merita.* In the order of execution merit must indeed come first; but in the order of divine decrees election of certain individuals to eternal life takes precedence, and thereupon follows the bestowal of efficacious graces from

---

[23] Ibid. 321, 324.　　　　　　[24] ML. 125, 55 sqq.

which merit results through the free coöperation of the human will. Hence the Synod of Valence makes the unqualified statement: *In electione tamen salvandorum misericordiam Dei praecedere meritum bonum.* Another statement of the same Synod, namely, that Christ did not die for all, was corrected in the sense that God sincerely desired the salvation of all men, even after Adam's fall into sin.[25]

B — Teaching of the Scholastics

It was in this condition that the Scholastic theologians found the doctrine of predestination when they began to systematize the theological teaching of preceding ages. They developed it considerably, but mostly along lines of subordinate importance. The solution of the real difficulty connected with predestination lay beyond the reach of even their giant intellects. Nor could it be otherwise; for when all is said, only God knows why He deigns to save the one and suffers the other to perish. The following brief outline of Scholastic teaching on the subject of predestination will suffice for our purpose. In presenting this outline we shall follow the chronological order, as that will enable us to notice more readily what development took place.

The first theologian to be considered in this connection is St. Anselm, who sets forth his views in a work entitled, *De Concordia Praescientiae Dei cum Libero Arbitrio.* In the first part of this treatise he endeavors to show that the eternal and infallible prevision of God does not interfere with the actions of man's free will, while in the second part he brings his conclusions to bear upon predestination. He sums up the result of his inquiry in regard to this latter point as follows: " Just as foreknowledge in God, which is not deceived, does not foreknow anything else than the truth precisely as it will be in its future existence, flowing either from a necessary or free cause; so in like manner does predestination, which is not changed, not predestine anything else than what is contained in God's foreknowledge. And as that which is fore-

[25] Cfr. Hinkmar, De Praedest. c. 26.

known, although unchangeable in its eternal prevision, may nevertheless admit of change in time before it comes to pass; so it is also with regard to predestination." [26]

This obviously makes the final status of free beings, as foreknown and fore-ordained by God, dependent upon their own free actions under the influence of divine grace. Hence, according to St. Anselm, both predestination and reprobation follow upon God's prevision of each one's merits or demerits; so that both are *post praevisa merita*. In this sense the author uses the term predestination in reference to the reprobate as well as to the elect; for he says: "It must be understood that there is not only a predestination of the good, but also of the wicked; just as God is said to cause evil, not that He really causes it, but He permits it to come to pass. For He is said to harden a person's heart when He does not soften it, and to lead some one into temptation when He does not free him therefrom. It is therefore no impropriety of language when God in this manner is said to predestine the wicked, and also their evil deeds, since He does not correct the one or impede the other. But He is said in a special sense to foreknow and predestine what is good, because He effects that it is good; in regard to what is evil, on the other hand, He is indeed the cause of its physical entity, but not of its being evil.[27]

Peter Lombard follows closely in the footsteps of St. Augustine, and states the problem in this way: "Predestination bears reference to all that is connected with salvation, and is said of men who are to be saved. For as St. Augustine says: Predestination signifies the preparation of grace, which is impossible without foreknowledge on the part of God. However, foreknowledge is possible without predestination. By predestination indeed God foreknew what He would do at any future time; but He also foreknew what He would not do, that is, all the evils that ever come to pass. He predestined those whom He had chosen; but the others He reprobated, that is, He foreknew the eternal death of

---

[26] Op. cit. c. 3. [27] Ibid. c. 2.

sinners." [28] Hence the author seems to regard reprobation as a simple passing by on the part of God when He chose His elect.

The effects of predestination have a bearing upon both the good and the bad; but in a different way, as is thus explained by the author: "While predestination is the same as the preparation of grace, that is, a divine election by which God chose before the foundation of the world whomsoever it pleased Him to choose; reprobation, on the contrary, must be understood as a divine foreknowledge of the wickedness of some, and as a preparation of eternal punishment for their evil deeds. For just as the effect of predestination is the grace by which we are justified in the present life, and are enabled to live virtuously and to persevere in good; so reprobation on the part of God, who from all eternity rejected some by not choosing them, has a twofold effect, one of which He foreknew and did not prepare, that is, their wickedness; the other He foreknew and prepared, namely, their eternal punishment." [29]

Developing the subject still further, the author finally comes to the conclusion that the predestination of the elect is without any merit of theirs, while the reprobation of the wicked is consequent upon their iniquity as foreknown by God. He sums up in these terms: "Just as predestination on the part of God is, properly speaking, God's foreknowledge and His preparation of divine favors, by reason of which the elect are most certainly saved; so reprobation on the part of God is the same as His foreknowledge of the never ending wickedness of some, and the consequent preparation of everlasting punishment. And as the effect of predestination is the bestowal of grace, so in a manner the effect of eternal reprobation seems to consist in the obduration of the sinner. Not that God effects this obduration by the causing of malice, but rather by not bestowing His grace; as indeed they are not worthy to receive it." [30]

Alexander of Hales examines the question of predestina-

---

[28] Sent. I, d. 40, n. 1.   [29] Ibid. n. 4.   [30] Ibid. n. 4.

tion under a threefold aspect. First he inquires what the name itself imports; next he tries to determine the formal concept of predestination; lastly he investigates what it is in itself — *secundum rem.* The name, he says, imports two things: priority and destination. By reason of priority, predestination is eternal; under the aspect of destination it is a divine decree in reference to some good that is to be conferred in time. Considered in its formal concept, predestination is in the order of divine knowledge of good pleasure or approbation — *in genere scientiae beneplaciti sive approbationis.* In itself it is the preparation of grace for the present and of glory for the future.[31]

Hence, predestination necessarily implies an act of foreknowledge and an act of the divine will. The relation of these two acts is thus explained by the author: " Divine knowledge is the same with regard to all men: the divine will by itself is also the same in regard to all: but the divine will in conjunction with foreknowledge is not the same in respect to all men. However, this is not owing to any difference that results in the divine foreknowledge from the aforesaid conjunction; but it arises from the fact that we are not all in the same condition as known by God. Hence, predestination does not stand for the will of God alone, but for the will as guided by foreknowledge of the use which men will make of His gifts. Consequently, as John Damascene remarks, we must distinguish two wills in God: one that is antecedent and another that is consequent. By His antecedent will God wills all men to be saved; for this will regards the rational creature as capable of salvation: but by His consequent will, which is guided by His foreknowledge of the use which rational creatures will make of His gifts, He does not will all men to be saved, but only the elect. And in this sense the will of God is said to be rational; for if He willed the final salvation of one who abused his freedom of choice, He would not be just." [32]

Then examining the question whether a person's merits

---

[31] Sum. I, q. 28, m. 1, 2, 3.   [32] Ibid. q. 28, m. 2.

are the cause of his predestination, he comes to this conclusion: "The terms predestination and reprobation signify several different things. For in predestination is included not only foreknowledge, but also grace and glory, which are the effects of predestination. So too are there three things to be considered in reprobation: foreknowledge, present wickedness, and future punishment. Hence, when we find it stated in the writings of saints that predestination and reprobation depend on the merits of the persons in question, we must make this distinction. If predestination be considered precisely as it is in God, it is not caused by the merits of those who are predestined; but if it be considered as it is in the persons themselves, it is the result of their merits. However, even in this latter case there is a difference between predestination and reprobation. For predestination, in so far as it is in God or signifies the bestowal of grace, is not of merit; but it is of merit only in so far as the conferring of final glory comes in question. Now in reprobation the matter is different: for there we have the act of reprobation itself as it is in God, the present iniquity of the sinner, and his future punishment. The first of these is not caused by the demerits of the reprobate, since it is identified with God's essence; but the other two are caused by these same demerits." [33]

St. Bonaventure repeats this reasoning of his master almost word for word, and makes it his own.[34] Then he proceeds to show that the fact of predestination and reprobation does not interfere with the freedom of man's will in regulating his moral conduct. He sums up in these terms: "The divine foreknowledge is of such a kind that God knows from all eternity what each one of us is able to think and to will, and together with this He sees in what direction our choice lies, and what manner of works we perform in the course of our lives. And because He sees all this together, what we can accomplish, what we actually choose, and what we do; hence it is that He cannot be deceived. Consequently, as

[33] Ibid. q. 28, m. 3.
[34] In Sent. I, d. 40, a. 1, q. 1; q. 41, a. 1.

predestination includes divine foreknowledge, it must be in conformity with our free will." [35]

Finally, touching the heart of the mystery, namely, why God elects one to eternal life and passes by the other, he says: " Care must be taken lest, while we desire to exalt the will of God, we rather dishonor it. For if there were no reason why He chose the one and not the other, except that it so pleased Him, there surely would be nothing hidden about the divine judgments; on the contrary, all would be manifest, since every one can understand that reason. Nor would the divine judgments be in any way wonderful, but merely arbitrary. Consequently, it must be held, as St. Augustine points out, that the eternal decree of predestination and the divine will are most reasonable, and are based upon the best of reasons; and as they are from all eternity, so too is there for them an eternal reason — not as regards the act itself in God, but in respect of its term in the creature. . . . And this may be shown by an example. Thus if it be asked, why does God wish that it should rain in winter rather than in summer, the answer is: Because in winter there is a greater abundance of watery vapor than there is in summer. In a similar way, if it be asked, why did God wish that Peter should be saved rather than Judas, we answer: Because Peter gathered merits for heaven, but Judas laid up punishment for hell." [36]

Albertus Magnus gives substantially the same exposition as the preceding two. " By His antecedent will," he says, " God wills the salvation of all men. . . . But by His consequent will, which takes account of our deeds, He wills the good to be saved and the wicked to be condemned. And this is the will that reference is made to in the definition of predestination; for it is by this that He wills only the good to be saved, because they alone are pleasing to Him." [37] And again: " Two things are to be noted: divine foreknowledge of those who are to be saved and the will of God predestinating just so many to salvation. This will of God has regard

---

[35] Ibid. d. 40, a. 2, q. 1.
[36] Ibid. d. 41, a. 1, q. 2.

[37] Sum. I, tr. 16, q. 63, a. 2, 1.

to our works, because He wills to save as many as make a good use of His grace, and not more; but if more were to make a good use of that same grace, then He would also from all eternity have willed that they should be saved." [38]

St. Thomas first shows that it belongs to the providence of God to direct created beings toward their proper end, and then points out that predestination is a part of Providence. He reasons in this way: "The end towards which created things are disposed by God is twofold: one that exceeds all proportion and faculty of created nature; and this end is life eternal, consisting in the beatific vision, which is above the nature of every creature. The other end is proportionate to created nature, and this end created beings can attain according to their natural powers. To that, however, which a creature cannot attain by the power of its own nature, it must be directed by some one else; thus an arrow is shot by the archer towards a mark. Hence, properly speaking, a rational creature, capable of eternal life, is led towards it, as it were, directed by God. The reason of that direction pre-exists in God; as in Him is the plan of the order of all things towards an end, which we proved above to be Providence. The plan of something to be done, existing in the mind of the doer, is a certain pre-existence in him of the thing to be done. Hence the plan of the above-mentioned direction of a rational creature towards the end of life eternal is called predestination. For to destine, is to direct or send. Thus it is clear that predestination, as regards its object, is a part of Providence." [39]

As predestination is a part of Providence, it is, properly speaking, "not anything in the person predestined; but only in the person who predestines. . . . It is a kind of plan of the ordering of some persons towards eternal salvation, existing in the divine mind. The execution, however, of this order is in a passive way in the predestined, but actively in God." [40] And as it is in God, predestination is from all eternity, although its effects belong to time. [41] Neither grace nor glory come into the definition of predestination, as some-

[38] In Sent. I, d. 40, a. 11.   [40] Ibid. a. 2.
[39] Sum. Theol. I, q. 23, a. 1.   [41] Ibid. a. 2 ad 3ᵐ.

thing belonging to its essence; but they are related to it as effect to cause and object to act.[42]

To the predestination of the just corresponds the reprobation of the wicked. This too is a part of Providence. For to Providence it belongs to permit certain defects in those things which are directed towards their end. " Thus, as men are ordained to eternal life through the providence of God, it likewise is part of that providence to permit some to fall away and be lost. This is called reprobation. . . . Therefore, as predestination includes the will to confer grace and glory; so also reprobation includes the will to permit a person to fall into sin, and to impose the punishment of damnation of account of that sin." [43] However, " reprobation acts quite differently in its causality from predestination. This latter is the cause both of what is expected in the future life by the predestined — namely, glory — and of what is received in this life — namely, grace. Reprobation, on the other hand, is not the cause of what is in the present — namely, sin; but it is the cause of abandonment by God. And so too is it the cause of what is assigned in the future — namely, eternal punishment. But guilt proceeds from the free will of the person who is reprobated and deserted by grace." [44]

The predestination of some and the reprobation of others necessarily implies election on the part of God. He chooses some whom He will save, and passes by others whom He suffers to be lost. From this, however, it must not be inferred that He does not sincerely desire the salvation of all men. In this connection the author brings in the distinction between the antecedent and consequent will of God. " God wills all men to be saved by His antecedent will, which is not to will absolutely but relatively; but not by His consequent will, which is to will absolutely." [45]

St. Thomas considers the relation of merit to predestination under the heading, whether God's foreknowledge of future merits is the cause of predestination. After rejecting several obviously false views, he answers with this distinc-

---

[42] Ibid. a. 2 ad 4m.
[43] Ibid. a. 3.

[44] Ibid. a. 3 ad 2m.
[45] Ibid. a. 4 et ad 3m.

tion: "We must say, therefore, that the effect of predestination may be considered in a twofold light — in one way,
in particular; and thus there is no reason why one effect of
predestination should not be the reason or cause of another;
a subsequent effect of a previous effect, as regards the final
cause; and the previous of those that follow, as regards the
meritorious cause, which is reduced to the disposition of the
matter; as if we were to say that God preordained to give
glory on account of merit, and that He preordained to give
grace to merit the glory. In another way, the effect of predestination may be considered in general. And so considered,
it is impossible that the whole of the effect of predestination
should have any cause as coming from us; because whatsoever is in man disposing him towards salvation, is all included under the effect of predestination; even the preparation for grace. For neither does this happen otherwise than
by divine help, according to the Prophet Jeremias: 'Convert us, O Lord, to Thee, and we shall be converted.' Yet
predestination has in this way, in regard to its effect, the goodness of God for its reason; towards which the whole effect of
predestination is ordained as to an end, and from which it
proceeds as from its first moving principle." [46]

From this it is quite obvious that according to St. Thomas
predestination in its adequate sense is not caused by the merits
of the predestined. Nor is any other view possible; because
considered adequately, predestination includes all graces, even
the first, and without grace no one can merit. On the other
hand, it is equally obvious that according to St. Thomas predestination in an inadequate sense, in so far as it signifies the bestowal of graces subsequent to the first and of final glory,
may be merited. And this he teaches in many other places,
as for instance in his *Commentary on the Sentences*, where
he says: "In regard to final glory, predestination is in the
order of distributive justice, and therefore we may say that
God gives glory to this one and not to that one, because the
former merited it and the latter did not; and in like manner
does He will that this one should have glory and the other

[46] Ibid. a. 5.

should not, because this one was worthy and the other was not." [47] Many Thomists, however, refer all this exclusively to the order of execution, while on the other hand they limit predestination to the order of intention, and thence they conclude that St. Thomas taught predestination *ante praevisa merita*.[48]

In regard to the reprobate, St. Thomas makes some statements from which it has been inferred that he held negative reprobation. Thus he says: " God wills to manifest His goodness in men; in respect of those whom He predestines, by means of His mercy, by sparing them; and in respect of others, whom He reprobates, by means of His justice, in punishing them. This is the reason why God elects some, and rejects others. . . . Why He chooses some for glory, and reprobates others, has no reason; except the divine will." [49] And again: " Although anyone reprobated by God cannot acquire grace, nevertheless that he falls into this or that particular sin comes from the use of his free will. Hence it is rightly imputed to him as guilt." [50]

Others, however, contend that all these statements refer to positive reprobation, which follows upon the prevision of sin. And this they prove from the author's own teaching. Thus he states quite clearly: " As far as in Him lies, God is ready to give grace to all; for He wills that all should be saved and come to a knowledge of the truth. And those only are deprived of grace who put an obstacle in its way; and this is imputed to them as guilt, just as in the case of a person who shuts his eyes while the sun is shining and thereby causes some harm to follow: he is guilty by his own action, although without the sunlight he cannot see." [51] Again: " It must be held that those conditions by reason of which man fails to attain his end, and under which God does not will him to be saved, are of man's own making, and therefore all that follows is imputed to him as a sin." [52]

Duns Scotus takes a somewhat different view of predes-

---

[47] Op. cit. I, d. 41, q. 1, a. 4 ad 2m.
[48] Cfr. Gotti, I, tr. 6, q. 3.
[49] Sum. Theol. I, q. 23, a. 5 ad 3m.
[50] Ibid. a. 3 ad 3m.
[51] Contra Gent. III, c. 159.
[52] In Sent. I, d. 46, q. 1, a. 1 ad 5m.

tination. He is above all concerned about safeguarding the liberty of God to ordain what He pleases. This is entirely in harmony with the superiority of the will as compared to the intellect, both in the divine and the created order of things. Hence he is inclined to favor predestination *ante praevisa merita*.[53] But he staunchly defends the freedom of the' human will in regulating its own choice. He also contends that sufficient grace is given to all,[54] and that no one is cast off by God except in view of final impenitence.[55] After trying to refute the opinion of Henry of Ghent, which is substantially the same as that of St. Bonaventure noted in a preceding paragraph, he concludes in these terms: "Therefore, lest one in his search of these deep matters plunge beyond his depth, it is better for him to choose that opinion which finds greater favor with him, making certain, however, that through it divine liberty suffer no injustice and that God's bounty in preëlecting be given just play. Should one make choice of any other view (than the one here proposed), he must meet the difficulties which have been urged against it." [56]

In regard to other points more or less intimately connected with predestination there was hardly any difference of opinion among the Scholastics. Thus all are agreed that no one can be certain of his being among the predestined, unless he receives a special divine revelation to that effect.[57] They are also agreed that predestination is unchangeable, and that therefore no one of the predestined can ever be lost.[58] However, this does not make prayers and good works useless; because it is only they that can make our salvation certain, as on account of them salvation is ultimately conferred.[59] According to the more common opinion the number of the predestined is absolutely fixed by God, so that when this number is actually saved the world will come to an end.[60] What this number is, no one can tell. St. Thomas speaks of it as fol-

[53] In Sent. I, d. 41.
[54] Ibid. q. 46, n. 3.
[55] Ibid. d. 41, n. 11.
[56] Ibid.

[57] Cfr. Thomas, In Sent. I, q. 23, a. 1 ad 4m.
[58] Sum. Theol. q. 23, a. 6.
[59] Ibid. a. 8.
[60] Ibid. a. 7.

lows: "Concerning the number of all the predestined, some say that so many men will be saved as angels fell; some, however, so many as there were angels left; others, in fine, so many as the number of angels who fell, added to that of all the angels created by God. It is, however, better to say that to God alone is known the number for whom is reserved eternal happiness, as the prayer for the living and dead expresses it." [61]

[61] Loc. cit.

CHAPTER IV

THE BLESSED TRINITY [1]

All that is essential in the doctrine of the Blessed Trinity was already clearly taught in the Patristic age — the unity of the divine nature, the trinity of persons, the generation of the Son, the procession of the Holy Spirit, and the nature of the divine hypostases as *relationes subsistentes*.[2] On these points the East and the West were in full doctrinal agreement, although in course of time a difference arose in regard to the *principium quod* in the procession of the Holy Spirit.[3] When the Scholastics began their great work of doctrinal synthesis, the Church's teaching on this fundamental mystery of the Christian faith was almost fully developed, so that little remained to be done save along the lines of properly co-ordinating the different parts of the doctrines. However, along with this, there were a number of subordinate points that admitted of still further development, and these were investigated and discussed by nearly all the theologians of the Middle Ages. The following brief review of mediæval teaching on the mystery of the Blessed Trinity will be sufficient to bring out what is of special interest to the history of dogmas.

1. *Existence of the Mystery.*— In order to prove the truth that in the unity of the Godhead there are three persons, the Scholastics use two distinct series of arguments, one of which is drawn from Holy Scripture and tradition, and the other from the principles of natural reason. The former series is regarded by them as absolutely conclusive, so that the truth thus established is held to be of faith; whilst the latter is

[1] Cfr. Schwane, Histoire des Dogmes, t. IV, p. I, c. 2; De Regnon, Etudes sur la Trinite, t. II, III; Hefele, Conciliengeschichte, V.
[2] Cfr. vol. I, p. 260 sqq.
[3] Ibid. p. 490 sqq.

looked upon as having only suasive force, confirming in a manner by reason what is already known by revelation. The truth in question is, therefore, by all of them considered as a mystery in the strict sense of the term — a truth, that is, whose existence cannot be discovered by unaided reason, and whose intimate nature cannot be understood even when its existence is made known by revelation. It is in this sense that St. Thomas writes: " By natural reason we can know what belongs to the unity of essence, but not what belongs to the distinction of persons. Whoever, then, tries to prove the trinity of persons by natural reason, derogates from the faith." [4] And St. Bonaventure: " The trinity of persons can in no way be known by reasoning from the creature to God." [5] Even Abelard, who frequently speaks of this mystery as if it were a natural truth, explicitly states that the arguments drawn from reason cannot produce supernatural faith, but can only make the teaching of faith more acceptable.[6]

2. *Errors of Some Early Scholastics.* — The very concept of the Trinity, according to the teaching of the Church, implies not only distinction of persons, but also numerical identity of nature. This last point was denied by Roscelin, canon of Compiègne, who towards the end of the eleventh century taught in that city, and also at Besançon and Tours. His own writings, with the exception of a letter to Abelard,[7] have not been preserved, but his teaching on the point in question can be gathered from the refutation of it by St. Anselm,[8] Abelard,[9] John of Salisbury,[10] and Otto of Freising.[11]

Being a Nominalist in philosophy, he logically maintained that the idea of person can be realized only in an individually existing nature, distinct from all others of its kind, not only in personality, but also in substance. Hence he argued: " If there are in God three persons and only one substance (*una res*), and not three substances, each one separately by

---

[4] Sum. Theol. I, q. 32, a. 1.
[5] In Sent. I, d. 3, p. 1, q. 4.
[6] Introd. ad Theol. II, c. 3.
[7] Opp. Abelard. t. II, ed. Cousin.

[8] De Fide Trin. c. 1.
[9] Ep. 21.
[10] Metalog. II, 17.
[11] De Gest. Fred. I, c. 47.

itself, even as in the case with three angels or three souls, yet in such a manner that they are altogether the same by way of power and will, then the Father and the Holy Spirit have become incarnate together with the Son." [12] And again: "Whoso says that the Father is the Son, and that the Son is the Father, as he necessarily must if he holds that the three names signify the same substance, he confounds the persons. For all names of one and the same individual thing are predicated of one another. . . . The substance of the Father is nothing else than the Father, and the substance of the Son is nothing else than the Son, even as the city of Rome is Rome and the creature of water is water. Hence as the Father begot the Son, the substance of the Father begot the substance of the Son. Hence as the substance of him who begets is one and the substance of him who is begotten is another one, the one must be different from the other; . . . and therefore we cannot avoid making a separation in the substance of the Holy Trinity." [13]

This teaching, which is tritheism pure and simple, was condemned by the Council of Soissons (1093), which had been convened by Archbishop Raynold of Rheims. Roscelin retracted his error under the pressure of popular indignation, but shortly after he relapsed, as appears from his letter to Abelard. There he cites a large number of extracts from the writings of the Fathers, all of which, he contends, show that Christian antiquity never understood God to be only one being, numerically one nature subsisting in three persons. His error was thoroughly refuted by St. Anselm in his work *De Fide Trinitatis,* which was primarily written for that purpose.

About the same time Abelard fell into error by going to the other extreme, in as much as he seemed to identify the three divine persons with the attributes of power, wisdom, and goodness. In his *Introductio ad Theologiam,* he states the problem in this way: Christian faith teaches that there is only one God — not several gods — one Lord of all, one

---

[12] Cfr. Anselm, De Fide Trin. c. I. [13] Ep. ad Abelard., op. cit. p. 799, 800.

Creator, one Principle, one Supreme Good. Hence the two questions: What distinction is there between the three persons in the one divine nature? How is the trinity of persons compatible with the unity of nature?

He answers: The names of the three persons seem to express the perfection of the Supreme Good. The name of Father stands for power, that of Son for wisdom, and that of Holy Ghost for goodness or love. These are three fundamental concepts of the Divine Being. In their unity and distinction consists the Trinity. This, however, must not be so understood that the Father only is power, the Son only is wisdom, and the Holy Ghost only is goodness; but these attributes are peculiar to the three persons respectively, and so are distinctive of the same. The Father is power, because He is the unbegotten and absolute principle; the Son is wisdom, because He is the Word; the Holy Ghost is love or goodness, because He is the fountain of divine grace: yet the Son and the Holy Ghost, though derived from the Father, are also power.[14]

Then, to illustrate his teaching by examples, he makes use of expressions and comparisons which caused him to be accused of Modalism. A piece of brass, he says, upon which an artist engraves the likeness of the king, is essentially the same as the image, and the image is essentially the same as the brass; yet they are distinct in their properties as metal and image. Something very similar to this we find in the Trinity. For even as the seal is of the brass and has in a certain sense its origin therein, so has the Son His being of the substance of the Father, and in so far is He begotten of the Father. Then, as regards the Holy Spirit, some ecclesiastical teachers indeed hold that He is also of the substance of the Father, in as much as He is of one substance with Him; but this is not strictly true. Because if it were true, it would follow that He was begotten by the Father and the Son, whereas He only proceeds from them.[15] Since, then, both the Son and the Holy Spirit are of the Father —

[14] Introd. ad Theol. I, 5–10.
[15] Ibid. II, 13, 16; cfr. Theol. Christ. IV.

the one begotten, the other proceeding — generation differs from procession in this, that He who is begotten is of the very substance of the Father, as it is in the nature of wisdom, that is, of being, that it should be a certain power; whereas the effect of love is classed as goodness rather than as power.[16]

The first one in France to oppose Abelard was William of St. Thierry, who was soon joined by St. Bernard, Hugh of St. Victor, and others. St. Bernard sums up the errors in question as follows: " *Denique constituit Deum Patrem plenam esse potentiam, Filium quamdam potentiam, Spiritum Sanctum nullam potentiam: atque hoc esse Filium ad Patrem, quod quamdam potentiam ad potentiam, quod speciem ad genus, quod materiatum ad materiam, quod hominem ad animal, quod aereum sigillum ad aes."* [17] These errors were condemned by the Council of Soissons (1121), and again by the Council of Sens (1141), which at the same time deprived Abelard of his license to teach.[18]

3. *Definition of Person.* — Early in the sixth century, Boethius had defined person as an individual substance of a rational nature — *Persona est naturae rationalis individua substantia.* Some of the early Scholastics found fault with this definition as applied to the three persons in the Godhead. Thus Richard of St. Victor argued, since the divine nature is an individual substance, it ought, according to the Boethian definition, be a person; yet this conclusion runs counter to the teaching of the Church. Hence to make the definition applicable to divine persons, it should be modified in this way: *Persona divina est divinae naturae incommunicabilis existentia* — a divine person is the incommunicable existence of the divine nature.[19] Alexander of Hales views the matter in practically the same light; hence he gives the following defintion: *Persona est existentia incommunicabilis intellectualis naturae vel existens per se solum secundum quemdam modum existendi.*[20] The same definition is later

---

[16] Introd. ad Theol. II, Martène, 1085.
[17] Tract. de Error. Abelard. c. 1, 2.

[18] Mansi, 21, 568; Hefele, V, 476.
[19] De Trin. IV, c. 22; cfr. c. 21.
[20] Sum. I, q. 56, m. 4.

on given by Scotus, who points out that incommunicability, taken as the *ratio formalis* of personality, implies not merely a negation of actual and aptitudinal communication, but a positive repugnance to the same; and therefore the concept of personality is not negative, but positive.[21]

However, the greater number of Scholastics accepted the Boethian definition, but in their application of it to the three divine persons they explained the two terms *substantia* and *individua*. The former term, they say, is taken in a general sense, prescinding from first and second, or singular and universal; whilst the other is added to restrict this general signification and at the same time to convey the idea of incommunicability.[22]

This more common view is thus expressed by St. Thomas: " In the opinion of some, the term substance in the definition of person stands for first substance, which is the hypostasis; nor is the term individual superfluously added, for as much as by the name of hypostasis or first substance the idea of universality and of part is excluded. For we do not say that man in general is an hypostasis; nor the hand, since it is only a part. But where individual is added, the idea of assumptibility is excluded from person; for the human nature in Christ is not a person, since it is assumed by a greater, that is, by the Word of God. It is, however, better to say that substance is here taken in a general sense, as divided into first and second, and when individual is added, it is restricted to first substance." [23]

4. *Principles of Divine Processions.*— According to the unanimous teaching of Patristic writers, the Son is begotten of the substance of the Father, and the Holy Spirit proceeds of the substance of the Father and the Son. In view of this teaching, Peter Lombard opens his treatise on the Trinity with the question, " Whether the Father begot the divine essence, or whether the divine essence begot the Son, or whether

---

[21] In Sent. I, d. 23, n. 4; ibid. III, d. I, q. I, n. 10.

[22] Halens. Sum. p. I, q. 56, m. 3; Bonavent. In Sent. I, d. 25, a. I, q. 2;

Thom. Sum. Theol. I, q. 29, a. I ad 2m; Albert. Magn. Sum. p. I, tr. 10, q. 44, m. 2.

[23] Sum. Theol. loc. cit.

the essence begot the essence, or whether the essence neither begot nor was begotten.[24] His answer is: " In full agreement with Catholic writers on this subject, we say that the Father did not beget the divine essence, nor did the divine essence beget the Son, nor did the divine essence beget the divine essence," [25] but the Father begot the Son, and the Father and the Son breathed forth the Holy Spirit.

This teaching was attacked by some of Peter's contemporaries, and among others by Abbot Joachim de Floris. He contended that thus there was a fourth term introduced into the Trinity, which would necessarily result in a quaternity. The contention was settled by the Fourth Lateran Council, held in 1215. The Council sustained the Lombard, whom it mentioned by name, and defined that the essence " is neither begetting, nor begotten, nor proceeding; but it is the Father who begets, the Son who is begotten, and the Holy Spirit who proceeds." [26]

Taking this definition as their starting point, all subsequent Scholastics held that the *principium quod* — that which begets or breathes — is not the divine essence as such, but as it is found in the persons concerned, or rather the persons themselves to whom the productive actions are attributed. But there remained the further question about the *principium quo* — the power by which the persons are constituted productive principles. Is this something absolute or relative? Peter Lombard had already pointed out that it could not be anything purely absolute, but must in some way include a relation — *posse generare dicit quid, sed secundum respectum ad aliquid.* Others, among them William of Auxerre and Durandus of Saint Pourçain, considered it to be something purely relative. In his *Summa*, St. Bonaventure pronounces this last view as more probable,[27] but in his *Prologus ad II Sent.* he declares himself in favor of the Lombard. This latter position is also taken by Albertus Magnus, who holds that the *potentia generativa* is something intermediate between what is essential and what is per-

[24] Sent. I, d. 5.
[25] Ibid.
[26] Mansi, 22, 982; DB. 431.
[27] D. 7, a. unic. q. 1.

sonal.[28] St. Thomas expresses the same view, when, after a somewhat lengthy disquisition on the point, he concludes: " And therefore the power of begetting signifies the divine nature directly, but the relation indirectly." [29] Finally, Scotus thinks that the different views on this subject may be brought into agreement, and that the chief difference consists in the terms employed.[30]

A further question is, what is the *principium quo* of the two divine processions in itself, and how does it differ in the generation of the Son and the procession of the Holy Spirit? Leaving aside the peculiar view of Richard of St. Victor, who looked upon divine love as the common source of the Son and the Holy Spirit, the unanimous answer of the Scholastics to this question is that the Son is begotten by way of nature or intellect, and that the Holy Spirit proceeds from the divine will. On this they are all agreed, but in their explanation of this answer there is manifest a considerable difference of views. Thus Alexander of Hales makes the act of the notional intellect merely concomitant to the fecundity of the divine nature. Hence he says: *Cum ergo dicitur, intelligendo generat, vel intelligere est speciem generare, intelligitur per concomitantiam.*[31] Very much the same view is taken by St. Bonaventure.[32] St. Thomas, on the other hand, places a special emphasis on the divine intellect. " Procession," he says, " always supposes action, and as there is a procession *ad extra* corresponding to the act tending to external matter, so there must be a procession *ad intra* corresponding to the act remaining within the agent. This applies most conspicuously to the intellect, the action of which remains in the intelligent agent. Whenever we understand, by the very fact of understanding there proceeds something within us, which is a conception of the object understood, a conception issuing from our intellectual power and proceeding from our knowledge of that object. This conception is signified by the spoken word, and it is called

[28] In Sent. I, d. 7, a. 2.
[29] Sum. Theol. I, q. 41, a. 5.
[30] Report. d. 7, q. 1.
[31] Sum. q. 42, m. 2.
[32] In Sent. I, d. 6, a. unic.

the word of the heart signified by the word of the voice." [33]
In this manner the Son " proceeds by way of intelligible action, which is a vital operation." [34]

Scotus adopts the terminology of St. Bonaventure, stating
that the divine processions are *via naturae* and *via voluntatis*.[35] In opposition to St. Thomas, he denies that the act
of simple cognition, even in so far as it connotes paternity,
constitutes the generation of the Son. That generation, he
contends, is logically posterior to cognition and proceeds from
the *memoria fecunda,* that is, from the intelligence already
in possession of its essential object.[36] Furthermore, whilst
St. Thomas holds that the Son proceeds from the intellect
in so far as it is expressive of all that is knowable,[37] Scotus
restricts the generative action of the intellect to its cognition
of the divine essence and attributes, including probably also
a quasi abstract cognition of the persons.[38]

There is a similar difference of views with regard to the
procession of the Holy Spirit. All are agreed that the Holy
Ghost proceeds by way of the will, and that this is a procession of love. St. Thomas describes it as follows: "We
must consider each procession similarly. For as when a
thing is understood by any one, there results in the intelligent
agent a conception of the object understood, which conception we call word; so when any one loves an object, a certain impression results, so to speak, of the thing loved in
the affection of the lover. And by reason of this the object
loved is said to be in the lover, as also the thing understood
is in the one who understands; so that when any one understands and loves himself he is in himself, not only by real
identity, but also as the object understood is in the one who
understands, and the thing loved is in the lover." [39]

Scotus admits this reasoning in so far as it affirms that
the Holy Spirit proceeds from an act of love, but he divides
that love into two formally distinct acts. The first follows

[33] Sum. Theol. I, q. 27, a. 1.
[34] Ibid. a. 2.
[35] In Sent. I, d. 2, q. 7, n. 18–33.
[36] In Sent. I, d. 2, q. 7, n. 2–16.

[37] Sum. Theol. I, q. 34, a. 3; cfr.
Cont. Gent. IV, c. 13.
[38] In Sent. I, d. 10; Report. I, d.
6, q. 2; In Sent. II, d. 1, q. 1, a. 2.
[39] Sum. Theol. I, q. 37, a. 1.

upon God's essential cognition and precedes both the generation of the Son and the procession of the Holy Spirit. The second corresponds to the *memoria fecunda* in the generation of the Word, and constitutes the active spiration which is common to the Father and the Son.[40] Moreover, God's love of Himself is both free and necessary. It is free in so far as it comes within the scope of God's power and dominion, and it is necessary in as much as its object is infinite.[41]

That the Holy Spirit proceeds both from the Father and the Son was conceded by all to be an article of faith, as it had been authoritatively inserted in the Creed at the beginning of the eleventh century.[42] On account, however, of the opposition of the Greeks, both St. Anselm and St. Thomas wrote special treatises in support of the doctrine. Moreover all were agreed that the Father and the Son constitute only one principle of spiration, yet so that there are said to be two persons of whom the act of spiration is predicated.[43] St. Thomas puts his explanation in this form: " If we consider the spirative power, the Holy Ghost proceeds from the Father and the Son as they are one in the power of spiration, which in a certain way signifies the nature with the property. . . . Nor is there any reason against one property being in two subjects that possess one common nature. But if we consider the subjects — *supposita* — of the spiration, then we may say that the Holy Ghost proceeds from the Father and the Son as distinct; for He proceeds from them as the unitive love of both." [44]

The teaching here set forth was thus defined by the Council of Lyons, held in 1274: " We profess that the Holy Spirit proceeds eternally from the Father and the Son, not as from two principles, but as from one principle, not by two spirations, but by one spiration. . . . But because some, through ignorance of the aforesaid irrefragable teaching, have

---

[40] Report. I, d. 6, q. 11.
[41] In Sent. I. d. 2, q. 7 ; Report. I, d. 10, q. 3 ; Quodl. 1, 16.
[42] Cfr. vol. I, p. 497.
[43] Cfr. Halens. Sum. p. I, q. 70, m. 3 ; Bonavent. In Sent. d. 11, a.

unic. q. 1, 2 ; Albert. Magn. In Sent. d. 11, a. 3, 4, 5 ; Henr. Gand. Sum. a. 54, q. 6 ; Thom. In Sent. d. 11, q. 1, a. 2 ; Scot. In Sent. d. 12, q. 1.
[44] Sum. Theol. I, q. 36, a. 4 ad 1m.

fallen into various errors, we, wishing to close the way to these errors, with the approval of the sacred Council, condemn and reprobate those who presume to deny that the Holy Spirit proceeds eternally from the Father and the Son; and also those who temerariously assert that the Holy Spirit proceeds from the Father and the Son as from two principles, and not as from one." [45]   A similar definition was given by the Council of Florence in 1439,[46] both definitions being occasioned by the attempted reunion of the Greek Church with the Holy See.

5. *Divine Relations.*— As there are processions in God, it necessarily follows that there are also divine relations. For, says St. Thomas, " when something proceeds from a principle of the same nature, then both the one proceeding and the source of procession agree in the same order; and then they have real relations to each other." [47]   Now as there are two processions in the Godhead, each involving a principle and a term, there must be four relations, two of origination and two of procession. The former two are paternity and spiration, the later filiation and procession.[48]   These relations are, on the one hand, really identified with the divine essence; yet, on the other hand, as relations they are really distinct from one another.[49]   Their real identity with the divine essence was affirmed by the Council of Rheims against Gilbert de la Porrée, who held that they were merely assistant or externally affixed to the nature of the Godhead; while their real distinction from one another is necessarily implied in the distinction of the persons. However in regard to both points there was some difference of views among the Scholastics, as there is among theologians to-day.

The first point is thus explained by St. Thomas: " It is manifest that relation really existing in God is really the same as His essence; and only differs in its mode of intelligibility, in as much as it imports regard to its opposite which is not expressed in the name of essence." [50]   Hence he holds a

---

[45] Mansi, 24, 81B; DB, 460.
[46] Mansi, 31, 765E; DB, 691.
[47] Sum. Theol. I, q. 28, a. 1.

[48] Ibid. a. 4.
[49] Ibid. a. 3.
[50] Ibid. a. 2.

virtual distinction, which is based upon the different modes of intelligibility as proper to the essence and the relations. St. Bonaventure conceives the matter in very much the same way, but he contends that the distinction is more than merely virtual. He calls it a distinction of attribution, in as much as the concept of relation adds to the concept of essence a regard to something else.[51] Scotus introduces here his formal distinction — *distinctio formalis ex natura rei*,[52] which, according to some, is only a logical development of the *distinctio attributionis* of St. Bonaventure. The Nominalists, on the other hand, rejected all virtual distinction, contending that essence and relations, as also all absolute perfections in the Godhead, are distinguished only mentally — *distinctione rationis ratiocinantis*. This view, which St. Bonaventure and Alexander of Hales attribute also to Praepositivus, Chancellor of the Paris University early in the thirteenth century, was rejected by all the other Scholastics. And, in fact, it cannot be admitted without destroying the foundation of the real distinction of the divine persons.

The second point at issue, that the relations are really distinct from one another, was held by all Scholastics outside the Nominalist School. It is precisely the relations that constitute the distinction between the divine persons. For according to the fundamental law of the Trinity, first definitely formulated by St. Anselm [53] and later formally approved by the Council of Florence, in the Godhead all perfections are identical save where there is relative opposition — *in divinis omnia sunt unum ubi non obviat relationis oppositio*.[54] The reason for the distinction is thus given by St. Thomas: " The idea of relation necessarily means regard of one to another, according as one is relatively opposed to another. So as in God there is real relation, there must also be real opposition: but the very nature of relative opposition includes distinction. Hence there must be real distinction in God; not, indeed, according to that which is

<hr/>

[51] In Sent. d. 26, a. unic. q. 1.
[52] In Sent. d. 2, q. 7, n. 41; Quodl. 5.

[53] Monol. c. 2.
[54] Decret. pro Jacob.; Mansi, 31, 1735D; DB, 703.

absolute — that is the essence, wherein there is supreme unity and simplicity — but according to that which is relative." [55]

6. *Divine Persons.*— That the Father, the Son, and the Holy Spirit are in a true sense divine persons, was accepted by the Scholastics as clearly contained in the teaching of the Church. This point had been firmly established by the great Fathers of the fourth century, and, in fact, had always been a matter of faith. Furthermore, that the divine persons are not something absolute but relative, was also admitted without controversy. In keeping with the teaching of St. Augustine, it was generally assumed that the persons in the Godhead are subsisting relations — *relationes subsistentes.* Hence St. Thomas writes: " Relation in God is not as an accident in a subject, but is the divine essence itself; and so it is subsistent, for the divine essence subsists. Therefore, as the Godhead is God, so the divine paternity is God the Father, who is a divine person. Therefore a divine person signifies a relation as subsisting. And this is to signify relation by way of substance, and such a relation is a hypostasis subsisting in the divine nature, although in truth that which subsists in the divine nature is the divine nature itself." [56]

However, as the divine relations may be viewed either in their origin or in themselves, the question arose, under what aspect are they constitutive and distinctive of the persons? Are the persons constituted and distinguished from one another solely by their origin, or by the relations themselves, or by the two together? On this point the Scholastics entertained different views.

Praepositivus and others, whose view appears acceptable to the Lombard, held the divine persons to be distinguished by their origin only, so that the relations must be regarded as mere manifestations of the distinction already presupposed. St. Bonaventure also approves of this view, although he modifies it somewhat before he makes it his own. The persons are distinguished, he says, by their origin *inchoative,* and by the relations *formaliter;* or, which comes to the same, they

[55] Sum. Theol. I, q. 28, a. 3.   [56] Ibid. q. 29, a. 4.

are distinguished by each separately, but only in so far as the
one includes the other.[57]

St. Thomas rejects the opinion of Praepositivus and his
followers " for two reasons: Firstly, because, in order that
two things may be understood as distinct, their distinction
must be conceived as resulting from something intrinsic to
both; as in created things it results from their matter and
form.   But origin of a thing does not designate anything intrinsic; it means the way from something or to something.
. . . Secondly, because the distinction of the divine persons
is not to be so understood as if what is common to them all
is divided, because the common essence remains undivided;
but the distinguishing principles themselves must constitute
the things which are distinct.   Now the relations or the properties distinguish or constitute the hypostases or persons, in
as much as they are themselves the subsisting persons; as
paternity is the Father, and filiation is the Son, because in
God the abstract and the concrete do not differ.   But it is
against the nature of origin that it should constitute hypostasis or person.   For origin taken in an active sense signifies
proceeding from a subsisting person, so that it presupposes
the latter; while in a passive sense origin, as nativity, signifies the way to a subsisting person, and as not yet constituting the person." [58]   Hence he concludes: " It is therefore
better to say that the persons or hypostases are distinguished
by relations rather than by origin." [59]

Scotus also rejects the opinion of Praepositivus, and holds
with St. Thomas that the divine persons are constituted and
distinguished by the relations.[60]   However, as he regards incommunicability, in which he places the formal reason of
personality, as something absolute, he holds that in so far
even the absolute properties may be considered as constituting the divine persons.[61]

The fact that there are only three persons in the Godhead
is, of course, an article of faith; for therein consists the

[57] In Sent. d. 26, a. unic. q. 3.   [60] In Sent. I, d. 26; Report. I, d.
[58] Sum. Theol. I, q. 40, a. 2.   2, q. 7.
[59] Ibid.   [61] In Sent. I, d. 26, n. 23–40.

mystery of the Blessed Trinity. But the Scholastics went beyond the mere fact and inquired into the reasons why there can be only three divine persons. Almost without exception, they find the explanation in the processions themselves. Only two processions are possible in the Godhead, because there are only two immanent actions in God from which divine processions can be derived — that of the intellect and will.[62] From these two processions there can result only three really distinct and subsisting relations, because real distinction between divine relations supposes relative opposition. This opposition is found between paternity and filiation, and between active and passive spiration. But active spiration is common to the Father and the Son, and hence, although it is a relation, it is not a personal property and therefore does not constitute a person. Consequently, there can be only three really distinct and subsisting relations — paternity, filiation, and procession; and these are respectively the Father, the Son, and the Holy Spirit.[63] Furthermore, as the acts of God's intellect and will are infinite, each procession necessarily exhausts the fecundity of its own principle, both proximate and remote.[64]

From the nature of the divine processions it necessarily follows that the three divine persons are at once really distinct, consubstantial, and intimately present to one another. This threefold consequence is usually expressed by the term *circumincessio;* or as modern usage seems to prefer, by the term *circuminsessio.* "In the divine order," says St. Bonaventure, "there is a perfect circumincession. And the meaning of circumincession is this, that one is in the other and conversely. Properly speaking and in its perfection, this can have place only in God; because circumincession implies both distinction and unity. And because in God alone is found the most perfect unity together with distinction — so that the distinction is without confusion and the unity with-

---

[62] Thom. Sum. Theol. I, q. 30, a. 2; Scot. Report. I, d. 2, q. 7: Quodl. q. 2; Albert. Magn. In Sent. I, d. 10, a. 12; Halens. Sum. I, q. 45, m. 7.

[63] Ibid.

[64] Cfr. Thomas, Sum. Theol. I, q. 41, a. 6: Scotus, Report. I, d. 2, q. 7; Quodl. q. 2.

out distinction — hence it is that in God alone perfect circumincession can be found. The reason of this is obvious; because the formal concept of circumincession implies identity of essence and real distinction of persons." [65]

St. Thomas uses somewhat different terms, but comes to substantially the same result. Answering the question, whether the Son is in the Father and conversely, he says: " There are three points of consideration as regards the Father and the Son: the essence, the relation, and the origin; and according to each the Son and the Father are in each other. The Father is in the Son by His essence, forasmuch as the Father is His own essence, and communicates His essence to the Son not by any change on His part. Hence it follows that as the Father's essence is in the Son, the Father Himself is in the Son; likewise, since the Son is His own essence, it follows that He Himself is in the Father in whom is His essence. . . . It is also manifest as regards the relations, each of two relative opposites is in the concept of the other. Regarding origin also, it is clear that the procession of the intelligible word is not outside the intellect, in as much as it remains in the utterer of the word. What also is uttered by the word is therein contained. And the same applies to the Holy Ghost." [66]

[65] In Sent. I, d. 19, p. 1, a. unic. q. 4.
[66] Sum. Theol. I, a. 42, a. 5.

CHAPTER V

CREATION OF THE WORLD

The Church's teaching on the origin of the world, like that on the mystery of the Blessed Trinity, was bequeathed to the Scholastics of the Middle Ages in an almost fully developed state. The absence of a material cause, the unity of the efficient cause, and the transcendence of the final cause of creation were as fully understood and as clearly demonstrated by the theologians of the Patristic period as by their successors during the golden age of Scholasticism. Much work still remained to be done by way of synthesis and proper evaluation of the various subordinate parts of the doctrine, but the doctrine itself stood in no need of further elucidation.[1]

Still on the very threshold of Scholasticism the doctrine of creation was attacked by a man who was perhaps the most original thinker of his time. This was John Scotus Erigena, *" vir per omnia sanctus, qui potuit errare, haereticus esse noluit."* Most probably a native of Ireland, he was towards the middle of the ninth century called to the court of Charles the Bald, where, besides being placed at the head of the palace school, he was asked by his royal patron to translate the works of Pseudo-Dionysius and of Maximus Confessor. Having accomplished this, he composed several original works, the most important of which is his treatise *De Divisione Naturae*. It is practically a reconstruction of Neo-Platonism, with little more than a mere veneering of Christian teaching. His views touching the origin of the world, as there expressed, are plainly pantheistic. God, he says, is the essence of all things, because He alone has existence in the true sense of the term. The being of all things is the supereminent being of the Godhead.[2] Hence when we hear it

---

[1] Cfr. vol. I, p. 284 sqq.   [2] Op. cit. c. 3.

said that God made all things out of nothing, we must not
understand this in any other sense than that God is in all
things, that is, He subsists as the essence of all things." [3]
Some have tried to interpret these and many similar expressions in an orthodox sense, but the whole trend of the book
militates against such an interpretation.[4]

However this teaching of Erigena found no followers in
the schools, except in that of Chartres, and there only indirectly and to a very limited extent. It is true, many of the
Scholastics, and among them St. Thomas himself, speak of
creation as a *processio vel emanatio creaturarum a Deo;* they
say that the universe proceeded from God even as a river
flows from its source, as a shadow is cast by the substance,
as an image is reflected in a mirror: but at the same time they
are careful to insist that God can in no sense be regarded
as the material cause of creatures, and that no reality passes
from the Creator into the created object. Even St. Anselm,
whose realism in philosophy might easily have led him into
error on this point, is a staunch defender of creation in the
strict sense of the term. He holds, indeed, that creatures
had a certain preëxistence in the mind and power of God,
but only in so far as the Creator is the exemplary and efficient
cause of all that exists. Before their creation all finite beings
were simply nothing in the order of their own reality — *non
erant quod nunc sunt, nec erat ex quo fierent.*[5]

The principal points to be considered in the Church's teaching on the origin of the world are the following: The creative act, the efficient cause, the exemplary cause, the final
cause, creation in time, creation and conservation.

1. *The Creative Act.*— The two definitions of creation
given by St. Thomas — creation is the production of being
as being, and, creation is the production of the whole substance of a thing, with nothing presupposed [6]— were, with
some slight verbal modifications, defended by all Scholastics.[7]

---

[3] Op. cit. c. 72.
[4] Cfr. W. Turner, The Irish
Theological Quarterly, October,
1910, p. 391–401.

[5] Monol. c. 8, 9; cfr. c. 3, 4.
[6] Sum. Theol. I, q. 44, a. 2; Ibid.
q. 65, a. 3.
[7] Cfr. Halens. Sum. p. II, q. 6, m.

The two definitions are essentially the same, and both emphasize the most fundamental concept of creation — the production of something from nothing, or of being from not-being.
This constitutes the specific difference between the creative
act and all other modes of production.   In creation there is
no transition from one mode of real being to another; there
is simply an inception of the reality itself in obedience to the
command of an omnipotent will.   As St. Bonaventure words
it: " The world was called into being, not only in its entirety,
but in respect of its intrinsic principles, which are not from
something else, but from nothing." [8]

St. Thomas, comparing creation to other modes of productions, describes it in this way: " We must consider not
only the emanation of a particular being from a particular
agent, but also the emanation of all being from the universal
cause, which is God.   Now what proceeds by particular
emanation, is not presupposed to that emanation; as when
a man is generated, he was not before, but man is made from
not-man, and white from *not-white.*   Hence if the emanation
of the whole universal being from the first principle be considered, it is impossible that any being should be presupposed
before this emanation.   For nothing is the same as no being.
Therefore as the generation of a man is from the *not-being*
which is *not-man,* so creation, which is the emanation of all
being, is from the *not-being* which is *nothing.*" [9]

The creative act has for its proximate principles the divine
intellect and will, the one as directive and the other as execu-
tive principle.   The ultimate principle is the divine nature,
with which the act itself is identified.   On this all Scholastics
are agreed, though with some slight shades of difference in
their views respecting the function of the intellect.   But on
two other points there was considerable difference of opinion,
namely, whether the creative act should be called immanent,
or transient, or a mere relation; and, whether the dependence

I, 2; Scotus, In Sent. II, d. I, q. 2;   [8] Loc. cit.
Bonavent. In Sent. II, d. I, p. I, a.   [9] Sum. Theol. I, q. 45, a. I.
I, q. I.

of the creature on the Creator must be conceived as something superadded to its being.

In answer to the first question, all state that the creative act is not transient in the sense that there is any change or imperfection in the Creator. Hence some call the act simply immanent; while others prefer to regard it as formally immanent and virtually transient, because whilst the action itself remains entirely in God, its term is placed *ad extra*.[10] St. Thomas words his explanation somewhat differently, although his view does not seem to differ materially from the second one here given. " Creation," he says, " places something in the being created according to relation only; because what is created is not made by motion or by change. For what is made by motion or by change is made from something preëxisting. And this happens, indeed, in the particular productions of some beings, but cannot happen in the production of all beings by the universal cause of all beings, which is God. Hence God by creation produces things without motion. Now when motion is removed from action and passion, only relation remains. . . . Hence creation in the creature is only a certain relation to the Creator as to the principle of its being." [11]

There was a similar difference of views with regard to the second question. Some there were who regarded the relation of the creature to the Creator as something really distinct from the created essence. This view is also taken by St. Thomas, who says that it is a relative accident superadded to the substance of the creature.[12] St. Bonaventure holds that it is really identical with the essence, but formally distinct from it as a relation.[13] Scotus, after a lengthy discussion of the point, comes to the same conclusion, holding that this is an instance where his *distinctio formalis ex natura rei* finds its proper application.[14]

---

[10] Cfr. Bonavent. loc. cit. a. 3, q. 2; Albert. Magn. Sum. I, tr. 13, q. 53, m. 2.

[11] Sum. Theol. I, q. 45, a. 3.

[12] In Sent. II, q. 1, a. 2 ad 4^m; De Potent. q. 3, a. 3 ad 3^m.

[13] In Sent. II, d. 1, p. 1, a. 3, q. 2.

[14] In Sent. II, d. 1, q. 2; Report. II, d. 1, q. 5, 6.

As creation is thus not a *processus physicus,* but simply an act of the divine will *ad extra,* God was free to create or not to create, to create this world or any other world, according to His own good pleasure. This was denied by Abelard, who contended that God was necessitated by His own goodness and perfection, not only to create, but to create the best possible world.[15]

This teaching of Abelard was immediately attacked by William of Saint Thierry, St. Bernard, and Hugh of St. Victor, and together with his many other errors was condemned by the Council of Sens. Alexander of Hales, discussing the matter of freedom in reference to the creative act, points out that God cannot be dependent on anything outside Himself, and therefore it follows that He was free in creating the world and in giving it what perfection He pleased; but having once decreed to call the world into being, the manner of accomplishing His work was most perfect.[16] Albertus Magnus distinguishes betwen the order of the universe as a whole and the perfection of individual creatures: in the former sense the world is most perfect, but not in the latter.[17]

The view of St. Thomas on this matter may be summed up as follows: In the first place, we must distinguish between the idea of the world in the mind of God and its realization in the order of things. The former has a necessary existence, since it is identified with God's essence; but the latter depends on God's free determination, since He is sovereignly independent of all that can have existence outside Himself. Then, as God creates by an act of His free will, He can communicate His goodness and perfections in whatever degree He chooses, and consequently create a world more

[15] He put his teaching in this form: "Necessario itaque Deus mundum esse voluit ac fecit, nec otiosus extitit, qui eum, priusquam fecit, facere non potuit, quia priusquam fecit, fieri eum non oportuit. Si enim prius fecisset, utique et prius eum fieri oportuisset, quia facere quidquam nisi opportunum non potest, immo nisi optimum, id est, tam bonum quantumcumque convenit, quod suo alto reservatur consilio" (Theol. Christ. V; cfr. Introd. ad Theol. III, c. 5).

[16] Sum. II, q. 21, m. 3, a. 1, 2.

[17] Sum. I, tr. 19, q. 77, m. 3, a. 1.

or less perfect according to His own good pleasure. Moreover, a world that could in no sense be more perfect, a *mundus absolute optimus,* would be a contradiction in terms.[18]

This careful analysis of the creative act, under all its different aspects, was at the time of great importance. For although the Neo-Platonic pantheism of Scotus Erigena had been condemned by the Church,[19] there was danger of a similar error finding its way into the schools through the Arabian philosophers, especially Avicenna (+1036) and Averroes (+1198), who were held in great esteem during the twelfth and thirteenth centuries. It was especially through a corrupted text of Aristotle that they propagated their pantheistic views. Postulating the existence of eternal matter, they at the same time explained the origin of the world by a series of emanations from the Supreme Intelligence, thus completely setting aside the idea of creation as contained in the teaching of the Church.[20] St. Thomas wrote special treatises to refute Averroes, but for all that he spoke of him with great respect and used his *Grand Commentary on Aristotle* as his model.

2. *Efficient Cause of Creation.*— That God is the author of all things, visible and invisible, is a truth that was defined by the First General Council. It was, moreover, fully explained and proved by many of the Fathers, especially St. Augustine, in their struggles against Manichaeism. In the early Middle Ages it was again denied by the Cathari, an heretical sect which under various names gained a strong foothold in France and Italy. In regard to creation they revived the Manichaean teaching that there are two First Principles, one being the author of what is good in the world, and the other of what is evil. They were condemned by several local synods, and finally by the Third and Fourth Lateran Councils. The latter thus defines Catholic teaching on the point in question: " We believe that there is one sole true God, . . . three persons indeed, but one essence, sub-

---

[18] Sum. Theol. I, q. 14, a. 8; q. 19, a. 4; q. 46, a. 6; q. 104, a. 3; QQ. DD. 3, a. 15.

[19] Mansi, 22, 1211.
[20] Cfr. Albert. Magn. In Sent. II, d. 1.

stance, or nature altogether simple, . . . one principle of all things, creator of all things visible and invisible, spiritual and corporeal, who by His omnipotent power, simultaneously with the beginning of time, created a twofold nature, spiritual and corporeal, namely, the nature of the angels and that of material things, and then human nature, which partakes of both, in that it consists of soul and body. For the devil and other demons were indeed good in their nature as created by God, but they made themselves bad by their own conduct; man sinned at the suggestion of the devil." [21]

The position of the Scholastics in this matter is clearly revealed by the following characterization of the Manichaean error by St. Bonaventure: "Every system of philosophy condemns the fundamental principle of this error — that there are two First Principles of things. For this being admitted, the order of the universe is destroyed and the power of God is limited; . . . and thence it follows that God is not God, and that there is nothing good." [22] In addition to this they pointed out that whatever is good in creatures comes from God, and what is bad results either from the limitation of finite natures or from the abuse of a created free will.[23]

As creation proceeds *ad extra,* the *principium quod* of the creative action is the whole Trinity, but so that there is only one Creator. St. Thomas explains this as follows: " To create is, properly speaking, to cause or produce the being of things. And as every agent produces its like, the principle of action can be considered from the effect of the action; for it must be fire that generates fire. And therefore to create belongs to God according to His being, that is, His essence, which is common to the three persons. Hence to create is not proper to any one person, but is common to the whole Trinity. . . . Nevertheless the divine persons, according to the nature of their procession, have a causality respecting the creation of things. For . . . God is the cause of things by His intellect and His will, just as a craftsman is the cause of things by his craft. Now the craftsman works

[21] Mansi, 22, 982; DB. 428.
[22] In Sent. II, d. 1, p. 1, a. 2, q. 1.
[23] Cfr. St. Thom. Sum. Theol. I, q. 49.

through the word conceived in his mind, and through the love of his will regarding some object. Hence also God the Father made the creature through His Word, which is the Son; and through His love, which is the Holy Ghost. And so the processions of the persons are the *rationes* of the productions of creatures in as much as they include the essential attributes, knowledge and will." [24]

What St. Thomas here says about the part of the persons in the creative act because of the processions, is denied by Scotus, who regards the essential attributes of intellect and will as the proximate principle of the creative act, in so far as they are common to the three persons. Hence the mode of all production *ad extra* is independent of the processions.[25]

In connection with their speculations on the efficient cause of creation, the Scholastics considered the subordinate question, whether God can make use of instrumental causes in the creation of things. All admitted that creative power is exclusively proper to God, and also that God did not employ instrumental causes in creating the world; but in regard to the possibility of it opinions were divided. Thus an affirmative answer was given by Peter Lombard and some others; [26] whilst Durandus contended that the impossibility of a creature acting as the instrumental cause of creation cannot be demonstrated by any conclusive argument, so long as there is question only of some particular effect.[27] The more common view, however, subscribed to by Alexander of Hales,[28] St. Bonaventure,[29] St. Thomas,[30] and Scotus,[31] denies that creative power can in any sense be communicated to creatures. The principal reason of this denial is based upon the nature both of instrumental causality and of the creative act. St. Thomas, refuting the opinion of the Lombard, puts his view in this way: " The secondary instrumental cause does not participate in the action of the superior cause, except as much as by something proper to itself it acts

[24] Ibid. q. 45, a. 6.
[25] In Sent. II, d. 1, q. 1, n. 19–23.
[26] Sent. IV, d. 5, n. 3.
[27] In Sent. II, d. 1, q. 4.

[28] Sum. p. 2, q. 9, m. 7, 8.
[29] In Sent. II, d. 1, p. 1, a. 2, q. 2.
[30] Sum. Theol. I, q. 45, a. 5.
[31] In Sent. IV, d. 1, q. 1, n. 28.

dispositively to the effect of the principal agent. . . . Now the proper effect of God creating is what is presupposed to all other effects, and that is absolute being. Hence nothing else can act dispositively and instrumentally to this effect, since creation is not from anything presupposed, which can be disposed by the action of the instrumental agent. So therefore it is impossible for any creature to create, either by its own power, or instrumentally, that is, ministerially." [32]

3. *Exemplary Cause of Creation.*— That God is the exemplary cause of all things created is the common teaching of the Scholastics. They usually treat the subject in connection with the question of divine ideas. " As the world was not made by chance," says St. Thomas, " but by God acting by His intellect, . . . there must exist in the divine mind that form to the likeness of which the world was made." [33] This form or idea is, of course, identical with the divine essence, but as it is in the divine mind it exhibits the various modes in which that essence may be imitated in creatures. St. Thomas explains this by saying: " The divine essence is not called an idea in so far as it is that essence, but only in so far as it is the likeness or type of this or that created thing. Hence ideas are said to be many, in as much as many types are understood by the self-same essence." [34] The substance of this explanation is admitted by all Scholastics, but there is among them a considerable difference of opinion concerning points of minor importance.[35]

4. *The Final Cause of Creation.*— The final cause of a thing, taking the term in the strict sense, is that which the agent intends to attain and by which he is moved to act. In this sense there can be no final cause of creation, as God can be moved to act neither by His own goodness nor by any good apart from Himself. But taking cause in a wider sense,

[32] Sum. Theol. I, q. 45, a. 5.
[33] Ibid. q. 15, a. 1.
[34] Ibid. a. 2 ad 1m.
[35] Cfr. Halens. Sum. p. 1, q. 23, m. 4, a. 1; Albert. Magn. Sum. p. 1,

tr. 13, q. 55, m. 2, a. 4; Bonavent. In Sent. I, d. 35, a. unic. q. 1; Scotus, In Sent. I, q. unic.; Durand. Sent. I, d. 36, q. 3.

as a sufficient reason for an end freely willed, the term is applicable to God in respect of His creative work. Not only did He ordain the attainment of His own extrinsic glory as the end to which all creation is directed, but He had a sufficient reason for willing this end. With the exception of Durandus,[36] all Scholastics are at one on the question so understood. And as such a sufficient reason they assign God's own goodness or glory — not to be acquired or increased, but to be manifested. As St. Thomas words it: " Every agent acts for an end; . . . but it does not belong to the First Agent, who is agent only, to act for the acquisition of some end; He intends only to communicate His perfection, which is His goodness; . . . Therefore the divine goodness is the end of all things." [37]

Subordinated to this primary end, and materially identified with God's extrinsic glory, is the utility and happiness of rational creatures. In this sense St. Bonaventure writes: " The principal end of things created is God's glory or goodness, rather than the utility of creatures. . . . Therefore on account of His own glory did He create — not, indeed, that He might augment His glory, but that He might manifest and communicate it; and in this manifestation and participation consists the highest good of His creatures, namely, their glorification and beatitude." [38] Six hundred years later the doctrine thus set forth was defined in almost identical terms by the Vatican Council.[39]

5. *Creation in Time.*— Whether the world existed from all eternity, or was created in time, was during the Middle Ages a very live question; because the disciples of Avicenna and Averroes, who followed in this the teaching of pagan philosophers, stood strongly for the eternity of the world, at least in its material substratum. The Scholastics, with the exception of Abelard, were agreed on two points: First, that the created world is not necessarily from all eternity; secondly, that this world was de facto created in time. The first conclusion they derived from the freedom of the creative act, which is by

---

[36] Sent. II, q. 2, a. 1.
[37] Sum. Theol. q. 44, a. 4.

[38] In Sent. II, d. 1, p. 2, a. 2, q. 1.
[39] Cap. 1, can. 5; DB, 1783, 1805.

its very nature independent of time as well as of material causes. The second they proved directly from revelation, although the majority held that the same conclusion could also be derived from the principles of reason, as brought to bear upon the world in its concrete reality.

But there was a third question involved, namely, the possibility of eternal creation. On this point a sharp controversy was carried on for many years. Alexander of Hales,[40] St. Bonaventure,[41] Albertus Magnus,[42] Henry of Ghent,[43] Richard of Middleton,[44] and the vast majority of Scholastics denied absolutely that eternal creation was possible; whilst St. Thomas,[45] Scotus,[46] Durandus,[47] Biel,[48] and many Nominalists held that the impossibility of eternal creation could not be demonstrated with any degree of certainty. Most of these latter, however, limited their discussion to beings that are not subject to motion or change. St. Thomas is usually interpreted as holding the possibility of eternal creation in regard to changeable beings as well.

The arguments commonly adduced to show the impossibility of eternal creation are of two kinds. First, the very nature of finite beings is such that they cannot be from all eternity. For their very finiteness involves succession, and whatever involves succession is temporal in its beginning.[49] Secondly, creation is a *productio ex nihilo,* so that being necessarily follows upon not-being, and therefore creatures cannot be co-extensive in duration with the Creator.[50]

St. Thomas examines these arguments very carefully, and then points out how they fail to prove the contention of the *Murmurantes.* The first argument, he says, would be conclusive in regard to changeable things, if it were evident that an infinite number is repugnant to reason; but as this is not

[40] Sum. p. 1, q. 12, m. 8; p. 2, q. 14, m. 1, a. 1; q. 9, m. 9.
[41] In Sent. II, d. 1, p. 1, a. 2, q. 2.
[42] Quodl. 1, q. 7.
[43] Sum. p. 2, tr. 1, q. 4, m. 2, a. 5.
[44] In Sent. II, d. 1, q. 3, a. 4.
[45] Cont. Gent. II, c. 18, c. 31–38; Sum. Theol. I, q. 46, a. 1, 2.

[46] Report. d. 1, q. 4; In Sent. II, q. 3.
[47] In Sent. II, d. 1, q. 4, a. 1.
[48] In Sent. II, d. 1, q. 3.
[49] Cfr. Albert. Magn. Sum. tr. 1, q. 1, a. 3.
[50] Cfr. Middl. In Sent. II, d. 2, a. 3, 1, 4.

evident, the argument has no force. The other contention, that in creation being follows upon not-being, rests upon the false supposition that this order of succession necessarily implies on the part of not-being priority of duration. This supposition is false, because priority of nature is quite sufficient to establish the required order of succession. Hence both arguments are inconclusive.[51]

With this reasoning Scotus was in full agreement, and in some ways even went beyond it, in as much as he held that reason cannot prove that the present world, with all its various changes, was created in time.[52] Subsequently most Thomists followed the teaching of St. Thomas on this point, but the greater number of theologians and philosophers preferred the view of Albertus Magnus and St. Bonaventure. The fact of creation in time or with time was defined by the Fourth Lateran, and more recently by the Vatican Council.[53]

6. *Creation and Conservation.*— There was also some difference of views on the nature of God's conservative action as distinguished from His productive act. All, indeed, admitted the fact and necessity of conservation; but whilst some regarded the conservative action of God as a mere continuation of His creative activity, others made a real distinction between the two. The matter is thus explained by St. Thomas: " As, then, it is impossible that the production of a thing should continue, when the action of the agent producing it ceases; so is it impossible that the being of the thing should continue, when the action of the agent ceases: for that action is not only the cause of the production of the thing, but of its being itself." [54] . . . " However, the conservation of things by God is not by way of a new action, but is a continuation of the action by which He gave existence to things; for that action is without motion and time, even as the conservation of light in the air is effected by a continued activity exercised by the sun.[55]

[51] Opusc. 22.
[52] Oxon. II, d. 1, q. 3.
[53] DB, 428, 1783.

[54] Sum. Theol. I, q. 104, a. 1.
[55] Ibid. a. 1 ad 4[m].

Alexander of Hales,[56] St. Bonaventure,[57] Albertus Magnus,[58] and Scotus[59] took practically the same view; but Henry of Ghent,[60] Durandus,[61] Richard of Middleton,[62] and others argued that if conservation and creation were not different actions in so far as they terminate at creatures, created beings would always be in a state of being produced, which is against common sense. As an ultimate reason for this conclusion they assign the fact that in created beings essence and existence are identified *in re,* and only *ratione* distinct.

[56] Sum. p. 2, q. 13, m. 3, 4.
[57] In Sent. II, d. 47, a. 1, q. 2.
[58] Sum. II, tr. 4, q. 3, m. 3, a. 2.
[59] In Sent. II, d. 2, q. 1, n. 3 sqq.

[60] Quodl. 10, q. 7; Quodl. 1, q. 9.
[61] In Sent. II, d. 1, q. 2.
[62] In Sent. II, d. 1, a. 2, q. 1-4.

CHAPTER VI

ANGELOLOGY

In their teaching on the angels, the Scholastics developed to a considerable extent what had been handed down to them in the writings of the Fathers. Yet, with the exception of a few points, all this development remained more or less a matter of speculation. Nothing has been defined in regard to the angels that was not already of faith before the end of the Patristic age. Their existence, their creation by God, the spirituality of their nature, the fact that some fell into sin and were lost, whilst others remained faithful and were saved; and the further fact that the fallen angels are bent upon bringing about man's ruin, whereas the good angels are appointed by Providence to be his faithful guardians — these points constitute the sum-total of the explicit teaching of the Church in reference to this part of God's creation. And all of these truths, except the spirituality of the angelic nature as now understood, were universally believed in the earliest ages of the Church. The Scholastics took these same truths as the starting points of their speculations and deduced from them conclusions of varying degrees of certitude. Some of the more important, together with the reasoning that led up to them, may here be briefly stated.

1. *Creation of the Angels.*— That the angels were created by God is usually touched upon only in connection with the question of creation in general. No special treatise was devoted by the Scholastics to this subject. Some, however, gave considerable space to the consideration of the subordinate question, at what particular time the angels were created. Nothing very definite had been established with regard to this point

by Patristic writers.[1] Nor did the Scholastics come to any general agreement, except that the angels were not created from all eternity. And this was defined by the Fourth Lateran, chiefly to counteract the growing influence of Averroism in Christian schools. St. Thomas states this point of doctrine as follows: " God alone, Father, Son, and Holy Ghost, is from eternity. Catholic faith holds this without doubt, and everything to the contrary must be rejected as heretical. For God so produced creatures that He produced them from nothing; that is, after there had been nothing." [2]

The more common opinion among the Scholastics was that the angels were created at the same time as the material universe. This view was based partly upon authority and partly upon reason. The authority specially appealed to was the statement of Holy Writ, that God " created all things together," [3] which expression was incorporated in the definition of the Fourth Lateran Council. However, neither Holy Scripture nor the Council seem to use the expression in reference to time. The principal argument from reason is thus stated by St. Thomas, in his answer to the question whether the angels were created before the corporeal world: " There is a twofold opinion on this point to be found in the writings of the Fathers. The more probable one holds that the angels were created at the same time as corporeal creatures. For the angels are part of the universe; they do not constitute a universe of themselves; but both they and corporeal natures unite in constituting one universe. This stands in evidence from the relationship of creature to creature; because the mutual relationship of creatures makes up the good of the universe. But no part is perfect if separate from the whole. Consequently, it is improbable that God, whose works are perfect, . . . should have created the angelic creature before other creatures. At the same time the contrary is not to be deemed erroneous; especially on account of the opinion of Gregory Nazianzen." [4]

2. *Elevation of the Angels.*— The only two points on which

[1] Cfr. vol. I, p. 293 sqq.
[2] Sum. Theol. I, q. 61, a. 2.
[3] Eccli. 18, 1.
[4] Sum. Theol. I, q. 61, a. 3.

all the Scholastics were agreed, as regards the elevation of the angels, are these: First, that they were all created for eternal happiness; secondly, that they had at least sufficient actual graces to merit heaven. On everything else widely different opinions were entertained. However, leaving aside the peculiar view of a few of the earlier Scholastics, all these opinions turn about the question whether the angels received sanctifying grace at the moment of their creation or some time later, after they had disposed themselves for its reception. The two different views held at the time are thus indicated by St. Thomas in his *Commentary on the Sentences:* " On this point there are two opinions: Some there are who say that the angels were not created in the state of grace, but of natural perfection only, and this opinion is the more common. Others, however, say that the angels were created in the state of grace. Which of these two views is the truer one, cannot be shown by any conclusive reason." [5] However he adds that the second view, according to which the angels were created in the state of grace, pleases him more, though without prejudice to the other.

The first opinion, that the angels were created in the state of natural perfection only, was defended by Peter Lombard,[6] Alexander of Hales,[7] Henry of Ghent,[8] St. Bonaventure,[9] Richard of Middleton,[10] and not a few others. The principal advocates of the other view, besides St. Thomas,[11] were Albertus Magnus,[12] Durandus,[13] and Dionysius the Carthusian.[14] Scotus considered both opinions as probable.[15]

Those who held that the angels were created in the state of merely natural perfection, rested their view chiefly on two principles: First, that rational creatures must dispose themselves, under the influence of God's special assistance, for the

---

[5] II. d. 4, q. unic. a. 3.
[6] Sent. II, d. 4.
[7] Sum. p. 2, q. 19, m. 2.
[8] Quodl. 8, q. 10.
[9] In Sent. II, d. 4, a. 1, q. 2.
[10] Sent. II, d. 4, a. 2, q. 2.
[11] In Sent. loc. cit.; Sum. Theol. I, q. 62, a. 3.

[12] In Sent. II, d. 3, a. 12; Sum. p. 2, tr. 4, q. 18, m. 1.
[13] In Sent. II, d. 4, q. 2.
[14] In Sent. II, d. 4, q. 2.
[15] In Sent. II et Report. d. 4, q. unica.

reception of sanctifying grace; secondly, that in the very act of being created such a disposition is impossible on the part of the creature. For the disposition must be positive, and for that there is need of free election, which necessarily presupposes actual existence. Hence at least one moment must elapse after the creative act, before sanctifying grace can be infused according to God's ordinary law of sanctification.

St. Thomas and his followers grant the first contention, but they point out that free election on the part of the creature may be simultaneous with creation. No priority of time is required in this matter, but only of nature; so that, at the very moment of its creation, the free will, supported by actual grace, turned deliberately to God as its supernatural end. The positive reasons for this second view are thus stated by St. Thomas: "Although there are conflicting opinions on the point, some holding that the angels were created only in a natural state, while others maintain that they were created in grace; it seems more probable, however, and more in keeping with the sayings of the Saints, that they were created in sanctifying grace. For we see that all things which, in the process of time, were produced by the work of Divine Providence, the creature operating under the direction of God, were produced in the first fashioning of things according to seedling forms, as Augustine says, such as trees, and animals, and the rest. Now it is evident that sanctifying grace bears the same relation to beatitude as the seedlike form in nature does to the natural effect; hence in the First Epistle of John (3, 9) grace is called the seed of God. As, then, in Augustine's opinion it is contended that the seedlike forms of all natural effects were implanted in the creature when corporeally created, so straightway from the beginning the angels were created in grace." [16]

On the further question, whether the fallen angels as well as those who remained faithful received sanctifying grace, there was likewise a difference of opinion, though not to the same extent as on the preceding point. All those who held

[16] Sum. Theol. I, q. 62, a. 3.

that the angels were created in the state or grace, gave an affirmative answer. Those, however, who favored the other opinion generally taught that Lucifer and his followers fell into sin before they had disposed themselves for the reception of sanctifying grace, and consequently never received that gift of God intended for all. This latter view has been set aside by most subsequent theologians.

3. *Nature of the Angels.*— Both the Fathers and the Scholastics are at one in teaching that the angels are spirits endowed with intellect and free will. However the term " spirit " was not by all of them taken in the same sense in which it is understood in this connection to-day. Not a few Fathers taught that the angels had bodies, which were composed of some kind of ethereal substance, ordinarily invisible to human eyes.[17] This view was taken over by many of the earlier Scholastics, whose teaching on the angels was little more than a restatement of what they found in Patristic writings. Rupert of Deutz,[18] St. Bernard,[19] and Peter Lombard [20] are quite definite on this point. Robert Pulleyn [21] and Hugh of St. Victor,[22] on the other hand, contended that the angels must be regarded as pure spirits.

During the first part of the thirteenth century this latter view became more common, possibly owing to the position taken by the Fourth Lateran Council. The doctrine was not directly defined, but as the Council divided all creatures into three classes — spiritual beings, beings composed of spirit and matter, and purely material beings — its mind on the point in question was made sufficiently clear. However the Franciscan school, represented by Alexander of Hales,[23] St. Bonaventure,[24] and Scotus [25] still continued to ascribe bodies to the angels, but in a somewhat different sense. Their position is most clearly explained by Scotus, who brought the theory to its last stage of development.

[17] Cfr. vol. I. p. 293 sqq.
[18] De Victoria Verbi, I, c. 28; ML. 169, 1262.
[19] Serm. 5 in Cant. n. 2; ML, 182, 790.
[20] Sent. II, d. 8.

[21] Sent. II, c. 2.
[22] De Sacram. c. 7.
[23] Sum. p. 2, q. 20, m. 2; q. 61, m. 1.
[24] In Sent. II, d. 3, p. 1, q. 1 et 2.
[25] De Rerum Principiis, q. 7, 8.

According to Scotus all created beings — angels, human souls, and material substances — are composed of potency and act. This potency, which he calls a *potentia passiva,* is material in its nature. It is of three kinds, designated respectively as *materia primo prima, secundo prima, tertio prima.* The *materia primo prima* is absolutely indeterminate, and is in a condition to be ultimately the foundation or subject of any form whatever. In material substances it receives the *forma corporeitatis,* and together with this constitutes the *materia secundo prima.* When still further determined by a specific form, either spiritual or material, the result is the *materia tertio prima,* which exists in the natural order of things as a complete substance, and is not further determinable except by accidental forms.[26]

Now it is the *materia primo prima* that enters into the composition of angels and of human souls. As it is thus not completed by the *forma corporeitatis,* neither angels nor human souls are corporeal; they are spirits, but at the same time they are composed of matter and form. Hence according to Scotus, and the same is true in respect of the others mentioned above, God alone is a pure spirit. All other beings are in one way or another fashioned out of matter by the hand of God.[27]

The more common view, however, which had as its chief advocates Albertus Magnus,[28] St. Thomas,[29] Henry of Ghent,[30] Durandus,[31] Ægidius Romanus,[32] and Dionysius the Carthusian,[33] was entirely in favor of the spirituality of the angels in the strict sense of the term. All these writers re-

[26] De Rerum Principiis, q. 7, a. 1, 2, 3.
[27] Thus all creation is closely bound together by the *materia primo prima,* as he himself describes it in the following passage: "Mundus est arbor quaedam pulcherrima, cujus radix et seminarium est materia prima, folia fluentia sunt accidentia; frondes et rami sunt creata corruptibilia; flos rationalis anima; fructus naturae consimilis et perfectionis natura angelica. Unicus autem hoc semi-narium dirigens et formans a principio est manus Dei" (Ibid. q. 7, a. 4, n. 30).
[28] Sum. tr. 1, q. 3, m. 3, a. 2; q. incid. 4.
[29] In Sent. II, d. 3, q. 1, a. 1; Sum. Theol. q. 50, a. 2; q. 75, a. 5; Cont. Gent. II, c. 50; De Spiritual. Creat. a. 1; De Substant. Separat. c. 5–8.
[30] Quodl. 4, q. 16.
[31] In Sent. II, d. 3, q. 1.
[32] In Sent. d. 3, p. 1, q. 1, a. 1.
[33] In Sent. II, d. 3, q. 1.

garded *materia prima* as a constitutive principle that is essentially limited to bodily substances. They did not admit the distinction between *materia primo prima* and *materia secundo prima,* and consequently destroyed the foundation upon which the Scotist reasoning was based. Their principle was : *Materia et forma dividunt substantiam materialem —* material substances, and material substances only, are composed of matter and form.

St. Thomas, after giving an exposition of the opinion held by the Arabian philosopher Avicebron, which is essentially the same as that of Scotus, refutes it in this way : " One glance is enough to show that there cannot be one matter of spiritual and of corporeal things. For it is not possible that a spiritual and a corporeal form should be received into the same part of matter, otherwise one and the same thing would be corporeal and spiritual. . . . It is, further, impossible for an intellectual substance to have any kind of matter. For the operation belonging to anything is according to the mode of its substance. Now to understand is an altogether immaterial operation, as appears from its object, whence any act receives its species or nature. For a thing is understood according to its degree of immateriality; because forms that exist in matter are individual forms which the intellect cannot apprehend as such. Hence it must be that every intellectual substance is altogether immaterial." [34] " In material things there is one thing which determines to a special grade, and that is the form; and another thing which is determined, and this is the matter; . . . whereas in immaterial things there is no separate determinator and thing determined; each thing by its own self holds a determinate grade of being." [35]

However, " although there is no composition of matter and form in an angel, yet there is act and potentiality." For " there still remains the relation of the form to its very existence, as of potentiality to act. And such a kind of composition is understood to be in the angels; and this is what some say, that an angel is composed of that *whereby he is*

[34] Sum. Theol. I, q. 50, a. 2.   [35] Ibid. a. 2 ad 1m.

and that *which is,* or *existence* and *essence,* as Boethius says.
For essence is the form itself subsisting; and existence is that
whereby the substance *is,* as the running is that whereby the
runner runs.   But in God *existence* and *essence* are not different. . . . Hence God alone is pure act." [36]

The discussion about the spirituality of the angels led to
another inquiry, namely, what is the relation of the angels to
place?   As they have no bodies, at least not in the strict sense
of the term, can they be said to be in a place?   To this question all Scholastics gave an affirmative answer, and St. Thomas
considered the contrary opinion as heretical.[37]   However, this
local presence is not circumscriptive, as is that of bodies; it
is a definitive presence, which is indeed limited to a certain
portion of space, but without correspondence of parts to parts.
The whole substance is in the whole place, and the whole is in
every part thereof.   This presence, moreover, the Scholastics
derive, not from the exigencies of the angelic substance itself,
but rather from the free ordination of the Creator.   As the
angelic substance is without extension, it is of its own nature
outside the category of space.   Hence its relation to place
must ultimately come from the will of God.[38]

On these several points there was hardly any difference of
views among the Scholastics; but on the further question, in
what precisely does this relation to place consist, opinions differed.   St. Thomas, with many others, held that it must be
reduced to an application of the angelic power.   Comparing
the local presence of angels to that of bodies, he says: " A
body is said to be in a place in such a way that it is applied
to it according to the contact of dimensive quantity; but there
is no such quantity in the angels, for theirs is a virtual one.
Consequently an angel is said to be in a corporeal place by
application of the angelic power in any manner whatever to
any place.   Accordingly there is no need for saying that an
angel can be deemed commensurate with a place, or that he
occupies a space in the continuous; for this is proper to a

[36] Ibid. a. 2 ad 3[m].
[37] In Sent. I, d. 37, q. 3, a. 1.
[38] Cfr. Albert. Magn. In Sent. I,

d. 37, a. 26; Scot. In Sent. II, d. 2,
q. 6; Bonavent. In Sent. II, p. 2, a.
2, q. 1.

located body which is endowed with dimensive quantity. In similar fashion it is not necessary on this account for the angel to be contained by a place; because an incorporeal substance virtually contains the thing with which it comes into contact, and is not contained by it; for the soul is in the body as containing it, not as contained by it. In the same way an angel is said to be in a place which is corporeal, not as the thing contained, but as somehow containing it." [39]

Scotus, on the other hand, favored the opinion defended by Richard of Middleton, that the formal reason of this presence in a particular place is neither the angelic substance nor its operation, but a sort of local simultaneity (*simultas*), even as the formal reason of the application of a body to a place is its circumscription.[40] This view also had a considerable number of advocates, but none of them give a clear exposition of what the *simultas* really is in itself.

4. *Knowledge of the Angels.*— With the exception of Durandus, William of Auxerre, and some Nominalists, the Scholastics were agreed that the angels know things apart from their own being by means of *species* or intellectual representations, and not directly by way of their own essence. As regards the origin of these *species* there was some difference of opinion. All admitted that the angels received infused knowledge of things at the moment of their creation, and that this knowledge consisted in the intelligible species of the things known. But whilst many held with St. Thomas that the angels are incapable of acquiring new intelligible species through their own intellectual activity, St. Bonaventure, Scotus, and others contended that the acquisition of such new species on the part of the angels must necessarily be admitted. The ultimate reason of this difference of views is based upon the difference of concepts in regard to the angelic nature, about which something was said in the preceding number. Presupposing that difference of concepts, the two views of angelic cognition may here be briefly stated.[41]

[39] Sum. Theol. I, q. 52, a. 1.
[40] In Sent. I, d. 37, a. 2, q. 1.
[41] Cfr. Halens. Sum. p. 2, q. 24, m.
2, 3; Bonavent. In Sent. II, d. 3, p. 2, a. 2, q. 1; Scotus, In Sent. II, d. 30, q. 10, 11; d. 9, q. 2; Thom. In

As St. Thomas holds that the angels are pure spirits, as was explained above, he establishes an absolute difference between angelic and human cognition. All human cognition is ultimately derived from sense perception, and the proper object of the human intellect is the essence of material things, considered in its universality and necessary predicates. Hence in man there is an active and a passive intellect. The active intellect abstracts the intelligible idea from the sensible representation of material things as contained in the phantasm, while the passive intellect receives the idea thus abstracted and expresses it immanently in the form of knowledge. On the other hand, the proper object of the angelic intelligence is wholly immaterial, being necessarily in the same order with the nature of the angelic substance. Hence in the angels there is no active intellect, nor can they abstract any intelligible species from the material world. But neither is there in them a passive intellect, in the sense that they are sometimes understanding only in potentiality the things which they naturally apprehend. Their knowledge is always actual, in virtue of the intelligible species of things which they received from God together with their intellectual nature; and it is the more universal in proportion as the perfection of their being is more exalted.[42]

In accord with these fundamental principles, St. Thomas outlines the contents of angelic cognition as follows: The angels have actual knowledge of their own being and, in the natural order, also of God, by means of their essence, without needing any intelligible species. They know each other by the help of intelligible species infused by God at the moment of creation. In the same way they also know human souls and material objects, both in their individual existence and in their universal concepts. But they have no natural knowledge of future free actions, nor of the secrets of hearts, nor of the mysteries of grace. Their knowledge is not discursive, but intuitive. They apprehend in one glance all the principles and

Sent. II, q. 3, a. 1, 2, 3; Sum. Theol. I, q. 55, 56; Albert. Magn. In Sent. d. 3, q. 5, 6.

[42] Sum. Theol. I, q. 54–56; Cont. Gent. I, c. 95–100; De Verit. q. 8, a. 8, 9.

particular applications of universal propositions. However their knowledge of things is not simultaneous, in the sense that they actually know all things at once or by one idea. They know objects successively, by actuating any intelligible species they choose. In regard to the proper objects of their natural knowledge they cannot fall into error; but whilst they were *in via* they could err in reference to truths belonging to the supernatural order. This possibility of error, of course, still obtains in the case of the fallen angels.[43]

From this exposition of angelic cognition as given by St. Thomas, that of Scotus and his school differs considerably. Scotus also holds that there is a specific difference between angels and human souls, but not in that absolute sense insisted on by St. Thomas. His *materia primo prima* runs through the whole of God's creation. This brings the angelic and the human natures much closer to each other. He admits with St. Thomas the infusion of intelligible species, by reason of which angels have a much greater and higher natural knowledge than is attainable by man; but with regard to every other point he takes opposite views. According to him, the proper object of the human intellect is being itself, without connotation of particular or universal,[44] and this is also the proper object of the angelic intelligence. As there is a passive and an active intellect in man, so is there in angels. Hence they can abstract intelligible ideas from particular things; not by means of phantasms, but simply by making these things the object of their intelligence.[45] Moreover, angelic cognition is not necessarily intuitive; it may also be discursive. Nor is it limited to things present and past, and to future events that proceed from necessary causes; but it extends to all free acts of the present, to the secrets of hearts, and to all past and present mysteries of grace.[46] The knowledge of the fallen angels, however, is less extensive; not on account of any natural incapacity, but because in regard to some things, as

[43] Sum. Theol. I, q. 54–58; Cont. Gent. I, c. 95.
[44] In Sent. III, d. 14, q. 7; IV, d. 45, q. 3; Quodl. q. 13, n. 9; In Metaphys. VII, q. 15, 22.
[45] In Sent. II, d. 9, q. 2, n. 439, 130.
[46] In Sent. II, d. 1, q. 5, n. 3; Ibid. d. 9, q. 2, n. 27.

the secrets of hearts, God withholds His *concursus* from such cognition.[47]

5. *Volition of the Angels.*— As angels are intellectual beings created by God for the attainment of eternal happiness as a reward of their merit, it necessarily follows that they are endowed with free will. About this there never was any difference of opinion among the Scholastics. Views began to differ only when the nature of angelic volition came up for consideration. And in regard to this the same two schools of thought were opposed to one another as on the subject of angelic knowledge. In fact, one difference is necessarily connected with the other, and both harken back to a different conception of the angelic nature, as was indicated above. It will be sufficient here to indicate a few of the more important points.

St. Thomas and his school conceive the will as a natural tendency towards good, which finds expression in love. In human beings this tendency is of a higher and lower order, in keeping with man's composite nature; but in angels only the higher spiritual tendency is found, and this has for its object the universal good.[48] There exists in angels both a natural love and a love of choice. The former has for its proper object their own happiness as their last end, which they will and love by a necessity of their nature; the latter is directed towards the means by which their last end is attained, and in regard to them they enjoy freedom of election.[49] They can not turn away from their last end in the natural order, but they can turn away from their supernatural last end. Hence, whilst they were still on probation, they could sin by seeking their own good in opposition to the order established by God.[50] As they apprehend by one glance both their last end and the means thereto, any sin committed by them was necessarily opposed to their last end, and therefore mortal.[51] Their first choice, whether for good or for evil, determined their fate for all eternity; because their will attached itself to the object

[47] In Sent. IV, d. 10, q. 8, ad 3m.
[48] Sum. Theol. I, q. 60.
[49] Ibid. a. 1, 2, 3.
[50] Ibid. a. 1 ad 3m; De Malo, q. 16, a. 5.
[51] Ibid. ad 4m; Sum. Theol. I. II, q. 89, a. 4.

of their choice with full knowledge, uninfluenced by passion, very much the same way as the intellect attaches itself to evident first principles in the order of truth. Hence those who fell were thereby confirmed in evil, and irrevocably lost; while those who remained faithful were by that one act forever established in good, and forthwith admitted to eternal beatitude. In their present state, the good angels love God necessarily, and the bad angels hate God necessarily; hence in neither case is there further room for merit or demerit.[52]

The view of Scotus is opposed to this in nearly every particular. He holds that there is in the angels both a higher and a lower tendency towards good, as there is in human beings.[53] Moreover their will enjoys freedom of choice with regard to every object, and their free will must direct their natural inclination in its tendency towards good.[54] Their eternal condition was not irrevocably decided by one act. The fallen angels committed many sins, of which they might have repented whilst still *in via*.[55] They retained their free will even after they had been condemned to eternal punishment; but their inveterate malice prevents them from doing any good.[56] Conversion is indeed impossible for them, not because they haven't the exercise of their free will, but because God has decreed that there should be no conversion after the final sentence was passed; hence He now withholds His grace.[57] A similar condition obtains in the case of the good angels. Although they are in possession of their last end, nevertheless they still remain free. There is, however, no longer room for merit or demerit in either case, because the time of probation is past.[58]

6. *Mutual Relation of the Angels.*— Following the teaching of the Pseudo-Areopagite, the Scholastics commonly held that the nine choirs of angels, which are mentioned in Holy Scripture, constitute a celestial hierarchy, corresponding to the ec-

[52] Ibid. I, q. 62, a. 8; q. 63, a. 2; De Malo, q. 16, a. 5; Sum. Theol. I, q. 62, a. 8; q. 60, a. 5 ad 5ᵐ.
[53] In Sent. III, d. 35.
[54] In Sent. II, d. 6, q. 2, n. 8, 9; Report. II, d. 6, q. 2, n. 9.

[55] In Sent. II, d. 6, q. 2, n. 16.
[56] Ibid. n. 24.
[57] In Sent. II, d. 6.
[58] Ibid. d. 7, q. unic. n. 28.

clesiastical hierarchy on earth. There are three divisions, each comprising three choirs. To the highest division belong the Seraphim, Cherubim, and Thrones; to the second, the Dominations, Virtues, and Powers; to the third, the Principalities, Archangels, and Angels. The principle underlying this division is variously assigned by the different authors. The more common opinion points to the relation of the angels to God in respect of their ministry and to the imparting of knowledge by the higher to the lower orders. However all this is more or less a matter of speculation; the only certain point is that there is a division into choirs, although even this has not been defined.[59]

In connection with this grouping of the angelic host into certain divisions, the Scholastics also speculated about the specific difference of the angels. St. Thomas, assigning quantified matter — *materia signata* — as the principle of individuation, consequently held that each angel constitutes a distinct species, whereas Scotus and others contended that the principle of individuation must be either the concrete nature itself or a perfection formally distinct from nature, and hence in either case several individual angels may belong to the same species.[60]

There was a similar difference of opinion about *illumination* and *locution*. All were agreed that one angel can communicate with another, and therefore impart knowledge and reveal his own mind after the manner of speech; but they differed considerably in their explanation of the admitted fact. Illumination, in the sense of instruction, was commonly restricted to the higher orders in respect to the lower; while locution was held to be common to all. It was particularly this latter which they found difficult to explain. St. Thomas makes locution exclusively a matter of the will. The mere fact that one angel wishes to communicate with another arouses the intellectual attention of the angel so addressed, no matter in

[59] Cfr. St. Thomas, Sum. Theol. I, q. 108, 106, 107; Scotus, In Sent. II, d. 9, q. 2; Report. d. 9, q. 2.

[60] Sum. Theol. I, q. 50, a. 3; In Sent. II, d. 3, q. 7.

what part of space he may happen to be.[61]   St. Bonaventure agrees with this in so far as locution depends on the will of the speaker, but thinks that distance must be taken into consideration.[62]   Others require, over and above a simple act of the will, some kind of spiritual sign, capable of attracting the attention of the one spoken to.[63]   Scotus holds that angels can read one another's mind independently of any act of the will; but for locution, in the proper sense of the word, it is required that the speaker produce in the mind of the one addressed a concept of the matter he wishes to communicate. And this the angels can do in the same way as they produce a concept in their own mind.[64]

7. *Ministry of the Angels.*— That the good angels are the ministers of God in the government of the world is a matter of faith, and was accepted as such by the Scholastics.   It is also a matter of faith that some angels are deputed by God to be the guardians of men, for the purpose of protecting and assisting them in the attainment of their last end.   Neither of these truths has been defined by the Church, but both are clearly contained in Holy Scripture and tradition.   That each and every person has his own special guardian angel is not of faith, but the doctrine was commonly held by the Scholastics.[65]   St. Thomas states this common teaching as follows: " In this life man is on his way to heaven, along which way he is threatened by many dangers, both interior and exterior. . . . And thus in the same manner as guards are given to a wayfarer who must travel along dangerous roads, so to each human being, whilst still on the way, a guardian angel is assigned; but when the end of the journey is reached, he will no longer have a guardian angel; instead, if in heaven, he will have an angel reigning with him in glory, or, if in hell, a demon inflicting punishment." [66]

[61] Sum. Theol. I, q. 107, a. 1; In Sent. II, q. 2, a. 3.

[62] In Sent. II, d. 10, a. 3, q. 2.

[63] Cfr. Richard of Middleton, In Sent. II, d. 9, a. 2, q. 1.

[64] In Sent. II, d. 9, q. 2, n. 27; Ibid. n. 15, 28, 24.

[65] Cfr. Halens. Sum. p. 2, q. 41, m. 4, a. 1, 3; Bonavent. In Sent. II, d. 11, a. 1, q. 1; Scotus, In Sent. II, d. 11, q. unica; Thomas, In Sent. II, d. 11, q. 1.

[66] Sum. Theol. I, q. 113, a. 4.

As guardian angels are the ministers of Divine Providence
in behalf of their wards, they assist those entrusted to their
care in various ways.   They are indeed incapable of acting
in opposition to the laws of nature, and therefore unable to
work miracles, nevertheless they have the power of acting
upon both body and soul.   By an application of their natural
activities to bodies, they can move them locally, cause alter-
ations in their composition, and thus use them for the production of effects that lie beyond the power of man.   They can
also act upon the imagination, and thereby indirectly enlighten
the mind and fortify the will.   Besides, God permitting, they
may on occasions assume bodies and so appear in visible
forms, without, however, informing these bodies after the
manner of human souls.[67]

A similar influence upon human affairs can also be exerted
by evil spirits, who are always intent upon bringing about
man's ruin.   By their action upon the senses they can suggest
temptations, obscure man's spiritual vision, and thus incline
his will to evil.   On rare occasions God permits them even
to take possession of men's bodies, and cause the unfortunate
victims of their malice to act as if they were bereft of reason.
When their power thus exercised extends to the whole bodily
organism, it is called possession; when only to a part, it is
termed obsession.   However in neither case do the evil spirits
have direct power over man's will; hence although they can
cause him to utter blasphemous and indecent expressions,
and to perform actions that are materially sinful, they can
never force him to sin.   He is still the object of a wise and
loving Providence; and although his body be given over to
Satan, his soul ever remains in the hands of God.[68]

[67] Ibid. q. 111, a. 1–4; Scotus, In
Sent. II, d. 11, q. unica; Report. II,
d. 11, q. 1; Halens. Sum. p. 2, q. 41,
m. 4; Albert Magn. In Sent. d. 11,
a. 6.

[68] Halens. Sum. p. 2, q. 100, m. 1,
2; Bonavent. In Sent. II, d. 8, p. 2,
a. unic. q. 1–4; Thom. In Sent. II,
d. 8, a. unic. q. 5; Albert. Magn.
Sum. p. 2, tr. 7, q. 29.

CHAPTER VII

ANTHROPOLOGY

In their dissertations on the creation of man, the Scholastics were agreed on the following three points: First, man was made to the image and likeness of God; second, the soul of the first man owed its origin to a creative act; third, man's body was the immediate result of a divine operation. These points are all contained in Holy Scripture, and the Scholastics, following the example of the Fathers, accepted them according to the obvious meaning of the sacred text.

In reference to the first point, that man is the image of God, they distinguish between image and trace — *imago et vestigium*. The latter is found in all creatures, in as much as they are the effects of a divine causality; for every effect is assimilated to its cause. But the concept of image implies over and above mere similarity an express intention in the agent to make the effect a formal representation of his own nature and personal being. This is called a specific likeness. Now this specific likeness to God can be realized only in rational beings — angels and men. God made them of express purpose like unto Himself in that He gave them being, life, and the power of understanding.[1]

Moreover, man is not only the image of the divine nature, but also of God as He exists in three persons — of the Blessed Trinity. St. Thomas explains this as follows: " Some effects represent only the causality of the cause, but not its form; as smoke represents fire. Such a representation is called a trace; for a trace shows that some one has passed by but not who it is. Other effects represent the cause as regards the similitude of its form, as fire generated represents fire gen-

[1] Sum. Theol. I, q. 93, a. 2.

129

erating; and a statue of Mercury represents Mercury; and this is called the representation of image. Now the processions of the divine persons are referred to the acts of intellect and will, as was said above. For the Son proceeds as the word of the intellect; and the Holy Ghost proceeds as the love of the will. Therefore in rational creatures, possessing intellect and will, there is found the representation of the Trinity by way of image, in as much as there is found in them the word conceived, and the love proceeding." [2]

Scotus words this somewhat differently, though he comes to practically the same result. Man is the image of the Trinity, he says, not only in so far as he has an intellect and will, but also because the first man, at the first instant of his existence, elicited an act of understanding and love; and so in the fecundity of his nature, through his intellect and will, he represented the Father, the Son, and the Holy Spirit. These three, the memory — *memoria fecunda* — the intellect, and the will, are consubstantial on the part of the soul, yet they are distinct in their acts. [3]

The creation of the first soul is necessarily implied in the creation of all things by God, and about this there was no difference of views among the Scholastics. The production of the human body by a special divine operation was also commonly accepted. Some of the Franciscan school still harked back to the *rationes seminales* made rather much of by St. Augustine, but even they attributed the formation of the body of Adam to the immediate operation of God. [4] St. Thomas explains the statement of St. Augustine, that the body of the first man was produced according to its *causales rationes* in the work of the six days, in this way: "That which is said to exist in creatures according to their causal reasons may be understood in two ways. One way in respect of active and passive potency, so that there is not merely an objective possibility of something being produced from preëxisting matter, but that there also preëxists a creature which can produce

[2] Ibid. q. 65, a. 7.

[3] In Sent. I, d. 3, q. 9.

[4] Cfr. Bonavent. In Sent. II, d.

18, a. 1, q. 3, Scholion — Quaracchi Ed.

this something. Another way in respect of passive potency only, so that this something can be produced from preëxisting matter by God alone; and in this way does St. Augustine say that the body of man preëxisted in the works already produced according to its causal reasons." [5]

His own reasons for the production of the first human body by God Himself he states in this way: "The formation of the human body could not be effected by any created power, but only by the immediate intervention of God. . . . For as God alone by His omnipotent power can create matter, He alone can produce a form in matter without the help of any preceding material form. And hence it is that the angels cannot so change bodies as to fit them for any particular form, except in so far as the form already preëxists by way of seed. Consequently, since there was not as yet a human body, in virtue of whose generative power a similar body might be formed, it was necessary that the first human body should be formed immediately by God." [6] However "it may well be that the angels performed some ministerial function in the formation of the body of the first man, as they will also do in the final resurrection, by gathering together the dust." [7]

Closely connected with the question of man's origin is that of his essential constitution. For clearness' sake, the subject may here be divided into these three points: First, the essential identity of the rational and sensitive soul in man; secondly, the origin of individual souls; thirdly, the union of soul and body.

1. *Essential Identity of the Rational and Sensitive Soul.*— This question, about which there had been some difference of views in Patristic times, was to all intents and purposes closed by the Eight General Council, held in 869. For in its eleventh canon, the Council declares that both the Old and the New Testament, and also the Fathers of the Church, teach that man has only one "rational and intellectual soul"; and then it condemns those who foolishly maintain that "he has two souls." It anathematizes not only the authors and propagators

5 Sum. Theol. I, q. 91, a. 2 ad 4m.   7 Ibid. a. 2 ad 1m.
6 Ibid. a. 2.

of " this impiety," but also all others who entertain similar
views.[8]

Whether this declaration of the Council was directly intended as a definition of the essential identity of the rational
and sensitive principle in man, or merely of the oneness of
the rational soul, is not altogether clear.   Some theologians
think that we have here nothing more than a condemnation
of Manichaean dualism; while others are of opinion that the
absolute oneness of the human soul was defined, but that there
are no proofs to establish the fact as a certainty.   Aside from
this, however, the doctrine itself is sufficiently certain from an
earlier definition of the Church, which was directed against
the Origenists and Apollinarians.   In it Christ as man is declared to be consubstantial with us, being composed of a rational soul and a body.[9]   Hence the rational soul is evidently
assumed to be the only vital principle in man.

And this was accepted by the Scholastics as the teaching of
the Church.   Several of them defended the doctrine against
the error of Averroes, according to which all men have numerically the same rational soul, so that only the sensitive soul is
multiplied in individuals.   Under a somewhat different form,
this teaching of Averroes was condemned by the Fifth Lateran
Council, which sat from 1512 to 1517.[10]

Although the intellectual soul is thus the sensitive and
vegetative principle, it is nevertheless incorruptible.   St.
Thomas gives three reasons for this.   First, the soul is a pure
spirit, in the sense that it is not composed of matter and form.
It is, therefore, a subsisting form; and as a form cannot be
separated from itself, it is impossible that the soul should be
subject to corruption.   Secondly, although some hold that the
soul is in a manner composed of matter and form, yet even
so it must be incorruptible.   For corruption can only result
from contrary elements, and from the intellectual soul as such
contrary elements are necessarily excluded.   This is manifest
from its highest operation, which is altogether spiritual.
Thirdly, as the intellect apprehends being under an absolute

---

[8] Mansi, 15, 403B, 432C; DB, 338.   [10] Mansi, 32, 842A; DB, 738.
[9] Mansi, 9, 533A.

form, the soul naturally desires to exist forever; and as this natural desire cannot be of anything unattainable, its very presence indicates that the soul is an incorruptible substance.[11]

2. *Creation of Individual Souls.*— In Patristic times, the question of the creation of individual souls was regarded as still open for discussion, although the weight of authority was in favor of Creatianism.[12] But when the Scholastics began to write their *Summae* and *Commentaries,* all discussion of the matter had come to an end. This was owing, in part at least, to the position taken by the Church, as indicated by the symbol which Leo IX, in 1050, presented to Bishop Peter of Antioch for subscription. It contains this confession of faith concerning the point in question: " I believe and profess that the soul is not a part of God, but is created out of nothing, and that, without baptism, it is in original sin." [13] As the soul " in original sin " is said to be created, the Pope evidently refers, not to the soul of Adam, but to individual souls.

Hence, although a few of the earlier Scholastics still regarded Creatianism as only more probable, the general consensus was that the creation of individual souls could not be called in question. Thus Peter Lombard states quite definitely: " The Church teaches that souls are created at their infusion into the body." [14] St. Thomas is still more emphatic; for he says: " It is heretical to say that the intellectual soul is transmitted by way of generation." [15] Others do not give the same theological note to the doctrine of creation as here set forth, but they entertain no doubt regarding its truth.

St. Thomas thus indicates the various opinions that had been held on the subject at different times: " Regarding this question various opinions were expressed in times past. Some held that the soul of the child is propagated by the soul of the parent, just as the body is propagated by the body. Others said that all souls are created apart; but maintained that they were all created together in the beginning, and afterwards

11 Sum. Theol. I, q. 75, a. 6.
12 Cfr. vol. I, p. 299 sqq.
13 Mansi, 19, 662B; DB, 348.
14 Sent. II, d. 18, n. 8.
15 Sum. Theol. I, q. 118, a. 2.

were united to procreated bodies, either by their own free
volition, or, as others would have it, by the command and
action of God.   Others, again, declared that the soul at the
moment of its creation is infused into the body.   Though for
a time these several views were upheld, and though it was
doubtful which came nearest the truth, . . . nevertheless the
Church subsequently condemned the first two, and approved
the third." [16]

3. *Union of Soul and Body.*— On this point there was considerable discussion, and also some difference of opinion,
among the Scholastics. All agreed, however, in rejecting
Plato's theory of a merely mechanical union *per modum
motoris.*   And to this they were necessarily led by their teaching on the oneness of the vital principle in man.   For not only
man's thoughts and volitions, but also his sensations are immanent actions, and consequently there must be an intrinsic
union between soul and body.   It is indeed true that intellectual activity is intrinsically independent of the bodily organism; but that is owing to the fact that the soul is a subsistent form, which in being and activity transcends the limitations of material substances.   By reason of its sensitive powers
the soul constitutes with the body one principle of action; and
by reason of its spiritual faculties it forms a principle of
action by itself, except in so far as it needs the presence of
phantasms for its spiritual operations.   The one does not interfere with the other.[17]

As the intrinsic union of the soul with the body requires
that the material element be specifically determinable, all Scholastics admitted some kind of *materia prima;* but there was no
agreement in regard to its nature.   Alexander of Hales, St.
Bonaventure, Scotus, and the whole Franciscan school held
that both soul and body are composed of potency and act, or
of matter and form; while Albertus Magnus, St. Thomas,
and very many others denied the composition of both soul
and body.   This point has already been touched upon in the
preceding chapter, where a short explanation is given of the

[16] De Potentia, q. 3, a. 9.
[17] Cfr. St. Thom. Sum. Theol. q. 76, a. 1.

Scotistic view on the nature of the angels. The same principles there set forth are applied by the Franciscan school to the two constitutive elements of human nature. Hence a few extracts from their writing will here suffice to give us a fair understanding of their teaching on the subject now under consideration.

Alexander of Hales, speaking of the human soul, thus states his view regarding its nature: " It must be held that the human soul is composed of matter and form; but it can in nowise be said that it has matter and form in the same sense as bodies have. . . . For corporeal matter is the foundation of magnitude; not so spiritual matter. . . . Still nothing can be the agent and the receiver of one and the same thing in itself. Hence as to act is proper to the form and to receive is proper to matter, it follows that the human soul, which performs both functions, is composed of matter and form.[18] . . . Besides, it seems very probable that all corporeal substances, as regards their matter, were produced in the six days of creation; hence for the same reason the soul also, as it is not entirely simple, was then produced as regards its matter: but that matter can only be spiritual, and therefore the soul was then produced as regards its spiritual matter." [19]

Then, referring to the union of soul and body, he says: " It must be noted that there is a first form whose function it is to perfect matter; as, for instance, elementary forms; and in their case the form directly perfects the whole matter and its every part. . . . But the soul has something over and above its own matter, which cannot be said of the first form; hence the soul does not actuate the matter of the body, but the natural body itself already complete in respect of its natural form: and this form is called the corporeal form — *forma corporalis.*" [20]

St. Bonaventure followed the teaching of his master, and expresses it in almost identical terms. The soul, he says, is a something that acts and is acted upon, that moves and is moved, and therefore there is in it a material principle from

[18] Sum. II, q. 61, m. 1.
[19] Sum. II, q. 60, m. 2, a. 1.
[20] Ibid. q. 63, m. 3.

which it has its existence, and a formal principle from which it has its being.   However, that material substratum is outside the category of extension, and above all tendency to privation and corruption; and therefore it is called spiritual matter.[21] In regard to the union of the soul with the body he states: " Although the rational soul is composed of matter and form, nevertheless it has a tendency to perfect corporeal nature; similarly as the organic body, composed of matter and form, has a tendency to receive the soul." [22]

Henry of Ghent defended the same doctrine, and advanced a number of theological arguments in support of his view. Thus he pointed out, that, if the *forma corporeitatis* be admitted, it is much easier to explain the identity of Christ's body during the *triduum mortis,* to defend Mary's title of Mother of God, and to give a reasonable exposition of other facts belonging to the faith.[23]

Scotus, as was explained in the preceding chapter, divides the material elements of things into *materia primo prima, materia secundo prima,* and *materia tertio prima.*   The first is pure potency devoid of all forms, and as such it is the substratum of all created beings.   The second is actuated by a substantial form, the *forma corporeitatis,* which determines it quantitatively and makes it a fit substratum for specific organic and inorganic beings.   The third is the complete substance, specifically determined by an ultimate substantial form. This is not subject to further determination, except by way of accidental forms.[24]

It is, therefore, the *materia secundo prima* which constitutes the body of which the rational soul is the substantial form.   It has already been placed in the order of bodies by the *forma corporeitatis,* but it becomes a human body by being still further determined by the spiritual soul.   So determined, it constitutes together with the soul the *compositum humanum,* which is truly an *unum per se.*   The soul does not communicate to this body being simply, but specific being; and in so far only can it be called the substantial form of the body.

[21] In Sent. II, d. 17, a. 1, q. 2.   [23] Quodl. 4, q. 13.
[22] Ibid. q. 2 ad 6^m.   [24] De Rerum Princ. q. 8, a. 3.

Over against this somewhat theoretical exposition, which is still advocated by many, stands the more direct and simple explanation of Albertus Magnus and St. Thomas. Both of them follow closely the teaching of the Stagirite, but neither of them simply transcribes his thoughts. The views of Albertus on the matter now under consideration may be reduced to the following points. 1. The soul is essentially simple, and therefore not composed of a really distinct act and potency.[25] 2. The rational soul is immediately united to the body as its substantial form.[26] 3. The soul gives to the body its specific, numerical, and substantial unity.[27] 4. The soul is the *actus corporis* in the sense that it communicates to the *materia prima* the *esse corporis* as well as the *esse vivum et sensitivum*.[28]

St. Thomas takes this teaching of his master and develops it in his own inimitable way. " To seek the nature of the soul," he says, " we must premise that the soul is defined as the first principle of life in those things which live: for we call living things animate (souled); and not-living things inanimate (soulless)." [29] Now, " it must necessarily be admitted that the principle of intellectual operation, which we call the soul, is a principle both incorporeal and subsistent." . . . For it " has an operation of its own apart from the body. But only a self-subsisting thing can have an operation of its own; for nothing can operate but what is actual." [30] Moreover, " the intellectual soul itself is an absolute form, and not something composed of matter and form. For if the intellectual soul were composed of matter and form, the forms of things would be received into it as individuals, and so it would know only the individual; just as it happens with the sensitive powers which receive forms in a corporeal organ. . . . It follows, therefore, that the intellectual soul, and every intellectual substance which has knowledge of forms absolutely, is exempt from composition of matter and form." [31]

25 Sum. II, tr. 12, q. 2, m. 2.
26 Ibid. q. 72, m. 2.
27 De Creat. II, tr. 1, q. 4, a. 5.
28 De Hom. tr. 1, q. 7, a. 1.

29 Sum. Theol. I, q. 75, a. 1.
30 Ibid. a. 2.
31 Ibid. a. 5.

Again, " it is well to remark that if anyone holds that the soul is composed of matter and form, it would follow that in no way could the soul be the form of the body. For since the form is an act, and matter is only a potentiality, that which is composed of matter and form cannot be the form of another by virtue of itself as a whole. But if it is a form by virtue of some part of itself, then that part which is the form we call the soul, and that of which it is the form we call the primary animate." [32]   Yet " we must assert that the intellect, which is the principle of intellectual operation, is the form of the human body. For that whereby primarily anything acts is a form of the thing to which the act is to be attributed. . . . But the soul is the primary principle of our nourishment, feeling, and local movement; and likewise the primary principle whereby we understand. Therefore this principle by which we primarily understand, whether it be called the intellect or the intellectual soul, is the form of the body." [33]

This excludes, first of all, Plato's idea of a merely extrinsic union *per modum motoris*. " For that which is moved is neither generated by the application of the moving power, nor does it corrupt by the withdrawal of that power; because there is no dependence in respect of being, but only in respect of movement. If, therefore, the soul be united to the body only in the function of mover, it follows that in the union of soul and body there is no generation, nor in their separation is there corruption; and thus death, which consists in the separation of soul and body, does not mean a corruption of the animal nature; which is obviously false." [34]

Hence the union of soul and body is necessarily intrinsic; and this follows obviously from the nature of the *compositum* that is formed by their union. " For to be and to act is not predicated of the form alone, nor of the matter alone, but of the composite resultant: to be and to act is attributed to both in common, in so far as the one discharges the functions of form and the other that of matter. For we say that a man is healthy in respect of his body and health, and that he is

[32] Ibid. q. 76, a. 1.   [34] Cont. Gent. II, 57.
[33] Ibid.

wise in respect of his soul and wisdom; in which predication
wisdom is taken as the form of him who is wise, and health
as the form of him who is healthy. But to live and to feel
is attributed to soul and body; for we are said to live and to
feel by reason of our soul and our body, but so that the soul
is the formal principle of life and sensation. Therefore the
soul is the form of the body," and this by intrinsic union.[35]

From this intrinsic union of soul and body it necessarily follows that " it is impossible for another substantial form besides the soul to be found in man." . . . For " the substantial
form gives simple existence; therefore by its coming a thing is
said to be generated simply; and by its removal to be corrupted
simply." . . . But, " if besides the intellectual soul there pre-
existed in matter another substantial form by which the subject of the soul were made an actual being, it would follow that
the soul does not give existence simply; and consequently that
it is not the substantial form: and so at the advent of the soul
there would not be simple generation, nor at its removal simple
corruption; all of which is clearly false. Whence we must
conclude, that there is no other substantial form in man besides the intellectual soul; and that, as the soul virtually contains the sensitive and nutritive souls, so does it virtually contain all inferior forms, and itself alone does whatever the imperfect forms do in other things." [36]

A little later, Peter John Olivi, a Franciscan and opponent
of St. Thomas, explained the union of soul and body in a
manner that induced the Council of Vienne to define at least
one part of the teaching set forth in the preceding paragraphs,
namely, that the rational soul is of itself and essentially the
true form of the body — *per se et essentialiter vera forma corporis*. Whether the Council meant also to define the essential
identity of the rational and sensitive soul, is not quite clear;
although many theologians interpret the definition in this
sense.

The principal difficulty experienced in determining the full
meaning of the definition given by the Council arises from the

[35] Ibid.   [36] Sum. Theol. I, q. 76, a. 4.

uncertainty about the exact import of Olivi's teaching.   There
are no Acts of the Council, and Olivi's own works have per-
ished.   However some years ago a copy of his *Quodlibeta* was
found, and from them some idea may be obtained as regards
the general trend of his thoughts on the point in question.
Speaking of the union of soul and body, he says: " Their union is intimate, but not immediate; because by the mediation
of the sensitive soul they are inclined to one another, and so
they are united. . . . But how this union can be understood
and be consubstantial in such a way as not to be formal,
may easily be gathered from this, that the sensitive soul is
united with the intellectual soul in a common spiritual matter;
or, so to speak, in one subject of the rational soul." [37]

This can hardly mean anything else than that the rational
and sensitive soul in man are really distinct; and so Olivi's
teaching was understood by Scotus, who was practically his
contemporary.   He does not mention Olivi by name, but he
cites his words and then points out that they imply a real distinction between the rational, sensitive, and vegetative principles in man.[38]   Most modern theologians give the same interpretation.

Against this teaching, whatever way it was then understood,
the Council of Vienne, convened in 1311, issued the following
definition: " Whosoever shall hereafter pertinaciously presume to assert, defend, or teach, that the rational or intellectual soul is not *per se* and essentially the form of the human
body, shall be considered a heretic." [39]   This definition
clearly lays down three points.   1. That the rational soul is
in a true sense the substantial form of the body.   It is not an
accidental or mere assistant form.   2. It is the form of the
body *per se;* that is, of itself, and not through the instrumentality of the sensitive or vegetative soul.   3. It is the form
of the body essentially, or by reason of its essence; not merely,
therefore, through some accidental influence it may be said to
exercise on the body.   In more recent years the definition was

[37] Cfr. Palmieri, De Deo Creante,
p. 772 sqq; Zigliara, De Mente Concilii Viennensis, p. 115 sqq.

[38] De Rerum Princ. q. 9, a. 2, s. 1.
[39] Mansi, 25, 410E; DB, 481.

interpreted by Pius IX in the sense that there is only one principle of life in man, and that this is the rational soul, " from which the body also receives movement and life and every sense." And this teaching, he declares, " is in such wise connected with the dogma of the Church, that it is its only legitimate and true interpretation, and consequently cannot be denied without an error in faith." [40]

It must be noted, however, that the Council did not touch the further question, whether the rational soul, as the form of the body, is united to the *materia prima* in the Thomistic or Scotistic sense of that term. It did not condemn the teaching of Scotus and his Franciscan brethren on the *forma corporeitatis.* In the definition the rational soul is said to be the *forma corporis,* not the *forma materiae primae.* It remains for theologians to determine what is meant by *corpus* in this connection.

[40] Ep. "Dolore haud mediocri," ad Episc. Wratislaviensem, 30 Apr. 1860; DB, 1655, note I.

CHAPTER VIII

STATE OF ORIGINAL JUSTICE

In reference to the primitive condition of our first parents, the early Scholastics did little more than restate the teaching of the Fathers. Thus St. Anselm followed closely the lines of thought marked out by St. Augustine, and hardly anywhere reached beyond the results already achieved by that profound thinker. Both regarded original justice primarily as a supernatural rectitude of the will, which manifested itself in a fixed tendency towards God as the object of eternal blessedness. This rectitude, however, they conceived to be based upon a gratuitous intrinsic gift, which by its own nature and by the will of the Giver permanently inhered in the soul, yet could be preserved only by the free subjection of the creature to the Creator. It was the *gratia justitiae,* or sanctifying grace, whereby human nature was elevated to a condition of divine sonship.[1]

Furthermore, along with this rectitude of the supernaturally elevated will, Adam received, according to both authors, certain prerogatives that perfected his lower nature, and made his existence on earth a life of singular blessedness. Among these prerogatives were especially freedom from inordinate concupiscence, immunity from bodily infirmities, and immortality of the body. And all these gifts were bestowed upon Adam, not only as a personal possession, but as a sacred heirloom of the whole race, which it was his duty to transmit intact to his posterity. This transmission, however, as also his own permanent possession of these prerogatives, was made dependent on Adam's fidelity to his Creator.[2]

Practically the same view was taken by Hugh of St. Victor,

[1] De Conc. Grat. et Lib. Arbit. 13.   [2] De Conc. Virg. 2.

142

except that he entertained some doubt as to whether Adam had infused charity before the fall, although he held that the moral virtues were certainly connected with the other gifts received by our first parents.[3] By way of knowledge, moreover, Adam was gifted with an intuition of divine things, a power of contemplation which held a middle place between faith and the beatific vision. By this intuition Hugh seems to have understood that enlightened knowledge of God and divine things which the mystic school in general looked upon as the special privilege of perfect souls.[4]

Peter Lombard restated and somewhat developed the same doctrine. With Hugh of St. Victor, he held that Adam enjoyed the privilege of contemplating God in a very special manner; by a vision, not indeed so perfect as that of the blessed in heaven, but neither so imperfect as that which is granted to us here on earth.[5] When speaking of the graces that were bestowed upon Adam, he follows St. Augustine's exposition step by step. Adam was made right, and by the grace of his state he could live without sin, although he needed another grace in order to merit eternal life.[6]

Great progess along these lines was made by Alexander of Hales, who considered the state of original justice under all its different aspects. Accepting the teaching of his predecessors as regards the fact of original justice, he inquired more deeply into its inmost nature. Our first parents, he notes, were free from inordinate concupiscence,[7] immune from bodily sufferings and death,[8] and endowed with a high degree of the knowledge of God.[9] It was in these prerogatives that original justice properly consisted. But along with them, though not as forming an essential part of original justice, our first parents also received the *gratia gratum faciens,* or sanctifying grace, which must be considered as a gratuitous gift of God, exceeding all natural exigencies and capacities of human nature. In order to preserve this grace, there was

[3] De Sacr. VI, c. 17.
[4] Ibid. c. 14.
[5] Sent. II, d. 23, n. 4.
[6] Ibid. d. 24, n. 1.

[7] Sum. II, q. 87, m. 1.
[8] Ibid. q. 88, m. 1–4.
[9] Ibid. q. 92, m. 1–4.

placed at their disposal the *gratia gratis data,* which, besides the virtues proper to their state, included also a special help of God, enabling them to persevere in good and to merit eternal life.[10]

Sanctifying grace the author speaks of as a *sublimatio creaturae rationalis* — an elevation of the rational creature above its own nature. Referring to the complacency which the Creator takes in the creatures of His hands, he says that this complacency is of three degrees. First, all creatures are acceptable to God in as much as by their nature they are all good; secondly, rational creatures are more acceptable to God, precisely in so far as they are rational; thirdly, rational creatures are in a very special and most proper sense acceptable to God because they are consecrated to Him, so that they are His temple, His children, and united to Him as His spouses. " And this sublimation of the rational creature," he continues, " is a *supra naturale complementum* — a perfection that is above the nature of the recipient; and therefore neither the aforesaid consecration, nor the adoption, nor the assumption, is effected through the instrumentality of anything that belongs to nature, but by means of a gift that is superadded to nature, which consecrates the soul, makes it into a temple, assimilates it to God, to the end that it may be His son or daughter — links or unites it to God through conformity of the will, so that it may be His spouse." [11]

This sanctifying grace was possessed by our first parents in the state of original justice, but not from the very beginning. It was not communicated to them at the moment of their creation, but only some time before their fall into sin. On this point, the author says, there were two contrary opinions in his day. His own words are: " Some hold that the first man was created in the state of sanctifying grace. And the reason which moves them to hold this view is God's perfect liberality and man's sufficient disposition. Others hold that he was created only in his natural state, not in the state of sanctifying grace; and this opinion is to be adopted rather than the other,

[10] Ibid. q. 91, m. 1, 2.   [11] Ibid. q. 91, m. 1, a. 2 ad 1m.

because it is more in conformity with reason, is supported by
the weight of authority, and manifests more clearly the divine excellence." [12] God could indeed have adorned human
nature with sanctifying grace at the moment of its creation;
but it was more in harmony with His general way of acting in
the supernatural order, that He should require some kind of
positive disposition produced by man's free coöperation with
actual grace.[13]

For the necessity of grace, both actual and habitual, Alexander assigns these two reasons: First, human nature, because of its animal proclivities, does not readily and expedi-
tiously tend toward God as its last end, even in the natural
order; secondly, as man was destined for a supernatural end,
he had need of supernatural means. " He could, indeed, reach
out to the things that were within the order of nature; but he
could do nothing towards attaining the end that was above
nature." [14] For that he needed a *bonum ultra terminos naturae sive supra omnem naturam* — a help that was strictly
supernatural.[15]

Along with sanctifying grace, Adam received also the infused virtues of faith, hope, and charity, as without them it
would have been impossible for him to merit heaven. The
knowledge of God is twofold: natural and supernatural. The
former we gather from God's creatures around us, and by
it we apprehend God as the highest natural good; the latter
comes to us by way of revelation, and leads us to some understanding of the inner life of God. And so is there a twofold
love of God: one that is natural, in as much as it flows from
our natural knowledge of God; and another that is supernatural, and this has its source in the supernatural knowledge
of faith.[16] Unlike the Lombard and Scotus, Alexander
places a real distinction between charity and sanctifying grace.

St. Bonaventure follows rather closely the lines of thought
traced out by his master. Like him, he understands by the
justitia originalis the gift of integrity, in virtue of which hu-

[12] Ibid. q. 90, m. 1, a. 1.
[13] Ibid.
[14] Sum. II, q. 91, m. 3, a. 2.

[15] Ibid. m. 2, a. 3.
[16] Ibid. q. 92, m. 1, 2.

man nature was, in all its faculties and powers, properly disposed in itself and in reference to God as its last end. This gift consisted principally in the prerogatives of bodily immortality and of freedom from concupiscence.[17] They were not strictly supernatural, since there is an aptitude for them in nature; but they were nevertheless a largess of grace —*quantum ad aptitudinem fuit (immortalitas) a natura, quantum ad complementum fuit a gratia.*[18] Together with these prerogatives, Adam possessed a special knowledge of God, which was more perfect than the knowledge derived from creatures and less perfect than the knowledge of vision. The author calls it *scientia apparitionis et contemplationis.* Owing to the perfection of his state, Adam did not have the knowledge of faith.[19]

In his explanation of the *gratia gratum faciens* which was conferred upon our first parents, St. Bonaventure uses the identical terms employed by Alexander. Through it the soul is consecrated as a temple of the Godhead, is adopted as God's own child, and is received by Him as His spouse. Thus the soul is intrinsically sanctified, is made like unto God, and endowed with a most surpassing spiritual beauty. In itself this sanctifying grace is a *supra naturale complementum omnis creaturae* — a gratuitous gift that is in no sense due to any created nature.[20] Without it man is neither acceptable to God in the supernatural order, nor can he merit eternal life. However, this gift was not bestowed at the moment of creation, but only after our first parents had disposed themselves for its reception by faithful coöperation with God's helping grace.[21]

Albertus Magnus also distinguished between the *justitia originalis* and the *gratia gratum faciens,* understanding by the former a preternatural order and harmony of all the faculties and powers of human nature, and by the latter an elevating principle whereby Adam became capable of supernatural merit.[22] The gift of integrity or original justice was con-

[17] In Sent. II, d. 19, a. 3, q. 1, 2.
[18] Ibid. q. 1.
[19] Ibid. q. 23, a. 2, q. 1, 3.

[20] Ibid. d. 29. q. 1; cfr. d. 26, a. unic. q. 1.
[21] Ibid. d. 29, q. 2.
[22] Sum. II, tr. 14, q. 85.

ferred at the moment of creation, and if Adam had remained
faithful it would have been bestowed upon all his descendants;
but sanctifying grace was not given until Adam had disposed
himself for its reception.[23]   However, he received it before
the fall, and thus was placed in a condition in which he could
have remained faithful to God and merited eternal life.[24]
Sanctifying grace is a universal habit or quality, which inheres
both in the soul and all its faculties; although in the latter
it inheres rather by reason of the accompanying virtues.[25]
These virtues are intimately connected with sanctifying grace,
as are also the gifts of the Holy Spirit.[26]

St. Thomas developed this teaching of his predecessors in
his own clear way, and on some points departed from their
views.   Speaking of original justice and sanctifying grace, he
says: " It must be noted that in relation to the first man there
is question of a twofold justice: The one is original justice,
which bears reference to the due subordination of the body
to the soul, and of the lower powers to the higher, and of the
higher powers to God.   In the primitive state, this justice
was by the divine goodness conferred upon human nature itself; and therefore, if Adam had remained faithful, he would
have transmitted it to his descendants.   There is also another
gratuitous justice, which is the principle of supernatural merit;
and in regard to this there is a twofold opinion." [27]

This " twofold opinion " refers both to the time when sanctifying grace was bestowed on Adam and to its transmission
to his posterity.   He states the two views in this way: " Some
say that the first man was created only in the state of perfect
nature, and not in the state of grace.   The reason assigned
for this view is, that for the reception of such a grace there
was need of a personal preparation on the part of the recipient.
As a necessary consequence, in this opinion the grace thus
conferred was a personal gift to the soul, and therefore would
in no sense have been transmitted, except in so far as there
would have been an aptitude in all to receive it.   But others

23 Ibid. q. 90, m. 1.   26 Ibid. tr. 14, q. 90, m. 4, 5.
24 Ibid. m. 3.   27 In Sent. II, d. 20, q. 2, a. 3.
25 Ibid. tr. 16, q. 98, m. 4.

say that man was created in the state of grace, and according to this view the gift of grace was conferred on human nature itself: hence grace would have been transmitted together with nature." [28] This latter view St. Thomas definitely adopted in his *Summa Theologica*, where he says: "But since the root of original justice, which conferred righteousness on the first man when he was made, consists in the supernatural subjection of reason to God, which subjection results from sanctifying grace, . . . we must conclude that if children were born in original justice, they would also have been born in grace." [29]

Hence St. Thomas established a much closer connection between sanctifying grace and the preternatural gifts of original justice than any of his predecessors had attempted. Alexander of Hales and Albertus Magnus considered these gifts as standing by themselves; and the same view was taken by St. Bonaventure: while St. Thomas makes them rest upon sanctifying grace as their supernatural foundation. Hence he gives this reason for holding that Adam received sanctifying grace at the moment of creation: " The very rectitude of the primitive state, wherewith man was endowed by God, seems to require that, as others say, he was created in grace. . . . For this rectitude consisted in his reason being subject to God, the lower powers to reason, and the body to the soul: and the first subjection was the cause of both the second and the third." . . . For " if the loss of grace dissolved the obedience of the flesh to the soul, we may gather that the inferior powers were subject to the soul through grace existing therein." [30]

The following is a brief outline of the teaching of St. Thomas on the various perfections with which Adam was endowed in the state of original justice. He studies successively the perfections of the intellect, of the will, and of the body.

1. *Perfections of the Intellect.*—" The first man did not see God through His essence if we consider the ordinary state of that life; unless, perhaps, it be said that he saw God in a vision, when God cast a deep sleep upon Adam. . . . Nevertheless he

[28] Ibid. q. 1, a. 1.
[29] Op. cit. I, q. 100, a. 1 ad 2m.
[30] Sum. Theol. I, q. 95, a. 1.

knew God with a more perfect knowledge than we do. Thus in a sense his knowledge was midway between our knowledge in the present state and the knowledge we shall have in heaven, when we see God through His essence." And the reason for this higher knowledge must be sought in the fact that " the first man was not impeded by exterior things from a clear and steady contemplation of the intelligible effects which he perceived by the radiation of the first truth, whether by a natural or by a gratuitous knowledge." [31]

Adam's knowledge was intended not only for his own personal ends, but also for the instruction and government of others; hence he " was established by God in such a manner as to have knowledge of all those things for which man has a natural aptitude. And such are whatever are virtually contained in the first self-evident principles, that is, whatever truths man is naturally able to know. Moreover, in order to direct his own life and that of others, man needs not only those things which can be naturally known, but also things surpassing natural knowledge; because the life of man is directed to a supernatural end: just as it is necessary for us to know the truths of faith in order to direct our own lives. Wherefore the first man was endowed with such a knowledge of these supernatural truths as was necessary for the direction of human life in that state. But those things which cannot be known by merely human effort, and which are not necessary for the direction of human life, were not known by the first man; such as the thoughts of men, future contingent events, and some individual facts." [32] However, " as long as the state of. innocence continued, it was impossible for the human intellect to assent to falsehood as if it were truth," even as regarded things to which man's knowledge did not extend; for such possibility of deception would not have been befitting the integrity and rectitude of the primitive state.[33] Hence, " although the woman was deceived before she sinned in deed, still it was not till she had already sinned by interior pride." [34]

[31] Ibid. q. 94, a. 1.
[32] Ibid. a. 3.
[33] Ibid. a. 4.
[34] Ibid. a. 4 ad 1m.

2. Perfections of the Will.— As the lower powers were subject to the higher, and the higher powers were subject to God, the will of the first man, so long as he continued in the state of innocence, was never disturbed or weakened by the influence of passions. In their actual tendency towards their proper object, they existed only as consequent upon the judgment of reason. And even in this sense there were no passions save those only that " are ordered to what is good "; " such as joy and love, desire and hope that casteth not down." [35] Hence the will could always exercise its full power in the pursuit of virtue.

The perfection of the primitive state required also that the first man should in a certain sense possess all the virtues. For " the virtues are nothing but those perfections whereby reason is directed to God, and the inferior powers are regulated according to the dictate of reason." Here, however, a distinction is to be made as regards habit and act. Some of these virtues involve no imperfection in their nature, such as faith, hope, charity, and justice; and they existed " in the primitive state absolutely, both in habit and in act. But other virtues are of such a nature as to imply imperfection either in their act, or on the part of the matter. If such imperfection be consistent with the perfection of the primitive state, the virtues necessarily existed in that state; as faith which is of things not seen, and hope which is of things not yet possessed. For the perfection of that state did not extend to the vision of the divine essence, and the possession of God with the enjoyment of final beatitude. . . . But any virtue which implies imperfection incompatible with the perfection of the primitive state, could exist in that state as a habit, but not as to the act; for instance penance, which is sorrow for sins committed; and mercy, which is sorrow for another's misery; because sorrow, guilt, and misery are incompatible with the perfection of the primitive state." [36]

As man in the state of innocence had a free will, and also the assistance of God's grace, he could perform meritorious

[35] Sum. Theol. I, q. 95, a. 2.   [36] Ibid. a. 3.

actions. In one sense these actions were more meritorious than corresponding actions in the state of reparation, and in another sense they were less so. For merit as regards degree may be gauged either by the grace and charity of the agent, or by the proportionate difficulty of the action. " We conclude therefore that in the state of innocence man's works were more meritorious than after sin was committed, if the degree of merit on the part of grace be considered; which would have been more copious as meeting with no obstacle in human nature: and in like manner, if we consider the absolute degree of action; because, as man could attain to greater virtue, he would perform greater actions. But if we consider the proportionate degree, a greater reason for merit exists after sin, on account of man's weakness; for a small deed is more beyond the capacity of one who works with difficulty than a great deed is beyond that of one who performs it easily." [37]

3. *Perfections of the Body.*— The chief perfections of man's body in the primitive state were immortality and impassibility. The former was a *posse non mori* — the perpetual preservation from death of a mortal nature. Man did not possess the natural incorruptibility of the angels, nor the incorruptibility of glory enjoyed by the blessed in heaven; but an incorruptibility of a lower order gratuitously conferred on him by his Creator. " For man's body was indissoluble not by reason of any intrinsic vigor of immortality, but by reason of a supernatural force given by God to the soul, whereby it was enabled to preserve the body from corruption so long as it remained itself subject to God. This entirely agrees with reason; for since the rational soul surpasses the capacity of corporeal matter, . . . it was most properly endowed at the beginning with the power of preserving the body in a manner surpassing the capacity of corporeal matter." [38]

Impassibility is divided by St. Thomas into two kinds, according to the nature of the passion or suffering it excludes from its subject. " For passion may be taken in two senses.

[37] Ibid. a. 4.   [38] Sum. Theol. I, q. 97, a. 1.

First, in its proper sense, and thus a thing is said to suffer when changed from its natural disposition. For passion is the effect of action; and in nature contraries act on, or suffer from, one another, accordingly as one thing changes another from its natural disposition. Secondly, passion can be taken in a general sense for any kind of change, even if belonging to the perfecting process of nature. Thus to understand and to feel are said in a sense to be passive. In this second sense, man was passible in the state of innocence, and was passive both in soul and body. In the first sense man was impassible, both in soul and body, as he was likewise immortal; for he could curb his passion, as he could avoid death, so long as he refrained from sin." [39]

Scotus agreed with this teaching of St. Thomas in its main outlines, but departed from it on some minor points. He held that Adam was created in the state of original justice, and this state was not merely a condition of natural rectitude, but was the result of preternatural prerogatives gratuitously bestowed on human nature by the Creator. It consisted in a perfect tranquillity of the soul and all its powers, so that man's inferior nature did not tend to go contrary to the dictate of reason; or if of itself it was inclined so to do, it could easily be regulated and reduced to order, without causing any difficulty to his higher nature, or any sadness to his lower nature. [40]

The proximate cause of the condition of perfect tranquillity was a *complexus habituum* — so many particular gratuitous gifts, which resided in the will and the other faculties. Thus the will was so disposed by an inherent power, that it could withdraw itself with pleasure from any object craved by the lower appetite. [41] These permanent dispositions of the faculties must, however, not be confounded with the infused virtues; nor with habitual grace. They were special virtues, entirely proper to the state of innocence. Hence the state of original justice as such was independent of sanctifying grace. In fact, however, sanctifying grace was an integral part of

[39] Ibid. a. 2.   [40] In Sent. II, d. 29, n. 2, 4.

that state as ordained by God.[41]   Whether Adam was created in sanctifying grace, is not clearly stated by Scotus. Some interpret his teaching in this sense, although he is usually cited as an authority for the contrary view.[42]

In explaining man's bodily immortality in the primitive state, Scotus rejects the teaching of St. Thomas, that its proximate cause was an intrinsic power of the soul over matter, communicated to it by God.   According to him, Adam always retained the *potentia ad mori,* but by a special intervention of Providence that *potentia* could not be reduced to act, so long as the state of innocence continued.   Hence in his own being Adam was simply mortal; but whilst he remained faithful, God warded off all danger to his life, and before the time of natural dissolution approached, He would have taken him up to heaven.[43]

Finally, all these prerogatives of original justice were intended for the entire human race, although their transmission was made dependent on Adam's fidelity.   Each human being was to have received them at the moment of birth, not as an inheritance from Adam, but as a free gift of God.   However, all would have been subjected to a probation, with the same chances of failure that proved the undoing of the first man.[44]

Comparing now the teaching of the most representative Scholastics, as outlined in the preceding paragraphs, we may put down the following points as common to all.

1. Man's primitive condition was a state of righteousness, which resulted from certain gifts of God not due to human nature.

2. These gifts affected both soul and body, and all man's faculties.   They included enlightenment of the intellect by infused knowledge, steadfastness of the will under the influence of grace, a perfect harmony between man's higher and lower nature through immunity from concupiscence, immortality of the body, and a corresponding freedom from suffering.

[41] Ibid. n. 5; I, d. 32, n. 19.
[42] Cfr. In Sent. II, d. 29, q. unic. n. 7; Report. q. 2.

[43] In Sent. II, d. 19.
[44] Ibid. d. 20, q. 1.

3. Over and above these preternatural gifts, the first man received sanctifying grace, which is strictly supernatural. Through it he became an adopted son of God, with the right and title to an eternal inheritance. By it he was also placed in a position to perform meritorious actions, to persevere in his happy state, and finally to claim heaven as his reward. With sanctifying grace were connected all those virtues that were not repugnant to the state of innocence, and also a right to necessary actual graces.

4. In one sense all these gifts and graces were bestowed upon Adam as personal favors, in as much as he could enjoy and use them for his own advantage; but in another sense they were the property of the whole human race, since by the intention of the Giver Adam was to transmit them, with the one exception of infused knowledge, to all his descendants. Their bestowal upon Adam was absolute, yet their continuance in his own case and their transmission to his posterity was conditioned by his own fidelity.

These four points, leaving aside all explanations as regards details, constitute the common teaching of the Schoolmen. They had been taken over by the Scholastics from the works of the Fathers, and somewhat later, at the Council of Trent, they received the solemn approval of the Church.[45]

[45] Sess. 5, Decretum de Pecc. Originali; Mansi, 33, 27A sqq.; DB. 787 sqq.

CHAPTER IX

ORIGINAL SIN

The existence of original sin had been defined against the Pelagians of the fifth century,[1] and no subsequent theologian called it in question. Nor was there among the Schoolmen any serious doubt in regard to its being a sin in the strict sense of the term. Abelard, indeed, held that nothing was transmitted by Adam to his posterity except the *reatus poenae* — a mere liability to punishment; but his view was condemned by the Council of Sens, in 1141, and also by Pope Innocent II.[2] There was, however, among the Scholastics no agreement about the precise nature of this sin, nor about the manner of its transmission. The following outline will be sufficient to indicate the historical development of the doctrine in question.

1. *The Nature of Original Sin.*— St. Augustine had defined original sin as a *reatus concupiscentiae* — the guilt of concupiscence, without making it altogether clear in what objective reality or condition this guilt must be conceived to consist. This guilt, moreover, he held to be transmitted through concupiscence, which accompanies the act of procreation.[3] His teaching was restated in practically the same terms by Pope Gregory I, and thenceforth it was universally accepted and defended by Western theologians until the end of the eleventh century.

The first one to break with this traditional teaching, and to place the nature of original sin in a somewhat clearer light, was St. Anselm. He subjected the whole question of original sin to a thorough examination in his treatise *De Conceptu Virginali et Peccato Originali,* in connection with the sinless

---

[1] Cfr. vol. I, p. 358.
[2] Mansi, 21, 568C; DB. 376.
[3] Cfr. vol. I, p. 364 sqq.

conception of the Savior. Setting aside the teaching of St. Augustine, without, however, mentioning his name, he thus proposes his own view: " By original sin, then, I understand nothing else than the sin that is in the child as soon as it has a rational soul. . . . And this sin, which I call original, I cannot understand in these children in any other sense than that it is a privation of original justice, brought about by the disobedience of Adam. Through this privation all are children of wrath, because the deliberate casting off of justice rendered guilty the nature which God had made in Adam." [4]

This view of the matter places the essence of original sin in the privation of original justice, in so far as that justice had been conferred by God as a prerogative of human nature itself. Original justice, however, is here not taken as designating sanctifying grace, but as standing for the preternatural prerogatives which formally constituted the state of innocence.[5] Hence the author defines justice, in this connection, as a rectitude of the will preserved for its own sake — *rectitudo voluntatis propter se servata*. In this rectitude Adam was created, and God willed that it should be the prerogative of Adam's posterity. Hence the privation of it is against the will of God, and constitutes in every one of Adam's descendants a sin in the strict sense of the term. " In Adam the person made human nature sinful, because when Adam sinned, man sinned. . . . In children it is human nature that makes the person sinful," because that nature is against the will of God deprived of original justice.[6] " In this manner the person despoiled human nature of justice in Adam; and thus despoiled, human nature causes all persons, whom it begets of itself, to be sinful and unjust." [7]

Hence St. Anselm's formal concept of original sin differs considerably from that of St. Augustine, but it also differs considerably from that of present day theologians. He made a great advance over his predecessors by placing the essence of original sin in the privation of justice, but he retarded, and to some extent rendered futile, his own advance, by failing to

[4] Op. cit. c. 27.
[5] C. 3, 5, 7, 19.
[6] Ibid. c. 23.
[7] Ibid.

make this justice chiefly consist in sanctifying grace. Hence he experienced the same difficulty, as did St. Augustine before him, in explaining the blotting out of original sin by baptism. He states the difficulty in this way: " I said that the inability of possessing justice does not excuse the injustice of children. Hence some one will perhaps ask: If sin, that is injustice, is in the child before baptism, and the child's inability of possessing justice, as you say, is no excuse, and yet in baptism no sin is remitted except that which existed before, then, since the child after baptism, so long as it is a child, is without justice, nor can be understood to preserve justice, how is it not still unjust, although it has been baptized?" [8]

This is a fair statement of the difficulty, which was necessarily involved in his theory on the nature of original sin. If original sin is a privation of some perfection that God willed to be in human nature, then it can be removed only by supplying that perfection. Yet baptism does not restore original justice, hence it would seem that baptism does not remove original sin.

St. Anselm's answer is this: " I answer this question by saying that the sins which existed before baptism was received, are entirely blotted out by baptism. Hence the original inability of possessing justice is not imputed as a sin to those who are baptized, as it was imputed to them before. Just as the inability of not possessing justice did not excuse its absence before baptism, because this absence was real guilt; so it does altogether excuse the same after baptism, because it remains without any guilt. Hence it is that the justice which was demanded of children before baptism, without admitting any excuse on their part, is not exacted of them after baptism as something which they owed." [9] This answer, as is obvious, really explains nothing. It makes the blotting out of original sin consist in a mere non-imputation of guilt.

Anselm's teaching on original sin was taken but little notice of by the theologians of the twelfth century. Only two of them, Odo of Cambrai ($+$ 1113) and Honorius of Autun

<hr>

[8] Ibid. c. 29.　　　　　　　　[9] Ibid.

(1150), adopted his views. All the other more notable writers of that period, such as Robert Pulleyn,[10] Hugh of St. Victor,[11] Peter Lombard,[12] and Pope Innocent III,[13] followed the lead of St. Augustine. They all regarded original sin as a *reatus vel vitium concupiscentiae,* which is propagated *per libidinem,* in some mysterious way stains the *semen,* and then in a still more mysterious way infects the soul at its union with the body. Thus the Lombard writes: " What, then, is original sin? It is the touch-wood of sin, namely, concupiscence or the concupiscible power, which is called the law of the members, or the languor of nature, or the tyrant which is in our members, or the law of the flesh." [14] It is not the act of concupiscence, but the habit — a radical vice that inclines to evil. " And that this vice exists as a corruption in the flesh before its union with the soul is proved by the effect produced in the soul upon its infusion into the body; for it is stained by the corruption of the flesh — just as it is known that there was impurity in the vessel, when the wine which is poured into it becomes sour." [15]

A slight change was introduced into this teaching by Alexander of Hales, who sought to combine the views of St. Anselm and St. Augustine. With this object in view, he writes: " Original sin is guilt which consists in the privation of a justice that is due, or a certain deformity by which the soul itself is deformed. Concupiscence is the punishment of sin, . . . original sin is the privation or absence of a justice that is due." [16] " This definition," he says, " is formal, drawn from the efficient cause ; while the other definition usually given — original sin is a vice resulting from the corruption of the *semen* in man — is material or taken from the material cause.[17] Here appears for the first time the famous distinction between the formal and material element of original sin, which finally enabled the Scholastics to get away from the view of St.

[10] Sent. VI, 1.
[11] De Sacr. I, p. 7, c. 28; Sent. III, 11.
[12] Sent. II, d. 30, c. 7; d. 31, c. 6.
[13] In VII Ps. Poenit. 4; ML, 218, 1058.

[14] Sent. II, d. 30, c. 7.
[15] Ibid. d. 31, c. 6.
[16] Sum. II, q. 106, m. 2, n. 1, 3.
[17] Ibid.

Augustine, without placing themselves in open contradiction with his theory.

The distinction thus introduced was taken up by St. Bonaventure, who tried to explain the nature of original sin by comparing it to actual sin. " As actual sin," he says, " does not consist exclusively in privation, since it is not only an aversion but also a conversion, . . . so the same must in its own way be held in regard to original sin. . . . Thus original sin is said to be in a person, not only because he is deprived of original justice, but also because he has a certain inclination to evil and is under the power of concupiscence. . . . Hence when it is asked, what is original sin? it is perfectly correct to answer that it is concupiscence; and it is also perfectly correct to answer that it is the privation of original justice: for the one answer is contained in the other; although the one emphasizes the inclination to evil that is in original sin, and the other that of privation. . . . Hence it must be conceded that original sin is concupiscence, not any concupiscence whatever, but the concupiscence that includes the privation of original justice." [18]

It must be noted, however, that St. Bonaventure, like St. Anselm, the Lombard, and Alexander of Hales before him, understands by original justice merely the aggregate of preternatural gifts proper to the state of innocence, without including sanctifying grace. Hence his difficulty in explaining the blotting out of original sin by baptism. In regard to this he writes: " Hence it is that, as the Master says, in baptism original sin passes away as to its guilt, but remains as regards its reality — *transit reatu et remanet actu;* because although concupiscence remains, yet it does not remain in so far as it implies guilt and a liability to punishment. . . . When, therefore, original sin is blotted out, it is not blotted out in such a way that it does not at all exist, but only in such wise that it is not a sin. . . . Nor must it be imagined " that original justice itself is restored, but rather that a certain compensation is made by way of conferring sanctifying grace." [19]

[18] In Sent. II, d. 30, a. 2, q. 1.   [19] In Sent. II, d. 32, a. 1, q. 1.

Albertus Magnus made a similar attempt to reconcile the two opposite views, although his dissertation on the nature of original sin is almost entirely taken up with its material element.   He defines original sin as " a proneness to evil which includes the privation of a justice that is due." [20]   And of concupiscence, as found in the members of the body, he says: " This concupiscence is in the body as a punishment only, for the reason that the body is not a rational substance and therefore not susceptible of guilt.   And hence when concupiscence infects a subject that is susceptible of guilt, the latter is immediately present together with the former.   Thus it is that the soul becomes infected, and is made subject both to guilt and punishment." [21]

As will have been noted, all the writers thus far mentioned, with the sole exception of St. Anselm, conceived original sin to consist in some kind of physical stain, which is first in the body and then in some inexplicable way transmitted to the soul. That this was a fundamentally wrong concept is sufficiently obvious; for the soul, as a spiritual substance, cannot be defiled by a bodily stain.   Concupiscence is indeed also in the soul, but it is there independently of the body.   Hence it was necessary to eliminate this theory of defilement by contact, before real progress could be made in the rational exposition of the nature of original sin.   And this elimination was effected by St. Thomas, who subjected the whole question of original sin to a very thorough investigation.   The following is a brief summary of his views on the nature of original sin.

He first rejects the view of his predecessors, that original sin is connected with a physical stain in the body, whereby the soul is contaminated.   All such explanations, he says, are necessarily insufficient, since the stain in question, whatever may be said about its transmission to the soul, lacks the formal element of sin, which is obviously a deordination in the moral order.[22]   Next he gives a general definition of original sin, pointing out that it must in some way be a *habitus,* in as much as it is a certain inordinate disposition, resulting from the

[20] In Sent. II, 30, 3.   [22] Sum. Theol. I. II, q. 81, a. 1.
[21] Ibid. a. 1.

dissolution of that harmony in which original justice consisted. In this sense, original sin is called a languor of nature.[23] It is not an infused habit; nor one that is personally acquired, except on the part of our first parent: but it is inborn in us because of our vitiated origin.[24]

After this general description of original sin, he proceeds to an investigation of its intrinsic constituents. He accepts the definition given by St. Augustine — *Concupiscentia est reatus peccati originalis,* but he explains it in his own way. "The species of a thing," he says, " is taken from its form. Now, as was said above, the species of original sin is derived from its cause; hence it follows that, what is formal in original sin, must be derived from the cause whence this sin originated. But of opposites there are opposite causes; and therefore it must be noted that the cause of original sin is bound up with the cause of original justice, but by way of opposition. Now the orderly condition of original justice had its source in this, that the will of man was subject to God. And the whole sub-jection was first and chiefly brought about by the will, whose function it is to direct all other powers to their proper end. Hence, because of the turning away of the will from God, there followed a corresponding insubordination in all the other powers of the soul. Thus, therefore, the privation of original justice, through which the will was subject to God, is the formal element in original sin; and every other kind of in-ordination of the powers of the soul belongs to the material element. But the inordination of the other powers of the soul consists chiefly in this, that they tend inordinately to-wards the attainment of what is passing and changeable; and therefore this inordination may well be called concupiscence. And thus original sin, considered in its material element, is concupiscence; but considered in its formal element, it is the privation of original justice." [25]

Now the material element of original sin, which is here said to be concupiscence, may be considered in one of two ways: either as something consequent upon the formal element, or

---

[23] Ibid. q. 82, a. 1.
[24] Ibid. a. 1 ad 3m.

[25] Sum. Theol. I. II, q. 82, a. 3.

as a constituent part of original sin itself.   In what sense the
term is used by St. Thomas is not altogether clear.   His modern followers usually hold that he took it in the former sense,
and the text cited above may well be adduced in support of
that interpretation.   For it was " because of the turning away
of the will from God that there followed a corresponding insubordination in all the other powers of the soul "; and " this
insubordination may well be called concupiscence."   But in
not a few other texts he speaks of concupiscence as if it were
a constituent part of original sin.   Thus, for instance, he
says: " Just as in artificial things . . . the matter is predicated of the whole, so that one may say, the knife is iron;
even in such wise is concupiscence said to be original sin." [26]
Again: " Ignorance and the inclination to evil are the material element in original sin, just as the turning to a changeable good is the material element in actual sin." [27]   And still
more explicitly: " Concupiscence in the newly born is the
cause of original sin by way of matter, which is of the essence
of a thing." [28]   Hence all his followers before the Council of
Trent, among them Capreolus, Ferrariensis, and Cajetanus,
interpreted him as having taken the material element in the
strict sense of the term, or as a constituent part of original
sin.

There is also some difficulty in connection with the formal
element, in so far as it is at first sight not clear what exact
meaning St. Thomas attached to the term " original justice,"
as used in this connection.   All his predecessors had taken it
in an exclusive sense, as distinct from sanctifying grace; and
he himself, in those places where he explicitly treats of the
nature of original sin, seems to prescind from sanctifying
grace altogether.   However this difficulty is more apparent
than real.   For according to him, sanctifying grace is the root
and foundation of original justice, so that all other supernatural gifts in the state of innocence depended for their continuance upon the presence of sanctifying grace in the soul.
Hence he says quite explicitly: " The root of original justice,

[26] In Sent. II, 30, q. 1, a. 3.   [28] Ibid. q. 4, a. 2.
[27] De Malo. q. 3, a. 7.

in whose rectitude man was made, consists in a supernatural subjection of his reason to God, and this is brought about by sanctifying grace." [29] And again: "Hence if the loss of grace dissolved the obedience of the flesh to the soul, we may gather that the inferior powers were subjected to the soul through grace existing therein." [30] Consequently, he must have held that the formal element of original sin consisted ultimately in the privation of sanctifying grace, although he does not state this explicitly in his exposition of the nature of original sin. At all events, he laid down the principles which were adopted by the Council of Trent, and which enabled later theologians to work out a consistent theory on this difficult matter.

Still further progress was made by Scotus, who likewise adopted St. Anselm's view as his own. Rejecting the opinion of those who held that original sin consisted in concupiscence, he says: "In regard to this matter there is another way, which was followed by Anselm in the whole first book of his work *De Conceptu Virginali,* where he treats the subject of original sin. . . . I say, therefore, that original sin, which is the privation of original justice, is nothing else than the privation of a justice that is due. And if it be objected that some saints seem to say that original sin is concupiscence, my answer is this: Concupiscence in the sensitive appetite cannot in itself be sin; and concupiscence in the will is a merely material element of sin." [31] And this material element can only be taken as such in a wider sense of the term, as simply an inordinate disposition of the will resulting from original sin. The material element in the strict sense is the obligation man is under to possess justice — *debitum habendi justitiam.* Hence "in the constitution of original sin two elements concur: The privation of justice as its formal element, and the obligation of possessing justice as its material element; just as in the constitution of other privations, there is a concurrence of the privation itself and of the aptitude for the opposite perfection." [32]

[29] Sum. Theol. I. II, q. 100, a. 1.
[30] Ibid. q. 95, a. 1.
[31] In Sent. II, d. 32, n. 7.
[32] Ibid. n. 15, 7.

Thus Scotus definitely eliminated concupiscence as a constituent element of original sin, and this was a decided step forward. But his teaching on the nature of the privation in which original sin formally consists is less satisfactory. Instead of adopting the view of St. Thomas, he returned to that of St. Anselm. Although he admitted, as was shown in the preceding chapter, that in its adequate sense original justice included sanctifying grace, yet in connection with original sin he took it inadequately, as exclusive of the *gratia gratum faciens*. This appears especially in his exposition of the effect of baptism, where he says: "I say that in baptism the obligation of possessing original justice is taken away, and is commuted into an obligation of having an equivalent gift, namely, sanctifying grace. And this second obligation thereafter always remains, nor does the first ever return; and he who is without the second gift, thus due to him, sins more grievously than he who is without the first; but he is not now a sinner because of original sin, for the obligation of possessing that justice does not return." [33]

2. *The Transmission of Original Sin.*— In reference to the transmission of original sin, the followers of St. Augustine assumed the principle that it is not generation but actual concupiscence which transmits original sin — *non generatio sed libido transmittit peccatum originale*. This *libido* was supposed to stain the *semen* in the act of procreation, and that stain would in some way defile the soul on its union with the body. This view was defended by Hugh of St. Victor, Robert Pulleyn, Peter Lombard, Henry of Ghent, and Pope Innocent III. The last named writes: "Therefore of the defiled and corrupt seed a corrupt and defiled body also is conceived, and when the soul is finally infused into this, it likewise becomes corrupt and defiled. . . . Just as a liquid is corrupted when it is poured into an unclean vessel." [34] It was at best a very unsatisfactory theory, and its abandonment was only a question of time.

St. Anselm, consistently with his view on the nature of

[33] Ibid. n. 16.   [34] In VII Ps. Poenit. 4; ML, 218, 1058.

original sin, offered a better explanation. Setting aside the *libido* as a cause of transmission, he had recourse to the connection which exists between the person of Adam and human nature on the one hand, and human nature and the persons of Adam's descendants on the other. The person of Adam despoiled human nature, and that despoiled human nature made all his descendants sinners. Generation was thus conceived as a *conditio sine qua non* of transmission, a bond that links Adam and all his descendants together in the common misery of sin. In the last instance, of course, it was the will of God that ordained the law of transmission; but in this matter the will of God is the final explanation of every other law that one may try to establish.[35] God so ordained that Adam should transmit the prerogatives of original justice to all his descendants by way of generation, and hence when he had despoiled himself of these gifts, he transmitted a despoiled nature by the same way.[36] And this despoiled nature, because of its spoliation, is infected with original sin.

Alexander of Hales cites the definition given by St. Anselm, that original sin is the privation of a justice which by the will of God was due to human nature, and in connection with that gives this exposition of the way in which original sin is transmitted: " The reason underlying the transmission of original sin seems to be this: The prohibition was put upon Adam in as far as he contained the whole human nature in himself, since all others were to descend from him by way of generation. And thus the prohibition extended not to him alone, but also to those others who were seminally contained in him." [37] Hence Adam was the head of the whole race, not only in the physical but also in the moral order. His disobedience, therefore, was not merely a personal act; it was the disobedience of the entire human race as seminally contained in him. Just as the obedience of Christ, the moral head of mankind in the order of redemption, was the obedience of all.[38]

Thus the ultimate reason for the transmission of original

[35] Op. cit. c. 23; cfr. c. 29.　　[37] Sum. II, 105, m. 3.
[36] Ibid. c. 10.　　　　　　　　　[38] Ibid.

sin is the divine decree which constituted Adam the moral head
of his descendants.   But the means or the instrumental cause
of the transmission is the act of procreation.   This the author
explains in his answer to the question, whether original sin is
transmitted through the flesh.   He says: "As original sin
involves both guilt and punishment, it is transmitted in a different way in regard to each of the two.   In so far as it
involves punishment it results from the defilement which is
in the flesh; for as soon as the soul is infused into the defiled
flesh, so soon is itself defiled; just as wine becomes corrupt
through the impure condition of the vessel into which it is
poured.   But in so far as it involves guilt, it proceeds from
the privation of that justice which should have been in the
nature thus generated." [39]

Practically the same position was taken by St. Bonaventure,
who took special pains to explain the connection between the
defilement of the flesh and the resultant guilt in the soul.   "In
order to understand," he says, "how from the defilement of
the flesh there can arise a culpable corruption in the soul, these
three points must be presupposed as evidently true: First,
that the defilement of the flesh can cause the body to rise in
rebellion against the spirit; secondly, that the soul united to
the body either lifts it up or is dragged down by it, on account
of the intimate union that exists between the two; thirdly, that
the soul by its own power cannot rule the rebellious flesh,
unless it be assisted by divine grace.   From these three pre-
suppositions it necessarily follows, that if the soul be united
to a body thus defiled, it is dragged down by it and is through
concupiscence inclined to evil.   But being inclined to evil is
nothing else than being in a state of perversion; and perversion in a rational substance, which is capable of possessing
justice, is nothing else than injustice and guilt.   From this,
therefore, it is clear that the defilement which is in the flesh
can bring it about that the soul, united to it, is sinful.   And
because this defilement is derived from the first parent, from
whom all his descendants have their origin according to the

[39] Sum. II, q. 105, m. 4.

law of propagation, hence it is that by way of the flesh original sin is transmitted to all." [40]

The most serious drawback of this teaching is the undue emphasis it places upon concupiscence in the transmission of original sin. Concupiscence in the parent defiles the flesh in the child, and the flesh thus defiled in its turn through concupiscence defiles the soul. The whole process of transmission is thus limited to the physical order. Excepting St. Anselm, all these theologians commit themselves to the same untenable view. And to some extent, this is also true of St. Thomas, especially in his earlier works. Thus in his *Commentary on the Sentences* he says: "The soul is not infected by the infection of the body, in the sense that the body acts upon the soul; but by way of the intimate presence of the one to the other." [41] For the rest he gives the following very clear exposition of the law of transmission.

"The guilt of original sin comes from this, that the gift which was gratuitously conferred on Adam, namely, original justice, was not conferred on him personally, but in so far as he had such a nature; so that all those in whom the same nature should exist as derived from him, should be entitled to the same gift; and hence original justice should have been propagated together with the flesh. Hence it was in the power of nature always to preserve original justice in itself; and therefore the want of it, considered in reference to that nature, constitutes guilt in all those who derive their nature from the person who sinned. Now as this want of justice, together with the nature itself, is through the origin of the flesh derived by way of generation, hence the person is said to have infected nature. But because in these other persons original sin is present as derived from the first person who generated, it does not have the formality of guilt from themselves, since they do not incur this sin by their own personal will, but it has this formality only in so far as they receive the nature together with the guilt. Hence it is, in the second place, that the person is said to infect the nature." [42]

[40] In Sent. II, d. 31, a. 2, q. 1. [41] In Sent. II, d. 30, q. 1, a. 2 ad
[42] In Sent. II, d. 31, q. 1, a. 1. 5ᵐ; cfr. De Malo, IV, 6 ad 16ᵐ.

In his *Summa Theologica* he places a much stronger emphasis upon the solidarity of human nature as the proximate reason of the transmission of original sin by way of generation. After eliminating altogether the physical transmission of guilt, he continues: " Hence we must proceed along another way, which comes to this, that all men, who are born of Adam, can be considered as one man, in so far as they have a common nature which they received from their first parent; on the same principle as in the civil order all men belonging to the same community are considered as one body, and the whole community as one man. . . . Thus, therefore, many human beings have descended from Adam as so many members of one body. But the act of any one bodily member, as for instance the hand, is not voluntary by the will of the hand itself, but by the will of the soul, which imparts motion to the member; and hence homicide, committed by the hand, is not imputed to the hand as a sin, if the hand be considered in itself as distinct from the body; but the homicide is imputed to it in so far as the hand is a part of man which is moved by the first motive principle of man. . . . And just as actual sin, which is committed by some member, is not the sin of that member, except in so far as that member is a part of the man himself, on account of which connection it is called a human sin; so is original sin not the sin of the person, except in so far as that person received his nature from the first parent: hence it is called the sin of nature." [43]

He further emphasizes the fact that only those contract original sin who descend from Adam by way of the active principle of generation — *per virtutem activam in generatione*. This is what is understood by being seminally contained in Adam. " But if any one were formed from human flesh by divine power, it is manifest that in such a case the active principle of generation was not derived from Adam; and hence that person would not contract original sin." [44]

Scotus viewed the law of transmission in a somewhat different light. The inclusion of human nature as a whole in

[43] Op. cit. I. II, q. 81, a. 1.   [44] Ibid. a. 4.

Adam, emphasized both by St. Anselm and St. Thomas, according to him does not explain anything. " For this numerical nature which is in the child was not in Adam, although there was in him a nature of the same species. Therefore that particular nature was not endowed with original justice; and therefore it cannot be held responsible for its loss." [45] His own explanation is this: " When the gift (of original justice) was made to the will of Adam, it was made in such a way, that by the same act of giving, so far as it came in question, it was made likewise to every single will of all his descendants, with the proviso that no obstacle should be put in the way of its being actually received by them." [46]

He rejects very definitely the teaching of St. Bonaventure, Alexander of Hales, and others in regard to the part played by concupiscence in the transmission of original sin. He accepted and used the expression, *anima contrahit mediante carne,* but he explained it in his own way. Thus he writes: " It is said that the soul contracts original sin by way of the flesh, but this is not to be understood as if the flesh, through a certain quality caused in it, were the cause of original sin; but in this other sense, that from the flesh conceived under the influence of concupiscence there is formed an organic body, into which the soul is infused and thereby constitutes a person, which person is the child of Adam; and for this reason said person is under obligation of possessing original justice, which was given to Adam himself for all his descendants, and yet is deprived of it. I say, then, that original sin does not result from the action of the flesh upon the soul. . . . From the flesh nothing else results in the child than the relation of being by nature the son of Adam; and upon this relation is consequent the obligation that was imposed by the divine law." [47]

Thus the teaching of the Scholastics on the subject of original sin ran through its successive stages of development. One by one its inconsistent elements were eliminated, divergent views were drawn more closely together, obscure concepts

[45] In Sent. II, d. 32, n. 9.   [47] In Sent. II, d. 32, n. 4-11.
[46] Ibid. d. 33, n. 18.

were clarified, the various details were duly coördinated, and so there finally resulted a theory that satisfied the demands of reason and was in perfect harmony with the data of revelation. All the essential parts of the doctrine thus retained in its ultimate development — the nature of original sin as a privation of justice, its presence in every one as his own proper sin, its voluntariness as derived from the will of the first parent, its transmission by way of generation, Adam's moral headship of the race — all these were incorporated by the Council of Trent in its decree on the nature and propagation of original sin.[48] Some minor points still remained involved in obscurity, as for instance the *vulneratio humanae naturae in naturalibus,* but all that is essential was clearly set forth and firmly established for all times.

[48] Sess. V, Mansi, 33, 27A sqq.; DB, 787 sqq.

CHAPTER X

CHRISTOLOGY

SOME CHRISTOLOGICAL ERRORS: CHRISTOLOGY OF THE SCHOLASTICS

There is no doctrine of our holy faith that was so thoroughly investigated during Patristic times as that of the Incarnation. And for this fact two reasons may be assigned. First, the doctrine is so fundamental that with it Christianity must either stand or fall. Secondly, no other doctrine was so fiercely and so constantly attacked by men of heretical tendencies, who called in question now one now another truth connected with this central mystery of Christian belief. As a consequence, when the Patristic age came to a close, Christology had been fully developed, and at the same time there seemed to be no room left for new heresies to spring up along the lines of Christological teaching. Nor did really new heresies arise in this matter during all the centuries that followed, but some old errors were revived and presented in a new form. One or two of them may be briefly noted, before we proceed to review the Christology of the Scholastics.

A — SOME CHRISTOLOGICAL ERRORS

Spanish Adoptionism, which was really a recrudescence of the Nestorian heresy,[1] was condemned by the Council of Frankford in 794. However, in one form or another, traces of it continued to appear for hundreds of years after its formal condemnation. Thus Roscelin contended that, as nature and person are identical, one must necessarily admit a human person in Christ, since it is of faith that He has a human nature.

[1] Cfr. vol. I, p. 498 sqq.

171

His error, which is Nestorianism pure and simple, was combatted by St. Anselm, in his treatise *De Fide Trinitatis*.[2] "The Word made flesh," St. Anselm argues, "assumed another nature, not another person. For when the term man is used, it signifies the nature which is common to all men; but when we denominate in the concrete this or that man by the name of Jesus, we designate the person, having together with nature an aggregate of properties by which man, taken in a general sense, becomes an individual and is distinguished from other individuals."[3]   And Christ is only one such individual; hence He is only one person.

However, it was principally by Abelard and his school that Adoptionism was revived.   This revival seems to have been the outcome of a wrong conception of the hypostatic union, through which the humanity of Christ was assumed into the unity of person.   According to Abelard, the hypostatic union is neither intrinsic nor substantial.   A truly substantial union, he contends, would lead to an identification of the humanity with the Godhead of the Word, and thus introduce a created and finite person into the Trinity.   Hence such expressions as God is man, this man is God, must always be taken in an improper or figurative sense.[4]   The connection between subject and predicate in these propositions is purely accidental; it does not imply a communication of properties in any true meaning of the term.

It was this misconception of the nature of the hypostatic union that gave rise to the doctrinal error known in history as *Christological Nihilism*.   Its teaching is summed up in the phrase, *Christus in quantum homo non est aliquid* — Christ as man is not anything.   It was not meant as a denial of the reality of Christ's body or soul, but of the substantial union between His human nature and the person of the Word, by reason of which the one can in the concrete be predicated of the other.   The Word took a real body and a real soul, but did not assume them into the unity of person.   They are

[2] Op. cit. c. 6.
[3] Ibid.

[4] Introd. ad Theol. III; ML. 178, 1107; cfr. Bach, Dogmengeschichte, II, p. 391–395.

realities, but not a substantial reality of the Word Incarnate. They are in the Word, but not one with the Word. The Son of God clothed Himself with the humanity as with a garment, that He might appear to men; He used the humanity as an instrument, that He might perform human actions. Hence the expression, *Deus factus est homo,* can only mean, *Deus accepit hominem;* and the corresponding expression, *Deus est homo,* merely stand for, *Deus est habens hominem.*[5]

Furthermore, the better to uphold this peculiar view of the hypostatic union, not a few of its defenders denied that Christ's human soul and body were united so as to form a complete human substance. For the result of such a union would necessarily be an individual substance of rational nature, and therefore a person. But in Christ there is no human person, and consequently there can be no complete human substance. The two constituent elements of such a substance are there, but in a state of separation. Hence the Word Incarnate is in no sense a new reality; He is only the recipient of a new *modus — habitu inventus ut homo.*[6]

Logically this view of the humanity of Christ excludes all filiation, so that Christ as man is neither the Son of God by nature nor by adoption; and not a few theologians of the school of Abelard drew that inference. If the humanity was not even a complete rational substance, adoption in the true sense of the word was obviously out of the question. For adoption means the free assumption of an extraneous person to the right of inheritance; but where there is no complete rational substance, there is no person.[7]

Although this Christological error was most widespread in France, owing to the many disciples and admirers of Abelard, it found followers also in other countries of Europe. Abbot Gerhoh of Reichersberg, who was one of its most formidable opponents, relates that when he visited Rome under Honorius II (1124–1130), he met there a certain Luitolf who openly taught that Christ as man was the adopted son of the Father;

---

[5] Epitome, c. 27; ML, 178, 1737; cfr. Bach, op. cit. II, 391–395.

[6] Cfr. John of Cornwall, Eulogium; ML, 199, 1047.
[7] Cfr. Sum. Sent.; ML, 176, 76.

and also a canon of the Lateran by the name of Adam, who held that Christ was partly God and partly man.[8] In Germany similar views were defended by Folmar, Abbot of Triefenstein near Wuerzburg, who went even so far as to assert that Jesus Christ was neither the Son of God nor equal to God, and that it would be unlawful to accord Him divine honors. It was against Folmar that Gerhoh wrote his treatise *De Gloria et Honore Filii Hominis,* in which he goes to the other extreme of teaching that the divine attributes had been communicated to the humanity of Christ, not only by way of predication, but in reality and in being, that is, in a Eutychian sense.[9]

These Adoptionist errors, propagated by the disciples of Abelard, were discussed at the Council of Tours in 1163, and again at the Council of Sens in 1164; but without definite results. A few years later, however, Pope Alexander III, condemned them in three successive letters, in the last of which, addressed to William of Champeaux, then archbishop of Rheims, he says: " Since Christ is perfect God and perfect man, it is strange that some should go so far in their temerity as to assert that Christ as man is not anything (*non sit aliquid*). In order that such an abuse may not creep into the Church of God, we, by these Apostolic Letters, command Your Fraternity to interdict under anathema, by Our Authority, the presumptuous assertion that Christ is not anything; because as He is true God, so is He also true man, subsisting in a rational soul and human flesh." [10]

This condemnation put an end to all theological discussion on the controverted point, and the last traces of Adoptionism gradually disappeared. Later Scholastics qualified the statement, *Christus in quantum homo non est aliquid,* simply as heretical; [11] and *a fortiori* that as man He is not the natural Son of God. However in the fourteenth century another form of Adoptionism made its appearance, which seems to

[8] Ep. ad Coll. Card.; ML, 193, 576.
[9] ML, 184, 1174; cfr. Pez, Thesaur. Anecdot. ML, 193, 478.
[10] Mansi, 21, 1081C; DB, 393.
[11] Cfr. Thomas, Sum. Theol. III, q. 2, a. 6.

have been originated by Durandus. He admitted that, in virtue of the eternal generation of the Word, Christ as man was the natural Son of the Father; but he thought that over and above this, in view of the rights conferred on the humanity of Christ by the hypostatic union, He might also be called the adopted son of God.[12] Similar views were held by Gabriel Biel and other Nominalists. Although never condemned by the Church, these peculiar opinions are generally regarded as untenable.

B — CHRISTOLOGY OF THE GREAT SCHOLASTICS

Nearly all the most eminent writers of the golden age of Scholasticism built their systems of theological thought upon the foundation laid by Peter Lombard, in his famous *Sententiarum Libri Quatuor*. In regard to Christology, however, this foundation was in many respects unsatisfactory. It was wanting both in depth of thought and in systematic arrangement of the subject-matter. In fact, what he has on the subject is little more than a faint echo of Patristic teaching, supplemented by not a few rather doubtful opinions that were current in his day. Still, on account of the great authority which he enjoyed in the schools, it will be helpful to give in this connection a brief summary of his Christological teaching, as contained in the third book of his Sentences.

Although any one of the three divine persons might have become incarnate, nevertheless it was more befitting to the Son than to the Father or the Holy Spirit; because as in the Godhead He is the Son of God, so was it becoming that in the humanity to be assumed He should become son of man.[13] The Incarnation is the work of the whole Trinity, but it is rightly attributed to the Holy Spirit; because He is the charity and the gift of the Father and the Son, and it was through the ineffable charity of God that the Word became man.[14] The Son assumed the entire human nature, body and soul, for the reason that the entire nature had been corrupted by sin.

[12] In Sent. III, d. 4, q. 1.　　[14] Ibid. d. 4.
[13] Op. cit. d. 1.

However He assumed an individual nature, not human nature in general.[15]   Both soul and body were united to the Godhead, but the body *mediante anima*.[16]

He took real flesh of the Virgin, who had been purified from all stain before His conception. He was conceived and born without sin, and although a descendant of Adam, he was free from all concupiscence.[17]   He took upon Himself not sin, but the punishment of sin.[18]

In Peter's time it was a much mooted question, whether the nature of the Word or the person had become incarnate. His answer is: " The person of the Son assumed human nature, and the divine nature was united to the human nature in the Son. . . . For although it is said that the Son alone took the form of a servant, nevertheless by this the divine nature is not excluded, but only the persons of the Father and the Holy Spirit." [19]   However it is not proper to say that the divine nature became flesh, because this would seem to do away with the distinction of the two natures.[20]   Nor can it be said that the Word assumed a human person; because, although soul and body were united so as to form a human nature, that nature had no personality of its own: they were united in their assumption by the Word.[21]   As the human soul, which is indeed an individual substance of rational nature, is not a person when united to the body, though it is a person when separated from it by death; so is the human nature of Christ not a human person in its union with the Word.[22]

In connection with the foregoing question, he considers the meaning of the expressions, God became man, God is man. He first states the three different views then current. He words them as follows: " There are some who say that in the very incarnation of the Word an individual man was formed, consisting of a rational soul and human flesh, as every other true man, and that this man began to be God — not indeed the divine nature, but the person of the Word; and that God began

[15] Ibid. d. 2.
[16] Ibid. n. 2.
[17] Ibid. d. 3.
[18] Ibid.

[19] Ibid. d. 5.
[20] Ibid. n. 3.
[21] Ibid. n. 4, 5.
[22] Ibid. n. 5.

to be that man. . . . And there are others who in part agree
with the aforesaid, but who besides contend that the man,
who is thus said to be God, consists not only of a rational soul
and a body, but of the human and the divine nature, that is, of
three substances, the divinity, the body, and the soul; and this
Jesus Christ they hold to be only one person, but so that before the Incarnation the person was simple, while in the Incarnation the same person became composite, being made up
of the divinity and the humanity. . . . And others there are
who not only deny that in the incarnation of the Word there
took place a composition of the natures in respect of the person,
but also that there was formed an individual man or any
other substance, composed of soul and body. These two,
soul and body, were united to the person or nature of the Word
in such a way that from the two or the three no nature or person resulted; but rather in such wise that the Word of God
was clothed with the soul and the body as with a garment,
so that He might in a becoming manner appear to mortal
eyes." [23]

In his critical review of these three opinions, he brings forward objections against the first and the second without giving
a definite and final answer. If the first be admitted, he says,
then God is now a substance which was not always God, and
a substance is God without being divine. If the second be accepted, then God and man are each a part of the person of
the Son, and before the Incarnation that person was not complete, but was completed and perfected in the union. Against
the third opinion he urges no objections, and in so far he
seems to make it his own.[24]   However, he concludes by asking
the reader to give the matter still further study, and meanwhile to hold firmly that God assumed human nature in such a
way that man was not changed into God, nor God into man.[25]

Next he examines the question, whether it can be said that
the divine nature, which became incarnate, was born of the
Virgin. He answers in the negative, and assigns as a reason
for his answer that the divine nature was not born of the

[23] Ibid. d. 6.   [25] Ibid. n. 14.
[24] Ibid. d. 7.

Father. It was only the person of the Word that was generated by the Father, and this alone can properly be said to have been born of Mary.[26] However Christ has two nativities, the one eternal according to His Godhead and the other temporal according to His manhood; and in this sense He was twice born.[27]

In regard to the worship that is due to the humanity of Christ, he simply states the two opposite views that were held at the time. Some thought that Christ as man should only be venerated as are the saints of God, but in a higher degree; while others maintained that even as man He must be worshiped with divine honors. The author does not decide the question, but he seems to be in favor of the latter view.[28]

Although Christ as man is not a human person, He is nevertheless a rational substance composed of body and soul; and therefore the statement, *Christus in quantum homo non est aliquid,* is false.[29] According to His human nature He was predestined to be the Son of God, not by nature but by grace.[30] Yet, although the Son of God only by grace, He is not an adopted son; because He never was a person extraneous to the Godhead. His divine sonship, in so far as He is man, is based upon the grace of union.[31] Nor can He be called a creature, except in a figurative way. His human nature is indeed a created substance, but He to whom that nature is united is the Creator Himself.[32] Neither is it proper to say that He had a beginning, for it was only His humanity that began to exist in time.[33] That humanity could have been produced by a creative act, but it was more becoming that it should have its origin by generation from the race of Adam, of which Christ was to be the Redeemer.[34]

In consequence of the hypostatic union, the soul of Christ received from the first moment of its existence grace and knowledge without measure.[35] Although it is said in Holy

[26] Ibid. d. 8.
[27] Ibid. n. 2.
[28] Ibid. d. 9.
[29] Ibid. d. 10.
[30] Ibid. n. 3.

[31] Ibid. n. 4.
[32] Ibid. d. 11.
[33] Ibid. d. 12.
[34] Ibid. n. 2.
[35] Ibid. d. 13.

Scripture that the child Jesus increased in wisdom and grace, yet this cannot be understood in the sense that He did not already possess the plenitude of both. It only means that He manifested His wisdom and grace more fully as He advanced in years.[36] His human will was free, but because of its union with the Word it was confirmed in grace and made impeccable.[37] His human intellect was endowed with infused knowledge, so that Christ as man knew all that He knew as God, but not in the same excellent and perfect way.[38] However as man He could not do all that He could do as God, because human nature is incapable of receiving unlimited power.[39] Moreover His human nature was passible both in soul and body, and therefore as man He was subject to all the infirmities of a passible nature, in so far as these infirmities did not involve sin and were not unbecoming to the dignity of the God-Man.[40]

Upon this foundation, laid by the *Magister Sententiarum,* most of the Scholastics based their system of Christological thought. However, they added much of their own, and at the same time sought to develop what the Sentences contained only in germ. In the following survey it will be best to gather the views of the most prominent Schoolmen under certain headings, so that one may see at a glance what was more or less common to all and what was peculiar to each.

1. *Preliminary Questions.*— Nearly all the great Scholastics consider by way of introduction a number of questions whose solution is intended to prepare the way for a thorough study of the mystery itself. These questions deal chiefly with the possibility, the fitness, and the final cause of the Incarnation. A few remarks in reference to each will be sufficient to indicate the general trend of thought which they involve.

The possibility of the Incarnation is, of course, implied in the accomplished fact as set forth by the teaching of the Church; and in so far it was presupposed by the Scholastics. But they made it a subject of special inquiry for the purpose

36 Ibid. n. 2–5.   39 Ibid. n. 2, 3.
37 Ibid. d. 12, n. 3, 4.   40 Ibid. d. 15.
38 Ibid. d. 14.

of forestalling objections and making the mystery acceptable to reason.   Hence they point out that the Incarnation is but one of the many ways in which God may communicate His goodness to His creatures.[41]   As it is not a change of God into the creature, nor of the creature into God, but only an extension of the divine personality to human nature, it lies entirely within the sphere of omnipotence.   For since one divine nature subsists in three persons, there appears no reason why it should be impossible for two natures to subsist in one person.[42]   And as the person of the Son was from all eternity an hypostasis in respect of the divine nature, why could not the same in time become also the hypostasis of a human nature? [43] For neither is its terminating power in itself limited, nor is human nature incommunicable to a higher personality.[44]   All this can indeed not be demonstrated by positive arguments, because there is question of a mystery; but it can at least be shown not to imply an evident contradiction.[45]

The fitness of the Incarnation all these writers prove by pointing to the striking manifestation of God's various attributes in this mystery — of His power which brought together the highest and the lowest into so intimate a union; of His mercy which had so tender a compassion on man's weakness and misery; of His wisdom which found so excellent a way of repairing the ravages of sin; of His justice which demanded from human nature the full payment of the debt it had incurred; of His goodness which communicated His own being in the highest possible measure to the creature He had made.[46] And it was especially befitting that the person of the Son should become incarnate, although the Father and the Holy Spirit might also have assumed human nature.[47]   The reasons

[41] Thomas, Sum. Theol. III, q. 1, a. 1.
[42] Id. In Sent. III, d. 1, q. 1, a. 1.
[43] Bonavent. In Sent. III, d. 1, a. 1, q. 1.
[44] Scotus, In Sent. III, d. 1, q. 1, n. 1.
[45] Cfr. Halens. Sum. III, q. 2, m. 1, 2; Albert. Magn. In Sent. III, d. 1, a. 1; Bonavent. loc. cit.; Thomas, loc. cit., et Cont. Gent. IV, c. 39, 40; Scotus, loc. cit., et Report. III, d. 1, q. 1.
[46] Halens. Sum. III, q. 2; Thomas, In Sent. III, d. 1, q. 1, a. 2; Bonavent. Ibid. a. 2, q. 1; Albert. Magn. Ibid. a. 1.
[47] Halens. loc. cit. m. 5; Thomas, Sum. Theol. III, q. 3, a. 5; Bonavent. In Sent. III, d. 1, a. 1, q. 4.

for this special fitness are thus given by St. Thomas: Man was created through the Word; therefore it was becoming that after the fall he should be restored by the Word. Man was predestined to become the son of God by adoption; therefore it was fitting that he should possess this dignity through Him who is Son of God by nature. Man strayed from God by an inordinate thirst for knowledge; therefore it was proper that he should be led back to God by the eternal Wisdom.[48]

The final cause of the Incarnation, as of anything else, is the end to be attained. This is ultimately the manifestation of God's glory. On this point all the Scholastics were necessarily agreed, as it was evidently contained in the teaching of the Church. Their discussions turned about the proximate final cause, or the chief reason why God decreed to manifest His glory through the Incarnation. In trying to solve this question, they generally spoke with great reserve. St. Thomas says that it is a matter which He alone knows who was born and offered up for our redemption because He willed it.[49] However He ventures the opinion that the redemption must be regarded as the chief motive of the Incarnation. For " since everywhere in Holy Scripture the sin of the first man is assigned as the reason of the Incarnation, it is more in accordance with this to say that the work of the Incarnation was ordained by God as a remedy for sin; so that, had sin not existed, the Incarnation would not have been. However, the power of God is not limited to this; hence even if sin had not existed, God could nevertheless have become incarnate." [50]

The same view is taken by St. Bonaventure, who says that " the principal reason of the Incarnation seems to have been the redemption of mankind, although with this principal motive there were connected many other reasons of fitness.[51] Alexander of Hales gives no definite solution, but simply states: " It may be said without prejudice to truth, that, if human nature had not fallen into sin, the Incarnation would still have been befitting.[52] Albertus Magnus solves the ques-

[48] Sum. Theol. III, q. 3, a. 8.
[49] In Sent. III, d. 1, q. 1, a. 3.
[50] Sum. Theol. III, q. 1, a. 3.

[51] In Sent. III, d. 1, a. 2, q. 2.
[52] Sum. III, q. 2, m. 13.

tion in the same way as St. Thomas,[53] while Richard of Middleton gives arguments for both sides, without coming to a decision on the point at issue.[54]   Scotus, on the other hand, holds that the redemption of mankind can be considered only as a secondary motive of the Incarnation; while the primary motive was the manifestation of God's glory in this mystery of divine love.   Hence, although he does not positively assert that the Word would have become incarnate even if human nature had not fallen into sin, nevertheless the general import of his teaching points to that conclusion.[55]   And in this view he has always had many followers, even outside the Franciscan school of theology.

2. *The Person Assuming Human Nature.*— When speaking of the assumption of human nature by the Word, nearly all Scholastics consider these three questions: Whether to assume is proper to a divine person?   Whether the divine nature can assume?   Whether one person can assume without the others?   In connection with these questions they also speculate about other points, such as the incarnation of the three divine persons in the same human nature, and in different natures; the assumption of irrational creatures, and other matters of a similar import: but all this may here be passed by, as it has little or no dogmatic value.   It will be sufficient to make a few observations in reference to the first three questions mentioned above.

The term, "to assume," as Richard of Middleton explains, may be taken in three different meanings.   In the first it signifies simply to take and unite; in the second, to take and unite to oneself; in the third, to take and unite to one's person.[56]   In accordance with this threefold meaning of the term, the Scholastics teach that in the first sense the assumption is common to all three persons, because the Trinity united human nature with the person of the Son; in the second sense the assumption belongs to the divine nature, in as much as it caused the human nature to be together with itself in the same

[53] In Sent. III, d. 20, a. 4.
[54] Ibid. a. 2, q. 4.
[55] Ibid. d. 7, q. 3; Report. ibid. q. 4–6.
[56] In Sent. d. 5, a. 1, q. 1.

person; in the third sense the assumption is proper to the person of the Son, since it is to His person alone that the human nature is united.[57]

St. Thomas formulates this common teaching as follows: " The act of assumption proceeds from the divine power, which is common to the three persons, but the term of the assumption is a person. . . . Hence, what has to do with action in the assumption is common to the three persons; but what pertains to the nature of the term belongs to one person in such a manner as not to belong to another; for the three persons caused the human nature to be united to the person of the Son." [58] Again: " To be the principle of the assumption belongs to the divine nature itself, because the assumption took place by its power; however to be the term of the assumption does not belong to the divine nature in itself, but by reason of the person in whom it is considered to be. Hence a person is primarily and more properly said to assume, but it may be said secondarily that the nature assumed a nature to its person. And after the same manner the nature is said to be incarnate, not that it changed to flesh, but that it assumed the nature of flesh." [59]

3. *The Human Nature Assumed by the Person of the Word.* — It is a matter of faith that Christ has a true and complete human nature, composed of body and soul, each one of which has its own proper faculties and senses. In accordance with this teaching of faith, the Scholastics point out that the Word assumed human nature not in the abstract, but in the concrete;[60] not as multiplied in many, but as individualized in one.[61] Abstract human nature, representing the species, could not be thus assumed; for, as St. Thomas argues, " this assumption is terminated in a person, and it is contrary to the nature of a common form to be thus individualized in a

---

[57] Halens. Sum. III, q. 5, m. 1, 2, 3; Thomas, In Sent. III, d. 5, q. 2, a. 1, 2; Bonavent. Ibid. a. 1, q. 1–3; Albert. Magn. Ibid. a. 1, 3, 4, 6; Scotus, Ibid. 1, 1.

[58] Sum. Theol. III, q. 3, a. 4.

[59] Ibid. a. 2.

[60] Halens. Sum. III, q. 4; Bonavent. In Sent. III, d. 5, a. 2, q. 1; Albert. Magn. Ibid. a. 5.

[61] Bonavent. Ibid. d. 2, a. 1, q. 3; Thomas, Ibid. q. 1, a. 2.

person." [62]　Nor would it have been befitting " for human nature to be assumed by the Word in all its supposita.　First, because the multitude of supposita of human nature, which are natural to it, would have been taken away. . . . Secondly, because this would have been derogatory to the dignity of the incarnate Son of God, as He is the First-born of many brethren.　Thirdly, because it is fitting that as one divine suppositum is incarnate, so He should assume one human nature, so that on both sides unity might be found." [63]

Thus the Word assumed all the essential parts of human nature.　He assumed a real body, made up of flesh and blood; for that belongs to the essence of man, and it would not have been becoming Him to have anything fictitious in His work; besides this is the teaching of Holy Scripture.[64]　And He assumed a rational soul, through which the body received its specific being.　This appears both from the Sacred Writings and from the purpose and truth of the Incarnation.[65]　Moreover soul and body were substantially united, so as to form a complete and individual human nature.[66]　However the body was assumed *mediante anima,* in the sense that it was made assumable by its relation to the rational soul, and that the soul, on account of its higher dignity, occupies a middle place between it and God; but not in the sense that the soul is the formal bond of union.[67]

However, although the Word thus assumed a complete and individual human nature, He did not assume a human person. This is evident for three reasons:　First, if the human person existed before its assumption, the Word would not have been conceived by Mary; secondly, if only in its assumption, it would have been consumed rather than assumed; thirdly, if it continued to exist after the assumption, there would be two

---

[62] Sum. q. 4, a. 4.
[63] Sum. Theol. III, q. 4, a. 5.
[64] Halens. Sum. III, q. 4, m. 4; Bonavent. In Sent. III, d. 2, a. 2, q. 1; Thomas, Ibid. q. 1, a. 3; Albert. Magn. Ibid. a. 1, q. 1; Scotus, Ibid. q. 2, 3.
[65] Cfr. Ibid., et Rich. Middleton,

In Sent. III, d. 2, a. 1, q. 1; Ægid. Rom. Ibid. q. 1, a. 1.
[66] Cfr. Thomas, Sum. Theol. III, q. 2, a. 4, 6.
[67] Halens. Sum. III, q. 4, m. 5; Albert. Magn. In Sent. III, d. 2, a. 9, 10; Bonavent. Ibid. a. 3, q. 1; Thomas, III, q. 6, a. 1; Scotus, In Sent. Ibid. q. 2, n. 5.

persons in Christ, which it is heretical to say.[68]   Hence, while complete in every other respect, the human nature as assumed by the Word was without its own proper personality.

4. *Definition of Human Personality.*— Nearly all Scholastics accepted the Boethian definition of person, so that they regarded a human person as an individual substance of a rational nature.   It is true, Richard of St. Victor, Alexander of Hales, and Duns Scotus, as was pointed out in the chapter on the Blessed Trinity, modified this definition somewhat; but that modification did not introduce any substantial change. They all insist that a substance, in order to be properly denominated as a person, must be separated from others of its kind by a threefold distinction — of singularity, incommunicability, and dignity.   A substance is said to be singular when it is undivided in itself, and divided from every other substance.   It is incommunicable, when it has no natural aptitude to become in any sense a part of another being.   These two distinctions constitute the substance in question a *suppositum.*   When to these is added the distinction of dignity, which consists in rationality or intellectuality, there results a *person.*   Here it must be noted, however, that in every rational subject the suppositum and the person are identical.   Hence a human person is a rational suppositum.[69]

On these points the Scholastics were agreed, except that a few of them placed a distinction between the suppositum and the person in the same subject.[70]   But in regard to the further question, what is it precisely that distinguishes the person from the rational nature, or what does personality add to rational nature so as to make it a person, their agreement was not so perfect.   The question is in itself purely philosophical, and as such they did not give to it any special consideration; but they incidentally indicate their views regarding it when speaking of the hypostatic union.   Although even in that connection hardly any of them state explicitly in what the formal reason of personality consists.

[68] Cfr. Bonavent. loc. cit. d. 5, a. 2, q. 2.

[69] Cfr. Thomas, Sum. Theol. III, q. 2, a. 3.

[70] Ibid.

Thus Alexander of Hales, after explaining the threefold distinction noted above, goes on to say that if a rational nature is created so as to exist by itself, it is a person; but if at the moment of creation it is united to another personality, it is not a person, although it is a complete rational nature.[71] Hence he seems to imply that the formal reason of personality, presupposing a complete rational nature, is nothing else than the fact of independent existence. The same view is taken by St. Bonaventure, who says that the human nature of Christ is not a person, simply because it is united to the person of the Word.[72] Scotus is somewhat more explicit. He holds that personality is the ultimate complement whereby a rational nature, complete in itself, is made actually incommunicable; but this complement adds nothing to the complete nature except the double negation of actual and aptitudinal communication. "That negation of dependence . . . actual and aptitudinal, constitutes the formal reason of personality." [73] Henry of Ghent, though not quite so explicit, gives a similar explanation.[74] Hence although the concept of personality is fundamentally positive, in as much as person is the same as a separately existing complete rational nature; still formally considered it is negative, since it implies no physical reality distinct from the complete nature itself.

St. Thomas looks at the matter in a somewhat different light, but according to many of his interpreters comes to practically the same result. "Person," he says, "has a different meaning from nature. For nature . . . designates the specific essence which is signified by the definition. And if nothing was found to be added to what belongs to the notion of the species, there would be no need to distinguish the nature from the suppositum of the nature, which is the individual subsisting in this nature. . . . Now in certain subsisting things we happen to find what does not belong to the notion of the species, namely, accidents and individuating principles, which appear chiefly in such as are composed of matter and form. Hence in such as these the nature and the suppositum really

[71] Sum. III, q. 4, m. 6.
[72] In Sent. d. 5, a. 2, q. 2.
[73] In Sent. III, d. 1, q. 1, n. 9.
[74] Quodl. 5, q. 8.

differ, not indeed as if they were wholly separate, but because in the suppositum is included the nature, and certain other things outside the species are added. . . . And what is said of a suppositum is to be applied to a person in rational or intellectual creatures; for a person is nothing else than an individual substance of rational nature, according to Boethius." [75]

From this exposition many have inferred that St. Thomas regarded personality as something positive, really distinct from the complete nature — either a *modus realis* or the *actus existendi*. But that such was not his mind appears from his solution of such difficulties as were drawn from the acknowledged fact that Christ's human nature is a complete rational substance. Thus when the objectors urged that Christ's human nature answers the Boethian definition of person, he replied: " We must bear in mind that not every individual in the genus of substance, even in rational nature, is a person, but that alone which exists by itself, and not that which exists in some more perfect thing. . . . Therefore, although this human nature is a kind of individual in the genus substance, it has not its own personality, because it does not exist separately, but in something more perfect, namely, in the person of the Word." [76] And to the statement, that the Word assumed whatever perfection He had sown in our nature, and therefore human personality, he replied: " Its proper personality is not wanting to the nature assumed through the loss of anything pertaining to the perfection of human nature, but through the addition of something which is above human nature, namely, the union with a divine person." [77] Hence whatever physical perfection is found in human nature existing by itself apart, is also found in the human nature assumed by the Word; and the only reason why it is not a human person is the fact that it does not exist apart. And this the author expressly states in answer to another difficulty, when he says: " If the two natures together with their properties were separated, there

[75] Sum. Theol. III, q. 2, a. 2. [77] Ibid. q. 4, a. 2 ad 2^m.
[76] Sum. Theol. III, q. 2, a. 2 ad 3^m.

would be on both sides that totality which is required by the notion of person; but while they are united there is only one totality, and therefore only one person." [78]

In the light of these and similar texts, the other statements of St. Thomas, that person and nature are really distinct, that person adds something to nature, evidently bear reference only to specific nature, or to nature in the abstract; not to nature in the concrete. Hence, if according to his teaching, as some of his followers contend, the formal notion of personality is something positive in itself, it is at most a *modus*, not positively, but only negatively distinct from the complete nature. And this was also the teaching of Albertus Magnus. " Were Christ," he says, " to lay aside His humanity, that which was so laid aside would be an individual substance of rational nature, and therefore a person. And if some one were to ask, what conferred upon it the personality which it did not have before, the answer would be that it was the singularity which it did not have before, or the incommunicability, as others say; for properly speaking it is singularity that causes rational nature to be a person. And if it were asked still further, what gave it singularity, one would have to answer that it was division which gave it *per accidens*. For although *per se* division removes something, still *per accidens* it causes that which is divided to be one and separate from the other, and that is singularity." [79]

On the other hand, Durandus and the Nominalists went still farther than Scotus in their identification of nature and person. According to them the distinction between the two is merely a matter of concept; it is in no sense real. [80] This, however, ill accords with the oneness of person in Christ, and hence their view is commonly rejected as untenable.

5. *The Hypostatic Union.*— When the Scholastics began their speculations regarding the mystery of the Incarnation, two fundamental points in reference to the union itself had been clearly defined: First, that the union resulted in oneness

[78] In Sent. III, d. 5, q. 1, a. 3 ad 3^m.
[79] Ibid. d. 5, a. 12.
[80] Durand. Ibid. q. 2; Biel, Ibid. d. 5, q. unica.

of person; secondly, that in spite of this oneness of person, the two natures with all their properties remained really distinct in the union.[81] Hence it is the common teaching of the Scholastics that the union between the divinity and the humanity of Christ is hypostatic or personal. The human nature is united to the divine nature, but in the person of the Son.[82]

This hypostatic union they, first of all, try to illustrate by various examples found in nature; but they are careful to point out that all these examples fall short of a real explanation. The one most commonly used is that of grafting. The inserted shoot becomes in a manner one suppositum with the tree upon which it is engrafted, yet the natures of the two remain really distinct; they do not form a new or third nature.[83] A similar example is found in the union of soul and body, which had already been employed in the Athanasian Symbol. It is true, soul and body form not only one person, but also one nature; still in that nature the one constituent element is not changed into the other, and in so far the example illustrates the hypostatic union. St. Thomas thought it was the best example that could be found in created things.[84]

In the next place they inquire whether anything intervenes between the two extremes of the union, or between the person of the Word and the human nature. On this point they restrict their inquiries to the question of grace; that is, whether habitual grace can in any sense be considered as a medium in which the union took place. With the exception of Alexander of Hales, they all answer the question in the negative.[85] Alexander taught that grace must be considered as a necessary disposition of the human nature, in order that it might fittingly be assumed by the Word. Hence he called it the grace of union.[86] The others also admitted that the human nature of

[81] Cfr. vol. I, p. 396 sqq.; 404 sqq.
[82] Halens. Sum. III, q. 4; Bonavent. In Sent. III, d. 5, a. 1; Thomas, ibid. q. 2; Scotus, ibid. q. 1.
[83] Halens. Sum. III, q. 7. m. 1, a. 1; Bonavent. In Sent. III, d. 6, a. 2, q. 1; Thomas, ibid. d. 1, q. 1, a. 1.

[84] QQ. DD. de Unione Verbi, a. 1.
[85] Bonavent. In Sent. III, d. 2, a. 3, q. 2; Middleton, ibid. a. 2, q. 3; Dionys. Carth., ibid. q. 5; Scotus, ibid. q. 2, 3; Ægid. Rom., ibid. q. 2, a. 3.
[86] Sum. III, q. 7, m. 2, a. 1.

Christ was adorned with sanctifying grace, but held that it was consequent upon the union *in ordine naturae*, if not in point of time.

The common teaching on the point in question was thus formulated by St. Thomas: " In Christ there was the grace of union and habitual grace. Therefore grace cannot be taken to be the means of the assumption of the human nature, whether we speak of the grace of union or of habitual grace. For the grace of union is the personal being that is given gratis to the human nature in the person of the Word, and it is the term of the assumption. While the habitual grace pertaining to the spiritual holiness of the man is an effect following the union. . . . But if by grace we understand the will of God doing or bestowing something gratis, the union was effected by grace, not as a means, but as the efficient cause." [87]

Considered in itself, the hypostatic union consists in the relation which resulted from the act of assumption, and in so far it is something created. " The union of which we are speaking," says St. Thomas, " is a relation which we consider between the divine and the human nature, in as much as they came together in one person of the Son of God. Now . . . every relation which we consider between God and the creature is really in the creature, by whose change the relation is brought into being; whereas it is not really in God, but only in our way of thinking, since it does not arise from any change in God. And hence we must say that the union of which we are speaking is not really in God, except only in our way of thinking; but in human nature, which is a creature, it is really. Therefore we must say it is something created." [88]

Although the hypostatic union thus formally consists in a created relation, it is nevertheless the most intimate of all unions. except that of the nature and persons in the Blessed Trinity. In respect of the distance of the terms brought together, of the power that united them, of the term in which the union resulted, of the indissoluble perpetuity of its duration —" in respect of all these conditions," says St. Bonaventure, " there

[87] Sum. Theol. III, q. 6, a. 6.   [88] Sum. Theol. III, q. 2, a. 7.

is no other union that is at all similar to it; because it exceeds all nature and all ordinary graces; for it is the indissoluble union of the divine and human nature in one person brought about by the power of God." [89] St. Thomas derives the intimate nature of the union chiefly from its term; " for the unity of the divine person, in which the two natures are united, is the greatest." [90] And as this unity " is greater than the unity of person and nature in us, hence also the union of the Incarnation is greater than the union of soul and body in our nature." [91]

It is because of this intimate union that Christ is strictly one — one person, one suppositum, one being, although the natures remain distinct and retain their own properties.[92] In itself the person or hypostasis of Christ is altogether simple; yet as one subsisting being in two natures, He is in so far said to be a composite person.[93] Hence one nature may in the concrete be predicated of the other, so that in view of the union it is perfectly correct to say, God is man, man is God.[94] One may also say, God became man; but its converse, man became God, would be an error in predication.[95] And as the two natures may thus be predicated of one another, so also may the attributes of the natures when taken in the concrete. Hence it is perfectly orthodox to state that the immortal is mortal, the passible is impassible. The justifying reason of these and similar predications is the oneness of person; because it is always the person that forms the proper subject of predication in the concrete.[96]

6. *Consectaria of the Union.*— As the human nature is united to the Godhead in a personal union, it necessarily shares in such properties of God the Son as are communicable to a creature. The first of these is divine sonship. Not only Christ as God, but also Christ as man is the natural Son of God. Nor can He in any sense be called God's adopted son. Some

[89] In Sent. III, d. 6, a. 2, q. 2.
[90] Ibid. a. 9.
[91] Ibid. a. 9 ad 3ᵐ.
[92] Halens. Sum. III, q. 6, m. 2; Bonavent. In Sent. III, d. 6, a. 1; Thomas, ibid. a. 2; Scotus, ibid. q. 2.
[93] Loc. cit.
[94] Cfr. Thomas, Sum. Theol. III, q. 16, a. 1, 2.
[95] Ibid. a. 4, 5.
[96] Ibid.

of the earlier Scholastics fell into error on this point, as was indicated in the first section of this chapter; but their successors were at one in defending Christ's natural sonship. Filiation, they insisted, is a personal property; and as there is only one person in Christ, so can there be only one filiation.[97] Scotus, indeed, called in question the principle that filiation is exclusively a personal property; but he accepted the doctrine of one sonship in Christ from the teaching of the Church.[98]

Since Christ as man is thus the natural Son of God, it necessarily follows that He must be adored with the adoration of *latria,* which has for its formal object God's uncreated excellence. On this point there was no dissension after the time of the Lombard. But it was a moot-question whether the humanity might at the same time be venerated with the cult of *dulia,* which is due to created beings on account of their supernatural excellence. St. Bonaventure and others regard the question as purely theoretical and then solve it in the affirmative;[99] while St. Thomas considers it as practical, and also gives an affirmative answer. Thus he writes: "Adoration is due to the subsisting hypostasis: yet the reason for honoring may be something non-subsistent on account of which the person, in whom it is, is honored. And so the adoration of Christ's humanity may be understood in two ways. First, so that the humanity is the thing adored: and thus to adore the flesh of Christ is nothing else than to adore the incarnate Word of God, just as to revere a king's robe is nothing else than to revere a robed king. And in this sense the adoration of Christ's humanity is the adoration of *latria.* Secondly, the adoration of Christ's humanity may be taken as given by reason of its being perfected with every gift of grace. And in this sense the adoration of Christ's humanity is the adoration not of *latria* but of *dulia.* So that one and the same person of Christ is adored with *latria* on account of His divinity, and with *dulia* on account of His perfect humanity." [100]

[97] Halens. Sum. III, q. 10; Bonavent. In Sent. III, d. 8, a. 2; Albert. Magn. ibid. a. 2; Thomas, Sum. Theol. III, q. 35, a. 5.

[98] In Sent. III, d. 10, q. unica.
[99] Ibid. d. 9, a. 1, q. 1.
[100] Sum. Theol. q. 25, a. 1, 2.

Strictly consequent upon the hypostatic union are certain created perfections, which are found in the faculties of Christ's human soul — in his will and intellect. These were treated by the Scholastics under the headings of grace and knowledge. Only a few of the more important points can here be indicated.

In the matter of grace, aside from the grace of union and substantial sanctity, they held that Christ as man was endowed with habitual grace, and also with gratuitous graces, or *gratia gratis data*. The former was in Him the same as in other just men, only He possessed it in an incomparably higher degree. Though finite in itself, it did not admit of an increase as possessed by Him.[101] With it were connected all the virtues and gifts, excepting such as in their formal concept conflicted with the perfection of the state of personal union. To this latter class belong faith and hope, when taken in their full significance; because Christ's human soul enjoyed from the first moment of its existence the beatific vision.[102] He also possessed all the gratuitous graces that may be communicated to human nature, and that in the highest possible degree.[103] And all these graces and gifts were proper to Him both as an individual man and as the head of the Church.[104] Under the latter aspect they are called the *gratia capitis*.

Although in Christ as man there was thus the fullness of all graces, nevertheless His human will remained free; not in regard to final beatitude of which His soul was already in possession, but in reference to the choice of good actions which He performed during His life on earth.[105] At the same time, however, it was so determined to good that the very possibility of sinning was excluded. For this impeccability three reasons are assigned — the fullness of grace, the beatific vision, and the hypostatic union.[106] Scotus, however, did not

---

[101] Halens. Sum. III, q. 8. m. 3; Bonavent. In Sent. III, d. 13, a. 1; Albert. Magn. ibid. a. 1; Scotus, ibid. d. 18, q. 3.
[102] Thomas, Sum. Theol. III, q. 7.
[103] Ibid. a. 7, 8; Bonavent. In Sent. III, d. 13, a. 2.
[104] Ibid.

[105] Cfr. Thomas, Sum. Theol. III, q. 18, a. 4.
[106] Halens. Sum. III, q. 5, m. 2, a. 2; Bonavent. In Sent. III, d. 12, a. 2; Albert. Magn. ibid. a. 4-6; Thomas, ibid. q. 2, a. 1; Scotus, ibid. q. unica.

admit that the hypostatic union necessarily excluded the possibility of sin.[107] In this he was followed by Durandus, who held that if the humanity had been assumed without being perfected by grace, Christ could have sinned and even lost his soul.[108]

In the human intellect of Christ the Scholastics recognized a threefold knowledge — *scientia beata, infusa, acquisita.* The first is the intuitive vision of God, which Christ's human soul enjoyed from the first moment of its existence; the second was produced in the intellect by a special divine operation, also at the first moment of His earthly life; the third was acquired by a natural use of His faculties during His sojourn on earth. By the knowledge of beatific vision " the soul of Christ knows in the Word all things existing in whatever time, and the thoughts of men," but not all those possibles that " are in the divine power alone." [109] By the infused knowledge " the soul of Christ knew: First, whatever can be known by the force of man's active intellect, as, for example, whatever pertains to human sciences; secondly, all things made known to man by divine revelation, whether they belong to the gift of wisdom or the gift of prophecy, or any other gift of the Holy Ghost; . . . Yet He did not know the essence of God by this knowledge, but by that of vision alone." [110]

Coexisting with these perfections of intellect and will, there were in the soul and body of Christ " those defects which flow from the common sin of the whole nature, yet are not repugnant to the perfection of knowledge and grace." [111] Hence He experienced hunger, thirst, pain, and the agony of death. All these defects or infirmities were proper to the nature assumed by the Word; for that nature was passible and did not as yet enjoy all the effects of the beatific vision.[112]

In this brief outline are contained the chief points discussed by the Scholastics in their Christological teaching. Comprehensive and thorough as that teaching was, it did nevertheless

[107] Loc. cit.
[108] Ibid. q. 2.
[109] Cfr. Thomas, Sum. Theol. III, q. 10, a. 2.
[110] Ibid. q. 11, a. 1.
[111] Ibid. q. 14.
[112] Ibid.

not add very much to the development of dogmas connected with the mystery of the Incarnation. And the reason is that nearly all of them had received their full development during Patristic times.[113]   When the Scholastics began their speculations, the oneness of person in Christ, the duality of natures, faculties, and operations, His natural sonship as God and as man, and His title to divine worship, had all been defined as so many dogmas of the faith; and to these nothing really new was added by later definitions.   But the studies of the Schoolmen did excellent service in making these various dogmas, and many important points of doctrine connected with them, more accessible to reason.

[113] Cfr. vol. I, p. 308 sqq.; p. 387 sqq.; p. 498 sqq.

CHAPTER XI

SOTERIOLOGY

SOME SOTERIOLOGICAL ERRORS: SOTERIOLOGY OF THE SCHOLASTICS

The teaching of the Fathers on the redemption of the world not only emphasized the fact that Christ was sent by God as the Savior of our fallen race, but also set forth with considerable attention to details the nature of the redemptive work. They regarded the incarnation of God's own Son as a deification of our vitiated nature, and in His sufferings and death they recognized a superabundant satisfaction for all the sins of the world. He was to them the second Adam, who by His perfect obedience undid the harm that had been wrought by the disobedience of the first Adam. He overcame Satan, conquered death, opened up the sources of divine grace, and in all things acted as mediator between sinful men and their offended God.[1] This teaching was taken over in its entirety by the Scholastics; and, excepting a few minor points, was without further development incorporated in their theological system.

A — SOME SOTERIOLOGICAL ERRORS

In a previous chapter it was pointed out that Abelard and his school fell into a very serious error regarding original sin. They looked upon it not as a moral stain implying guilt, but as a mere liability to punishment. Human nature, according to them, was not intrinsically vitiated, and therefore stood in no need of restoration. Nothing was required but a remission of the punishment which rested heavily upon the race on account of the sin committed by the common ancestor. And for this the Son of God need not have become man.[2]

Such a view of original sin necessarily led to a misappre-

[1] Cfr. vol. I, p. 316 sqq.　　　[2] In Epist. ad. Rom. c. 5.

hension of the redemptive work of the Savior.   It was the example of right living that mankind needed, not the healing touch of a divine physician.   And this formed the burden of Abelard's soteriological teaching, as appears from many parts of his works.   Thus he writes: " It seems to us that in this we are justified and reconciled to God, in the blood of Christ, that, through a singular grace conferred on us, the Son took our nature, and persevered in instructing us by word and example even till death, drawing us so closely to Him by the bonds of love, that, inflamed by the thought of so great a benefit of divine grace, we might in our charity not be afraid to bear all for His sake. . . . Hence our redemption is that exceeding great love of Christ which He showed forth in His sufferings; for thereby we were not only set free from the servitude of sin, but also acquired the true liberty of the children of God; so that now we do all things, not through fear but through love." [3]

The enlightenment that comes to us from Christ's instructions, the encouragement afforded by His heroic example, the graces obtained for us by His prayer — these, according to Abelard, constitute the work of redemption.   " When God caused His Son to become man, He made Him subject to the law which was common to all men.   Hence it was necessary that He should love His neighbor as Himself, and infuse into us the grace of His charity, both by instructing us and by praying for us." [4]

These vagaries of Abelard were at once strongly attacked by William of Saint Thierry and by St. Bernard.   William went to the root of the error by pointing out that original sin is in the true sense of the term a vitiation of human nature, and that the nature so vitiated needed more than example and instruction to raise it from its moral degradation.   It was the death of the God-Man that wrought the redemption.[5]   Christ's death was a vicarious satisfaction for sin.   He was in truth the second Adam, by whom spiritual life was restored to the fallen race.[6]

[3] Loc. cit.; cfr. Theol. Christ. I, 4.   [5] Ænigma Fidei, p. 111.
[4] Loc. cit.   [6] Ibid. p. 123.

St. Bernard's refutation follows the same line of thought. "The original fault," he says, "was in truth a grievous sin, which infected not only the person of Adam but the entire race."[7] God thought it proper that the redemption should be wrought by the outpouring of blood. "Why, you ask, should He effect by the outpouring of blood what He could have effected by instruction? Ask Him. For me it is enough that so it was decreed."[8] Yet it was not death as such, but rather the obedient will that was efficacious: "Not death, but the ready will of Him who died was acceptable; and so by that death He overcame death, effected our salvation, and restored us to innocence."[9] Christ accepted His sufferings and death freely; but we had urgent need of them for our redemption. "For human perversity can indeed kill, but it has no power to restore life. . . . He alone could in such wise lay down His life, who by His own power rose from the dead."[10]

Another erroneous conception of the redemption is usually ascribed to St. Anselm; not in regard to the nature of the redemptive work in itself, but in reference to its necessity. He develops his theory of the redemption in the treatise which he entitled, *Cur Deus Homo?* The following outline will suffice to make clear his views on the subject.

His fundamental thought on the point in question is this: Every reasonable creature is bound to obey God; "this is the sole and entire honor which we owe our Maker.[11] Whosoever does not give to God this honor which is His due, takes away from Him what is His own, and thereby dishonors Him."[12] Now the human race by committing sin disobeyed God, and therefore deprived Him of the honor to which He had a right; it took away from God what was His own. Consequently, "so long as man does not restore what he snatched away, he remains guilty. Nor is it sufficient to restore that only which was thus unjustly taken from God; but, on account of the affront implied in that unjust action, even more than

---

[7] In IV Hebd. Sanct. n. 7.
[8] De Error. Abelard. c. 5.
[9] Ibid.

[10] In IV Hebd. Sanct. n. 3.
[11] Op. cit. I, 11.
[12] Ibid.

was taken away must be given by way of restoration." [13]
This, then, was the position of the fallen race. Might its
disobedience have been forgiven, without demanding satisfaction? No: "because all God's ways are well ordered; and
right order demands that sin not satisfied for be punished.
For it is by punishment that God subjects the recalcitrant
sinner to Himself." [14] Hence " it is necessary that every sin
be followed either by satisfaction or by punishment." [15] But
the punishment and consequent loss of all mankind would
interfere with the purpose which God had in view when He
created man; " for He intended that human nature, which He
created free from sin, should fill up the number of the angels
who had fallen away." [16] Besides " it was not becoming that
what God had proposed concerning man should be entirely
frustrated." [17]

Hence satisfaction was necessary. But man could not make
due satisfaction: First, because he already owed God everything; secondly, even if he did not, he could never make satisfaction in proportion to the gravity of the sin committed.[18]
If you doubt this, " you have not considered what the weight
of sin is." [19] Due satisfaction for sin is " something far
greater than every conceivable thing besides God." [20] Hence
God's goodness must complete the work which it began in
the act of creation.[21] And because no one can give due satisfaction except God, and no one must give it except man, hence
it was necessary that it should be given by a God-Man.[22]
This is the answer to the question, *Cur Deus homo?* God became man that He might in His human nature render satisfaction for the sins of men.

Through Christ a way was opened for the sinful race to
effect its reconciliation with God. He was in a position to
make atonement for all the sins of the world, and to do so
through His human nature. For although as man He owed

[13] Ibid.
[14] Ibid. I, 12; I, 15.
[15] Ibid. I, 15.
[16] Ibid. I, 16.
[17] Ibid. I, 4.

[18] Ibid. I, 20.
[19] Ibid. I, 21.
[20] Ibid. II, 6.
[21] Ibid. II, 5.
[22] Ibid. II, 6.

God obedience, yet He was under no obligation to suffer and
to die as He did. He accepted death freely, and by His
ready obedience fulfilled all justice.[23] Hence one can truly
say: *" Illum tale quid sponte dedisse Deo ad honorem illius,
cui quidquid, quod Deus non est, comparari non potest, et
quod pro omnibus omnium hominum debitis recompensare
potest."* [24] God alone can be compared to what He gave, and
therefore it was an adequate compensation for the sins of
men.

Such a gift, coming from Christ, necessarily called for a
reward; " but as Christ did not stand in need of anything, He
graciously allowed His followers, to whom by dying He gave
an example of dying for justice's sake, to become sharers in
His merit; so that what they owed for their sins might be
canceled, and what was wanting to them on account of their
sins might be given to them," namely, the grace of God.
" Nothing more reasonable, nothing sweeter, nothing more
desirable, could the world ever conceive." [25] In this the mercy
of God, so to speak, exhausted itself. " So great do we find
this mercy, so perfectly in accord with the demands of justice,
that neither a greater nor one more just can be conceived." [26]

This, then, is Anselm's theory: Redemption through the
incarnate Son of God was necessary; because it was unbecoming that God should either forgive man's sins without requiring satisfaction, or that He should allow all mankind to
perish forever; and, on the other hand, man was altogether
incapable of rendering due satisfaction: therefore the redemption must be brought about by the expiatory death of the God-
Man. It must, however, be borne in mind that the author
bases his reasoning exclusively on natural principles, without
reference to revelation. Hence Boso, his interlocutor, says
very much to the point: *" Sic probas Deum fieri hominem ex
necessitate, ut etiam, si removeantur pauca, quae de nostris
libris posuisti (ut quod de tribus personis Dei et de Adam
tetigisti), non solum Judaeis, sed etiam paganis sola ratione
satisfacias."* [27]

[23] Ibid. I, 9; II, 19.　　[25] Ibid. II, 20.　　[27] Ibid. II, 23.
[24] Ibid. II, 19.　　　　　[26] Ibid. II, 21.

B — Soteriology of the Scholastics

In their soteriological discussions the Scholastics enter into so many details and side issues that it is impossible even to mention them in a compendious work like the present. Nor is such an enumeration at all necessary; for many of the points discussed are mere speculations, and are not likely to develop at any future time into dogmas of the faith. In the following outline, therefore, only such questions will be briefly touched upon as are more or less essential to a full understanding of the redemptive work of Christ as set forth by the Schoolmen.

1. *Necessity of the Redemption.*— It is sometimes said that St. Anselm had no followers among the Scholastics in his theory on the necessity of the redemption. This statement is true in so far as his theory is interpreted as implying necessity in the strict sense of the term, and on the part of God. But not a few of the Scholastics gave a different interpretation of it. Thus St. Bonaventure says that it must be understood *in quantum est ex parte nostra, praesupposita dispositione divina, qua nos sic, et non alio modo, liberare decrevit.*[28] And the same interpretation is given by St. Thomas: *Anselmus loquitur quantum est ex parte nostra, supposita Dei ordinatione.*[29] If this interpretation be correct, which does however not appear very probable, it must be said that St. Anselm had nearly all the most representative Scholastics on his side. For, with the exception of Scotus and a few others, they are all agreed that man was entirely unable to make due reparation for his sins, and that therefore in the present order of Providence redemption by the God-Man was necessary. They usually bring out the following points.

Due satisfaction for sin must imply a twofold reparation: First, of God's personal honor which was outraged by sin; secondly, of the loss sustained by God in the corruption of the human race. Now whatever may be said about the possibility of a creature, assisted by grace, repairing the loss caused by sin; no creature whatever, even the holiest, could possibly

[28] In Sent. III, d. 20, a. unic., q. 6 ad 2^m.
[29] Ibid. a. 4 ad 2^m.

repair the injury done to God's honor. That injury is measured by God's infinite dignity, and in this sense the evil of
sin is infinite; whereas the moral value of any satisfaction that
might be rendered by a creature is necessarily finite. Hence
in the supposition that God demanded adequate satisfaction
from human nature, there was no other means of redemption
besides the incarnation of God's own Son.[30]

However with this more common teaching of the most representative Scholastics, Scotus, Durandus, and the Nominalists
generally, do not agree. They deny the very foundation upon
which it is made to rest, namely, that sin is in any real sense
an infinite moral evil. It is true, God's offended majesty is
infinite, but that infinity, they say, has only an extrinsic relation to sin. Hence they hold that human nature endowed with
the fullness of grace, but without being hypostatically united to
the Godhead, might have made adequate reparation for all
sins and thus have redeemed mankind. It is true, God would
have been under no obligation to accept this satisfaction, but
neither was He under obligation to accept the satisfaction
rendered by Christ.[31]

On the other hand, all are at one in holding that God might
have been satisfied with an inadequate reparation, such as it
was in the power of man to make. The common teaching on
the point is thus set forth by St. Thomas. " Satisfaction may
be said to be sufficient in two ways: First, perfectly, in as
much as it is condign, being adequate to make good the fault
committed, and in this way the satisfaction of a mere man cannot be sufficient for sin, both because the whole of human nature has been corrupted by sin, whereas the goodness of any
person or persons could not make up adequately for the harm
done to the whole of the nature; and also because sin committed against God has a kind of infinity from the infinity of
the divine majesty; for the greater the person we offend, the
more grievous the offence. Hence for condign satisfaction it

[30] Halens. Sum. III, q. 1, m. 6;
Bonavent. In Sent. III, d. 20, a.
unic., q. 3; Albert. Magn. ibid. a. 6,
7; Thomas, ibid. a. 2; Sum. Theol.
III, q. 1, a. 2.
    [31] In Sent. d. 20, q. unic. n. 3
sqq.; Durandus, ibid. q. 2.

was necessary that the act of the one satisfying should have an infinite efficiency, as being of God and man. Secondly, man's satisfaction may be termed sufficient imperfectly, that is, in the acceptation of him who is content with it, even though it is not condign, and in this way the satisfaction of a mere man is sufficient." [32] Scotus, however, as was pointed out in the preceding paragraph, held that this " imperfectly sufficient satisfaction " might have been accepted by God as condign.

Furthermore, all are agreed that God might have freed mankind from sin without requiring any satisfaction whatever; for the manner of forgiveness rests with the person who is offended by sin. " If He had willed to free man from sin without any satisfaction," argues St. Thomas, " He would not have acted against justice. For a judge, while preserving justice, cannot pardon faults without penalty, if the faults have been committed against another. . . . But God has no one higher than Himself, for He is the sovereign and common good of the whole universe. Consequently, if He forgive sin, which has the formality of fault in that it is committed against Himself, He wrongs no one: just as any one else, overlooking a personal trespass, without satisfaction, acts mercifully and not unjustly." [33] However such forgiveness, they all hold, would have been less in accord both with God's perfections and the needs of man.[33]

2. *The Atonement.*— It is the common teaching of the Scholastics that Christ merited during the whole time of His earthly existence, from His conception till His death; and in that sense every action of His life contributed to the atonement for man's sins.[34] However, they ascribe the atonement in a special sense to His passion and death, as it was through them that God wished to effect the full redemption of the world. In themselves neither sufferings nor death would have been necessary to render God condign satisfaction; but there were special reasons of congruity why He wished the redemption

[32] Sum. Theol. III, q. 1, a. 2 ad 2m.
[33] Ibid. q. 46, a. 2 ad 3m.
[34] Halens. Sum. III, q. 16, m. 2;

Bonavent. In Sent. III, d. 18, a. 1; Albert. Magn. ibid. a. 6; Thomas, ibid. a. 3; Scotus, ibid. q. unica.

to be accomplished in this way. "That man should be delivered by Christ's passion," writes St. Thomas, "was in keeping with both His mercy and His justice. With His justice, because by His passion Christ made satisfaction for the sin of the human race; and so man was set free by Christ's justice: and with His mercy, because since man of himself could not satisfy for the sin of all human nature. . . . God gave him His Son to satisfy for him." [35]

Then there were special reasons on the part of man, besides deliverance from sin. Those commonly given by the various writers are thus summarized by St. Thomas: "In the first place, man knows thereby how much God loves him, and so is stirred up to love Him in return, and herein lies the perfection of human salvation. . . . Secondly, because thereby He set us an example of obedience, humility, constancy, justice, and the other virtues displayed in the passion, which are requisite for man's salvation. . . . Thirdly, because Christ by His passion not only delivered man from sin, but also merited justifying grace for him and the glory of bliss. . . . Fourthly, because man is all the more bound to refrain from sin, when he bears in mind that he has been redeemed by Christ's blood. . . . Fifthly, because it redounded to man's greater dignity, that as man was overcome and deceived by the devil, so also it should be a man that should overthrow the devil: and as man deserved death, so a man by dying should vanquish death." [36]

The moral value of Christ's sufferings and death are thus indicated by St. Bonaventure, in answer to an objection that the Savior's passion was not sufficient to blot out all sins: "This one passion of Christ was not only sufficient to satisfy for the sin of Adam, but also for the vast number of all other sins. Hence the death of Christ was of avail also for His slayers, if they were willing to be converted; for the merit of the suffering Christ was infinitely greater than the sin of Judas who betrayed Him, than the sin of the Jews who instigated the Gentiles to crucify Him; because the goodness of Christ far exceeded their malice." [37]

[35] Sum. Theol. III, q. 46, a. 1.
[36] Ibid. a. 3.
[37] In Sent. III, d. 20, a. unic., q. 5 ad 6m.

In another place the same author states that the merit of Christ is of infinite moral value, and this arises from the fact that " His soul is united to a divine person, on account of which union not only man but God Himself is said to die; whence it follows that His merit is infinite, not by reason of created grace, but because of the infinite dignity of His person." [38] St. Thomas expresses this view in almost identical terms, when he says: " The dignity of Christ's flesh is not to be estimated solely from the nature of flesh, but also from the person assuming it — in as much as it was God's flesh, the result of which was that it was of infinite worth." [39]

It was, however, not exclusively from the dignity of Christ's person that the satisfactory worth of His sufferings and death was derived. Other elements also contributed thereto, as is thus stated by St. Thomas: " He properly atones for an offence who offers something which the offended one loves equally, or even more than he detested the offence. But by suffering out of love and obedience, Christ gave more than was required to compensate for the offence of the whole human race. First of all, because of the exceeding charity with which He suffered; secondly, on account of the dignity of His life which He laid down in atonement, for it was the life of one who was God and man; thirdly, on account of the extent of the passion and the greatness of the grief endured. . . . And therefore Christ's passion was not only a sufficient but a superabundant atonement for the sins of the human race." [40]

Hence in estimating the moral value of the satisfaction rendered by Christ, two distinct sources must be considered. The first is the physical goodness of the action, as derived from its productive principle, its circumstances, and its object. The second is the same goodness as elevated in the moral order by the dignity of the person of whom the action is predicated. Under the first aspect, the satisfaction of Christ has a finite moral value; because its productive principle — Christ's human nature — its circumstances, and its object are all finite. Un-

[38] Ibid. d. 13, a. 1, q. 3.
[39] Sum. Theol. III, q. 48, a. 2 ad 3m.
[40] Ibid. a. 2.

der the second aspect its moral value is infinite; because the person of the Word, as its elevating principle, is of infinite dignity. Nor is this infinite moral value, as derived from the person of the Word, something merely extrinsic to Christ's human actions; because in virtue of the hypostatic union, the dignity of the person is communicated to the human nature in such wise that its actions are in a true sense the actions of God. Hence it is perfectly correct to say that the satisfaction of Christ is intrinsically of infinite moral value.[41]

On this last point, however, different views were entertained by some of the Scholastics. Thus Scotus maintained that the satisfaction of Christ, and His merit in general, must be considered simply as finite. He states his view in these precise terms: "I say that the merit of Christ was finite: because it essentially depended on a finite principle, and therefore, even considering all its circumstances, its relation to the person of the Word, its connection with the end to be obtained, it was simply finite; for all these relations were finite."[42] Still he admits that in its relation to the person of the Word it may be termed extrinsically infinite; because on account of this relation it was of such a nature that it might be accepted by God as of infinite value. This was also the view taken by the Nominalists, who laid down the general principle: "*Meritum quodcumque tantum et pro tantis potest acceptari passive, quantum et pro quantis vult tota Trinitas active.*"[43]

3. *Effects of the Atonement.*— From what has been said in the preceding paragraphs, it is clear that the Scholastics looked upon the satisfaction rendered by Christ as a compensation offered to God's offended majesty for the dishonor and loss caused by man's sins. This concept, though occurring quite often in the writings of the Fathers, was first fully developed by St. Anselm, as was pointed out at the beginning of this chapter. The later Scholastics adopted it as developed by him, and made it the central idea of their soteriological system. Hence, according to them, the first effect of Christ's redemptive work is the reconciliation of the sinful world with God.

[41] Cfr. Thomas, Sum. Theol. III, q. 46, a. 4, 12.

[42] In Sent. III, d. 19, n. 7.

[43] Cfr. Biel, ibid. note 3.

Christ placated God by restoring that which sin had unjustly taken away.   This is the proper effect of the redemption taken in the sense of atonement or satisfaction.   It directly terminates in God, and has only an indirect bearing upon the redeemed world.

However this placation of God must not be understood in the sense that God was at enmity with the world, but rather that the world was at enmity with God.   God loved the world even when buried in sin, and hence He sent His own Son to pay the price of redemption demanded by His justice; but without the payment of that price He would not grant the graces that were necessary for the world's salvation.   Hence whilst the redemption is in one sense a compensation made to God, it is in another sense a source of merit both for the Redeemer Himself and for all those who were redeemed by Him. It is more particularly under this second aspect that the Scholastics consider the effects of the redemption in detail.   In this connection they inquire what the Savior merited for Himself, and what for those whom He had come to save.

That all the requisite conditions for merit were found in Christ's actions, is thus briefly pointed out by St. Thomas: " For merit three things are required: A person who can merit, a meritorious action, and a reward. . . . Now all three of these are found in the case of Christ.   For although in one sense He was *in termino,* namely, in regard to those operations of His soul by reason of which He enjoyed the beatific vision; nevertheless there was still something wanting to Him in respect of glory, namely, in so far as He was passible both in soul and body and was subject to bodily death: and therefore in this respect He was a *viator,* in the state of acquiring something further.   In like manner all His actions were meritorious by reason of charity; and again, He had dominion over His actions on account of the liberty of His will; and therefore He merited by every one of His actions." [44]   Lastly, the third condition, that there was a reward in store for Him, is necessarily implied in the preceding two; since the merit of

[44] In Sent. III, q. 18, a. 2.

His actions was in proportion to any reward that God could bestow.[45]

The common teaching of the Scholastics regarding the object of Christ's merit for Himself is thus formulated by the same author: "Since all perfection and greatness must be attributed to Christ, consequently He must have by merit what others have by merit; unless it be of such a nature that its want would detract from His dignity and perfection more than would accrue to Him by merit. Hence He merited neither grace nor knowledge nor the beatitude of His soul, nor the Godhead, because, since merit regards what is not yet possessed, it would be necessary that Christ should have been without these at some time; and to be without them would have diminished Christ's dignity more than His merit would have increased it. But the glory of the body, and the like, are less than the dignity of meriting, which pertains to the virtue of charity. Hence we must say that Christ had by merit the glory of His body and whatever pertained to His outward excellence, as His ascension, veneration, and the rest." [46]

In regard to the first point, however, William of Auxerre and a few others maintained that Christ also merited for Himself life eternal, although His soul was in possession of the beatific vision from the moment of His conception.[47] This view was regarded by Albertus Magnus as probable.[48] The second point was admitted by all, except that Scotus held that Christ merited the glory of His body only indirectly. According to him the direct object of Christ's merit in this respect was the cessation of the miracle by which the glorification of the body was withheld during the Savior's earthly life.[49] St. Thomas and others look upon this withholding of glory from Christ's body as a special dispensation, "in order that He might procure His bodily glory with greater honor, when He had merited it by His passion." [50]

---

[45] Ibid.; cfr. a. 3, 4.
[46] Sum. Theol. III, q. 19, a. 3.
[47] Sum. Aurea, III, tr. 1, c. 7.

[48] In Sent. III, d. 18, a. 4.
[49] Ibid. q. 1, n. 15.
[50] Sum. Theol. q. 19, a. 3 ad 3m.

The object of Christ's merit in our regard includes all the graces and favors that come to us in the supernatural order of our existence. The Scholastics usually gather them under these heads: Deliverance from sin, from the power of the devil, from the debt of punishment; reconciliation with God; opening of the gates of heaven.[51] However the various benefits here enumerated are not the immediate results of Christ's redemptive work; they can be realized in individual souls only by a faithful use of the spiritual graces merited by Christ. Hence the first effect of the redemption in our regard consists in the grace of God, freely offered to us as a means of working out our eternal salvation.

By deliverance from sin the Scholastics understand forgiveness of all sins, original and personal, obtained by an application of the merits of Christ through the ordinary channels of grace. "The passion of Christ," writes St. Thomas, "is the proper cause of the forgiveness of sins in three ways. First of all, by way of exciting our charity, because . . . it is by charity that we procure the pardon of our sins. . . . Secondly, Christ's passion causes forgiveness of sins by way of redemption. For since He is our head, . . . He delivered us as His members from our sins, as by the price of His passion. . . . Thirdly, by way of efficiency, in as much as Christ's flesh, wherein He endured the passion, is the instrument of the Godhead, so that His sufferings and actions operate with divine power for expelling sin." [52] Or as St. Bonaventure puts it: "*Justificatio nostra attribuitur passioni Christi per modum meriti intervenientis, exempli provocantis et exemplaris dirigentis.*" [53]

Deliverance from the power of the devil is effected in three ways: First, "in as much as the passion is the cause of the forgiveness of sins"; secondly, "in as much as it reconciled us with God"; thirdly, "in as much as in Christ's passion he exceeded the limit of power assigned him by God, by conspir-

---

[51] Halens. Sum. III, q. 17, 18; Bonavent. In Sent. d. 19, a. 1; Scotus, ibid. q. unic.; Albert. Magn. ibid. a. 1.

[52] Sum. Theol. III, q. 49, a. 1.
[53] In Sent. III, d. 19, a. 1, q. 1.

ing to bring about Christ's death, who, being sinless, did not deserve to die." [54]

We were delivered from the debt of punishment both directly and indirectly. Directly, " in as much as Christ's passion was sufficient and superabundant satisfaction for the sins of the whole human race; but when sufficient satisfaction has been paid, then the debt of penalty is abolished. Indirectly, in so far as Christ's passion is the cause of the forgiveness of sin, upon which the debt of punishment rests." [55]

There are also two ways in which we may be said to have been reconciled to God. First, because Christ's passion " takes away sin by which men became God's enemies." Secondly, because " it is a most acceptable sacrifice to God. Now it is the proper effect of sacrifice to appease God; just as man likewise overlooks an offence committed against him on account of some pleasing act of homage shown him." [56]

Lastly, by Christ's passion the gates of heaven were opened, in the sense that by the forgiveness of sin, obtained through the merits of the Savior, the obstacle to the intuitive vision of God was removed. For this obstacle was the twofold sin which prevented men from entering into the kingdom of heaven — original sin and personal sin. " Now by Christ's passion we have been delivered not only from the common sin of the whole human race, both as to its guilt and as to its debt of penalty, for which he paid the penalty on our behalf; but, furthermore, from the personal sins of individuals, who share in His passion by faith and charity and the sacraments of faith. Consequently, the gates of heaven's kingdom are thrown open to us through Christ's passion." [57]

From the foregoing exposition of the redemptive work of the Savior, which was accomplished by His human nature as united to the person of the Word, it necessarily follows that Christ is mediator between God and men. For, as St. Bona-

[54] Thomas, Sum. Theol. III, q. 49, a. 2.

[55] Ibid. a. 2; cfr. Halens. Sum. III, q. 17, m. 4; Bonavent. In Sent. III, d. 19, a. 1, q. 4; Scotus, ibid. d. 14, q. 1.

[56] Thomas, Sum. Theol. III, q. 49, a. 4.

[57] Ibid. a. 4; cfr. Bonavent. In Sent. III, d. 18, a. 2, q. 3.

venture says, a mediator is a link that unites two extremes and exercises the function of reconciliation.[58]   Christ is both God and man, and thus unites in Himself the offended Godhead and human nature gone astray from its Maker.   As man He physically performs the actions which are required to pay the debt; as God He communicates to these actions an infinite moral value, so that the payment may be adequate.   Thus as God-Man He brings about the reconciliation of man with God. Hence the mediatorship of Christ is not based upon His human nature alone, nor upon His Godhead alone; but upon the two united in the one person of the Word.[59]   However, to be mediator properly belongs to Him as man, and not as God; for as God He does not differ from the Father and the Holy Ghost either in nature or in power of dominion, while as man He differs from God in nature and from men in dignity of both grace and glory.[60]

Furthermore, to be a mediator between God and men is proper to the office of priesthood; therefore Christ is not only our mediator but also our eternal high priest.[61]   And as He offered Himself as a sacrifice for our salvation, He is at the same time a victim immolated in our behalf — a victim for sin, a peace-offering, a perfect holocaust.[62]   His priesthood, moreover, He communicates to others in such wise that He " is the fountain-head of the entire priesthood: for the priest of the Old Law was a figure of Him; while the priest of the New Law works in His person." [63]

4. *The Death of Christ.*— For the fitness of the death of Christ St. Thomas gives these five reasons: " First of all that He might satisfy for the whole human race, which was sentenced to die on account of sin. . . . Secondly, that He might show the reality of the flesh assumed. . . . Thirdly, that by dying He might deliver us from the fear of death. . . . Fourthly, that by dying in the body to the likeness of sin — that is, to its penalty — He might set us the example of dy-

[58] Ibid. d. 19, a. 2, q. 2.
[59] Ibid.
[60] Ibid. cfr. Thomas, Sum. Theol. III, q. 26, a. 2.

[61] Ibid. q. 22, a. 1.
[62] Ibid. a. 2.
[63] Ibid. q. 22, a. 1.

ing to sin spiritually. . . . Fifthly, that by rising from the
dead, and manifesting His power whereby He overthrew death,
He might instil into us the hope of also rising again." [64]

In His death, Christ's soul and body were separated from
one another, but both remained united to the divinity.[65]
Hence, on the one hand, Christ truly died, and in consequence
He was no longer man in the strict sense of the term; and,
on the other hand, the hypostatic union continued uninterrupted. With regard to the first point, however, Peter Lombard and a few others held that Christ's soul, whilst separated
from the body, was truly a person.[66] The second point, which
was admitted by all, is thus explained by St. Bonaventure:
" Speaking of the union in its active and passive sense, it is
to be held that the body and soul were united to the Word by
one union; but speaking of the same union as a relation, it
must be said that before death there was one union actually
and several potentially, while after death there were actually
several unions." [67]

After death Christ's soul, united to His divinity, descended
into hell, by which place the Scholastics understand the *Limbus
Patrum,* where the souls of the just were detained till the
opening of heaven's gates.[68] This descent was real, and nearly
all are agreed that Christ admitted the holy souls immediately
to the beatific vision. Durandus, however, maintained that
Christ's descent into hell was only virtual, it being nothing
more than an exercise of His power in that place of waiting.[69]
The same view had been held by Abelard, whose teaching on
that point was condemned by the Council of Sens. The doctrine of the real descent was confirmed by the Fourth Lateran,
when it declared against the Albigenses: *Descendit in anima
et resurrexit in carne.*[70] Some held, furthermore, that Christ
also appeared to the poor souls in purgatory, and freed them

[64] Ibid. q. 50, a. 1.
[65] Halens. Sum. III, q. 19; Thomas, In Sent. d. 21, q. 1; Bonavent.
ibid. a. 1, 2; Scotus, ibid. q. unica.
[66] Sent. III, c. 2.
[67] In Sent. III, d. 21, a. 1, q. 3.

[68] Bonavent. In Sent. III, d. 22,
a. unic. q. 4; Thomas, ibid. q. 2;
Albert. Magn. ibid. a. 4.
[69] Ibid. q. 4.
[70] Mansi, 22, 982; DB. 429.

from their sufferings; but this view was commonly regarded as improbable.[71]

These are the chief points in the soteriological teaching of the Scholastics. Most of them are directly or indirectly a matter of faith, and taught as such by the Church. Thus the Fourth Lateran restated the article of the Creed, that Christ " suffered and died on the wood of the cross for the salvation of the human race, and descended into hell." [72] Pope Clement VI, in 1343, declared that, because of the hypostatic union, the merits of Christ are an " infinite treasure." [73] The Council of Trent defined that Christ is the meritorious cause of our justification; and declared that He merited justification for us by His most holy passion on the wood of the cross, that we are justified by the merits of the one Mediator, and that all those are anathema who say that men are justified without the justice of Christ, by which He merited our justification.[74] Moreover all these points, as was indicated at the beginning of the present chapter, were already clearly contained in the teaching of the Fathers; and in so far there was little or no development in the doctrine of the redemption as presented by the Scholastics.

[71] Cfr. Thomas, Sum. Theol. III, q. 52, a. 8.
[72] Loc. cit.
[73] DB. 550.
[74] Decretum de Justificatione, DB. 799 sqq.

CHAPTER XII

THE CHURCH OF CHRIST: THE PAPACY

St. Augustine, in his contentions with the Donatists, had frequent occasion to set forth and also to develop the traditional teaching on the Church — on her constitution, her powers, and distinguishing marks. Hence, at the time of his death, Latin ecclesiology presented a fairly complete system of theological thought, which needed only a few finishing touches to bring it to its final stage of development.[1] This system was taken over by the Scholastics of the Middle Ages, and then was handed down by them, practically in the same condition in which they had received it, to their successors who came after the Council of Trent. A few points, indeed, were somewhat further developed, but that was owing to incidental causes rather than to the systematic labor of theologians. Most of the Scholastics touched the subject only in connection with other matters, and even then merely in a passing way. However, the following summary of what may be gathered from their writings will be of some help to the student in determining the general trend of dogmatic development along these lines.

A — THE CHURCH OF CHRIST

Some interesting remarks on the Church and her relation to the State are made by Hugh of St. Victor, who touches the subject in his treatise *De Sacramentis*. According to to him, the Church is the assemblage of all the faithful, forming together one body, of which Christ is the head and the Holy Spirit the

[1] Cfr. vol. I, p. 323 sqq.

vivifying principle.[2]   The unity of this body is conserved by faith under the guidance of the Holy Spirit.[3]

The Church and the State are the two powers instituted by God for the right government of the people.   Each of them is entitled to make its own laws, and to enforce their observance by means proportionate to the end to be attained.   Both are monarchical in constitution, and therefore the supreme power resides in one individual, who communicates it in varying degrees to many others for the good of all.   Compared to the State, the Church is the higher power; because she must lead men to their eternal salvation, while the State provides for their temporal welfare.   The State has the king as its head; but the head of the Church is the Pope.[4]

As both powers are immediately from God, and as the spiritual power is the higher of the two, the Pope can be judged only by God Himself.   On the other hand, the temporal power, in so far as it is vested in a particular person, may be constituted and judged by the spiritual.   However, the spiritual power cannot proceed arbitrarily in this matter, but must be guided by the true interest of the people.[5]

As there are thus two powers constituted by God, so are there also two classes of people, each with its own well defined rights and duties.   The first of these two classes comprises all the clerics, who are consecrated or deputed to the service of God; the second is made up of laics, to whatever state in life they may belong.   The two together form the walls of the Church; both were prefigured in the Old Testament, the clerics by the tribe of Levi, and the laics by the other eleven tribes.[6]

Peter Lombard has a few scattered remarks on the Church in his commentaries on the Epistles of St. Paul, but practically

---

[2] He says: "Caput enim est Christus; membrum Christianus. Caput unum, membra multa: et constat unum corpus ex capite et membris, et in uno corpore Spiritus unus" (Op. cit. c. 1).

[3] His words are: "Ecclesia sancta corpus est Christi uno spiritu vivificata, et unita fide una et sanctificata. . . . Quid est ergo Ecclesia nisi multitudo fidelium, universitas Christianorum?" (Ibid. c. 2).

[4] Ibid. c. 4.

[5] Ibid. c. 4.

[6] Ibid. c. 3.

omits the subject in his four books of the Sentences. As this work later on became the textbook of the schools, it was most likely owing to his example that subsequent theologians barely touched the various doctrines concerning the Church.

Alexander of Hales devotes a few articles of his *Summa* to a consideration of the Church, but has nothing of value. According to him, the Church of Christ began with Abel, whose faith in the future Redeemer was manifested through his sacrifice. He also prefigured the sanctity of the Church in his exemplary life, and was the first to suffer martyrdom for the sake and the name of Christ. Of this Church, which formed then as now Christ's mystical body, Christ was even then the chief and the head. The fact that the Church is the mystical body of Christ, and also His spouse, necessarily implies that she is indefectible. Her power may wax or wane according to the varying conditions and circumstances of time and place, but she shall never be vanquished by evil or cease to exist till the end of time. Furthermore, this indefectibility is assured to her by Christ's own promise, as recorded in the Gospel: " Lo, I am with you all days, even to the consummation of the world." [7]

A somewhat lengthier exposition is found in the Summa written by Moneta of Cremona (+ 1250), against the Cathari and the Waldensian heretics. He proves the Apostolic origin of the Church of Rome, her freedom from error, the uninterrupted succession of her bishops, her legislative power, her right to own temporal possessions for the attainment of her God-appointed end, and other points of a kindred nature.[8] However, he does not contribute anything of special value to the further development of ecclesiological teaching.

St. Thomas has some very valuable points on the Church, but he too treats the matter only in passing. He specially emphasizes the importance of unity, both among the members themselves and between the members and the head. That unity is essential in as much as the Church is an individual organism, an organized community, the kingdom of God,

[7] Sum. IV, q. 2, m. 4.   [8] Op. cit. L. V.

whose members must hold fast to the truth as an object of faith, and must ever live together in the spirit of love and peace.[9]   The visible Church on earth is a copy of the invisible Church in heaven, and has for its chief and head the visible representative of the invisible Christ, even as the blessed have for their head the glorified God-Man Himself.[10]

Protestants not rarely blame the Scholastics for having unduly emphasized the external and visible element of the Church, almost to the entire neglect of the interior spirit which escapes the eyes of man.   But this accusation is based upon an entire misunderstanding of their viewpoint.   The very fact that they regarded the Church as a living organism, vivified by the Holy Spirit, sufficiently shows that they looked upon the interior and spiritual element as the fountainhead of all true ecclesiastical life.   Nor did they fail to point this out when occasion offered.   Thus, for instance, St. Thomas states quite definitely: " The beauty and perfection of the Church consists chiefly in what is interior, and to the same also belong all her outward actions, in as much as they proceed from the interior spirit, and are directed towards the preservation of the beauty that is from within." [10a]   What the soul is to the body, that the spiritual gifts and endowments, together with the Holy Spirit Himself, are to the Church.

The truth is that the Scholastics, in this matter as in all others, followed the golden mean in the expression of their views.   They maintained, indeed, that the Church was intended by her divine Founder to be a visible institution — visible in her regimen, in her sacraments, in her cult; but they also taught that to this visible institution must ever correspond a spiritual reality perfectly known to God alone.   In this sense they admitted even an invisible Church, made up of all those who are actually united to God in faith and love and in the fervent practice of perfect virtue.   Yet, on the other hand, in maintaining this, they were far removed from the later Protestant idea of the invisibility of the Church of Christ; and also from the unreasonable contention of Wiclif and Hus that the Church

[9] Cont. Gent. IV, 76.   [10a] In Sent. IV, d. 15, q. 3, a. 1.
[10] Ibid.

of Christ consists only of the predestined. For, as St. Thomas points out, the invisible Church is nothing else than a perfect realization of the visible Church in its individual members, and is essentially dependent on it for all its perfection.[11]

In their relation to the faithful, the Apostles and their successors must be regarded as the vicars of Christ. They must foster the life of the Church in her members by preaching the faith and by administering the sacraments. St. Thomas speaks of them as follows: " It is to be held that the Apostles and their successors are the vicars of God, in so far as the government of the Church, the preaching of the faith, and the administration of the sacraments come in question. Hence, as it is not lawful for them to found another church, neither is it lawful for them to preach another faith, or to institute other sacraments; but through the sacraments that flowed from the side of Christ, as He was hanging on the cross, is the Church said to have been established and built up." [12]

In virtue of her divine institution, the Church has full administrative powers over all the treasures of grace which Christ intended to communicate through external rites. She has not, it is true, the power of absolute authority in this matter — *potestas auctoritatis,* for that belongs to God alone; nor does she have the power of excellence —*potestas excellentiae,* since that is proper to Christ the author of our redemption; but she has a ministerial power — *potestas ministerii,* communicated by the Founder of the Church to the Apostles and their successors, and exercised under the direction of the Pope as the supreme pastor of all the faithful. This comprises the power of orders and the power of jurisdiction. The former has for its chief object the true or Eucharistic body of Christ, and as such is shared in equal degree by priests, bishops, and the Pope. The latter is exercised over the mystical body of Christ, or the faithful as constituting the Church, and is possessed in all its fullness only by the Pope, in a limited degree by bishops, and with still greater limitations by priests. It finds application both in the internal and external forum,

[11] Ibid. d. 19, q. 1.   [12] Sum. Theol. III, q. 64, a. 2.

according as it is used in the administration of the sacraments or in the enactment of laws and whatever is connected therewith by way of enforcement or dispensation.[13]

The power of jurisdiction, as already stated, resides primarily in the Sovereign Pontiff, and it is conferred on him not by sacramental consecration, but in virtue of his election to the primatial dignity. Upon other prelates it is conferred by way of declaration on the part of their superiors.[14] Jurisdiction *in foro interno*, for the absolution of penitents, can be given to all priests; but jurisdiction *in foro externo*, that is, for the purpose of governing, making laws, judging, and punishing, belongs to the bishops under the authority of the Pope, and to such as have been legitimately delegated by him.[15]

This brief outline contains the gist of the ecclesiological teaching of St. Thomas, and comprises practically all that is found in the writings of his predecessors and contemporaries. The matter was somewhat further developed in the *Summa de Ecclesia* of Torquemada, who, as cardinal of the Roman Church, took part in the Council of Constance, and also in that of Basle and Florence. But the work was not published until the middle of the sixteenth century.

B — The Papacy

At the beginning of the Middle Ages, that is, from the ninth century forward, the Papacy was for some time in a deplorable condition. Unworthy Popes, like Benedict IX, brought disgrace upon the See of Peter and were a cause of scandal to the Christian world. However, towards the middle of the eleventh century a reform movement began, which resulted in the election of a succession of Sovereign Pontiffs who proved themselves in every way worthy of their high station. The first of these was the saintly Leo IX, who defended the prerogatives of the Roman See against Michael Cerularius, the chief author of the Greek schism. He displayed great zeal in laboring for the reformation of morals and the cor-

---

[13] In Sent. IV, d. 7, q. 3, a. 1; d. 13, q. 1, a. 1.   [14] Ibid. d. 24, q. 3, a. 2.
[15] Ibid. d. 19, q. 1, a. 3.

rection of abuses both among the clergy and laity. His immediate successors, Victor II and Nicholas II, continued the work which he had so well begun. But it was especially Gregory VII (1073-1085) who restored to the Papacy all its ancient splendor, although he died in exile for justice' sake. The full result of his labors became apparent only under Innocent III (1198-1216), who was "the living embodiment of Papal power at its apogee." With occasional slight yieldings, this position was maintained till the death of Boniface VIII (1303), when a new decline set in that was considerably accelerated by the secularizing influence of the Renaissance.

From this brief sketch it will be seen that the golden age of Scholasticism coincided with the period when Papal power was at its highest. And to this coincidence the theological writings of the time bear no uncertain testimony. The supreme power of the Pope, not only in matters ecclesiastical, but to a considerable extent also in secular affairs of worldwide interest, stands out most prominently. It is not referred to as something that needs to be proved, but as a universally acknowledged fact, which may be used as a source of arguments for the confirmation of other doctrines. Or if occasionally a proof is introduced, it is only by way of assigning the reason for a fact that is accepted by all. In the following summary we shall first present an outline of what was held by the Scholastics in regard to the spiritual supremacy of the Pope, and then add a few remarks in reference to the relation of Church and State as commonly understood and accepted in those times.

1. *Spiritual Supremacy of the Pope.*— The position of the Church during Patristic times, in regard to the supremacy of the Pope, appears most clearly from the formula subscribed to by the Eighth General Council, held in 869. It reads as follows: "It is impossible to set aside the ordination of our Lord Jesus Christ, who said: 'Thou art Peter, and upon this rock I will build my Church.' The truth of these words has been abundantly proved by subsequent events, because by the Apostolic See the Catholic religion has always been preserved

immaculate, and sound doctrine has ever been taught. There-fore, not wishing in any way to be separated from its faith and teaching, and following in all things the example of the Fathers, and particularly the ordinations of the Pontiffs of the Apostolic See, we anathematize all heresies." [16]

This testimony of the Eastern Church, all the more valuable because it was given at a time when the schism was already in preparation, also voiced the firm belief of the West. Only a few years before the Eighth General Council was held, Rabanus Maurus bore witness to that belief in these terms: " We see that the authority of the Roman Pontiff extends itself to all the churches of Christ, so that all bishops acknowl-edge him as their head, and that all ecclesiastical transactions are subject to his judgment; hence according to his decision, what has been established remains in force, what has been done amiss is corrected, what needs to be enacted is approved. . . . The decrees of the Roman Pontiffs are sent to all the churches, both in the East and the West, and they are received and observed by the faithful as having the force of ecclesias-tical laws." [17]

The Popes themselves also took the same view of their posi-tion in the Church of Christ. Thus Leo IX stated the su-premacy of the Roman See in no uncertain terms, when, on the occasion of the Greek schism, he wrote to Michael Cer-ularius: " Is it not true that by the See of the Prince of the Apostles, namely by the Roman Church, both through the same Peter and through his successors, the lying inventions of all heretics have been laid bare and condemned? " And farther on: " Just as a hinge, remaining itself immovable, opens and shuts the door, so Peter and his successors exercise judiciary authority over the whole Church, and their firm position no one must attempt to shake; because the Supreme See is judged by no one — *quia Summa Sedes a nemine judicatur.*" [18]

This is the teaching faithfully echoed by the Scholastics in their more or less casual remarks on the subject, as suggested

[16] Mansi, 8, 351.
[17] Cont. Graec. 11, 4; cfr. ML. 121, 343.

[18] Ep. 55, ad Michaelem Cerula-rium et Leonem Acridanum, c. 7 et 32; cfr. Mansi, 19, 638 B sqq.

by other matters that claimed their attention at the moment. Thus Alexander, while speaking of the priest's power to absolve from sin, points out how the use of this and other powers is subject to the authority of the Pope. " It is to be held," he says, " that this subordination was intended for the good of the Church. For God willed that certain persons in authority should have power over many others; and over these, others in smaller number should have authority; and so on until we arrive at one, namely the Pope, who is subject immediately to the Lord, according to the saying of Ecclesiastes: ' He that is high hath another higher.' . . . And besides, there is a king who commandeth the whole earth, namely the Pope, who calls himself the servant of the servants of God; so that, just as the Church triumphant is one, so also the Church militant, and the body of the Church triumphant together with that of the Church militant is united in one under the Supreme Head." [19]

Albertus Magnus regards the supremacy of the Pope in all things ecclesiastical as the very foundation of that unity which is an essential mark of the Church. It was for the preservation of this unity that Christ committed the keys to one individual, " so that in him might be found the plenitude of power, and that from him all others should derive their authority in keeping with the charge committed to their care." [20]

Hence the Pope is bishop of bishops as well as of the faithful in general, and he exercises immediate jurisdiction over all without exception. Albertus expresses his views in these terms: " A superior has either limited powers or he has the plenitude of power; this latter is the prerogative of the Pope, who is the ordinary of every one of the faithful. . . . Hence as the ordinary of all, he has power over his subjects independently of their consent; because he holds the place of God on earth." [21]

Furthermore, as head of the Church, the Pope is infallible in deciding questions of faith. For speaking of the common

[19] Sum. IV, q. 79, m. 6, a. 3.
[20] De Sacrific. Missae, tr. 8, c. 6, n. 9.
[21] Sum. Theol. II, tr. 24, q. 141, m. 3.

usage of reserving to the Pope the granting of plenary indulgences, the author says: " It is in no way to be admitted that
the head of the Church could lead anyone into error, when
there is question of matters that the whole Church receives
and approves. Yet it is known to all that he preaches, and
causes to be preached by others, that indulgences are valid before God." [22]   Here it must be noted that the phrase, " what
the whole Church receives and approves — *quae tota Ecclesia
recipit et approbat,*" is not intended to make the Pope's infallibility dependent on the approbation of his teaching by the
universal Church; but, as is clear from the author's own explanation, it is meant simply to indicate a prerequisite condition of infallibility, namely, that the Pope must speak as the
supreme teacher of the whole Church. The same condition
was also put down by the Vatican Council.[23]

St. Thomas reasons about the supreme power of the Pope
in this way: " As the Church is a living organism, essentially
one and visible, she must have one head living visibly among
men; her oneness, moreover, demands that this head have supreme authority in matters of faith, so that he may decide
questions and solve difficulties connected therewith. Then, as
the Church is expected to be governed in a perfect manner, hers
must be a monarchical constitution; finally, as she is an image
of the Church triumphant in heaven, of which Christ is the
head, the one who holds the supreme power must be the representative of Christ here on earth." [24]

What appears thus so reasonable from the very nature of
the Church, is, furthermore, also clearly taught in Holy Scripture. Christ, argues the author, is indeed the invisible head
of the Church, as He is also the author of grace; yet, as in the
administration of the sacraments He wished to be represented
by a visible minister, so too in the government of the Church
did He wish to be represented by a visible head. Hence He
appointed Peter to the office of chief pastor, and in Peter all
his successors. It was to signify the prerogative of Peter that
He gave the keys to him, and that He confirmed him in the

[22] In Sent. IV, d. 20, a. 17.   [24] Cont. Gent. IV, 76; In Sent. IV,
[23] DB. 1839.   d. 24, q. 3.

faith.   Consequently, as the Sovereign Pontiff is the successor
of Peter, he has by divine right full jurisdiction over the whole
Church, and holds the place of Christ in regard to pastors and
flock alike.[25]

This supreme jurisdiction of the Pope extends itself to everything that concerns the welfare of the Church — the administration of the sacraments, legislative enactments, matters of
discipline and dispensations.   In consequence, he has power
over all that is merely accidental in the administration of the
sacraments; he can depute simple priests to give confirmation
and confer minor orders; he can restrict their power of absolving from sin, reserve certain cases to himself, and grant
indulgences.[26]   He can also for a reasonable cause abrogate
Apostolic enactments — *agere contra Apostolum*,[27] and has
power to dispense from vows and oaths.[28]

In regard to the faithful, this supreme jurisdiction is immediate, so that he can act as their bishop and their parish priest
by a direct exercise of his power.   That this is really the case
is quite obvious; for bishops and priests derive their jurisdiction from him; hence if in particular cases he wishes to exercise
that jurisdiction personally, there is nothing to prevent him
from so doing.[29]

As sovereign lawgiver, the Pope does not fall under the
penal laws which he enacts; consequently these laws are for
him merely directive norms.[30]   Nevertheless, like any one else,
he is subject to fraternal correction; and when he publicly
endangers the faith, this correction too may be administered
in public.[31]

Speaking of the value of indulgences before God, St.
Thomas touches incidentally the question of the Church's infallibility in matters of faith, and points out that it is ultimately a
prerogative of the Sovereign Pontiff as supreme teacher of
the whole Church.   He says: " The universal Church cannot

[25] Ibid. q. 3, a. 2 ad 1m.
[26] Ibid. d. 7, q. 3, a. 3; d. 20, q. 1,
a. 4; Sum. Theol. III, q. 72, a. 12.
[27] In Sent. IV, d. 20, q. 1, a. 4.
[28] Sum. Theol. II. II, q. 88, a. 12;
q. 89, a. 9.

[29] In Sent. IV, d. 24, q. 3, a. 2;
d. 17, a. 3 ad 3m quint. quaest.
[30] Ibid. d. 19, q. 2, a. 2.
[31] Sum. Theol. II. II, q. 33, a. 4
ad 2m.

fall into error: because He who in all things was heard for His reverence said to Peter, upon whose confession the Church was founded: ' I have asked for thee, that thy faith may not fail.' But the universal Church approves indulgences: therefore indulgences are of value before God." [32]

It is because of this infallibility that opposition to the teaching of the Church causes a person to be regarded as a heretic. And this is also borne witness to by the practice of all past ages. For we find that " after anything pertaining to the faith had been decided by the authority of the universal Church, and some one opposed that decision, he incurred forthwith the stigma of heresy. Now this authority resides chiefly in the Sovereign Pontiff." [33] Again: " It belongs to the Sovereign Pontiff to determine those things that are of faith, so that they may be firmly believed by all." [34]

St. Thomas also considers the Pope's relation to general councils. He sets forth his view in the following terms: " Just as a subsequent council has the power of interpreting a symbol drawn up by a preceding council, and of adding thereto by way of explanation, as appears from what has been said; so in like manner can the Roman Pontiff do the same by his own authority. Furthermore, it is only by his authority that a council can be convened, and it belongs to him to confirm the decisions of the council. Finally, it is lawful to appeal from the council to him. All this is evident from what was done at the Council of Chalcedon. Nor is it even necessary to convene a general council for matters of this kind, as in times of war it would be impossible to do so." [35] Hence, according to the teaching of St. Thomas, not only is the Pope's authority above that of a general council, but it is also from him as head of the universal Church that general councils derive their infallibility in deciding questions of faith.

The infallible teaching authority of the universal Church, and consequently of the Pope, has for its proper object all revealed truths that must be believed by the followers of Christ.

[32] In Sent. IV, d. 20, q. 1, a. 3.
[33] Sum. Theol. II. II, q. 11, a. 2 ad 3ᵐ.
[34] Ibid. q. 1, a. 10.
[35] QQ. DD. De Potentia Dei, q. 10, a. 4.

" This," St. Thomas argues, " follows from the ways of Divine Providence, which directs the Church by the Holy Spirit, so that she may not fall into error; and the same was also promised by Christ, when he said that the Holy Spirit would come and teach all truth in matters necessary for salvation. Hence it is plainly impossible that the judgment of the universal Church should err in those things that pertain to the faith; and as it belongs to the Pope to decide questions of faith, his decisions have greater weight than the views of all men whatever, no matter how well versed in Holy Scripture they may be." [36]

That the Pope enjoys the same infallibility in regard to questions and facts connected with faith, is, according to St. Thomas, a matter of pious belief. To this category belongs the canonization of saints. Having pointed out that the Pope may err in other cases where his decision depends on the truth of human testimony, he proceeds: " The canonization of saints holds a middle place in regard to inerrancy. However, as the honor which we pay the saints is in a way a profession of faith, in as much as we believe that they have attained to glory, it is to be piously believed that in this matter also the judgment of the Church is not subject to error." [37]

Hence, as appears from the foregoing citations, the teaching of St. Thomas on the supremacy of the Pope may be summed up in these points: 1. The Pope is the primate of all bishops. 2. He has preëminence over the whole Church. 3. In the Church he has plenitude of power. 4. He has the same power that Christ gave to Peter. 5. The final decision in matters of faith rests with him. 6. Submission to the Pope in things spiritual is required of all.— As a mere glance suffices to show, this teaching is in all essentials identical with the doctrine defined by the Vatican Council just six hundred years later.

St. Bonaventure advances substantially the same views. Like St. Thomas, he points out that the supremacy of the Pope is necessary for the well-being of the Church, and especially for

[36] Quodl. 9, c. 16.   [37] Ibid.

the maintaining of unity.[38]   Hence it was that Christ appointed Peter as the prince of the Apostles and chief of the whole world, and provided also that this plenitude of power should be possessed by Peter's successors, the canonically elected bishops of Rome.[39]

The power thus conferred on the head of the Church is threefold: " First, the Sovereign Pontiff alone has the whole plenitude of authority which Christ gave to His Church; secondly, he can exercise this authority in any and all particular churches in the same way as he does at Rome; thirdly, from him all authority and jurisdiction possessed by other dignitaries throughout the whole Church are derived, just as in heaven all glory of the saints flows from the one fountain of infinite goodness, which is Christ Jesus." [40]   It is true, bishops have by divine right full power in their own dioceses, in as much as Christ instituted the episcopal office and dignity; but this power they enjoy only so long as they are in communion with the Pope, and at the same time the Pope has immediate jurisdiction over the faithful in every diocese.[41]

St. Bonaventure explains the infallible teaching authority of the Church in the same way as does St. Thomas, as will appear with sufficient clearness from one or two citations.   Thus, speaking of religious poverty, he says: " If at the time of the legal priesthood it was morally wrong to contravene the judgment of the high priest, and was punished with death; how much more is not this the case under the dispensation of revealed truth and grace, when it is known that the plenitude of power has been entrusted to the vicar of Christ.   Hence this evil is in no way to be tolerated, that in matters of faith and morals any one should teach what is contrary to his decisions; approving what he has reprobated, building up again what he has torn down, defending what he has condemned." [42]

He also points out that the infallibility of the Pope extends to the approbation of religious orders and their rules.   " It is

[38] In Expos. Regul. c. 9.
[39] In Sent. IV, d. 25, a. 1, q. 1.
[40] Opusc.: Quare Fratres Minores praedicent.
[41] Ibid.
[42] Apol. Paupert. c. 1.

manifest," he argues, "that the sixth rule of St. Francis was approved and confirmed by Pope Honorius. But if he fell into error in giving this approbation, he has led the whole Church into error; for it is well known that the universal Church, throughout the world, receives such religious orders as are approved by the Pope; and therefore the whole Church was deceived and led into error by her divinely constituted head." [43] Of course, the conclusion is inadmissible; therefore also the premise from which it follows, namely, that the Pope fell into error when he approved the aforesaid rule.

Duns Scotus is equally emphatic in his statements regarding the universal jurisdiction and infallible teaching authority of the Pope. To the Sovereign Pontiff alone, he says, does it belong to fulminate a sentence of major excommunication, which entirely cuts off the delinquent from the Church.[44] The infallible teaching authority of the Pope is identified with that of the universal Church, and dogmatic decrees of the Sovereign Pontiffs have the same force as those of general councils. All decisions regarding doubtful points in Holy Scripture and tradition are reserved to the Pope, in the sense that his decision alone is binding.— These various points Scotus brings out repeatedly in his teaching on the sacraments.

What has been said in the foregoing paragraphs represents in substance the common teaching of the Scholastics on the rights and prerogatives of the Holy See in the sphere of religion. On only one point was there some difference of opinion, namely, whether the jurisdiction of bishops is derived immediately from Christ or mediately, that is, through the Pope. This latter view was defended by Alexander of Hales, St. Bonaventure, St. Thomas, and nearly all representative Scholastics; while the former was held by Henry of Ghent and a few others.[45] But even with regard to this point, all admit that no bishop can exercise his jurisdiction without the consent of the Pope. Hence the view of some later Nominalists, which prevailed at the Council of Constance (1431–1434), that the jurisdiction of a general council is above that of the Pope,

[43] De Paupert. Christi, a. 2.   [45] Quodl. 9, q. 22.
[44] Report. IV, d. 19, q. 1.

was directly opposed to the teaching of mediæval theologians.

The chief points set forth in this section, namely, the primacy of the Roman See, the universal jurisdiction of the Pope, his right to decide questions of faith and morals, and his position of supreme judge to whom appeal may be made by any one of the faithful throughout the world, were all embodied in the profession of faith exacted from Michael Palaeologus by the Second Council of Lyons, held in 1274.[46] It is true, the Council did not directly define the Pope's infallibility in matters of faith and morals; but it indicated its mind quite clearly on the subject, when it stated: "As he, before all others, is bound to defend the faith, so in like manner does it belong to him, when questions of faith arise, to decide them according to his own judgment." [47]

2. *Relation of Church and State.*— That during the Middle Ages the State was regarded as subject to the Church in all spiritual matters need not be pointed out; for that follows necessarily from the universally accepted idea of the supremacy of the Pope, as set forth in the preceding section. As head of the Church, the Pope was believed to have full jurisdiction in all things spiritual, not only over individuals, but also over every form and kind of society made up of Christians, and therefore over the Christian commonwealth. Hence the point now at issue regards solely the relation of Church and State in temporal matters.

Protestants quite commonly accuse the Popes of the Middle Ages of having dominated, or tried to dominate, over temporal sovereigns to such an extent that no king or emperor enjoyed untrammeled freedom in carrying on the government committed to his charge. To all intents and purposes, as they see it, the Popes aimed at nothing less than to establish themselves as feudal overlords of the whole Christian world. They not only exacted the payment of tribute from many countries which they regarded as papal fiefs, but without their good will no king or emperor ever felt quite safe on his throne. By the terrible weapon of excommunication any sovereign could be

---

[46] Mansi, 24, 70 A sqq.   [47] Ibid.; cfr. DB. 466.

brought to his knees, as was Henry IV of Germany when
forced to implore the mercy of Gregory VII at Canossa.[48]
In confirmation of these and similar statements, Protestant
writers not only adduce certain facts of history, such as the
case of Henry IV just referred to, but also cite the teaching
of Popes and theologians to the same effect. As regards the
teaching of the Popes, it is especially the *Dictatus Papae,*
sometimes ascribed to Gregory VII, and the Bull, *Unam sanctam,* of Boniface VIII, that are made to do service.

That these charges are grossly exaggerated need hardly be
pointed out; still there is sufficient truth in them to make
them plausible. The fact of the matter is this: The Christians of the Middle Ages knew from bitter experience that in
certain contingencies they had no protection against the tyr-
anny and arbitrary violence of wicked rulers, except such as
might be afforded them by the Sovereign Pontiff. Hence in
most cases they were more than willing to acknowledge him as
their overlord, in so far as he used his spiritual power to check
the excesses of their kings or emperors. Again, rulers of
smaller countries, who had always more or less reason to dread
attacks from their more powerful neighbors, not rarely considered it a privilege to enfeoff their domains to the Holy See,
so that for the payment of the nominal tribute they might enjoy its powerful protection. Consequently, if in this sense the
Popes were to some extent feudal lords, the position was not of
their own seeking; it was thrust upon them by the condition of
the times or the devotion of the people.

Nor did they claim the power and privilege of appointing
or dethroning temporal rulers; but they did claim the right to
cut them off from ecclesiastical communion, if against the
laws of the land they misused their authority to the destruction of the Christian commonwealth and obstinately refused
to be corrected by gentler means. But this only shows that
they considered the high and the low to be on an equal footing
in the Church of God. If either of them chose to lead a life
unworthy of the Christian name, he must be satisfied to be ex-

---

[48] Cfr. Hinschius-Sehling, Real-encyklpaedie fuer Protestantische Theologie und Kirche, 14, 663.

cluded from the benefits of the Christian Church. It is true, such an excommunication, if persistently disregarded, might in the case of princes lead to the loss of their throne, because it was usually understood to release subjects from their oath of allegiance; but on the part of the Popes this was no more than an acknowledgment of the people's natural right to defend themselves against an unjust aggressor. No doubt, this power of excommunication might be abused, and perhaps sometimes was abused; but so is every other power under the sun.

Beyond what is conceded in the two preceding paragraphs, neither Popes nor theologians made any claims in regard to the subjection of the temporal power to the spiritual. Even if the *Dictatus Papae* were certainly the " sayings " of Gregory VII, which they most probably are not; or if they faithfully reflected the attitude of the mediæval mind on this matter, which in regard to most of the " sayings " may be conceded; even then, nothing could be proved from them beyond what has been admitted. In fact, only two of them have any bearing on this matter at all. They read as follows: 1. *Quod illi liceat imperatores deponere* — That it is lawful for him (the Pope) to depose emperors. 2. *Quod a fidelitate iniquorum subjectos potest absolvere* — That he (the Pope) can absolve the subjects of wicked (princes) from their oath of allegiance.[49] If these " sayings " be taken in the sense explained above, both may be admitted to be genuine expressions of the mediæval mind on the matter in question; on the other hand, if they be interpreted to imply the claim of arbitrary power by the Pope, there is not a shred of evidence to support the interpretation.

The same is true of the Bull, *Unam sanctam,* of Boniface VIII. In it occurs the sentence: *Porro subesse Romano Pontifici omni humanae creaturae declaramus, dicimus, definimus et pronuntiamus omnino esse de necessitate salutis* — Furthermore, We declare, say, define and pronounce that it is necessary, by way of salvation, for every human being to be

[49] Ep. 55; Mansi, 20, 168.

under (the power of) the Roman Pontiff.— As it stands, this looks rather sweeping, but it need not mean that the Pope claimed direct power over the temporal affairs of princes. In fact, when Louis the Fair of France interpreted it in this sense, Boniface declared without hesitation: "It is now forty years since We began to be versed in the law, and We know that there are two powers established by God: who, then, ought or can believe that such fatuity, such foolishness, ever entered Our head?" [50]

The teaching of theologians on this subject is neatly summarized by Hugh of St. Victor, who was practically a contemporary of Gregory VII. He says: "The Church and the State are the two powers instituted by God for the right government of the people. Each of them is entitled to make its own laws, and to enforce their observance by means in keeping with the end to be attained. . . . Compared to the State, the Church is the higher power; because she must lead men to their eternal salvation, while the State provides for their temporal welfare. . . . As both powers are immediately from God, and as the spiritual power is the higher of the two, the Pope can be judged only by God Himself. On the other hand, the temporal power, in so far as it is vested in a particular person, may be constituted and judged by the spiritual. However, the spiritual power cannot proceed arbitrarily in this matter, but must be guided by the true interest of the people." [51]

In regard to the deposition of princes by the Pope, St. Thomas reasons as follows: "When a Christian prince falls away from the faith, he may be punished by a judicial sentence; and the proper punishment in such a case would be to deprive him of the power to rule over Christian subjects; for if he continues to rule over them, there is imminent danger of his turning them also away from the faith. Hence, as soon as the sentence of excommunication has been pronounced against an apostate prince, his subjects are by that very fact freed from his dominion and released from their oath of allegiance." [52]

[50] Cfr. DB. 468, note.
[51] De Sacr. c. 4.
[52] Sum. Theol. II. II, q. 12, a. 2.

As is obvious, this power of excommunication can not be used against sovereigns who have never been baptized. And hence St. Thomas remarks: "Infidelity in itself is not incompatible with the right to rule; because that right was introduced by the law of nations, which is a human law — *jus humanum*." [53]   No, it is not infidelity as such that justifies the Pope to proceed against any sovereign; but the infidelity of one who had a right to the crown only because he was supposed to be a Christian.

[53] Ibid. q. 12, a. 2.

CHAPTER XIII

ACTUAL AND SANCTIFYING GRACE: JUSTIFICATION AND MERIT

Patristic teaching on the subject of divine grace was mostly concerned with its supernatural character and its absolute necessity for the attainment of eternal life. What was its precise nature, what its various divisions, what its mode of operation, were questions that received only a passing attention as occasion demanded.[1] It is chiefly on these points that Scholastic speculation supplements the teaching of the Fathers as regards the question of grace. The following is a brief summary of what was thus accomplished by the most representative of the Schoolmen.

A — Actual and Sanctifying Grace

A fair outline of Scholastic teaching on the subject of grace is presented by Peter Lombard, whose brief statements were afterwards developed by his commentators. On some points, however, as will be noted in the proper place, his views were set aside as untenable.

Referring to the teaching of St. Augustine, whom he follows rather closely, he first points out the need we all have of a special divine help in order to work out our salvation. " The will of man," he says, " when left to its natural resources, has not the power either to will efficaciously what is supernaturally good, or to accomplish it. For this it needs the grace of God, by which it is liberated and assisted. It is liberated in this sense, that stirred up by grace it really wills; and it is assisted in the sense that it successfully accomplishes the work to be done." [2]

[1] Cfr. vol. I, p. 369 sqq.   [2] Sent. II, d. 25, n. 16.

This grace of God, which is given for the performance of supernaturally good works, may be considered in itself or in its relation to the action of the will. In the first case it is called operating grace — *gratia operans;* for the reason that it exerts an influence on our intellect and will, and disposes these faculties for the eliciting of salutary acts. In the second it is termed coöperating grace — *gratia cooperans;* because it concurs with the actions of our faculties as prepared by its supernatural influence.[3] Hence the operating grace of God is in us without our own doing; it anticipates the salutary action of our will and makes it possible, and hence it is also called preventing or prevenient grace. It is purely a gift of God's gratuitous mercy.[4] However, strictly speaking, this is true only of the first grace that is given us, which is the gift of faith; for if we coöperate with that, we can merit the bestowal of other graces and thus with God's help work out our salvation.[5] Hence we are bidden to pray for the further help of God; so that what He has begun in us, He may also accomplish.[6]

Entitatively considered, preventing and helping grace — *gratia operans et cooperans* — are the same. They are one and the same gratuitous gift of God, but bear a different relation to the activity of the will in respect of supernatural actions. Preventing grace calls forth that activity by soliciting the will to act and making it capable of so doing; while coöperating grace acts together with the will in exerting its activity for the attainment of a supernatural end. Consequently, grace and free will constitute one principle of action, which is at the same time supernatural and free — supernatural, because of grace; free, because of the free coöperation of the will.[7]

When it comes to the heart of the question, namely, what actual grace really is in itself, the author is not very definite. In the first place, he points out that it cannot be a movement of

---

[3] The author's own words are: "Haec est gratia operans et cooperans. Operans enim gratia praeparat hominis voluntatem ut velit bonum; gratia cooperans adjuvat ne frustra velit" (Ibid. d. 26, n. 1).
[4] Ibid. n. 1, 2.
[5] Ibid. n. 3, 4, 5.
[6] Ibid. n. 5.
[7] Ibid. d. 26, n. 9; ibid. n. 3.

the faculties — *motus vel affectus mentis* — in so far as that might be said to have its origin from the faculties themselves; for if it were, grace would not be the gift of God. Next he considers the opinion of some who hold that grace is a supernatural quality or form of the soul — *bonam mentis qualitatem sive formam, quae animam informat.* And this, he thinks, is about all that can be said concerning so abstruse a matter. Hence he concludes by stating: *Et illa gratia virtus non incongrue nominatur, quia voluntatem hominis infirmam sanat et adjuvat.*[8]

Finally, although grace is necessary for salutary actions, nevertheless, even after the fall, man's free will retains the power of performing naturally good works. Thus, if a Jew or a bad Christian were to give an alms to a poor man, with the intention of relieving the sufferings of a fellow human being, his action would be praiseworthy; but, unless moved thereto by the grace of God, it would have no bearing upon eternal life.[9]

The question of sanctifying grace is touched only incidentally by the Lombard, and what he does say about it is very unsatisfactory. As will be pointed out in the following chapter, he identified the virtue of charity with sanctifying grace, and then both with the Holy Spirit. Not indeed in the sense that the Holy Spirit might be said to inhere in the soul as an intrinsic form, but rather that He must be conceived to dwell therein as the efficient and exemplary cause of the soul's supernatural life." [10] The special indwelling of the Holy Spirit in the souls of the just is, of course, admitted by all theologians; but the Lombard's inference that this same indwelling is identical with sanctifying grace finds no defenders, and was unanimously rejected by his own commentators.

Alexander of Hales begins his treatise on grace with a very complete division of the various supernatural gifts in one way or another designated by that term. He proceeds as follows: " Grace therefore, according to the common acceptation of the term, is either an uncreated gift, or a concreated gift, or a

8 Ibid. d. 27, n. 1–3.   10 Cfr. Sent. I, d. 17, n. 1–6.
9 Ibid. d. 41, 3.

superadded gift.   Again, there is a grace that makes us pleasing to God, and a grace that is the first supernatural power in the soul, and a grace that is the first effect of grace after the fall, and a grace that signifies certain spiritual prerogatives, and a grace that is a sign of grace, and a grace that is the reward that follows upon grace.[11]

These various graces he divides into two distinct classes: the first contains the *gratia gratum faciens* or sanctifying grace; and the other, the *gratia gratis data*.   By this latter term he designates, not only the *charismata*, as we do to-day, but also all actual graces and infused virtues.   This use of the term was quite common in the schools up to the time of St. Thomas.

In his division of actual graces he follows the Lombard, who, it may be noted in passing, had taken his terminology and principle of division from St. Augustine.   " The free will of man," he says, " may be considered in reference to grace in two different ways: as the subject that receives grace and as the faculty that is moved to act."   As received into the will, grace is called operating or preventing grace; as acting with the will, it is termed coöperating grace.   Then he continues: " In the reception of grace, that is, when grace prepares the will, the action of grace is first; thereupon follows the consent of the free will, or its coöperation in yielding its consent to the movement of grace; and for this reason grace is called operating or prevenient.   But the free will is said to coöperate with grace when it performs the good action through grace; because the action proceeds from the power of the free will as assisted by grace: and therefore the free will itself is said to act, while grace contributes its help to it as the coöperating principle." [12] The two act together, yet the entire effect is attributable to each.[13]

[11] Sum. III, q. 61, m. 1.
[12] Sum. III, q. 61, m. 3, a. 2 ad 2m.
[13] In this exposition he closely follows St. Bernard, who, in his treatise *De Gratia et Libero Arbitrio,* puts the matter very clearly in these terms: " Sic autem ista cum libero arbitrio operatur, ut tantum illum in primo praeveniat, in ceteris comitetur; ad hoc utique praeveniens, ut sibi deinceps coöperetur. Ita tamen, quod a sola gratia coeptum est, pariter ab utroque perficiatur; ut mixtim, non singillatim; simul, non vicissim, per singulos profectus operentur. Non partim gratia, partim liberum arbitrium, sed totum singula opera

Like the Lombard, Alexander holds that preventing and co-operating grace are entitatively the same, and he gives this reason: " Because both are related to the will as its moving cause." [14] Preventing grace is in the will both as a super-natural disposition and as an impulse to action, and when the will yields to this impulse, the same grace acts together with the will and is then properly termed coöperating grace.[15] It may be noted here, that the author does not restrict the term, preventing grace, to the first indeliberate acts of the faculties that result, so to speak, from the divine touch; but extends it to the whole process by which the faculties are elevated and prepared for salutary action. Hence, in this connection, he does not use the two terms, *praeveniens* and *operans,* as synonymous.[16]

The *gratia gratum faciens,* or sanctifying grace, is some-thing objective and permanent in the soul. He speaks of it as follows. " It must be held that the grace by which one be-comes pleasing to God, necessarily places something super-natural in the person, which is the reason of his being thus pleasing to God. And this particular something is the same as that by which a person becomes deiform or is made like unto God; and hence a person is said to be pleasing to God when he is like unto Him." [17]

Furthermore, this grace is both increate and created. For he continues: " It must be maintained that in the just there is a created grace and an increate grace. The increate grace is the Holy Spirit: and the Holy Spirit is called grace in as much as He is a gift; and He is termed a gift in as much as He is love: for by way of appropriation the Holy Spirit is said to

individuo peragunt. Totum quidem hoc, et totum illa; sed ut totum in illo, sic totum ex illo" (Op. cit. c. 14).

[14] Loc. cit. a. 1.
[15] Ibid.
[16] He explains the terms as fol-lows: "Eadem est gratia operans et praeveniens, sed differenter; quia utraque comparatur respectu liberi arbitrii ut causa movens ip-sum; sed praeveniens dicitur in quantum semper praesto est ut causa bonae voluntatis, etsi in ef-fectu non causet; operans vero efficit bonam voluntatem. Unde gratia praeveniens et operans di-cuntur causa bonae voluntatis, sed praeveniens dicit causam secundum habitum, operans vero dicit causam secundum actum" (Ibid. m. 3, a. 2).
[17] Ibid. m. 2, a. 1.

be love. . . . Since therefore the Holy Spirit is love, . . . hence it is that when He is given to us, He transforms us into a special divine likeness, so that our soul itself is made like unto God. But besides this increate grace, we must also hold that there is a created grace, which is a certain divine likeness and supernatural disposition on the part of the rational soul, and by reason of this the soul is pleasing to God and is made like unto Him. Hence there is in the soul a transforming form, and this is increate grace; and there is in like manner also a transformed form, which remains permanently in the soul as the effect of the aforesaid transformation, and this is created grace." [18]

The question whether sanctifying grace, as distinct from the Holy Spirit, is an accident or a substance, he answers with a distinction: " It is to be held that created grace has a twofold relation to the soul: First as regards the essence of the soul, or its nature; secondly, as regards the perfection of the soul in the supernatural order. In its first relation, I say that grace is an accident; because it is superadded to the soul when already complete in its essential perfection. In its second relation, grace is a substantial disposition; nevertheless it is not a substance." [19] Hence sanctifying grace is a supernatural quality, which permanently inheres in the soul and is the foundation of all other divine gifts. It is in this sense that the author favors the opinion of those who hold that the relation of sanctifying grace to the infused virtues is the same as that of the soul to its faculties. [20]

St. Bonaventure does little more than reproduce the teaching of Alexander, and hence there is no need of examining his

[18] Ibid. m. 2, a. 2.
[19] Ibid. m. 2, a. 3.
[20] Ibid. m. 2, a. 4. Besides the citations in the text, the following may also be noted: " Gratia duplex est, scil. gratum faciens et gratis data, et haec non est gratum faciens, sed tamen disponens. . . . Gratia gratis data proprie dicitur donum infusum rationali naturae sine meritis, . . . disponens ad salutem propriam, vel aedificationem alterius. . . . Ad differentiam gratiae gratum facientis, quae non est sicut dispositio ad salutem, quasi distans, sed est dispositio salutis, quia habens illam dignus est salute aeterna; immo gratia gratum faciens est ipsa salus, ad quam disponit gratia gratis data" (Loc. cit. m. 6, a. 3 ad 1m; ibid. q. 63, m. 2, 3).

views in detail. He gives the same division of grace into *gratia gratum faciens et gratis data,* and uses the latter term to designate all divine gifts distinct from sanctifying grace. He refutes Peter Lombard who denied that sanctifying grace must be considered as a permanent created gift, really distinct from the indwelling of the Holy Spirit. The opinion of those, he says, who maintain that sanctifying grace is a created gift, a permanent supernatural accident of the soul, is safer and more reasonable. It is safer, because it is commonly held in the schools — *Doctores enim Parisienses communiter hoc sentiunt et senserunt ab antiquis diebus.* It is more reasonable, because it is unintelligible how supernatural effects, such as we observe in the just, should be produced by the soul without an inherent supernatural form.[21]

Sanctifying grace purifies the soul, elevates it to the supernatural state, makes it like unto God, and is the principle of all supernatural merit.[22] It is not merely a superficial ornament of the soul, but penetrates its very being and faculties, vivifying all the infused virtues, and making their actions meritorious for heaven. In regard to this last effect he compares sanctifying grace to material light, which brings out all the beautiful colors inherent in the objects of sense.[23]

Unlike Alexander, who considered the increase of sanctifying grace to consist in an intensification of its power and in the conferring of a more perfect likeness to God,[24] St. Bonaventure explains it by an addition of new degrees, which result in a quantitative augmentation of sanctifying grace. Moreover the increase of grace is not merited *de condigno,* nor *de congruo,* but by a sort of intermediate merit.[25] This last kind of merit was not generally admitted in the schools.

Albertus Magnus gives substantially the same exposition as

---

[21] In Sent. II, d. 26, a. unic. q. 2.
[22] Breviloq. V, 3, 4.
[23] His own words are: "Quemadmodum enim color qualitas est corporis terminati, quae a praesentia luminis influxi venustatur et completur, ut possit movere visum, sic virtus, quae est habilitatio potentiae, absque gratia gratum faciente informis est sicut color sine lumine; sed ea adveniente, ex qua tota anima in se et in suis potentiis decoratur, formari et vivificari dicuntur virtutum actus et effici Deo accepti" (In Sent. II, d. 27, a. 1, q. 2; cfr. ibid. d. 26, q. 2).
[24] Sum. q. 69, m. 2.
[25] In Sent. II, d. 27, a. 2, q. 2.

Alexander and St. Bonaventure. In regard to sanctifying grace he points out that its relation to the infused virtues resembles that which exists between the soul and its faculties, and that therefore it has only a mediate influence upon salutary acts. " It is evident," he says, " that sanctifying grace is primarily not a perfection of the potencies, but of the essence of the soul, and through this only does it exercise its influence upon these same potencies." [26]

St. Thomas, in keeping with his customary mode of procedure, draws largely on the known facts of nature, when he comes to consider the various questions connected with the subject of grace. In the order of nature God is the first cause: as creator, He produces all secondary causes; as preserver, He sustains them in being; as ruler, He directs them to their proper end. He concurs with all their activities in such a way, that the effects depend on Him as well as on these secondary causes themselves. And the same is also true in the supernatural order. Grace is the result of His goodness and mercy; He infuses it into the soul or its faculties, and through it He moves man to the practice of virtue and the final attainment of Life eternal.

The activity of grace is exercised in a two-fold manner. First, it serves as a remedy against the moral weakness caused by sin, and in so far it is of a medicinal nature. Secondly, it confers a mode of action that lies beyond the reach of man's natural powers in any state, and as such it is a principle of supernatural merit. Taken in the first sense, grace belongs properly to the state of fallen nature; in the second, it is a necessary complement of the powers of every rational creature destined for a supernatural end. [27]

In his classification of grace, St. Thomas uses the same terms as Alexander of Hales, St. Bonaventure, and Albertus Magnus; but he attaches to them a different sense. Thus by the term *gratia gratum faciens* he designates all supernatural helps and gifts conferred for the recipient's own sanctification, comprising both habitual and actual graces. On the other

[26] In Sent. II, d. 27, a. 1, q. 1; Sum. II, tr. 16, q. 101.
[27] Sum. Theol. I. II, q. 109, a. 2.

hand, the term *gratia gratis data* he restricts to such gratuitous gifts or charismata as are intended for the good of others rather than for that of the recipient. He puts his division in these terms: "According to this, there are two kinds of grace: one, namely, through which the recipient himself is united to God, and this is called a grace that makes one pleasing to the Giver — *gratia gratum faciens;* another, again, through which one person assists others, for the purpose of leading them back to God; and a gift of this kind is termed a grace gratuitously bestowed — *gratia gratis data."* [28] In another sense, however, both kinds of grace are gratuitous gifts, excluding not only all natural merit, but also rising above the exigencies of human nature.[29]

Again, the *gratia gratum faciens* is also of two kinds: habitual and actual. "For the right ordering of his life," he says, "man needs a two-fold help of God: one by way of a permanent gift, through which corrupted human nature is healed, and when healed is elevated, for the purpose of performing actions that are meritorious of life eternal, and ·that exceed the powers of unaided nature. In another way man needs the help of grace in order that he may be moved by God to perform actions that are necessary for the attainment of salvation." [30] This latter help is called actual grace.

Actual grace is a movement of the faculties produced by God; habitual grace is a supernatural quality infused into the soul. He describes both in these terms: "It was said above that man is gratuitously assisted by God in two ways: one way, in as much as man's soul is moved by God to know something, or to will, or to act; and when assisted in this way, the gratuitous effect produced in man is not a quality, but a certain movement of the soul; for the act of him that moves is movement in him who is moved. In another way, man is assisted by the gratuitous will of God in the sense that a permanent gift is infused by God into his soul. And this gift is infused into the soul because it would be unbecoming that God should be less generous to creatures destined for a supernatural

---

[28] Ibid. q. III, a. I.   [30] Ibid. a. 9.
[29] Ibid. a. I ad 2ᵐ.

end than to those destined merely for a natural end. For to these latter He not only imparts the requisite movements in respect of their natural actions, but He also endows them with permanent forms, and certain powers, which are so many principles of action in accordance with the movements which He imparts. In this way the movements produced in them by God are connatural to these creatures, and render easy the exercise of their powers, according to the saying of Wisdom : ' He disposed all things sweetly.' With far greater reason, therefore, does He infuse certain forms, or supernatural qualities, into those creatures that He directs towards the attainment of a supernatural and eternal good, so that in accordance with them they may be moved by Him to the acquisition of the aforesaid eternal good both sweetly and promptly. And in this sense, grace is a certain quality." [31]

This quality, in which habitual grace consists, is distinct from the infused virtues. And the reason is that the infused virtues presuppose a permanent elevation of the soul to the supernatural order, just as the acquired virtues presuppose the soul's essence. Hence sanctifying grace is related to the infused virtues very much the same way as nature is related to its potencies.[32]

As a logical consequence, sanctifying grace has for its immediate subject of inhesion, not the faculties, as is the case with infused virtues, but the substance of the soul itself. " It follows therefore," he argues, " that as habitual grace is prior to the virtues, it has for its subject something that is prior to the potencies of the soul ; and this is the soul's substance. For just as man by reason of his intellectual faculty participates in divine cognition through the virtue of faith, and by reason of his volitional faculty participates in divine love through the virtue of charity ; so does he by reason of the substance of his soul participate according to a certain similitude in the

[31] Ibid. q. 110, a. 2.

[32] He sums up his argument in these terms : " Sicut igitur lumen naturale rationis est aliquid praeter virtutes acquisitas, quae dicuntur in ordine ad ipsum lumen naturale; ita etiam ipsum lumen gratiae, quod est participatio divinae naturae, est aliquid praeter virtutes infusas, quae a lumine illo derivantur, et ad illud lumen ordinantur " (Ibid. a. 3).

divine nature through a spiritual regeneration and supernatural elevation." [33]

Both actual and habitual grace are divided into operating and coöperating grace. He explains the division in this way: " Considered in either sense, grace is properly divided into operating and coöperating grace. For the operating or producing of an effect is not attributed to the thing moved but to the mover thereof; hence in the production of that effect in respect of which our mind is moved and not moving, but God alone is moving, the operation is attributed to God; and in this sense the movement is termed operating grace: but in the production of that effect in regard to which our mind is both moving and moved, the operation is attributed not only to God, but also to the soul; and in this sense the movement is called coöperating grace." [34] However, habitual grace does not act effectively, but formally: " just as whiteness is said to make the surface of a body white." [35] Operating and coöperating graces are entitatively the same, but they are distinguished in their relation to the effect produced.[36]

As operating or preventing grace stands exclusively for the operation of God in the soul, it is obvious that in relation to this grace there can be no question of freely accepting or rejecting it. Precisely because it is preventing or prevenient grace, hence it comes to us without our own deliberate concurrence — *est in nobis sine nobis*. But the question is, how does it affect the will? Does it leave the will free to make it coöperative, so that the efficacy of connection, as it is called, comes from the free will prepared by grace? Or does it contain that same efficacy in itself, so that in its presence the will is not free to withhold its coöperation? How does St. Thomas answer this very fundamental question?

In one sense it may be said that he did not answer it at all, in as much as he never proposed the question in that particular form. But in another sense he answered it very fully, in so far, namely, as he laid down principles from which it necessarily follows that in his view the efficacy of connection comes

[33] Ibid. a. 4.
[34] Ibid. q. III, a. 2.
[35] Ibid. a. 2 ad 1m.
[36] Ibid. a. 2 ad 4m.

from man's free will. Thus, for instance, he says that God
" acts upon man's free will in such a way as to impart to it
the power of acting, and to bring it about that the will acts together with Him; without, however, interfering with the free
determination of the will in respect of the action to be performed and the end to be attained.   Hence the will retains the
dominion over its own action." [37]   And again: " Man's will
would not be free unless it belonged to him to determine the
course of his own actions, and to choose by his own proper
judgment either the one or the other." [38]   Statements of this
kind are met with over and over again in the writings of St.
Thomas, and therefore the only possible inference is that he
held the efficacy of connection to come from man's free will
and not from grace.   Nor is this inference at all weakened by
the fact that in many other texts he ascribes the consent of the
will to the action of grace; for they need mean no more than
that grace prepares the will to give its free consent when it
still may withhold the same.   Hence the contention of later
Thomists, that the Angelic Doctor taught anything like their
praemotio physica, is absolutely without foundation in fact.

Duns Scotus proposes practically the same doctrine as regards actual grace, and is quite definite in asserting the freedom
of the human will as moved by God.   That freedom is not
merely a matter of terms, but it implies the power of freely
choosing either the one or the other of two opposite actions at
the very instant when the choice is made.[39]   Grace and free
will act together in producing the same effect, and that effect
may be impeded by the withdrawal of either of the two
causes.[40]   Hence the efficacy of connection is derived immediately from the free will, and mediately from grace; in as
much, that is, as grace prepares the will to give its free consent.[41]

On the other hand, the teaching of Scotus on sanctifying
grace is, to say the least, peculiar.   In the first place, he identi-
fies sanctifying grace with the theological virtue of charity.

[37] In Sent. II, d. 25, q. 1, a. 1 ad
3[m].
[38] Ibid. d. 28, q. 1, a. 1.

[39] Ibid. I, d. 39, n. 16.
[40] Ibid. II, d. 37, n. 14.
[41] Ibid.

" The Holy Ghost," he says, " does not move the will to the meritorious love of God by a habit distinct from charity, nor does He by a habit distinct from charity dwell in the soul; and this habit is grace, and grace itself is charity." [42] Thus sanctifying grace and charity are essentially the same; nevertheless as referred to God they are distinct, but only *distinctione formali*.[43]

Next he holds that sanctifying grace has for its immediate subject of inhesion, not the substance of the soul, but the will; for the will is the immediate subject of charity, and charity is the same as grace. Furthermore, although the will through charity participates in divine love, and the intellect through faith participates in divine knowledge; yet the soul through sanctifying grace is not made a partaker of the divine nature. The reason he assigns for this is twofold: First, because the divine nature so far transcends all created beings that it cannot be represented in them by a proper image of itself, such as participation implies; secondly, this participation would necessitate the inhesion of sanctifying grace in the substance of the soul; and this is against the well known fact that the loss of grace manifests itself first in the loss of love, which is in the will.[44]

In this reasoning the author obviously loses sight of two facts pointed out by St. Thomas: First, that the participation of the divine nature through sanctifying grace is only analogous, consisting as it does in a certain accidental likeness to God; secondly, that the infused virtues do not flow physically from sanctifying grace, and consequently there is no necessary connection between the loss of grace and of the virtues. Charity is indeed lost together with grace, but that is because of its essential opposition to every mortal sin.

B — JUSTIFICATION AND MERIT

According to the common teaching of the Scholastics, justification is effected through the infusion of sanctifying grace

[42] In Sent. II, d. 27, n. 35.   [44] Ibid. d. 26, n. 1.
[43] Ibid.

into the soul by God. In its final term it is an instantaneous change, which offers four distinct points for consideration. Alexander of Hales describes it in the following manner: " In justification there are two terms: the term whence and the term whither — *a malo ad bonum*. Hence on the part of God there is something required in regard to the term whence, and also in regard to the term whither: in like manner there is something required on our part in regard to each. . . . Now on the part of God there is required, in respect of the term whither, the infusion of sanctifying grace; and in respect of the term whence, the forgiveness of sin. On our part, in reference to the term whither, is required the turning of our free will to God through faith; and in reference to the term whence, contrition or the detestation of sin." [45]

This exposition, as is obvious, presupposes that the person to be justified has attained to the use of reason; for in infants justification is entirely the work of God, and as such comprises only the infusion of grace and the remission of original sin. The matter is treated in the same way by St. Bonaventure,[46] and also by St. Thomas.[47] In fact, as regards the four points themselves, enumerated by Alexander, there is no difference of opinion among the Scholastics. All admit that without true conversion of heart on the part of man, and the infusion of grace together with forgiveness of sin on the part of God, there can be no justification of the adult sinner. A mere imputation of the justice of Christ, such as was excogitated by the sixteenth-century Reformers, is never referred to by them as even thinkable. But there is not the same agreement among them when the above-mentioned four points are considered in their relation to one another. In the order of time they are simultaneous, but in the order of nature priority of one to the others must be admitted. Which of them has the precedence? It is on this that opinions differ. A few words must suffice to indicate the nature of the contention.

St. Thomas answers the question of priority in this way: " It is to be held that the aforesaid four points, which are re-

[45] Sum. IV, q. 17, m. 4, a. 6 ad 4ᵐ. [47] Sum. Theol. I. II, q. 113, a. 6.
[46] In Sent. IV, d. 17, p. 1, a. 2, q. 1.

quired for the justification of the sinner, are indeed simultaneous in time — because justification is not successive; but in the
order of nature one comes before the other. And in this
order, first of all occurs the infusion of grace; next comes the
turning of the free will to God; then the free will turns against
sin; and in the fourth place is granted the remission of guilt." [48]
This order, he argues, must be observed because in the matter
of justification God takes the initiative, and He acts through
the infusion of grace. It must be noted, however, that in this
explanation he considers justification under its formal aspect.
Hence in another place he says that the ultimate disposition required for justification, or the act of contrition, proceeds from
sanctifying grace then and there infused into the soul; *quia
secundum ordinem causae formalis, efficientis et finalis infusio
gratiae natura prior est.* On the other hand, if justification be
considered with reference to the material cause — *secundum
ordinem causae materialis* — the forgiveness of sin precedes
the infusion of grace, and is in its turn preceded by the turning
of the will to God and away from sin; because this is required
by way of disposition on the part of the soul, which is related
to grace as matter to its form. [49] Hence, in the view of St.
Thomas, sanctifying grace is the formal reason of the expulsion of sin from the soul.

Alexander of Hales and St. Bonaventure conceive the matter somewhat differently. According to them, the production
of grace in the soul is indeed prior to the expulsion of sin; but
the expulsion of sin, in its turn, is prior to the information and
sanctification of the soul by grace. In a similar manner, the
act of contrition on the part of the subject precedes the infusion
of grace and the expulsion of sin, but only as attrition; the moment that grace is infused, it becomes contrition in the strict
sense of the term, and then sin is expelled by grace. [50] Hence
in their view also, sanctifying grace expels sin formally from
the soul. The whole process of justification is beautifully described by St. Bonaventure in his *Breviloquium.* [51]

[48] Ibid. q. 113, a. 8. [50] Loc. cit.
[49] In Sent. IV, d. 17, q. 1, a. 4; [51] Op. cit. V, 3.
De Verit. q. 28, a. 8.

Duns Scotus regards justification in an altogether different light. He conceives it to consist in two divine operations: the forgiveness of sin and the interior renovation of the soul through sanctifying grace. The two are simultaneous in time, but in the order of nature the forgiveness of sin precedes the infusion of grace.[52] Hence grace does not expel sin formally from the soul, but only by way of moral exigency, in as much as its presence in the will is a cogent reason why God should forgive sin. It is, therefore, absolutely possible that mortal sin and sanctifying grace should be in the soul at one and the same time.[53] Conversely, of course, mortal sin does not formally expel sanctifying grace, but only by way of demerit.[54] This peculiar view of Scotus on justification is based upon an equally peculiar view on the nature of habitual sin, that is, of sin as it exists in the soul after the sinful act has ceased. Such a sin, according to him, does not consist in the privation of sanctifying grace, nor in anything positive in the soul; but simply in a liability to punishment — *nihil aliud nisi ista relatio rationis, scilicet ordinatio ad poenam.*[55]

Closely connected with the question of justification is that of merit. For, in the first place, although justification in its ultimate term is an instantaneous operation, nevertheless the whole process consists of many acts of the will elicited under the influence of actual grace; and in regard to these acts the question immediately arises whether they have any meritorious value. In the next place, justification is not intended for its own sake, but is meant as a preparation for the attainment of eternal life; hence the same question of merit recurs in regard to actions performed after justification. Hence the following few points in the teaching of the Scholastics on the subject of merit may be added to what has been said on the question of justification and grace.

The first point that deserves consideration in this connection is the possibility of merit. For merit, as St. Thomas

[52] In Sent. I, d. 17, q. 2; Report. IV, d. 16, q. 2, n. 23.
[53] Report. IV, d. 16, q. 2; cfr.

Mastrius, Scotus Academicus, IX, tr. 3, d. 3, q. 2, 3.
[54] In Sent. IV, d. 1, q. 6.
[55] Ibid. d. 16, q. 2.

observes, is in the order of justice; and as God cannot be under obligation of justice in regard to His own creatures, it would seem that merit on the part of man is impossible. He solves the difficulty by distinguishing between justice according to absolute equality and justice according to a certain proportion. The former can indeed have no place between man and God, but the latter may; in so far, namely, as man does what in him lies to comply with the demands of God in using the powers given him for the attainment of a certain end. Hence, in this connection, merit presupposes a divine ordination in virtue of which certain actions are entitled by way of reward to an equivalent of their moral value in the eyes of God.[56]

In regard to the conditions put down for merit, presupposing the divine ordination just mentioned, there is no disagreement. All postulate the *status viae,* freedom of choice, and the assistance of divine grace. Thus St. Thomas, after pointing out the necessity of grace, says very briefly: *Quia creatura rationalis seipsam movet ad agendum per liberum arbitrium; unde sua actio habet rationem meriti.*[57] And Scotus defines meritorious actions in these terms: *Actus potentiae liberae et secundum inclinationem gratiae elicitus, acceptus a Deo ut praemiabilis beatitudine.*[58] Furthermore, when there is an equality of proportion between the meritorious action and the reward, merit is said to be condign — *de condigno;* when that equality is wanting, but still there is a certain fitness that the action should receive some remuneration, merit is termed congruous — *de congruo.* Both kinds of merit are admitted by the Scholastics.

The object of merit varies with the conditions of the person who performs the meritorious action. In the first place, if he is in the state of mortal sin, he is incapable of meriting *de condigno;* because no one is entitled to a reward who is not united to God through sanctifying grace.[59] Secondly, if he is in the state of grace, he can merit *de condigno* both an increase of sanctifying grace and life eternal. In regard to the

[56] Sum. Theol. I. II, q. 114, a. 1.
[57] Ibid.
[58] In Sent. I, d. 17, q. 3, n. 25.

[59] Cfr. Thomas, Sum. Theol. I. II, q. 114, a. 5.

second point, namely, that life eternal can be merited *de condigno,* there never was any difference of opinion among the
Scholastics; they all admitted that heaven was promised not
only as an inheritance but also as a reward. On the other
hand, with regard to the increase of sanctifying grace opinions
were divided. Thus, for instance, St. Bonaventure contends
that although such an increase may be merited, still the merit
in question can only be *de congruo.* And the reason is that
there is a want of proportion between the lower degree of
grace, which is the foundation of merit, and the higher degree
which is conferred as a reward. But at the same time it is
fitting that the good works of the just should be rewarded by
an increase of grace, and hence there is room for merit *de
congruo.*[60]

St. Thomas solves this difficulty by distinguishing between
the quantity of grace and its power of meriting. "The increase of grace," he argues, "is not above the meriting power
of the grace already existing in the soul, although it exceeds
that same grace in quantity. And this may be illustrated by
an example taken from the growth of a tree; for although the
tree exceeds the seed in quantity, nevertheless it was evidently
not beyond the power of the seed to produce it."[61] And in
keeping with this solution he makes the general statement,
that the object of merit comprises everything for which grace
is given; and grace is given not only for the actual attainment
of eternal life, but also for the growth in sanctity as implied
in a proper preparation for that life. And in this sense the
increase of sanctifying grace falls under merit *de condigno.*[62]

The object of merit in a wider sense of the term, or of merit
de congruo, may comprise even the spiritual good of others.
Thus a just man by his prayers and good works may merit the
conversion of sinners, or an increase of perfection for those
who are already in the state of grace. Of course, what is
merited in this case is not sanctifying grace itself, but the
bestowal of actual graces that lead to the end intended.

[60] In Sent. II, d. 27, a. 2, q. 2.   [62] Ibid. a. 8.
[61] Sum. Theol. I. II, q. 114, a. 8
ad 2m.

Hence, although no one can merit the first grace for himself, he may merit it for others. St. Thomas argues the point in this way: "Because a just man fulfills the will of God, hence it is fitting that God also, in consideration of their mutual friendship, should have regard to his will in reference to the conversion of others." [63]

The chief points contained in the present chapter, especially those referring to actual grace and justification, were incorporated by the Council of Trent in its dogmatic decree on the justification of sinners.[64] Further particulars regarding the definition of the points in question will be given in another chapter.

[63] Ibid. a. 6.   [64] Cfr. DB. 793 sqq.

CHAPTER XIV

INFUSED VIRTUES: THEOLOGICAL AND CARDINAL

Most of the Scholastics treat the subject of infused virtues in connection with Christology. Peter Lombard introduces it in these terms: "As we have shown above that Christ was full of grace, it will not be out of place here to inquire whether, besides charity, He had also faith and hope. For if He was without these, it seems that He did not have the plenitude of grace. Now, in order to make this matter clear, we must consider each of these two virtues by itself."[1] Then he gives a brief dissertation on faith and hope, and points out in what sense they were found in Christ. After this he presents an outline of his views on the four cardinal virtues, justice, fortitude, prudence, and temperance,[2] to which he adds a somewhat fuller exposition of the seven gifts of the Holy Ghost.[3]

This arrangement and disposition of the subject-matter was retained by his commentators, but they expanded his brief statements into numerous and lengthy articles. However, in so doing they did not indulge in profitless speculations; on the contrary, they contributed very much to the development of a doctrine which had only been touched upon in a general way by Patristic writers. The following points may be put down as constituting the more important results of their laborious investigations.

1. *Nature of Infused Virtues.*— Alexander of Hales terms the infused virtues *gratiae gratis datae,* to distinguish them from the *gratia gratum faciens* or sanctifying grace;[4] while Peter Lombard and most of his commentators speak of them as gratuitous habits — *habitus gratuiti.* They agree

[1] Sent. III, d. 23, n. 1.
[2] Ibid. d. 33.
[3] Ibid. d. 34.
[4] Sum. III, q. 63.

253

with acquired habits in this, that they are permanent dispositions of their proper subject in the order of operation. But
they are distinguished from them in their origin, in their
sphere of activity, and in their relation to the end for the
attainment of which they are intended. Acquired habits are
the result of a repeated and systematic exercise of man's
natural faculties; of themselves they operate exclusively in
the natural order, and tend towards the more ready attainment of a natural end. As a consequence, they may be either
good or bad, according as they incline the will to what is
morally good or morally evil. Infused habits, on the other
hand, are a free gift of God, and as such they are produced
in their subject without any operation on its part; their purpose is not to facilitate but to make possible the connatural
production of supernatural acts, and their tendency is always
towards a supernatural end. Hence they are necessarily good,
and have no part in the doing of evil.[5] It is because of
this that they are called virtues; because a virtue is defined as
" a habit that perfects a human potency in respect of good
acts." [6]

As these gratuitous habits have thus an essential relation to
activity, their proper subject is not the substance of the soul,
but the faculties through which the soul exerts its own activity
as a rational being.[7] Hence they reside in the intellect and
will, and are *ad modum potentiae*. St. Thomas, however,
holds that they may also reside in the sensitive potencies
" *sed secundum quod sunt rationales per participationem, ut
obedientes rationi*.[8] Scotus says that they immediately perfect the soul.[9]

Although the infused habits, or virtues, are really distinct
from one another, yet they are all connected among themselves, and with sanctifying grace. On this general statement
all Scholastics are agreed, but they are at variance in regard

---

[5] Cfr. Thomas, In Sent. III, d.
23, q. 1, a. 1–5; Bonavent. ibid. a.
1; Halens. Sum. III, q. 68, m. 3.
[6] Thomas, In Sent. III, d. 23, q. 1,
a. 4.
[7] Halens. loc. cit. m. 3, 8;

Thomas, loc. cit. q. 2, a. 3; Albert.
Magn. In Sent. III, q. 23, a. 6;
Bonavent. Ibid. a. 1, q. 2.
[8] Sum. Theol. I. II, q. 50, a. 3.
[9] In Sent. III, d. 34, n. 6.

to some particular aspects of the point in question. The Lombard and a few others seem to hold that grace and the infused virtues are essentially the same, but their position in reference to this matter is not very clear.[10] St. Bonaventure expresses his view in these terms: " Because of its perfection, by reason of its dignity and eminence, grace confers on man all the habits that constitute the integrity of justice in relation to the various acts and objects, conditions and opportunities, which are found *in statu viae.*" [11] However this " conferring " does not imply efficient causality on the part of grace; it denotes only a certain concomitant exigency, in view of which God produces the virtues in the soul.[12] In this sense they have their origin in grace, and in so far grace may be regarded as their source.[13] They have each their own proper form which bears a relation to specifically different acts, and hence they are essentially and formally distinct.[14]

St. Thomas teaches practically the same. " Just as the potencies," he says, " which are certain principles of action, flow from the essence of the soul; so also do the virtues flow from grace into the potencies of the soul, which are thereby moved to their own proper acts." [15] And again: " Grace is reduced to the first species of qualities; however it is not the same as virtue, but is by way of habitude, which is presupposed to the infused virtues as their principle and root." [16]

Alexander of Hales develops these points at considerable length, while the others touch upon them more or less incidentally. He points out the distinction between sanctifying grace and the infused virtues; their relation to one another and to salutary acts; their connection with the gifts of the Holy Spirit, and their distinction from the same. On all these questions his teaching is essentially the same as that set forth in the preceding paragraphs.[17]

2. *Division of Infused Virtues.*— Infused virtues, writes

[10] Sent. d. 26, n. 4.
[11] In Sent. III, d. 34, p. 1, a. 2, q. 3.
[12] Ibid. II, d. 27, a. 1, q. 2 ad 1m.
[13] Ibid. III, d. 34, p. 1, a. 1, q. 2.
[14] Ibid. d. 33, a. unic. q. 2.

[15] Sum. Theol. I. II, q. 110, a. 4 ad 1m.
[16] Ibid. a. 3 ad 3m.
[17] Sum. III, q. 62–64.

Alexander of Hales, are classed according as they are *in finem* or *ad finem*. To the former class belong the three theological virtues of faith, hope, and charity; to the latter, the four cardinal virtues of prudence, justice, fortitude, and temperance.[18] This is the same division as that given by the Lombard, and was adopted by most of the Schoolmen. By some, however, it was rejected as unduly multiplying the number of infused virtues. Thus Scotus denies that any solid reason can be assigned for holding that moral virtues are infused by God; because the acquired virtues under the influence of faith and charity are quite sufficient to regulate man's moral conduct.[19] The same position was taken by Henry of Ghent,[20] Durandus,[21] and most of the Nominalists.

The necessity and nature of the theological virtues is thus indicated by St. Thomas: " Man is perfected by virtue in respect of the acts that place him in due relation to beatitude. . . . Now man's beatitude or happiness is twofold: One that is in proportion to human nature, and to which man can attain by the proper use of his natural principles of action; another that exceeds man's nature, and which he can reach only through divine power by way of a certain participation of the divinity. . . . And because this beatitude exceeds the capacity of human nature, hence man's natural principles of action . . . are not sufficient to place him in due relation to it; and therefore it is necessary that other principles be divinely bestowed on him, by which he is so disposed in respect of supernatural beatitude, as he is disposed by natural principles of action in regard to his connatural end, though not without the assistance of divine grace. Now these principles are called theological virtues; both because they have God for their object, in as much as by them we are placed in the proper relation to God; and because they are infused into us by God alone; and also because their existence is known to us only by divine revelation as contained in Holy Scripture." [22]

These theological virtues are really distinct from intellec-

18 Ibid. q. 68.
19 In Sent. III, d. 36, n. 28.
20 Quodl. 6, q. 12.

21 In Sent. III, d. 33, q. 6.
22 Sum. Theol. I. II, 62, a. 1.

tual and moral virtues. Because "habits are distinguished according to the formal difference of their objects; but the object of the theological virtues is God Himself, the ultimate end of things, in so far as He exceeds the cognition of our reason; while the object of intellectual and moral virtues is something that can be comprehended by human reason: therefore the theological virtues are specifically distinct from intellectual and moral virtues." [23]

There are only three theological virtues — faith, hope, and charity. This follows from their very nature, since they are in us as so many permanent dispositions towards God as our last end. For in every one who strives to attain an end, two prerequisites must be found before he can act — knowledge of the end and an intention of attaining the end. But in order to have such an intention, two further prerequisites are necessary: First, the possibility of attaining the end, for no one is moved to strive for what is impossible; secondly, the goodness of the end, because no one intends except what is good. Therefore faith is required in order to make the end known; hope is necessary to give confidence of attaining the end; charity is needed to incline the agent to the end as his own good. And besides these nothing else is requisite by way of placing man in a proper relation to the attainment of his last end, which is God. [24]

However, as these theological virtues have God for their object, there must be other infused virtues whose object consists in the things that lead us to God; and these are the infused moral virtues. They bear the same relation to the theological virtues as the acquired intellectual and moral virtues bear to our natural principles of action. [25] They are in the same general order of operation as the acquired moral virtues, but they are specifically distinct from them; because their formal object is different, in as much as they regulate man's activity according to the supernatural norm of rectitude. [26]

3. *The Virtue of Faith.*— Faith, says St. Bonaventure, is not only a virtue, but it is the pilot or helmsman of all virtues;

[23] Ibid. a. 2.
[24] In Sent. III, d. 33, q. 1, a. 5.
[25] Sum. Theol. III, q. 63, a. 3.
[26] Ibid. a. 4.

because without faith there is no knowledge of God as our
supernatural end, and without such knowledge no infused virtue could exert its activity along its own proper line of operation.[27]   It is a virtue that captivates the intellect in the obedience of Christ and clings to the First Truth on account of
Itself and above all things.[28]   In regard to it, authority takes
the place of reason; not any authority whatever, but the Supreme Authority, God Himself, who is infallible in His testimony to the truth.[29]

Most of the Scholastics evolve the definition of faith given
by St. Paul — *Now faith is the substance of things to be hoped
for, the evidence of things that appear not.*[30]   " This designation of faith," writes St. Thomas, " is a most complete definition; not that it is put in the accustomed form of a definition,
but in it all those things are touched upon which are required
for a definition of faith." [31]   Here we have the material object of faith in the *things that appear not;* the act of faith in
the *evidence* of the same things; and the end of faith in the
substance of things to be hoped for.[32]   Or as St. Bonaventure
puts it: " The habit of a virtue must be designated with respect to two things — its end and its object.   The end of faith
consists in eternal beatitude, which we hope to attain, and
therefore in the *things to be hoped for;* the object of faith consists in the truth that is not seen, and therefore in the *things
that appear not."* [33]

In connection with this definition of faith given by the
Apostle, St. Thomas defines the virtue of faith as a " habit
of the mind, by reason of which eternal life has its inception
in us, in as much as it causes the intellect to give its assent to
things that are not seen." [34]   In substance this definition is
admitted by the other representative Scholastics, although they
use somewhat different terms.   In the first place, they are all
agreed that faith, whether it is considered in one and the same
individual or in several, is specifically one virtue; because a

[27] In Sent. III, d. 23, a. 1, q. 1.
[28] Ibid.
[29] Ibid. ad 3m.
[30] Hebr. 11, 1.

[31] De Verit. q. 14, a. 2.
[32] Ibid.
[33] In Sent. III, d. 23, a. 1, q. 5.
[34] Loc. cit.

virtue is specified by its principal act, and the principal act in its turn is specified by its proper object, and the proper object of faith is one — the First Truth.[35] Furthermore, all are at one in assigning the intellect as the subject of the virtue of faith; but there is some difference of opinion among them as to whether faith is properly in the speculative or practical intellect. The latter view is taken by Albertus Magnus,[36] Richard of Middleton,[37] and a few others. St. Thomas holds that the virtue of faith " is in the speculative intellect, although it is there as the remote occasion of operation; hence operation is not attributed to it except as under the influence of charity. However it must be noted that it is not in the speculative intellect absolutely, but in so far as the latter is subject to the dictate of the will." [38] The matter is viewed in practically the same light by St. Bonaventure;[39] while Alexander of Hales holds that if faith be considered materially it must be said to be in the speculative intellect, but if taken formally it is in the practical intellect.[40]

The object of faith is twofold — material and formal. The former consists in the truths that must be believed; the latter, in the reason upon which this belief is made to rest. The Scholastic teaching on both points may be given in a few words.

In the first place, all admit that the material object of faith comprises in a general way all the truths revealed by God, in the sense that belief in them can be made to rest upon the infallible authority of God's word.[41] In so far there is full agreement of views; but this agreement ceases when the question is asked, whether truths that are clearly apprehended by man's natural reason may at the same time be an object of faith. On this there are the following two sets of opinions.

---

[35] Bonavent. In Sent. III, d. 23, a. 1, q. 3; Albert. Magn. ibid. a. 12; Middleton, ibid. a. 4, q. 3; Halens. Sum. III, q. 68, m. 4.
[36] Loc. cit. a. 6.
[37] Loc. cit. a. 6, q. 2.
[38] De Verit. q. 14, a. 4; In Sent. III, d. 23, q. 2, a. 3.

[39] In Sent. III, d. 23, a. 1, q. 1.
[40] Sum. III, q. 68, m. 3.
[41] Halens. loc. cit. m. 7, a. 6; Bonavent. loc. cit. q. 2; Thomas, Sum. Theol. III, q. 1, a. 1; Scotus, In Sent. III, d. 23, n. 6.

The question is answered negatively by St. Thomas, who expresses his view in these terms: " A thing may be credible in two ways: First, simply, in the sense that it exceeds the capacity of all men whilst they are *in statu viae* — such as the truth of the Trinity, and others of the same kind. Concerning these it is impossible that any man should have natural knowledge; hence, everyone of the faithful gives his assent to them because of the testimony of God, to whom they are ever present and known. Secondly, a thing may be credible not simply, but only in respect of some particular person; for the reason that it does not exceed the capacity of all men, but of some only; such as the truths that can be known by demonstration. Of this kind are the truths that God is one and incorporeal, and others of the same nature. In regard to them there is no reason why they should not be known to some by way of demonstration, and believed by others who for one reason or another do not perceive the force of the demonstration: but it is impossible that they should be both known and believed by the same person." [42] The position thus taken by St. Thomas was endorsed by Scotus,[43] and is defended by many modern theologians, although the majority reject it as untenable. On the other hand, St. Bonaventure,[44] Alexander of Hales,[45] Albertus Magnus,[46] Richard of Middleton,[47] and Durandus,[48] took the opposite view. St. Bonaventure argues the point in this way: " The reason why such knowledge is compatible with faith in regard to the same object, so that the one cognition does not expel the other, is this, because knowledge which results from the light of reason, although it affords some certainty and evidence in reference to divine things, does nevertheless not make that certainty and evidence quite clear so long as we are on the way to God. For although we may be able to show by conclusive reasons that God exists and that God is one, still we are not able to see the divine essence itself, nor the unity of God, nor

[42] De Verit. q. 14, a. 9.
[43] In Sent. III, d. 23, n. 17.
[44] Ibid. a. 2, q. 3.
[45] Loc. cit. m. 7, a. 3.

[46] In Sent. III, d. 15, a. 9.
[47] Ibid. d. 24, q. 5.
[48] Ibid. q. 1.

how that unity does not exclude the plurality of persons, unless we are purified by the justice of faith. . . . Hence, as was pointed out above, just as faith is compatible with external vision, because something remains hidden about the person of Christ; so must it also be understood in regard to the habit of faith and this manner of knowing, namely, that they are compatible with each other in the same person and in respect of the same material object." [49]

The truths to be believed are in the present order of Providence unchangeable, so that the material object of faith admits neither of increase nor diminution. However men's knowledge of what is contained in the material object of faith grows with the lapse of time; " because what at one time was believed only implicitly, as involved in some article of the faith, was later on explained and thereupon became an object of explicit belief." [50] In this sense, therefore, faith may also be said to grow objectively; not by addition to the truths revealed, but by a clearer exposition of them as occasioned by the circumstances of time. [51]

The formal object of faith, as was stated above, is the reason upon which supernatural faith is based. This reason, according to the common teaching of the Scholastics, is the Supreme Truth bearing witness to Its truthfulness and authority in the revelation made to men. Thus St. Bonaventure, answering the objection that to believe without reason is worthy of blame, says: " This is very true in cases where authority does not supply the place of reason. But where authority does supply the place of reason it is not blameworthy but commendable. Thus it is in faith; for although no reason presents itself to the intellect on account of which it ought to give its assent to the truth, nevertheless there is present to it the authority of the Supreme Truth which exerts its suasion on the heart; and we know that the Supreme Truth cannot lie, and therefore it is impious not to believe Its testimony." [52]

[49] In Sent. III, d. 24, a. 2, q. 3.
[50] Ibid. d. 25, a. 2, q. 1.
[51] Albert. Magn. ibid. q. 1; Thomas, ibid. q. 2, a. 2; Middleton, ibid. a. 5, q. 1; Scotus, Report. III, d. 25, q. 1; In Sent. IV, d. 11, q. 3, n. 5.
[52] In Sent. III, d. 23, a. 1, q. 1.

Or as Scotus puts it very briefly: *"Fides infusa assentit
alicui revelato, quia credit Deo, vel veracitati Dei asserentis
illud."* [53]   And St. Thomas: *"Ratio assentit alicui ex hoc
quod est a Deo dictum."* [54]

However the intellect does not give its assent precisely as
compelled by the evidence of the revealed truth; faith is a free
act and depends partly on the bidding of the will as moved by
divine grace. "Faith," says St. Thomas, "is not in the intellect except in so far as commanded by the will, . . . Hence
although the act of the will can be said to be accidental to the
intellect, yet it is essential to faith." [55]   On the other hand,
the act of the mind is not a blind assent; the light of faith
itself makes it reasonable.[56]   The intellect is elevated and enlightened by the First Truth, and so disposed, it is inclined by
the will, also elevated by divine grace, to yield its assent to the
truth proposed.[57]

The certainty of faith, therefore, is not in proportion to the
light of evidence, but to the weight of God's authority.   St.
Thomas presents this aspect of faith as follows: " Certainty
imports two things: First, firmness of the assent given, and
in this respect faith is more certain than all cognition and
knowledge; because the First Truth, which causes the assent
of faith, is a more powerful cause than the light of reason
which causes the assent in natural cognition.   Secondly, certainty imports also the evidence of that to which assent is
given, and in this respect there is no certainty in faith." [58]

St. Bonaventure puts the same teaching in a somewhat different form.   Speaking about the action of grace in the matter of faith, he says: " Since man must give credence to the
truth, and greater credence to the greater truth, and the greatest credence to the greatest truth; and since the truth of the
First Principle is infinitely greater than all created truth, and
infinitely more luminous than all the light of his intellect, it
necessarily follows that his intellect, in order to show itself

[53] Ibid. d. 23.
[54] De Verit. q. 14, a. 2.
[55] Ibid. a. 3 ad 10m.
[56] Ibid. corp.

[57] Bonavent. In Sent. III, d. 23,
a. 1, q. 1 ad 3m.
[58] De Verit. q. 14, a. 1 ad 7m.

properly disposed in the matter of belief, must give greater
faith to the first Truth than to itself, and thus yield itself to
the obedience of Christ, so that he not only believes those
things that appear to be in conformity with reason, but also
those that are above reason and in opposition to the experience of the senses. If he refuses to do this, he fails to show
the proper reverence that is due to the Supreme Truth, pre-
ferring as he does the judgment of his natural reason to the
dictate of the Eternal Light." [59]

Hence the certainty of faith consists in only one thing — in
the firmness with which the mind clings to the First Truth.[60]
From this it naturally follows that faith does not necessarily
exclude from the mind involuntary doubts in regard to the
truths that are believed, although its certainty is of a higher
order than that which can be found in any natural knowledge;
because in faith " the intellect is not in the quiescent state that
results from the evidence of vision." [61]

4. *The Virtue of Hope.*— Hope is defined by the Lombard
as " a virtue by which spiritual and eternal things are hoped
for, that is, are looked forward to with confidence." [62]   " This
expectation," comments St. Bonaventure, " consists in a certain reaching out to the· good things of eternity, which arises
from the confidence with which the soul, in all the abandon of
its strength, leans upon God Himself." [63]   Almost the same
terms are used by St. Thomas, when he says that " hope implies a certain reaching out of the appetite to what is good." [64]

All are agreed that hope is a theological virtue, and nearly
all that it is really distinct from faith and charity.[65] Its real
distinction from the other two theological virtues was called
in question by a few obscure writers, whose view, Scotus says,
" is opposed to the authority of the saints as based upon the

[59] Breviloq. V, 7.
[60] Bonavent. In Sent. III, d. 23,
a. 1, q. 3.
[61] Thomas, ibid. q. 2, a. 2, sol. 3
ad 2m.
[62] Sent. III, d. 26, c. 1.
[63] In Sent. III, d. 26, a. 1, q. 3
ad 4m.

[64] Sum. Theol. I. II, q. 40, a. 2.
[65] Albert. Magn. In Sent. III, d.
26, a. 2; Bonavent. ibid. a. 1, q. 2,
3; Thomas, ibid. q. 2, a. 3; Middleton, ibid. a. 3, q. 3; Durandus, ibid.
q. 2.

teaching of St. Paul." [66] The reason why hope is to be considered as a theological virtue is thus given by St. Bonaventure: "Hope must undoubtedly be classed as a theological virtue; and the reason for this assertion is taken both from the object and the subject of hope. From the object, because, just as faith in the act of believing gives its assent to God as dictating what is true, so does hope rely upon Him as promising what is great. Hence just as the object of faith, which acts by way of motive, is something uncreated, which is God, and for that reason faith is counted among the theological virtues; so the same must be said and understood in regard to hope. From the subject also a similar reason may be taken; because as the superior part of the soul must be perfected by the theological virtues, and as hope is one of the virtues that perfects this part of the soul, it follows necessarily that hope is a theological virtue." [67] St. Thomas puts this very briefly, when he says: "Hope has God for its object, and therefore it is a theological virtue." [68] And it is distinct from faith and charity, because while faith simply gives knowledge of man's last end, and charity embraces it as the highest good, hope tends to it as attainable. [69]

The material object of hope, according to the Scholastics, is God Himself to be possessed in eternal beatitude. "The good we must properly and chiefly hope for from God," says St. Thomas, "is infinite and in proportion to God's assistance; and this is life eternal, consisting in the fruition of God Himself." [70] And St. Bonaventure: "Whatever hope expects, it expects not only from God but also in God, so that possessing God it may possess all that is good." [71] Hence the material object of hope does not consist in formal beatitude, which is something created, and finite, but in beatitude taken objectively, which is God Himself as the object of blessed fruition. The only one of the Scholastics who held a different view on this point was Durandus, in as much as he made formal beatitude, or the fruition of God apart from God Him-

---

[66] Ibid. q. unic. n. 2; cfr. n. 10.
[67] In Sent. III, d. 26, a. 1, q. 3.
[68] Ibid. q. 2, a. 2.

[69] Ibid. q. 2, a. 3.
[70] Sum. Theol. II. II, q. 17, a. 2.
[71] In Sent. III, d. 26, a. 1, q. 2.

self, the immediate object of the virtue of hope.[72] Scotus is sometimes cited as holding that objective and formal beatitude together constitute the material object of hope, but he states quite distinctly and definitely that hope tends to a good which is infinite and eternal, and this is God Himself.[73]

However, as is quite obvious, since no one can hope to possess God except by the help of divine grace, the material object of hope must also include the means that are necessary for salvation. Hence these means constitute the secondary object of hope. In this sense Scotus writes: " We expect an infinite good from God, who liberally communicates Himself to us in view of the graces previously conferred." [74] In the same sense also St. Thomas writes: " Hope looks chiefly to eternal beatitude, and in reference to it all other things are asked of God " [75] And this is the common teaching of the Schoolmen.

The formal object of hope, if taken in a general sense, is the possession of God regarded under the aspect of possibility. However, as the possession of God is difficult of attainment, the formal object of hope is commonly designated as *summum bonum in quantum summum arduum* — it is the Supreme Good as possible of attainment indeed, but not without great difficulty. This is the explanation given by St. Thomas, who says: " Hope implies a motion of the appetite towards a good that is commensurate with the strength of him that hopes: for it neither regards a good that is unattainable, nor a good that is esteemed as nothing; but such a good only as can be attained, yet the attainment of which is difficult. For this reason it is termed a *bonum arduum*." [76] Others use practically the same terms, though some of them attach a slightly different meaning to the term *arduum*.[77]

From the fact that hope has the attainment of good for its object, it necessarily follows that it is a virtue which resides in the will. On this point all Scholastics are agreed.

---

[72] Ibid. q. 2.
[73] Ibid. d. 26, n. 11.
[74] Loc. cit.
[75] Sum. Theol. II. II, q. 17, a. 2 ad 2m.

[76] In Sent. III, q. 26, a. 2.
[77] Cfr. Bonavent. In Sent. III, d. 26, a. 2, q. 4.

But there is no strict agreement as regards the number of potencies that must be distinguished in the will. Some few hold that the irascible part of the will constitutes a distinct potency, and is therefore really distinct from the concupiscible part. Others identify the irascible and concupiscible parts so completely as to make them absolutely one potency of the rational soul.[78] Others, again, distinguish the two, but maintain that the irascible part, as referred to the rational soul, must be taken in an improper sense. The concupiscible and the irascible parts constitute really one potency, which is the rational will; but they imply different tendencies of the will towards its object. This is the more common view, and is defended by St. Thomas,[79] St. Bonaventure,[80] Scotus,[81] and many others.

However, notwithstanding this diversity of views in regard to the potencies of the will, there is found a general agreement among the Scholastics in reference to the proper subject of hope. They all maintain that the virtue of hope resides primarily in the irascible part of the will. The *summum arduum*, which they regard as the formal object of hope, in one way or another implies difficulties that must be overcome; and it is to the irascible part of the will that the overcoming of difficulties properly belongs. However, as hope also looks forward to the fruition of the *summum bonum*, in so far it may be said to reside secondarily in the concupiscible part of the will.[82]

Although the act of hope is essentially an act of the will, since the virtue resides in the will as its proper subject, nevertheless the more representative Scholastics hold that hope has a certainty of its own, distinct from that of faith. " It is, however, a difficult thing," says St. Bonaventure, " to define in what this certainty consists." [83]   St Thomas puts his explanation in this form: " The certainty of faith and hope differ in four respects: First in this, that the certainty of faith is in the intellect, whereas the certainty of hope is in

[78] Cfr. Henry of Ghent, Quodl. I, q. 13.
[79] In Sent. III, d. 26, q. 2, a. 3.
[80] Ibid. d. 26, a. 2, q. 5.
[81] Ibid. d. 34, n. 13.
[82] Loc. cit.
[83] In Sent. III, d. 26, a. 1, q. 5.

the affections; secondly, because the certainty of faith can never fail, while the certainty of hope may fail *per accidens;* thirdly, because the certainty of faith is *de complexo,* whereas the certainty of hope is *de incomplexo,* which is the object of the appetite; fourthly, because the certainty of faith is opposed to doubt, while the certainty of hope is opposed to diffidence or hesitation." [84] This certainty of hope comes ultimately from God.

5. *The Virtue of Charity.*—All Scholastics are at one in holding that charity is a theological virtue, but there is no agreement regarding its distinction from sanctifying grace. Scotus,[85] Durandus,[86] Henry of Ghent,[87] and nearly all the Nominalists follow the view taken by the Lombard, that charity and sanctifying grace are essentially the same, although there is between them a *distinctio rationis.* "The same *habitus,*" says Scotus, "which is grace is also charity." [88] And again: "By the same *habitus* by reason of which the Holy Spirit dwells in our soul, the will is inclined to its own meritorious acts." [89] Henry of Ghent is even more explicit, when he says: "Grace and charity do not really differ; nay, that which in the essence itself is grace, in so far as it is considered absolutely or by way of essence, the very same is there also charity, in so far as it is considered under the aspect of potency." [90]

On the other hand, St. Thomas,[91] Albertus Magnus,[92] Ægidius Romanus,[93] and some others maintain that charity and sanctifying grace are really distinct. Their relation to one another is somewhat like that of potency and essence, if the terms be taken in a wider sense. St. Thomas points out that in the natural order of things there are three requisites for the attainment of any given end: A nature that is in proportion to the end proposed; an appetitive inclination towards its attainment; and an actual tendency in its direction.

[84] Ibid. q. 2, a. 4 ad 5^m.
[85] In Sent. II, d. 27, q. unic.
[86] Ibid. d. 26, q. 1.
[87] Quodl. 4, q. 10.
[88] In Sent. II, d. 27, n. 35.
[89] Ibid. I, d. 17, q. 3.

[90] Quodl. 4, q. 10.
[91] In Sent. II, d. 26, a. 4; Sum. Theol. I. II, q. 110, a. 3.
[92] In Sent. II, d. 26, a. 11.
[93] Ibid. q. 2, a. 1.

By analogy, then, it follows that similar requisites must be found in the supernatural order, so that man may be enabled to attain the end that lies beyond the reach of his natural powers. This being premised, the author continues: "Hence it is necessary that something be bestowed upon man by reason of which he is not only enabled to strive for the end, or has an inclination thereto, but his nature itself is elevated to a certain degree of dignity, so that it be in proportion to the supernatural end; and for this purpose grace is bestowed; but for the purpose of inclining the will to the same end, charity is given; while for the performance of actions by which the end is actually attained, other virtues are infused. And therefore just as in the natural order of things nature is distinct from its inclination to the end and from its operation, so likewise in the supernatural order is grace distinct from charity and other virtues." [94]

Between these two opposite views there is a third, advocated among others by St. Bonaventure [95] and Alexander of Hales.[96] According to this, there is not merely a *distinctio rationis* between charity and sanctifying grace, but neither is there between them a *distinctio realis*. They are distinguished not *per essentiam,* but only *comparatione* and *secundum esse.* St. Bonaventure illustrates his distinction as follows: "Just as the productive principle in man, because of its great perfection in giving natural life, not only causes life *in actu primo* but also *in actu secundo,* which consists in operation; so likewise does the principle of reparation give life to the spirit in the supernatural order, both as regards the life itself and the operation that follows." [97] Hence in the supernatural order, sanctifying grace is the remote principle of action; just as nature is the remote principle of action in the natural order: hence grace compared to charity, even as light compared to color, " is not different in essence, but only by way of comparison and in its mode of existence." [98]

The proper subject of the virtue of charity is simply the

[94] De Verit. q. 27, a. 2.
[95] In Sent. II, d. 27, a. 1, q. 2.
[96] Sum. II, q. 61, m. 2, a. 4.

[97] Breviloq. V, c. 4.
[98] In Sent. II, d. 27, q. 2.

rational will itself, though a few of the Scholastics assigned as its subject the concupiscible part of the will. Concerning these latter St. Thomas says: " Some say that charity resides in the concupiscible part, but this cannot be; because the concupiscible part belongs to the sensitive appetite. And if it be said that the concupiscible part is human, this is not true except because of its being under the direction of reason; unless perhaps they intend to call, by way of equivocation, the will itself an irascible and concupiscible potency." [99] And this some of them did intend, as for, instance, St. Bonaventure, who, on the one hand, held that the virtues of hope and charity reside in the rational will, and yet, on the other hand, assigned as their respective subjects the irascible and concupiscible part of the will. [100]

The material object of charity is in a way twofold: primary and secondary. The primary object is God Himself, the Supreme Good, to be possessed in eternal beatitude. The secondary object comprises all rational creatures in so far as they are capable of possessing God. [101] Hence the fallen angels and lost souls are not properly included in the secondary object of the virtue of charity. [102]

The formal object of charity is God as the absolute and supreme good, to be loved for His own sake. " Faith and hope," says St. Thomas, " do indeed reach out to God, but only in so far as from him comes the knowledge of what is true and the possession of what is good; whereas charity embraces God Himself for the purpose of resting in Him, and not that thence any advantage may accrue to us." [103] Hence charity is first and foremost a love of benevolence, because it intends the good of the beloved; but as the possession of God constitutes our eternal beatitude, it in so far also includes the love of concupiscence. [104]

Although the virtrue of charity, like that of faith and of

[99] In Sent. III, d. 27, q. 2, a. 3.
[100] Ibid. a. 1, q. 1; d. 26, a. 2, q. 5.
[101] Cfr. Bonavent. ibid. d. 27, a. 2, q. 4; Thomas, Sum. Theol. II. II, q. 23, a. 5; q. 25, a. 1; Albert. Magn. In Sent. III, d. 27, a. 7.

[102] Cfr. Thomas, In Sent. III, d. 28, q. 2, a. 5; Bonavent. ibid. a. unic. q. 2.
[103] Sum. Theol. II. II, q. 23, a. 6.
[104] Id. In Sent. III, d. 29, q. 1, a. 4; Bonavent. ibid. d. 27, a. 2, q. 2.

hope, is really distinct from sanctifying grace; yet unlike them, it does not remain when grace is lost. This difference is owing to the different opposition of the three theological virtues to mortal sin. Thus faith is opposed only to the sin of infidelity, either partial or total; hope, to the sin of presumption and despair; but charity is opposed to all mortal sins. Hence, while faith and hope may exist in a soul that is deprived of grace, charity cannot.[105] Finally, while faith and hope cease on the threshold of heaven, in the sense that they issue respectively into vision and possession; charity remains formally as it is, only it blossoms into greater perfection. This, however, does not necessarily imply that whatever perfection there is in the virtues of faith and hope is lost; but only that all imperfection has been removed from their corresponding acts.[106]

6. *The Cardinal Virtues.*—" The general purpose of virtue," says St. Bonaventure, " is twofold: First, that they may give a right direction to the powers of the soul by counteracting man's natural obliquity of inclination; secondly, that they may strengthen these same powers against the difficulties that must be overcome." [107] Now man has a threefold relation — to God, to himself, and to the neighbor. The right ordering of his relation to God is affected by the three theological virtues; but as they do not touch his relation to himself and the neighbor, other supernatural virtues must be infused for this purpose. These are the moral virtues: justice, fortitude, prudence, and temperance. The last three regulate man's conduct in respect to himself, while the first orders his relations with his neighbor. Each one of these four has other moral virtues connected with it, and therefore they are called principal or cardinal virtues. They have their own proper object, and are distinct from corresponding acquired habits.[108] Scotus, however, as was pointed out above, does not admit the existence of infused moral virtues.[109]

---

[105] Ibid. q. 4; Albert. Magn. ibid. a. 3.

[106] Loc. cit. d. 31, a. 3, q. 1; Thomas, ibid. q. 2, a. 1.

[107] In Sent. III, d. 33, q. 1.

[108] Cfr. Thomas, QQ. DD., De Virt. Cardinal.; Bonavent. In Sent. III, d. 33; Dionys. Carth. ibid. q. unica.

[109] The relation of all these vir-

The principal points in this teaching of the Scholastics on the infused virtues have been embodied by the Council of Trent in its decree on justification, and by the Council of the Vatican in its definitions of matters pertaining to faith, as will be pointed out in a later chapter. It must be noted, however, that the declarations of these two councils bear almost exclusively on the existence and nature of the theological virtues; the moral virtues are referred to only in passing, without even any direct affirmation of their existence. Hence the view taken by Scotus and his followers is free from all ecclesiastical censure, but it is rejected by most modern theologians. The Council of Vienne, held in 1311–1312, left the question still open, whether sanctifying grace and the virtues are infused in the baptism of children; [110] but the Council of Trent decided it in the affirmative, by defining in a general way that justification is obtained in baptism, and that in justification the virtues of faith, hope, and charity are infused together with sanctifying grace.[111]

tues to sanctifying grace, and their connection with one another, is thus beautifully described by St. Bonaventure: "De ramificatione igitur gratiae in habitus virtutum haec tenenda sunt, quod una sit gratia gratificans animam, septem tamem sunt virtutes gratuitae, quibus regitur vita humana: tres quidem theologicae, scilicet fides, spes et caritas: quatuor cardinales, scilicet prudentia, temperantia, fortitudo et justitia, quae uno modo est virtus communis et generalis, alio modo specialis et propria. Haec autem septem virtutes, licet sint distinctae et proprias excellentias habentes, sunt tamen connexae et aequales ad invicem in eodem; et licet sint gratuitae per gratiam informatae, possunt tamen fieri informes per culpam, sola caritate excepta, et iterum reformari per poenitentiam adveniente gratia, quae est habituum virtualium origo, finis et forma" (Breviloq. V, c. 4).

[110] Cfr. BD. 583.
[111] Cfr. Ibid. 800.

CHAPTER XV

THE SACRAMENTS IN GENERAL

DEFINITION AND EFFICACY OF THE SACRAMENTS

St. Augustine, when speaking of baptism, states that a sacrament consists of two things: a material or sensible element and the word — *accedit verbum ad elementum et fit sacramentum*.[1] By the word he most likely understood, not only the prayer used in the consecration of the material element, but also the sacramental form. The combination of the word and the element he designated on various occasions as a *visible word, a sacred sign, the sign of a sacred thing, a sign of grace,* or simply as a *sacrament.* In his usage of them, all these terms stand for the outward sacramental rite. Then, with this outward rite he connected an inward effect, a *res sacra* or *gratia,* which he usually called the power of the sacrament — *virtus sacramenti.* The production of this inward effect he attributed to the Holy Spirit, as operating in and through the sacramental rite.[2]

These fundamental concepts, considerably clarified though not all first introduced by St. Augustine, were looked upon as a sacred heirloom by most subsequent theologians. Up to the twelfth century, and even till somewhat later, sacramental theology did not pass beyond that stage of development to which it had been advanced by the labors of Augustine in his contention with the Donatists. Then his studies of the sacramental system were taken up again with renewed ardor, and for nearly three hundred years continued to be a subject of special interest to the greatest of the Schoolmen. What he had barely touched upon they subjected to a searching inquiry, with the result that they rounded out and completed the sys-

[1] Ad Catech. 3.   [2] Cfr. vol. I, p. 347 sqq.

tem in all its parts.   The contents of the present and the following chapter will give us some idea of the fruitfulness of their labors.

1. *Definition of a Sacrament.*— During the ninth and tenth centuries, St. Augustine's definition of a sacrament as a sacred sign had been, to a great extent, replaced by that of St. Isidore of Seville, according to which a sacrament is a sacred secret or a mystery.   But with the advent of Scholasticism the Augustinian definition came again into favor.   Abelard expanded it somewhat, without, however, introducing any substantial modification.   " A sacrament," he says, " is a visible sign of the invisible grace of God." [3]   This definition, as is obvious, may be applied to any sacred ceremony, and for that reason it was soon found to be of little practical value to the scientific study of the sacraments.

About the same time, Hugh of St. Victor defined a sacrament as " a corporeal or material element, which in its outward application is perceptible by the senses, by its similitude represents some invisible spiritual grace, by reason of its institution signifies that grace, and because of its sanctification contains the same." [4]   This is a rather cumbersome definition; and, moreover, it is applicable only to those sacraments that are partly made up of a "corporeal or material element," which is not the case with penance, orders, and matrimony.   Besides, when the author says that a sacrament " contains " grace, he seems to hold that grace is stored up in the sanctified element as in a vessel; and this he actually asserts a little further on.[5]

A better definition is found in the *Summa Sententiarum,* which in the past was commonly ascribed to Hugh of St. Victor but is now considered by many to be the work of some unknown twelfth-century writer.   Discussing the Augustinian definition, he says: " A sacrament is a visible form of the invisible grace conferred in it, which grace the sacrament itself confers.   For a sacrament is not merely a sign of a sacred thing, but also exerts efficiency in its respect.   And this is the

[3] Introd. ad Theol. I, 2.   [5] Ibid. c. 4.
[4] De Sacram. I, p. 9, c. 2.

difference between a sign and a sacrament: in order to be a sign nothing is required except that it signifies the thing of which it is a sign, without in any way bestowing the same; but a sacrament furthermore also bestows that of which it is a sign or expression." [6]

This marks an immense advance over the definition given by Hugh. It places an essential distinction between sacramental rites and all other sacred ceremonies, by attributing to the former an efficacy in the production of grace which is denied to the latter. Practically the same definition is found in the *Sentences of Magister Bandini.* He puts it in this form: " That is properly said to be a sacrament which signifies grace in such a way as also to confer it. And by this the difference between the old and the new sacraments is clearly manifested: for they only promised and signified, whereas these signify and give grace." [7]

Almost the same terms are used by Peter Lombard in the definition which in one form or another recurs in the works of all his commentators. After briefly explaining the various kinds of signs and their purport, he states that a sacrament is not a natural but a conventional sign, but of such a kind that it bears the likeness of the thing signified; and then he proceeds: " For that is properly said to be a sacrament which is in such a manner a sign of the grace of God and a form of invisible grace, that it bears its image and is its cause. It was not therefore merely to signify grace that the sacraments were instituted, but also to confer sanctification." [8] It is this that distinguishes the sacraments of the Old and the New Law: the former " only promised and signified, the latter give salvation." [9] Hence every sacrament is indeed a sign, but not every sign is a sacrament. [10]

Later Scholastics frequently shortened the definition given by the Lombard, but they all kept its essential elements. Thus St. Thomas states briefly: " A sacrament is a sign of a sacred thing in so far as it sanctifies men." [11] It is its objective con-

---

[6] Op. cit. tr. 4, c. 1.
[7] Op. cit. IV, d. 1.
[8] Sent. IV, d. 1, c. 4.

[9] Ibid.
[10] Ibid.
[11] Sum. Theol. III, q. 60, a. 2.

nection with grace that differentiates a sacrament from all other sacred rites and ceremonies. This, therefore, is the specific difference that restricts the generic term, " sacred sign " or " sign of a sacred thing," in its signification, and limits it to a particular class of sacred signs, which finally came to be exclusively designated as sacraments.

While the Scholastics thus gradually succeeded in working out a satisfactory definition, they also investigated the nature and composition of the external rite or sign. They soon recognized that the " element " and the " word," spoken of by St. Augustine, are not only found in every sacrament, but bear a very definite relation to one another in the constitution of the " sacred sign." The element is always more or less indefinite in its signification, and this indefiniteness is taken away by the words used in its application. Thus water, which is the " element " in baptism, may be employed either for cooling or cleansing purposes; but when the " word," I baptize or wash thee, is added, the purpose of the ceremony is definitely determined. And so proportionately in all other sacramental rites, even in those which do not consist of a corporeal element and formal words. The analogy between this observed fact and the constitution of bodies, as explained by the Scholastics, was too striking to remain long unnoticed. Hence early in the thirteenth century, William of Auxerre originated the theory of matter and form as applied to the sacramental sign.[12] Alexander of Hales adopted the terms in his exposition of the sacramental rite,[13] and after him St. Thomas permanently introduced them into the theological language of the Schoolmen. What formerly went by the general name of thing, was thenceforth spoken of as matter; and what till then had been designated as words, was thereafter simply called form.[14]

This theory was still further developed by Duns Scotus, who distinguished two kinds of matter: remote and proximate. The remote matter, according to his distinction, is the indefinite element in itself; as, for instance, the water used in baptism or the chrism employed in confirmation. While the prox-

---

[12] Cfr. Schanz, Die Lehre von den heiligen Sacramenten, p. 103.

[13] Sum. IV, q. 5, m. 3, a. 1.
[14] Sum. Theol. IV, q. 60, a. 6, 7, 8.

imate matter is the application of the indefinite element or
remote matter to the recipient of the sacrament; as ablution
and chrismation in baptism and confirmation respectively.[15]
All this, as is obvious, introduced no real change in sacramental theology, but it was helpful towards clarifying ideas.
Scotus, it may here be noted, made some reservation in applying the theory of matter and form to the sacrament of penance,
in so far as he did not consider the acts of the penitent constituent parts of the sacrament.

2. *The Efficacy of the Sacraments.*— St. Augustin, in his
contention with the Donatists, had already clearly pointed out
that the Christian sacraments produce their effects independently of the moral disposition of the minister; and had also
made it clear that the sanctification of the subject is objectively connected with the sacramental rite.   It was this teaching, called to mind at a time when violent discussions were carried on regarding the validity of sacraments conferred by
excommunicated ministers, that introduced the phrase *opus
operatum* into sacramental theology.   It was at first used to
distinguish the sacramental rite, as objectively posited, from
the action of the minister considered subjectively, although
later on it became customary to apply the same distinction also
to the actions of the recipient.   Its earliest use is thus indicated by Peter of Poitiers, who died in 1205: *Baptizatio dicitur actio illius qua baptizat, quae est aliud opus quam baptismus, quia est opus operans, sed baptismus est opus operatum,
ut ita liceat loqui.*[16]   A few years later Pope Innocent III used
the term in a similar connection.   Speaking of the administration of the sacraments by an unworthy minister, he says:
*Quamvis igitur opus operans aliquando sit immundum, semper
tamen opus operatum est mundum.*[17]

After the middle of the thirteenth century, the two terms,
ex opere operato and *ex opere operantis,* were also quite generally used to indicate the difference between the Christian
sacraments and the Mosaic rites.   As already pointed out

[15] In Sent. IV, d. 7, q. 1; cfr. ibid.
d. 3, q. 3.
[16] Sent. V, c. 6.

[17] Cfr. Pourrat, Theology of the
Sacraments, p. 163.

in a preceding paragraph, the difference between the two was held to consist chiefly in their connection with grace. It is true, some of the Scholastics, among whom was Peter Lombard,[18] went so far as to assert that the sacraments of the Old Law were of no spiritual benefit whatever, even to those who used them piously; but the majority of mediæval theologians regarded them in some way as means of grace, although not in the same sense as the Christian sacraments. According to Hugh of St. Victor and a few others, their connection with grace was objective but indirect, in the sense that they foreshadowed the sacraments of the New Law, and by this foreshadowing caused grace in the recipient.[19] St. Thomas, on the other hand, and indeed the greater number of the Scholastics, denied them all objective efficacy and held that they sanctified the recipient because of the faith and charity with which he received them. Hence their efficacy was entirely *ex opere operantis,* whereas that of the Christian sacraments is *ex opere operato.*

From this use of the term, *ex opere operato,* it is sufficiently clear that the Scholastics ascribed some kind of causality to the sacraments of the New Law. And this appears also from the definition of the sacraments as signs that sanctify, signs that signify and cause grace. But what kind of causality did they have in mind? In precisely what sense must the Christian sacraments be considered as causes of grace? On this point there was no agreement, even at the time of St. Thomas; for he says: " All are forced to admit that the sacraments of the New Law are in some manner causes of grace; for this is the express teaching of authority. But different men regard that causality in a different way."[20] These different views held by different theologians during the Middle Ages, are usually reduced to three distinct systems of sacramental causality. The following is a brief outline of them, as gathered from the works of the most representative Scholastics.

The first is the system of *occasional causality,* which was most ably defended by St. Bonaventure and Duns Scotus. The

[18] Sent. IV, d. 1, c. 4.
[19] Sum. Sent. tr. 4, c. 1, 2.
[20] In Sent. IV, d. 1, a. 4.

former speaks of it in these terms: " There is also the opinion
of other great men, who say that, in the sense of quality or
absolute property, there is no causality in the sacraments, nor
any power productive of grace, either by way of efficiency or
disposition; but that grace is produced by reason of a certain
divine assistance. For they say that the divine power, which
is the cause of grace, is present in the sacrament, and that the
faith and devotion of the recipient act by way of disposition
for the reception of grace. And this they explain by an example: At the word of Eliseus, Naaman, washing himself,
was cleansed of his leprosy; in this case the divine power effected the cure, and the devotion and obedience of Naaman
acted by way of disposition, but there was no causality either in
the word of Eliseus or in the water of the Jordan. Now, if the
Lord had so decreed that at the word of Eliseus, not only
Naaman himself, but also all others coming for this purpose
to the Jordan should be cured, and then by a kind of covenant
had promised His perpetual assistance, that water would be
said to cure and heal leprosy, and also to be the cause of such
cures and to have the power of healing. And so, they say,
it is in the case of the sacraments; so that, at the uttering of the
word, the divine power is present in the water and thus infuses grace and regenerates the recipient, while he submits
himself by a profession of faith and by obedience. In this
sense, they hold, the sacraments are said to have power, to be
causes, to produce effects, on account of the divine power
which is present." [21]

Then, after explaining more in detail how all these terms,
power, efficiency, causality, are taken in a wider sense — *ex-
tenso nomine* — when applied to the sacraments, and how
grace is produced entirely in virtue of a divine ordination that
became effective at the time when the sacraments were instituted, he concludes by saying: " To this position the piety of
faith is not opposed, and reason gives its approval." [22] In
another place he assigns as his reason for adopting this view
the fact that the efficiency of the sacraments, taken in the

[21] In Sent. IV, d. 1, p. 1, a. unic.   [22] Ibid.
q. 4.

strict sense of the term, in regard either to the production of grace or of a disposition thereto, is unintelligible.[23]

Scotus explains his position in practically the same terms. The sacraments, he says, are not the cause of grace by reason of any intrinsic form or property; but they may be said to produce grace by a kind of concomitance, in as much as, in consequence of the order established by God, they induce a natural condition in the subject on account of which God causes grace in the soul. Hence their efficacy in relation to grace is not raised above the natural order, and even this dispositive efficacy is the result of a divine agreement, or compact, as the author calls it, by which God bound Himself to impart His grace to all those who receive the sacraments with the proper disposition. A sacrament, therefore, is merely the occasion on which God recalls His promise, and then on account of His promise produces grace in the soul.[24] This occasional causality of the sacraments, as it is usually called, was also defended by Durandus,[25] Ockam[26] and the Nominalists generally.

Another explanation of the efficacy of the sacraments was outlined by Alexander of Hales, and afterwards further developed by St. Thomas. Like Peter Lombard, Alexander distinguished two effects produced in the reception of the sacraments — the *sacramentum et res* and the *res tantum*. By the former he understood the sacramental character, or, when there was question of sacraments that do not imprint a character, a spiritual ornament produced in the soul; by the latter he designated the grace conferred in the administration of the sacraments. The character or the ornament of the soul, as the case might be, he conceived to be efficiently produced by the sacraments, with a view to dispose the soul for the reception of grace;[27] while grace itself, thus called for by the dis-

---

[23] In Sent. III, d. 40, dub. 3.

[24] In Sent. IV, d. 1, q. 4, 5; Report. IV, d. 1, q. 4, n. 8.

[25] In Sent. IV, q. 4.

[26] Ibid. IV, q. 1, 6.

[27] His own words are: " Sine praejudicio melioris sententiae opin-ando dico, nihil asserendo, quod sacramenta sunt causae alicujus effectus in anima, non dico solum disponendo, sed efficiendo; efficiunt enim simpliciter characterizando et ornando. Unde dico, quod singula sacramenta aliquo modo ornant

position effected in the soul through the sacramental rite, must be caused directly and exclusively by God.[28]   Hence the sacraments act directly only as dispositive causes of grace.   Thus their causality is indeed saved, but it has only an indirect bearing on the production of the grace which they are said to confer.

This view was adopted by St. Thomas, at least in his earlier works; for in his *Commentary on the Sentences* he says: " Others there are who maintain that in the reception of the sacraments two things are effected in the soul; one is the *sacramentum et res,* as the character, or an ornament of the soul in the case of sacraments that do not imprint a character; the other is the *res tantum,* as grace.   In respect of the first effect the sacraments are in some way efficient causes; but in respect of the second they are dispositive causes, inducing such a disposition as necessitates the infusion of grace, unless there be an impediment on the part of the recipient.   And this view seems more in conformity with the teachings of theologians and the sayings of the saints." [29]

However, as there appears to be an insuperable difficulty in the supposition that a physical and material rite produces a supernatural and spiritual effect, whether that effect be sanctifying grace or merely a disposition thereto, St. Thomas found himself under the necessity of introducing here the distinction between principal and instrumental causes.   The principal cause of the sacramental character or ornament of the soul, as well as of sanctifying grace, is God, whose causality alone bears a due proportion to the effect produced; but the instrumental causes of this same effect are the sacraments, in so far as they are subservient to God's power and intentions.   Thus he says: " In so far as they are the instruments of the divine mercy which justifies man, they produce instru-

animam, vel imprimendo characterem, vel alio modo signando " (Sum. IV, q. 5, m. 3, a. 5 ad 1[m]).

[28] " Solus Deus operatur gratiam et animae infundit: sed sacramenta Novae Legis disponunt ipsum susceptibile, efficiendo aptiorem ad gratiae susceptionem et faciunt, quod gratia efficax sit " (Ibid. a. 5 ad 2[m]).

[29] In Sent. IV, d. 1, q. 1, a. 4.

mentally in the soul some effect that bears a direct proportion to the sacraments, such as the character or something of that kind.   But to the ultimate effect, which is grace, they do not attain even instrumentally, except by way of disposition strictly as such.   Hence what the sacraments directly produce is a disposition that necessitates, so far as it comes in question, the infusion of grace." [30]

Then, in order to show the possibility of this instrumental causality as predicated of the sacraments, he enters into a rather minute discussion on the difference between the action of principal and instrumental causes.   " The power of acting," he says, " is always in proportion to the agent.   Therefore it is necessary to suppose one kind of power in the principal agent, and another in the instrumental agent.   The principal agent acts always according to the exigencies of his own form, and therefore his active power is some form or quality that is complete in the order of nature.   But the instrument acts only as moved by another, and hence it must have power in proportion to this movement.   Now movement is not a complete entity, but is the way to it, holding a middle place between pure potency and complete actuality. . . . Hence, as the sacraments are instrumental agents, their spiritual power is not a complete entity, but is incomplete." [31]   And again: " In a corporeal thing there cannot be a spiritual power that is complete in itself; but it can be there by way of intention, just as art is said to exist in the instruments employed by the artist." [32]

This view of St. Thomas was adopted by many of his followers, and up to the sixteenth century it was commonly defended as his genuine and exclusive teaching.   Then, however, owing to the sharp criticism of Cardinal Cajetan,[33] it was by many set aside in favor of another view, which St. Thomas apparently defended in his *Summa Theologica*. Whether he really did change his mind is even now a matter of dispute, but all indications are that he did.   For in the

[30] Ibid.
[31] Ibid.
[32] Ibid. a. 4 ad 4ᵐ.
[33] In Sum. III, q. 62.

Summa, which is the last work he wrote, he puts aside the distinction between the *sacramentum et res* and the *res tantum,* and states without any modification whatever that the sacraments are the instrumental causes of grace. Furthermore, he answers the objection that grace, being a participation of the divine nature, can be produced only by God without the concurrence of a created instrument, by explaining how the effect is assimilated not to the instrumental but to the principal cause, and that consequently the nature of grace does not make impossible the instrumental causality of the sacraments.[34] Some writers, like Cardinal Billot, maintain that this teaching of the *Summa* should be interpreted by what St. Thomas holds in his *Commentaries on the Sentences;* but modern Thomists generally contend that the Angelic Doctor changed his mind with advancing years.

According to this latter interpretation, then, St. Thomas finally decided in favor of the system that advocates the physical perfective causality of the sacraments, in the sense that the sacraments are physical instrumental causes, not merely of a disposition to grace, but of grace itself. By virtue of a divine power, in some way transiently communicated to them, they exercise an immediate physical influence on the production of grace in the soul. However, that the sacraments, according to the teaching of St. Thomas, are physical instrumental causes is not conceded by all those of his genuine followers who admit that he finally abandoned the idea of dispositive causality. In various places, they point out, there occur expressions which indicate that he was rather in favor of causality in the moral or intentional order. Thus he says that the sacraments are causes by way of signification,[35] that their causative virtue is present after the manner of intention — *per modum intentionis,*[36] and that in baptism the water produces its spiritual effect in the soul in so far as it is recognized by the intellect as a sign of supernatural cleansing.[37] Expressions of this kind occur quite frequently in his writings, and their import seems to be that the causality of

[34] Sum. Theol. III, q. 62, a. 1, 4.
[35] QQ. DD., q. 27, a. 4 ad 18m.
[36] In Sent. IV, d. 1, a. 4 ad 4m.
[37] QQ. DD., q. 27, a. 4 ad 2m.

the sacraments belongs to the moral or intentional rather than to the physical order. At all events, it is not likely that a unanimous verdict on the teachings of St. Thomas in regard to sacramental causality will ever be reached.

CHAPTER XVI

THE SACRAMENTS IN GENERAL

SACRAMENTAL GRACE: THE CHARACTER: NEED OF INTENTION: THE NUMBER SEVEN: INSTITUTION OF THE SACRAMENTS

Since all the sacraments have the same essential definition, it necessarily follows that they have certain properties in common. The more important of them will be briefly outlined in the present chapter.

1. *Sacramental Grace.*— St. Bonaventure cites three different views on the nature of the grace conferred by the sacraments, each one of which had its defenders among the Scholastics. Those who held the first view maintained that sacramental grace did not differ intrinsically from ordinary sanctifying grace, the term sacramental being applied to it simply for the purpose of indicating its origin. Others, who defended the second view, contended for an essential difference between the two kinds of grace. Ordinary sanctifying grace, according to them, has for its object the performance of good works, whereas sacramental grace is primarily intended to repair the ravages of sin. Hence there may be two different kinds of sanctifying grace in the soul. St. Bonaventure himself took a middle stand, holding on the one hand that all sanctifying grace is essentially the same, and on the other that sacramental grace connotes different effects because of the purpose for which it is given.[1]

The position of St. Thomas in this matter is not quite clear. In his *Commentary on the Sentences* he says that the grace conferred by the sacraments is distinct from the grace of virtues and gifts, or from ordinary sanctifying grace;

[1] In Sent. IV, p. 1, a. unic., q. 6.

and also that sanctifying grace is of one kind in so far as it is in the essence of the soul, and of another kind in so far as it perfects the potencies.[2]   On the other hand, in the *Summa* he seems to hold that sanctifying grace is essentially the same whatever be its origin, and that the grace derived from the sacraments merely connotes different helps intended for the attainment of the end proper to each sacrament.[3]   Practically the same indefinite position had been taken by Alexander of Hales.[4]   However, the opinion defended by St. Bonaventure finally gained the day.

According to the common teaching of the Scholastics, sacramental grace is ordinarily conferred at the time when the sacraments are received; however, if there be an obstacle in the recipient, which on the one hand does not invalidate the sacrament and on the other impedes its effect, the bestowal of grace is deferred until the obstacle has been removed.   This deferred bestowal of grace is now known as the *reviviscence* of the sacraments.   The doctrine of *reviviscence* is clearly taught by St. Thomas in respect of the three sacraments that imprint a character.[5]   Scotus refers to it only when speaking of baptism, and then he says that as soon as the obstacle is removed by proper penance, baptismal grace is conferred in virtue of the baptism already received.[6]

2. *The Sacramental Character.*— The doctrine of the sacramental character, and also of the consequent initerability of the sacraments by which it is imprinted, was brought to practically its full development by St. Augustine.   His teaching on this point was accepted by the whole Western Church, and remained a directive norm till about the end of the seventh century.   But from that time on, at least so far as appearances go, little attention seems to have been paid to the doctrine of the sacramental character.   Owing to the disorder caused by schism, moral corruption, and the encroachment of the civil authority upon the rights of the Church, theological learning was at a low ebb, and in places practices sprang up

[2] Op. cit. IV, d. 1, q. 1, a. 5.
[3] Op. cit. III, q. 62, a. 2.
[4] Sum. IV, q. 5, m. 4, a. 2.

[5] In Sent. IV, d. 4, a. 2.
[6] Ibid. IV, q. 5, n. 2, 3.

that were directly opposed to the teaching of Christian antiquity. Among these abuses was that of reordaining persons upon whom orders had been conferred by simoniac or deposed bishops, or of declaring their orders null and void. In the contentions that thereupon ensued, little or no reference was ever made to the fact that an indelible character imprinted by the sacrament of orders would make such reordinations sacrilegious. And hence the logical inference seems to be that the doctrine of the sacramental character had more or less fallen into oblivion.[7]

However, the correctness of this inference is not clearly established. Even to what extent the practice of reordination was carried is historically uncertain. Saltet appears to take an extreme view when he states: " In the struggle of the Church against simoniacs and intruders, until the twelfth century, the chief instrument of warfare, sometimes of the enemies of the Church, sometimes too, nay most often, of the best sons of the Church and of several Popes, was simply to declare void and to repeat ordinations that were certainly valid." [8]

At all events, during the twelfth century the doctrine of the character was thoroughly familiar to theological writers. This appears clearly from the manner in which Innocent III answered the question, whether those who had been baptized whilst asleep, or whilst out of their mind, had received the sacramental character. Neither the question nor the answer admits of any doubt regarding the doctrine that in baptism a character is impressed on the soul. The only point on which the questioners were in doubt touched the validity of baptism under the given conditions. And this doubt the Pope solved by saying that, if the persons in question had previously intended to be baptized, the sacrament so administered was valid.[9] Hence the contention of some Protestant writers, that Innocent III introduced the doctrine of the sacramental character, only shows that either they have not read or else must have misinterpreted his answer to the proposed question. And

[7] Cfr. Morin, De sacris Eccl. ordinat. III, exerc. 5, c. 5.

[8] Bulletin de litt. eccl. 1901, p. 229, 230.

[9] DB. 441.

the same must be said with regard to some fourteenth-century theologians, among whom were Scotus and Durandus. The former admitted the existence of the sacramental character only because it was taught by the Church in his day,[10] while the latter based his acceptance of the doctrine on the prevailing opinion of the schools.[11]

In the early part of the thirteenth century, the Scholastics began to inquire into the nature of the character, as imprinted on the soul by baptism, confirmation, and orders. On this point there was quite a diversity of opinion. Thus William of Paris thought that the sacramental character must be regarded as a certain kind of sanctity, somewhat like that which results from the consecration of churches, altars, and liturgical vessels.[12] In maintaining this view, he had no followers except Durandus, who, about a century later, described the sacramental character in these terms: *Character non est aliqua natura absoluta, sed est sola relatio rationis, per quam ex institutione vel pactione divina deputatur aliquis ad sacras actiones.*[13]

Peter Lombard barely refers to the sacramental character, but Alexander of Hales gives a full exposition of the doctrine. According to him, the character imprinted by the sacraments is an objective and absolute reality that adheres to the soul. It belongs to the first species of qualities, which is termed *habitus*. Its primary purpose is to dispose the soul for the reception of grace, and to mark it as belonging to the flock of Christ. Each of the three characters is the foundation of a peculiar relation to the Savior. That of baptism makes the recipient like unto Him as Head of the Church; that of confirmation produces a somewhat similar likeness to Him as King of the sacred hosts; while that of orders assimilates the newly ordained to Him as Sovereign Priest. Its proximate subject is not the substance of the soul, but the potencies, and through them it inheres in the soul itself. It is especially attributed to the intellect, as that faculty is more expressive of the divine image in man. By divine ordination it is indeli-

[10] In Sent. IV, d. 6, q. 9, n. 14.   [12] De Sacrament. c. 3.
[11] Ibid. d. 4, q. 1.   [13] In Sent. IV, d. 4, q. 1.

ble, and therefore will remain in the soul for all eternity.[14]

St. Bonaventure gives the same exposition, both as regards the nature and purpose of the sacramental character and its proximate subject. He explicitly refutes five different views on the nature of the sacramental character, which were held in his day. The first regarded the character as a mere consecration of the soul; the second, as a potency; the third, as a passible quality; the fourth, as a form or figure; the fifth, as some unclassified infused quality. After giving the reason for rejecting these views, he establishes his own, holding with Alexander that the sacramental character is an indelible *habitus,* which, residing proximately in the faculties, disposes the soul for the reception of sanctifying grace.[15]

Albertus Magnus takes practically the same position, except that he favors the opinion which makes the intellect the proximate subject of the sacramental character.[16] St. Thomas, on the other hand, looked at the matter in quite a different light. In the first place, he set aside the opinion, rather common in his day, that the character is a *habitus;* and the reason he gives for this is that no virtuous habit, such as the character would have to be if it were a *habitus,* can be used indifferently for good or evil, as is the case with the sacramental character. Then, as the character is permanent and indelible, it can evidently not be a *passio,* which is a merely transient modification; hence he concludes that it is a *potentia.*[17]

This conclusion, moreover, he reasons out by a consideration of the end for which the sacraments were instituted. Their purpose is not only to serve as a remedy against sin, as was commonly held at the time, but furthermore to perfect the soul in those things which pertain to the service of God according to the Christian manner of life. Hence some sacraments imprint a character, in order to fit man for this service.[18] Now, divine service consists either in receiving something sacred for oneself or in giving it to others; and for both purposes a certain power is required, passive in one case

[14] Sum. IV, q. 8, m. 8, a. 1.
[15] In Sent. IV, d. 6, p. 1, a. unic. q. 1, 2.
[16] Ibid. d. 6, a. 3, 4.
[17] Sum. Theol. III, q. 63, a. 2.
[18] Sum. Theol. III, q. 63, a. 1.

and active in the other. Consequently, the sacramental character imparts a certain spiritual power, whose direct object is the service or worship of God. Still, this power, and therefore the character itself, is, properly speaking, not in any genus or species, but is reducible to the second species of quality, and in this sense it is a *potentia*.[19]

Considered in relation to its primary purpose, the sacramental character is a participation in the eternal priesthood of Christ, whence the Christian manner of worship is derived. Hence every one of the faithful, by the very fact of his baptism, is clothed with a priesthood like that of the eternal High Priest. This likeness is perfected in confirmation, and brought to its highest perfection in the sacrament of orders.[20] On the other hand, the sacramental character may also be considered as a configuration or resemblance of the soul to the Blessed Trinity, but only through Christ, who is the brightness of God's glory and the figure of His substance.[21]

Finally, as the sacramental character is a *potentia,* and is primarily imprinted for the purpose of fitting the recipient for rendering God due service, either by receiving the sacraments himself or by administering them to others, its proximate subject is not the substance of the soul but its faculties.[22] And as, moreover, the reception and administration of the sacraments is in a certain manner a profession of faith, the character is properly said to reside in the intellect.[23]

For a time this teaching of St. Thomas gained many followers, but later theologians, with the exception of the Thomists, quite generally set it aside as being more or less arbitrary. For whatever be said about the baptismal and sacerdotal character in this respect, it seems quite obvious that the character bestowed in confirmation does not confer any power, either active or passive, which is not already possessed in virtue of baptism. And this is admitted by St. Thomas himself. Hence, outside the Thomistic school, it has become the common teaching of theologians that the character is simply

[19] Ibid. a. 2.
[20] Ibid. a. 3.
[21] Ibid.

[22] Ibid. a. 4.
[23] Ibid. a. 4, ad 3m.

a supernatural quality which places the soul in a special relation to Christ, and in view of its sacramental origin entitles man to those abundant helps to salvation which the sacraments were intended to confer.[24]

A word may here be added in reference to the rather peculiar position of Duns Scotus. After rejecting the arguments of St. Bonaventure and St. Thomas, which were advanced by these authors for the express purpose of proving that the sacramental character must be regarded as an absolute quality, he states his own view in the following terms: " Notwithstanding these reasons, which do not conclude, it may be said that the character is only some kind of extrinsic relation of the soul itself, caused directly by God in the reception of the sacraments that are initerable; for putting the matter in this way, all that is commonly said about the character is perfectly safe." [25] This extrinsic relation is supposed to be real, and has the will for its proximate term.[26] Hence the view of Scotus regarding the sacramental character is different from that of Durandus, but its drawbacks are hardly less serious; for it is impossible to conceive a real relation of this kind without some absolute quality as its foundation in the soul. For this reason modern followers of Scotus usually interpret his teaching on the sacramental character as postulating such an absolute quality; yet, to all appearances, he himself did not consider it necessary.

3. *Need of Intention.*— That neither sanctity nor faith is required for the valid administration of the sacraments is the common teaching of the Scholastics.[27] But not the same unanimity is found in their statements regarding the need of intention. Thus Rolandus held that baptism would be valid even if the minister had no intention whatever, provided he administered the sacramental rite according to the prescription of the Church.[28] Hugh of St. Victor, on the other hand, regarded this view as absurd.[29] So did the author of the

---

[24] Cfr. Pesch, Praelect. Dogm. VI, n. 189 sq.
[25] In Sent. IV, d. 6, q. 10, n. 2, 13.
[26] In Sent. IV, d. 6, q. 11.

[27] Cfr. Thomas, Sum. Theol. III, q. 64, a. 5, 9.
[28] Sent. Gietl, p. 206.
[29] De Sacr. II, 6, 13.

Summa Sententiarum,[30] and Peter Lombard.[31] But Robert
Pulleyn, at the beginning of the thirteenth century, tried to
refute the arguments of Hugh, and stated in very explicit
terms: " Baptism is valid when the rite is outwardly performed in its entirety, whatever be the inward intention of him
who baptizes or of him who is baptized." [32]

A little later Alexander of Hales formulated a rule in regard
to baptism which was generally adopted by later Scholastics,
and applied to other sacraments as well. He expresses it in
this way. " Whenever anyone uses the proper words and
has the intention of doing what the Church does, although he
understands not what that may be — that is, he intends to
do what the Church has been accustomed to do — that baptism is valid." [33] Yet, even he admitted that the want of intention on the part of the minister might be supplied by Christ,
at least in the case of those sacraments that are necessary for
salvation.[34] Some also interpret a passage in the works of St.
Thomas as upholding this view, but others understand it in a
different sense.[35] Innocent IV is frequently cited in favor of
the opinion that there is no need of an interior intention; but
without just reason. He treats the question of the validity of
baptism in his commentary on the third book of *Decretals,*
which he wrote before his elevation to the pontifical chair; and
although he maintains that the minister need not " bear in
mind to do what the Church does," or " may even have the
contrary in mind," still in this contention he refers merely to
the minister's understanding of the end intended, not to the
fact of an interior intention as such. Hence his further
statement: " The baptism is valid, provided he intends to
baptize." [36]

At all events, the general teaching of the thirteenth-century
and later Scholastics is that an interior or mental intention is
required on the part of the minister for the valid administration of the sacraments. The principle underlying this teach-

[30] Sent. IV, d. 6, 5.
[31] Op. cit. tr. 6, 9.
[32] Sent. V, c. 16.
[33] Sum. IV, q. 8, m. 3, a. 1.

[34] Loc. cit.
[35] In Sent. IV, d. 6, q. 1, a. 2.
[36] Tit. 42, c. 2; cfr. Pesch, Praelect. Dogm. VI, p. 120.

ing is thus stated by St. Thomas: " When a rite is of such a nature that it may indifferently signify many things, it must be determined in its signification by something else. Now, the sacramental rites are of this kind; thus ablution in baptism may have for its end either bodily cleanness, or bodily health, or mere enjoyment, or many other things of a similar kind; and therefore it is necessary that it be determined by the intention of the minister to signify one of them, that is, to signify the sacramental effect." [37] And that he understands this intention to be interior or mental, the author indicates in his answer to an objection drawn from the distractions that may occur during the performance of the sacramental rite; for he says: " If, while making ready to baptize, the priest intends to do in baptism what the Church does, then, even if during the rite his thoughts wander to something else, the sacrament is valid in virtue of the intention which he actually had before he began to baptize." [38] This teaching had already been embodied in the profession of faith which Innocent III required of converts from the Waldensian error.[39]

A similar intention was also required in the recipient of the sacraments. Hence the same Pope decided that those who approach baptism induced by fear of punishment, and those who are baptized while unconscious or asleep, do not receive the sacrament unless they have an actual or habitual intention to that effect.[40]

4. *The Number Seven.*—Before the number of the sacraments could be determined, there was need of an exact definition which marked off the sacramental rites from all other sacred ceremonies. Such a definition was worked out in the twelfth century, and it was at that time that seven religious rites began to be exclusively designated as sacraments. All of them had been known to Patristic writers, and the Church had used them from the beginning of her existence; but so long as there was no strict definition of a sacrament, the term was applied indiscriminately to all rites and ceremonies that had a religious character. Hence, what the Scholastics achieved

[37] Sum. Theol. III, q. 64, a. 8.   [39] DB. 424.
[38] Ibid. a. 8 ad 3m.   [40] Ibid. 411.

was not the invention of sacramental rites, but their proper classification by means of an exact definition. It was this classification that the unknown author of the *Summa Sententiarum* had in mind when he wrote: " A sacrament is not merely a sign of a sacred thing, but it also exerts efficacy in its respect. And this is the difference between a sign and a sacrament: in order to be a sign nothing is required except that it signifies the thing of which it is a sign, without in any way bestowing the same; but a sacrament furthermore also bestows that of which it is a sign or expression." [41]

The work of classification itself proceeded slowly, even after the principle upon which it was to rest had been clearly enunciated. This was partly owing to the want of proper terms for sacred rites that were not productive of grace. It was not until Alexander of Hales coined the term *sacramental* that the name *sacrament* could be used in an exclusive sense. Hence the earliest attempts at classification distinguished between *sacramenta majora* and *minora,* that is, between sacred rites that were held to be of great importance because of their intimate connection with salvation, and others that were considered of less importance. That distinction is already found in the works of Abelard,[42] of Hugh of St. Victor,[43] and Alger of Liege,[44] all of whom wrote in the first half of the twelfth century. They, however, enumerate only five sacraments among the *majora:* Eucharist, baptism, confirmation, matrimony, and extreme unction; or as Alger gives them: Eucharist, baptism, chrisma (confirmation), confession, and orders.[45]

At the same time, or perhaps a little later, the author of the *Summa Sententiarum* speaks about " all the sacraments," and then treats of baptism, confirmation, the Eucharist, penance, anointing of the sick, and matrimony; thus leaving out the sacrament of orders; but to that he refers in connection with the keys which are given at the consecration of the priest.[46] Meanwhile in Abelard's own school penance and

---

[41] Op. cit. tr. 4, c. I.
[42] Epit. Theol. Christ. 28.
[43] De Sacr. I, 9, II, 9, 1.
[44] De Misericord. et Just. I, 62–70.
[45] Loc. cit. ML, 180, 884.
[46] Op. cit. tr. 5–7.

orders, which he himself had passed by, were also counted
with the other five. Thus Rolandus [47] and Omnebene [48]
speak first in a general way of the *sacramentum Incarnationis*,
and then of baptism, confirmation, the sacrament of the body
and blood of Christ, penance, the conferring of the keys, and
matrimony. At the same time, however, all these authors
still apply the name sacrament also to other religious rites;
and so too did the Third Lateran, 1179, and a synod of London held in 1237.[49] It was Peter Lombard who first enumerated the seven sacraments in their present order, and
designated them exclusively as sacraments; [50] but it took some
little time before his terminology was universally accepted.

From the foregoing brief statements it appears sufficiently
clear that the classification of seven religious rites as sacraments did not result from the individual speculation of the
Lombard, as is frequently maintained by Protestant writers.
He merely gave the finishing touch to a development that had
been going on for generations. Nay, it seems that even independently of his speculations the same classification resulted spontaneously from the traditional teaching of the
Church. For in a sermon which was written down at the very
latest towards the middle of the twelfth century, we find this
striking passage: " As I am about to depart from you, I deliver to you what was delivered unto us by the Lord, a pledge
of the holy faith between you and God, namely, the seven
sacraments of the Church, as the seven sanctifying gifts of
the Holy Spirit. . . . For your sake I deem it proper to enumerate them once more, and to point out which they are —
baptism, confirmation, the anointing of the sick, the Eucharist,
the reconciliation of sinners, matrimony, and orders. . . .
Wherefore retain them with all honor and reverence, love and
revere them; teach them to your children, so that they may
know them by heart and diligently guard them for all future
generations." [51]

After the twelfth century theologians no longer inquired

[47] Cfr. Gietl, 157 sqq.
[48] Cfr. Denifle, ALKG, I, 467.
[49] Mansi, 22, 221; 23, 448.

[50] Sent. IV, d. 2, 1.
[51] Cfr. Bolland. I, Jul. 396;
Monum. Germ. Hist. Script. 20, 732.

into the number of the sacraments, but they displayed considerable ingenuity in thinking out reasons why there should be seven. They were convinced that Christ had given seven sacraments to His Church, neither more nor less; but why seven? In answer to this question they advanced a great variety of divergent views. Thus Albertus Magnus thought that the sacraments were instituted as so many remedies against the seven capital sins.[52]   St. Bonaventure coördinated them with the three theological and the four cardinal virtues.[53] St. Thomas pointed out the evident correspondence that is found between man's natural and supernatural life, and thence derived reasons of congruity as to why there should be five sacraments to provide for man's spiritual needs in so far as he is an individual human being, and two others to be of help to him in his relation to society.[54]   It must be noted, however, that as all these authors presuppose the existence of seven sacraments, the various reasons advanced by them are not intended to prove anything else than the fitness of the divine institution.

5. *Institution of the Sacraments.*— The traditional teaching of the Church in regard to the institution of the sacraments was thus formulated by a fourth- or fifth-century writer, to whom the treatise *De Sacramentis* is attributed: " The author of the sacraments? Who is he, if not the Lord Jesus? The sacraments have come down from heaven." [55]   This traditional view, in so far as it merely asserts that the sacraments were in some way instituted by Christ, was universally adopted by the Scholastics. But on the further question, whether Christ instituted the sacraments immediately, in person, or through the agency of others, there was no absolute agreement. Thus Hugh of St. Victor and Peter Lombard held that extreme unction was instituted by the Apostles; [56] and the same was taught by Alexander of Hales [57] and St. Bonaventure.[58]   The latter expressed a similar view with re-

[52] In Sent. IV, d. 2, a. 1.
[53] Breviloq. VI, 3.
[54] Sum. Theol. III, q. 65, a. 1.
[55] Op. cit. ML, 16, 439.

[56] Hugh, De Sacr. II, 15, 11; Lomb. Sent. IV, d. 23, c. 3.
[57] Sum. IV, q. 9, m. 1, 2.
[58] In Sent. IV, d. 23, a. 1, q. 2.

gard to confirmation,[59] while the former attributed the institution of that sacrament to the Council of Meaux, held in 845. Before that time, he contended, the Holy Ghost had been imparted to the faithful without the medium of any sacramental rite.[60]

St. Bonaventure, however, seems to have changed his mind towards the end of his life. For in his *Breviloquium* he says: "Christ instituted the aforesaid sacraments in different ways. Some of them he instituted by confirming, approving, and perfecting what already existed, as matrimony and penance; some others, by insinuating and initiating them, as confirmation and extreme unction; others again, by initiating, consummating, and receiving them Himself, as the sacrament of baptism, the Eucharist, and orders. These three He instituted fully, and He was also the first to receive them." [61] Even Alexander states in one place that all the sacraments were instituted either by Christ Himself or by the Apostles, in virtue of His authority.[62]

Albertus Magnus,[63] St. Thomas,[64] and Duns Scotus [65] attribute the institution of all the sacraments immediately to Christ, so that the Apostles simply used and promulgated what Christ had established. St. Thomas, while speaking of extreme unction, expresses his view in these terms: "In regard to this sacrament there are two opinions. Some there are who say that Christ did not institute extreme unction and confirmation in person, but commissioned the Apostles to institute them; because these two, on account of the fullness of grace which is conferred in them, could not be instituted before the final sending of the Holy Spirit. . . . Others say that Christ instituted all the sacraments in person; but that He personally promulgated only those which present greater difficulty in the way of belief, while He left it to the Apostles to promulgate the others, such as extreme unction and confirmation. And this opinion appears all the more probable

[59] Ibid. d. 7, a. 1, q. 1.
[60] Loc. cit. m. 1.
[61] Op. cit. VI, c. 4.
[62] Op. cit. q. 5, m. 2, a. 1.

[63] In Sent. IV, d. 7, a. 1-3 .
[64] Ibid. q. 1, a. 1-3.
[65] Ibid. d. 2, q. 1.

as the sacraments belong to what is fundamental in the New Law, and therefore their institution pertains to the Lawgiver Himself." [66] And where he speaks of the sacraments in general, he simply states that they were instituted by God *potestate auctoritatis,* and by Christ *potestate excellentiae.*[67]

After the time of St. Thomas the immediate institution of the sacraments by Christ was universally taught in the schools, and not until the seventeenth century was the mediate institution of some of the sacraments again defended by theologians. Then, however, the question was proposed in a different form, namely, whether Christ determined the sacramental rite *in genere* only or also *in specie.* Thus put, the question is still waiting for a solution.

The principal points contained in the foregoing two chapters, which set forth the teaching of the Scholastics on the sacraments in general, were embodied by the Council of Trent in its various definitions of doctrines then under discussion. The septenary number of the sacraments, their institution by Christ, their efficacy *ex opere operato,* the conferring of grace, the impression of a character by baptism, confirmation, and orders; the difference between the sacraments of the Old and New Law, the need of an intention on the part of the minister, the validity of the sacraments conferred by ministers in the state of mortal sin — all these points were clearly defined and proposed for the acceptance of the faithful.[68] It is true, not all of the doctrines thus defined had been brought to their full development by the labor of the Scholastics; but in no other field of theological inquiry did the Schoolmen achieve more satisfactory results than in sacramental theology.

[66] Sum. Theol. Suppl. 29, a. 3.   [68] DB, 844–856.
[67] Ibid. III, q. 64, a. 2, 3.

CHAPTER XVII

BAPTISM: CONFIRMATION

After considering the points that are common to all the sacraments, or at least to several of them, the Scholastics proceed to investigate each sacrament in particular. They inquire into the time and circumstances of its institution, its nature, effects, and the manner of its administration. In this study they are, as a general rule, rather diffuse, considering not only dogmatic questions, but also such as have an exclusively moral bearing. Hence in the following chapters it will be impossible to do more than give the barest outline of their teaching, setting forth only such points as are of more particular interest and importance in the history of dogmatic development.

A — BAPTISM

Peter Lombard describes baptism in these terms: " Baptism is called a dipping in — *intinctio* —, that is, an external washing of the body done while pronouncing a prescribed formula. For, if the washing be not accompanied by the pronouncing of the words, no sacrament is had, but when the washing in the water is accompanied by the pronouncing of the words, it becomes a sacrament; the water itself does not, indeed, become a sacrament, but the washing in the water." [1]

Hence the sacrament of baptism consists of two parts: a bodily ablution with water and a prescribed form of words. The bodily ablution was considered by the Scholastics both under an active and a passive aspect. Under its active aspect they understood by it the action of the minister in so far as he applies the baptismal water to the subject and pronounces the

[1] Sent. IV, d. 3, c. 1.

prescribed form. Under its passive aspect they considered the ablution precisely as received by the subject. From this distinction arose the question, under which of these two aspects does the ablution properly constitute the sacrament of baptism? Some answered this question by saying that the sacrament is properly in the person who is regenerated by it, and therefore it is the ablution in its passive sense that constitutes the sacrament.[2] Others made a distinction between the sacrament as a sign of grace and a cause of regeneration. In the former sense the sacrament was said to consist in the ablution as applied by the minister; in the latter, as received by the subject.[3] Others, again, argued that the sacrament is primarily an efficacious sign of grace, and therefore it is the ablution taken in an active sense that properly constitutes its essence.[4]

In connection with this discussion a distinction was made between the remote and proximate matter of baptism, and thereby different definitions were more or less reconciled. The remote matter is the water itself that is to be used in the sacramental rite; and it was with this before his mind that Hugh of St. Victor said: " Baptism is the water that is sanctified for the blotting out of sin." [5] The proximate matter is the application of the baptismal water to the subject, or the bodily ablution taken in an active sense; and referring to this the Lombard defined baptism as a bodily ablution under a prescribed form of words.[6]

Again, in the same connection a distinction was made between the sacrament only, the sacrament and the thing, and the thing only — *sacramentum tantum, sacramentum et res, res tantum.* The first is the sacramental rite in itself, the second is the character, the third is sacramental grace. In reference to this St. Bonaventure states: " Baptism is sometimes denominated a sacrament from the *sacramentum et res,* which is the character; hence the Damascene writes: ' Bap-

[2] Cfr. William of Auxerre, Sum. IV, tr. 3, c. 2.
[3] Cfr. Bonavent. In Sent. IV, d. 3, p. 1, a. 1, q. 2.
[4] Cfr. Thomas, Sum. Theol. III, q. 66, a. 1.
[5] De Sacr. III, p. 6, c. 2.
[6] Loc. cit.

tism is the principle of spiritual life, a seal and safeguard and an illumination of the mind.' " [7] And thus the various definitions are substantially the same, only they refer to different aspects of baptism.

Regarding the form of baptism, all the Scholastics were agreed that in their day the invocation of the Blessed Trinity was of obligation. The majority also held that the Trinitarian form was necessary for the validity of the sacrament. However, Hugh of St. Victor [8] and Peter Lombard [9] were of opinion that baptism administered in the name of Jesus might still be considered valid. On the other hand, they all held that baptism in the name of Jesus, without an explicit invocation of the Blessed Trinity, had been both valid and licit in the first ages of the Church. To this conclusion they argued from what they found in the Acts of the Apostles,[10] from a statement of St. Ambrose,[11] and from a decision given by Pope Nicholas I.[12] They pointed out, however, that the primitive usage rested upon a special dispensation from the general law of baptism under the explicit invocation of the Blessed Trinity. And the reason for this dispensation they found in the fact that in the beginning the name of Jesus was still unknown, or where known it was generally despised; and therefore, in order to cause this name to become known and honored, it was ordained that for some time it alone should be used in the administration of the baptismal rite.[13]

That according to the ordinary law of baptism an explicit invocation of the Blessed Trinity is essential, is thus taught by St. Thomas, with whom St. Bonaventure and others are in full agreement. " The sacraments," he says, " have their efficacy from the institution of Christ. And therefore if any of those things be omitted which Christ instituted in regard to any one of the sacraments, it is without efficacy; except when the omission occurs in virtue of a dispensation granted

[7] In Sent. IV, d. 3, p. 1, a. 1, q. 1.
[8] De Sacr. II, p. 6, c. 2.
[9] Sent. IV, d. 3, c. 4.
[10] Op. cit. 2, 38; 8, 16; 10, 48.
[11] De Spirit. Sanct. c. 3.
[12] Ad Bulgaros, DB. 335.
[13] Thomas, Sum. Theol. III, q. 66, a. 6 ad 1m; Bonavent. In Sent. loc. cit. a. 2, 1, 2 ad 3m.

by Him who connected His own power with the sacramental rite. Now Christ ordained that the sacrament of baptism should be conferred under the invocation of the Trinity; and therefore if anything be wanting to the full invocation of the Trinity, the integrity of baptism is thereby destroyed. Nor is this conclusion invalidated by the fact that in the name of one person that of another is understood (thus in the name of the Father the Son is understood), or that he who names one person only can have the right faith concerning the three: because just as sensible matter is required for the sacrament, so likewise is there required a sensible form. Hence a mere understanding of the doctrine or interior faith in the Trinity does not suffice for the validity of the sacrament, unless the Trinity be also mentioned in words that can be perceived by the senses." [14]

Besides the three holy names, the form of baptism must also express the act of baptizing. The reason for this is thus given by St. Bonaventure: " As stated by Alexander, the word expressing the act of baptizing is essential to the form. And the reason for it is the institution of the sacrament itself. Furthermore, the reason why the sacrament was thus instituted is this, because in administering the sacrament there is need of an intention; then, too, this sacrament is necessary for salvation and is conferred on some one distinct from the minister. Hence to avoid the danger of not having the proper intention, it is necessary that this intention be expressed by a proper word in the form." [15]

St. Thomas gives a different reason. " Baptism," he says, " is consecrated by its form. . . . Therefore it is necessary that in the form of baptism the cause of baptism be expressed. Now the cause is twofold: the one is the principal cause, from which baptism has its power, and this is the Blessed Trinity; the other is the instrumental cause, namely, the minister, who confers the exterior sacrament. Hence it is necessary that in the form of baptism mention be made of both. Now the ministerial cause is mentioned by saying: I baptise thee; and

[14] Sum. Theol. III, q. 66, a. 6.   [15] In Sent. IV, d. 3, p. 1, a. 2, q. 1.

the principal cause, by saying: In the name of the Father, and of the Son, and of the Holy Ghost." [16]

The manner of baptizing was still in a state of transition, from immersion to affusion. Peter Lombard mentions immersion only, but later writers refer to both as being in use simultaneously in different churches. St. Bonaventure states that although baptism by affusion is customary in some places, the Roman Church still baptizes by immersion.[17] Albertus Magnus considers baptism by immersion more praiseworthy,[18] and St. Thomas speaks of baptism by affusion as being more or less exceptional.[19] However the general rule laid down was, that the custom of the place where baptism was administered should be observed.

In regard to the effect produced by baptism it was customary to make a threefold distinction. In the first place, all hold that baptism imprints an indelible character on the soul, and this effect is produced by every valid baptism.[20] Secondly, all are agreed that in a properly disposed subject sin and the punishment due to sin are entirely blotted out.[21] Thirdly, they are also agreed that when adults are baptized, and are properly disposed, they receive sanctifying grace together with the infused virtues and the gifts of the Holy Spirit.[22] The amount of grace, however, in the case of adults, varies according to the different dispositions with which the sacrament is received. The person who is better disposed receives more grace, and the one who is less well disposed receives less grace.[23]

When there is question of the baptism of infants, all teach that a character is imprinted on the soul and that original sin and its punishment are blotted out; but there is some difference of opinion in regard to infusion of grace and the accompanying virtues. St. Thomas speaks of this diversity of

[16] Loc. cit. a. 5; Sent. d. 3, c. 7.
[17] In Sent. d. 3, p. 2, a. 2, q. 1.
[18] Ibid. a. 5.
[19] Op. cit. q. 66, a. 7.
[20] Cfr. Bonavent. Op. cit. d. 6, p. I, a. unic. q. 4; Thomas, op. cit. q. 69, a. 8.

[21] Cfr. Thomas, In Sent. IV, d. 4, q. 2.
[22] Bonavent. op. cit. d. 4, p. I, a. I, q. 3.
[23] Ibid.; Thomas, Sum. Theol. III, q. 69, a. 8.

opinion as follows: " Some of the older teachers held that in the baptism of children grace and the virtues were not infused, but that the character of Christ was imprinted on their souls, in virtue of which, when arrived at the age of reason, they received grace and the virtues. But this appears to be false for two reasons: First, because children, the same as adults, are in baptism made members of Christ; and hence it is necessary that they receive from the Head an influx of grace and virtue. Secondly, because according to this, children dying after baptism would not attain eternal life, as it is said that *the grace of God is life everlasting;* and thus it would be of no benefit to them to have been baptized. The cause of the error lay in this, that they did not know how to distinguish between the virtues and their acts; and hence seeing that children are incapable of eliciting acts of virtue, they thought that after baptism they in no way had the virtues themselves." [24]

The question had already been referred to by Innocent III in 1201, but was left undecided.[25]   Clement V took the matter up again at the Council of Vienne, held in 1311, and gave his decision in these terms: " The second opinion, which holds that in baptism sanctifying grace and the virtues are conferred on children as well as on adults, is more in harmony and concord with the sayings of the saints and the teaching of modern theologians; and therefore, with the approval of this holy Council, we have thought proper to give it the preference." [26]   This view was adopted as certain by the Council of Trent.[27]

In the case of adults, the principal effect of baptism, that is, the infusion of grace and the blotting out of sin, may also be obtained by the baptism of desire, which consists in an act of perfect contrition and the intention of receiving the sacrament at an opportune time. " God," says St. Bonaventure, " obliges no one to do the impossible, . . . and therefore it must be admitted that the baptism of desire without the baptism of water is sufficient, provided the person in question has the

[24] Sum. Theol. III, q. 69, a. 7.   [26] Mansi, 25, 410; DB. 483.
[25] DB. 410.   [27] DB. 800.

will to receive the baptism of water, but is prevented from doing so before he dies." [28] Or as St. Thomas words it:
"Although the effect depends on the First Cause, nevertheless
the Cause exceeds the effect and is not dependent thereon.
And for that reason one may obtain the effect of the sacrament
aside from the baptism of water, namely through the sufferings of Christ, in so far as one becomes conformable to Him
in suffering for His sake. . . . And for the same reason one
may also obtain the effect of baptism through the power of the
Holy Spirit, not only without the baptism of water but also
without the baptism of blood; namely, in so far as anyone's
heart is moved by the Holy Ghost to believe and to love God,
and to do penance for his sins; hence it is also called the
baptism of penance." [29]

What St. Thomas here says about the baptism of blood, that
it justifies before God without the baptism of water, is the
common teaching of the Scholastics, and was taught by the
Church from the beginning. Still they generally point out
that *per se* it frees from venial sins only; because mortal sins,
if there be any, must be blotted out by charity, without which
even martyrdom "would be of no avail unto salvation." [30]

There is no complete agreement among the Scholastics in
regard to the time when baptism was instituted. "Concerning the institution of baptism, as regards the time," says the
Lombard, "there are various opinions. Some say that baptism was instituted when Christ said to Nicodemus: *Unless
a man be born again of water and the Holy Ghost, he cannot
enter into the kingdom of heaven.* Others hold that the institution of baptism took place when He said to the Apostles:
*Go, teach all nations, baptizing them in the name of the Father
and of the Son and of the Holy Ghost.*[31] Alexander of
Hales [32] and Albertus Magnus [33] make a distinction between
formal and material institution. Baptism, they say, was
formally instituted after Christ's resurrection, when He sent

[28] In Sent. IV, d. 4, p. 2, a. 1, q. 1.
[29] Sum. Theol. III, q. 66, a. 11.
[30] In Sent. IV, d. 4, p. 2, a. 2, q.
1; Cfr. Thomas, II. II, q. 124, a. 2
ad 2m.

[31] Sent. d. 3, n. 5.
[32] Sum. IV, q. 8, m. 2, a. 3.
[33] In Sent. d. 3, a. 8.

His Apostles to baptize all nations; it was materially instituted when Christ Himself was baptized by John. However, according to the more common view, held by St. Bonaventure,[34] St. Thomas,[35] and Duns Scotus,[36] the sacrament was instituted before Christ's sufferings and death, and probably at the time of His own baptism.

The obligation of receiving baptism did not come into force until after the death of Christ, as is admitted even by those who hold that the sacrament was instituted before He suffered; but on the further question, how soon after His death that obligation arose, there is no agreement. St. Thomas [37] and Albertus Magnus [38] consider it probable that it began immediately, so that after Christ had died for the sins of the world, baptism became forthwith the ordinary means of justification for all men. On the other hand, Alexander of Hales,[39] St. Bonaventure,[40] Richard of Middleton,[41] and Scotus [42] hold that the obligation to receive baptism did not begin until the law had been sufficiently promulgated; which promulgation took place gradually, up to the fall of Jerusalem.

B — CONFIRMATION

In regard to confirmation comparatively little is said by the Scholastics. The Lombard puts all he has to say on the subject in two short paragraphs. The form, he says, is known to all; the sacrament can be administered only by a bishop; it must be received by all Christians; it confers the Holy Spirit, and for that reason it is of a higher dignity than baptism; it cannot be repeated.[43] These few points were taken by his commentators and made the headings of so many distinct questions or articles, to which were usually added a few subordinate considerations by way of clearer and fuller exposition.

Although in olden times confirmation was intimately connected with baptism, yet most Scholastics simply assume that

34 Ibid. p. 2, a. 1, q. 1.
35 Ibid. q. 1, a. 3.
36 Ibid. q. 4, n. 2.
37 Ibid. q. 1, a. 5.
38 Ibid. a. 6.

39 Op. cit. q. 8, m. 2, a. 3.
40 Loc. cit. a. 3, q. 1.
41 Ibid. a. 5.
42 Ibid. q. 4.
43 Sent. d. 7, n. 2.

it is a distinct sacrament. St. Thomas, however, thinks it proper to give a proof to that effect. He proposes it in these terms: " The sacraments of the New Law were instituted for the production of special effects in the order of grace. Hence, wherever a special effect of grace is produced, there we must admit a distinct sacrament. . . . Now it is manifest that in man's bodily life a certain perfection is acquired when he arrives at mature age, and in consequence is capable of performing perfect actions; . . . and hence it is that besides generation, from which he receives bodily life, there is also the movement to augmentation, by which he is brought to a perfect state. And so man receives spiritual life through baptism, which is a spiritual regeneration; but in confirmation he attains to a certain maturity in the spiritual life. . . . And therefore it is manifest that confirmation is a special sacrament." [44]

The external rite of confirmation, according to all the Scholastics, comprises the anointing of the forehead with consecrated chrism and the verbal form: *Consigno te signo crucis, et confirmo te chrismate salutis, in nomine Patris, et Filii, et Spiritus Sancti.*[45] The previous consecration or blessing of the chrism by a bishop is regarded as essential, so that without it the sacrament would not be valid. The reason usually assigned for the necessity of this consecration is that Christ Himself did not consecrate the matter of this sacrament by His own use. For He did not receive confirmation, and so He did not impart a blessing to its material element. Yet, on the other hand, only consecrated material elements can be used in the administration of the sacraments; hence, as the bishop cannot consecrate chrism by simply using it, he must do so by a previous blessing.[46]

Furthermore, according to Alexander of Hales and St. Bonaventure, as was pointed out in the preceding chapter, Christ did not designate the matter and form of confirmation, although the efficacy of the sacrament must in the last instance be attributed to Him. Hence these authors regard

[44] Sum. Theol. III, q. 72, a. 1.   [46] Cfr. ibid. a. 3; Bonavent. In
[45] Ibid. a. 4.   Sent. IV, d. 7, a. 1, q. 2.

the sacramental rite of confirmation as having a purely ecclesiastical origin, and consequently as needing a special consecration, so far as its material element comes in question, before it may be used to confer the Holy Spirit. St. Thomas and others set aside this aspect of the question. They hold that Christ not only instituted the sacrament of confirmation in the sense that He is the author of the grace conferred thereby, but that He also designated the very matter and form that were used in after ages. Hence, according to them, the Apostles usually administered confirmation not by a mere imposition of hands and a suitable prayer, but by the use of chrism and a corresponding form.[47] Thus the historical difficulty arising from an apparent change of matter and form, which exercised the ingenuity of later theologians, had practically no existence for these writers.

The ordinary minister of confirmation is the bishop, and the bishop only, although the Pope, in the plenitude of his power, may at times depute a simple priest to administer the sacrament.[48] St. Bonaventure assigns two reasons why it is that bishops alone can confirm in virtue of their ordinary power. The first is that it was so in the beginning; for then confirmation was reserved to the Apostles, and it is only the bishops who are properly speaking their successors. The second consists in the fact that the bishops are the highest prelates in the Church, and it is their office to provide such things as are necessary for the defense of their flock.[49] The same reasons are also given by St. Thomas.[50] But as St. Bonaventure remarks, many others might be assigned, as this is a matter of fitness rather than of necessity.[51]

The effect of confirmation is twofold: it confers sanctifying grace and imprints a sacramental character. Concerning the former St. Bonaventure remarks: " Theologians agree in this, that confirmation confers sanctifying grace. But it must be noted that grace is termed sanctifying in two ways: First, when it makes one pleasing to God who before was not pleas-

---

[47] Loc. cit. a. 2.
[48] Ibid. a. 11; Bonavent. op. cit. d. 7, a. 1, q. 3.
[49] Loc cit.
[50] Loc. cit.
[51] Loc. cit.

ing to Him; and such is the grace of baptism and of penance. Secondly, when it makes one who is already pleasing to God more pleasing to Him; and such is the grace of confirmation, which augments and confirms the grace already present in the soul." [52]   St Thomas infers the bestowal of sanctifying grace in confirmation from the fact that the Holy Spirit is given — *missio seu datio Spiritus Sancti non est nisi cum gratia gratum faciente.*[53]   And this grace is not given for the blotting out of sin, as is that of baptism; but for the increase and greater stability of justice.[54]   Hence confirmation is a sacrament of the living, and consequently it must always be received in the state of grace.   However, if any one receives confirmation in the state of mortal sin, of which he is not conscious and for which he is not perfectly contrite, grace is nevertheless given him by the sacrament, provided he is sincere in receiving it under these conditions.[55]

Connected with sanctifying grace, as bestowed in confirmation, are certain special helps which enable the recipient to profess his faith boldly under difficult circumstances.   Hence the phrase commonly used by the Scholastics in this connection: *Spiritus Sanctus datur ad robur.*   It is to indicate both the strength thus imparted and the obligation assumed that the recipient is anointed on the forehead.[56]

Confirmation, like baptism, imprints an indelible character on the soul; and this follows from the very end and purpose of the sacrament.   For in confirmation the Christian becomes a soldier of Christ, and as such he must have his badge of special allegiance and service.   In virtue of this character, says Scotus, man is permanently enrolled in the spiritual militia of Christ, for the purpose of defending the grace merited for him by the Saviour of the world.[57]   Or as St. Thomas puts it: "In baptism man receives the power of working out his salvation in so far as he lives an individual life; but in confirmation he receives power to carry on a spiritual warfare against the

---

[52] In Sent. IV, d. 7, a. 2, q. 1.
[53] Sum. Theol. III, q. 72, a. 7.
[54] Ibid. ad 1m.

[55] Ibid. ad 2m.
[56] Ibid. a. 9.
[57] In Sent. IV, d. 7, q. 1, n. 4.

enemies of the faith. . . . And hence it is manifest that the sacrament of confirmation imprints a character." [58]

Although confirmation is not strictly necessary for salvation, as all Scholastics are agreed, nevertheless, unless they have a valid excuse, the faithful are under obligation to receive the sacrament. " It is the law of the Church," argues St. Bonaventure, " that all must receive this sacrament, so that they may be brave in the battle of life: and therefore if anyone, to whom place and time and opportunity are not wanting, contemptuously neglects to receive confirmation, he exposes himself to danger." [59] And again: " The grace of confirmation is not such that one absolutely cannot be saved without it; but it is such that without it one is not prepared to battle for salvation." [60] St. Thomas derives the necessity of confirmation chiefly from the fact that God intends all men to reach spiritual perfection, for which it is necessary that they be assisted by the grace of confirmation, as thereby they grow in holiness and are firmly established in justice.[61]

Nearly all the chief points contained in the foregoing summary of Scholastic teaching on baptism and confirmation were later on embodied in the *Decretum pro Armenis,* which Pope Eugenius IV issued while the Council of Florence was in session, 1438–1445. That document can indeed not be said to contain new definitions of the faith, yet it offers at least an authoritative declaration of the accepted teaching of the Church.[62] Furthermore, what touches the nature of the two sacraments, their matter and form, their institution by Christ, and their principal effects, was defined by the Council of Trent.[63]

[58] Loc. cit. a. 5.
[59] Op. cit. d. 7, a. 3, q. 2.
[60] Ibid. ad 3m.

[61] Sum. Theol. III, q. 72, a. 8.
[62] DB. 695 sqq.
[63] DB. 844 sqq.

CHAPTER XVIII

THE HOLY EUCHARIST

THE REAL PRESENCE: TRANSUBSTANTIATION: THE MANNER OF CHRIST'S PRESENCE: THE ACCIDENTS OF BREAD AND WINE

The Eucharist was from the beginning the central point of Christian faith and worship. Christ had indeed ascended into heaven, yet He had not thereby deprived the earth of His personal presence. He was no longer visible to the bodily eyes of His followers, but He continued to be discernible by the eyes of faith in His mysterious presence under the Eucharistic veil. There the faithful still felt the enduring love of His human heart; there they still recognized the shrouded majesty of His incarnate Godhead. Christ risen from the dead dieth no more: true indeed, but Christ risen from the dead is forever an immolated victim on the altar of sacrifice. Around that altar gathered the martyrs of old; around the same altar gathered the believers of all succeeding ages. Without Christ there is no Christianity; without the Eucharist there is no Christian worship.

All this was from the very first so clearly and thoroughly realized that during the seven centuries of Patristic theology, which were for the most part centuries of great religious strife, no one ever thought of calling in question the Church's teaching on the sacrament of Christ's love. The Church used the Savior's own words in the celebration of the Sacred Mysteries — *this is my body, this is the chalice of my blood* — and these words were understood by all His followers in their literal sense. That sums up the faith of the Patristic age in regard to the Blessed Eucharist.[1]

[1] Cfr. vol. I, p. 352 sqq.; 472 sq.

And this simple faith was taken over by the Scholastics of the Middle Ages. They accepted the teaching of the Fathers on this point practically without comment, and incorporated it in their general system of theology. Most of them treat the subject with considerable attention to detail, but even in so doing they contribute little by way of doctrinal development. If we except the nature of the Eucharistic change, which they set forth with remarkable clearness, there is hardly any aspect of the Blessed Sacrament that received a more definite treatment in the works of the Scholastics than in those of the Fathers. And the reason is that the doctrine was almost fully developed before the Apostles laid down their lives for the faith which they had delivered to their successors in the teaching office of the Church.

In their work of systematizing the teaching of the Fathers on this matter, the Scholastics say very little about the sacrificial aspect of the Eucharist. But that need not appear strange; for they speak of this mystery of our holy religion almost exclusively in connection with the other sacraments, and so it was more or less natural that its sacramental aspect should chiefly engross their attention. It is for the same reason that they discuss the Eucharist as a sacrament before they consider the doctrine of the Real Presence. In their day it was perfectly safe to assume Christ's presence on the altar as something that was admitted by all, and from that assumption to proceed without delay to an exposition of the sacrament. At the present time his could hardly be done, and therefore in the following resumé the teaching of the Scholastics on the Real Presence is put in the first place. It must be noted, however, that this inversion of their order of treatment introduces no change whatever in the exposition of their doctrine.

1. *The Real Presence.*— It is quite commonly assumed by Protestant writers that the ninth-century Eucharistic controversy, carried on principally by Radbertus and Ratramnus, both of Corbie in Picardie, was concerned with the real presence of Christ's body and blood in the Holy Eucharist. But this assumption is altogether false. The one point at issue was, whether Christ's Eucharistic body and blood, which both

contestants held to be real, must be conceived as subject to the laws of space in the same way as was His historic body whilst tarrying here on earth. While Radbertus gave an affirmative answer, and in this sense contended that Christ's Eucharistic body is the same as that which was born of the Virgin Mary, Ratramnus answered the question in the negative, and in consequence maintained that in respect of its relation to space the historic body of Christ is not present in the Eucharist. The issue appears at times confused, owing to the inappropriate terms that were employed in the controversy; but at no time was the reality and truth of Christ's presence called in question.[2]

It was nearly two hundred years after the death of Radbertus and Ratramnus that the real presence of Christ's body and blood in the Holy Eucharist was attacked, and then the attack was made in the interest of dialectics. It was Berengarius of Tours (+1088) who first tried to set aside the traditional teaching of the Church, and contended for a merely virtual presence. In discussing the mystery of the Eucharist, he put forward the principle: *Maxime plane cordis est ad dialecticam confugere, quia confugere ad eam ad rationem est confugere.*[3] He belonged to the school of Fulbert of Chartres (+1028), and through him was connected with Gerbert, afterwards Pope Sylvester III. Besides a few letters and some fragments from an early controversial work, his treatise *De Sacra Coena adversus Lanfrancum* and the *Acta Concilii Romani in Causa Berengarii* are the only two of his works that have come down to us.

His error in regard to the Eucharist appeared first in a letter to Lanfranc, written in 1050. He professed to follow the teaching of Ratramnus, but wholly misinterpreted the views of that author. Ratramnus had designated Christ's sacramental body as a figure of His historic body, intending thereby merely to indicate that its presence in space was not the same as that which is proper to His body in heaven; whereas Berengarius

[2] Cfr. Bach, Dogmengeschichte des Mittelalters, I, p. 166 sqq.; 192 sqq.   [3] De Sacra Coena, ed. Vischer, 101.

took the term " figure " in its literal sense, and thence argued to a purely symbolic or virtual presence in the Eucharist. At Easter of the same year he was condemned by a synod then held in Rome, and a few months later by another synod which convened at Vercelli. However, he continued to defend his view, until in 1059 Nicholas II forced him to recant. On that occasion he accepted the following formula, presented to him by Cardinal Humbert: *Panem et vinum, quae in altari ponuntur, post consecrationem non solum sacramentum, sed etiam verum corpus et sanguinem Domini nostri Jesu Christi esse (confiteor) et sensualiter, non solum sacramento, sed in veritate manibus sacerdotum tractari, frangi, et fidelium dentibus atteri.*[4]

Although Berengarius attacked the formula which he had been induced to sign, still for about ten years after the Council he abstained from open controversy, and even enjoyed the protection of Hildebrand, afterwards Pope Gregory VII. But in 1069 he returned to his former position and published a controversial treatise against Nicholas II and Cardinal Humbert, which is no longer extant. He was answered by Hugh, bishop of Langres,[5] Lanfranc, archbishop of Canterbury,[6] Guitmund, a pupil of Lanfranc,[7] and others. In answer to Lanfranc, Berengarius wrote his still extant work *De Sacra Coena,* which was published towards the end of the year 1076. For some time no measures were taken against him, but at a synod held in Rome during the Eastertide of 1079, Gregory VII required him to confess: *Panem et vinum, quae ponuntur in altari, per mysterium sacrae orationis et verba nostri Redemptoris substantialiter converti in veram et propriam et vivificatricem carnem et sanguinem Jesu Christi.*[8] On his return to France, he repudiated his profession of belief in the Real Presence and returned to his old error. However, a year later he made a final retractation, and eight years later died in peace with the Church.

[4] Lanfranc, De Corpore et Sanguine Domini, 2.
[5] Tractatus de Corpore et Sanguine Domini.
[6] Op. cit.
[7] Libri Tres de Corporis et Sanquinis Christi Veritate.
[8] Mansi, 19, 762 E.

As appears from the formulas which were presented to him for subscription, Berengarius not only denied the conversion of the Eucharistic elements into the body and blood of Christ, but also defended a purely intellectual or spiritual presence. And the same may be inferred from various statements found in his works.[9]   Protestant writers usually contend that he simply restated the teaching of St. Augustine, which had fallen into oblivion; but that contention rests entirely upon a misinterpretation of St. Augustine's doctrine.[10]

These discussions contributed considerably towards the clearing up of certain hazy concepts, which are met with in not a few writers of the period.   Thus, to rectify a rather common misconception in reference to persons who communicate in the state of mortal sin, Lanfranc pointed out that they truly receive the body and blood of Christ, but only to their spiritual detriment.[11]   Guitmund showed that at the consecration the bread and wine are converted in such a way that the whole Christ is in the entire species and also in each single part thereof.[12]   He further called attention to the fact that the changes to which the accidents of bread and wine are subject do not affect the body and blood of Christ present under the consecrated species.[13]   St. Anselm explained the doctrine of concomitance, showing that the whole Christ is received under each separate species, whether it be that of bread or of wine.[14] While Gregory VII, in the formula presented for subscription to Berengarius, indicated that the Eucharistic conversion is effected by the words which our Savior used in the institution of the Holy Eucharist.[15]

The thirteenth-century Scholastics touch these discussions only incidentally, while affirming the Real Presence as based upon the faith of the Church and the words of our Savior. Thus St. Thomas, after citing a number of texts from the writings of the Fathers and from Holy Scripture, concludes his article on the Real Presence with this brief statement:

[9] Ep. ad Adelman, fragm. 3.
[10] Cfr. vol. I, p. 352.
[11] Op. cit. 20.
[12] Op. cit. I; ML. 149, 1434 B.
[13] Op. cit. III.
[14] Epp. IV, 107; ML. 159, 255.
[15] Loc. cit.

" Some, not bearing in mind what is here said, held that the body and blood of Christ are not present in this sacrament except figuratively — *in signo* —, which opinion must be rejected as heretical, because it is opposed to the words of Christ. Hence, also Berengarius, who was the first author of this error, was compelled to retract his erroneous teaching and to confess the truth." [16]   And St. Bonaventure briefly remarks: " As the Master says in passing, it was the opinion of some, and a most wicked error it was, that Christ is present on the altar only *in signo,* and that to eat His body means simply to eat the sign of His body. . . . But this is the worst of errors and opposed to the piety of faith." [17]

2. *Transubstantiation.*— From their brief references to the Real Presence the Scholastics pass on to the question of Eucharistic conversion or transubstantiation. This, again, they treat not as something new, but as a doctrine that was clearly contained in the teaching of the Church. Still there were some different views on the matter, four of which are thus indicated by the Lombard: 1. *Substantia panis fit corpus Christi . . . sicut farina fit panis.* 2. *Illud quod erat panis . . . post consecrationem est corpus.* 3. *Ubi erat panis, nunc est corpus Christi . . . substantia panis in nihilum redigitur.* 4. *Substantia panis remanet et ibidem corpus Christi est.*[18] The first and the fourth of these views he rejects as absolutely inadmissible, and then argues from the promise of the Savior, as contained in the sixth chapter of St. John, that in the consecration the bread is changed into the identical body which Christ has in heaven. However, he does not enter into any speculations as regards the intimate nature of this change, but contents himself with the statement that after the consecration nothing remains of the bread and wine except their accidents.[19]

St. Bonaventure mentions some other views, which, he says, had come into vogue since the time of the Lombard. Some hold that as the accidents of bread and wine remain, the matter

---

[16] Sum. Theol. III, q. 75, a. 1.
[17] In Sent. IV, d. 10, p. 1, a. unic. q. 1.
[18] Sent. IV, d. 11, c. 3, 4.
[19] Op. cit. d. 11, c. 4.

of their substance must also remain, although the form is
changed. Others, on the contrary, seeing that the accidents
have an operation of their own, contend that the substantial
forms of bread and wine remain, and that the matter alone is
changed. He rejects both of these views as utterly untenable,
and then continues: " It is the common teaching of theologians that the whole substance is converted into the whole body
and blood of Christ — *totum transit in totum* —, and that for
a necessary and useful reason the accidents alone remain. And
therefore, setting aside the first opinion which denies the conversion of the matter, and also the second which denies the
conversion of the form, we hold as more Catholic that the
whole bread is converted into the whole body of Christ, and
this conversion is most aptly called transubstantiation." [20]

The discussion of St. Thomas proceeds along the same lines.
He first rejects the opinion of those who hold that the substance of bread and wine remain on the altar together with the
body of Christ. If the bread and wine remain, he reasons,
then the truth of the sacrament is destroyed. For there is no
sacrament unless the body and blood of Christ be really present, and yet they can become present only by way of conversion.[21] Then he refutes the view of those who assert that
the substantial form of the elements remains. If this were
true, he says, the bread would not be changed into the whole
body of Christ, but into its matter only; and then the form of
the sacrament, *This is my body,* would be false.[22] In the consecration, he argues, " the whole substance of the bread is
converted into the whole substance of the body of Christ, and
the whole substance of the wine is converted into the whole
substance of the blood of Christ. Hence this conversion is
not formal but substantial; nor is it contained in any species
of natural changes, but is denominated by its own proper term
of transubstantiation." [23]

The technical term " transubstantiation," which is used by
all the later Scholastics to designate the Eucharistic conversion,

[20] In Sent. IV, d. 11, p. 1, a. unic.
q. 3.
[21] Sum. Theol. III, q. 75, a. 2.
[22] Ibid. a. 6.
[23] Ibid. a. 4.

is of uncertain origin. As far as can now be determined, it occurs for the first time in a sermon formerly attributed to Hildebert of Lavardin, archbishop of Tours (+1133), but now usually ascribed to Peter Comestor, who died after 1170.[24] It occurs also in the *Tractatus de Sacramento Altaris,* which was written either by Stephen I or Stephen II of Autun. The former died in 1139, and the latter in 1189. Shortly after the middle of the twelfth century the term seems to have been in common use in the schools, as it is found again and again in theological treatises belonging to that period.[25] Likely enough it originated in the discussions with Berengarius, but there is no documentary evidence to prove that it did.

Most of the Scholastics proved the doctrine of transubstantiation from the words of institution, pointing out that these words would not be true except on the supposition that the whole substance of the bread and wine are changed into the body and blood of Christ. Duns Scotus, however, did not consider this argument conclusive, if used independently of the traditional teaching of the Church. His final conclusion is: " It is therefore to be held that the substance of the bread ceases to be there in virtue of a conversion, and that its ceasing to be is a conversion into the body of Christ. And this I hold principally on account of the authority of the Church, which cannot fall into error regarding those truths that belong to the faith." [26] This was also the position taken by the Nominalists. Thus Ockam,[27] D'Ailly,[28] Gabriel,[29] and others of the same school, personally favored the impanation theory, namely, that the substance of the bread and wine remain on the altar together with the body and blood of Christ; but on account of the clear teaching of the Church they professed their belief in transubstantiation.

---

[24] The passage in which it is used reads as follows: " Cum profero verba canonis et verbum transsubstantiationis, et os meum plenum est contradictione et amaritudine et dolo, quamvis eum honorem labiis, tamen spuo in faciem Salvatoris " (Serm. 93; ML, 21, 776).

[25] Cfr. Dictionnaire de Theologie Catholique, t. 5, col. 1290 sqq.
[26] Report. IV, d. 11, q. 3, n. 13.
[27] In Sent. IV, q. 6 D.
[28] In Sent. IV, q. 6 E.
[29] Exposit. Can. Missae, lect. 41 J; cfr. In Sent. IV, 11, q. 1, a. 1, note 1.

It is, then, in virtue of the consecration that Christ is really and personally present on the altar, because thereby the substance of bread and wine are changed into His body and blood; but in what precise manner does the conversion thus effected bring about Christ's personal presence? All Scholastics are agreed that the Eucharistic conversion does not effect a local change in Christ. And this is quite obvious: for although He becomes truly present on the altar, yet He ever remains unchanged in heaven. But aside from this one point, which is a matter of faith, there is no agreement among mediæval theologians in reference to the proposed question. A few remarks about the two principal views entertained by them must here suffice.

In the first place, Alexander of Hales,[30] St. Bonaventure,[31] and St. Thomas [32] maintain that the reason of Christ's presence on the altar lies in the fact that the Eucharistic conversion is a productive action, in the sense that it is equivalent to the production of an already existing term or reality. They do not actually use the term *production* in this connection, but that is obviously what they have in mind. Thus St. Bonaventure compares the conversion of the bread and wine to the act of creation and to other productive changes, although, as he remarks, in some particulars it differs from each and all.[33] St. Thomas explains that the body of Christ becomes present through the conversion of the substance of the bread into itself; [34] and, again, that the entity of the one is changed into

[30] Sum. IV, q. 10, m. 7, a. 3 ad 6[m].
[31] In Sent. IV, d. 11, p. 1, a. unic. q. 2.
[32] Sum. Theol. III, q. 75, a. 4.
[33] His words are: "Dicendum, quod haec est mutatio singularis, quae nullum simile plenum habet; assimilatur tamen in aliquo. Quia enim in hac mutatione nihil commune manet; assimilatur creationi. Quia vero principium initiale non est nihil, sed aliquid; ideo dissimilis est creationi et similis generationi. Quia vero terminum finalem non habet aliquid de novo factum, sed prius existens; ideo est dissimilis generationi et similis augmento. Quia vero corpus Christi ex hoc non crescit, sed in pluribus locis existit; ideo dissimilis augmento et similis loci mutationi. Quia vero in alio loco existit et a proprio non recedit, sed aliquid in ipsum transit; ideo omni motui et mutationi dissimilis est et est prorsus mutatio singularis" (Loc. cit.).
[34] Answering the question whether the bread is converted into the body of Christ, the author says: "Cum in hoc sacramento sit verum

the entity of the other.[35] True, the reproduction of an already existing reality is something that baffles all human understanding, but so does everything else that is attempted by
way of explanation in reference to the question under discussion. In this matter one feels inclined to rest satisfied with
the saying of Pope Innocent III: *Ego nescio quomodo
Christus accedit; sed et quomodo recedit, ignoro. Novit ille
qui nihil ignorat.*[36]

Duns Scotus brings forward many arguments against the
view taken by St. Thomas and St. Bonaventure, and then attempts an explanation of his own. Transubstantiation, he
holds, is not the formal reason of Christ's sacramental presence; that presence can be explained only by postulating such
a change in the body of Christ that in virtue of it there results
a new relation to place, yet without any local change properly
so called.[37] As interpreted by his commentators, he distinguishes between passive and active transubstantiation. By the
former he understands the substance which ceases to be and
that which succeeds it, together with their mutual relations of
terminus a quo and *terminus ad quem;* by the latter he designates the conversive action of the agent, which is in itself
neither productive nor adductive, but simply expresses the
order and relation of change. But concomitantly this action
may be either productive or adductive, according as a new term
is produced or merely a new presence of an already existing
term. Similarly the term of transubstantiation is twofold.
The one formal, namely, the substance of the body of Christ

corpus Christi, nec incipit ibi esse
de novo per motum locale-n, cum
etiam nec corpus Christi sit ibi
sicut in loco, ut ex dictis patet,
necesse est dicere quod incipiat ibi
esse per conversionem substantiae
panis in ipsum" (Loc. cit.).

[35] To the objection, "non potest
esse quod haec materia panis fiat
haec materia qua individuatur corpus Christi," he replies by saying:
" Ad tertium dicendum, quod virtute
agentis finiti non potest forma in
formam mutari, nec materia in ma-

teriam sed virtute agentis infiniti
(quod habet actionem in totum ens)
potest talis conversio fieri, quia utrique formae et utrique materiae est
communis natura entis; et id quod
est entitatis in una potest auctor entis convertere in id quod est entitatis
in altera, sublato eo per quod ab illa
distinguebatur" (Loc. cit. ad 3[m]).

[36] De Sacro Altaris Mysterio, 4,
16.

[37] In Sent. IV, d. 10, q. 1, n. 5
sqq.; q. 3.

already existing; the other concomitant, namely, the new relation to place of that same body.　In the former there is no
production, as the same body of Christ which is in heaven is
also on the altar; in the latter there is a new presence, by reason of which Christ's body is really and truly in the Holy
Eucharist.　Hence, Christ is present on the altar not by way
of reproduction, but by way of simple adduction.[38]

Apparently this is a much more rational explanation than
that offered by St. Thomas; yet the difficulties involved in it
are hardly less formidable.　For if this new presence is something real, a real *ubi intrinsecum,* there is a real though accidental change in the body of Christ, which theologians are
unwilling to admit; if it is not something real, a mere *ubi
extrinsecum,* how can it be adductive in respect of the body
of Christ?　And so in either case, there seems to be no way
out of the difficulty, and one feels again inclined to say:
Novit ille qui nihil ignorat.

3. *The Manner of Christ's Presence.*— In regard to the
manner of Christ's presence on the altar, the Scholastics first
of all teach that He is whole and entire under the species of
bread, and whole and entire under the species of wine.　In
virtue of the consecrated words, they point out, only the body
of Christ is under the species of bread, and only the blood
under the species of wine; but by reason of a natural and real
concomitance, the whole Christ is under each separate species.
" Because the bread has a likeness only to the body," says St.
Bonaventure, " therefore it was ordained to be converted only
into the body; and the sanctifying word, namely: *This is my
body,* signifies that it is converted into the body; neither into
the divinity, nor into the soul, nor into the blood, is anything
of the bread·converted.　Neither, however, is the body in the
sacrament without them; for although they are not there on
account of the conversion, still they are there because of their
inseparable connection or indivisible conjunction.　For the
blood is there by reason of its commingling, the soul by reason
of its conjunction, the divinity by reason of its union." [39]

[38] Cfr. Rada, Controvers. p. 4,　　　[39] In Sent. IV, d. 11, p. 1, a. unic.
controv. 6.　　　　　　　　　　　　q. 4.

St. Thomas gives the same explanation, and then adds: "The blood of Christ is now no longer separated from the body, as it was at the time of His suffering and death; hence if the Eucharist had then been celebrated, under the species of bread would have been the body without the blood, and under the species of wine would have been the blood without the body, just as body and blood were then separated in reality." [40]

As the whole Christ is present in the Eucharist, it follows that His body and blood are there with their own proper quantity; and this is the common teaching of the Scholastics, against Durandus [41] and a few Nominalists. However the secondary effects of quantity, such as actual extension and impenetrability, are impeded; and hence the quantity of the body and blood of Christ is present after the manner of substance — ad modum substantiae. Consequently Christ is in the Eucharist totus sub toto et totus sub qualibet parte.[42] In this sense, therefore, He is definitely present; yet, on the other hand, as His presence is not limited to the space occupied by the consecrated species, it is not properly speaking definitive but sacramental.

St. Bonaventure, citing Pope Innocent III, gives this exposition of Christ's presence in the Eucharist: "As Innocent words it, ' just as the Son of God has a threefold presence according to His divinity, in as much as He is in all things by His essence, in the just by His grace, in Christ through the hypostatic union; so the body of Christ is locally in heaven, personally in the Word, sacramentally on the altar.' According to this third manner of presence, he says, Christ is in many places; because there are many consecrated species under which He is contained. Hence properly speaking, as an individual He is in only one place, in which He is contained; but because many (substances of bread and wine) are converted into Him, and they are in different places, consequently He Himself is in different places after that manner

---

[40] Sum. Theol. III, q. 76, a. 2.   [42] Thomas, loc. cit. a. 4.
[41] In Sent. IV, d. 10, q. 2.

of presence according to which they are converted into Him, and thus He is in the sacrament." [43]

The objection that Christ must be in the Eucharist either definitively or circumscriptively, is thus answered by St. Thomas: "I reply that the body of Christ is not present definitively in this sacrament; because in that case it would not be anywhere else except on the altar where the sacrament is consecrated, whereas it is in its proper form in heaven, and under the sacramental species on many altars. In like manner it is also plain that the body of Christ is not circumscriptively present in this sacrament; because it is not there after a manner commensurate with its own proper quantity, as was said in the body of this article. The fact that the body of Christ is limited in its sacramental presence to the consecrated species, and is not in any other place on the altar, is no indication that it is present either definitively or circumscriptively, but results from the fact that there only did it begin to be in virtue of the consecration and conversion of the bread and wine." [44]

Because the whole Christ is thus sacramentally present under the entire species, hence it follows that He is present in the same way under each part independently of actual division. On this point there seems to have been some differences of opinion among the Scholastics, which is thus referred to by St. Thomas: "It is manifest that the whole Christ is present under each part of the species of bread, even while the host remains entire, and not only when it is broken, as some say. They argue from the example of an image in a mirror, which is only one so long as the mirror remains whole; but when it is broken, the image is multiplied according to the number of parts. Now in this there is no parity; because the multiplication of images results from the different reflections as caused by the different parts of the mirror; whereas in the Eucharist there is only one consecration by reason of which the body of Christ is present in the sacrament." [45]

4. *The Accidents of Bread and Wine.*— According to the

[43] Loc. cit. d. 10, a. unic. q. 3.   [45] Sum. Theol. III, q. 76, a. 3.
[44] Loc. cit. a. 5 ad 1^m.

common teaching of the Scholastics, as was pointed out above, the substance of bread and wine ceases to be by being converted into the body and blood of Christ. On the other hand, the accidents of bread and wine, as all admit, remain unchanged. Hence the question arises, how do they exist? They can obviously not inhere in the body of Christ, as that in its sacramental presence is without extension. Nor can they naturally exist without inhering in some subject, as their very essence implies an exigency to inhere. Consequently, their separate existence must be based on some special intervention of God's wisdom and power.

On this point all the Scholastics are agreed, but they do not all take the same view of the nature of God's special intervention. "Some there are," says St. Thomas, "who hold that the accidents inhere in the circumambient air as their subject. But this cannot be; first, because the air cannot receive accidents of this kind; secondly, the accidents are not in the same place as the air, and even expel the air when moved about; thirdly, accidents cannot pass from one subject to the other and remain numerically the same; fourthly, the air has its own proper accidents and it cannot have others along with these. Nor can it be said that this is effected miraculously in virtue of the consecration; because the words of consecration do not signify this, and they effect only what they signify." [46]

Then he continues: "It remains therefore that the accidents in this sacrament are without a subject of inhesion, and this indeed can be brought about by divine power. For since the effect has a greater dependence on the first cause than on the second, God, who is the first cause of substance and accident, can by His divine power conserve the accident in being, after withdrawing the substance through which it was conserved as through its proper cause; and this He can do in the same way in which He also produces other effects of natural causes independently of these same causes, as when He formed a human body in the womb of the Virgin without the concurrence of a male agent." [47]

[46] Ibid. q. 77, a. 1.   [47] Ibid.

St. Bonaventure uses almost the same terms, when he says: " It is to be held that the accidents can, by way of miracle, exist without a subject or substance. For since they differ essentially from their subject of inhesion, there is no repugnance in their being separated from it by divine power." [48] Then rejecting the same opinion referred to by St. Thomas, he states : " It is the common teaching of theologians that the Eucharistic accidents exist without a subject." [49] With this common teaching Scotus is in full agreement; but he points out that as absolute accidents have their own proper essence, they must also have their own proper existence, and so divine power can, without any contradiction, cause them to exist outside the subject in which they naturally inhere. [50]

With the exception of Durandus and some Nominalists, who deny all distinction between quantity and quantified substance, the Scholastics are at one in holding that the Eucharistic accidents inhere proximately in the quantity of bread and wine, and that this is sustained in being by the power of God. Hence when they are said to exist without a subject of inhesion, it is the remote subject, or the substance, that is referred to. [51] However, even with this, the question still remains, how does God sustain them in being? Does He miraculously provide some permanent mode, which takes in their regard the place of substance? Or are they sustained in being by His direct efficient intervention?

St. Thomas seems to favor the former of these two possible suppositions. For replying to a difficulty bearing on that point, he says: " While inhering in the substance of bread and wine, these accidents, like all others of a similar kind, did not have their own proper existence; but it was through them that their subjects were of such or such a kind, just as snow is white by reason of its whiteness: but after the consecration these same accidents, which remain, have existence, and hence they are then composed of existence and that which exists, as it was said in the first part in respect of the angels;

[48] In Sent. IV, d. 12, p. 1, a. 1, q. 1.
[49] Ibid. q. 3.
[50] Report. IV, d. 12, q. 1, n. 3–9.
[51] Cfr. Bonavent. In Sent. IV, d. 11, p. 1, q. 2.

and together with this there is in them the composition of quantitative parts." [51a] This seems to imply that the new *esse* is some kind of permanent mode, by reason of which the accidents exist apart from their proper subject. And the same reasoning he repeats a little farther on in regard to quantity, the proximate subject of these accidents. [52]

Scotus, on the other hand, rejects this permanent mode, and holds that the accidents are sustained in being by the direct efficient influence of divine power. Together with the quantity of bread and wine, all the absolute qualities naturally inherent therein constitute a physical complexus, and to this God's sustaining power is efficiently applied. [53] St. Bonaventure seems to favor the same view, although he does not express himself clearly on the point. [54]

While thus existing in a state of separation from their proper subject, the accidents are capable of producing all their natural effects, both physical and chemical. They act and are acted upon in the same way as if the substance of bread and wine were present. It is by reason of them that the sacramental body and blood of Christ can be moved from place to place; [55] it is they that are touched and broken and divided, not the body and blood of Christ; [56] it is they that corrupt under the influence of external agents, and thereby cause Christ's sacramental presence to cease; [57] it is they that nourish the flesh, while Christ's body and blood refresh the spirit. [58]

In regard to this last point there was considerable discussion among the Scholastics. "Some hold," says St. Bonaventure, "that the Eucharistic accidents do not nourish the body in any way; but this is against the testimony of our senses. Others maintain that, when the Real Presence ceases, the accidents already in a state of corruption are converted into

[51a] Sum. Theol. III, q. 77, a. 1 ad 4ᵐ.
[52] Ibid. a. 2, ad 1ᵐ.
[53] In Sent. IV, d. 12, q. 1.
[54] Ibid. p. 1, a. 1.
[55] Cfr. Thomas, Theol. Sum. III, q. 76, a. 3; ibid. q. 77, a. 3.
[56] Cfr. Halens. Sum. IV, q. 10, m.

9, a. 1, 2; Scotus, In Sent. IV, d. 12, q. 4.
[57] Cfr. Halens. op. cit. m. 7, a. 1; Albert Magn. In Sent. IV, d. 12, a. 16.
[58] Cfr. Henry of Ghent, Quodl. 8, q. 36; Albert. Magn. op. cit. d. 13, a. 9, 10.

the same substance into which bread and wine would have
been converted if they had been present, and thus they nourish
the body. This opinion is sufficiently probable. Others,
again, contend that the accidents are not converted into substance, but that the substances of bread and wine return, when,
owing to the corruption of the accidents, the sacramental
presence ceases. This is the explanation given by Innocent
III, and I consider it probable and safe, especially on account
of his great authority." [59]

St. Thomas refers to these different explanations in his
Commentary on the Sentences,[60] without definitely stating his
own view; but in the *Summa* he says: "It seems preferable
to hold that in the consecration the accident of quantity becomes the primary subject of all subsequent forms, and as
this is proper to matter, quantity thereby becomes capable of
discharging all the functions of matter in its natural condition." [61] Scotus rejects all these explanations and holds that
God directly supplies the substance which ought to be there
in the natural process of decomposition to which the accidents
are subjected.[62]

There was a similar discussion in regard to the breaking
of Christ's body — *fractio corporis Christi*. In the formula
of Cardinal Humbert, which Berengarius was ordered to subscribe, it is said in reference to the body of Christ, *non solum
sacramento, sed in veritate manibus sacerdotum tractari,
frangi, et fidelium dentibus atteri*. Some took this in a literal
sense, but the common interpretation of the Scholastics was
that all these expressions can be directly applied only to the
consecrated species. " The body of Christ," argues St. Bonaventure, " is truly taken into the stomach, and there it remains
so long as the consecrated species are incorrupt; but it is not
masticated, nor is it broken." [63]

---

[59] In Sent. IV, d. 12, p. 1, a. 2,
q. 1.
[60] Op. cit. d. 12, q. 1, a. 2.

[61] Op. cit. q. 77, a. 5.
[62] In Sent. IV, d. 12, q. 7.
[63] Loc. cit. a. 3, q. 1.

CHAPTER XIX

THE HOLY EUCHARIST

THE FORM OF CONSECRATION: THE MATTER OF CONSECRATION: THE CONSECRATING MINISTER: THE EUCHARIST AS A SACRAMENT: THE EFFECTS OF THE SACRAMENT: THE EUCHARIST AS A SACRIFICE

As Christ becomes present on the altar in virtue of the consecratory action of the priest, the Scholastics enter into considerable detail regarding the consecration of the bread and wine. They investigate both its formal and material element, and in the same connection study the sacramental and sacrificial aspect of the Eucharist. The following is a brief summary of what they accomplished along these lines.

1. *The Form of Consecration.*— There is a general agreement among the Scholastics that the form of consecration consists of the words of institution, exclusive of the *epiclesis* or invocation of the Holy Spirit. For the consecration of the bread they assign the four words, *Hoc est corpus meum;* and for the consecration of the wine they designate the corresponding form, *Hic est calix sanguinis mei.* In regard to this latter, however, St. Thomas seems to hold that the words which follow it in the Roman missal — *novi et aeterni Testamenti, mysterium fidei, qui pro vobis et pro multis effundetur in remissionem peccatorum* — are also necessary;[1] but whether he considers them as belonging to the substance of the form, so that without them there would be no consecration, is not quite certain.

There was some difference of opinion in regard to the manner of reciting these words. In the first place, Innocent

[1] Sum. Theol. III, q. 78, a. 3.

III [2] and Præpositivus [3] seem to have held that they should be spoken by way of recitation only, in as much as the consecrating priest simply states the historic fact that Christ spoke them " the day before He suffered." This view is rejected by St. Thomas,[4] St. Bonaventure,[5] Scotus,[6] and the Scholastics generally, who hold that the words of consecration must be spoken both in a recitative and assertive way. The priest uses them not only as having once been spoken by Christ, but also to indicate the effect which they here and now produce. The two forms are not merely speculative propositions; they are practical, effecting what they signify.

In the second place, there was considerable discussion in reference to the truth of these propositions. What meaning must be attached to the pronouns *hoc* and *hic,* as they are spoken at the beginning of the two forms? What the priest holds in his hands at the moment when he utters them is simply bread, or the chalice containing wine; while at the completion of the forms the bread has been changed into the body of Christ, and the wine has been changed into the blood of Christ. What, therefore, do these pronouns indicate if they are used by way of assertion?

St. Thomas, after adverting to the fact that the forms are practical propositions, and that transubstantiation is effected instantaneously when the last syllable is pronounced, maintains that the pronouns *hoc* and *hic* indicate in an indeterminate way what is common to the terminus *a quo* and the terminus *ad quem.* Hence, in the consecration of the bread, the sense of the proposition is: *That which is contained under these species is my body;* and in the consecration of the chalice the corresponding proposition signifies: *That which is contained under these species is my blood.*[7]

[2] De Sacro Altaris Mysterio, c. 17.
[3] Sum. p. 4.
[4] In Sent. IV, d. 8, q. 2, a. 1.
[5] Ibid. p. 2, a. 1, q. 1.
[6] Ibid. d. 8, q. 2, n. 12 sq.
[7] " Sic ergo hoc pronomen *hoc* neque demonstrat terminum ad quem transubstantiationis determin- ate, . . . neque iterum demonstrat terminum a quo determinate. Relinquitur ergo quod demonstret hoc quod est commune utrique termino indeterminate. . . . Communia sunt accidentia sensibilia. . . . Unde sensus est: 'Hoc contentum sub his speciebus est corpus meum '" (Loc. cit).

St. Bonaventure regards this explanation as probable, but does not consider it quite satisfactory. The chief objection to it, he says, is that the pronoun thus really points out, not the body of Christ, but the substance of bread in so far as it is perceptible by reason of its accidents. To escape this difficulty, he holds that the pronoun in the form of consecration appeals partly to the senses and partly to the intellect. In so far as it appeals to the senses it points out the substance that is to be converted; in so far as it appeals to the intellect it designates the body or blood of Christ which are the terms of this conversion, and of which the bread and wine are sensible signs.[8] With some slight modifications the same view is also defended by Alexander of Hales [9] and Richard of Middleton,[10] while Scotus is in favor of the explanation given by St. Thomas.[11]

In regard to the causality of the forms of consecration there existed the same difference of opinion as in reference to sacramental causality in general, concerning which an explanation has been given in a previous chapter. While some ascribed an instrumental efficacy to the words, others considered them merely as a *conditio sine qua non* of the effect produced by the omnipotence of God.[12]

2. The Matter of Consecration.— The proper matter for consecration, according to the common teaching of the Scholastics, is wheaten bread and wine of the grape — *panis triticeus et vinum de vite.* To this conclusion they reason from the fact that Christ consecrated bread and wine, and that, in the common acceptation of the terms, bread is supposed to be made of wheaten flour and wine to be pressed from the grape. St. Thomas, after referring to some antiquated heretical views, says: " All these and similar errors are excluded by the fact that Christ instituted this sacrament under the species of bread and wine." [13] And then to the question, whether bread must be made of wheat flour, he replies: " The kind of bread to be used is determined by

8 In Sent. IV, d. 8, p. 2, a. 1, q. 1.   11 Ibid. q. 2, a. 1.
9 Sum. IV, q. 10, m. 4, a. 2.   12 Op. cit. d. 10, p. 2, a. 1, q. 3.
10 In Sent. IV, d. 8, a. 3, q. 1.   13 Sum. Theol. III, q. 74, a. 1.

the more common meaning attached to the term as employed by men. Now people more commonly use wheaten bread; for other kinds of bread seem to be mere substitutes for it." [14] In a similar manner he reasons about the wine.[15]

The bread, moreover, should be unfermented; but this is not necessary for the validity of the sacrament. St. Thomas states the accepted views of theologians on this point as follows: "It is necessary indeed that the bread should be wheaten; for otherwise the sacrament would be invalid. But it is not necessary for the validity of the sacrament that the bread should be either unfermented or fermented. . . . It is, however, proper that each one should observe the rite of the church in which he celebrates." [16] Nor is it necessary for the validity of the sacrament that a small quantity of water should be mixed with the wine, although it is enjoined under grave obligation. By the water thus added is typified the people of God, who share in the sacrament; and thereby is also recalled the flowing of water from the side of Christ as He hung upon the cross.[17]

3. *The Consecrating Minister.*— That the priest alone has power to consecrate the Eucharist is assumed by all Scholastics as a matter that admits of no discussion. "Only priests can consecrate," says St. Bonaventure, "and if any one else attempts it, he accomplishes nothing. This is the teaching of our faith, which we have received from the Apostles." [18] But on the further question, whether all priests can consecrate, there is found among them some difference of opinion. Thus Hugh of St. Victor,[19] Peter Lombard,[20] and the author of the *Summa Sententiarum,*[21] hold that excommunicated priests are deprived of the power of consecrating. Peter Lombard assigns this reason for his view: *Illi vero, qui excommunicati sunt, vel de haeresi manifeste notati, non videntur hoc sacramentum posse conficere, licet sacerdotes sint; quia nemo dicit in ipsa consecratione offero, sed offerimus, quasi ex persona Ec-*

[14] Ibid. a. 3.
[15] Ibid. a. 5.
[16] Ibid. a. 4.
[17] Ibid. a. 7.

[18] In Sent. IV, d. 13, a. 1, q. 2.
[19] In Ep. S. Pauli, q. 102.
[20] Sent. d. 13, c. 1.
[21] Op. cit. tr. 6, c. 9.

clesiae.   Et ideo, cum alia sacramenta extra Ecclesiam possint celebrari, de hoc non videtur.[22]

Later Scholastics, on the other hand, unanimously reject this reasoning and hold that the power of consecrating, which is received in ordination to the priesthood, cannot be lost. St. Thomas answers the difficulty, noted above, in this way: " In the prayers of the Mass the priest speaks indeed in the person of the Church, to the unity of which he belongs, but in the consecration he speaks in the person of Christ, whose place he holds through the power of ordination.   And therefore when an excommunicated priest celebrates Mass, he truly consecrates by changing bread and wine into the body and blood of Christ; because he has not lost the power received in his ordination.   But because he is separated from the unity of the Church, hence his prayers have no efficacy." [23]   Then, speaking of priests who have been degraded from their priestly rank, he says: " The power of consecrating the Eucharist pertains to the sacerdotal character.   Now the character, because conferred by a certain consecration, is indelible. . . . Hence it is manifest that the power of consecrating is not lost through degradation." [24]

In this connection the Scholastics also consider the question, whether a Mass celebrated by a good priest is of greater value than a Mass celebrated by a bad priest.   The answer had already been given by Innocent III, who embodied this clause in the profession of faith required of the Waldensians: *In quo (sacrificio) nihil a bono majus, vel a malo minus perfici credimus sacerdote, quia non in merito consecrantis, sed in verbo efficitur Creatoris et in virtute Spiritus Sancti.*[24a]   The common teaching of the Scholastics on the point in question is thus formulated by St. Bonaventure: " Speaking of the Mass, we must first of all consider what is its substantial value, namely, the consecration of the body and blood of Christ, and this is the same in all cases; because one and the same thing is in this regard effected by all priests.   Next

[22] Loc. cit.
[23] Sum. Theol. III, q. 82, a. 7, ad 3m.
[24] Ibid. a. 8.
[24a] DB. 424.

there are in the Mass certain accidentals, such as petitions, prayers, impetrations, and fervor; in respect of these the Mass of a good priest is of greater value, because they lead to greater devotion in those who assist. And if any one would rather hear Mass when celebrated by a more devout priest, I believe that he does well; provided, however, that he at the same time believes that there is no difference as regards the substantial value. Otherwise he would fall into a dangerous error." [25]

4. *The Eucharist as a Sacrament.*— According to the teaching of the Scholastics, the Holy Eucharist is a sacrament in the true sense of the term, but at the same time it is in some respects different from all other sacraments. The common view is thus presented by St. Thomas: " A religious rite is called a sacrament from the fact that it contains something sacred. Now a thing may be sacred in one of two ways: absolutely or relatively. And this is the difference between the Eucharist and other sacraments that are partly made up of sensible matter: the Eucharist contains something that is absolutely sacred, namely, the very body of Christ; whereas baptism, for instance, contains something that is sacred only in relation to something else, namely, the power of sanctifying: and the same is to be said in regard to confirmation and other similar sacraments. Hence the sacrament of the Eucharist is completed in the very consecration of the matter, while other sacraments are completed only in their application to the one who is to be sanctified. And from this also another difference arises: for in the sacrament of the Eucharist that which is the *res et sacramentum* is found in the matter itself; and that which is the *res tantum* is in the recipient, namely, the grace which is conferred: in baptism, on the other hand, both are in the recipient; namely, the character, which is the *res et sacramentum,* and the grace of justification, which is the *res tantum.* And it is the same in the case of the other sacraments." [26]

Hence the sacrament of the Eucharist does not consist pre-

[25] In Sent. IV, d. 13, a. 2, q. 1.   [26] Sum. Theol. III, q. 73, a. 1.

cisely in the words or action of transubstantiation, as St. Thomas was inclined to hold when he wrote his *Commentary on the Sentences;* but it is essentially constituted by the consecrated species of bread and wine, in so far as they connote and contain the body and blood of Christ.   The species, which naturally indicate bodily sustenance, in virtue of the consecration signify the presence of spiritual sustenance — the body and blood of Christ — and this in its turn signifies the grace to be conferred in the reception of the sacrament.   Substantially the same explanation is given by Alexander of Hales,[27] Albertus Magnus,[28] St. Bonaventure,[29] and Scotus.[30]

Although the Eucharist consists of two distinct species, that of bread and wine, it is nevertheless only one sacrament. This is the teaching of the most representative Scholastics, such as Alexander of Hales,[31] St. Bonaventure,[32] Duns Scotus,[33] and St. Thomas.[34]   The reason given by them is, that the two species together represent one spiritual refection. " A thing is said to be one," argues St. Thomas, " not only because it is indivisible, or continuous, but also because it is perfect — as one house and one man.   Now a thing is one in the order of perfection by reason of all those integrating parts that are necessary for the attainment of its end.   Thus man is integrally made up of all the members that are required for the operation of his soul, and a house of all those parts that are necessary to fit it for a habitation.   And in like manner this sacrament is said to be one; because it is intended for a spiritual refection, which is conformable to bodily refection in that it consists of food and drink." [35]

On the other hand, from the fact that the two species constitute but one sacrament, it does not follow that the Eucharist must be received by all under both species.   During the thirteenth century the practice of the Church in regard to lay communion was in a state of transition.   In some places the

[27] Sum. IV, q. 10, m. 3, a. 3.
[28] In Sent. IV, d. 8, a. 12.
[29] Ibid. p. 2, a. 2, q. 1.
[30] Ibid. q. 1.
[31] Loc. cit. a. 1.

[32] Loc. cit. q. 2.
[33] Loc. cit. q. 1, n. 4.
[34] Ibid. q. 1, a. 1.
[35] Sum. Theol. q. 77, a. 2.

laity still received under both species, and in others only under
the species of bread. St. Thomas, who gives the common
teaching on the point in question, presents the matter in these
terms: " Regarding the use of the sacrament two points may
be considered: one in reference to the sacrament itself, and one
in reference to those who receive it. As regards the sacrament itself, it is indeed becoming that both be received, that
is, the body and the blood, because the perfection of the
sacrament consists of both; and therefore, as it belongs to the
priest to consecrate and complete the sacrament, he must in
no way receive the body of Christ without also receiving His
blood.

" But on the part of those who receive it, there is required
the greatest reverence and caution, lest something should happen that would desecrate so great a mystery. This is especially
the case with regard to the receiving of the blood, which, if
taken without proper caution, might easily be spilled. And
because in the ever increasing multitude of Christians there
are old people and young, and children, many of whom have
not the necessary discretion, nor take the proper precautions,
in receiving this sacrament, hence it has been very wisely
ordained in some churches that the laity do not receive
communion under the species of wine, but the priest
only." [36]

5. *Effects of the Sacrament.*—" This sacrament produces
no effect," says St. Bonaventure, " except in him who receives
it worthily; and he alone receives it worthily who prepares
himself for its reception as he ought." [37] Then to the question, whether it has any efficacy in the sinner, he replies:
" We do not wish to put limits to the generosity of God, who
may and perhaps sometimes does grant the remission of all
sins in this sacrament; but it must be said that in accordance
with the common law and general reason for its institution,
this sacrament is intended as food for those who are in the
body of Christ, and all such have charity; therefore it exerts
its efficacy only in the just. And its effect in the just is libera-

[36] Ibid. q. 80, a. 12.   [37] In Sent. IV, d. 12, p. 2, a. 1,
                                         q. 1.

tion from venial faults and preservation from mortal sin." [38]
A little farther on he shows how this general effect is attained
by a most intimate union with Christ.[39]

St. Thomas considers the matter somewhat more in detail.
This sacrament produces grace, because it contains the author
of grace; it represents the sufferings of the Savior; it is
given as spiritual food; it is the sign of union with the God-
Man.[40]   Mortal sin is an impediment to its reception, because
food is not for the dead.[41]   However, if a person receives in
good faith, not being conscious of the fact that he is in mortal
sin, and at the same time is sorry for whatever sins he may
have committed, he receives forgiveness through the sacrament.[42]

6. *The Eucharist as a Sacrifice.*— Alexander of Hales,[43] St.
Thomas,[44] and some other Scholastics give a detailed and
minute description of the Mass, but none of them examine
into the intimate nature of the Eucharistic sacrifice. Their
remarks about it are incidental, and hardly ever touch the
points that caused so much discussion in later centuries. The
following statements of St. Thomas contain practically all
that can be gathered from their writings.

" This sacrament," he says, " is both a sacrifice and a sacrament. It is a sacrifice in so far as it is offered to God; it is
a sacrament in so far as it is received by men. Hence it has
the effects of a sacrament in him who receives it; and the effects of a sacrifice in him who offers it up, or also in those
for whom it is offered." [45]

In another connection he gives this descriptive definition of
a sacrifice in the proper sense of the term: *Sacrificia proprie
dicuntur, quando circa res Deo oblatas aliquid fit; sicut quod
animalia occidebantur, et comburebantur: quod panis frangi-
tur, et comeditur, et benedicitur; et hoc ipsum nomen sonat,
nam sacrificium dicitur ex hoc, quod homo facit aliquid
sacrum: oblatio autem directe dicitur, cum Deo aliquid offer-*

38 Ibid. q. 2.
39 Ibid. q. 3.
40 Sum. Theol. III, q. 79, a. 1.
41 Ibid. a. 3.

42 Ibid.
43 Sum. IV, q. 10, 11.
44 Op. cit. q. 83.
45 Op. cit. q. 79, a. 5.

tur, etiamsi nihil circa ipsum fiat; sicut dicuntur denarii offerri, vel panes in altari, circa quos nihil fit: unde omne sacrificium est oblatio, sed non convertitur.[46]

Applying this to the Eucharistic rite, he says that it may be considered as an immolation of Christ as He becomes present under the sacramental species. And this for two reasons: First, because the rite is representative of the sufferings and death of Christ on the cross, when He was truly immolated for the sins of the world. Secondly, because through the Eucharist we are allowed to share in the effects of Christ's true immolation.[47] Again: " The celebration of this sacrament is a certain representative image of the passion of Christ; and therefore it is said to be an immolation of Christ Himself." [48] Hence too, the Christian altar represents the cross, whereon Christ was immolated.[49]

Furthermore, this representation of Christ's immolation on the cross is verified in the consecration itself, and therefore it is not lawful to consecrate the body without the blood.[50] This rite is a sacrifice precisely in so far as it represents the passion of Christ, in which He offered Himself to God as a victim for sin.[51] In the Eucharistic sacrifice as well as in the sacrifice of the cross, Christ Himself is both priest and victim; the officiating priest is merely His ministerial representative, acting in His name and person.[52] Hence, although the Eucharist is celebrated in many different places, and by many different priests, it is nevertheless only one sacrifice — a renewal and representation of the one sacrifice offered up on the cross.[53]

With this teaching of St. Thomas Duns Scotus agrees in so far as he also holds that the sacrifice of the Mass is an objective representation of the sacrifice of the cross,[54] that therein Christ is both victim and priest,[55] and that the officiating priest acts in His name and person; but he differs from it when he places the essence of this sacrifice, not in the

---

[46] II. II, q. 85, a. 3 ad 3ᵐ.
[47] Sum. Theol. q. 83, a. 1.
[48] Ibid.
[49] Ibid. a. 1 ad 1ᵐ.
[50] Ibid. q. 80, a. 12 ad 3ᵐ.

[51] Ibid. q. 79, a. 7.
[52] Ibid. q. 83, a. 1 ad 3ᵐ.
[53] Ibid.
[54] Quodl. q. 20, n. 22.
[55] Ibid. n. 22, 2.

consecration itself, but in the oblation that follows.[56] He also points out that, although the value of the Eucharistic sacrifice is in itself infinite, nevertheless as offered by the Church it is finite in its application to the faithful.[57]

Of the several points touched in these two chapters, some have been defined by the Church, others represent the common teaching of theologians, while still others are little more than theological speculations. To the first class, with which we are here more directly concerned, belongs the Real Presence, transubstantiation, the existence of the accidents of bread and wine independently of their natural subject of inhesion, the form and matter of consecration, the power of every priest to consecrate, the freedom from mortal sin as a necessary disposition for a worthy reception, the increase of sanctifying grace in the worthy recipient, and the fact that the Holy Eucharist is both a sacrament and a sacrifice. It must be noted, however, that nearly all these definitions were occasioned by the cavils of heretics, and that they simply formulate in a clear and definite way what had always been held to be an object of faith.

[56] In Sent. IV, d. 13, q. 2.   [57] Quodl. 20, n. 22.

CHAPTER XX

PENANCE

PRACTICE OF THE EARLY MIDDLE AGES: TEACHING OF THE SCHOLASTICS

In a certain sense, penance is to the fallen Christian what baptism is to the unregenerated heathen — a plank of safety out of the shipwreck. And as such has it always been regarded in the Church of Christ. In fact, the comparison was already a commonplace in the third century. And so, too, was all that is essential in the doctrine and administration of penance. On the other hand, in the matter of accidental details many changes were introduced in the course of time. Some of these appear at first sight so striking that not a few thoughtless critics have been led to deny the continuity of the penitential rite itself. Such a denial is, of course, without warrant; for while in the course of many centuries the external form of penance has undergone various changes, the essentials of both doctrine and practice have always remained the same. The following remarks on the penitential practices of the early Middle Ages will make this sufficiently clear.

A — Practice of the Early Middle Ages

During Patristic times, penance as administered by the Church was of two kinds: private and public. In private penance both the confession of sins and the rite of reconciliation were secret; in public penance sacramental confession was also secret, but the works of satisfaction enjoined and the final reconciliation were public. Moreover, under ordinary circumstances, reconciliation was not granted until due satisfaction had been made. It was chiefly in regard to public penance that changes were gradually introduced. These changes were determined partly by altered social conditions and partly by the varying attitude of the faithful in regard to public penance. And rightly so: for as public penance was in great part merely a matter of discipline, it was quite proper that the Church should accommodate her regulations in this respect to the needs of the times and the greater good of those whom she desired to benefit. Hence we find that in some countries public penance was never in force. This was the case in England, and probably also in Ireland. In regard to the former country the *Poenitentiale Theodori* explicitly states: *Reconciliatio ideo in hac provincia publice statuta non est, quia et publica poenitentia non est.*[1]

It was principally since the seventh century that public penance began to be discontinued in the various countries in which it had been in vogue during Patristic times. Thus in France, during the disorders of the Merovingian period, it fell into almost complete desuetude. And this state of things continued even after public order had been restored, as is evident from a statement of the Synod of Chalons, held in 813. The statement reads as follows: *Poenitentiam agere juxta antiquam canonum institutionem in plerisque locis ab usu recessit.*[2] The same Synod, however, passed this decree: *Si quis publice peccat, publice mulctetur poenitentia et secundum ordinem canonum pro merito suo excommunicetur et reconcilietur.*[3] During the next two centuries this legislation was regarded as the general norm of procedure — public penance was to be imposed upon public sinners, at least in cases where the sin had caused considerable scandal. At the same time, however, excommunication was not inflicted except when the sinner refused to do penance. Similar conditions obtained also in other countries.

A further mitigation was introduced in regard to the time of reconciliation. For many centuries reconciliation was ordinarily granted only after the penance enjoined had been duly performed. Practically the only exceptions to this rule

---

[1] Op. cit. 13, 4; cfr. Hadden and Stubbs, Councils, III, 187.

[2] Mansi, 14, 98.

[3] Ibid.

were those in favor of the dying. To them immediate reconciliation was granted even if they had put off doing penance,
although in that case its effectiveness was not rarely called in
question. Thus, in the sixth century, St. Cæsarius of Arles
stated in reference to such persons : " If any one, when in
danger of death, asks to be admitted to penance, and, the
favor having been granted, he departs this life after being thus
reconciled, I confess, we do not deny him what he asks, but
at the same time we do not presume that he has died well." [4]
With reference to the dying in general, Rabanus Maurus, towards the middle of the ninth century, gives this direction
to his clergy : " In regard to those who are at the point of
death, account must be taken of their sincere conversion rather
than of the time still left them for doing penance." [5]   And
even before this, immediate reconciliation was already extended to those in health; for the *Statuta Bonifatii* contain this
general direction : " Let every priest see to it that penitents be
reconciled immediately after their confession." [6]   However,
as appears from the *Libri Poenitentiales,* this did not apply to
cases of great public scandal. By the beginning of the
eleventh century immediate reconciliation had become the
general rule, even in the case of public sinners; and thereafter public penance practically disappeared.

During all these centuries, private penance, including
sacramental confession, was much insisted upon. Confession
was considered to make even the most grievous sins venial,
that is, easily forgiven. Thus Alcuin states: " Believe me,
whatever sin you may have committed becomes venial, if you
are not ashamed to confess it and to do penance. . . . The
Lord is waiting for the sacrifice of your confession, so that
He may show you the sweetness of His mercy; for He wishes
all men to be saved and desires no one to perish." [7]   And
again: " God desires our confession, so that He may have
a just reason for granting pardon." [8]   In the sacred tribunal
of penance the priest is at once intercessor, advocate, and

[4] ML. 67, 1082 C.
[5] Poenit. 14; ML. 110, 483.
[6] Mansi, 12, 386.

[7] De Confess. Pecc. 2; ML. 101, 622.
[8] Ibid. 622 A.

physician. He reconciles the sinner to God, and, in virtue of
the authority conferred upon him by the Church, loosens the
bonds of sin.[9] The form of absolution was still deprecatory,
and the declarative form did not come into common use until
about 1200.[10] Even then some Scholastics still disputed the
lawfulness of its use.[11] However, the final acceptation of
this form shows that it had always been the common per-
suasion that the priest really absolved from sin, even if he
granted absolution in the form of a prayer.

How the sacrament of penance was regarded in the early
Middle Ages appears most clearly from the Pseudo-Augustin-
ian treatise *De Vera et Falsa Poenitentia*. This work was
probably composed at the beginning of the eleventh century,
although Gratian, about 1140, regarded it as a genuine work
of St. Augustine. The points of most interest in the present
connection are the following:

1. The proper object or matter of the sacrament of penance
are mortal sins: *Sunt quaedam peccata venialia, quae oratione
Dominica cotidie solvuntur, . . . alia vero, quae sunt ad
mortem, non sic, sed per fructum poenitentiae solvuntur.*[12]
Agenda est poenitentia, ut deleantur crimina.[13]

2. However venial sins may also be confessed; and when
they are frequently committed, confession is very advisable:
*Ista assidua et quodam modo necessaria assidua laventur con-
fessione, assidua restaurentur confessione;*[14] *est enim
poenitentia assidue peccantibus assidue necessaria.*[15]

3. The confession of sins by catechumens is not necessary:
Poenitentia baptizandis non est necessaria.[16]

4. The life of a Christian is necessarily a penitential life:
*Quantum sit appetenda gratia poenitentiae . . ., omnis
bonorum vita conatur ostendere;*[17] *fides fundamentum est
poenitentiae.*[18]

5. This penance may be repeated as often as seems good;[19]

9 Ep. 112; ML. 100, 337, sqq.
10 Regino, De Ecclesiast. Discipl.
I, 300; ML. 132, 252.
11 Morinus, 8, 9, 23; p. 537 sq.
12 Op. cit. 4, 10: ML, 1116.
13 Ibid. 8, 22; 1121.

14 Ibid. 8, 21; 1120.
15 Ibid. 8, 20; 1119.
16 Ibid. 8, 19; 1119.
17 Ibid. 1, 1; 1113.
18 Ibid. 2, 3; 1113.
19 Ibid. 3, 5-15.

but if public penance must be done, that may be performed only once.[20]

6. Normally all men are at one time or another guilty of mortal sin; hence, referring to John 8, 7–9, the author says: *Nullus erat sine peccato. In quo intelligitur omnes crimine fuisse reos, nam veniale semper remittebatur per cerimonias; si quod igitur peccatum in eis erat, criminale erat.*[21]

7. True penance consists first of all in a contrite confession of the sins committed: *Quem igitur poenitet . . . representet vitam suam Deo per sacerdotem, praeveniat judicium Dei per confessionem. . . . Ex misericordia enim hoc praecepit Dominus, ut neminem poeniteret in occulto. . . . Fit enim per confessionem veniale, quod criminale erat in operatione.*[22]

8. If no priest be at hand, and there is danger of death, it is advisable to confess even to a layman: *Tanta itaque vis confessionis est, ut si deest sacerdos, confiteatur proximo; . . . fit dignus venia ex desiderio sacerdotis.*[23]

9. The priest acts as the messenger of God — *nuntius Dei;*[24] he exercises the power of a judge — *in potestate judicis;*[25] he is vested with judicial power — *judiciaria potestas.*[26]

10. For secret sins private penance suffices, but for public sins public penance is proper: *Si peccatum occultum est, sufficiat referre in notitiam sacerdotis. . . . Docemur publice peccantibus non proprium, sed ecclesiae sufficere meritum; . . . qui enim multos offendit peccando, placare multos oportet satisfaciendo.*[27]

11. In order to satisfy completely for one's sins, one must be assiduous in performing works of penance: *Qui perfectam vult consequi gratiam remissionis, fructificet in poenitentia.*[28]

12. True penance shows itself in mortification, sorrow of heart, and alms-giving: *Abstineat a multis licitis, . . . semper offerat Deo mentis et cordis contritionem, deinde et*

---

[20] Ibid. 11, 26.
[21] Ibid. 20, 36; 1129.
[22] Ibid. 10, 25; 1122.
[23] Ibid.
[24] Ibid.

[25] Ibid. 15, 30; 1125.
[26] Ibid. 20, 36; 1129.
[27] Ibid. 11, 26; 1123.
[28] Ibid. 15, 31; 1126.

quod potest de possessione, ut semper puniat se ulciscendo, quod commisit peccando; poenitere enim est poenam tenere.[29]

13. Those who neglect to do penance here on earth shall be punished in purgatory: *Prius purgandus est igne purgationis, qui in aliud saeculum distulit fructum conversionis.*[30]

14. If any one dies without repenting of his sins, he is condemned to the pains of hell: *Qui autem impoenitens moritur, omnino moritur et aeternaliter cruciatur.*[31]

The same general outlines of early mediæval teaching on penance might also be drawn up from the sermons of St. Peter Damian, who died in 1072. Of those who contritely confess their sins he says: *In fide Ecclesiae credat sibi peccata dimitti.*[32] It is only after the *oris confessio,* sacramental confession, that works of penance are in place.[33] If sufficient satisfaction for sins is not rendered here on earth, the penitent must submit to the pains of purgatory: *Cum in purgatoriis ignibus perficiendum sit, quidquid hic minus feceris, quia dignos poenitentiae fructus quaerit Altissimus.*[34] He calls penance the sacrament of confession — *sacramentum confessionis.*[35] It is the ordinary means of sanctification for saint and sinner alike: *Via communis ad Deum, fons tam justis quam peccatoribus patens.*[36]

From the foregoing summary it ought to be sufficiently clear that private sacramental penance did not grow out of monastic practices, as is so frequently contended by Protestant writers on the subject. It was in vogue all over the Christian world, and the obligation of submitting to it was insisted upon by the secular clergy as well as by the monks. Nor were the clergy themselves exempt from this obligation, although they usually were exempt from the obligation of submitting to public penance. Much less can it be held, as many Protestants do hold, that the obligation of sacramental confession had its origin in the legislation of the Fourth Lateran Council, convened in 1215 under Innocent III. All that the Council did was to

[29] Ibid. 10, 25; 1122.
[30] Ibid. 18, 34; 1128.
[31] Ibid.
[32] Serm. 58; ML, 144, 832 D.
[33] Ibid. 832 D; 833 A.
[34] Ibid. 831 A.
[35] Serm. 69; ML, 901 A.
[36] Ibid. 901 A.

prescribe certain limits, beyond which the faithful must not
neglect to confess their sins.[37]   The obligation itself had existed from the beginning of the Church, but it was only when
the faithful had become careless in this respect that the Church
found it necessary to enforce it by a general law.   Moreover
local synods had passed similar laws centuries before, but the
Fourth Lateran legislated for the whole Church.

B — Teaching of the Scholastics

Most of the Scholastics consider penance under two distinct heads: penance as a virtue and penance as a sacrament.
But they do not all follow the same order of treatment.   Some
discuss first the virtue of penance and then pass over to its
sacramental aspect; while others first explain what belongs to
the sacrament and thereupon treat of the virtue in connection
with the effects and acts of penance.   The former arrangement
seems the more logical, and will be followed in this brief review of their teaching.

1. *The Virtue of Penance.*— The question whether penance
must be regarded as a virtue is variously answered by the
Scholastics.   St. Bonaventure enumerates four different views
on this point, each one of which had its defenders among the
Schoolmen.   " Some there are," he says, " who hold that
penance is not a virtue, but an act of virtue; not of one virtue
in particular, but of all together — they all concur in the production of that act.   Just as the chords of the lyre give out
one musical note when touched in accord with the rules of the
musician's art, so do the virtues produce this one act under
the direction of prudence. . . . Others say that penance is a
habitus, not of virtue but of grace; nor does it refer only to
the substance of grace, but also to its act.   As the grace of
baptism is called innocence, so is the grace of justification
called penance. . . . A third opinion admits that penance is a
virtue, but only in the wider sense of the term.   For virtue
in the proper sense directs the agent towards good, while
penance recalls him from evil. . . . The last view is that pen-

[37] DB. 437.

ance is a habit of virtue — *habitus virtutis* — and of virtue in its proper acceptation, not merely in a general sense. And this, I believe, is the more probable view." [38]

This " more probable view " was held by nearly all the most representative Scholastics,[39] Albertus Magnus being the only one of note who considered penance as a virtue in the wider sense of the term.[40] Then the further question arose whether penance must be regarded as a special virtue distinct from all others. In respect to this there was again some difference of views, in as much as a few identified penance with justice, while all the others held it to be a special virtue. Thus St. Thomas argues: " Habits are distinguished according to the specific difference of their acts; hence where there are specifically different praiseworthy acts, there it must be admitted that they are elicited by a special virtue. Now it is manifest that in penance there is found a specifically different praiseworthy act, namely, to bring about the destruction of past sin in so far as it is an offence against God, which does not belong to any other virtue. Hence it necessarily follows that penance is a special virtue." [41] St. Bonaventure words his reasoning somewhat differently, but comes to the same conclusion. " Penance," he says, " is a special virtue, because it has a bearing upon evil as committed against God, whereby man has made himself deserving of punishment." [42]

However, although penance is thus a special virtue, it is nevertheless reducible to the cardinal virtue of justice, of which it is a part. On this point nearly all were agreed, only a few contending that penance must be reduced to charity. The more common view is thus set forth by St. Thomas: " Penance is a special virtue not only for the reason that it causes grief for sins committed, because for that purpose charity would suffice; but rather for the reason that the penitent

[38] In Sent. IV, d. 14, p. 1, a. 1, q. 1.
[39] Cfr. Halens. Sum. IV, q. 12, m. 1, a. 1; Thomas, in Sent. IV, d. 14, q. 1, a. 1; Scotus, ibid. q. 2; Middleton, ibid. a. 1, q. 1.
[40] Ibid. a. 3.
[41] Sum. Theol. III, q. 85, a. 2.
[42] In Sent. IV, d. 14, p. 1, a. 1. q. 2.

grieves for sins committed in so far as they are an offence
against God, and at the same time resolves to make
amends. Now to make amends for an offence committed against some one does not consist merely in a cessation of the offence; but furthermore requires that a certain
compensation be made to the person offended, just as sin demands punishment. . . . But compensation and punishment
belong to the matter of justice, because there is a commutative
aspect in both. Hence, it is manifest that penance, in so far as
it is a special virtue, is a part of justice." [43]   However, as it is
the virtue of an inferior in respect of his superior, it is not
commutative justice in the strict sense of the term; because
that has no place except between equals.[44]

Again, as penance is a part of the virtue of justice, its proper
subject is the will. Hence, too, repentance is an act of the
will, although it usually also manifests itself in the affections.[45]
Its proper act consists in the detestation of sin and the firm
purpose of amendment, so that thereby due compensation may
be made to God for the offence that resulted from past sins.[46]

Penance as a virtue is infused by God. This is the common
teaching of the Scholastics against Scotus.[47]   Considered as
an act, penance arises from a variety of motives. The whole
process of repentance is thus described by St. Bonaventure:
" First it is necessary to know God's goodness and justice, to
which every sin is an offence and as such calls for punishment
— and one must be conscious of having done something that is
displeasing to God's goodness; this is the consciousness of
guilt, and thence results the apprehension of punishment as
inflicted by divine justice. It is also necessary to know God's
mercy, by reason of which He is prepared to grant forgiveness
to everyone who sincerely repents of his sins. From the first
knowledge arises fear; from the second hope of forgiveness:
then from the two together springs the desire and the determination of returning to God, of becoming reconciled to Him,

[43] Sum. Theol. III, q. 85, a. 3.   [46] Ibid.
[44] Ibid.   [47] Cfr. supra, " Infused Virtues."
[45] Ibid. a. 4; Bonavent. In Sent.
IV, d. 14, p. 1, a. 2, q. 1.

and of rendering Him due satisfaction by sorrow of heart and other penitential works. If a person thus starts out to do what in him lies, he is disposed for justification." [48]

This is substantially the common teaching of the Scholastics, though not by all of them expressed in the same terms. St. Thomas, for instance, puts it this way: "Of penance we can speak in two ways: one way in as much as it is a *habitus* and as such it is immediately infused by God, we only contributing thereto by way of disposition; another way in as much as it is an act, in which we coöperate with God through penance. Of these acts the first principle is God's operation in so far as He converts the heart, according to Lament. ult., 21: 'Convert us, O Lord, to Thee, and we shall be converted.' The second is an act of faith; the third is an act of servile fear, by which one is drawn away from sin through the fear of punishment; the fourth is an act of hope, by which one in expectation of forgiveness resolves upon amending one's life; the fifth is an act of charity, by which one detests sin as it is in itself and not merely for fear of punishment; the sixth is an act of filial fear, by which one through reverence for God freely offers to make amends. And thus it is clear that the act of penance proceeds from servile fear as the first movement of the affections ordained to this end; but from filial fear as its immediate and proper principle." [49]

If a person is truly repentant and prepared to comply with all the conditions laid down by God for justification, he infallibly obtains the grace of God, no matter what sins he may have committed.[50] In connection with this they usually inquire into the measure of sanctifying grace that one receives in thus rising from grievous personal falls. By mortal sin sanctifying grace is lost, by penance it is recovered; but in what measure is it recovered as compared to the grace possessed before sin was committed? Obviously, three suppositions are

---

[48] In Sent. IV, d. 14, p. 1, a. 2, q. 2.

[49] Sum. Theol. III, q. 85, a. 5.

[50] The common teaching of the Scholastics on this point is thus formulated by St. Bonaventure: "Concedendum igitur, quod omnis agens poenitentiam super culpam secundum assignationem praedictam, quantumcumque peccaverit, invenit gratiam" (In Sent. IV, d. 14, p. 2, a. 2, q. 1).

possible. First, that penance places man in the same position
where he was before he sinned; so that he has the same amount
of sanctifying grace and the same merits for heaven. Secondly, that penance restores the full amount of grace and all
the merits possessed before sin was committed, and adds
thereto whatever is due to the supernatural acts of penance itself; whence it would follow that the sinner after his conversion possesses a higher degree of grace and more merits
for heaven than he did before he sinned. Thirdly, that penance does not restore the grace and merits lost through sin,
and that therefore the penitent after his conversion has only
that degree of grace and those merits which correspond to the
supernatural acts involved in the process of his repentance.

Different answers are given to the question by different
Scholastics. Some hold that penance restores the same grace
that was lost by sin; others say that penance restores the grace
that was lost and besides adds thereto in proportion to the
fervor of repentance; others, finally, maintain that the grace
conferred by penance is simply in proportion to the disposition
of the penitent, and that all lost merits are merely the cause
of accidental glory in heaven. This last seems to be the view
of St. Thomas, for he says: " The penitent who rises from
his sins in a lower degree of charity, will indeed obtain an
essential reward in proportion to the degree of charity which
he is found to possess; nevertheless he will have greater joy on
account of the good works which he did in his first charity,
over and above that which results from the works he performed after his conversion; and this belongs to his accidental
reward." [51] The same is also held by Alexander of Hales [52]
and Richard of Middleton.[53] In this view, therefore, the
merits lost by sin do not revive through penance.

On the other hand, St. Bonaventure [54] and Duns Scotus [55]
are in favor of a full restoration of all previous merits. The
former says: " It is the common opinion of theologians that

[51] In Sent. III, d. 31, a. 4, quaestiunc. 1, 2, 3; Sum. Theol. III, q. 89,
a. 5 ad 3ᵐ.
[52] Sum. IV, q. 12, m. 4, a. 5.

[53] In Sent. III, d. 31, a. 1, q. 2.
[54] In Sent. IV, d. 14, p. 2, a. 2,
q. 3.
[55] Ibid. d. 22, q. unic. n. 8, 9, 10.

works which were at first meritorious, because they were performed in the state of grace and therefore deserving of an eternal reward, become dead through sin — because as long as there is guilt they are on account of the person's sinful condition no longer deserving of reward — but when grace returns and makes the penitent worthy of life eternal, these same works also deserve a reward, and are therefore restored and vivified." [56]   Scotus points out that if these meritorious works are not restored at the moment of conversion, on account of the penitent's imperfect disposition, then they are restored later on when his disposition is more perfect; or at all events at the moment of death.[57]

2. *The Sacrament of Penance.*—" The perfection of penance," argues Peter Lombard, " consists of three things: sorrow, confession, satisfaction — *compunctio cordis, confessio oris, satisfactio operis.*" [58]   These three are essential on the part of the penitent, and when to them is added the absolution of the priest, there results the sacrament of penance.   True, actual satisfaction is not a constituent part of the sacrament, but by way of satisfaction the penitent must at least have the sincere will to perform the penance enjoined by the confessor. In this sense, satisfaction as well as sorrow and confession is an indispensable requisite for a valid absolution.   Moreover, sorrow for sins must necessarily include a firm purpose of amendment; for without such a purpose, either expressed or implied, it would not be true sorrow.   Hence the sacrament of penance comprises five distinct parts: sorrow for sins, a purpose of amendment, confession, satisfaction, and absolution.   The first four of these must obviously be supplied by the penitent, and the last just as obviously by the priest who receives the confession.

So far all are agreed; but if it be asked whether all these parts enter the constitution of the sacrament, so that they in some way belong to its essence, there is some diversity of opinion.   Scotus and his followers contend that the acts of the penitent are indeed necessary conditions for a valid absolu-

---

[56] Loc. cit.
[57] Loc. cit.

[58] Sent. IV, d. 16, c. 1.

tion, but deny that they enter the constitution of the sacrament.
Scotus himself gives this definition of the sacrament of penance : *Absolutio hominis poenitentis, facta certis verbis, cum
debita intentione prolatis, a sacerdote jurisdictionem habente,
ex institutione divina efficaciter significantibus absolutionem
animae a peccato.*[59]   According to his view, it is the absolution alone that constitutes the sacramental sign.   And this he
expressly states, when he says in another place : *Hoc sacramentum non habet nisi unum signum ut verba prolata, habet
tantum formam et non proprie materiam.*[60]   Or again :
*Poenitentia, sacramentum, nihil aliud est quam forma audibilis
verborum prolatorum super poenitentem a sacerdote.*[61]   Hence
he says in regard to the acts of the penitent : *Sunt quaedam
dispositiones congruae praeambula convenientia ad susceptionem congruam poenitentiae sacramenti.*[62]   Sorrow for sins,
a purpose of amendment, confession, and satisfaction are all
necessary; but only as requisites for absolution, not as parts
of the sacrament.   Substantially the same explanation is given
by Durandus.[63]

However, the greater number of the Scholastics took a different view of the point in question.   The matter is most
clearly set forth by St. Thomas, who begins his treatise on
penance with a brief consideration of the sacramental rite.
He first points out that penance is a true sacrament of the New
Law, since the acts of the penitent and the absolution of the
priest together constitute a sacred sign which was instituted
for the sanctification of men.[63a]   Then to the objection that
there is no corporeal element in penance as there is in baptism,
he replies : " By the term corporeal things, taken in a wider
sense, are also understood exterior actions which can be perceived by the senses, and in this sacrament they take the place
of water in baptism or of chrism in confirmation.   But it must
be noted that in those sacraments which confer a more excellent grace, a grace which surpasses the reach of all human
acts, some corporeal matter is used by way of exterior appli-

[59] In Sent. IV, d. 14, q. 4, n. 2.   [62] In Sent. IV, d. 16, q. 1, n. 13.
[60] Report. IV, d. 16, q. 6, n. 6.   [63] Ibid. d. 16, q. 1.
[61] Ibid. n. 12.   [63a] Sum. Theol. III, q. 84, a. 1.

cation; thus in baptism, which confers a full remission of sins, both as to guilt and punishment; and in confirmation, which gives the fullness of the Holy Spirit; and in extreme unction, which bestows perfect spiritual health, flowing from the power of Christ as from a certain extrinsic principle. Hence, if in such sacraments there occur any human acts, they do not belong to the essence of the sacramental rites, but are merely requisite dispositions for the proper reception of those sacraments. Whereas in those sacraments which produce effects corresponding to human acts, these sensible human acts themselves constitute the matter of the same sacraments, as happens in penance and matrimony." [64]

From the fact that the acts of the penitent constitute the matter of the sacramental rite, it necessarily follows that in this sacrament the minister does not apply the matter to the recipient. These acts are inspired by God, are then presented by the penitent in the tribunal of penance, and thereupon receive their sacramental character from the absolution of the priest.[65] In a certain sense, the sins confessed by the penitent may be considered as the remote matter of the sacrament of penance; for it is upon them that the acts of the penitent, as the proximate matter of the sacrament, are made to bear.[66] And these sins comprise all personal sinful acts, venial and mortal, although it was chiefly for the forgiveness of mortal sin that the sacrament of penance was instituted.[67]

The form of the sacrament of penance consists in the words, *Ego te absolvo;* all that precedes these words by way of prayer is simply intended to obtain the grace of a proper disposition for the penitent. This form is taken from the promise which our Savior made to Peter, when He said: *Quodcumque solveris super terram, etc.*[68] It was then that He determined what should be required on the part of the minister, although He did not indicate its efficacy and the origin of its power until after His resurrection.[69]

As regards the power of the keys, which the priest uses in

[64] Sum. Theol. III, q. 86, a. 1.
[65] Ibid. a. 1 ad 2m.
[66] Ibid. a. 2.
[67] Ibid. a. 1 ad 3m.
[68] Ibid. a. 3.
[69] Ibid. q. 84, a. 7.

sacramental absolution, there is no perfect agreement among
the Scholastics.　In this matter two things must be distinguished: guilt and punishment.　According to some, the priest
in giving absolution simply declares that the guilt, or sin itself,
has been taken away by God, and then remits part of the punishment due to sin.　This is the view taken by Peter Lombard,[70] Richard of St. Victor [71] and probably also by St. Bonaventure.　The latter holds that the power of the keys extends
itself to the forgiveness of sin by way of prayer, but not by
way of imparting pardon for sin.[72]　Prayer, he says, obtains
grace; but absolution presupposes it.[73]　In accordance with
this view, he interprets the words of our Lord, *whose sins you
shall forgive, etc.,* as having been spoken merely *quantum ad
ostensionem, vel quantum ad poenam.*[74]

However, by far the greater number of Scholastics understood the power of the keys in a different sense.　Thus St.
Thomas, refuting the view of the Lombard, according to whom
the words, *ego te absolvo,* signify, *ego te absolutum ostendo,*
states very clearly:　" It must be said that the interpretation
of *I absolve thee,* as *I declare thee to have been absolved,* is
indeed partly true, but not altogether.　For the sacraments of
the New Law not only signify, but also effect what they signify.　Hence, just as the priest when he baptizes some one
declares by his words and actions that the recipient is interiorly cleansed, not only significatively but effectively; so likewise when he says I absolve thee, does he declare the penitent
to be absolved, not merely significatively but effectively.　Nor
does he say this in any uncertain way; for just as the other

---

[70] Sent. d. 18, n. 4, 5.
[71] De Potest. ligandi et solvendi.
[72] " Si ergo quaeratur, utrum potestas clavium se extendat ad
delendam culpam, dicendum, quod
bene potest se extendere per modum
deprecantis et impetrantis: et illud
significatum est in benedictione
sacerdotum, Numero sexto; sed
per modum impertientis non.
Quoniam ergo potestas sonat per
modum activi et impertientis ex se;

hinc est quod potestas clavium,
proprie loquendo, non se extendat
supra culpam" (In Sent. IV, d. 18,
p. 1, a. 2, q. 1).
[73] " Deprecatio gratiam impetrat,
sed absolutio praesupponit. Nun-
quam enim sacerdos absolveret
quemquam, de quo non praesumerat,
quod esset absolutus a Deo"
(Ibid.).
[74] Ibid. q. 1, ad 1m.

sacraments of the New Law have of themselves an infallible effect because of the passion of Christ, although that effect can be impeded on the part of the recipient; so it is also in the case of this sacrament. . . . Consequently, a better interpretation is this: *I absolve thee,* that is, *I impart to thee the sacrament of absolution."* [75]

True, the action of the priest in giving absolution is only ministerial, but so it is in the administration of all other sacraments. Hence the objection that God alone can forgive sins, St. Thomas answers by saying: " It is to be held that God alone can absolve from sin by His own authority, and thus remit sin; nevertheless priests do both by reason of their ministerial office, and that in as much as the words of the priest in this sacrament operate as the instrument of divine power, just as in the other sacraments. For it is the divine power that operates interiorly in the case of all sacramental signs, whether they are things or words, as was said above. Hence, our Lord mentioned both, the absolving from sin and the remission of sins; for in Matthew He says, *whatever you shall loosen upon earth, etc.,* and in John, *whose sins you shall forgive, they are forgiven them.* Nevertheless, the priest says, *I absolve thee,* rather than, *I remit thy sins,* because this is more in accord with the words used by our Lord when He conferred the power of the keys by which priests absolve. However, since it is only as God's minister that the priest absolves, it is fitting that something expressive of God's authority be added, namely, that he say: *I absolve thee in the name of the Father and of the Son and of the Holy Ghost,* or, *by the power of the passion of Christ,* or, *by the authority of God.* . . . Still, since this is not determined by the words of Christ, as it is in baptism, the addition is left to the judgment of the priest." [76]

The sacrament of penance is necessary for salvation, but not in the same sense as baptism. The latter is necessary for all alike, whereas the former is necessary only for those who after baptism have fallen into mortal sin.[77] Nor is it even for them absolutely necessary, but only on the supposition that

[75] Sum. Theol. III, q. 84, a. 3 ad 5m.

[76] Ibid. q. 84, a. 3.
[77] Ibid. a. 5.

they have an opportunity of receiving it; for where there is a good will and true sorrow, and a sincere desire to confess, God is always able and willing to forgive sins without the sacrament.[78]

The effect of the sacrament of penance, presupposing the good disposition of the penitent, consists in the remission of all sins truly repented of, and in the canceling of the eternal punishment due to sin.[79] Temporal punishment may also be canceled, but that depends on the degree of coöperation on the part of the penitent.[80]

For the worthy reception of the sacrament of penance, as was remarked above, three things are required on the part of the penitent: true sorrow for sins, including a firm purpose of amendment; confession of all mortal sins, in so far as he can call them to mind by diligent examination of conscience; and the will to render due satisfaction according to the judgment of the confessor. In regard to these requisites there is substantial agreement among the Scholastics, and a few remarks will suffice to indicate the trend of their teaching.

In the matter of sorrow for sins, or contrition, they distinguish between perfect and imperfect contrition; or also between contrition and attrition. However, they do not always take this distinction in precisely the same sense as do modern theologians. Both agree in attributing to perfect contrition the power of blotting out sin, and for that reason they call it perfect; while they regard imperfect contrition as being merely a disposition thereto, and in so far they consider it imperfect. But besides this, the Scholastics frequently use the two terms in reference to the presence or absence of sanctifying grace in the soul of the penitent. Thus taking one and the same act of sorrow, so long as the penitent is without sanctifying grace, they call it imperfect contrition or attrition; and the moment he receives sanctifying grace, they term it simply attrition. In this sense St. Thomas says: *Omnis dolor de peccato in habente gratiam est contritio.*[81] And in the same sense St. Bonaventure states: *In contritione gratiae est contritio ad*

---

[78] Ibid. q. 86, a. 2.
[79] Ibid. a. 1, 4.

[80] Ibid. a. 4 ad 2m.
[81] De Verit. q. 28, a. 8.

generandum vas novum et solidum per humorem gratiae et lacrymarum; et ideo recte dicitur contritio, non attritio, quia partium tritarum est unio.[82]

The perfection or imperfection of contrition depends ultimately on the motives by which sorrow for sin is inspired. Thus perfect contrition is conceived to flow from the consideration of sin precisely as it is an offense against God, who is infinitely good and deserving of all our love; while imperfect contrition is held to proceed from a less perfect motive, such as the intrinsic deformity of sin, the loss of eternal happiness, or even the fear of positive punishment. In reference to this St. Thomas says that the act of penance, which leads to the forgiveness of sin, takes its rise from servile fear, but has filial fear as its immediate and proximate principle.[83]

The question, what kind of contrition, perfect or imperfect, is required for a worthy reception of the sacrament of penance, is variously answered by the Scholastics, in keeping with the different views they entertain in respect to the power of the keys. In the first place, those who hold that the confessor merely declares the penitent to be absolved from his sins by God, consequently maintain that ordinarily perfect contrition is required. Thus St. Bonaventure compares penance in this respect to the reception of the Eucharist. In both cases, he says, the recipient must have at least probable reasons for believing that he has perfect charity, in order to be properly disposed for a worthy reception of the sacraments.[84]

On the other hand, those who hold that the priest really absolves from the guilt of sin, although only as the instrument

---

[82] In Sent. IV, d. 16, p. 1, a. 1, q. 1.

[83] Sum. Theol. III, q. 85, a. 5.

[84] He proposes his view in these terms: " Sicut dictum est, quod non tenemur ad Eucharistian accedere cum caritate secundum veritatem, sed sufficit, quod secundum probabilitatem; sic dico, quod ad sacramentum poenitentiae non est necesse, quod accedat habens caritatem vel dispositionem ad caritatem sufficientem secundum veritatem, sed sufficit secundum probabilitatem. Haec autem dispositio attritio est, quae frequenter ob confessionem superadjunctam et absolutionem sacerdotis formatur per gratiam, ut fiat contritio " (Ibid. d. 17, p. 2, a. 2, q. 3). Hence it is only by way of exception that attrition suffices for a worthy reception of the sacrament of penance.

of God, contend that attrition is always sufficient for a worthy reception of the sacrament of penance; provided, of course, that it flows from some supernatural motive. Hence, when St. Thomas defines contrition in so far as it is necessary for sacramental absolution, he derives its origin from only two motives: fear and hope. Fear, he says, is the principal motive, and with this is associated hope of forgiveness; for without hope, fear would degenerate into despair.[85] He adduces five different definitions of contrition as found in the works of the Fathers, and in not one of them is there question of perfect charity. As an example take the definition he quotes from St. Isidore of Seville: *Contritio est compunctio et humilitas mentis cum lacrimis, veniens de recordatione peccati et timore judicii.* Or that cited from St. Gregory the Great: *Contritio est humilitas spiritus, annihilans peccatum inter spem et timorem.* Both are identical with our definition of attrition. And these definitions St. Thomas makes his own.[86]

This more common view is also defended by Duns Scotus. He defines contrition in a general way as a detestation of past sins — *displicentia de peccato commisso,*[87] which includes or has connected with it a firm purpose of amendment — *propositum cavendi de caetero.*[88] Without such an act of contrition there is no forgiveness; because as sin turns man away from his last end, so must contrition turn him back to that same end.[89] When distinguishing between perfect and imperfect contrition, he uses the terminology rather common at the time, according to which contrition was denominated perfect from the presence of sanctifying grace in the soul, whereas it was called imperfect in so far as it preceded the advent of sanctifying grace.[90] In reference to this use of terms, he distinguishes two kinds of attrition: one that merits justification *de congruo* without the actual reception of the sacrament, and another that justifies only when the sacrament is actually received.[91] In substance, this latter kind of attrition is identical

---

[85] Sum. Theol. III, Suppl. q. 1, a. 1.
[86] Ibid.
[87] In Sent. IV, d. 14, q. 2.
[88] Ibid. q. 4, n. 9.

[89] Ibid. n. 18.
[90] Ibid. n. 14, 15.
[91] In reference to this second kind of attrition he says: " Ita ut parum attritus, attritione quae non habet

with that required by St. Thomas, as explained in the preceding paragraph.

In regard to the second requisite on the part of the penitent, namely, confession, there is practically no disagreement among the Scholastics. The common teaching is thus set forth by St. Thomas: "There is a twofold obligation to confess our sins. The first arises from the divine law which made confession a medicine for sin; and by this law not all are bound, but those only who commit mortal sin after baptism. The second obligation results from an ecclesiastical law, enacted in a general council under Innocent III, and by this all are bound. The purpose of the law is to bring all to a realization of their sinfulness, since we all have sinned and need the grace of God; a further purpose is to prepare the faithful for a proper reception of the Eucharist; and finally, to enable pastors to know their subjects, and so to discover the wolves that may lie hidden among the flock." [92]

Here it must be noted that St. Thomas extends the obligation of confession even to those who are guilty of only venial sins, because of the law passed by the Fourth Lateran in regard to yearly confession. This was the more common interpretation of that law during the Middle Ages. Hence, St. Bonaventure says in regard to venial sins: *Venialia igitur non tenetur quis confiteri propter vinculum peccati, sed hoc solum est propter obligationem praecepti, quae obligat unumquemque ad confitendum. Et ideo, si non habeat nisi venialia, tenetur illa confiteri; unde si haberet mortalia, quae confiteretur, non teneretur ad venialia.*[93] However, St. Thomas admits the other interpretation as probable, even from the wording of the law, which says that *all* sins must be confessed; for no one can call to mind *all* his venial sins. Hence, he concludes, if a person has no mortal sins to confess, he complies with the law by

rationem meriti ad remissionem peccati, . . . recipiat effectum sacramenti, scilicet gratiam poenitentialem, non quidem ex merito, quia dispositio interior non erat sufficiens per modum meriti, sed ex facto Dei assistentis sacramento suo" (Ibid. n. 14).

[92] Suppl. q. 6, a. 3.

[93] In Sent. IV, d. 17, p. 2, a. 2, q. 1.

presenting himself to his pastor and informing him of his immunity from mortal sin.[94]

All mortal sins must be confessed *in specie;* or as St. Bonaventure words the common teaching of that time: *Omnis peccati mortalis differentiam necesse est confiteri, sive sit latens, sive manifestum, sive sit cordis, sive sit oris.*[95] In regard to the circumstances that accompany mortal sin, a distinction is made by the Scholastics between those that simply aggravate the guilt and those that change the species or kind of the sin committed. According to some, both kinds of circumstances must be confessed, while others hold that there is no obligation to confess merely aggravating circumstances. This latter seems to be the more common view among the Scholastics, and is expressed by St. Thomas in these terms: " To confess all circumstances is impossible, yet there are some which it is necessary to confess: but in this matter there is a difference of opinion. Some hold that all circumstances which add notably to the gravity of sin must be confessed, if they occur to the mind of the penitent. Others contend that it is not necessary to confess the circumstances of sins committed, except when they are such as to change one sin into another; and this is the more probable opinion: but it must be added, that even then confession of the circumstances is necessary only when the second sin is also mortal. And the reason of this is, that there is no obligation of confessing venial sins, but such only as are mortal." [96]

Sacramental confession can be made only to priests who have jurisdiction over the penitent: for they alone can absolve from sin. But merely as an act of virtue, one may confess his sins to any one, lay or cleric, from whom it is reasonable to expect advice or the help of prayer. And in case of necessity this is very advisable, although the obligation of afterwards confessing to a priest still remains.[97]

On the part of the priest, confession induces the obligation

[94] Suppl. q. 6, a. 3.
[95] In Sent. IV, d. 17, p. 3, a. 2, q. 2.
[96] Ibid. d. 16, q. 3, a. 2, quaestiunc. 5.
[97] Cfr. Bonavent. op. cit. d. 17, p. 3, a. 1, q. 1, 2; Thomas, Suppl. q. 8, a. 2–6.

of the *sigillum* or seal of secrecy.[98] This extends itself directly only to the sins that have been confessed, but indirectly also to other things, the revelation of which would be to the detriment of the penitent or bring odium upon the sacrament.[99]

The last requisite on the part of the penitent is satisfaction. The purpose of satisfaction is partly to satisfy the justice of God for the debt of temporal punishment that may still be due after the guilt of sin has been blotted out, and partly to be of spiritual benefit to the penitent himself. Under this latter aspect it is intended both as a medicine against past sins and as a preservative against future falls.[100] The general concept of satisfaction, as found in the works of the Scholastics, is thus presented by Duns Scotus: *Operatio laboriosa vel poenalis voluntarie assumpta ad puniendum peccatum commissum a se et hoc ad placandam divinam offensam.*[101] However, the two terms, *poenalis* and *voluntarie,* are taken in a rather wide sense, as it is commonly admitted that any good work and inevitable afflictions may serve the purpose of satisfaction.[102]

The different kinds of satisfactory works are commonly reduced to these three: alms-giving, fasting, and prayer. St. Thomas shows their appropriateness in this way: " Satisfaction ought to be such that through it we deprive ourselves of something for the honor of God. Now we have only three kinds of goods, namely, goods of the soul, goods of the body, and goods of fortune, that is, external goods. We deprive ourselves of the goods of fortune by alms-giving, and of the goods of the body by fasting; yet of the goods of the soul we ought not to deprive ourselves of anything in regard to their essence, so that they are thereby diminished, for it is through them that we are acceptable to God; but in this way, that we submit them entirely to God; and this we do through prayer." [103]

In connection with the sacrament of penance, the Scholastics

[98] Cfr. Thomas, op. cit. q. 11, a. 1–5.
[99] Ibid.
[100] Ibid. q. 12, a. 3.
[101] In Sent. IV, d. 15, q. 1, n. 11.
[102] Cfr. Thomas, op. cit. q. 15, a. 1, 2.
[103] Ibid. a. 3.

also treat of ecclesiastical censures, as the inflicting of them implies the power of the keys *in foro externo*. The subject does not properly belong to the history of dogmas, except in so far as the power of the Church to inflict censures comes in question. And on this point there was no difference of opinion in the Middle Ages.[104]

[104] Cfr. Thomas, op. cit. q. 21, 22.

CHAPTER XXI

INDULGENCES

HISTORICAL DEVELOPMENT: THEOLOGICAL EXPOSITION

It was the common teaching of the Scholastics, as it had been of the Fathers before them, that the remission of sin does not necessarily include the remission of all punishment due to sin. In this matter they distinguished between eternal and temporal punishment. Eternal punishment as such, they said, does not remain when the guilt of mortal sin is blotted out: it is either commuted into temporal punishment, as some contended; or it is simply canceled, as others taught. But of the temporal punishment, either resulting from commutation or due for other reasons, a part usually remains, which must be expiated by works of penance. It is the removal of this punishment, which remains after sin itself has been remitted, that forms the end and object of indulgences. Hence an indulgence essentially consists in the remission of temporal punishment due to sin, after the guilt of sin has been forgiven, either through an act of contrition or the sacrament of penance.

As will be pointed out farther on in this chapter, the remission of temporal punishment, as gained by means of an indulgence, is not directly due to the works of penance a person may perform; nor, on the other hand, is it purely the effect of absolution pronounced by competent ecclesiastical authority. It is effected by an authoritative substitution of the satisfactory merit of Christ or His saints, made dependent for its efficacy on the fulfillment of certain conditions. When there is question of indulgences for the living, these conditions must be complied with by the beneficiary himself; when indulgences are applicable to the dead, there is required a vicarious fulfillment of the conditions laid down. These conditions always consist in the performance of some work of piety, either by way of prayer, penance or alms-deed. In regard to indulgences as thus understood, two points come up for consideration: the historical development of the doctrine, and its theological exposition. Both may be briefly outlined as follows.

A — Historical Development

Most Protestant writers, when referring to indulgences, date both doctrine and practice from the early Middle Ages. In Patristic times, they say, indulgences were unknown. It was only when the faithful had lost their fervor, and could no longer be induced to perform the severe penances imposed for certain sins, that recourse was had to the expedient of redemptions and commutations; and from these, towards the middle of the twelfth century, developed that ill-begotten progeny of sloth and covetousness which found a place in later Catholic theology under the name of indulgence. In their view, consequently, an indulgence is a purely human invention; an invention, moreover, that is evil in root and branch.[1]

Passing by for the present the moral aspect of the doctrine in question, we shall in this section trace its origin and development, in so far as that is possible, by making a critical use of the historic data at our disposal. And for this purpose we shall divide the centuries to be considered into several periods of time, so that it may appear at a glance what development or change there was as the one passed into the other. The division commonly adopted, and the one that seems most reasonable, is the following. First period: from the first century to the seventh. Second period: from the seventh century to the twelfth. Third period: from the twelfth century to the Council of Trent, in the sixteenth. After that the question is of no further historical interest, because the doctrine had reached its full development.

[1] Cfr. *Lea, A History of Auricular Confession and Indulgences, vol. III; *Brieger, Das Wesen des Ablasses am Ausgange des Mittelalters.

1. *From the First Century to the Seventh.*— This period, as will be noted, embraces practically the whole Patristic age. During all these centuries, we are told, indulgences were unknown. In one sense this statement is true; in another it is false. Indulgences were unknown as general ecclesiastical grants in favor of all who cared to comply with certain fixed conditions for obtaining the remission of temporal punishment due to sin; but they were quite well known as particular grants in favor of individuals who for one reason or another appeared deserving of leniency in the matter of penance. By the beginning of the third century it was a well established custom to remit part of the imposed canonical penance at the instance of those who had suffered for the faith. In these cases it was the bishop who granted the remission, but in consideration of the intercession and sufferings of some particular member of the Church. And the remission thus granted was believed to be valid before God, so that the temporal punishment due to sin was canceled. To this belief St. Cyprian, among many others, bears witness. " Those," he says, " who have received the benefit of a martyr's intercession, are thereby enabled to satisfy the justice of God." [2]

Now, if we look only to what is essential in the matter of indulgences, namely, the authoritative substitution of the satisfactory merit of Christ or His saints, we have here an indulgence in the strict sense of the term. It was the satisfactory merit of the martyr, substituted by the authority of the bishop for the canonical penance still to be performed, that was believed to satisfy the justice of God and thereby cancel the temporal punishment due to sin. Whether that belief was well founded has for the present nothing to do with the case. The only point at issue now is the historical fact that indulgences were known and granted in the primitive Church. And from what has been said, that point appears to be beyond reasonable doubt.

Nor is this the only form of indulgence we meet with in the early centuries. More than one council acknowledged the

[2] Ep. 18 (H 2, 523 sq.) ; cfr. Tertul. Ad Martyr. c. 1; ML, 1, 621.

right of bishops to shorten the time of canonical penance for any reasonable cause, and thereby show mercy to well disposed penitents.[3] Yet any one who is familiar with the spirit that guided the primitive Church in her dealing with penitents, or with her valuation of things temporal and eternal, must understand that this "mercy" was not supposed to consist in a mere relaxation of canonical penance as such; but in a remission of punishment before God. Neither councils nor bishops considered it a "mercy" to be spared suffering in this world and to be made liable to it in the world to come. On the contrary, the chief reason why such severe penances were enjoined was the well founded hope of thereby saving penitents from the necessity of enduring much greater sufferings after death. And hence dispensation from these penances, without a corresponding remission of punishment, would have been the very opposite of "mercy."

In this sense, therefore, it is historically certain that indulgences were as well known in the early ages of the Church as they are to-day. Perhaps they were not as freely granted as they are now, but that is not to the point. The doctrine that the Church has power to grant indulgences was firmly established in Patristic times. It was not invented by theological speculation during the Middle Ages, but it is an heirloom of Apostolic preaching faithfully transmitted by the primitive Church.[4]

2. *From the Seventh Century to the Twelfth.*— During this second period indulgences appear mostly in the form of commutations and redemptions. And in so far the statement of Protestant writers, as noted above, is true to facts. Penances as then imposed were almost as severe as those that had been in use during the early centuries of the Church. In fact, when there was question of public penance, they were substantially the same. They went by the name of canonical penance, because they were in conformity with the canons or rules established in past ages. Yet under the changed con-

---

[3] Cfr. Conc. Ancyr. can. 2, 5; Conc. Nicaen. can. 12; Conc. Arelat. I, can. 12.

[4] Cfr. Hefele, Conciliengeschichte, I, 226, 415.

ditions of society, and partly also because there was a lack of fervor on the part of penitents, it was not always feasible to exact the rigorous performance of penances thus imposed. Hence, when in individual cases there appeared sufficient reason for so doing, these penances were commuted or changed into others of a less burdensome nature or of shorter duration. Sometimes the penance thus substituted consisted in prayers to be recited or some good work to be performed; at other times in the payment of a certain sum of money to be used for a religious or charitable purpose. In the first case we have what is technically called a commutation; in the second, what is technically known as a redemption.

This practice seems to have originated in Ireland, where it existed as early as the seventh century. Thus the *Canones Hibernenses,* dating from about that time, recognize the established custom of changing long fasts and other severe penances into the singing of psalms or good works more in keeping with the strength of the penitent.[5] A little later the same practice appears among the Franks. In some places the custom crept in of allowing the penitent to hire a person who would perform the imposed penance in his stead. Thus the *Poenitentiale Cummeani* contains the following direction: " If a penitent does not know the psalms or is unable to fast, let him choose some pious person who is willing to perform the penance enjoined, and for this let him pay an equivalent either in money or labor." [6] However, this was generally looked upon as an abuse, and hence in the *Poenitentiale Merseburgense* we read: " If any one has received payment for fasting, in case he did it through ignorance, let him fast so long for himself as he promised the other, and let him give to the poor what he received for his promise. Furthermore, whosoever thus takes the sins of another upon himself, is not a true Christian." [7]

Commutations to the payment of money for some charitable purpose came into vogue about the same time. Thus in the

[5] Op. cit. II; cfr. Wasserschleben, p. 139.

[6] Op. cit. Prolog.; cfr. Wasserschleben, p. 463.

[7] Op. cit. 44.

Pseudo-Beda, a *Poenitentiale* that dates from the beginning of the eighth century we read: " If perhaps some one is not able to fast, let him pay a redemption if able to do so. If he be rich, let him pay twenty solidi instead of fasting for seven weeks. But if he has not sufficient means, let him give ten solidi; and if he is very poor, let him give three. . . . At the same time, let each one well understand for what purpose he must make his contribution; whether it is to be given for the redemption of captives, or for the sanctuary, or for the poor of Christ." [8]   That this practice was open to abuse is quite obvious, and hence it was at times strongly opposed by theologians. In fact, the Council of Chalons, held in 813, stigmatized some of these penitential manuals as utterly untrustworthy, " filled with errors concocted by unknown authors — *quorum sunt certi errores et incerti auctores.*" [9]

On the other hand, it had the support of men of undoubted learning and approved sanctity. Thus St. Peter Damian, about the middle of the eleventh century, laid down the principle that relaxation of penance might be conceded in proportion to the alms given by the penitent. He says: *Cum a poenitentibus terras accipimus, juxta mensuram muneris eis de quantitate poenitentiae relaxamus.*[10] And a provincial council held in 895 gives the following rule to be adhered to in the reconciliation of those who have committed murder. The penance to be imposed on such a person is to last for seven years. During all this time he remains excluded from divine service; but already during the first year of his penance, if on a journey or sick, he can be dispensed from fasting on Tuesdays, Thursdays, and Saturdays. However, instead of fasting he must give each day one-twelfth of a solidus by way of alms. During the second and third year he is, on the days mentioned, entitled to a redemption without further condition. Finally, from the fourth to the seventh year included, he is obliged to keep every year three lents of forty days each; but at other times he is dispensed from fasting

[8] Op. cit. c. 41.
[9] Conc. cit. can. 38; Mansi, 14, 101.

[10] Ep. 12, ML, 144, 323 C.

on Tuesdays, Thursdays, and Saturdays, while on Mondays and Wednesdays he is entitled to a redemption.[11]

When this remission of penance by way of commutation and redemption became general, indulgences as at present understood had come into existence.   For the substituted work was understood to be effective in removing the punishment still due to sin, and therefore it was not merely a relaxation of canonical penance.   At the same time there was no longer question of particular grants to individual penitents, as had been the case in Patristic times and also in the seventh and eighth centuries; but certain conditions were put down on the fulfillment of which penitents, otherwise disposed, gained either a partial or a full remission of whatever temporal punishment might still remain after they had duly confessed their sins.   In this we have not only the essential requisites of an indulgence as understood to-day, but also its outward form.

At what precise time this last development took place is not certain.   The ruling of Tribur, referred to in a preceding paragraph, indicates the transition.   It is general, but only in regard to one class of penitents.   About a century later the development seems to have been accomplished.   For in an old document, bearing the signature of Archbishop Pontius of Arles (995–1030) and of his successor Raimbaldus, we meet with an indulgence in its modern form.   It is granted to all those who visit the monastery of Mons Major and there contribute an alms for the erection of a church.   The grant reads as follows: " If a penitent comes to the aforesaid church, on the day of its dedication or once a year, and there holds vigil and gives an alms to promote the building of the Church of Holy Mary, which is now in course of construction, . . . let him be absolved from a third part of the penance imposed on him for the greater sins: and this remission is to be reckoned from the very day on which he holds his vigil to the same day the next year. . . . Then, in the case of those who have confessed less grievous sins and received penance for the

[11] Conc. Tribur. c. 56–58; Mansi, 18, 157.

same, if they come to the dedication, . . . we absolve them
from one half of the penance received." [12]

A few years later indulgences of this kind began to multiply.
They were usually granted by bishops for the building of
churches or monasteries, or for the promotion of similar pious
works. They were all partial indulgences, and the alms was
supposed to bear some proportion to the means of the giver —
tale sit, quatenus possunt.[13] However, a plenary indulgence
was granted by Pope Alexander II, in 1063, to all Christians
who would take up arms against the Saracens in Spain. The
grant reads: " We release them from their penance and concede them the remission of their sins — *Poenitentiam eis
levamus et remissionem peccatorum facimus.*"[14] In 1095
Urban II granted similar indulgences to the Crusaders;[15] and
a century later, Innocent III extended the privilege of gaining
these indulgences to all those who in any way contributed to
the recovery of the Holy Land.[16]

3. *From the Twelfth Century to the Council of Trent.*—
During the twelfth century the practice of granting indulgences increased very rapidly. But this was owing almost entirely to the action of individual bishops; for the Holy See,
as even Protestant writers admit, constantly exercised a re-
straining influence in this matter.[17] The reason for the stand
thus taken by the Sovereign Pontiffs was the fear that by an
undue multiplication of indulgences the Church's penitential
discipline would be relaxed. This is clearly stated by the
Fourth Lateran Council, held under Innocent III. The
practice, it says, is to be restricted, " because by the granting
of indiscreet and superfluous indulgences . . . the keys of the
Church are brought into contempt and sacramental satisfaction loses its force."[18] And in accordance with this, the
Council enacted the following law: " When a church is dedi-
cated, the indulgence granted must not exceed one year,

[12] D'Archery, Spicilegium, VI,
427 sq.
[13] Ibid. 428.
[14] Cfr. Loofs, Dogmengeschichte,
p. 494. The expression, *remission-*

em peccatorum, will be explained
farther on.
[15] Mansi, 20, 816 E.
[16] Mansi, 22, 1067 D.
[17] Cfr. Brieger, Realencyk. 9, 79.
[18] Mansi, 22, 1050.

whether one bishop be present at the dedication or several; and the indulgence granted on the anniversary of the dedication must not exceed forty days of the penance that had been enjoined." [19] Besides, forty days is to be the limit for all indulgences that may be granted by a bishop on other special occasions. [20]

The first Jubilee was published by Boniface VIII in 1300. It was a plenary indulgence which could be gained by all those who visited Rome in the course of that year, and during fifteen days performed their devotions in the Basilicas of the Apostles. The Jubilee itself was termed " the year of full remission and of the reconciliation of the human race — *annus plenariae remissionis et reconciliationis humani generis.*" This indulgence was at first intended to be repeated only once every hundred years, but Clement VI reduced the term to fifty years, Urban VI to thirty-three, and Paul II to twenty-five years. Since the fifteenth century the Jubilee indulgence may be gained even without a visit to Rome, but usually a year after it has been proclaimed in Rome itself.

In this connection a word must be said about the expression, " a plenary indulgence of punishment and guilt "— *indulgentia plena a poena et culpa* — which occurs in some Papal documents. The phrase, as it stands, is ambiguous, and it has proved a stumbling block to both Catholics and Protestants. Some of the former, when brought face to face with it refused to believe that it was authentic. This position was taken by Maronis, a Scholastic who wrote at the beginning of the fourteenth century. " Such an indulgence," he says, " never was granted by the Holy See, nor ought it to be taught as legitimate." [21] He had many followers, and among them Cardinal Cusa, who held that the expression was simply an interpolation introduced by some irresponsible indulgence preacher. Protestants, on the other hand, eagerly seized upon it as an irrefutable piece of evidence that the Popes were carrying on a most shameless traffic in pardons for sins. [22]

Although there is perhaps no direct proof for the genuine-

[19] Ibid. can. 62.
[20] Loc. cit.

[21] In IV Sent. d. 19, q. 3.
[22] Cfr. Brieger, RE, 9, 84 sqq.

ness of the phrase as it stands, still its equivalents occur again and again, and that in connections which exclude all suspicion of interpolation. Thus in the Bull of Martin V, *Inter cunctas,* is found the expression, " indulgences for the forgiveness of sin "— *indulgentias in remissionem peccatorum.*[23] It is true, the meaning is clear enough from the context: because one of the conditions required for the gaining of such indulgences, as is there stated, consists in contrite confession; but the ambiguous expression is certainly genuine. And so it is admitted to be in other Bulls, even where the meaning is not so clear. However, it was never used in the sense ascribed to it by Protestant writers, namely, that the indulgence itself was supposed to effect the forgiveness of sin. And this is now commonly admitted by those who have studied the documents in question at first hand.[24]

A very clear explanation of this whole matter is given by John of Palts, who preached the Jubilee under Alexander VI. He was a fellow religious of Luther, and his exposition is accepted as correct even by Brieger, a most rabid and bigoted Protestant writer on the question of indulgences. " Properly speaking," writes Palts, " in virtue of an indulgence no one is ever absolved from punishment and guilt, but from punishment only. However, it is commonly said that during the Jubilee one is absolved from both — *a poena et culpa.* And that saying is true, because a Jubilee is more than a mere indulgence; it includes authority to confess and absolve and together with this the power to remit punishment by way of indulgence. In this way it includes the sacrament of penance and together with it an indulgence properly so called. For the clearer understanding of the aforesaid, it must be noted that the term indulgence may be taken in one of two ways. In one way, in so far as it properly signifies the mere remission of punishment, and in this sense it does not imply the remission of guilt; and in another way, in as much as in a wider sense it stands for the Jubilee, or for the letter including the Jubilee, and then it extends itself to the remission

[23] Mansi, 27, 1211 B; DB, 676.   [24] Cfr. Brieger, loc. cit.

of sin. And the reason is that usually when the Pope grants
a Jubilee, he does not concede a simple indulgence, but also
the faculty of confessing and absolving from all sins. And
in this way the guilt is taken away by the sacrament of penance,
which there intervenes; while the punishment is canceled by
the indulgence, which is there granted." [25]

That indulgences may also be applied to the dead, simply
by way of help, without the exercise of ecclesiastical jurisdiction in the strict sense of the term, seems to have been commonly held by mediæval theologians. But, as far as can now
be ascertained, the first authoritative reference to this matter
occurred only in the fifteenth century. Then Pope Sixtus IV
granted an indulgence that could be applied to the souls in
purgatory. On that occasion he used the expression " by way
of help "— *per modum suffragii* — which seems to have caused
a great deal of discussion as to its precise meaning. Hence
a few years later, in 1477, he published a Bull in which the
term was explained. He says that he makes use of the
treasure of the Church, which consists of the merits of Christ
and the saints, and this is of benefit to the poor souls if applied to them by those who fulfill the conditions on which
the indulgence is granted. *Per modum suffragii,* therefore,
means that the indulgence is offered as a help; it is not a canceling of the temporal punishment by an act of jurisdiction. [26]

This may be said to complete the development of the doctrine on indulgences. And if we now gather together what
has been brought out more or less clearly in the preceding
paragraphs, we come to the following result. 1. In the early
centuries the substance of the doctrine was well known, but
it was presented under a different form. An indulgence then
consisted in a relaxation of canonical penance, which was
believed to be valid before God, and in that sense to remit
temporal punishment due to sin. This relaxation was always
a matter of individual concession. 2. From the seventh century forward, simple relaxation gave place to commutation

[25] Quoted by Brieger, op. cit. 88.   [26] Ibid. 92.

and redemption. This transition implied no change of principle, but only a variation of form. The difference between the severer penance first imposed and the lighter into which it was changed, corresponded to the relaxation of earlier times. Here, too, the application was to individuals. 3. During the first half of the eleventh century there was a further transition from individual to general concessions, so that any penitent might shorten his penance by the fulfillment of certain fixed conditions. In this transition the modern form of indulgences first appeared.

As regards indulgences under this new form, these further points may be noted. 1. Like the commutations and redemptions, the earliest indulgences of this kind were episcopal, and were granted to those who visited a certain church, either on the day of its dedication or at some other fixed time, and there made an offering for some pious purpose. 2. Originally they were all partial indulgences, one-half, or one-third, or one-fourth of the imposed penance being remitted. 3. During the eleventh century there was as yet no technical term for these indulgences. 4. Up to the twelfth century they affected ecclesiastical life very little; but after that they seem to have seriously interfered with the spirit of penance, so that the Popes found it advisable to restrict the power of the bishops in the matter of granting indulgences. 5. Plenary indulgences were usually granted by the Pope, and as a general rule but sparingly. 6. It was never taught by those in authority that an indulgence, in the proper sense of the term, was equivalent to a remission of sin.

B — THEOLOGICAL EXPOSITION

Indulgences had practically no place in theology until the first half of the thirteenth century. Theologians accepted the fact of commutations and redemptions as explained in the preceding section, but seldom stopped to speculate concerning their precise nature. Even Peter Lombard passes them by with the vague remark that the prayers and alms of friends may be

accepted as a vicarious penance in the case of the dying.[27]
The first one to attempt anything like a theological exposition
of indulgences was Alexander of Hales.[28] He was followed
by St. Bonaventure and St. Thomas. The former of these
two copied him almost word for word, while the latter took
the substance of his teaching and presented it in his own way.
Even later Scholastics added little of their own, so that our
present theology of indulgences is little more than the teaching of Alexander arrayed in a modern garb.

The first question which he proposes to himself is, whether
indulgences or relaxations really remit temporal punishment
due to sin. He answers that there are two opinions concerning this matter. The first holds that indulgences are simply a
relaxation of the penance imposed by the Church, and that
therefore they are valid only in her forum and not in the forum
of God — *in foro Ecclesiae, non in foro Dei.* This view he
rejects as altogether untenable. And the reason is that the
universal Church has always taught the contrary; yet the universal Church cannot fall into error concerning matters of this
kind. Nor is there any doubt as regards the teaching of the
Church; because when the Apostle said, " what I have pardoned that Christ also hath pardoned," he referred also to
the remission of punishment by way of indulgence; and the
power of the Sovereign Pontiff is not less than that of the
Apostle. Moreover, as bishops share in the power of the
Church, it must be admitted that relaxations granted by them
are also valid before God.[29]

Then, in the body of the article, he explains how indulgences
may be granted without in any way failing to satisfy the demands of divine justice. Because, aside from the personal
satisfaction of the penitent, there is the satisfactory merit of
Christ and of the Church; and this is offered to God when a
relaxation of penance is conceded.[29a] Hence the penitent
really satisfies for his sins, but he does so by drawing on the
treasury of the Church.[30]

[27] Sent. IV, d. 20, c. 4.
[28] Sum. IV, q. 83.
[29] Ibid. m. I, a. I ad I[m].

[29a] Loc. cit.
[30] Ibid. a. I ad 4[m].

In connection with the foregoing, the author inquires whether one person can satisfy divine justice in place of another. He answers with a distinction. Sometimes, he says, penance is imposed by way of medicine; and then, of course, the penitent is bound to perform it in person. At other times it is enjoined as a compensation for the injury done to God by sin; and in that case it may be performed by some one else. For the Church is the mystical body of Christ, in which the members are all intimately united and mutually helpful the one to the other. However, this vicarious satisfaction is not a matter of individual choice; it is of value only when approved by lawful superiors. Moreover, in authorizing it, superiors must have due regard to the disposition of the penitent and the amount of penance that is to be imposed upon his substitute. On the part of the penitent there must be real need of this substitution; and then as regards the amount of penance, it must be borne in mind that vicarious penance is less efficacious than that performed by the penitent in person, and therefore it ought to be more severe in order to give the same satisfaction to divine justice.[31]

Touching the question of authority in the matter of granting indulgences, he teaches that it belongs exclusively to bishops and the Pope; so that neither priests nor prelates of the lower grades, such as priors and abbots, have any jurisdiction in this respect. And the reason is that indulgences are nothing else than an application of the supererogatory satisfaction of Christ and His saints. This satisfaction constitutes the spiritual treasury of the Church, which can only be at the disposal of those through whom the Church is espoused to Christ. It is through the Pope and the bishops that children are begotten unto Christ the Redeemer, and hence it is their exclusive right to dispose of the Church's spiritual treasures in favor of these same children.[32] Furthermore, the plenitude of this right and power is found only in the Sovereign Pontiff; because to him is entrusted the welfare of the whole Church, and therefore all others in a position of

[31] Ibid. a. 2.   [32] Ibid. m. 3.

authority depend for the exercise of their jurisdiction on his will and direction.[33]

The conditions on which the gaining of indulgences is made to depend, although they may be of various kinds, ought in some way to be connected with sacrifices in the material order. For, first of all, this follows from the usage established in the Church; in as much as indulgences are commonly granted on the condition that alms be given, pilgrimages be made, and visits be paid to churches and shrines. In the next place, indulgences are a relaxation of the penance that should be performed after the guilt of the sin has been forgiven; but this penance is always some exterior work, such as fasting, mortification, and so forth; consequently the conditions on which indulgences are granted should also be something exterior, or some sacrifice in the material order. Of this kind are alms for the building and beautifying of churches, taking part in the deliverance of the Holy Land, fasting, bodily austerities, and pilgrimages.[34]

Furthermore, other conditions are required, both on the part of the person who wishes to gain an indulgence and on the part of him who grants it. The former must be in the state of grace, believe in the efficacy of indulgences, and perform the prescribed works in a spirit of devotion. The latter must have a sufficient reason for disposing of the satisfactory merits that are in the spiritual treasury of the Church. Such a justifying reason is found, for instance, in the need there is of promoting works of piety. But in all cases there must be due proportion between the value of the indulgence granted and the difficulty of the conditions enjoined.[35] Finally, if there be a sufficiently grave reason, the Pope may grant a plenary indulgence, which cancels all temporal punishment due to sin.[36]

Indulgences may also be applied to the souls in purgatory, because the Sovereign Pontiff has the right to dispose of the spiritual treasure of the Church in favor of all who need it and who are in a condition to benefit by his liberality.

[33] Ibid. ad 2m.
[34] Ibid. m. 4.
[35] Ibid. m. 5.
[36] Ibid. m. 6.

Now when the poor souls departed this life, they were in communion with the Church, and they still are her children although suffering in another world. Hence they are in a condition to be helped by her in their present need. However, as they are no longer under the Pope's jurisdiction, he cannot grant them an indulgence by way of a judiciary sentence; but only by way of help and impetration — *per modum suffragii et impetrationis.*[37] It must be noted, therefore, that in regard to this one point alone — the manner of application — does an indulgence for the dead differ from that for the living.

St. Bonaventure, as noted above, made the teaching of Alexander his own. He insists very strongly that indulgences are valid before God, because if they were not, the Church's action in granting them would not be merciful but cruel, and she would make herself guilty of deceiving those whom she was commissioned by Christ to guide in the way of truth.[38] When speaking of indulgences for the dead, he is inclined to favor the opinion of those who hold that in granting them the Pope uses his judiciary power.[39] In this view he differed from his master.

Albertus Magnus adds nothing to the exposition given by Alexander. He calls attention to the following two definitions of indulgences given by contemporary theologians: *Magistri definiunt relaxationem sic: Est satisfactionis majoris in minorem competens et discreta commutatio. Alii sic: Relaxatio est poenae temporalis debitae promissa diminutio.*[40] This latter, he holds, is the more proper of the two; and so did many before his time, although the matter had been but little discussed in a speculative way.

St. Thomas puts the teaching of Alexander in a somewhat different form, but agrees with it on nearly every point. In his first article he shows that indulgences are not merely a relaxation of canonical penance, but are valid for the remission of temporal punishment due to sin. And this remis-

---

[37] Ibid. m. 5.
[38] In Sent. IV, d. 20, p. 2, a. unic. q. 2.
[39] Ibid. q. 5, concl. 4.
[40] In Sent. IV, d. 20, a. 16.

sion holds good for the dead as well as for the living. After calling attention to the fact that an indulgence can be gained only when the guilt of sin has been remitted, either by an act of contrition or in the sacrament of penance, he points out the reason why indulgences are effective in remitting temporal punishment. The chief reason, he says, is the unity of the mystical body of Christ, many members of which have gathered more satisfactory merits than they need for themselves, and to that body also belong the merits of Christ. Now, as one person may satisfy for another, it stands to reason that those who have need thereof may be benefited by this supererogatory merit. However, as neither the saints nor Christ made over their satisfactory merits to individual persons, but left them as a spiritual treasure to the Church, it is only the head of the Church who can dispose of them by reason of the authority received from Christ to this effect. This is in perfect accord with the practice of every other society of men. Community goods are distributed to individuals by the head of the community. Hence, just as one would obtain the remission of punishment if some one else were to satisfy the justice of God in his place, so does he obtain the same remission if the satisfaction of some one else is distributed to him by one who has authority to that effect.[41]

Hence an indulgence, even in case of the living, is not a simple act of absolution from the liability to punishment; but it is an authoritative substitution of one satisfaction for another. By a judiciary sentence, the penitent receives a designated amount of the spiritual treasure of the Church, and therewith he pays to that extent his indebtedness to God.[42] In itself every indulgence is of such value as is determined by the person who has authority to grant it, and in this sense it is independent of the disposition of the recipient. But, on the other hand, unless the recipient is united to Christ by charity, he does not fulfill the conditions required for the gaining of an indulgence; hence in so far the efficacy of the indulgence depends on his disposition. St. Thomas sums up

---

[41] Suppl. q. 25, a. 1.   [42] Ibid. a. 1 ad 1m et 2m.

this point as follows: "It must he held that the value of indulgences is that which is stated in their promulgation, provided, of course, the one who grants them has due authority and the one who receives them is endued with charity and the object of their granting is some pious cause, which embraces God's honor and the neighbor's advantage." [43]

The authority to grant indulgences resides in those who are entrusted with the government of the Church, that is, the bishops and the Pope. However, the Pope alone can make use of this authority as may seem good to him; while the power of the bishops in the matter of indulgences is limited by his ordinations.[44] The *pietas causae* is sufficiently verified if the end ultimately intended is of a spiritual nature; hence anything temporal may be included among the conditions on which an indulgence is granted, provided it be directed to a spiritual end.[45] If the conditions are not complied with, the indulgence is not gained; even if the want of compliance was the result of an oversight or of inability.[46]

Duns Scotus gives a similar exposition of the doctrine on indulgences. His teaching is neatly summed up in the following definition: "An indulgence is the remission of the temporal punishment due to the actual sins of the repentant and left standing after sacramental absolution, a remission granted for reasonable cause by ecclesiastical prelates out of the Church's treasury, that is, the merits of Christ and the saints.[47]

Nearly all the chief points brought out in the foregoing paragraphs were embodied by Clement VI in the Jubilee Bull of 1343. After explaining the meaning of the spiritual treasury of the Church, he proceeds: " (Christ), indeed, founded this treasury that it might be dispensed to the faithful unto their salvation through the offices of St. Peter, the key-bearer of heaven, and of his successors, Christ's vicars upon earth, always for proper and reasonable cause, now for the complete and now for the partial remission of the tem-

[43] Ibid. a. 2.
[44] Ibid. q. 26, a. 1–3.
[45] Ibid. q. 25, a. 3.

[46] Ibid. q. 27, a. 3.
[47] Quaest. Miscellan. q. 4, n. 4.

poral punishment due to sins — a treasury to be devoted mercifully in general as well as for particular occasion, as under God they deem expedient, to those who are truly contrite of heart and have confessed their sins." [48]

[48] Cfr. DB. 550–552.

CHAPTER XXII

HOLY ORDERS: EXTREME UNCTION: MATRIMONY

Concerning the last three sacraments of the New Law only a few remarks need be made in the present connection. Holy orders and extreme unction are treated rather briefly by the Scholastics themselves, and although a great deal is said by them about matrimony, still that is mostly in regard to impediments, with which we are not directly concerned in the history of dogmas. Hence the following brief outline of Scholastic teaching on the three sacraments now under consideration will suffice for our purpose.

A — HOLY ORDERS

A neat summary of what is to be held in regard to holy orders is thus given by St. Bonaventure in his *Breviloquium:* " This, in brief, is the doctrine to be held concerning the sacrament of orders, that it is a sealing (or sign) by which spiritual power is imparted to the one ordained. Orders, though but one of the seven sacraments, comprises nevertheless seven grades. The first is that of door-keeper, the second that of lector, the third that of exorcist, the fourth that of acolyte, the fifth that of subdeacon, the sixth that of deacon, the seventh that of priest. Preparatory to these, on the one hand, the clerical tonsure is given and also the office of psalmist; on the other hand, they find their complement in the added grades of episcopacy, patriarchate, and papacy. By persons enjoying these latter dignities orders are conferred, and they must be dispensed with due attention to the external sacramental signs, both as regards the matter and the form, and the proper solemnity should be observed as to time, place, office, and person." [1]

The first part of this extract contains the definition of holy orders as commonly given by the Scholastics, and is taken from the *Sentences of the Lombard*.[2] Order, as a sacrament, is a certain seal or sign, by which spiritual power is imparted to him who is ordained. As St. Thomas explains it. " The term *signaculum* is here not meant to designate the interior character, but signifies the external rite, which is at once a sign and the cause of interior power; and thus it is understood in the given definition. However, if it were taken for the sacramental character, it would not imply any impropriety of speech. For the division of a sacrament into those three — *sacramentum tantum, res et sacramentum, res tantum* — is not, properly speaking, a division into integral parts. Because that which is the *res tantum* is not of the essence of a sacrament, and that which is the *sacramentum tantum* passes away, while that which is the *sacramentum et res* is said to remain. Hence it follows that the interior character itself is essentially and principally the very sacrament of orders." [3]

That the rite of ordination is a true sacrament, at least when there is question of the major orders, is directly inferred from the fact that it is an external sign instituted for the sanctification of the recipient. " In the reception of orders," says St. Thomas, " there is a certain consecration imparted to man by means of visible signs, and hence it is obvious that order is a sacrament." [4] And that the rite confers sanctifying grace he proves from the fact that the spiritual power is conferred by it, which necessarily implies the grace requisite for its proper use. " Hence just as in baptism, through which man becomes capable of receiving the other sacraments, sanctifying grace is conferred, so likewise in the sacrament of orders, by which man is ordained for the dispensation of other sacraments." [5]

The sacrament of orders is one, but there are several sacra-

---

[1] Op. cit. VI, c. 12.
[2] Sent. IV, d. 24, c. 10.
[3] Suppl. q. 34, a. 2 ad 1m.

[4] Suppl. q. 34, a. 3.
[5] Ibid. q. 35, a. 1.

mental rites of ordination, in each one of which the definition
of a sacrament is verified.[6]   The matter is thus explained by
St. Thomas, and substantially the same explanation is also
given by most other Scholastics.   " The division of orders,"
he says, " is not that of an integral into its parts, nor that of
a universal, but that of a potestative whole; and the nature
of it is this, that the whole according to its complete perfection is in one, and that in others there is a certain participation of the same.   And so it is here: the whole plenitude of
this sacrament is in one order, namely, in the priesthood; but
in the others there is a certain participation of the same order.
. . . And for this reason all the orders are one sacrament." [7]
Or as St. Bonaventure puts it: " All grades of the orders together constitute one sacrament, nevertheless to each grade the
term order is applied." [8]

Scotus, however, looks at the matter in a somewhat different light.[9]   He holds that the term order, as designating one
of the seven sacraments, is taken in a generic sense; and that
consequently the different grades are so many specifically distinct sacraments.[10]

The generic unity of these specifically different sacraments
is derived from the common end for which they were all
instituted, namely, the worthy celebration of the Eucharistic
rite.[11]

The Scholastics distinguish seven different orders, which are
divided into two groups and are respectively designated as
sacred and non-sacred; or major and minor, as they are known
to-day.   Various reasons are assigned by them why the
number of orders should be neither more nor less than seven.

[6] Ibid. Cfr. DB. 958.
[7] Suppl. q. 37, a. 1 ad 2[m].
[8] In Sent. IV, d. 24, p. 1, a. 2, q. 4.
[9] He first gives this general definition of orders: "Ordo est gra-
dus eminens in hierarchia ecclesiastica, disponens ad congrue exse-
quendum aliquem actum excellentem in Ecclesia." And by the
"actum excellentem" he understands any act intimately connected
with the consecration of the Holy
Eucharist (Report. IV, d. 24, n. 8).
[10] Then he adds: "Sacramentum
ordinis est unum genere, habens
sub se plures species, . . . quae
sunt diversae rationis et alterius
speciei, non tantum ejusdem rationis et speciei, et diversae numero"
(In Sent. IV, d. 24, n. 13).
[11] Ibid. n. 14.

St. Bonaventure enumerates and rejects three different views, and then proposes his own. The priest, he says, in whom the sacrament of orders is found in all its fullness, has two different spiritual powers: one over Christ's true body in the Holy Eucharist, and another over Christ's mystical body as composed of the faithful. In the exercise of each of these powers he needs assistants. In the consecration of Christ's true body he is assisted by the deacon and the subdeacon, who provide the matter for the consecration. Hence the orders of these two as well as that of the priest, because of their close connection with the Holy Eucharist, are termed sacred orders. Then in the exercise of his power over the mystical body of Christ, the priest is assisted by the ostiarius, who admits the faithful to the place of worship; by the lector, who reads to them the sacred text; by the exorcist, who gives them aid against the inroads of the devil; by the acolytes, who edify the faithful by their good example as typified by the burning candles which they carry. All this is likewise referred to the Holy Eucharist, but only distantly, and hence the orders in question are called non-sacred.[12] The exposition given by St. Thomas differs somewhat in regard to the minor orders, but is based upon the same fundamental idea that the division of orders was made in reference to the Holy Eucharist.[13]

In this connection the question arises, whether all seven orders are to be regarded as sacraments, in the sense explained in a preceding paragraph. The Scholastics usually put the question in this form: Does each one of the seven orders imprint a sacramental character? In this they seem to take for granted that all are sacraments, so that the only question open for discussion is, whether in each ordination a character is imprinted. And nearly all of them give an affirmative answer, holding that this is to be considered as the more probable view. Durandus, however, contends that the priesthood alone is a true sacrament; all other orders must be considered as sacramentals.[14]

St. Thomas presents the more common view in these terms:

[12] In Sent. IV, d. 24, p. 2, a. 2, q. 4.

[13] Suppl. q. 37, a. 2.

[14] In Sent. IV, d. 24, q. 1, n. 9.

"Some there are who say that in the priesthood alone is a sacramental character imprinted; but this is not true, because no one except a deacon can licitly discharge the duties connected with that office, and thus it is quite manifest that he has a spiritual power in regard to the dispensation of the sacraments which others do not have. And for this reason others say that all the sacred orders imprint a character, but not so the minor orders. Yet this again is not to the point; because every order places the recipient above the laity in some grade of power respecting the dispensation of the sacraments. Hence, as the character is a sign whereby the recipient is distinguished from others, it follows that in all the orders a character is imprinted. And a further sign of this is the fact that these orders always remain, and are never repeated. This is the third opinion, which is more common." [15]

Of course, as all true sacraments of the New Law have been instituted by Christ, it follows from this " third opinion " that the minor orders were also instituted by Him. And so these authors commonly maintain. There is indeed the historical difficulty that the minor orders do not seem to have been in existence before the third century; but that is explained by saying that they were all contained in the diaconate. " In the primitive Church," says St. Thomas, " all the minor offices were entrusted to the deacons, because of the scarcity of ministers. . . . Nevertheless the aforesaid powers were all contained in the one power of the deacon. But later on divine worship developed more fully, and then the Church explicitly gave to different ministers the powers that were implicitly contained in one order." [16]

In this connection the question is also asked, whether the episcopate must be considered as a distinct order, and consequently as a true sacrament. Modern theologians answer the question in the affirmative, but in this they depart from the more common view of the Scholastics. With the exception of William of Auxerre,[17] Scotus,[18] and Durandus,[19]

---

[15] Suppl. q. 35, a. 2.
[16] Suppl. q. 37, a. 2 ad 2ᵐ.
[17] Sum. p. 5, tr. 8, q. 1.

[18] In Sent. IV, d. 24, q. unic. n. 5.
[19] Ibid. q. 6, n. 8.

practically all of them agree with St. Bonaventure, when he says: "The episcopate in so far as it implies the priesthood, is properly called an order; but as distinct from the priesthood, it signifies only a certain dignity or office connected with it, and is not properly an order, nor is a sacramental character imprinted by it, nor a new power given, but by it the power of the priesthood is amplified."[20] St. Thomas holds that the episcopate is a distinct order in respect of certain hierarchical powers over the mystical body of Christ, but not in respect of Christ's real body in reference to which orders constitute a true sacrament.[21]

Like all other sacraments of the New Law, that of holy orders is made up of matter and form. On this general fact all Scholastics are agreed; but there is a considerable difference of opinion as to what part of the ordination rite constitutes the sacrament of orders, and consequently as to precisely what part is the matter and what part is the form of the sacrament. Up to the ninth century, both the priesthood and the diaconate were conferred by the imposition of hands and an accompanying prayer, to which rite was later added the presentation of the chalice and paten.[22] Hence the early Scholastics, such as Hugh of St. Victor,[23] Peter Lombard,[24] and Innocent III,[25] commonly state that the power of orders is conferred by the imposition of hands and the prayer that accompanies it; while the fact of this power having been conferred is more distinctly expressed by the presentation of the chalice and paten. The same is taught by St. Bonaventure,[26] and as regards the diaconate also by Durandus.[27] These theologians, therefore, would regard the imposition of hands as the matter of the sacrament of orders, when conferred on the priest and the deacon, and the accompanying prayer as the form.

But towards the middle of the thirteenth century theological opinion in this respect began to undergo a change. The imposition of hands was indeed still regarded as being an in-

[20] Ibid. p. 2, a. 2, q. 3.
[21] Suppl. q. 40, a. 5.
[22] Cfr. Amalarius, De Eccl. Offic. II, c. 12; ML. 105, 1086.
[23] De Sacr. II, p. 3, c. 12.
[24] Sent. IV, d. 24, c. 9.
[25] De Sacro Altaris Myst. I, c. 9; ML. 217, 779.
[26] Op. cit. d. 24, p. 2, a. 1, q. 4.
[27] Ibid. q. 3, n. 6.

tegral part of the rite of ordination; but equal, if not greater, importance was attached to the tradition of the instruments — *traditio instrumentorum*. Hence, St. Thomas, although a contemporary of St. Bonaventure and on most other points agreeing with him in doctrine, refers only to the *traditio instrumentorum* when he explains the rite of ordination in respect to the different orders. After touching upon the relation of the sacrament of orders to the Holy Eucharist, he says in regard to the ordination of priests: *Et ideo cum ordinantur, accipiunt calicem cum vino, et patenam cum pane, accipientes potestatem conficiendi corpus et sanguinem Christi.* And then with reference to the deacon and subdeacon: *Et ideo accipiunt calicem de manu episcopi, sed vacuum, cum ordinantur.*[28] This *traditio instrumentorum* he regards as the matter of the sacrament of orders, while he considers the accompanying words, *Accipe* or *Accipite, etc.,* as the form.[29] By this rite alone is the character imprinted.[30]

This became practically the common view of the later Scholastics, and was embodied in the *Decretum pro Armenis,* issued by Pope Eugenius IV.[31] As to the doctrinal value of that decree, and also in regard to the intention of the Pope in issuing it, the opinion of theologians is divided; but they commonly agree that it was not intended as a definition in the strict sense of the term. The matter is too intricate to be dealt with here, nor is a discussion of it necessary for our purpose.

The valid reception of holy orders presupposes the baptismal character in the recipient,[32] but not necessarily that of confirmation; although it is unlawful to confer the sacrament on one who has not been confirmed.[33] Only a member of the male sex can be validly ordained.[34] For the licit reception of holy orders a certain definite age and adequate mental and moral fitness are required; but, excepting the episcopate, ordinations are valid even if conferred upon one who has not yet reached the age of discretion.[35]

[28] Suppl. q. 37, a. 2.
[29] Ibid. q. 34, a. 4.
[30] Ibid. q. 37, a. 5.
[31] DB. 701.

[32] Thomas, op. cit. q. 35, a. 3.
[33] Ibid. a. 4.
[34] Ibid. q. 39, a. 1.
[35] Ibid. a. 2-5.

The administration of the sacrament of orders belongs to the bishop; he alone has power to ordain priests and deacons, although simple priests may be delegated to confer minor orders.[36] The power to ordain is not lost either by heresy, simony, or any other crime.[37] Concerning this last point there was considerable discussion during the early Middle Ages, as was pointed out in a previous chapter; but during the twelfth century the matter was definitely settled by the decision of several councils.[38]

B — EXTREME UNCTION

All Scholastics definitely teach that extreme unction is a true sacrament of the New Law, but some call in question its immediate institution by Christ. Thus Hugh of St. Victor,[39] Peter Lombard,[40] Alexander of Hales,[41] and St. Bonaventure,[41a] expressly teach that extreme unction was instituted by the Holy Spirit through the Apostles. St. Thomas refutes the arguments advanced by these authors, and then states the more common view as follows: " For this reason others say that all the sacraments were instituted by Christ Himself; but some of them, because they presented greater difficulty to the belief of His followers, He also promulgated; while others, such as extreme unction and confirmation, He reserved for the Apostles to promulgate. And this view is all the more probable, because the sacraments belong to the very foundation of the law, and for that reason their institution pertains to the lawgiver; and again because it is from their institution that they have their efficacy, and this can only come from a divine source.[42]

The sacramental rite, according to all, consists in the anointing of the bodily senses with oil and the accompanying prayer said by the priest. Hence oil is the matter of the sacrament, and the prayer of the priest is its form. By oil, in this con-

[36] Cfr. Bonavent. In Sent. IV, d. 25, a. 1, q. 1; Thomas, op. cit. q. 38, a. 1.
[37] Ibid. q. 2, 3.; ibid. q. 38, a. 2.
[38] Mansi, 20, 1209; 19, 509.

[39] De Sacr. II, p. 15, c. 2.
[40] Sent. IV, d. 23, c. 2.
[41] Sum. IV, q. 9, m. 1, 2.
[41a] In Sent. d. 23, a. 1, q. 2.
[42] Suppl. q. 39, a. 3.

nection, they understand olive oil; for, says St. Thomas, that is the proper meaning of the term.[43]

Thus far all are agreed; but on two further points there is among them a difference of opinion. First, what is the effect of the consecration of the oil by the bishop? Secondly, is the form of this sacrament deprecatory or indicative?

In regard to the first point St. Bonaventure says: " There are some who hold that the oil itself is the matter of this sacrament, and that by the episcopal consecration of the oil the sacrament is constituted; then the anointing that follows is simply the use or dispensation of the sacrament. But this is contrary to the very name of the sacrament, and also to the common view of theologians. Hence, it is better to say that, just as in baptism, the matter of the sacrament is water, and in confirmation it is chrism, so in extreme unction it is oil consecrated by the bishop." [44] St. Thomas refers to the same difference of opinion, and gives the same solution as St. Bonaventure.[45] Moreover the consecration of the oil by a bishop is necessary for the validity of the sacrament.[46]

There is a similar but more pronounced difference of opinion in regard to the form. In the various liturgical books of the time, and in others of a later date, there is found a vast variety of forms, some of them deprecatory and others indicative.[47] Hence, as St. Bonaventure states, some theologians went even so far as to say that no definite form was required in extreme unction.[48] However, this view is rejected by nearly all Scholastics of any note. Yet there is no agreement among them as to what the proper form ought to be. Thus St. Thomas contends that the form must be deprecatory, and for this view he assigns the following reasons. First, because the deprecatory form is evidently indicated by the words of St. James; secondly, because it is the form used by the Church of Rome; thirdly, the nature of the sacrament itself requires it, since it is administered to the dying who are thereby recom-

[43] Ibid. a. 4.
[44] In Sent. d. 23, a. 1, q. 3.
[45] Suppl. q. 29, a. 5.
[46] Ibid. a. 6.

[47] Cfr. J. Kern, Tractatus de Extrema Unctione, c. 3.
[48] Loc. cit. q. 4.

mended to the mercy of God.[49]   The same view is also taken
by St. Bonaventure, who reasons about the matter in a similar
way.[50]

Albertus Magnus, on the other hand, while admitting that
the deprecatory form is valid, argues that the indicative form
ought to be used.   For he says, speaking of the Church in
Germany, " in this part of the world all the most ancient
liturgical books have the indicative form, and conclude the rite
by a prayer.   And these are the words written in those most
ancient books, which, because of their great antiquity, I can
heardly read: *Ungo hos oculos oleo sanctificato in nomine,
etc.;* to which is added: *Per istam sanctissimam unctionem et
suam piissimam, etc.*[51]   This appears really to be a mixed
form, but the author takes the first part only as the form
proper.   Richard of Middleton [52] and some others took a similar stand.

The subject of extreme unction is any person who has come
to the age of discretion and is in danger of death from sickness.   This sacrament, says St. Thomas, is a spiritual medicine, and as bodily medicine is not administered to those who
are in health, neither must this spiritual medicine.[53]   Furthermore, it is the last remedy against the ills of the soul that
the Church has at her disposal, and therefore it ought not to
be given to any one who is suffering from a slight ailment, but
to those only who are about to depart this life.   Hence, it is
properly called the sacrament of the dying.[54]   However, it
ought not be deferred till the last moment, but should be administered when it is reasonably supposed that the sickness
may prove fatal.[55]

As extreme unction does not imprint a character, it may be
repeated on given conditions.   Precisely what these conditions are is not so clear from the writings of the Scholastics.
Before the twelfth century it seems to have been more or less
customary, at least in many places, to repeat extreme unction

[49] Op. cit. q. 29, a. 8.
[50] Loc. cit.
[51] Ibid. a. 4.
[52] Ibid. a. 1, q. 4.

[53] Op. cit. q. 32, a. 1.
[54] Suppl. q. 32, a. 2.
[55] Ibid. a. 2 ad 1m.

in the same sickness and even in the same danger of death, if it so happened that the sick person appeared to be in need of special spiritual help.[56] Then a discussion arose concerning this practice, and thereafter most theologians decided that extreme unction ought not to be administered more than once in the same danger of death. Not a few, however, made an exception in favor of those who were grievously sick for more than a year.[57] In keeping with this, many Manuals for the use of priests in those times have this rule in regard to the repetition of extreme unction: *Potest iterari, sed non pro eadem infirmitate, nisi ultra annum protrahatur.*[58]

St. Thomas decides the question as follows: " In regard to the administration of this sacrament, one must not only consider the fact of sickness, but also the gravity of the sickness in question: for it ought not to be given except to those sick persons who, according to human judgment, seem to be nearing death. Now certain sicknesses are not of long duration; hence, if in these the sacrament be then administered when the patient seems to be in danger of death, it is reasonable to assume that he does not recover from that dangerous condition except by a cure of the illness itself, and thus he should not be anointed again. But if he suffers a relapse, that must be considered another sickness, and then he can again be anointed. Other forms of sickness, however, are of long duration, such as hectic fever, dropsy, and the like: in such cases extreme unction should not be given except when there appears to be danger of death; and when the patient recovers from that particular danger, the same sickness remaining, and then is again reduced to a similar condition, he can again be anointed; because it is a new state of sickness, although the sickness itself remains the same." [59]

St. Bonaventure looks at this matter in a somewhat different

[56] Cfr. Kern, op. cit. p. 331 sqq.

[57] Thus Hugh of Strasburg, a pupil of Albertus Magnus, writes: " Si saepe infirmatur quis ad mortem saepe potest inungi; sed in una infirmitate non debet quis bis inungi, nisi eadem infirmitas ultra annum protrahatur, ita quod in uno anno propter eandem infirmitatem nemo bis inungatur " (Opera B. Alberti, t. 34, p. 232).

[58] Cfr. Launoi, opp. t. 1, p. 553.

[59] Suppl. q. 33, a. 2.

light. According to him, the proper effect of extreme unction is the remission of venial sins, and as one may commit venial sins after having been anointed, it is obvious that the administration of the sacrament may be repeated. Still in the practical application of this fundamental idea, he comes to practically the same conclusion as St. Thomas. " When there is question of a protracted illness," he says, " some hold that extreme unction may be repeated after a year has elapsed; but that position is altogether absurd — as if the administration of the sacraments were to be regulated by the movements of the stars. It is therefore better to say that no sick person should be anointed except when he is presumably approaching his end; and this will be in such a state of his sickness that nature cannot long bear up under it, and so he will either overcome it or be overcome by it. If therefore he recovers somewhat and continues to live, although he is not really cured, still he is cured of an extremely dangerous condition; and hence, if his condition again becomes worse, he can and should receive the sacrament of extreme unction again, because he may again have fallen into venial sin." [60]

There is found among the Scholastics a similar diversity of opinion in regard to the principal effect of extreme unction, as distinct from sanctifying grace which is either conferred or augmented by every sacrament. St. Bonaventure, as stated in the preceding paragraph, holds that it is the remission of venial sins in so far as they would be an obstacle to the soul's immediate entrance into heaven. During life, he says, it is very difficult to avoid venial sins, and they may almost be regarded as an incurable evil; but when death draws nigh that evil can be cured in respect of its consequences, and so the merciful God has provided extreme unction as a means to take away the guilt of venial sins, and also part of the punishment due to them. " Hence," he continues, " this sacrament was principally instituted for the healing and alleviating of man's spiritual infirmity, that is, of venial sin; and secondarily also for

---

[60] In Sent. IV, d. 23, a. 2, q. 3 ad 3m.

the cure and alleviation of his bodily infirmity, by way of strengthening the soul which rules the body." [61]

He calls this the common view of theologians, and he defends it against the opinion of those who held that extreme unction was directly intended as a remedy against the consequences and remains of sin, both personal and original, and indirectly against the ills of the body as resulting from sin.[62] Substantially the same view as that of Bonaventure is taken by Alexander of Hales,[63] Richard of Middleton,[64] Duns Scotus,[65] Durandus,[66] and many others. However, it can hardly be termed the " common " view of the Scholastics, as not a few of them, among whom are Albertus Magnus [67] and St. Thomas,[68] defended the opinion rejected by St. Bonaventure. Pointing out that extreme unction was instituted by our Savior as a spiritual medicine, St. Thomas draws this conclusion: " The purpose of medicine is to expel sickness. Hence this sacrament was chiefly instituted to cure the sickness of sin. . . . Consequently it is intended as a remedy against those defects by reason of which man is spiritually infirm, in the sense that he does not have perfect vigor as regards the acts of grace during life or of glory after death. Now these defects are nothing else than a certain debility and ineptitude left in us as a consequence of actual or original sin; and against this debility man is strengthened through the sacrament of extreme unction." [69]

Hence, all the Scholastics are agreed that the sacrament of extreme unction is in one way or another a remedy against sin or its consequences; and as sin usually enters the soul through the senses of the body, it follows naturally that these senses should be anointed in the administration of the sacrament. And this appears to have been the common teaching of theologians during the Middle Ages. " The soul," says St. Bonaventure, " rules and guides the body by reason of a threefold power: that of sensation, procreation, and locomotion;

---

[61] Ibid. a. 1, q. 1.
[62] Ibid.
[63] Sum. IV, q. 5, m. 7, a. 2.
[64] In Sent. IV, d. 23, a. 1, q. 3.
[65] Ibid. q. unic.

[66] Ibid. q. 1.
[67] Ibid. a. 1, 14.
[68] Sum. Theol. III, q. 65, a. 1.
[69] Suppl. q. 30, a. 1, 2.

hence the organs of these powers should be anointed. And as there are five organs of sensation, namely, the mouth, the eyes, the nostrils, the ears, and the hands, and as the loins are for the purpose of generation, and the feet for the purpose of locomotion, it is these seven parts that are anointed." [70]

However, although there are thus seven distinct anointings, each with its own form, there is only one sacrament of extreme unction. For as all the members which are anointed constitute one nature, and it is for this one nature that the remedy is provided, the different anointings constitute one sacramental rite.[71] Or as St. Thomas puts it: " Although the sacramental actions in this case are many, nevertheless they are all united in one perfect action — the unction of all the external senses, which are the source of man's internal ills." [72]

C — MATRIMONY

" A sacrament," reasons St. Thomas when speaking of matrimony, " provides for man, by means of some sensible sign, a remedy of divine grace against sin; and as this is verified in the case of matrimony, the matrimonial rite must be numbered among the sacraments." [73] The conclusion is accepted by all Scholastics, although Peter Lombard [74] and Durandus [75] are sometimes adduced as denying that the sacrament of matrimony produces grace. And most probably even these two are accused unjustly, as both of them teach that matrimony provides a remedy against concupiscence, which remedy must finally be reduced to the grace of God.[76] However, some early canonists seem to have taken the position just mentioned, and it is probably to them that St. Bonaventure refers when he says: " Some there were who said that this sacrament does not confer any grace; and to the objection that all the sacraments of the New Law give grace, they replied by saying that this must be understood of the sacraments insti-

[70] In Sent. d. 23, a. 2, q. 3.
[71] Ibid. q. 3 ad 3m.
[72] Suppl. q. 29, a. 2 ad 2m.
[73] Ibid. q. 42, a. 1.

[74] Sent. IV, d. 2.
[75] In Sent. V, d. 26, q. 3, n. 12.
[76] Cfr. Pesch, Praelect. VII, p. 316, 317.

tuted in the New Law." [77] This answer implies the view, also held by some others, that matrimony, even as a sacrament, was already instituted in paradise.

That matrimony is a true sacrament according to the teaching of the Church, is thus stated by Scotus: *Communiter tenet Ecclesia sacramentum matrimonii esse septimum inter ecclesiastica sacramenta, et de sacramentis Ecclesiae non est aliter sentiendum quam sentit Ecclesia Romana.*[78] And he defines the sacrament of matrimony as follows: *Signum sensibile, ex institutione divina significans efficaciter gratiam conferri contrahentibus ad conjunctionem eorum in contractu perpetuo observandam.*[79] This definition embodies the common teaching of the Scholastics, although most of them define matrimony in reference to the union between man and woman. Thus Peter Lombard writes: *Sunt igitur nuptiae vel matrimonium viri mulierisque conjunctio maritalis inter legitimas personas, individuam vitam retinens.*[80] This union or *conjunctio,* as St. Thomas points out, consists primarily in a contract which unites two individuals in reference to the procreation and education of their offspring, and to common domestic life; then, consequent upon this, but not constituting the essence thereof, is the union of bodies and of souls between the contracting parties.[81] Consequently, matrimony is essentially complete without the act of procreation.[82]

Hence the external sign of the sacrament consists in the marital consent of man and woman, in so far as that consent signifies the union of Christ with His Church. " Since matrimony is a sacrament," argues the Lombard, " it is both a sacred sign and the sign of a sacred thing, namely, of the union of Christ with His Church, according to the teaching of the Apostle." [83] Thus the natural contract, which from the beginning of the human race constituted matrimony as an *officium naturae,* was elevated by Christ to the dignity of a sacrament. Viewed under its material aspect, therefore,

[77] Op. cit. d. 26, a. 2, q. 2.
[78] In Sent. IV, d. 26, n. 13.
[79] Report. IV, d. 26, n. 20.
[80] Sent. d. 37, c. 2.

[81] Suppl. q. 44, a. 1.
[82] Ibid. q. 42, a. 4.
[83] Sent. d. 26, c. 6.

Christian marriage is the same as that of pre-Christian times; only its formal aspect, or sacramental significance, is different.[84]

From this it follows that the ministers of the sacrament are the contracting parties themselves, and they are also the proximate efficient cause of the marital bond which results from the sacramental contract. However the remote efficient cause of that bond is God, who instituted the sacrament as the source of an indissoluble union between man and woman, and therefore its perpetuity depends on His will. As a consequence, when matrimony has been consummated by the bodily union of husband and wife, it is dissoluble only by the death of one of the parties; but so long as it has not yet been thus consummated, it may be dissolved by one of the contracting parties entering religion and taking the solemn vow of chastity. The former of these two conclusions follows from the very nature of Christian marriage,[85] and the latter is known from the teaching of the Church.[86]

The matter and form of this sacrament consist of the words or actions of the contracting parties by which their mutual consent is expressed. " Just as in the case of penance," argues St. Thomas, " the sacrament of matrimony is perfected by the acts of the persons to whom the sacrament is applied. And therefore, as in penance there is no other matter than that which consists in the acts of the penitent, which themselves hold the place of matter, so it is also in matrimony." [87] And again: " The words by which the matrimonial consent is expressed are the form of this sacrament; while the blessing of the priest is merely a sacramental, and in no wise the sacramental form." [88] However, not any kind of consent given with a view to marriage constitutes a matrimonial contract or a sacramental rite. It must first of all have a bearing upon marriage as here and now contracted; if it is merely given in reference to a future marriage, it results simply in an engage-

[84] Cfr. Thomas, Suppl. q. 42. a. 2; ibid. q. 45, a. 1; Bonavent. In Sent. IV, d. 26, a. 2, q. 1.
[85] Cfr. Ibid. d. 27, a. 3, q. 1; Thomas, Suppl. q. 62, a. 1-5.
[86] Ibid. q. 61, a. 1-3; Bonavent. loc. cit. q. 2.
[87] Suppl. q. 42. a. 1 ad 2m.
[88] Ibid. a. 1 ad 1m.

ment of the parties concerned.[89]   Secondly, it must be the
consent of persons who are in every way free and competent
to enter a matrimonial contract.   Nor is it sufficient that the
persons in question be naturally competent, but they must also
be free from all impediments that have been established by the
positive law, either divine or ecclesiastical.[90]

Finally, although all the Scholastics speak of matrimony
with due respect, and look upon it as a holy state, nevertheless
they are unanimous in placing perpetual virginity on a higher
level of Christian perfection.   This conclusion they derive both
from the example of Christ, the teaching of St. Paul, and from
the nature of the two states in respect to the service of God.
Matrimony is good, but perpetual virginity freely vowed to
God is better.[91]

[89] Ibid. q. 43, a. 1.
[90] Cfr. Thomas, Suppl. q. 50, a.
unicus; Bonavent. In Sent. IV, d.
36–42; Scotus, Ibid. d. 34–42.

[91] Cfr. Thomas, Sum. Theol. II.
II, q. 152, a. 4, 5; Bonavent. op. cit.
d. 39, a. 2; Middleton, ibid. a. 4, q. 2.

CHAPTER XXIII

MARIOLOGY

SANCTIFICATION BEFORE BIRTH: IMMACULATE CONCEPTION: DIVINE MOTHERHOOD: VENERATION

With the exception of a few subordinate points, dogmatic Mariology was fully developed during Patristic times. Mary was universally honored as the Virgin Mother of God, free from all stain of sin, full of grace, the holiest of God's creatures, conformable to her divine Son in His untold sufferings and the dissolution of death, but also sharing with Him the glory of His resurrection by being herself raised from the dead and assumed into heaven. All this was a matter of Catholic belief before the Scholastics began to systematize the teaching of the Fathers.[1] Hence there was little room for development in the Mariological teaching of the Church, except by way of setting forth certain details which had been only lightly touched upon by Patristic writers. And to this the Scholastics chiefly devoted themselves in their studies of the many privileges and prerogatives of the Mother of God.

A — SANCTIFICATION BEFORE BIRTH

" That the Blessed Virgin was sanctified in her mother's womb," writes St. Bonaventure, " is a matter which the Church holds to admit of no doubt. And this appears from the fact that the whole Church celebrates the feast of her nativity, which she would certainly not do if Mary had not been sanctified before her birth." [2] And then, to show the reasonableness of this teaching, he argues from the principle laid down by St. Bernard, who says: " That which we read to

[1] Cfr. vol. I, p. 441 sqq.   [2] In Sent. III, p. I, a. I, q. 3.

have been conferred on others, cannot be held to have been denied to the Virgin." Holy Scripture bears witness that the Prophet Jeremias and John the Baptist were thus privileged, and how much more should not this same privilege have been granted to the Virgin, who exceeded them both in purity and perfection of virginity? They indeed were distinguished for their virginity, but in her to perfect virginity was joined miraculous fecundity. They were sanctified in the womb because they were sent to announce the Holy of Holies, how much more, then, was it not becoming that she should be thus sanctified who was to bear God in her womb? [3]

This reasoning of the Seraphic Doctor summarizes the arguments that were commonly advanced by the Scholastics to prove the point in question. It is ultimately her divine motherhood to which Mary owes all her privileges, and as this is a dignity that exceeds all others ever granted to any creature, her privileges are in consequence the very highest that God can bestow. In this sense St. Thomas argues, when he says: " It is reasonable to believe that she, who brought forth the Only Begotten of the Father full of grace and truth, received greater privileges of grace than all others." [4]

This sanctification in the womb was so perfect, that in view of it the Blessed Virgin was preserved from all personal sin. On this point all Scholastics are agreed. St. Thomas outlines the common reasoning as follows: " God so prepares and endows those whom He chooses for some particular office, that they are capable of fulfilling it. . . . Now the Blessed Virgin was chosen by God to be His Mother. Therefore there can be no doubt that God, by His grace, made her worthy of that office. . . . But she would not have been worthy to be the Mother of God, if she had ever sinned. First, because the honor of the parents reflects on the child, . . . and consequently, on the other hand, the Mother's shame would have reflected on her Son. Secondly, because of the singular affinity between her and Christ, who took flesh from her: . . . Thirdly, because of the singular manner in which the Son of

---

[3] Ibid.   [4] Sum. Theol. III, q. 27, a. 1.

God, who is divine wisdom, dwelt in her, not only in her soul but in her womb. . . . We must therefore confess simply that the Blessed Virgin committed no actual sin, neither mortal nor venial; so that what is written is fulfilled: *Thou art all fair, O my love, and there is not a spot in thee."* [5]

To these reasons for belief in Mary's sinlessness, which are all taken from her relation to her divine Son, St. Bonaventure adds another which is based upon her relation to the fallen race and her triumph over the devil. " It was also becoming," he argues, " that the Blessed Virgin, through whom our disgrace was to be taken away, should conquer the devil so completely that she did not yield to him in the slightest degree. Hence, it is to her that St. Bernard and St. Augustine apply the verse in Genesis: *' She shall crush thy head.'* If then the suggestion of evil is the head of the devil, no suggestion of this kind ever found entrance into the mind of the Virgin, so that she was preserved from both mortal and venial sin. . . . Consequently, as the Blessed Virgin is the advocate of sinners, the glory and crown of the just, the spouse of God, the bridal bed of the whole Trinity, and in a most special manner the couch whereon the Son reposes, it was but right that, by a special grace of God, in her sin should have no place." [6]

In connection with Mary's preservation from all personal sin, the Scholastics discuss the question whether also the inclination to sin — the *fomes peccati* — was extinguished in her sanctification. On that point there is no agreement in their views. All indeed admit that Mary's natural inclinations were fully subject to reason assisted by grace, but there is a difference of opinion as to what this subjection really implied. In regard to the point in question, the Schoolmen usually distinguished a twofold sanctification of the Blessed Virgin: the first took place before her birth, as already indicated; the second was effected at the moment when she conceived her divine Son. This latter was regarded as a complement of the former, in the sense that it increased sanctifying grace in her soul and

[5] Ibid. a. 4.   [6] In Sent. III, p. 1, a. 2, q. 1.

thereby rooted her more firmly in her opposition to sin.   In accordance with this distinction, the following three views were formed in regard to the extinction of the *fomes peccati*.

Some there were, as St. Bonaventure testifies,[7] who denied the extinction of the *fomes* altogether, but held that it was put to sleep or fettered in the first sanctification, so that thereafter the natural appetite never rose in rebellion against the dictate of reason.   Then, in the second sanctification, this condition of inactivity on the part of the natural appetite was intensified by an increase of grace; but the *fomes* still continued to exist.

Others admitted the extinction of the *fomes,* but in this respect made a distinction between person and nature.   This was the view taken by Alexander of Hales.   In the first sanctification, he says, the *fomes* was extinguished as regarded the person of the Blessed Virgin, but in the second as regarded her nature.   In the first she was purified in such a way that she never fell into sin; in the second, so as to bring forth her child without sin.   In the first sanctification the *fomes* was extinguished in so far as it would have made her prone to evil; in the second, furthermore, in so far as it would have been an obstacle to good.[8]   This view St. Bonaventure terms unintelligible.[9]

Others, finally, held that in the first sanctification the *fomes* was fettered, and in the second it was extinguished.   This is the view taken by St. Thomas,[10] St. Bonaventure,[11] Albertus Magnus,[12] Richard of Middleton,[13] Ægidius Romanus,[14] and Durandus.[15]   St. Thomas puts it in this way: " In order to understand the question at issue, it must be observed that the *fomes* is nothing else than a certain inordinate, but habitual, concupiscence of the sensitive appetite; for actual concupiscence is a sinful motion.   Now sensual concupiscence is said to be inordinate, in so far as it rebels against reason; and this it does by inclining to evil, or hindering from good.   Consequently it is essential to the *fomes* to incline to evil, or

[7] In Sent. III, d. 3, p. 1, a. 2, q. 2.
[8] Sum. III, q. 9, m. 2, a. 5.
[9] Loc. cit.
[10] Sum. Theol. III, q. 27, a. 3.
[11] Loc. cit.
[12] In Sent. III, d. 3, a. 6.
[13] Ibid. a. 1, q. 4.
[14] Ibid. q. 1, a. 4.
[15] Ibid. q. 3.

hinder from good. Wherefore to say that the *fomes* was in the Blessed Virgin without an inclination to evil, is to combine two contradictory statements.

" In like manner it seems to imply a contradiction to say that the *fomes* remained as to the corruption of nature, but not as to personal corruption. For, according to Augustine, it is lust that transmits original sin to the offspring. Now lust implies inordinate concupiscence, not entirely subject to reason: and therefore, if the *fomes* were entirely taken away as to personal corruption, it could not remain as to the corruption of nature.

" It remains, therefore, for us to say, either that the *fomes* was entirely taken away from her by her first sanctification or that it was fettered. Now that the *fomes* was entirely taken away, might be understood in this sense, that, by the abundance of grace bestowed on the Blessed Virgin, such a disposition of the soul's powers was granted to her, that the lower powers were never moved without the command of reason; just as we have stated above to have been the case with Christ, who certainly did not have the *fomes* of sin; as also was the case with Adam, before he sinned, by reason of original justice: so that in this respect the grace of sanctification in the Virgin had the force of the primitive gift of righteousness. And although this appears to be part of the dignity of the Virgin Mother, yet it is somewhat derogatory to the dignity of Christ, without whose power no one had been freed from the first sentence of condemnation. . . . Consequently, just as before the immortality of the flesh of Christ rising again, none obtained immortality of the flesh, so it seems unfitting to say that before Christ appeared in sinless flesh, His Virgin Mother's or anyone else's flesh should be without the *fomes* which is called *the law of the flesh* or *of the members*.

" Therefore it seems better to say that by the sanctification in the womb, the Virgin was not freed from the *fomes* in its essence, but that it remained fettered: not indeed by an act of her reason, as in holy men, since she had not the use of reason from the first moment of her existence in her mother's womb, for this was the singular privilege of Christ: but by way of the abundant grace bestowed on her in her sanctification, and still more perfectly by Divine Providence preserving her sensitive soul, in a singular manner, from any inordinate movement. Afterwards, however, at the conception of Christ's flesh, in which for the first time immunity from sin was to be conspicuous, it is to be believed that entire freedom from the *fomes* redounded from the Child to the Mother." [16]

This view was commonly held by the more representative Scholastics up to the time of Scotus. He, however, was not satisfied with it; but instead defended the opinion, rejected by St. Thomas, that the *fomes* was entirely extinguished by the Virgin's first sanctification.[17] This has since become the common teaching of theologians, and is certainly more in keeping with the doctrine of the Immaculate Conception.

Along with the extinction of the *fomes,* the Scholastics also defend Mary's confirmation in grace. This they usually connect with the second sanctification; although even before that sanctification took place, Divine Providence preserved her from all personal sin. Hence, in a certain sense, Mary was impeccable. However, her impeccability differed both from that of Christ and of the blessed in heaven. Mary was a pure creature and still on her way to the state of final blessedness; hence she was rendered impeccable exclusively through the abundance of grace which she received. St. Thomas explains it in this way: " The power of sinning may be taken away in one of two ways: First, by the union of the free will with its last end, which so entirely fills it that no defect remains; and this is brought about by the vision of God in glory; hence, in no person who is still on the way to heaven is the power of sinning taken away in such a manner. . . . Secondly, the power of sinning may be removed by the infusion of such an abundance of grace that thereby all defects are expelled: and so it was removed in the case of the Blessed Virgin when she conceived the Son of God. All power of sinning was taken away, although the Virgin herself still remained in *statu*

---

[16] Sum. Theol. III, q. 27, a. 3.   [17] In Sent. II, d. 29, n. 4; d. 32, n. 4; III, d. 3.

viae." [18]   Or as St. Bonaventure briefly puts it: "Not only was sanctifying grace given to the Virgin in her second sanctification, but also the grace whereby she was confirmed in good; and this was granted to her because she was so closely united to her Son that He could in no way permit her to be separated from Himself." [19]

B — THE IMMACULATE CONCEPTION

Nearly all Patristic writers laid down principles from which belief in the Immaculate Conception flows as a natural consequence; although there is hardly one among them who taught the doctrine so explicitly that his words do not admit of a different explanation.[20]   The fact, too, that from the middle of the eighth century forward the feast of the Conception of the Virgin Mary was observed in ever widening circles, with at least the tacit acquiescence of the Church, is a sign that Christian consciousness was fast awaking to the truth of this doctrine.   The impulse came from the East, but it found a ready response among the faithful in western lands.

It was in this stage of its development that the doctrine of the Immaculate Conception was subjected to a thorough study by the Scholastics, and, strange to say, it was by nearly all of them set aside as not sufficiently in harmony with the Church's teaching on the universality of original sin and of the redemption.   St. Anselm, St. Bernard, Peter Lombard, Alexander of Hales, Bonaventure, Albertus Magnus, and St. Thomas, though tenderly devout to God's holy Mother and ever ready to defend her many privileges and prerogatives, nevertheless taught quite definitely that she was conceived in sin as all the rest of mankind.   Christ alone, they held, was immune from the original stain.— In this we seem to have a striking proof of the fact that sometimes the *sensus fidelium* is a safer guide in matters of faith, not yet clearly defined, than the prevailing views of theologians.

[18] In Sent. III, d. 3, q. 1, a. 2.   [20] Cfr. vol. I, p. 443 sqq.
[19] In Sent. III, d. 3, p. 1, a. 2, q. 3.

However, by way of explanation of the strange phenomenon just referred to, it must be noted that at the time there stood some serious difficulties in the way of a theological exposition and acceptance of the doctrine in question. First of all, most of the theologians of the day, as was shown in a previous chapter, had only an imperfect understanding of the nature and transmission of original sin. Secondly, a way had to be found of reconciling the doctrine of the universality of the redemption with the exemption from all sin of one who had descended from the fallen Adam. Thirdly, the biological fact of conception itself was not well understood, it being the common teaching at the time that the spiritual soul was not infused into the body of the child until the organism had sufficiently developed. In consequence, many interpreted the Immaculate Conception to mean either that the act of procreation was without sin on the part of the parents, or that the body of the child was preserved from contracting the original stain. Hence the strange question found in the works of nearly all Scholastics: "Whether the Blessed Virgin was purified from original sin before animation?" As is obvious, in such a confused state of things there is much to excuse the erroneous teaching to which even the greatest thinkers of the golden age of Scholasticism committed themselves.

With this premised, we may first give a brief résumé of the arguments usually advanced against the doctrine of the Immaculate Conception, and then indicate those that were urged in its favor.

Among the first who came out clearly against the Immaculate Conception, as then understood, was St. Bernard. His presentation of the question brings out strikingly the confusion of ideas referred to above. Protesting against the contemplated introduction of the feast in the church of Lyons, he asks: "Whence therefore comes the sanctity of the conception? Is she said to have been prevented by sanctification, so that she was holy when conceived, and for this reason her conception itself was holy, just as she is said to have been sanctified in the womb, and in consequence was holy in her birth? But she could not be holy before she existed; for in truth she had no existence before she was conceived. Or was there perhaps in the marital embrace of her parents sanctity communicated to the conception, so that she was at the same time sanctified and conceived? But how could there be sanctity without the sanctifying Spirit, or how could there be an association of the Holy Spirit with sin? Or surely, how was there no sin, where concupiscence was not absent? Unless perhaps some one would say that she was conceived of the Holy Ghost and not of man. But such a thing is hitherto unheard of."

From this it will be seen that the writer makes all manner of suppositions, except the right one — that her soul might have been sanctified by the infusion of sanctifying grace when united to the body. And in keeping with his false suppositions, he draws his false conclusion: "If therefore she could in no way be sanctified before her conception, because she did not yet exist; and neither in her conception on acount of the sin that was there; it remains that we must believe her to have been sanctified after her conception when already existing in the womb, and that in consequence the exclusion of sin caused her birth to be holy, but not her conception." [21]

St. Anselm, whose concept of original sin was substantially the same as that of modern theologians, and who stated so clearly that under God nothing could be conceived to be more pure than the Virgin Mother,[22] nevertheless fell into the same error concerning the Immaculate Conception. Thus when Boso, his interlocutor in the *Cur Deus Homo*, makes the statement that the Virgin was conceived in original sin, because she too had sinned in Adam, he answers: "We ought not to think it strange if we cannot see the reason why the wisdom of God so disposed matters, but we must admit with due reverence that in His hidden ways there is something we do not understand." [23]

Alexander of Hales, at the very beginning of his inquiry, enunciates the principle that whatever grace could be conferred upon the Blessed Virgin, was conferred upon her; but

[21] Ep. 174, n. 7.
[22] De Concept. Virgin. c. 18.
[23] Op. cit. II, c. 16.

among these possible graces he does not find that of the Immaculate Conception. He points out that she could not be purified before her conception, nor in her conception, nor before the infusion of her soul; but only after she had been conceived, as other saints had also been purified, and therefore her birth was holy.[24]

St. Bonaventure, in some respects, comes nearer to the point, but in the end he also decides against the doctrine. Putting the question whether the soul of the Blessed Virgin was sanctified before contracting original sin, he answers: " Some there are who say that in the soul of the glorious Virgin the grace of sanctification prevented the stain of original sin. And they assign this reason: It was becoming that the soul of the glorious Virgin should be sanctified in a more excellent manner than the souls of all other saints, not only as regards the abundance of sanctity, but also in respect of the acceleration of time; and therefore at the very instant of creation grace was given her, and in the same instant her soul was infused into the body." [25]

In this there is obviously no misunderstanding of the true doctrine; but though the doctrine is thus rightly understood, the author does not see his way towards making it his own. For he continues: " But the position of others is this, that the sanctification of the Virgin followed the contraction of original sin; and for this reason, that no one was free from the guilt of original sin save only the Son of the Virgin. For as the Apostle says in the third chapter of his Epistle to the Romans: *All have sinned and need the glory of God.* . . . And this manner of speaking is more common and more reasonable and more safe. More common, I say, because nearly all hold that the Blessed Virgin was infected with original sin. . . . More reasonable, because nature precedes grace, either in the order of time or in the order of nature; and hence St. Augustine says that one must first be born before one can be reborn. . . . Hence, it is necessary to hold that the infection of original sin preceded sanctification. More

---

[24] Sum. III, q. 9, m. 2.   [25] In Sent. III, d. 3, p. 1, a. 1, q. 2.

safe, because it is more in harmony with the piety of faith and the authority of the saints." [26]

Albertus Magnus summarizes his view on the subject in these terms: " It must be held that the Blessed Virgin was sanctified in the womb before her birth; but what precise day or hour this was accomplished, no man can know, except by way of revelation: unless one wants to hold that it took place shortly after animation." [27]

The same position is taken by St. Thomas, although since the end of the fourteenth century ever so many attempts have been made to show that he did not oppose the doctrine as rightly understood. He treats the subject in many different places, but the following extracts will suffice to indicate his mind on the point in question.

In his *Summa Theologica* he first gives several reasons why the Blessed Virgin could not have been sanctified before animation, and then gives this general argument: " And thus, in whatever manner the Blessed Virgin would have been sanctified before animation, she could never have incurred the stain of original sin: and thus she would not have needed redemption and salvation which is by Christ, of whom it is written: *He shall save His people from their sins.* But this is unfitting, through implying that Christ is not the Saviour of all men, as He is called. It remains, therefore, that the Blessed Virgin was sanctified after animation." [28] Then to the objection that " the purity of the Blessed Virgin would have been greater if she had never been stained by the contagion of original sin," he replies: " If the soul of the Blessed Virgin had never incurred the stain of original sin, this would be derogatory to the dignity of Christ, by reason of His being the universal Saviour of all. Consequently after Christ, who, as the universal Saviour of all, needed not to be saved, the purity of the Blessed Virgin holds the highest place. For Christ did not contract original sin in any way whatever, but was holy in His very conception, according to Luke 1, 35: *The Holy which shall be born of thee, shall be called the Son*

[26] Ibid.
[27] Ibid. a. 5; a. 3, 4.
[28] Op. cit. III, q. 27, a. 2.

of God. But the blessed Virgin did indeed contract original sin, but was cleansed therefrom before her birth from the womb." [29]

Then the further objection, that " no feast is celebrated except of some saint, and that some keep the feast of the Conception of the Blessed Virgin," he answers by saying: " Although the Church of Rome does not celebrate the Conception of the Blessed Virgin, yet it tolerates the custom of certain churches which do keep that feast; wherefore this is not to be entirely reprobated. Nevertheless the celebration of this feast does not give us to understand that she was holy in her conception. But since it is not known when she was sanctified, the feast of her Sanctification, rather than the feast of her Conception, is kept on the day of her conception." [30]

He proposes the same doctrine in his *Commentaries on the Sentences,* where he says: " The sanctification of the Blessed Virgin could not fittingly precede the infusion of her soul, because then she was not capable of sanctification; but neither could it take place at the very instant when her soul was infused into her body, so that through grace she was preserved from incurring original sin. For of all the human race Christ alone has this singular privilege that He does not need redemption, because He is our Head; but all others must be redeemed by Him. Now this could not be, if another soul were found that had never been infected with the original stain; and therefore this was not conceded even to the Blessed Virgin, nor to any one else besides Christ." [31]

The same reasoning recurs, almost word for word, in his *Commentary on the Epistle to the Romans,*[32] in his *Quodlibeta.*[33] in his *Expositio Salutationis Angelicae,*[34] and in his *Compendium Theologicum.*[35] Hence, any effort to make St. Thomas an advocate of the doctrine of the Immaculate Conception, or to show that he was not opposed to the doctrine as understood at the present time, is at best misdirected. His

[29] Ibid. ad 2m.
[30] Ibid. ad 3m.
[31] In Sent. III, d. 3, q. 1, a. 1, sol. 1 ad 1m.

[32] Op. cit. in V, 12.
[33] Op. cit. 6, a. 7.
[34] Op. cit. 1.
[35] Op. cit. c. 224 (al. 232).

arguments are not urged against a misinterpretation of the doctrine, but against the doctrine itself. This does not detract from his fame as a theologian, or as a devout client of the Mother of God; but only shows that even in theology there is such a thing as development.

However, although the most representative Scholastics prior to the fourteenth century were thus resolutely opposed to the doctrine of the Immaculate Conception, there were never wanting others, though of lesser fame, who with equal resolution defended Mary's prerogative by every means in their power. Among these was Vincent of Beauvais, a Dominican and contemporary of St. Thomas, who, referring to the feast of the Conception, says very definitely: " But now, because she is venerated by the authority of the whole Church, it is evident that she was preserved in every way from original sin, and by her was not only taken away the malediction of mother Eve, but all were filled with blessing. The Virgin was subject to no fault when she was born, nor did she contract original sin before she was sanctified in the womb." [36]

The doctrine was also defended by Eadmer, disciple and biographer of St. Anselm. He uses practically the same argument that was some two hundred years later employed by Scotus — *potuit, decuit, fecit.* " Could not God," he asks, " grant to the human body of which He prepared for Himself a temple, in which He dwelt corporeally, and of which He assumed human nature into the unity of person, that, although conceived amid the thorns of sin, it should nevertheless be altogether preserved from the sting of these thorns? He evidently could. If, then, He willed, He did. And indeed, whatever in the order of dignity He willed in regard to anyone apart from His own person, that, O Most Blessed of women, He surely willed in regard to thee. . . . Out of the sinful mass, therefore, He could preserve a human nature free from all stain of sin, and from it unite a human nature to His own person, so that He was a true man and yet in no way detract from the holiness of His divinity." [37]

[36] Laudes V. Mariae, c. 5, 6.   [37] De Conceptione Sanctae Mariae, n. 8.

Besides these two, there were many others who defended the doctrine of the Immaculate Conception, as is quite evident from the statement of St. Bonaventure referred to in a previous paragraph. However, it was reserved for Duns Scotus to turn the tide of theological opinion completely in its favor. This he did chiefly by removing the principal difficulty urged against it, namely, that such a privilege conferred on a pure creature would be derogatory to the dignity of Christ as the universal Savior; and secondarily also by clarifying the concept of original sin.

Assuming the principle upon which the adversaries of the Immaculate Conception built their arguments, namely, that Christ is the redeemer and mediator of all, he makes it the foundation of his own arguments for the doctrine. " The most perfect mediator," he argues, " has a most perfect way of mediating for any person in whose behalf he mediates. But Christ is the most perfect mediator. Therefore Christ had the most perfect way possible of mediating in behalf of any creature or person in respect of whom He was the mediator. But in respect of no person had He a more excellent way than in respect of Mary; therefore, etc. But this would not have been the case unless He merited for her preservation from original sin. And this I prove in three ways: First, in reference to God to whom He reconciled her; secondly, in reference to the evil from which He freed her; thirdly, in reference to the obligation under which He was in regard to the person whom He reconciled." [38]

Then, after completing the argument, he answers the objection that Mary was subject to the punishment consequent upon original sin, and therefore to original sin itself. His answer is: " A mediator can reconcile a person in such a manner that all useless punishment is taken away, while afflictions that are useful remain. Original guilt would not have been useful to Mary; but temporal pains were useful to her, because by bearing them she merited; therefore, etc." [39]

Finally he sums up the whole question in this way: " God

[38] In Sent. III, q. 1, n. 4 sqq.   [39] Ibid. n. 8.

could bring it about that she never contracted original sin; He could also have brought it about that she should have been in the state of original sin for only one instant; He could also have brought it about that she should have been infected with original sin for some time, and in the last instant of that time have been purified therefrom. . . . Which of these three possible ways He actually did choose, God knows. If it does not contravene the authority of the Church and of Holy Scripture, it seems probable that what is more excellent must be attributed to Mary." [40] Hence, he does not wish to decide the question on his own authority, but he makes it quite clear what he thinks of the doctrine under discussion.

The position taken by Scotus in favor of the Immaculate Conception proved decisive. His own order took up the defense without delay, in which it was soon joined by the Benedictines, the Cistersians, the Carmelites, and the Augustinians. The Dominicans alone held back, owing to the authority of St. Thomas, whom they all interpreted as being against the doctrine. At the same time the University of Paris censured a thesis which John de Montesa, a Dominican, had presented for his doctorate, and in which he stated: *Beatam Mariam Virginem et Dei Genitricem non contraxisse peccatum originale est expresse contra fidem;* and later on exacted from all candidates for the doctorate a promise under oath that they would defend the doctrine of the Immaculate Conception. In 1439, the Council of Basle, after it had become schismatical, declared that the doctrine was conformable to faith and reason, and prohibited all further arguing against it. Still the contention on the part of the Dominicans was continued, until Sixtus IV, in 1483, issued the Constitution *Grave nimis,* in which he reprobated all opposition to what had meanwhile become the accepted teaching of the Church. Thereafter it was regarded as a matter of reproach to speak against the Immaculate Conception, and finally, in 1854, the doctrine was defined by Pius IX, in the Bull *Ineffabilis Deus.*[41]

[40] Ibid. n. 9. [41] DB. 1641.

C — Divine Motherhood

Mary's right to the title, Mother of God, was proclaimed by Christian antiquity and solemnly defined by the Council of Ephesus.[42] The reason for the title is thus stated by St. Thomas: " Every word that signifies a nature in the concrete can stand for any hypostasis of that nature. Now, since the union of the Incarnation took place in the hypostasis, as was above stated, it is manifest that this word *God* can stand for the hypostasis having a human and a divine nature. Therefore whatever belongs to the divine and to the human nature can be attributed to that person: both when a word signifying the divine nature is employed to stand for it, and when a word is used signifying the human nature. Now, conception and birth are attributed to the person and hypostasis in respect of that nature in which it is conceived and born. Since, therefore, the human nature was taken by the divine person in the very beginning of the conception, as stated above, it follows that it can be truly said that God was conceived and born of the Virgin. Now, from this is a woman called a man's mother, that she conceived him and gave birth to him. Therefore the Blessed Virgin is truly called the Mother of God. For the only way in which it could be denied that the Blessed Virgin is the Mother of God would be one of these two: either that the humanity was first subject to conception and birth, before this man was the Son of God, as Photinus said; or that the humanity was not assumed into unity of the hypostasis or person of the Word of God, as Nestorius maintained. But both of these opinions are erroneous. Therefore it is heretical to deny that the Blessed Virgin is the Mother of God." [42a]

This is the common teaching of the Scholastics as regards the fact of Mary's divine motherhood; but there is some difference in their views in reference to her coöperation in the conception of her Son. St. Bonaventure puts the state of the question this way: " Since Mary is the Mother of Christ and truly conceived Him, it must be held without all doubt that

[42] Cfr. vol. I, p. 396 sqq.   [42a] Sum. Theol. III, q. 35, a. 4.

she truly coöperated with the Holy Spirit in the conception
of her Son, and this is commonly and generally held by teachers of theology.   But regarding the manner of coöperating
different men have different views.   Some prefer to say that
the Virgin Mary coöperated only by supplying the material
principle.   But others hold that she coöperated in the educ-
tion of the ultimate form and in the preparation of the matter, although not in the whole process.   And others, finally,
hold a view that is intermediate between these two." [43]

Then, after refuting the first and second opinion, he gives
his own in these terms: " Because the first opinion claims too
little and the second too much, hence their untenableness directs us in the way to the truth.   And for this reason it seems
preferable to hold the intermediate view, namely, that power
was divinely communicated to the Blessed Virgin, by which she
supplied the matter for the conception — the matter, I say,
not only in so far as it had the nature of matter or passive
potency, but also in the sense that it was disposed and suitable
for the production of the child.   However, as the operation
of this power was necessarily successive, and as the body of
Christ could not fittingly be produced by successive operation,
hence it was that the Holy Spirit by His infinite power brought
the matter to its ultimate perfection. . . . Hence the whole
substance of Christ's body was taken from His Mother; and
therefore if we wish to think and speak logically, we must
say that the Virgin was the Mother of Christ in a truer sense
than any other mother is the mother of her own child." [44]

St. Thomas also refers to the three different opinions mentioned above, and after a brief discussion of them adopts the
first, namely, that Mary was simply passive in the conception
of her Son.   And he takes this view, because in generation,
according to Aristotle, all activity is on the part of the father.
Hence he says: " Since, therefore, the Blessed Virgin was
not Christ's father, but His mother, it follows that it was not
given to her to exercise an active power in His conception.
. . . We must therefore say that in Christ's conception itself

[43] In Sent. III, d. 4, a. 3, q. 1.   [44] Ibid.

she did not coöperate actively, but merely supplied the matter thereof. Nevertheless, before the conception she coöperated actively in the preparation of the matter, so that it should be apt for the conception." [45] Hence " this conception had three privileges — that it was without original sin; that it was not of man only, but of God and man; that it was a virginal conception. And all three were effected by the Holy Ghost." [46]

In keeping with this difference of views, the Scholastics also differ in answering the further question, whether the conception of Christ was natural or miraculous. St. Bonaventure answers that under one aspect it was natural and under another it was miraculous. It was natural in so far as the Virgin had the natural power to prepare the matter for the conception; it was miraculous in so far as the Virgin had received the supernatural power to coöperate in the conception itself.[47] St. Thomas agrees that the conception was both natural and miraculous, but as he denies that the Virgin actively coöperated in the conception, he gives a different reason. He says: " Besides the union of two natures in one person, which was effected in the conception of Christ, and which is the miracle of all miracles, there was also this other miracle that the Virgin, remaining a virgin, conceived the God-Man. For in order that a conception may be said to be natural, it is necessary that it be affected by the agent in a natural manner, and by means of matter that is naturally apt for the conception. . . . Now the matter supplied by the Virgin was the same as that from which the body of man may be formed naturally; but the power forming the body was divine. Hence it must be said that the conception of Christ was simply miraculous, but natural in some respect." [48]

In the divine motherhood thus understood, the Scholastics recognized the source of all the graces and privileges bestowed on Mary. St. Thomas formulates the common teaching in this way: " In every genus, the nearer a thing is to the principle, the greater also is the part which it has in that principle; whence Dionysius says that angels, being nearer to God, have

[45] Sum. Theol. III, q. 32, a. 4.   [47] In Sent. III, d. 4, a. 3, q. 2.
[46] Sum. Theol. III, q. 32, a. 4.   [48] Ibid. q. 2, a. 2.

a greater share than men in the effects of the divine goodness. Now Christ is the principle of grace, authoritatively as to His Godhead, instrumentally as to His humanity: whence it is written: *Grace and truth came by Jesus Christ.* But the Blessed Virgin Mary was nearest to Christ in His humanity: because He received his human nature from her. Therefore it was due to her to receive a greater fullness of grace than others." [49] Hence, too, " there is no doubt that the Blessed Virgin received in a high degree both the gift of wisdom and the grace of miracles and even of prophecy, just as Christ had them. But she did not so receive them as to put them and suchlike graces to every use, as did Christ: but according as it befitted her condition of life." [50]

D — Veneration of Mary

The principle that underlies all true devotion to the Blessed Mother of God is thus neatly expressed by St. Bonaventure: " Whatever terms are used to set forth the Christian faith, they must be far removed from error and expressive of devotion; and this in a most special manner when they refer to the Virgin Mary. For by conceiving and bringing forth the Truth Itself, she has exterminated all heresy throughout the whole world, and also merited reconciliation for the entire race; and therefore devotion to her ought to burn with great intensity in the hearts of all Christians." [51]

And this is the common view of all the Schoolmen, nearly every one of whom manifested a tender devotion to the Mother of God. As Mother of the Redeemer, she was regarded as the cause of the world's salvation — a thought that had been expressed over and over again in the earliest ages of Christianity. Furthermore, as the recipient of the most extraordinary graces, among which shone in a special manner her virginal purity, she was endowed in her own person with an attractiveness that led all hearts captive, and bound them to herself in the most ardent love and tender devotion. Hence the many

[49] Sum. Theol. III, q. 27, a. 5.   [51] In Sent. III, d. 4, a. 3, q. 3.
[50] Ibid. a. 5 ad 3m.

panegyrics that were preached in her honor by the most learned men of the day, the numerous treatises composed to set forth her virtues, the multiplication of feasts and pious practices in every part of the Christian world. Those were the ages of faith, and faith gathers her children instinctively around the throne of God's own sweet Mother.

Yet all this devotion did not blind the Scholastics, nor the faithful in general, to the limitations that must necessarily be placed upon the veneration to which Mary can justly lay claim. " Although the honor which is paid her," argues Alexander of Hales, " is in some way referred to Him who became incarnate in her womb, nevertheless from this it does not follow that she may be honored with divine worship. Still the honor that is her just due has a special excellence of its own. Although paid to a pure creature, yet it is not shared in by any other saint. It is in a manner a disposition to divine worship, but not divine worship itself. When I worship the Mother of God because of her sublime dignity, I do not worship her as the creative cause of my being, and therefore I do not pay her divine honor; but because I worship her as the Mother of God, I honor her as the Mother of the Creator, and this on account of the Creator Himself. Hence the foundation of her honor is the honor of the Creator; but the honor itself is that which is due to a creature." [52]

St. Bonaventure uses almost the same terms. " The most Blessed Virgin Mary," he says, " is a pure creature, and therefore she does not rise to the height of divine honor and worship. But because she has the most excellent name, so that nothing more excellent can be bestowed on any mere creature, hence it is that she is not merely entitled to the ordinary honor of *dulia,* but to the singular honor of *hyperdulia.* And that most excellent name is this, Virgin Mother of God, which in truth is of such exalted dignity, that not only the wayfarers on earth but also the blessed in heaven, not only men but the angels also, reverence her by paying her the tribute of special honor. For by the fact that she is the Mother of

[52] Sum. q. 30, m. 3, a. 2 ad 2[m].

God, she is raised above all other creatures, and hence it is becoming that she be honored and venerated more than all. And this honor it has become customary among teachers to call *hyperdulia.*" [53]

Thus also St. Thomas reasons. " Since *latria* is due to God alone," he says, " it is not due to a creature so far as we venerate a creature for its own sake. . . . Since, therefore, the Blessed Virgin is a mere rational creature, the worship of *latria* is not due to her, but only that of *dulia;* but in a higher degree than to other creatures, in as much as she is the Mother of God. For this reason we say that not any kind of *dulia* is due to her, but *hyperdulia.*" [54] And again: " The honor due to the king's mother is not equal to the honor which is due to the king: but is somewhat like it, by reason of a certain excellence on her part." [55]

[53] In Sent. III, d. 9, a. 1, q. 3.   [55] Ibid. a. 5 ad 1m.
[54] Sum. Theol. III, q. 25, a. 5.

CHAPTER XXIV

ESCHATOLOGY

In their treatment of eschatological subjects the Scholastics are very diffuse. They indulge in lengthy speculations on points for the establishing of which neither reason nor revelation furnishes sufficient data. In these speculations we need not follow them, as it would be little to the purpose in a work that is concerned only with doctrines whose development is likely to issue into definite results along the lines of faith. Hence the following brief remarks on the four principal eschatological topics, the resurrection of the dead, the general judgment, the eternal blessedness of the elect, and the everlasting sufferings of the reprobate, must here suffice.

1. *The Resurrection of the Dead.*— The fact of the resurrection is treated by all Scholastics as an article of Christian belief, which from the earliest times found a place in the Creed. However they adduce various arguments to prove that the teaching of faith is acceptable to reason. Thus they point to the resurrection of Christ as the exemplar and promise of our resurrection. He is our Head, we are His members; and as the Head rose from the dead, so is it also fitting that the members should rise again.[1] They also argue that the fitness of a full eternal recompense, either by way of reward or punishment, makes the resurrection of the dead appear most probable even from the standpoint of reason. It was the whole man who practiced virtue or indulged in vice; and therefore it should also be the whole man who reaps the everlasting recompense of his mortal deeds.[2]

[1] Cfr. Bonavent. In Sent. IV, d. 43, a. 1, q. 1; Thomas, Suppl. q. 75, a. 1, 2; Scotus, In Sent. IV, d. 43, q. 1, n. 11.

[2] Cfr. Thomas, op. cit. a. 1–3; Bonavent. loc. cit. q. 1.

However the act of resuscitating the dead is supernatural, and implies the exercise of divine power.[3] St. Thomas holds that Christ as God-Man is both the efficient and exemplary cause of the resurrection of the dead, and that His sacred humanity acts in reference to the effect as the instrument of the Godhead.[4] Furthermore, as they all explain, in the resurrection there are three things to be considered: First, the gathering together of the material that constituted man's body during life; secondly, the disposing of that material for its union with the soul; thirdly, the actual reunion of soul and body. Of these three, only the last is strictly supernatural and as such must be effected by divine power.[5] " In regard to the other two," says St. Thomas, " God will make use of the ministry of the angels. But as the soul was immediately created by God, so shall it also, without the intervention of the angels, be again united to its body by the immediate action of God. And the same must be held with regard to the glorification of the body: God will glorify the body immediately, without the ministry of the angels; the same way as He immediately glorifies the soul." [6]

The resurrection will take place in one instant of time, at the moment when the angels have gathered the dust and disposed the body for its second union with the soul.[7] The resurrection will be universal, not only in the sense that all the dead shall rise again, but also that all must die before the second advent of the Lord.[8] Those who are already risen from the dead and are now with body and soul in heaven, as our Blessed Savior and His Holy Mother, will of course neither die nor rise a second time; but Henoch, Elias, and the saints that rose from their tomb on the occasion of our Savior's death, must probably be counted among those who shall rise on the last day.[9]

All shall rise numerically the same human beings as they

---

[3] Ibid. q. 5; Albert Magn. ibid. a. 4, 5; Scotus, ibid. q. 5, n. 7.

[4] Op. cit. q. 76, a. 1, 2.

[5] Cfr. Bonavent. loc. cit.; Middleton, ibid. a. 3, q. 3.

[6] Loc. cit. a. 3.

[7] Ibid. q. 77, a. 4; Scotus, Report. IV, d. 63, q. 5, n. 4-9.

[8] Cfr. Bonavent. In Sent. IV, d. 63, a. 1, q. 2; Thomas, ibid. q. unica, a. 1; Scotus, ibid. q. 1, n. 11.

[9] Ibid.

were before death.   The common teaching of the Scholastics
on this point is formulated by St. Thomas as follows: " The
necessity of admitting the resurrection arises from this, that
man may attain his last end for which he was created.   For
this end he cannot attain during the present life, nor while
his soul is separated from the body; and if he could in no
way attain it, he would have been created in vain.   And because numerically the same being that was made for a certain
end must attain thereto, lest it appear to have been made in
vain; hence it is that numerically the same man must rise
again.   And this is the case only when numerically the same
soul is united to numerically the same body; for unless identi-
cally the same man were restored, it would not be a resurrection in the proper sense of the term.   Hence to say that
numerically the same man shall not rise again, is heretical,
and derogates from the truth of Holy Scripture, which teaches
the resurrection of the dead." [10]

In the philosophical system of St. Thomas this numerical
identity is easily understood; for as according to it the immortal soul is the only substantial form, nothing further is
required than that this soul should again be united to the
same *materia prima* that was in the body during life.   And
this is all that St. Thomas postulates in his teaching on the
subject.[11]   But in the system of Scotus there appears a much
greater difficulty as regards the numerical identity of the
body.   For according to him, man's body does not result
from the union of the spiritual soul with prime matter; but
it is constituted as a body by the *forma corporeitatis,* and this
form is lost in the dissolution of the elements of man's body
after death.   Hence in the resurrection a new form must be
educed, and consequently the body thus constituted is not
numerically the same.   He meets the difficulty by stating that
the reproduction of numerically the same form is not impossible to God's omnipotence, and in this way there will be
identity of body as well as of soul.[12]

There is also found in the writings of the Scholastics some

[10] Suppl. q. 79, a. 2.   [12] Loc. cit. q. 3, n. 1-20.
[11] Ibid. a. 2 ad 3m.

difference of opinion in regard to the material elements that shall again be united to the soul in the resurrection. If the nourishment taken during life is converted into man's bodily substance, it is obviously impossible that the whole amount of substance, thus formed in the course of many years, should be made use of to constitute the risen body. Hence some hold, as Thomas points out,[13] that the human body consists, properly speaking, only of that portion of his bodily substance which each individual derived from his parents by way of generation, and consequently this alone will be taken up again by the soul on the last day. However, this view was commonly rejected as philosophically untenable, and most of the Scholastics hold that so much of each one's " true bodily substance " will be taken up again in the resurrection as suffices for a perfect body in the state of maturity.[14] In the case of infants God will supply additional matter, so that they too may rise in a state of perfect development.[15]

As the body is ultimately the handiwork of God, it will after the resurrection be possessed of all the perfections due to its nature;[16] and this, according to the more common opinion, will be the case even with the bodies of the reprobate.[17] The difference of the reprobate and the elect, as regards their respective bodies, arises solely from the different spiritual condition of their souls. Hence in the case of the former, the body remains grossly material, and although immortal, in the sense that it cannot die, it is susceptible of the same kinds of sufferings as it was during its earthly existence;[18] whereas in the case of the latter, the body after its own manner shares in the glory of the soul, and is thereby spiritualized and made independent of the laws of space and time by which it was bound down in the days of its sojourn on earth.[19] In regard to the glorified body, the Scholastics

[13] In Sent. II, d. 30, a. 1.
[14] Cfr. Bonavent. In Sent. IV, d, 64, a. 2, q. 1, 2; Thomas, ibid. q. 1, a. 2; Scotus, ibid. q. 1, n. 15.
[15] Ibid.
[16] Cfr. Thomas, Suppl. q. 81, a. 1, 2.

[17] Ibid. q. 86, a. 1; Bonavent. In Sent. IV, d. 44, p. 1, a. 3, q. 2.
[18] Ibid. a. 2, 3.
[19] Ibid. q. 82–85; Scotus, In Sent. IV, d. 49, q. 13–16.

restate and explain philosophically the teaching of St. Paul [20] and of St. Augustine,[21] without adding anything really new in the line of dogmatic development.

2. *The General Judgment.*— Immediately upon the resurrection of the dead follows the general judgment, which will mark the end of time for the race of man. In itself it is a public ratification of the sentence already passed at the moment of each one's death. Various reasons are adduced by the Scholastics for the fitness of such a general and public judgment. St. Thomas speaks of it as a detailed representation of the world's history, a mere glance at which will reveal to every one the justice, wisdom, and goodness of God in all His ways; and at the same time it is intended as a separation of the good and the bad, who shall then be known for what they really were during their life on earth.[22] It also serves the purpose of giving due honor to the Savior of mankind, whom so many despised or ignored when they should have given Him their undivided service.[23] Lastly, it will be a public justification of God's faithful servants so often misjudged by enemies and friends, and a public condemnation of that hypocritical holiness of life which sought only its own glorification.[24]

Hence there will be a general revelation of each one's deeds, both good and bad. On this point there is no difference of opinion, save only in regard to the sins of the elect that have been blotted out by sincere repentance. Thus Peter Lombard holds that these sins shall not be made known, as the evil done by them has been repaired;[25] but this view is commonly rejected as untenable. For, as St. Thomas argues, " from this it would follow that the penance done for these sins would not become known either, at least not perfectly; and that would detract much from the glory of the saints and from the praise due to God for having so mercifully freed them from their sins.[26] Furthermore, this revelation of their

[20] I Cor. 15.
[21] De Civit. Dei, 22, 9.
[22] In Sent. IV, d. 48, q. 1, a. 1.
[23] Cfr. Thomas, Suppl. q. 90, a. 2.

[24] Id. In Sent. loc. cit.
[25] Sent. IV, d. 45.
[26] Suppl. q. 87, a. 2.

sins will not be a cause of shame to the saints, as is quite obvious from the case of Mary Magdalene whose sins are publicly recited in the church.[27]

This revelation of each one's conscience, both to himself and to all others, is spoken of by the Scholastics as the reading of the book of life — *libri vitae.* It consists in an instantaneous cognition of all that was recorded by each one's conscience during life; and the efficient cause of this cognition is a special enlightenment of the intellect on the part of God.[28] There is some difference of opinion in regard to the reprobate, as to the manner in which they shall be enabled to read the book of life. Unlike the elect, they do not behold the essence of God, and therefore they do not seem to have an adequate means of instantaneous cognition; hence St. Thomas concludes: *Singula considerabunt, sed non in instanti, sed in tempore brevissimo.*[29]

As the reading of the book of life, so likewise the passing of the judicial sentence will most probably consist in an intellectual enlightenment, whereby each individual is made to understand his eternal condition as here and now irrevocably fixed. " In regard to this question," says St. Thomas, " nothing can be defined with certainty; nevertheless it is held to be more probable that the whole judgment, both as regards the examination, the accusation of the wicked, the commendation of the good, and the sentence passed upon each, is simply a mental process. For if the deeds of each one were to be recited by word of mouth, an immeasurable length of time would be required. . . . Hence it is probable that what is said in Matthew, c. 25, must be interpreted, not as a verbal, but as a mental process." [30]

The judgment will be general in the sense that all rational creatures of God will be present, and that each one shall receive a recompense according to his works. However most of the Scholastics take the term judgment in three different

[27] Ibid. a. 2 ad 3m.
[28] Cfr. Bonavent. In Sent. IV, d. 43, a. 2; Thomas, Suppl. q. 87, a. 1-3.
[29] Ibid. a. 3.
[30] Ibid. q. 88, a. 2.

senses, and in accordance with this distinction they make the judgment either general or limit it to certain classes. In the first sense it is merely a public manifestation of each one's spiritual condition and of the recompense that is his due; and so considered the judgment will be general in the full sense of the term. In the second sense it implies an examination of those to be judged and the passing of a sentence on the part of the judge; and under this aspect the judgment will not be general. " For some are judged and perish, others are not judged and perish; some are judged and reign, others are not judged and reign." [31]   In the third sense judgment means simply condemnation, and refers only to the wicked whose state is already fixed. These are of two classes: the evil spirits who were judged by God immediately after their fall, and infidels whose obstinate blindness here on earth was the beginning of their final judgment.[32]   Later theologians, however, usually reject this distinction, and hold that the judgment applies in the same sense to all who had the use of reason during life.

According to the common teaching of the Scholastics, the judgment will be presided over by Christ, the Redeemer of the world. " To judge," argues St. Thomas, " implies dominion in him who pronounces judgment. Hence Christ will be the judge in as much as He has dominion over men, in respect of whom it is chiefly that the final judgment will take place. Now, He is our Lord not only by reason of creation, . . . but also by reason of the redemption, which He wrought in His human nature. . . . And because through the redemption He restored not only mankind, but all creation, in as much as by reason of man's restoration all creatures were placed in an ameliorated condition; . . . hence it is that Christ through His passion merited to have dominion, not only over men, but over all creatures, and consequently to act as their judge." [33]   However, He will judge *ex virtute divinitatis.*[34]

[31] Cfr. Lombard, Sent. d. 47, c. 3.
[32] Cfr. Bonavent. In Sent. IV, d. 47, a. 1, q. 3; Thomas, op. cit. q. 89, a. 5-8.
[33] Suppl. q. 90, a. 1.
[34] Ibid. a. 1 ad 2ᵐ.

With Christ others will be associated in the judgment; not, however, as judges in the strict sense of the term. The common teaching of the Scholastics on this point is thus set forth by St. Bonaventure: " One is said to be a judge in a cause for one or other of two reasons: either because it pertains to him to pronounce judgment, or because he takes part in such pronouncement, in as much as some judges coöperate with and in some measure give counsel to the chief judge. He, therefore, who pronounces judgment is the chief judge; and such is Christ alone, as is clear from Matthew xxv, wherein is described the procedure of the judgment. Those, however, who coöperate, also partake of the title and dignity of judge; and such are those saintly men who have added to the works prescribed by the commandments the supererogatory perfection of the counsels. Now, such are chiefly the Apostles, as leaders, and their close followers. Their participation, however, will not be unto the giving of counsel, because the Lord hath no need of counsel; but it will be the honor of being near the judge, and, according to the word of the Lord, we can call this the honor of sitting in judgment with Him." [35] And the same honor will also be granted to the good angels.[36]

Christ will appear in His glorified humanity to the elect and the reprobate alike, but His divinity will be seen only by the elect. However, even the reprobate shall know with the utmost certainty that He is truly God, and they shall be forced to acknowledge this to their greater shame.[37] St. Thomas,[38] St. Bonaventure,[39] and nearly all Scholastic theologians hold that the facial vision of God on the part of the reprobate is impossible; whereas Scotus contends that it could be effected by God's absolute power.[40] Practically all Scholastics are of opinion that the judgment will take place in the early morning hours, at the time when Christ rose from the dead.[41] They also regard it as likely that Christ will ap-

[35] In Sent. IV, d. 47, a. 1, q. 1.
[36] Ibid. q. 2.
[37] Ibid. d. 48, a. 1, q. 2, 3; Thomas, loc. cit. a. 3; Halens. Sum. III, q. 25, m. 4.
[38] Loc. cit.
[39] Loc. cit. q. 2.
[40] In Sent. IV, d. 48, q. 1, n. 1–10.
[41] Cfr. Thomas, Suppl. q. 47, a. 3.

pear on Mount Olivet, and that those who are to be judged shall be gathered around Him in that neighborhood.[42]

Immediately after the last judgment there will be a universal conflagration in which all the works of man shall be destroyed. Animal and plant life shall then cease to exist, and the material elements shall all be renovated by a purifying flame, so that there results a new heaven and a new earth. Furthermore, according to St. Thomas, the terrestrial globe shall then be endowed with a peculiar brightness like that of the heavenly bodies, all movement shall come to an end, and thenceforth there shall be an everlasting calm.[43]

3. *The Punishment of Hell.*— St. Bonaventure mentions and refutes two antiquated heresies in regard to the eternity of hell, and then states the accepted teaching of the Church in these terms: "Therefore the third position is reasonable and in accordance with the teaching of faith, namely, that the punishment of the wicked is eternal; and this Holy Scripture manifestly declares, faith confirms, and right reason approves."[44] Then, as the teaching of Holy Scripture and of faith is quite obvious, he develops the argument from reason as follows. "First, by way of antithesis it is eminently fitting that as the virtuous receive an eternal reward, so the wicked should be condemned to everlasting punishment. Secondly, this is not only fitting, but also necessary; because justice requires that each one be recompensed according to his works. Now the wicked have sinned against an eternal and infinite good, and for that reason they deserve an eternal punishment. Furthermore, they are immovably fixed in their perversity, and therefore their guilt is everlasting; hence, as guilt and punishment must be in proportion, it follows that their punishment should be eternal."[45] The same argument had already been indicated by St. Augustine[46] and St. Bernard,[47] and was still further developed by St. Thomas.[48]

When speaking about the punishment of hell, the Scholas-

[42] Ibid. q. 48, a. 4
[43] Ibid. q. 91, a. 2.
[44] In Sent. IV, d. 44, p. 2, a. 1, q. 1.
[45] Ibid.
[46] De Civit. Dei, 21, 11.
[47] De Gratia et Lib. Arbitr. c. 9, n. 28.
[48] Suppl. q. 99, a. 1.

tics say practically nothing in regard to the pain of loss. They presuppose that this is most intense, as it is measured by the happiness that would have been theirs had they been faithful in the service of God.[49]   But presupposing this, they treat at great length of the positive pain, or the pain of sense, inflicted on the reprobate.   The following points may be briefly noted.

As the pain of loss corresponds to the sinner's turning away from God, so the pain of sense corresponds to his inordinate turning to creatures.   He made them, to all intents and purposes, his last end; and now they are converted by divine justice into instruments of the most exquisite torture.[50] Hence the pain of sense, argues St. Bonaventure, is caused by the four elements that constitute the material world — air, earth, fire, and water.[51]   Or as St. Thomas puts it: " According to St. Basil, in the last purification of the world there will be a separation of the elements, and whatever is pure and of a refined nature will remain in the higher regions for the glory of the blessed; but whatever is vile and filthy shall be cast into hell for the punishment of the damned: so that, as to the blessed every material creature shall be a source of joy, so in like manner to the damned all creatures shall be a cause of torment." [52]

It is the common teaching of the Scholastics that hell is a subterranean place, most probably situated at the center of the earth.   " Its arrangement," says St. Thomas, " is such as corresponds to the extreme misery of those detained therein. Hence there is both light and darkness, but in such a way as to intensify the torments of the lost.   In itself the seeing of things is a source of delight, . . . but under certain conditions it becomes a cause of suffering, namely, when we see things that are hurtful or repugnant to us.   And therefore the disposition of light and darkness in hell must be such that nothing is seen distinctly, but that those things which can afflict the heart are perceived as wrapt in a certain shadowy gloom.

[49] Cfr. Thomas, op. cit. q. 98, a. 9.   [51] In Sent. IV, d. 44, p. 2, a. 2,
[50] Ibid. q. 97, a. 1.   q. 2.
                                                         [52] Op. cit. q. 47, a. 1.

Hence, properly speaking, it is a place of darkness. Nevertheless, by divine disposition there is just sufficient light to make those things visible which can torture the soul: and this follows from the very position of the place; because in the center of the earth, where hell is said to be situated, there can be no fire except such as is dim and dull and smoky." [53]

The principal agent used by God in causing the pain of sense is material fire. This is the teaching of Peter Lombard.[54] Alexander of Hales,[55] Albertus Magnus,[56] St. Thomas,[57] St. Bonaventure,[58] Duns Scotus,[59] and all representative Scholastics. " Whatever may be said about the fire that tortures souls while separated from their bodies," argues St. Thomas, " the fire by which the bodies of the reprobate are tormented after the resurrection must be corporeal; because the body cannot be afflicted except by corporeal agents of pain." [60] Furthermore, the fire of hell is specifically the same as the fire that we use here on earth, although in some mysterious way it burns without consuming or being consumed.[61] The material nature of this fire was defended by the Scholastics against Avicenna and other Arabian philosophers who denied the resurrection of the body, and consequently contended that the term fire, when used in connection with the punishment of hell, must be taken in a metaphorical sense.

Again, it is also the common teaching of the Scholastics that this same material fire afflicts the evil spirits and human souls while in the state of separation from their bodies. But when they try to explain how this is possible, they severally advance somewhat different views. Thus Albertus Magnus practically contents himself with stating the fact as contained in Holy Scripture, and then affirming that God in His wisdom and power must have ways and means of afflicting spirits through the agency of matter.[62] St. Bonaventure admits that material fire as such cannot affect spiritual substances directly,

[53] Suppl. q. 97, a. 4.
[54] Sent. IV, d. 44, c. 6.
[55] Sum. II, q. 116, m. 4.
[56] In Sent. IV, d. 44, a. 37.
[57] Ibid. a. 4.

[58] Breviloq. VII, c. 6.
[59] Report. d. 44, q. 3, n. 19.
[60] Suppl. q. 97, a. 4.
[61] Ibid. a. 6.
[62] Loc. cit.

but it may do so in an indirect way; for divine justice may use it for the purpose of producing in the intellect and will a condition of fearsome apprehension and loathing repugnance, which results in unbearable mental and physical torture. Both evil spirits and disembodied souls may be shut up within the fire as in a prison, and thus be made to experience all the horrors that one naturally associates with earthly dungeons. Moreover, human souls always retain their sensitive faculties, by reason of which they can in some way be brought under the influence of material agents.[63]

St. Thomas examines three different views on this subject, and then rejects them as inadmissible. The first of these holds that spirits are terrified at the mere sight of fire; the second maintains that fire is apprehended by them as hurtful, and from this apprehension results an agony of dread and sadness; the third contends that spirits are physically afflicted by God Himself, who acts in the fire. After setting aside these explanations as insufficient, he gives his own in these terms: " It is necessary, therefore, to gather all these different ways together into one, so that it may become intelligible how a spirit can suffer from material fire. Let us say, then, that it is in accordance with the nature of fire for spirits to be united to it by way of location, just as any other thing localized is in a place; but over and above, in so far as the fire in question is an instrument of divine justice, it has also the power of holding these spirits bound to itself; and in this the fire is truly hurtful to the spirit, in as much as the soul, seeing that the fire is thus the cause of its involuntary detention, is tormented by the fire." [64]

Substantially the same explanation is given by Duns Scotus. In the first place, he says, the lost spirits are detained in one place by the fire; then they apprehend this detention; from this arises a repugnance to being thus detained; next this repugnance is vividly realized; finally, from the realization of their imprisoned condition, thus always before their minds, there results an intense agony of suffering and despair.[65]

[63] In Sent. IV, d. 44, a. 3, q. 2.
[64] Suppl. q. 70, a. 3.

[65] Report. IV, d. 44, q. 2, n. 9; cfr. In Sent. ibid. n. 11.

Morally the reprobate are in a state of unalterable perversion: they cling to their past sins, although they at the same time shrink from them as the cause of their torture;[66] they hate God, not as He is in Himself, but in so far as they experience the rigor of His justice;[67] they likewise hate all created beings, but more especially the blessed in heaven, whose happiness fills them with a most intense envy.[68]   Still, with all this, they do not sin; because their very condition of obduracy in evil is a punishment for their past misdeeds.[69]

4. *The Joys of Heaven.*— Heaven is a place where the elect see God face to face, as He is in Himself; and from this intuitive vision of the triune God results a state of ecstatic joy and unspeakable happiness.   On this point, considered as a mere fact, there never was a difference of opinion among the Scholastics.   Furthermore, nearly all of them are agreed that the elect are placed in full possession of their essential happiness as soon as they have satisfied the justice of God for their past sins.   Early in the fourteenth century, Pope John XXII, while still a simple theologian, advanced it as his private opinion that the intuitive vision of God's essence might be delayed even in the case of souls already perfectly pure in the sight of God; but his view met with strong opposition, as being out of harmony with the teaching of the Church.[70] Almost half a century before that unguarded statement was made, St. Thomas had stigmatized the opinion it expressed as heretical.[71]   And in 1336, Benedict XII thus defined the traditional teaching: *Homines pios plene purgatos vel justos ex hac vita decedentes statim consequi beatitudinem et visione Dei beatifica perfrui . . . definimus.*[72]

Most Scholastics divide beatitude into objective and formal. By the former they understand God Himself, who as the Supreme Good perfectly satisfies every rational tendency of the elect.   By the latter they designate that operation of the soul

[66] Cfr. Thomas, op. cit. q. 98, a. I, 2.
[67] Ibid. a. 5.
[68] Ibid. a. 7, 9.
[69] Ibid. a. 6.

[70] Cfr. Chartular Universit. Paris. t. II, n. 970–987.
[71] Suppl. q. 69, a. 2.
[72] Mansi, 25, 986 D.

or spirit by which God is possessed as the source of ecstatic fruition. In regard to objective beatitude there is no room for discussion, as apart from God there is no object the possession of which can be the source of perfect blessedness. Besides, on this point the teaching of Holy Scripture is so clear that it excludes all further development of doctrine. But matters look quite different when the question of formal beatitude comes up for consideration. For although it is a matter of faith that the blessed see God face to face, or as Benedict XII, defined it, *visione intuitiva et etiam faciali, nulla mediante creatura in ratione visi se habente,* nevertheless both the act of this vision itself and its relation to the essence of beatitude have always been a subject of discussion among theologians. Only a few passing remarks can here be made about the points in question.

As the intuitive vision of God is an act of the intellect, it must obviously be explained in terms of human knowledge. Now in human knowledge, according to the common teaching of the Scholastics, four things come up for consideration: the intellect, the object, the impressed species — *species impressa,* and the expressed species — *species expressa.* Of itself the intellect does not represent one object rather than another; and therefore, in order to represent a particular object, it must first be determined or modified by a likeness derived from that same object. This modification is called the *species impressa,* which is a virtual representation of the object in question. Thus modified, the intellect produces the *species expressa,* or the act of knowing, which is a vital and formal representation of the object as known.

Applying this exposition of the genesis of human knowledge to the beatific vision, the Scholastics studied the question in reference to the following three points: First, does the beatific vision postulate a *species impressa?* Secondly, does it postulate a *species expressa?* Thirdly, in whatever way the first two points be decided, must the intellect be supernaturally strengthened by the light of glory — *lumen gloriae* — in order to see God face to face?

Some of the older Scholastics, whom St. Bonaventure takes

occasion to refute,[73] identified the beatific vision with God's own eternal and uncreated knowledge, in a similar way as they identified sanctifying grace with the Holy Spirit. Somewhat like this is the opinion defended by Henry of Ghent, who distinguishes in the blessed a created and an uncreated beatitude. The former, he says, consists in acts of the intellect and will, which as such, even in this connection, do not imply proper knowledge of God; whereas the latter is an immediate communication of God, or of objective beatitude, to the soul by way of circuminsession — *per circuminsessionem vel illapsum*. It is in this that beatitude properly consists, and in so far it is not a perfection of the faculties, but of the soul's substance.[74]

St. Bonaventure defines formal beatitude as *influentia Dei in animam, quae est ipsa deiformitas et satietas*.[75] In his explanation of this definition he states that beatitude consists of two parts: the deification of the soul and its faculties which is a habit or quality, and the corresponding acts of the intellect and will. Hence it is neither a mere act, nor a mere habit, but a combination of the two; and thus it may be compared to a natural habit of knowledge which is always in act, or by which man always actually contemplates the object known.[76]

In none of these explanations is there a definite attempt made to analyze the act of knowledge in so far as it proceeds from the intellect. And hence the explanations themselves are vague and unsatisfactory. In this respect the exposition of St. Thomas is much more explicit. After setting aside the opinion of some Arabian philosophers as to the nature of human knowledge, he proceeds: "Since in all cognition there is need of some form by which the object is known or seen, the form by which the intellect is perfected, in order to have a cognitive vision of separated substances, is not the quiddity which the intellect abstracts from composite things, as is maintained by the first opinion; nor is it an impression of

---

[73] In Sent. III, d. 14, a. 1, q. 1.
[74] Quodl. 13, q. 12.
[75] In Sent. IV, d. 49, p. 1, a. unicus, q. 1.
[76] Ibid. q. 1 ad 5m.

the separated substance remaining in our intellect, as is held
by the second; but it is the separated substance itself which is
united to our intellect as a form, so that this substance itself
is both the object which is known and the form by which it
is known.

"But whatever may be said in regard to other separated
substances, this is undoubtedly the explanation to be accepted
in regard to the intuitive vision of God; because by whatever
other form our intellect be perfected, it necessarily remains
incapable of seeing God's essence. However the explanation
just given must not be understood in the sense that the divine
essence is properly the form of our intellect, or that from its
union with our intellect results a something that is strictly
one, as is the case when matter and form are united in the
natural order of things; but in this other sense, that the relation of the divine essence to our intellect is proportionately
the same as that of form to matter. . . . And that this suffices to make our intellect capable of seeing the divine essence
by means of that same essence, may be shown as follows. . . .
In the matter of knowledge, it is necessary to consider the
intellect itself as matter, and the intelligible species as its
form; hence the intellect in the act of knowing is composed
of the two. Consequently, given a self-subsistent being, which
is pure intelligibility, that being can of itself act as the form
by which the intellect knows. For since it is pure form,
without any admixture of matter, there is nothing to prevent
it from discharging the functions of form in regard to the
intellect; and thus become in a manner part of the composite,
which is the intellect in act. Because a thing is intelligible in
so far as it is in act. . . . Hence it follows that the divine
essence, since it is pure actuality, can be the form by which
the intellect knows; and this is the beatific vision." [77]

In this exposition, as is quite obvious, both the *species impressa* and the *species expressa,* as taken in the strict meaning
of the respective terms, are eliminated from the intuitive
vision of God. Their place is taken by the divine essence,

[77] Suppl. q. 92, a. I.

which unites itself immediately to the intellect, and through
this immediate union is seen face to face. The explanation
agrees perfectly with the definition of Benedict XII, issued
some sixty years later. It reads as follows: *Definimus:
quod secundum communem Dei ordinationem animae sanctorum omnium . . . vident divinam essentiam visione intuitiva et etiam faciali, nulla mediante creatura in ratione objecti
visi se habente, sed divina essentia immediate se nude, clare
et aperte eis ostendente, quodque sic videntes eadem divina
essentia perfruuntur.*[78]

It is true, neither St. Thomas nor Pope Benedict suppose
the intellect to be merely passive in the beatific vision; on the
contrary, they imply that the vision itself is an intellectual act;
but what they wish to exclude is the *species* as a created representation of the Godhead; for that representation would always be analogous, and as such it could not be nor lead to a
proper knowledge of God.   Substantially the same position is
taken by Duns Scotus.[79]   Hence, if the term *species expressa*
be understood in a wider sense, as simply designating an act
of knowledge, it may evidently be employed without prejudice
to the faith.

For this intuitive vision of God, in so far as it is a cognitive
act, the intellect must be disposed and strengthened by the
light of glory, which in some way corresponds to the light of
faith here on earth.   The fact is generally admitted by the
Scholastics, but most of them are rather vague when they
attempt to explain the nature of this light.   St. Thomas puts
his exposition this way: "Everything that is elevated to
what exceeds its nature, must be prepared by some disposition
above its nature; as, for example, if air is to receive the form
of fire, it must be prepared by some disposition for such a
form.   Now when any created intellect sees the essence of
God, the essence of God itself becomes the intelligible form
of the intellect.   Hence it is necessary that some supernatural
disposition should be added to the intellect in order that it
may be elevated to such a great and sublime height.   Since

[78] DB. 530.   [79] In Sent. IV, d. 49, q. 3, n. 6.

the natural power of the created intellect does not avail to enable it to see the essence of God, as was shown in the preceding article, it is necessary that the power of understanding should be aided by divine grace. This increase of the intellectual powers is called the illumination of the intellect, as we also call the intelligible object itself by the name of light or illumination." [80]

Again: " This light is required to see the divine essence, not as a similitude in which God is seen, but as a perfection of the intellect, strengthening it to see God. Therefore it may be said that this light is not to be described as a medium in which God is seen, but by which He is seen; and such a medium does not take away the immediate vision of God." [81] Furthermore, this light can in no wise be natural to any creature, but only to the divine nature; and therefore by it the rational creature is made deiform.[82]

At the time when St. Thomas wrote, no decision on this matter had yet been given by the Church; and hence a few later Scholastics, especially Durandus,[83] controverted his view, and argued that the mere fact of the divine essence being intimately present to the human intellect eliminates the necessity of the light of glory as a previous disposition. However, the Council of Vienne (1311–1312) decided against this teaching by rejecting a thesis in which it was stated, *quod anima non indiget lumine gloriae, ipsam elevante, ad Deum videndum et eo beate fruendum.*[84]

There was greater divergence of views among the Scholastics as regards the essence of beatitude. All were agreed that the blessedness of the elect must comprise at least three acts: an act of intuitive vision, an act of love, and an act of fruition or joy. The first of these is an act of the intellect, while the other two proceed from the will. In regard to them the question arose, and is still under discussion, what is their precise relation to the essence of beatitude? Are all three of them constitutive, so that if one be eliminated beatitude itself

---

[80] Sum. Theol. I, q. 12, a. 5.
[81] Ibid. a. 5 ad 1m.
[82] Ibid. a. 5 ad 3m.

[83] In Sent. IV, d. 49, q. 2, n. 24.
[84] DB. 475.

is destroyed? Or is only one of them essential, or at most two? And if so, which of them? Setting aside merely accidental and minor differences, the views of the Scholastics on this point may be reduced to the following three. First: Beatitude consists essentially in the intuitive vision of God, and from this flow the complementary acts of love and fruition. Second: The essence of beatitude comprises both the intuitive vision of God and an act of love, but in such a way that the intuitive vision is merely inchoative and receives its essential complement from the act of love. Third: Beatitude consists essentially in an act of love, to which the intuitive vision is presupposed as a necessary condition, and from which fruition flows as a connatural consequence.

The first of these three views is put forward by St. Thomas. Admitting that beatitude is the proper object of the will, since it is the possession of the Supreme Good, he holds that the act of the will does nevertheless not constitute the essence of beatitude. For, he argues, "that act is man's last end, taken subjectively, by reason of which he is placed in such a relation to God that the will rests perfectly satisfied in Him. But only the vision of God by the intellect is such an act; because by that only is there established a certain contact of God with the faculties — since everything that is known is in him who knows in so far as it is known; just as also bodily contact with something agreeable to the senses induces a quieting of the affections. And therefore man's last end consists in an act of the intellect; and thus beatitude, which is man's last end, is in the intellect as its proper subject. However, that which belongs to the will, namely, its resting in the end obtained, which may be termed delectation, is the formal complement of the essence of beatitude, as supervening upon the intuitive vision in which the substance of beatitude consists; so that thus there is attributed to the will both the first relation to the end, in as much as it desires its attainment, and also the last, in so far as it rests in the end already attained." [85]

The second opinion is defended by Richard of Middle-

[85] In Sent. IV, d. 49, q. 1, a. 1, sol. 2.

ton,[86] and also by St. Bonaventure.[87] Both of them teach that by way of genesis beatitude is first in the intellect, in as much as it has its inception in the intuitive vision of God; but it receives its essential perfection in the will, which is united to God in the act of love and possesses Him as the object of blessed fruition.

The third view is that of Scotus. He admits that both the intellect and will possess God as their immediate object; and also that by way of genesis beatitude is first in the intellect, in as much as without the intuitive vision there could be no immediate union of the will with the divine essence. But the essence of beatitude consists in only one operation — that of the will.[88] The will is man's noblest faculty, just as charity is the highest of virtues.[89] It is right, therefore, and obvious too, that the full and complete and perfect possession of man's end is an act of unitive love; not of a love of concupiscence, but of benevolence, which finds its perfect expression in this utterance: "The infinite goodness of God is to me an object of complacency, and by accepting Him and delighting in Him, I simply desire Him to possess all the goodness He does possess." [90]

After setting forth their views on the essential blessedness of the elect, the Scholastics usually enter into rather lengthy discussions of a number of subordinate points, more or less intimately connected with the state of eternal beatitude. The chief of these are the *dotes*, or spiritual dowry of the blessed; the *aureolae*, or special crowns corresponding to certain states in life and the perfect practice of certain virtues; the accidental happiness that arises from various created sources: the perpetuity of that blissful state; the impeccability of the elect; their social relations, and kindred subjects. But these discussions need not be reviewed in the present connection; because, with the exception of a few points, the subjects discussed are likely to remain a matter of speculation until we shall have attained the blessed vision of God.

---

[86] Ibid. a. 1, q. 6.
[87] Ibid. I, d. 1, a. 2, q. unica; II, d. 38, a. 1, q. 2; Breviloq. VII, c. 7.

[88] In Sent. IV, d. 49, q. 3, n. 6, 5; q. 4, n. 6, 5.
[89] Ibid. q. 4, n. 13–18.
[90] Ibid. q. 5, n. 4.

CHAPTER XXV

MEDIÆVAL HERESIES: MEDIÆVAL COUNCILS [1]

It was stated in the introduction to this volume that the development of dogmas during the Middle Ages was little influenced by the aberration of heretics and consequent decisions of councils. That this statement is perfectly correct must be evident from what has been said in the preceding chapters. Such heresies as did arise were either slight modifications of errors condemned centuries before, or they were simply momentary disturbances caused by individual fanaticism or indiscreet zeal for the purity of ecclesiastical life. With one or two exceptions, they did not spring from intellectual difficulties regarding any particular doctrine, as had been the case with all the great heresies of the fourth, fifth, and sixth centuries. Hence they led to little or no theological discussion, and consequently they did not affect the normal development of doctrine. It was owing to the ephemeral nature of these heresies that the numerous ecumenical councils held during the Middle Ages treated them only in passing. It was usually not for the purpose of giving dogmatic decisions that these councils were convoked, but rather for the sake of bringing about ecclesiastical reforms, or settling difficulties between the Church and the State. And this being the case, the following brief outline of mediæval heresies and councils will suffice for the proper understanding of the various questions that have thus far been treated in the present volume.

[1] Cfr. Hefele, Conciliengeschichte, V; Marion, Histoire de l'Eglise, II; Funk, Manual of Church History, I; Doellinger, Beitraege zur Sektengeschichte des Mittelalters.

438

A — MEDIÆVAL HERESIES

In regard to the errors of Gottschalk, Berengarius, Roscelin, Abelard, and Gilbert de la Porrée, nothing need be said on the present occasion, as a summary of them has been given in the preceding chapters.[2] It need only be added that their false views did not find favor with men of wide influence, and as a result they soon disappeared from the theological world. Some of them were indeed revived by later heretics, but of that it will be more convenient to say something in its own proper place. Hence at present we may devote our attention to such heretical vagaries and tendencies as have thus far either not been taken note of at all or else only in a passing way.

1. *Peter de Bruys and the Petrobrusians.*— Concerning the person and life of Peter de Bruys little is known. Practically our only source of information is a letter of Peter the Venerable, abbot of Cluny,[3] and a brief statement of Abelard in his *Introductio ad Theologiam.*[4] According to these authorities, he was a priest who had disgraced himself and in consequence was chased from his church by his own parishioners.[5] After that he traveled for about twenty years through Southern France and the neighboring countries, causing great disturbance by his fierce invectives against the Church and some of her doctrines. He was burnt to death at St. Giles in 1137, the enraged people having cast him into the fire which he himself had made of broken crucifixes.[6] His work was continued by the Cluniac monk Henry of Lausanne, who was condemned by the Council of Rheims in 1148.

From the statements of Peter the Venerable and Abelard, the teaching of these sectaries may be reduced to the following points:

(a) The baptism of children is invalid, because they are

[2] Cfr. cc. 1–4, 17.
[3] Epistola sive Tractatus adversus Petrobrusianos Hereticos, ML, 189, 719–850.
[4] Op. cit. II, c. 4.
[5] Cfr. ML, 189, 790.
[6] ML, 189, 723 A.

unable to make an act of faith; hence all those who have received the sacrament in childhood, must be rebaptized.

(b) God may be adored and worshiped anywhere, and
therefore it is unlawful to build churches; those that have been
built already should be torn down and destroyed.

(c) No veneration must be paid to crucifixes, because they
are instruments of punishment; hence wherever a crucifix is
found, it should be broken to pieces and cast into the fire.

(d) Christ changed bread and wine into His body and blood
only once, and He did not give the same power to His priests;
hence He is not really and personally present in the Eucharist.

(e) Prayers, alms-deeds, and other pious works for the departed are useless.   Church music, singing, and ecclesiastical
ceremonies generally should be abolished.   God simply laughs
at them: He is pleased only with the worship of the heart.

For the time being, Peter and Henry had many followers
and several synods were held to counteract their influence,
but after their death the sect to which Peter had given his
name slowly disappeared.

2. *Tanchelm and Eon de Stella.* — Tanchelm was an escaped
monk, who gathered around him a large following with which
he traveled from place to place in the Low Countries.   He
claimed to be the equal of Jesus Christ and to have received
as his special mission the reformation of ecclesiastical and religious life.   At the same time, however, his conduct was
shockingly immoral, and so was that of his immediate followers.   As he violently denounced the authority of the Church
and all priestly ministrations, he caused widespread disturbance wherever he went.   Finally, in 1115, he was slain by a
cleric.   Much of the harm wrought by him was repaired by
the zeal and prudence of St. Norbert.

Some twenty years later, a similar disturbance was caused
by Eon de Stella, a Breton nobleman.   He gave himself out
as the Son of God, the Judge of the living and dead.   His
extraordinary claim he tried to establish by an appeal to the
liturgical text: " *Per eum (Eon) qui venturus est judicare
vivos et mortuos et saeculum per ignem.*   He fiercely inveighed
against all worldly possessions on the part of the Church,

and also preached a kind of communism which secured him vast numbers of adherents. He was condemned by the Council of Rheims in 1148, and some years later died in prison.

About the same time, considerable agitation along these lines was carried on by Arnold of Brescia, who violently declaimed against the Church's possession of landed property, and also against the temporal power of the Pope. According to Otto of Freising, " he held that no cleric having property, no bishop holding fiefs, no monk who was not truly poor, could hope for salvation." [7] He was condemned by the Second Lateran Council, in 1139, but continued his propaganda for some time longer in France and Switzerland. In 1155 he was executed by Barbarossa, on account of his connection with the revolution which had broken out at Rome.

3. *Amalric of Bene and David of Dinant.*— Towards the end of the twelfth century, the Moorish commentaries on Aristotle gave rise to various false views among the professors of the University of Paris. Some held that what is true in philosophy may be false in theology, that authority alone cannot give full certainty, and that the Christian religion, like all others, contains both truth and falsehood. Others taught pantheistic doctrines, identifying the creature with the Creator. To this latter class belonged Amalric of Bene and David of Dinant. Amalric held that all Christians are members of Christ, in the sense that by way of identification they are all other Christs; while David maintained that God is primary matter, from which all other beings are derived by some kind of pantheistic evolution. The teaching of Amalric was condemned by the University of Paris in 1206, and also by Pope Innocent III, to whom he had appealed for an authoritative decision. Some years later, 1209 or 1210, a synod held at Paris renewed this condemnation and also ordered the writings of David to be committed to the flames.

However, the error of Amalric spread rapidly, both among the clergy and laity. In a few years after his death, which occurred in 1207, numerous adherents in France, Italy, Ger-

[7] Cfr. Hefele, op. cit. V, 861, 881.

many, and Switzerland proclaimed him as their prophet. They were known by various names, Amalricians, Brethren of the Free Spirit, or more generally, Beghards and Beguines. They held a threefold incarnation of God: of the Father in Abraham, of the Son in Christ, and of the Holy Ghost in each Christian. Because of this incarnation, each individual Christian is God in as true a sense as was Christ Himself. In their preaching they severely criticized the Church and the priesthood, and at the same time they claimed for themselves absolute freedom to indulge their sensual appetites. Their errors were repeatedly condemned by provincial synods, but it was only by the active intervention of the Inquisition that the sect was finally rooted out.

4. *The Cathari or Albigenses.*— These heretics are usually considered as the lineal descendants of the fourth-century Manichaeans, for whose conversion St. Augustine had labored with singular success. Since his time they had practically disappeared from the West, but in the seventh and eighth centuries they sprang up anew in the Eastern Empire, where they went by the name of Paulicians. Two centuries later they appeared under the name of Bogomiles among the Bulgarians, and thence made their way into Western Europe. In Italy they called themselves Patarini, while in the South of France they adopted the name of Cathari. In this latter country their stronghold was the city of Albi, and hence the French branch of the sectaries came to be known as the Albigenses.

Doctrinally these heretics belonged to two different schools. The Cathari of France were for the most part strict Manichaeans, who believed in the existence of two eternal principles, each of which was regarded as the creator of a different world. The Patarini of Italy, on the other hand, held the evil principle to be simply a fallen angel, whom they called Satan and identified with the God of the Old Testament. Aside from this fundamental difference in their belief, both parties were agreed on most other points of doctrine. They believed in the migration of souls, and as a consequence forbade the killing of animals. Their worship consisted chiefly in the recital of the Lord's prayer, and all ecclesiastical ceremonies, the sacraments, veneration of the saints, and the like, were rejected by them. Churches they regarded as useless, and therefore destroyed them wherever they could. They were opposed to all civil government; held oaths, capital punishment, and wars to be unlawful; disapproved of marriage, abstained from flesh-meat, and observed long fasts. However, these austerities were practiced only by the Perfect, who had received the *consolamentum* or spiritual baptism. The rank and file were allowed to indulge their sensual appetite to the fullest extent. For them it was sufficient to promise that they would receive the *consolamentum* at the hour of death.

As these sectaries caused great civil disorder as well as religious, and were moreover protected by powerful nobles, Pope Innocent III found it necessary to organize a crusade against them, and so come to the assistance of the persecuted Catholics. The conflict lasted for twenty long years, and led to much bloodshed on both sides. In the beginning milder measures had been used, and the prayers and preaching of St. Dominic had met with considerable success; but the awful ravages committed by the heretics made the use of force against them inevitable. Their power was at last broken, but only when the fair countryside had been changed to a desert. Even then many persevered in their error, and it was only the constant vigilance and severe measures of the Inquisition that finally succeeded in extirpating the sect completely.[8]

5. *The Waldensians.*— This sect, like so many others in the Middle Ages, sprang from the misdirected zeal of a well intentioned man. Its founder was a certain Waldes, a wealthy broker of Lyons in France. After reading the story of St. Alexius, he made up his mind to follow that holy man's example. Hence, about 1177, he disposed of his wealth, and became a poor preacher of penance. His object was to restore the simplicity of life which had distinguished the early Christians. In a short time he gathered around him numerous companions, and these he sent out to preach the gospel of poverty wherever they could get a hearing. Although ex-

---

[8] Cfr. Funk, op. cit. I, 350; Hefele, op. cit. V, 827 sqq.

pelled from Lyons, they were at first left unmolested by
ecclesiastical authority. However, in 1184, Pope Lucius III
excommunicated them together with other heretics. In this excommunication they are referred to as the Humiliati or Poor
Men of Lyons.

Unlike the early Christians, whom they professed to imitate,
these sectaries not only relinquished their possessions, but also
avoided all manual labor, and therefore depended for their
livelihood upon alms. But as their number increased very
rapidly, this mode of existence became too precarious, and so
they divided into two classes — the Perfect and the Believers.
While the former complied strictly with the demands of absolute poverty, the latter were allowed to own worldly possessions. The Perfect bound themselves by the vows of poverty,
chastity, and obedience, and thus in a manner constituted a
religious association. At the same time, they were doctrinally
unsound. They not only denied the lawfulness of oaths, of
military service, and of the death penalty for criminals; but
also rejected the doctrine of purgatory, of intercession for the
dead, and of indulgences. Moreover the Italian branch maintained that the value of the sacraments depended on the personal sanctity of the minister, a view that had been condemned
by the Church centuries before.

Under Innocent III serious efforts were made to reclaim
these deluded men, and large numbers returned to the Church,
but others persevered in their error. They were no longer
satisfied with claiming Waldes as their founder, but contended
that they were a remnant of the primitive Christians who had
remained faithful to Apostolic traditions when, through the
misdirected liberality of Constantine, the Church had fallen
a victim to the seduction of wealth and power. In the sixteenth century most of them threw in their lot with the Reformers, and through these Waldensians many Protestants
later on tried to establish their claim to Apostolic succession.[9]

6. *John Wiclif.*— Like many a self-constituted reformer
before him and since, Wiclif started out with the laudable in-

[9] Cfr. Hefele, op. cit. V, 726 sqq.

tention of counteracting certain tendencies that threatened the purity of ecclesiastical life. Many of the clergy in his day were more intent upon the accumulation of wealth than upon the saving of souls. Against these he preached the poverty of Christ and the Apostles. Then, to destroy the evil at its root as he conceived it, he began to attack the Church's right to possess property, and advocated a state-supported clergy. He was especially violent in his denunciation of religious orders, many of which possessed vast estates and great wealth. From these polemics against abuses, real or imaginary, he by degrees passed over to attacks on monasticism as an institution and finally on the Papacy itself. To such lengths, however, he did not go until after the outbreak of the Western Schism in 1378. From that time forward till his death in 1384, he fell into many doctrinal errors; and these he spread all through England by means of wandering preachers, historically known as Lollards, that is, sowers of tares.

The teaching of Wiclif was condemned by two synods held in London, the one in May and the other in November of 1382. At the first two lists of propositions drawn from the writings of Wiclif were examined and condemned. The most important of the condemned errors are the following: (a) The substance of bread and wine remain after the consecration. (b) The accidents of bread and wine do not exist without a subject. (c) In the Holy Eucharist Christ is not really and truly present in the same sense that He is in heaven. (d) A priest or a bishop who is in the state of mortal sin cannot consecrate, baptize, or administer any other sacrament. (e) If a person is truly sorry for his sins, he has no need of confession. (f) When the Pope leads a wicked life, he loses all his power except such as he received from the Emperor. (g) For clerics to own temporal possessions is against the teaching of Holy Scriptures. (h) It is a sin to found religious orders, whether they own property or not. (i) Whoever belongs to a religious order is by that very fact excluded from the communion of saints.[10]

[10] Cfr. Hefele, op. cit. VI, p. 954 sqq.

After the second of these synods, Wiclif retired to his vicarage at Lutterworth, where he spent his remaining days in writing his chief work, entitled *Trialogus*. In this he develops his erroneous views on predestination, the Church, and the Holy Eucharist. God predestines men to eternal life irrespective of their merit, the Church is made up only of the predestined, and the substance of bread and wine remain in the Holy Eucharist together with the body and blood of Christ. Forty-five propositions, taken partly from this book and partly from his other writings, were condemned by the Council of Constance and by Pope Martin V.[11]

7. *John Hus.*— Owing to the severe measures taken both by the ecclesiastical and secular authorities, Wiclifism practically disappeared from England soon after its author's death. But it found a home on the continent, and especially in Bohemia, where it was ardently defended by John Hus. He was at the time professor at the University of Prague, and an eloquent preacher. He took over the entire teaching of Wiclif, except his error on the Holy Eucharist. In opposition to that he firmly maintained the doctrine of transubstantiation as taught by the Church. In 1403, the University of Prague condemned a number of Wiclifite theses, but this had little effect upon Hus and his fellow admirers of the English heretic. Then, in 1411, he himself was excommunicated, and every community that presumed to harbor him was threatened with an interdict. He, however, continued to preach as before, and in his justification appealed from the Pope to a general council. He had a staunch supporter in his friend, Jerome of Prague.

On the 5th of November, 1414, the Council of Constance, convened for the purpose of terminating the schism, held its first session. Hus had secured a " safe conduct " from Emperor Sigismund, and came to the Council without any misgivings as to the favorable issue of the case against him. He seems to have been firmly convinced that he was perfectly orthodox in his teaching. However, after a preliminary examination, he was imprisoned in a Dominican monastery,

[11] Mansi, 27, 1207 sqq.

where he remained from the 6th of December till Palm Sunday. A formal charge of heresy was brought against him in a general congregation of cardinals and bishops on the 5th of June, and was thereafter discussed in four different sessions of the Council. These discussions led to the formulation of thirty propositions, which Hus was called upon to retract.[12] As he constantly refused to do so, on the plea that he had never taught heretical doctrines and that he could not retract the truth without offending God, he was degraded from his priestly rank and handed over to the secular arm. The Emperor ordered him to be burned at the stake, and this sentence was carried out on the 6th of July, 1415. Although his friend, Jerome of Prague, met the same fate eleven months later, it was not until after twenty years of civil war that the Husite troubles in Bohemia were finally settled.[13]

Protestant writers frequently state that Wiclif and Hus were Prereformers, who began the work that Luther was destined to perfect in the sixteenth century. But as Loofs [14] and other Protestant dogmatic historians point out, all these so-called Prereformers rejected every fundamental principle upon which Protestantism is based. They went astray on particular doctrines, but clung tenaciously to the Catholic concept of salvation through the ministerial intervention of the Church instituted by Christ. Neither the right of private judgment in the interpretation of Scripture, nor the doctrine of justification through faith alone, formed either an essential or an integral part of any heresy before the sixteenth century. Yet the two together make up the very essence of Protestantism.

B — MEDIÆVAL COUNCILS

What was said in the preceding section in regard to mediæval heresies, may here be applied to mediæval councils — they contributed very little to the development of dogma. Exclu-

---

[12] Ibid. 1209 sqq.
[13] Cfr. Hefele, op. cit. VII, 66–240.

[14] Dogmengeschichte, 635–658.

sive of the Council of Trent, which forms in a manner the
dividing line between mediæval and modern times, ten ecumenical councils were held during the Middle Ages, and of these
only five dealt to any considerable extent with doctrinal matter.
They are the following: The Fourth Lateran (1215); the
Second of Lyons (1274); the Council of Vienne (1311–
1312); the Council of Constance (1414–1418), and the Council of Florence (1438–1445). And even these five were not
convened for the purpose of giving dogmatic decisions; their
primary object was either the promotion of the crusades, the
settling of difficulties between Church and State, the reformation of discipline, the union of the East and West, or the
termination of schisms. Furthermore, as will be shown in the
following paragraphs, such dogmatic decisions as were given
amounted to little more than restatements of what was already
a matter of faith.

1. *The Fourth Lateran Council.*— In his letter of convocation, addressed to the bishops of Christendom, Pope Innocent
III stated the purpose of the Council in these terms: " Two
things I have especially at heart: The recovery of the Holy
Land and the reformation of the whole Church." The attainment of this twofold object, therefore, was to constitute the
chief topic of discussion and legislation. In accordance with
the Pope's wishes, on November 11, 1215, four hundred and
twelve bishops, some eight hundred abbots and priors, besides
numerous substitutes of absent prelates, gathered in the Lateran
Basilica to begin the work outlined for them by the Sovereign
Pontiff. Only three sessions were held, in which seventy
capitula were drawn up, containing definitions against heretics,
a decree in reference to the next crusade, and disciplinary
canons.[15] It is only of the first that a brief summary need be
given in the present connection.

The chief heretics in question were the Cathari and Waldensians, of whom a short account has been given in the preceding section. In opposition to them, the Council drew up a
creed which contained the Church's teaching on the various

[15] Cfr. Hefele, op. cit. V, 872 sqq.; Mansi, 22, 982 sqq.

points of doctrine either denied or distorted by the sectaries. The first part sets forth what is to be held in regard to the Blessed Trinity, and then specially emphasizes the fact that this triune God is the one sole principle of all created beings. All things whatsoever, material and spiritual, angels, men, and demons, were created by God; and as created by Him, they were all good; but some of them became evil through a perverse use of their free will.

The second part states the doctrine of the Incarnation, the properties of Christ's human nature, the work of the redemption, the Savior's death, resurrection and ascension into heaven. Then brief reference is made to the resurrection of the dead, the last judgment, and the eternity of heaven and hell.

The third part deals with the Church and the sacraments, which points were especially attacked by the Cathari. Particular mention is made of the Holy Sacrifice, in which Christ is both the sacrificing priest and the immolated victim. The bread and wine are " transubstantiated " into His body and blood, and this transubstantiation cannot be effected except by a duly ordained priest. In regard to baptism it is stated that the Trinitarian formula must be used, and that it is valid no matter by whom conferred. If any one falls into sin after baptism, he can always obtain forgiveness by means of true penance. Finally, the attainment of eternal life is possible, not only for those who observe virginal chastity, but also for all others who live in the married state.

In the second *capitulum* the teaching of Abbot Joachim on the Blessed Trinity is condemned. As was pointed out in another chapter,[16] Joachim contended against the Lombard that Father, Son, and Holy Ghost, are not one essence, one nature, or a *quaedam summa res*. The Council further defines that the Father is the *principium quod* as regards the generation of the Son, and that the Father and Son together are *principium quod* in respect to the procession of the Holy Spirit. This is followed by a rejection of the pantheistic

[16] Cfr. c. 4.

views of Amalric of Bene, as noted in the preceding section of this chapter. It is from this Council that the Inquisition dates its origin.

2. *The Second Council of Lyons.*— When Michael Palaeologus, in 1261, wrested Constantinople from its Latin Emperor Baldwin II, ecclesiastical union between East and West was again dissolved. It was principally to restore this union that Gregory X determined to convene a general council at which both the Greek and Latin Church should be represented, although ecclesiastical reform and recovery of the Holy Land were also to be considered. The Greek Emperor favored the plans of the Sovereign Pontiff, perhaps not so much from a desire of promoting the union as through hope of thereby obtaining much needed help against the dethroned Baldwin. At a synod held in Constantinople he succeeded in prevailing on the Greek bishops to subscribe to the following three points, which he considered essential to the union : Acknowledgment of the papal primacy, the right of appeal to Rome, and mentioning of the Pope's name in the liturgy. As regarded the *Filioque* clause of the Symbol, the bishops admitted that its dogmatic content could not be called in question, but its addition to the Symbol was against the ruling of the Council of Ephesus, and therefore was not to be tolerated.

On his part, the Pope sent a symbol of faith to the Emperor, in which, besides a general outline of Catholic teaching, were contained the various points of doctrine till then objected to by the schismatics. It stated the procession of the Holy Spirit from the Father and the Son, the unlawfulness of rebaptizing those who had already been baptized, the existence of purgatory and the efficacy of suffrages for the dead, the immediate reception into heaven of the departed who have fully satisfied for their sins, the septenary number of the sacraments, the validity of consecration whether fermented or unfermented bread is used, the lawfulness of second, third, or fourth marriages, and the indissolubility of the marriage bond during the lifetime of the contracting parties. Then followed a clear statement of the privileges of the Roman Church, the Pope's universal jurisdiction, and his competency to decide questions of faith.[17]

In his answer to the Pope, Emperor Michael declared himself ready to accept the symbol as a sincere expression of his own belief, and wished to submit to the authority of the Sovereign Pontiff. However, he asked as a favor that the Greek Church might be permitted to retain its own Creed, without the addition of the *Filioque* clause ; and also its ecclesiastical rites, such as they had been before the schism. Finally, he added, the legates had been instructed to repeat and explain his personal declaration at the Council.[18] A similar declaration was made by the archbishops of the Eastern Church, promising to accept the proposed union, and to yield the Pope that reverence and obedience which had been customary before the schism.[19]

The Council opened on May 7, 1274, in the Cathedral of St. John. There were present about five hundred bishops, and over a thousand inferior prelates. St. Thomas was to have taken part in the Council as a theologian, but died on his way thither, at the early age of forty-nine. St. Bonaventure, on the other hand, was present at the first four sessions, and rendered such valuable services that the success of the Council was largely due to his efforts. But before the sixth and last session of the Council, he also died. It was early Sunday morning, July 15, and on the same day he was buried in the church of his religious brethren, the Minorites of Lyons. It is sometimes stated that he presided at the Council, but this is obviously a mistake, since the Pope himself was present at all the public sessions.

The Greek representatives did not arrive at Lyons until June 24. They took part in the Council for the first time on July 6, when the fourth session was held. On that occasion they abjured the schism, and declared that they and those whom they represented returned freely to the obedience of the Roman Church, accepting in all its parts the symbol of faith

[17] Mansi, 24, 70 A sqq.
[18] Ibid. 67.
[19] Ibid. 74.

that had been submitted to their consideration before the Council.[20]   Thus the schism was healed, but only for a time. After the death of Emperor Michael, in 1282, the enemies of the union, of whom there were not a few both among the bishops and priests, brought his successor, Andronikus, over to their side and thereby the schism was renewed.

The Council closed with the sixth session, which was held on July 16.   The work of the Council was summed up in thirty-one canons, nearly all of which deal with matters of discipline and reform.   At the close of the last session, the Pope declared that two objects for which the Council had been convened had been attained — the union of Christendom and the taking of effective measures for the recovery of the Holy Land; but the third, the reformation of morals, was still in a very unsatisfactory condition.   Then, with a prayer and his blessing, he dissolved the Council.

3. *The Council of Vienne.*— The Council held its first session on October 16, 1311, in the Cathedral of Vienne in France. In his opening address, Pope Clement V assigned the following three objects for the attainment of which the Council had been convened.   1. the settlement of the question whether the Knights Templar should be suppressed; 2. the procuring of assistance for the Holy Land; 3. the reformation of morals and of the clergy.   The number of bishops present is uncertain.   From some sources it appears that there were as many as three hundred, while according to others there were only one hundred and fourteen.   The Pope himself presided.[21]

The suppression of the Knights Templar had been demanded by Philip the Fair of France.   His ostensible reason was that the order had fallen away from its original purpose, and was utterly corrupt both as regarded morals and faith. He brought forward many witnesses to prove his point, but his motives were justly suspected; and historically the true state of things is even now far from being clearly understood.   At all events, Pope Clement, with the concurrence of the Council, suppressed the order ·and assigned its temporalities to the

[20] Cfr. Hefele, op. cit. VI, 141.   [21] Cfr. Hefele, op. cit. VI, 515 sqq.

Knights of St. John. He took every possible measure to be just to all concerned, but the story of the suppression does not make pleasant or edifying reading.

The doctrinal decisions of the Council were occasioned by certain accusations brought against Peter John Olivi, and by the errors of the Beghards and Beguines. John Olivi was a learned and pious Franciscan, who put forward somewhat extreme and partly untenable views on religious poverty. This brought upon him the enmity of some of his own brethren, who in consequence accused him also of other doctrinal errors. The matter was first examined into by a commission appointed by the Superior General of the Franciscans, with the result that thirty-four propositions taken from Olivi's writings were censured as rash and dangerous. Olivi defended himself, and denied the authority of the commission to decide in matters of doctrine. Then the discussion was taken up by the Council, but only three of the thirty-four propositions were selected for further investigation. They are the following: 1, that Christ was still living when the soldier pierced His side with a spear; 2, that the rational soul is not of itself — *per se* — the form of the body; 3, that children do not receive sanctifying grace and the infused virtues in baptism. The first two were condemned, but the third was declared to be less probable than the contrary view.[22]

Against the Beghards and Beguines two canons were drawn up, the first of which condemns their manner of life, while the second points out and censures their errors. These are in substance as follows: 1. It is possible to acquire so high a degree of perfection here on earth as to become impeccable, and altogether incapable of further increase in sanctity. 2. Those who have acquired this degree of perfection are no longer bound to fast or pray, and can freely indulge the inclinations of the body. 3. Such persons are not subject to any authority, not even to that of the Church. 4. They enjoy here on earth the same happiness as the blessed in heaven. 5. Rational nature is of itself capable of enjoying the beatific

[22] Mansi, 25, 410 E sq.

vision, and needs not the light of glory in order to see God.
6. To practice virtue is a matter that belongs exclusively to
the imperfect.   7. To kiss a woman is a mortal sin, because
nature does not incline thereto; but to satisfy the lusts of the
flesh is not a sin, because that is according to nature.   8. It
is an imperfection to reverence the body of Christ when it is
elevated during Mass, because this interferes with the perfection of contemplation.[23]

4. *The Council of Constance.*— The primary purpose of this
Council was to terminate the Western Schism.   That schism
had grown out of the contested election of Urban VI, who succeeded Gregory XI on April 8, 1378.   As far as can now be
determined, the election was valid.   For although there was
during the conclave a great popular outcry for an Italian Pope,
still the freedom of the cardinals was not interfered with; and
when the election was over, all of them spontaneously offered
their homage to the new Pontiff.   It was not until several
weeks after the coronation, when Urban had already proved
himself a stern master, that some of the disappointed cardinals
began to feel that they had been unduly influenced in their
choice by fear of the people.   When it became evident that
Urban was bent upon carrying out his strict views, the majority
of the Sacred College repudiated his election as invalid, and on
September 20 chose Robert of Geneva as the new Pope.   He
took the name of Clement VII.

Although the greater part of Christendom remained faithful to Urban, nevertheless France and a few other countries
recognized Clement as the lawful successor of St. Peter, and
thus the schism was started.   When Urban died in 1389, he
was succeeded by Boniface IX; and when Clement died in 1394,
he received a successor in the person of Benedict XIII.   Thus
Rome and Avignon divided the Christian world into two
obediences.   Boniface was to all appearances the true Pope,
and so was Gregory XII who succeeded him in 1406; but many
learned and holy men yielded obedience to Benedict.   Matters
became even worse when the Council of Pisa, in 1409, at-

[23] Ibid. 410 A.

tempted to depose the two rivals and in their place elected Alexander V. As neither Gregory nor Benedict recognized the authority of the Council, the result was a third claimant of the Papal crown; and although Alexander died within a year after his election, his place was taken by John XXIII.

It was whilst ecclesiastical affairs were in this state of utter confusion that the Council of Constance was convened. The initiative was taken by the cardinals of all three obediences, whose plans for a reunion of Christendom were strongly supported by Emperor Sigismund. Of the three Popes, John alone had been induced to give a reluctant consent to the calling of a general council, while Gregory and Benedict steadfastly refused to countenance any movement in that direction. Hence if Gregory was the true Pope, as is practically certain that he was, the Council was simply an illegitimate gathering of prelates, who had no authority to legislate for the whole Church. It was only when after the resignation of Gregory, and the deposition of Benedict and John as doubtful Popes, Martin V was validly elected, that the Council became legitimate. By that time forty-two sessions had already been held, and several doctrinal decisions had been given, all of which were necessarily without force until approved by the new Pope.[24] The election of Pope Martin took place on November 8, 1417, just three years after the opening of the Council.

The doctrinal decisions above referred to bore chiefly on the errors of Wiclif and Hus, and they were embodied in the condemnation of these same errors by the Pope, as contained in the Bulls *Inter cunctas* and *In eminentis,* published February 22, 1418.[25] Hence there can be no doubt as regards their validity.

Considerable discussion was subsequently caused in regard to the proposition that a general council has its authority immediately from God, and that it is superior to the Pope. This view was adopted and promulgated in the fourth and fifth sessions, but at the time the Council was still illegitimate, and therefore incapable of defining matters of faith. Further-

[24] Cfr. Hefele, op. cit. VII, 66 sqq.; Salembier, The Great Schism of the West, 275 sqq.

[25] Mansi, 27, 1207 E sqq.

more, subsequent Roman Pontiffs always repudiated the doctrine as unorthodox; and Martin V, at the close of the Council, approved only in a general way what had been enacted by conciliar procedure in matters of faith — *in materia fidei conciliariter statuta*. It is, moreover, quite probable that the Council merely intended its declaration to meet a special difficulty, and therefore to have only temporary force.[26]

5. *The Council of Florence.*— One of the means chosen by the Council of Constance to bring about a reformation of morals, and also to counteract the ever increasing heretical tendencies of the times, was the frequent convening of general councils. It was determined that the next one should be called after five years, the one after that seven years later, and thereafter one should be held every ten years. This legislation had been agreed upon before the election of the new Pope, and it was obviously inspired by a distrust of the Papacy, which in its turn had been engendered by the sad experience of the forty years of schism before the Council. Although Pope Martin had bound himself by no personal pledge in this matter, he called a council at Pavia in 1423, which, owing to an epidemic, was shortly after transferred to Sienna. It accomplished practically nothing, and was dissolved in the spring of 1424.

The next council was convened at Basle, but before it met Martin V had passed away. He was succeeded by Eugenius IV. The Council held its first session in 1431, under the presidency of Cardinal Cesarini. But as nothing was accomplished, the Pope resolved to transfer it to an Italian city. This occasioned a restatement of the claim advanced at Constance, that general councils are superior to the Pope. Matters were allowed to drag on till 1437, when the Pope dissolved the Council. Its refractory members, however, continued to hold sessions, and in 1439 even elected an anti-Pope who took the name of Felix V. Meanwhile the Greeks had again applied for reunion, and to facilitate negotiations for this purpose, the Pope convened a council at Ferrara in 1438. After much useless discussion, which only showed the unwillingness of the

[26] Cfr. Funk, Kirchengeschichtliche Abhandlungen, I, 489 sqq.; Salembier, op. cit. 306.

Greeks to yield a whole-hearted submission to the Holy See, the
Council was transferred to Florence.

There the same discussion was taken up again, with the result that finally an agreement was reached which apparently
satisfied both parties. The Greeks admitted, as their fore-
fathers had done at the Second Council of Lyons, that the
Latin teaching on the procession of the Holy Spirit from the
Father and the Son was perfectly orthodox. An understanding was also reached on the four other points that had formed
a matter of controversy — purgatory, the commencement of
the beatific vision as soon as souls are purified from their sins,
the use of unleavened bread in the Eucharist, and the primacy
of the Roman Church. After this the union was once more
established, and the Pope embodied the five points referred
to in the Bull *Laetantur coeli,* which was published with the
concurrence of the Council, July 6, 1439. However, the union
was destined to be almost as shortlived as that which had
been established at Lyons, nearly two hundred years before.
It appears that the Greeks were animated by political motives
rather than by the desire of being in communion with the Holy
See. Hence, when the Turks, in 1453, took Constantinople,
the schism was renewed.[27]

After the departure of the Greek representatives, the Council
also received the submission of the Armenians and the Jacob-
ites, on each of which occasions a doctrinal decree was issued,
setting forth many points of teaching in regard to which conformity was required.[28] The Council was dissolved in 1445,
after it had been transferred from Florence to the Lateran
at Rome.

[27] Cfr. Hefele, op. cit. VII, 426   [28] Cfr. DB. 695 sqq.; 703 sqq.
sqq.

CHAPTER XXVI

THE PROTESTANT REFORMATION: THE COUNCIL OF TRENT [1]

Centuries before Luther was born, the reformation of the Church in her head and members had been earnestly desired and repeatedly attempted by Popes and councils. Side by side with the strong faith and genuine piety of the Middle Ages, there was a widespread corruption of morals and a corresponding laxity of discipline. There was urgent need of a reformation, and this need was universally felt; but it was to be a reformation of practice, not of belief. The faith of the Church had ever been preserved in its pristine purity, and at the time of Luther's revolt her teaching was orthodox in every respect. Unfortunately, it was precisely her faith and her teaching that were finally made the chief objects of attack, and consequently what was at first heralded as a reformation of her morals ended in a revolt against her authority. The genesis of this revolt and the checks opposed to it by the Church form the subject matter of the present chapter.

A — THE PROTESTANT REFORMATION

That at the beginning of the sixteenth century there was a combination of circumstances which favored a religious upheaval, or a breaking away from ecclesiastical authority, is today conceded by all impartial students of church history. In the first place, respect for the authority of the Pope had been considerably weakened during the forty years of the Western

[1] Cfr. Grisar, Luther, especially vol. I; Denifle, Luther und Luthertum; Moehler, Symbolism; *Gairdner Lollardy and the Reformation in England; *Schaff, Creeds of Christendom; Schwane, Histoire des Dogmes, VI; Hefele, Conciliengeschichte, VIII, IX; Swoboda, Das Concil von Trient.

Schism. The Papacy, which till then, in spite of the short-comings of individual Popes, had been universally regarded with the greatest reverence, lost much of its ancient prestige through the divided obedience of the Christian world. The unseemly spectacle of rival claimants anathematizing one an-other and clinging desperately to the entirely human ambi-tion of occupying the first place, did not a little towards shak-ing men's confidence in the divine shepherding of Christ's vicar on earth. Hence the growing tendency, first manifested at the Council of Constance, to subordinate the Pope's authority to that of a general council. The Pope was still re-garded as the vicar of Christ; but, in the opinion of not a few, he was a vicar who needed watching and from whose decisions one might appeal to a higher court.

Another factor that prepared men's minds for the sixteenth-century revolt is found in the decay of Scholasticism, and in the consequent low ebb of theological learning. This condition was not universal, but it was widespread. The idle specula-tions and senseless quibblings of the Nominalists had replaced the comprehensive and deep studies of St. Thomas and St. Bonaventure. Ockam, Gregory of Rimini, and Gabriel Biel were regarded by many as the highest authorities in the theological world; and they were at best unsafe guides. They discredited the ability of human reason to discern the truth even in its own legitimate sphere of mental activity, and in consequence they clung blindly to the teaching of the Church. As a result, when that authority was impugned, at least so far as it resided in the Pope, there was practically nothing left but recourse to the Scriptures read and interpreted by the individual under the guidance of the Holy Spirit. Thus the way was opened for the introduction of the fundamental prin-ciples of Protestantism, the right of private judgment in matters of faith.

As a third factor in bringing about a religious cataclysm, although of somewhat subordinate importance, we may assign the paganizing tendency of the Renaissance. The revival of classical learning brought with it a love of pagan ideals, and these ideals were all too often made the standard of moral

conduct.   They corrupted both mind and heart, and sapped the
very foundation of Christianity.   And what made the effect
all the more terrible and far-reaching, even if it did not directly
touch the masses, was the fact that many of those who fell
victims to the new paganism belonged to the ranks of the
clergy.   In the past not a few priests and bishops had given
scandal by their loose morality; but even they, as a general
rule, had preserved the faith; whereas now, where Humanism
had done its work, even faith was lost, and with the loss of
faith all respect for ecclesiastical authority was at an end.
This explains the numerous defections of the clergy when the
religious revolt was started.   It was not only immorality that
drove them into the camps of the innovators, although that
too had much to do with it; but also the fact that they had
already suffered shipwreck in the faith as taught by the
Church.

With the ground thus prepared, there was nothing strange
about the success that attended Luther's preaching of revolt
against ecclesiastical authority.   Whatever may have been his
personal motives at the beginning of his career as a reformer,
it was not a reformation of morals that constituted his life
work, nor a purifying of the faith from human accrescences,
as he tried to plead in his own justification; it was neither more
nor less than an attempt to substitute a new religion for the
Christianity that had been preached by the Apostles and handed
down by the Church.   And for such a substitution the ground
had been prepared by the various agencies briefly indicated in
the preceding paragraphs.

There is no need, in this place, of studying the psychological
processes by which Luther was led to the adoption of his two
fundamental principles; the right of private judgment in
matters of faith and justification by faith alone.   That belongs
rather to his personal history, and has been admirably done
by Hartmann Grisar in his monumental work referred to at
the beginning of the present chapter.   It suffices to state that
these two principles formed the doctrinal basis of the whole
movement, and were adopted by all other so-called reformers,
no matter how much they might differ from Luther's views

in regard to other points of doctrine.   It must be added, however, that the first principle — the right of private judgment — was admitted only to a limited extent.   Each particular leader claimed its unlimited use for himself, but at the same time he denied it to all others.   Hence the constant wrangling among the representatives of the reform movement, and the bitter invectives they hurled at each other in their doctrinal disputes.   On the other hand, the second principle — justification by faith alone — was admitted by all.

The root of this principle is found in the superficial and inaccurate views on justification defended by the Nominalists. While they admitted the teaching of the Church that man is justified by the infusion of sanctifying grace, and that good works performed in the state of grace are meritorious of a supernatural reward, they held that all this was simply the result of a positive ordination on the part of God.   In itself, according to their teaching, grace as understood by the Church is superfluous for salvation.   For everything depends on God's will, and it is only by reason of His acceptation that any action is deserving of a supernatural reward.

It was in this school of theological thought that Luther himself had received his training, and he pushed its principles to their last conclusion.   Only through the merits of Christ is justification possible, and that only in so far as God accepts them as our own.   This He will do if we place our full confidence in Him, and thus appropriate by faith what belongs to Christ.   No interior change is thereby wrought in us, save only as regards the attitude of our will towards God.   Hence neither the sacraments nor good works have any direct connection with justification; it is faith alone, in the sense of trust and confidence, that justifies us in the sight of God.

This view on justification had been worked out by Luther, at least in all its essentials, as early as 1516; but it was not until 1520 that he openly stated the final conclusion of his system in the words: " A Christian who believes cannot, even if he should so wish, lose his soul by any sin however great; since no sin, except unbelief, can damn him."   Meanwhile, in his ninety-five theses affixed to the door of the university church of Wittenberg, he had taken his public stand against the Church's teaching on indulgences. Ostensibly he aimed his attack merely at abuses connected with the preaching of indulgences, but in reality it was the doctrine itself that he had in view. Hence the statement made by him in course of the controversy that ensued: "Let us hold to this, that an indulgence is not what the Pope declares it; and if an angel from heaven says otherwise, he is not to be believed." And by way of argument he urged the claim advanced by St. Paul: "I have from God all I teach;" but unlike St. Paul, he had no way of establishing his claim.

When Leo X, who then occupied the pontifical chair, was informed of the threatening situation in Germany, he offered Luther the alternative of retracting, or of presenting himself for trial at Rome. However, through the intervention of Luther's friend and protector, the elector of Saxony, Cardinal Cajetan was sent to Germany with full power to decide the case. Luther was dissatisfied with the decision given, and appealed "from Leo ill informed to Leo better informed;" and a few days later, realizing the hopelessness of his case, he appealed to a future general council. Leo fully understood the gravity of the situation, but was anxious to avoid extreme measures; hence, when he published the Bull on indulgences, wherein he set forth the Catholic doctrine, he made no mention of Luther's name.

The following year, 1519, a doctrinal discussion was arranged to be held at Leipzig, between Eck, a professor of Ingolstadt, and Carlstadt, Luther's former teacher. Luther himself was also present, and in the course of the dispute denied that the primacy was of divine institution and that general councils were infallible. This he followed up with the publication of three pamphlets. The first of these was an appeal "To the Christian Nobles of the German Nation," which was intended to stir up the princes against the Church. The second was entitled, "On the Babylonian Captivity," and in it he rejected the Sacrifice of the Mass and all the sacraments except baptism and the Eucharist. The third contained a summary of his own teaching under the title, "Of Christian

Liberty." This latter he sent to the Pope, together with a flattering personal letter.

Leo's answer was the Bull *Exsurge Domine*, which condemned Luther's teaching and demanded a retraction within sixty days, threatening excommunication in case he failed to retract. When Luther received this bull, he publicly committed it to the flames at Wittenberg, with the words: " As thou hast troubled the saints of the Lord, so may the everlasting fire trouble and consume thee." Then he published the pamphlet entitled, " Against the Bull of Antichrist," in which he calls the Pope " a damned obstinate heretic." Summoned to appear before the imperial diet held at Worms in 1521, he was given another opportunity to retract; but, backed up by the revolutionary freebooters under Franz von Sickingen and Ulrich von Hutten, he refused. Then the ban of the empire was placed upon him, but he found safety in the Wartburg.

Thus the die was cast, and the religious revolution which was destined to drag away vast numbers from the Church of Christ had become an accomplished fact. Of the further development of that revolution only this much need be said in the present connection, that Luther's claim to a divine mission was advanced by many others, with the result that reformer was pitted against reformer, and thus the non-Catholic religious world became a veritable chaos. What one affirmed, the other denied; and soon there were almost as many opinions in the revolutionary camps as there were heads. Out of this chaos, however, three great Protestant bodies emerged, the Lutheran, the Calvinist, and the Anglican, which, together with a number of smaller sects, in course of time claimed the greater part of Northern Europe as their own. The chief points of their heretical teaching may be briefly outlined as follows.

1. *Holy Scripture.*— The only source of divine revelation is the written word of God as contained in the Bible. The Bible, moreover, does not include the deutero-canonical books, that is, those books whose divine origin and inspiration were at first called in question by some, but which were finally recognized by the whole Church as sacred, canonical, and inspired. However, later Protestants usually include in their

canon the deutero-canonical books of the New Testament. Furthermore, the Bible is to be interpreted, not according to the authority of the Church, but according to the private judgment of each individual believer, assisted by the direct inward illumination of the Holy Spirit.

2. *Original Sin.*— Our first parents were constituted in the state of original justice, which consisted of certain high and noble gifts wherewith the souls of Adam and Eve were endowed; but these gifts were natural and essential to perfect human nature.   Hence by the fall, in which original justice was lost, human nature was essentially corrupted and the soul was deprived of perfections that belonged to its natural integrity.   In consequence, original sin is an essential corruption of our nature, and as irremovable as that nature itself. Some of the Reformers defined it as " the very substance of fallen man," but the majority agreed with Calvin that it is " the hereditary depravity and corruption of our nature, which first made us worthy of God's wrath, and also produces in us works which Scripture calls works of the flesh." [2]

3. *Free Will.*— Luther asserted that man never had a free will, whereas Calvin maintained that free will was lost by the fall.   Moreover, according to both, the fall was due to an irresistible necessity and divine predestination.   As man has no free will, there is no room for merit; and so-called good works have no relation to man's eternal salvation.   Nay, in so far as they are the works of man, they are positively sinful — they are venial sins in the case of believers, and mortal sins in the case of unbelievers.   Moreover, the observance of the divine precepts, even by the just, is an impossibility.

4. *Grace and justification.*— As man's nature is essentially corrupt, grace and justification do not consist in an interior supernatural quality, but are simply the pardon of sin and the imputation of the merits of Christ.   Both are obtained by a firm confidence in the goodness and mercy of God, resulting in an absolute conviction and positive assurance that all sins have been forgiven.   According to Luther, justification

[2] Instit. I, 2, c. 1, n. 8.

is so completely the work of God that man is entirely passive; whereas Calvin admitted the active coöperation of man, but only under an irresistible and invincible divine impulse.

5. *Predestination.*— As justification is entirely the work of God, without free coöperation on the part of man, it necessarily implies the doctrine of absolute and unqualified predestination. And this doctrine was at first commonly admitted by the Reformers; but it was afterwards abandoned by all except Calvin. The latter made it a fundamental doctrine of his theological system. He defines it as follows: " We call predestination the eternal decree of God, by which He determined what He willed to be done with every man. For all are not created in a like condition, but to some is preordained eternal life, to others eternal damnation. Hence according as each one is created for one or the other end, we say that he is predestined to life or to death." [3]   Yet God is not unjust or cruel in regard to the reprobate; for " those whom He devotes to damnation are by a just and blameless but incomprehensible judgment shut off from all access to life." [4]   Hence they can have no real faith, nor are they ever justified, nor did Christ die for their salvation.[5]

6. *The Sacraments.*— From their erroneous concept of justification, the Reformers were logically led to the rejection of the sacraments as means or causes of grace. Hence they considered them only as pledges of the divine promises for the remission of sins, and means of confirming man's faith in this remission. Moreover, of the seven sacraments admitted by the Church, they retained only two: Baptism and the Lord's Supper. Furthermore, according to Calvin, the efficacy of these two sacraments is restricted to the elect. In regard to the Eucharist all were agreed that the doctrine of transubstantiation must be rejected. The Real Presence was also denied by all except Luther, who favored the theory of impanation; but even according to him, Christ is not really present in the Eucharist except at the moment of communion. The laity as well as the officiating minister must receive com-

[3] Op. cit. I, 3, c. 2, n. 5.   [5] Ibid.
[4] Ibid. n. 7.

munion under both kinds. The Eucharist is not a sacrifice, and therefore the Mass as a sacrificial rite must be abolished.

7. *The Church.*— As the Reformers rejected all the sacraments except baptism and the Eucharist, there is no Christian priesthood as understood by Catholics. On the other hand, every Christian is both priest and teacher; and it is only for the sake of order and greater efficiency that ministers are appointed. by the congregation. Hence the Church is not an hierarchical institution, but is simply an association of equals who acknowledge Christ as their head. Moreover, the real Church of Christ is invisible, or at least was so for centuries until the rise of Protestantism. The Pope, like any other minister, simply holds a place of honor; he has no jurisdiction over the faithful.

8. *The Communion of Saints.*— As justification is obtained by faith alone, there is no bond of prayer and helpfulness uniting all the children of God into one body. Hence neither must we pray for the dead nor invoke the saints. There is no other mediator besides Christ, and through Him each individual believer has direct access to God. Furthermore, as faith justifies man perfectly in the sight of God, there can be no purgatory, nor is there room for indulgences; all this must be swept away as so much popish invention.[6]

From this brief summary it will be seen that Protestantism differs from all preceding heresies. In the centuries that went before, heretics had denied one or other doctrine of the Church, but, with the sole exception of Arius, left the Christian religion as such untouched. The Reformers, on the other hand, brought about a fundamental change in that religion. Practically very little was retained of the Church's teaching aside from her doctrine on God, the Blessed Trinity, and the divinity of Christ. And in course of time, even in regard to these, errors sprang up that tended to sweep away the last vestige of Christianity. Nor was this merely an accidental outcome of the revolutionary movement initiated by Luther; it was the logical result of his rejection of ecclesiastical authority in matters of faith and morals.

[6] Cfr. Moehler, op. cit.

B — THE COUNCIL OF TRENT

Throughout their contention with Rome, Luther and his followers appealed from the Pope to a general council; but when after many difficulties and delays the council finally met, they refused to attend. Their excuse was, though not expressed in these precise terms, that they would not be allowed to act as judges of the faith. It was with them no longer a question of arriving at the truth on the points under discussion, but solely of how they might most effectively impose their views on the rest of Christendom. Hence if their own cause was judged in their absence, it was entirely their own fault.

The Council was convened by Paul III, and opened at Trent on December 13, 1545. After the eighth session, 1547, it was transferred to Bologna, where it was prorogued in 1549. In 1551, Pope Julius III transferred it back to Trent, but it was suspended the following year. Again reassembled at Trent in 1561, it concluded its sessions there in 1563 and was dissolved. The final decrees were signed by 252 members, whereas at the first session only 40 bishops had been present.

Protestant writers usually contend that the Council met for the sole purpose of counteracting the movement set on foot by the Reformers; but this contention is not based on facts as known to history. Its purpose was not only to condemn error, but also to define the truth. Hence not only its canons, but its capitula also contain definitions of doctrine. There was at the time need of a definite exposition of Catholic teaching, and that exposition was given in clear and explicit terms. Besides, the Council was also called to effect a thorough reformation of discipline and morals, which object was altogether independent of the disturbance caused by Luther and his associates. Hence the work of defining the faith and reforming discipline proceeded side by side from the beginning of the Council to the end. On the other hand, most of the definitions of the Council were occasioned by the errors of the day; but the contents of these definitions are simply a clear statement of Catholic teaching irrespective of all errors. They are the witness of the Holy Spirit to the cause of truth.

The various dogmatic and disciplinary decrees were passed in the 4th, 5th, 6th, 7th, 13th, 14th, 21st, 22nd, 23rd, 24th, and 25th sessions. With regard to matters of faith, which alone need be considered in the present connection, the particular doctrine in question is usually first stated in a positive form and embodied in a *capitulum* or chapter, and then the contrary errors are condemned in the canons that follow. A brief summary of the Council's teaching is here subjoined.

1. *Holy Scripture and Tradition* (sess. 4).— The Council first lays down the principle that the Catholic faith is contained both " in written books and in the unwritten traditions which were received by the Apostles from the lips of Jesus Christ Himself, or were transmitted, after a manner of speaking, from hand to hand by the Apostles themselves from the dictation of the Holy Ghost, and have come down to us." Next the Canon of Scripture is promulgated. It contains all the deutero-canonical books rejected by the Reformers, and is identical with that of Pope Damasus published at the end of the fourth century. Then the Council declares that it " receives and venerates with like sentiments of piety and reverence all the books of the Old and New Testaments, for the one God is the author of both; and also the traditions relating to faith and morals, as having been dictated either orally by Christ, or by the Holy Ghost, and preserved by an unbroken succession in the Catholic Church. Furthermore, all are anathematized who refuse to receive, as sacred and canonical, these books in their entirety and with all their parts, as they have been wont to be read in the Catholic Church and are found in the old Latin Vulgate edition." Lastly, it is stated that it is the exclusive right and duty of the Church to pass judgment on the true sense and interpretation of the Sacred Writings.

2. *Original Sin* (sess. 5).— Leaving undecided the dispute between the Thomists and Scotists, as to whether Adam was created in the state of grace or elevated thereto subsequent to his creation, the Council puts its teaching on original sin in the form of anathematisms, which state the Catholic doctrine and at the same time condemn the contrary errors. However, no clear definition of original sin itself is given, although

all the elements of such a definition are stated. The following are the most important points contained in the decree.

(a) "If any one does not confess that the first man, Adam, when he had transgressed the commandment of God in paradise, immediately lost the holiness and justice wherein he had been constituted; and that he incurred, through the offense of that prevarication, the wrath and indignation of God, and consequently death, with which God had previously threatened him, and, together with death, captivity under his power who thenceforth *had the empire of death, that is to say, the devil,* and that the entire Adam, through that offense of prevarication, was changed, in body and soul, for the worse; let him be anathema."

(b) "If any one asserts, that the prevarication of Adam injured himself alone, and not his posterity; and that the holiness and justice, received from God, which he lost, he lost for himself alone, and not for us also; or that he, being defiled by the sin of disobedience, has only transferred death, and pains of the body, into the whole human race, but not sin also, which is the death of the soul; let him be anathema."

(c) "If any one asserts, that the sin of Adam — which in its origin is one, and being transfused into all by propagation, not by imitation, is in each one as his own — is taken away either by the power of human nature, or by any other remedy than the merit of *one mediator, our Lord Jesus Christ, who hath reconciled us to God in his own blood, made unto us justice, sanctification, and redemption;* or if he denies that the said merit of Jesus Christ is applied, both to adults and to infants, by the sacrament of baptism rightly administered in the form of the Church; let him be anathema."

(d) "If any one denies that infants, newly born from their mothers' wombs, even though they be sprung from baptized parents, are to be baptized; or says that they are baptized indeed for the remission of sins, but that they derive nothing of original sin from Adam, which has need of being expiated by the laver of regeneration for the obtaining of life everlasting — whence it follows as a consequence, that in them the form of baptism, for the remission of sins, is understood to be not true, but false —; let him be anathema."

(e) " If any one denies, that, by the grace of our Lord Jesus Christ, which is conferred in baptism, the guilt of original sin is remitted; or even asserts that the whole of that which has the true and proper nature of sin is not taken away; but says that it is only canceled, or not imputed; let him be anathema. For in those who are born again, there is nothing that God hates; . . . so that there is nothing whatever to retard their entrance into heaven. But this holy Synod confesses and holds that in those who are baptized there remains concupiscence, or an incentive to sin; which while it is left as an occasion of struggle, cannot injure those who consent not, but resist manfully by the grace of Jesus Christ; yea, he who shall have *striven lawfully shall be crowned*. This concupiscence, which the Apostle sometimes calls sin, the holy Synod declares that the Catholic Church has never understood to be called sin, as being truly and properly sin in those born again, but because it is of sin, and inclines to sin. And if any one holds the contrary, let him be anathema."

(f) " The same holy Synod doth nevertheless declare, that it is not its intention to include in this decree, where original sin is treated of, the blessed and immaculate Virgin Mary, the Mother of God; but that the constitutions of Pope Sixtus IV, of happy memory, are to be observed, under the penalties contained in the said constitutions, which it renews." [7]

3. *Justification* (sess. 6).— As the Protestant error on justification was most fundamental, the Council discussed this point in all its details. Justification is described as " the transference of man from the state in which he is born as the son of the first Adam, to the state of grace and adoption of the sons of God through the second Adam, Jesus Christ, our Saviour." This transference is effected by means of the sacrament of baptism, received in deed or at least in desire.[8]

In the case of adults, the first motion towards justification is the work of God, who by His grace calls and moves the

[7] Cfr. DB. 787 sqq.   [8] Ibid. 796.

sinner to repentance; but man must freely coöperate with the grace that is given. Then God continues the work, in as much as He offers His grace, which enables the sinner to elicit acts of faith, holy fear, and hope; and also to begin to love God as the fount of all justice, to be sorry for his sins, and to resolve to be baptized and to begin a new life, having the firm purpose to observe all the commandments of God.[9]

After this preparation, justification itself takes place. It does not consist in the imputation of the merits of Christ, nor merely in the remission of sins, but in an inward sanctification and renewal through the reception of the gifts of habitual grace and the virtues of faith, hope, and charity. These gifts are infused into the soul by God through the merits of Christ and the instrumentality of the sacrament of baptism. They are permanent gifts, in the sense that they inhere in the soul until destroyed by sin. Faith alone does not justify, but it is the indispensable beginning, basis, and root of justification. If not accompanied by hope and charity, it is profitless and dead. It is, moreover, not identical with confidence in God's goodness or the assurance that our sins have been forgiven through the merits of Christ. Furthermore, we cannot know with the certainty of faith that we are in the state of grace; for we never have the absolute assurance that we complied in every respect with the conditions upon which our justification was made to depend.[10]

Once justified, man is capable of performing meritorious works, which lead to an increase of sanctifying grace and give him a title to an eternal reward. With God's help he is able to observe the divine precepts, and to this he is strictly obliged under pain of sin. By an abuse of his free will, he can refuse to coöperate with the grace of God, and thus again fall away from the state of justification. Moreover, without a special privilege, such as was granted to the Blessed Virgin, he cannot throughout his life avoid all venial sins. But, on the other hand, it is heretical to say that every good work of the just is in itself sinful, though not imputed to him unto

[9] Ibid. 797, 798; cfr. 813, 814, 818, 819.   [10] Ibid. 799, 802, 819, 824.

damnation. And it is an error to hold that good works are
vitiated by the hope of an eternal reward; or that the sorrow
for sins which springs from the motive of fear is not good and
praiseworthy.[11]

Even the just have no certain knowledge of their predestination to eternal life, or of their final perseverance, unless this
has been specially revealed to them by God. No one can
persevere without God's special help; but he must have confidence in the divine assistance, which he can always obtain
by prayer. The grace of justification is given, not to the elect
only, but to others also; nor has God predestined any one to
damnation.[12]

Justification may be lost, not only by the sin of infidelity,
but by any other grievous sin. It can be recovered in the
sacrament of penance, which was instituted as a remedy against
sins committed after baptism. The worthy reception of this
sacrament requires sorrow for sins, a purpose of amendment,
absolution, and the will to render satisfaction for the temporal
punishment which often remains due to sins after the guilt
and eternal punishment have been remitted. Sanctifying
grace is lost by every mortal sin; but faith is lost only by the
sin of heresy or infidelity. Those who have faith without
charity are yet to be regarded as Christians.[13]

4. *The Sacraments in General: Baptism and Confirmation*
(sess. 7).— As a means by which the grace of justification is
first bestowed, then increased, and also restored after having
been lost by sin, our Lord Jesus Christ instituted the seven
sacraments of the New Law; and these sacraments differ from
those of the Old Law, not only in their external rites and
ceremonies, but also in their efficacy. This efficacy is derived
from their institution, in as much as Christ meant them to be
practical signs or instrumental causes of grace. Hence they
do not merely excite the faith or devotion of the recipient,
but in a true sense confer the grace which God himself produces in the soul. Moreover, their efficacy is independent of
the faith and merit of the minister; grace is conferred *ex opere*

[11] Ibid. 803, 804, 818, 828–830.   [13] Ibid. 807, 808, 837–840.
[12] Ibid. 805, 806, 825–827, 832.

operato, through the merits of Christ. However, in the recipient certain dispositions are required in order to fit him for the reception of grace.[14]

Some sacraments are necessary means of grace for all; others only for certain classes of persons. However, even the former are not all of equal necessity; nor are all the sacraments of equal dignity. For their proper administration a duly appointed minister is required, on whose part nothing more is necessary, by way of validity, than the use of the essential rite instituted by Christ, with the intention of at least doing what the Church does.[15] Three sacraments, baptism, confirmation, and orders, imprint a character or indelible spiritual seal on the soul; hence they cannot be repeated.[16]

Baptism is necessary for salvation. The matter required for its validity is natural water. Christian baptism is essentially different from that of John the Baptist. It can be validly administered by heretics. Infants also must be baptized; nor may their baptism be repeated when they have reached the age of reason. They are truly enrolled among the faithful, and they are not at liberty later on to repudiate the obligations of their baptismal vows.[17]

Confirmation is not a mere empty ceremony that originated in the catechetical examinations to which Christian youths were of old subjected. It is a true sacrament in the strict sense of the term. A bishop only is its ordinary minister.[18]

5. *The Sacrament of the Holy Eucharist* (sess. 13).—" In the first place, the holy Synod teaches, and openly and simply professes, that in the august sacrament of the Holy Eucharist, after the consecration of the bread and wine, our Lord Jesus Christ, true God and man, is truly, really, and substantially contained under the species of these sensible things." The sacrament was instituted by the Savior when He was about to depart out of this world to the Father, that He might leave us a memorial of His passion, a sovereign remedy and pro-

---

[14] Ibid. 844–856.
[15] Ibid. 846, 853, 854.
[16] Ibid. 852.

[17] Ibid. 857–870.
[18] Ibid. 871–873.

tection against sin, and a most efficacious means of grace. It is the spiritual food and life of the soul, the symbol and bond of unity and charity, and a pledge of eternal glory.[19]

" The most Holy Eucharist has indeed this in common with the rest of the sacraments, that it is a symbol of a sacred thing, and is a visible form of an invisible grace; but there is found in the Eucharist this excellent and peculiar thing, that the other sacraments have then first the power of sanctifying when one uses them, whereas in the Eucharist, before being used, there is present the Author of sanctity Himself. . . . And this faith has ever been in the Church of God, that, immediately after the consecration, the veritable body of our Lord, and His veritable blood, together with His soul and divinity, are under the species of bread and wine; but the body indeed under the species of bread, and the blood under the species of wine, by the force of the words; but the body under the species of wine, and the blood under the species of bread, and the soul under both, by the force of that natural connection and concomitancy whereby the parts of Christ our Lord, *who hath now risen from the dead, to die no more,* are united together; and the divinity, furthermore, on account of the admirable hypostatical union thereof with His body and soul." [20]

" And because Christ, our Redeemer, declared that which He offered under the species of bread to be truly His own body, therefore has it ever been the firm belief in the Church of God, and this holy Synod doth now declare it anew, that by the consecration of the bread and of the wine, a conversion is made of the whole substance of the bread into the body of Christ our Lord, and of the whole substance of the wine into His blood; which conversion is by the holy Catholic Church suitably and properly called Transubstantiation." [21]

Hence divine worship is due to the Blessed Sacrament, and it should be reserved both for the adoration of the faithful and for the communion of the sick. The proper disposition for its reception presupposes the state of grace; and if one is in

[19] Ibid. 874, 875.
[20] Ibid. 876.

[21] Ibid. 877.

mortal sin, he must first have recourse to the sacrament of penance. Where the proper dispositions are found, it is the urgent desire of the Council that the Holy Eucharist be frequently received by the faithful.[22]

6. *The Sacraments of Penance and Extreme Unction* (sess. 14).— The sacrament of penance was instituted by Christ for the remission of sins committed after baptism, as appears from His own words: " Receive ye the Holy Ghost: whose sins you shall forgive, they are forgiven them: and whose sins you shall retain, they are retained." Sacramental absolution is a judicial act, and can be imparted only by a minister who has the priestly character. The fact that the absolving priest is in the state of mortal sin does not invalidate his absolution; but the want of jurisdiction does. On the part of the penitent are required, (a) supernatural sorrow; (b) confession, as complete as reasonably possible, of unconfessed mortal sins; (c) satisfaction for the temporal punishment that usually still remains to be expiated.[23]

Extreme unction was instituted by Christ and promulgated by St. James. It removes from the soul the remaining effects of forgiven sins, and gives a special grace to those in danger of death by sickness. If necessary, it even forgives sins; and as a secondary effect, restores health of body when God judges it expedient. The matter of this sacrament is olive oil blessed by a bishop; its form consists in the prayers used in the application of the matter to the various senses by a priest.[24]

7. *The Sacrifice of the Mass* (sess. 22).— The Holy Eucharist was instituted by Christ not only as a sacrament, but also as a true sacrifice, which must be offered to God continually in His Church by the Apostles and their successors in the priesthood. As a sacrifice it is the image of the great sacrifice of the cross, with which it is identical both in victim and in 'priest, differing only in the manner of offering. Through it are applied the merits of Christ's passion and death, both to the living and to the souls departed. Hence

---

[22] Ibid. 878, 879, 880.
[23] Ibid. 894–906.
[24] Ibid. 907–910.

it does not detract from the efficacy or the universality of the sacrifice of the cross.[25]

8. *The Sacrament of Orders* (sess. 23).— A true sacrifice presupposes a true priesthood. The Christian priesthood was instituted by Christ at the Last Supper, and its principal power and office is to consecrate and offer in sacrifice the true body and blood of Christ. The hierarchy, consisting of bishops, priests, and ministers, is divinely instituted. Bishops are superior to priests, and have the power to confirm and ordain. Orders are divided into major and minor; those below the priesthood are, as it were, preparatory to that dignity. The sacrament of orders imprints an indelible character; hence once a priest, always a priest.[26]

9. *The Sacrament of Matrimony* (sess. 24).— Christian marriage is a true sacrament, and as such it is subject to the jurisdiction of the Church. When consummated, it is absolutely indissoluble except by death; and a second marriage during the life of the first partner is by divine law null and void. The Church has the power to constitute impediments rendering marriage invalid.[27]

10. *Purgatory: Veneration of Saints and Images: Indulgences* (sess. 25).— The decree on purgatory affirms the existence of a place of purgation and the utility of prayers and other suffrages for the dead. It rules that all the more difficult and subtle questions, which do not contribute to edification, should be avoided by preachers in their sermons to the faithful.[28] In the same session, the veneration of the saints, of their relics, and of images, was declared lawful and beneficial.[29] Lastly, it was defined that Christ gave His Church the power to grant indulgences, that their use is salutary for the faithful, and the custom of granting them is to be continued in the Church.[30]

To the foregoing summary of Catholic teaching, as contained in the chapters and canons of the Council of Trent, may be added the doctrine on the Blessed Trinity, on the Incarna-

[25] Ibid. 939, 940, 948–956.
[26] Ibid. 957–968.
[27] Ibid. 969–982.

[28] Ibid. 983.
[29] Ibid. 984–988.
[30] Ibid. 989.

tion, the divine motherhood of Mary, and her perpetual virginity, as reaffirmed against the Socinians in the Constitution of Paul IV, *Cum quorundam,* August 7, 1555.[31] Also the declaration of the primacy of the Roman Church and of the Sovereign Pontiff as successor of St. Peter, which was embodied in the Tridentine profession of faith.[32] The teaching of the Council was somewhat later adapted for the use of parish priests in their instructions to the people, in the Roman Catechism, which was then published by order of Pius V. Thus a strong barrier was opposed to the revolutionary movement of the sixteenth-century Reformers, and the faith preached by the Apostles was once more set forth with that clear definiteness which is always the prerogative of truth.

[31] Ibid. 993.   [32] Ibid. 999.

CHAPTER XXVII

NEO-SCHOLASTIC THEOLOGIANS

The Council of Trent not only opposed a strong barrier to the revolutionary movement of the sixteenth-century Reformers, but it also laid the foundation of activities which in a short while produced splendid results along every line of ecclesiastical life. A succession of able and deeply religious Popes, a large number of earnest and profoundly learned theologians, a vast multitude of holy religious and many great saints, an inexhaustible supply of zealous preachers and self-sacrificing missionaries — all these worked together in bringing about a thorough reform of morals both among the clergy and laity and also in carrying the glad tidings of the Gospel to the uttermost ends of the earth. It was a marvelous revival of Catholic life, and a most convincing proof of the indefectibility of the Church as a divine institution for the salvation of the world. The evil seed sown by the Reformers indeed still bore its evil fruit, and sometimes even in Catholic circles; but the vigorous spirit of revived Catholicism ever devised effective remedies, and thus within the Church herself comparatively little harm resulted.

Most of these varied activities, however, supplied matter for church history rather than for the history of dogmas. True, during the latter part of the sixteenth century, and during nearly the whole of the seventeenth, there was displayed in many countries an intense theological interest, and much useful work was accomplished; but it was mostly by way of commenting on mediæval teaching in the light of the decisions given at Trent. On the other hand, while there was no want

[1] Cfr. Schwane, V, 24 sqq.; K. Werner, Franz Suarez und die Scholastik der letzten Jahrhun-derte; *Loofs, Leitfaden zum Studium der Dogmengeschichte; Hefele, The Life of Cardinal Ximenes.

of profound theological speculation, few of the topics dealt with were of a nature that promised definite and universally accepted results. They rather constituted so many school differences, and are apt to remain such for ages to come. Finally, though there was frequent occasion for authoritative pronouncements on the errors of the day, these pronouncements were for the most part little more than practical applications of dogmatic decisions given by previous councils. There are indeed exceptions to this, as will be pointed out below; but these exceptions are not as numerous as one might at first be led to believe when taking up the study of the documents in question. Hence, in a compendious work like the present, it seems advisable merely to summarize the more important points of post-Tridentine theology, without entering into any detail as regards the dogmatic developments which are still in course of formation. The following outline, therefore, must suffice for our present purpose.

In regard to the revival of theological studies after the Council of Trent, two points are especially deserving of notice. The first is the change of textbook employed in the schools; and the second is the shifting of the center of theological activities from France to Spain. This latter point is of interest chiefly because it marked the breaking away from the Nominalistic tendencies which since the middle of the fourteenth century had begun to dominate the University of Paris. The former, on the other hand, effected a general improvement in theological studies, both by providing a broader and more solid basis upon which to build, and by promoting clearness of thought and precision of reasoning. Up to the middle of the sixteenth century, the *Sententiarum Libri Quatuor* of the Lombard had been almost universally used as a text of Scholastic prelections; but thereafter this honor was accorded to the *Summa Theologica* of St. Thomas, except in the schools of the Scotists, where the·time-honored custom of commenting on the *Sentences* was retained.

This new theology, which was already in process of formation when the Council of Trent began its work, is usually designated as Neo-Scholasticism. Its first distinguished representative was Francis de Vittoria. He was born in 1488, and taught theology, first for some years at Valladolid, and then, from 1526 to 1544, at Salamanca. Being a member of the Dominican order, he took St. Thomas as his guide; and as not only his own younger brethren, but also many other religious and even seculars attended his lectures, he secured a large circle of admirers for the Angel of the Schools. Nor were his lectures merely a running commentary on the text of the *Summa,* but he adapted its principles and solutions to the needs of his own time. And even more than St. Thomas had done before him, he emphasized the positive aspect of theology, making an exensive use of Holy Scripture and the writings of the Fathers. Thus he replaced the idle speculations of decadent Scholasticism by a theological system that was at once thorough and comprehensive. In consequence he is justly regarded as the founder of Neo-Scholasticism, which is little else than the Scholasticism of the thirteenth century brought up to date and developed along positive lines.

Among the many distinguished disciples of Vittoria, Dominicus de Soto, Bartholomew Carranza, and Melchior Cano are deserving of special mention. All three were sent as theologians to the Council of Trent, and also ranked high as lecturers on theology, at Valladolid, Alcala, and Salamanca. Cano, however, considerably tarnished his fame by his unreasonable opposition to the Society of Jesus, whose growing success in the schools seems to have inspired him with envy. On the other hand, he gained immortal renown by his famous work *De Locis Theologicis,* which inaugurated a new era in the treatment of fundamental theology. Lucid in style and thorough in treatment, it is justly regarded as a model treatise on theological method. The author enumerates ten *loci,* or sources of theological arguments, each of which he treats in a separate book. These sources are, Holy Scripture, oral tradition, the Catholic Church, the councils, the Fathers, the Roman Church, the Scholastic theologians, natural reason as manifested in science, philosophy, and history. To these is added a final book that treats of the use and application of the *loci* in theological polemics.

The work thus begun by the Dominicans at Salamanca was ably continued by members of the same order during the second half of the sixteenth century. Thus Bartholomew de Medina, utilizing the writings of his predecessors in the theological chair, published two volumes of commentaries on the *Summa* of St. Thomas; and also a volume on moral theology, in which he defends the principles of probabilism. Towards the end of the century, Dominicus Bañez developed his doctrine of physical predetermination in reference to the action of efficacious grace, and thus became the founder of Neo-Thomism. His opposition to Molina's teaching on the *scientia media* was not only strong but violent, and largely on account of it he gave a decidedly forced interpretation of St. Thomas' doctrine on the foreknowledge of God. On both points he had numerous followers in his own order, as will be noted in the following chapter.

Besides the Dominicans, many other religious orders were established at Salamanca. Among them were the Augustinians, the Hieronymites, the Norbertines, and the Discalceated Carmelites. The last named published a large commentary on the *Summa* of St. Thomas, usually cited as *Salmanticenses*. The first edition, in nine folio volumes, appeared in 1631, under the title: *Collegii Salmanticensis fratrum discalceatorum B. M. de Monte Carmeto primitivae observantiae Cursus theologicus, Summam theologicam D. Thomae Doctoris Angelici complectens, juxta miram ejusdem Angelici Praeceptoris doctrinam et omnino consone ad eam, quam Complutense Collegium ejusdem ordinis in suo artium cursu tradit.* The last clause of this title refers to a work on the philosophy of Aristotle and St. Thomas, in five volumes folio, which had been published in 1624 at Alcala. The dogmatic standpoint of the *Salmanticenses* is strictly Thomistic, and to some extent also reveals the anti-Jesuit bias of Bañez and his followers.

The Scotist school of theology had also a number of distinguished representatives during the sixteenth and seventeenth centuries. Among them may be mentioned Gregory Ruiz, John Ovando, John of the Incarnation, Hugh Cavelli, and John Poncius. The last two were Irish Franciscans, but taught theology at the Ara Coeli in Rome. Their contemporary and brother in religion, Luke Wadding, published the works of Scotus in twenty-six folio volumes, together with a running commentary. The first volume appeared at Lyons in 1657. Unlike most other theologians of that time, the Scotists continued to use the *Sentences* of the Lombard as the text of their prelections, and to write commentaries on them as had been done by the Scholastics of the Middle Ages. Thus Mastrius, who died in 1673, wrote the *Disputationes Theologicae in 4 Libris Sententiarum,* which were published two years after his death. A few years later appeared the *Scotus Academicus* by Frassen, and the *Summa Theologiae Scotisticae* by Dupasquier. The latter work is regarded as the best presentation of the theology of Scotus. On the other hand, Bartholomew de Barberiis, Gaudentius of Brixen, and not a few others adhered closely to the teaching of St. Bonaventure.

By the side of the older religious orders, nearly all of which were intensely active in the fields of theology, the Society of Jesus took a distinguished position almost from its inception. Approved by Paul III in 1540, two of its first members, Salmeron and Laynez, were sent as the Pope's theologians to the Council of Trent, where both of them gave proof of their profound learning no less than of their religious fervor. However, it was with Toletus, later created cardinal, that Jesuit theology first made its way into the schools. He had received his theological training at Salamanca, and in 1559 was appointed to teach theology at the Roman College. He taught with great success, and wrote a valuable commentary on the *Summa* of St. Thomas. After his elevation to the cardinalate, he was succeeded in his chair of theology by Gregory de Valentia, who had previously taught at Dillingen. As this latter also had studied under the Dominicans at Salamanca, the theology of St. Thomas was naturally adopted by the Society as its own. This was entirely in accord with the wishes of St. Ignatius, who always had a great admiration for the Angel of the Schools.

While Toletus and de Valentia were establishing the theological reputation of the Society at Rome, Peter Fonseca and Louis Molina met with similar success at Evora in Portugal. The latter is best known as the author of a work on the *scientia media,* of which something will be said in the following chapter; but he proved his profound theological learning along other lines as well. Besides a commentary on the first part of the *Summa* and several historical treatises, he wrote a monumental work under the title, *De Justitia et Jure,* which secured for him an international reputation. From Evora, where he had taught dogmatic theology for twenty years, he was transferred to Madrid and appointed to the chair of moral theology. There he died in 1600, at the age of sixty-five.

About the same time two other Spanish Jesuits were making a name for themselves as distinguished lecturers and writers on theology. They were Gabriel Vasquez and Francis Suarez. Vasquez taught dogmatic theology for twenty-nine years, first at Alcala and then at the Jesuit college in Rome. He was both original and profound, and is sometimes called the Augustine of Spain. He wrote a large commentary of the *Summa* of St. Thomas, which has always been held in great esteem. Suarez, usually styled Doctor Eximius, lectured on philosophy at Avila and Segovia, and on theology at Valladolid, Rome, Alcala, Salamanca, and finally at the new university of Coimbra. In the latter place he taught from 1597 until his death in 1617. His fame as a professor of theology was so great that pupils flocked to Coimbra from far and near. He wrote voluminously both on philosophy and theology. His commentary on the *Summa* alone comprises twenty volumes.

In the first half of the seventeenth century, three other Jesuit theologians acquired great distinction, namely, Ruiz de Montoya, Martinez Ripalda, and John de Lugo, created cardinal by Urban VIII. De Montoya taught theology at Cordova and Seville, and published a work of remarkable depth of thought and closeness of reasoning on the omniscience and *scientia media* of God. He also wrote commentaries on parts of the *Summa.* Ripalda, professor of theology at Salamanca, is considered by many as one of the greatest theologians after the Council of Trent. His most celebrated work is entitled *De Ente Supernaturali*. In an appendix to this work he gives a thorough refutation of the errors of Baius. His treatise on redemption and grace made such an impression that he was called the Cyril of modern times. De Lugo lectured on theology at the Roman College from 1621 to 1641, when he was raised to the cardinalate. He won great renown as a moral theologian; but his dogmatic treatises on the Incarnation, the Holy Eucharist, and the sacrament of penance are also highly esteemed.

Most of the theological activity referred to in the preceding paragraphs was caried on in Spain, and nearly all the men concerned in it were of Spanish origin and training. However, other countries were also active in the same field, although not to the same extent. Thus Italy maintained theological schools of considerable importance at Padua, Naples, Pavia, and Pisa; while the colleges of the different religious orders in Rome were usually kept up to a high standard of efficiency. Many of the ablest professors were indeed drawn from other countries, principally Spain; but Italy supplied also some eminent men of her own, as, for instance, the Jesuits Bellarmine, Viva, and Zaccaria; the Franciscian de Rubeis, and Cardinal Gotti.

France also contributed a considerable number of able theologians, although the University of Paris had lost much of its ancient fame. Special mention may be made of the Jesuit Petavius, the author of a famous work on positive theology; the Oratorian Thomassin, who wrote a similar work; the Franciscan Frassen; the Dominican René Billuart, and the Sarbonne professors Gonet, Dupasquier, Habert, and Tournely. In Germany and Belgium a high degree of excellence was reached by Becanus, Lessius, and the authors of the *Theologia Wirceburgensis*.

Thus from the Council of Trent till well into the eighteenth century, theological studies were nearly everywhere in a flourishing condition. Besides, much excellent work was also done in canon law, exegesis, and church history. Then for a cen-

tury or more there was a constant decline, until some fifty
years ago the study of theology and kindred branches of learning was taken up again with renewed interest and considerable
success.

CHAPTER XXVIII

SCHOOL DIFFERENCES [1]

As the Council of Trent had been convened for the purpose
of extirpating heresy, and not with a view to decide controversies that happened to be carried on between Catholic theologians, it was but natural that the different theological schools
should continue to defend their own particular views on points
which had been in no way defined. Hence in regard to mere
school differences, practically no change was brought about
by the Council. In a few instances, indeed, particular opinions became untenable on account of their bearing upon defined
doctrines; but that was by way of exception. Generally speaking, the Dominicans, the Franciscans, the Augustinians, the
Scotists, and to some extent even the Nominalists, retained
all that was peculiar to their own particular schools of theological thought. Besides, in the course of a few years after the
Council, new differences arose; and these differences, in some
instances, caused divisions between theologians of one and the
same school. Again, differences were occasioned by the rise
of new religious orders, as in the case of the Jesuits; even if
they professed to follow the same guide as some older order.
To discuss all these various and divergent opinions would be
to no purpose in the present work, although a few of the more
striking of them may be profitably noted. The following are
perhaps the most important. They are so many later developments of mediæval teaching.

[1] Cfr. Schwane, VI, 57 sqq.; K.
Werner, Franz Suarez und die
Scholastik der letzten Jahrhun-
derte; De la Serviere, Theologie de
Bellarmin; Kleutgen, Die Theologie der Vorzeit; Turmel, Histoire
de la Theologie Positive; Regnon, Bañez et Molina, Histoire,
Doctrine, Critique metaphysique;
Schneemann, Controversiarum de
divinae gratiae liberique arbitrii
concordia initia et progressus;
*Loofs, Leitfaden der Dogmenge-
schichte.

1. *God's Foreknowledge of the Conditionally Free Acts of the Future.*— The fact of God's foreknowledge, even in regard to the conditionally free acts of the future, was unanimously taught by the Scholastics of the Middle Ages. On the other hand, hardly any attempt was made by them to determine more closely the particulars of this knowledge. Like St. Thomas, most of the Scholastics contented themselves with saying that God knows all future events, necessary or free, absolute or conditional, by reason of their eternal presentiality; yet in such wise that His own essence is the ultimate medium of cognition. As regards necessary events, or those free actions whose futurity is absolute, there is no great difficulty; for they presuppose in God at least a decree of concurrence with the finite agent, by reason of which they may be said to be present in the divine essence, and therefore knowable in the same. But there appears to be an insuperable difficulty in regard to future events that are conditioned by the free determination of the finite agent. For God's decree of concurrence presupposes definite knowledge of the absolute futurity of the event in question; and whence does God derive that knowledge so long as the event is regarded as conditioned? This view of the matter was not professedly investigated by the older Scholastics.

After the Council of Trent the solution of the difficulty became urgent for two reasons. First, because Socinus and other innovators denied that the conditionally free acts of the future were definitely known by God. Secondly, because God's foreknowledge of these acts is intimately connected with the freedom of man's will under the action of grace, which freedom was denied by the Reformers and defined by the Council. Hence a way had to be found of reconciling two apparently irreconcilable doctrines. It was not a mere penchant for speculation that introduced the difficult subject of God's foreknowledge into the field of theological discussion, but rather the urgent need of finding a reasonable solution of difficulties that were brought against the faith.

It was with this object in view that Molina worked out his theory of the *scientia media,* which in the scheme of divine knowledge holds a middle place between the *scientia simplicis intelligentiae* and the *scientia visionis,* till then commonly accepted as constituting a complete division of cognition on the part of God.   The idea itself of the *scientia media* was not new; for aside from the many Patristic texts which imply it more or less clearly, it had already been formulated by Fonseca, Molina's professor, who called it *scientia mixta.*   However, to Molina belongs the credit of having placed his professor's theory on a firm basis, and winning a place for it in the theological world.

As is quite obvious, all objects of divine cognition may be conceived to belong to one of these three classes: the purely possible, the actually existing, and possible events whose future occurrence is conditioned by the self-determination of a free agent.   The first class comprises the objects of the *scientia simplicis intelligentiae,* the second those of the *scientia visionis,* and the third those of the *scientia media.*   Hence the *scientia media* envisages its object as possible in itself and as actually existing on the supposition that certain conditions are fulfilled, and in so far it is intermediate between the other two kinds of divine knowledge.   It is from this intermediate position that it takes its name — *scientia media.*

An example of this kind of divine knowledge is found in Christ's declaration that Tyre and Sidon would have done penance in sackcloth and ashes, if they had witnessed the signs and miracles that were wrought in Corozain and Bethsaida. The conversion of these two cities was in itself purely possible; it would have become an actual occurrence had the aforesaid signs and miracles been wrought in presence of the inhabitants; and although they were not so wrought, and consequently the conversion did not take place, yet Christ knew its conditioned occurrence with absolute certainty.   Hence in regard to the mere fact of such a knowledge there can be no doubt.   It is only when the medium of cognition is considered that difficulties occur, and that views of theologians begin to differ.

Molina, in common with all other theologians, held that the ultimate medium of cognition is the divine essence, in so far as therein all objective truth is reflected. The fact that Tyre and Sidon, in the example given, would have been converted, was objectively true from all eternity, and as such it was like any other truth represented in the divine essence as a medium of cognition. This representation is independent of any decree of the divine will in regard to the occurrence in question; it is simply due to the perfection of God's essence as the mirror of all truth. Furthermore, God's knowledge, though determined by His own essence as the *medium in quo,* terminates at the object itself; and as His intellect is infinitely perfect, " He knows the most secret inclinations and penetrates the most hidden recesses of man's heart, and is thus enabled to foresee with mathematical certainty the free resolves latent in man's will." In this sense God may be said to know the conditionally free acts of the future even in their proximate causes. However, the certainty of this knowledge is in the last instance not derived from the object, which in itself is contingent; but from His own infinite perfection.

This represents the substance of Molina's theory as worked out by himself, and in the main also as it was adopted and defended by Suarez, Vasquez, Lessius, Becanus, and those who took part in the controversy with the Thomists. However, it was somewhat further developed by the introduction of two concepts which Molina had set aside as unnecessary. The first is derived from God's eternity. As St. Thomas teaches, God's eternal existence necessarily implies His co-existence with all His creatures, and this raises Him above and beyond all divisions of time. Hence the free self-determination of the will, even if it still lies in the future, is intimately present to His eternal essence. And therefore, looking at the matter from His point of view, He does not foresee but simply sees the future. Consequently, He knows future events as He knows those of the present; because to Him there is neither past nor future, but only the unchangeable *now* of eternal duration.

The second concept is taken from the obvious need and universally admitted fact of God's coöperation with the actions of His creatures. As no finite being can act except in so far as God sustains its activity and concurs with the same, every future action presupposes on His part the will to concur, and this will constitutes the medium of cognition. In regard to absolutely future actions, the will to concur is absolute; while in regard to conditionally future actions it is hypothetical; and this hypothetical will of concurrence is the medium in which God knows all future occurrences that are conditioned by the self-determination of a free agent. However, it must be borne in mind that the divine concurrence does not induce but merely presupposes the hypothetical self-determination of the agent's will; and therefore God's infallible knowledge of this self-determination belongs properly to the *scientia media*.

This theory of divine foreknowledge, as first formulated by Fonseca and Molina and then perfected by successive generations of Jesuit theologians, was fiercely attacked by the Dominicans, who denounced it as an unwarranted innovation. They, too, recognized the necessity of giving a more detailed explanation of the matter than could be found in the works of St. Thomas, but in trying to work out that explanation they proceeded along lines directly opposed to those followed by the Jesuits. God's knowledge, according to them, is of two kinds only: the knowledge of simple intelligence, and the knowledge of vision. The former has the purely possible for its object, while the latter extends to all other events and occurrences, even the conditionally free acts of the future. The reason why the knowledge of vision is so comprehensive lies in the fact that God knows things in so far as He is their cause, either as regards their absolute or their conditional existence. Even the self-determination of man's free will, although free, is possible only under the physical premotion of God's concurrence; hence in the divine decree of that concurrence the self-determination of the will is contained as an object of eternal vision. Hence there is neither need nor room for the *scientia media* of Molina.

This system, though to some extent based upon thoughts that are found in the writings of St. Thomas, received its first real development from Michael Bañez, a Spanish Dominican and author of Neo-Thomism. It was later on completed by Alvarez, Gonet, Gotti, Billuart, and others, who excogitated the theory of hypothetical decrees of the divine will. Hence Thomism no less than Molinism is the finished product of many minds, but in substance it has always remained what it was in the beginning — an explanation of divine foreknowledge by means of predetermining decrees.

A word of explanation may here be added in reference to the hypothetical decrees of the divine will. They are conceived as subjectively absolute and objectively conditioned. On the part of God there is a real decision concerning the occurrence of some future event, hence the decree is subjectively absolute; but the objective effectiveness of this decision is made dependent on the occurrence of something else, and therefore the decree is objectively conditioned. This something else is a condition the fulfillment of which is either entirely in the power of God, or partly also in the power of a created will. Hence there are two kinds of hypothetical decrees. Of the one kind the following is an example: " I decree that the inhabitants of Tyre and Sidon will do penance, if I send them the Messias "; of the other this is an instance: " I will that all men be saved, if they will coöperate with my grace." Still, precisely as mediums of divine cognition, both kinds are really the same; because even where the fulfillment of the condition is partly in the power of a created will, the decree of God's will predetermines the self-determination of the created free agent. Hence God knows what choice the free agent will make, because He Himself is the cause of that choice, though without interfering with the agent's freedom.

That Thomism thus offers a much clearer explanation of God's foreknowledge than can ever be attempted by Molinism, or by any other theory of divine cognition, is quite obvious. For as God Himself is said to predetermine the self-determination of the free agent, He knows conditionally free actions of the future in the same way as He knows future necessary actions, and in regard to these latter no one has ever found any difficulty. But the system has two very serious drawbacks. First, it necessitates an infinite number of hypothetical decrees, which seem more than unacceptable; secondly, to an unbiased person it appears impossible that these predetermining decrees should leave man's freedom untouched. It is especially on account of this latter difficulty that the system has found but little favor outside the Thomistic school.

2. *Controversies on Efficacious Grace.*— The relation of grace and man's free will is thus indicated by the Council of Trent, in its decree on justification: " The Synod furthermore declares, that, in adults, the beginning of justification is to be derived from the preventing grace of God, through Jesus Christ, that is to say, from His vocation, whereby, without any merits existing on their part, they are called; that so they, who by sins were alienated from God, may be disposed by His quickening and assisting grace to convert themselves to their own justification, by freely assenting to and coöperating with the aforesaid grace; in such a way that, while God touches the heart of man by the illumination of the Holy Ghost, man is not himself utterly without doing anything, while he receives that inspiration, forasmuch as he is also able to reject it; yet he is not able, by his own free will, without the grace of God, to move himself unto justice in His sight."

Hence in their discussions on grace and free will, all Catholic theologians regard two points as incontrovertible: First, that the influence of grace is necessary for every salutary act; secondly, that the human will remains free under the influence of grace. They, furthermore, also admit that there is a difference between merely sufficient grace and efficacious grace; but they are very much divided in their views when they come to assign the reason for this difference. In their efforts to demonstrate the mutual relations between grace and free will, which form the foundation of the difference between sufficient and efficacious grace, post-Tridentine theologians evolved two pairs of closely related systems, one of which takes grace for its starting point and the other the free will of man. To the former belong Thomism and Augustinianism; and to the latter, Molinism and Congruism. To these may be added a fifth system, known as Syncretism, which is eclectic and occupies a middle place between Thomism and Molinism. A few re-

marks in regard to each of the different systems will suffice
for our present purpose.

(a) *Thomism.*— According to Bañez and his followers,
every act of contingent causes is produced by an application
of their potentiality to the act under the physical premotion
of the First Cause.   By an influence that precedes all acts of
the creature, not in the order of time but in the order of causality, God moves every finite cause to its proper acts — the
necessary to necessary acts, and the free to free acts.   This is
true both in the natural and the supernatural order of things.
Hence the efficacy of grace is due to the intrinsic nature of
the grace bestowed, and is in no way dependent on the attitude
of man's free will in its regard.   Consequently, efficacious,
grace is intrinsically and of its very nature different from sufficient grace.   It has of itself an infallible connection with the
free correspondence of man's will, so that it not only gives
the power to act but causes the act itself.   On the other hand,
sufficient grace does not cause man to act, but merely gives
him the power of acting.   Nor is this power in itself sufficient
for the intended act, but it must be supplemented by another
grace which is intrinsically efficacious.   The grace is called
sufficient in the sense that it prepares the way for the supplementary grace, which would infallibly be given if the resist-
ance of man's free will to the first grace did not place an obstacle in its way.

The objections to this system are obvious.   For how does
the will remain really free, if it cannot refuse to act under the
premotion of efficacious grace?   To say that it could refuse
to act *in sensu diviso,* though not *in sensu composito,* appears
to be little more than a quibble.   Again, how can sufficient
grace, as explained in this system, with any propriety be called
sufficient?   For as the will cannot act except under the influence of physical premotion, it can obviously not do anything
else than resist whenever this physical premotion is wanting, as
it is wanting in sufficient grace.   Lastly, the system of physical
premotion seems to make God the originator of sinful acts.
For when God premoves man to the entity of the sinful act
and at the same time withholds the opposite premotion of effi-

cacious grace, it is hard to see how man can possibly avoid sin.

(b) *Augustinianism.*— As the name indicates, this system is professedly founded on the teaching of St. Augustine. In its elements it dates back to the Middle Ages, but it was fully developed only after the Council of Trent. This development is largely the work of Berti, Bellelli, Bertieri, Habert, and other seventeenth- and eighteenth-century theologians. According to the advocates of this system, grace is intrinsically and of its very nature efficacious or merely sufficient, as the case may be; but efficacious grace does not physically predetermine the will. Its efficacy implies a merely moral predetermination, which results from the victorious delight — *delectatio coelestis victrix* — produced by its action upon the free agent. On the other hand, merely sufficient grace produces a delight which is too weak to overcome the contrary motions of concupiscence. Hence the two kinds of grace are intrinsically and essentially different; but this difference arises ultimately from their respective relations to the perversity of fallen nature.

At first sight, this system has much in common with Jansenism, in regard to which something will be said in the following chapter. However, it can point to one very essential difference, which secures it against all suspicion of heresy. While Jansenism makes efficacious grace irresistible, Augustinianism does not. According to it, the will invariably and infallibly follows the stronger influence of grace or of concupiscence; but it does so without coercion or intrinsic necessity.

(c) *Molinism.*— It was chiefly to safeguard the freedom of the human will under the influence of efficacious grace that Molina worked out his theory of the *scientia media.* Hence he entitled his work on the subject, *Concordia Liberi Arbitrii cum Gratiae Donis, Divina Praescientia, Providentia, Praedestinatione et Reprobatione.* The views on the efficacy of grace defended in this book are directly opposed to the Thomism of Bañez, and they started a controversy between the Jesuits and the Dominicans that was terminated only by an order of Paul V, after the matter had been discussed for nine years before the *Congregatio de Auxiliis,* first convened by Clement

VIII in 1598. No decision was given for or against either of the two contending parties, but each was forbidden to censure the teaching of the other.

According to the teaching of Molina, there is no intrinsic and essential difference between efficacious and sufficient grace. Both have of their very nature the *efficacia virtutis,* in as much as they impart to man's free will the proximate power and aptitude to elicit a supernatural act.   Hence the difference between them in reference to the act in question, or the *efficacia connexionis,* comes *ab extrinsico,* from the attitude freely assumed by the will. If the will gives its consent, the grace becomes efficacious; if the will withholds its consent, the same grace remains merely sufficient.   However, in giving its consent, the will acts not merely as a natural power; for it is already prepared and placed in the supernatural order of activity by the presence in it of prevenient grace, and consequently the act that follows is the joint product of grace and free will. Yet in one sense this joint product is to be ascribed to grace rather than to free will; for it is not the will which by its free consent determines the power of grace, but it is grace which gives free will the power to act and coöperates with its action.   Hence there is absolutely no similarity between Molinism and Semi-Pelagianism, as most Protestant writers assert.

While the freedom of the human will under the influence of efficacious grace is thus preserved intact, the sovereign dominion of God in the distribution of efficacious graces is placed in safety by the intervention of the *scientia media.* For by reason of it God foreknows infallibly what particular graces will in any given instance secure the free consent of the human will, and what particular graces will not; and in accordance with this foreknowledge He can decree to bestow whatever graces answer the purpose of His own wise dispositions in the economy of salvation.   Thus infallibility of divine cognition is secured, to which, when there is question of efficacious graces, corresponds in the absolute order of things the infallibility of connection between grace and the subsequent act.

(d) *Congruism.*— When some of Molina's followers

pushed his principles to extremes by overemphasizing the power of free will, a reaction set in which led to the assertion of an intrinsic difference between efficacious and sufficient grace. This difference, however, was conceived to lie in the moral and not in the physical nature of grace. Efficacious grace, it was pointed out by Suarez, Vasquez, Lessius, Bellarmine, and others of the Society of Jesus, is a special gift of God and as such it has a higher moral value than merely sufficient grace. This higher moral value consists principally in the fact that the grace conferred is specially suited to the circumstances of the case, so that its congruity is a powerful factor in soliciting the consent of the will. Hence efficacious grace is called congruous grace — *gratia congrua* — whereas merely sufficient grace is termed incongruous grace — *gratia incongrua*. This view was strongly endorsed by Claudius Acquaviva, and by subsequent Generals of the Society. It must be noted, however, that the idea of congruous grace was already contained in the system as originated by Molina, only it was not emphasized by him to the same extent as it was by later theologians.

(e) *Syncretism.*— As the name indicates, this system resulted from the combination of elements taken from other systems then in vogue. However, the elements in question are really nothing else than Thomism on the one hand and Molinism on the other. The distinctive trait of Syncretism consists in the acceptance of two kinds of efficacious grace: one kind that is intrinsically and of its very nature efficacious, and another that derives its efficacy from the free consent of the will. The latter kind is given by God for the performance of less difficult good works, such as the resisting of slight temptations, devout prayer, and the like; then, if man accepts these graces and freely coöperates with them, God will give him an intrinsically predetermining grace for the performance of good works that are more difficult. Thus the freedom of the will is kept intact, the necessity of prayer is emphasized, and God's sovereign dominion in the matter of grace is vindicated.

The system was originated in the seventeenth century by Ysambertus, and later on developed by Duplessis, Habert,

Tournely, and others. It was endorsed by St. Alphonsus Liguori, and has not a few advocates among modern theologians. Yet there is little in it to make it acceptable. It has to solve all the difficulties that confront Thomism and Molinism, and offers no principle of so doing which is not contained in the one or the other of the two systems.

3. *Some Differences of Opinion Among Theologians.*— These differences are so numerous that it is practically impossible to give even the briefest outline of them in a compendious work like the present. Nor is there any need of it. Many of them are mere continuations of differences that arose among theologians in the Middle Ages, and as such have already been indicated in earlier chapters. Others have so little theological interest that an exposition of them would be out of place in a history of dogmas. Hence the following few points will suffice for our purpose.

(a) *The Hypostatic Union.*— The great theologians of the Middle Ages defended the fact of the hypostatic union, but did not evolve any very definite theory as to its ultimate explanation. This was attempted by their successors after the Council of Trent. All these theories are based upon different philosophical concepts of personality. Thus many Thomists hold that personality results ultimately from actual existence, between which and essence they place a real distinction. Hence, according to them, the hypostatic union consists in the fact that the personal existence of the Word supplies the actual existence of Christ's human nature. This view is taken, among others, by Cajetan, Gonet, Billuart, and more recently by Terrien and Cardinal Billot.

Not a few Jesuits, among them Suarez, Vasquez, De Lugo, and Ariaga, place personality in a physical mode, really distinct from existing human nature. And this mode, they contend, was impeded in the union, its place being taken by the personality of the Word. Some of them, like Suarez, furthermore postulate a *modus unionis,* in which the union formally consists. Others of the Society, as Molina, Petavius, Tiphanus, Cardinal Franzelin, Christian Pesch, and also many Scotists, place personality in a real mode which they hold to

be only negatively distinct from complete and actual existing
human nature.   Most of them, moreover, reject the Suarezian
modus unionis and contend that the union formally consists in
the extension of the hypostatic functions of the Word to the
humanity in Christ.

The Scotists as a school adhere to the view taken by Duns
Scotus, that personality consists in a real but negative perfection.   This perfection is identical with the complete and independently existing nature, in so far as it excludes both actual
and aptitudinal communication of the nature to another suppositum.   Hence as this perfection is impeded by the accession of the Word to the human nature of Christ, the personality of the Word must take its place.   In its last analysis, this
view seems to be really the same as the preceding.— Many
other theories have been excogitated, but these four suffice to
indicate the general drift of theological thought on the subject under consideration.

(b) *The Redemption.*— Omitting minor variations in the
soteriological teaching of post-Tridentine theologians, it is
necessary only to mention in this connection that the view of
Scotus on the primary motive of the Incarnation and on the
adequacy of Christ's satisfaction has still its many defenders,
even outside the Scotists' school of theology.   And this is
especially true in regard to the first point, although the weight
of theological opinion is still in favor of considering the redemption of the world as the primary motive of the Incarnation.   The necessity of the Incarnation, for the purpose of
rendering God condign satisfaction for the sins of mankind,
continued during all this time to be generally defended, but
was insisted on with special emphasis by the Salmanticenses.
This satisfaction is, according to all, in the order of justice, but
many theologians deny that it is *ad rigorem justitiae.*

(c) *Sanctifying Grace.*— Although the Council of Trent
defined that the created gift of sanctifying grace inhering in
the soul must be considered as the sole formal cause of justification, yet it did not indicate all the various functions of that
formal cause, and consequently there arose numerous discussions concerning them in the centuries that followed.   Does

sanctifying grace expel mortal sin physically from the soul as is held by most theologians, or only morally as is maintained by the Scotists? Is the participation of the divine nature merely in the moral-juridical order as the Scotists contend, or is it physical, though only analogous, as the greater number of other theologians maintain? Again, is sanctifying grace as a physical entity really distinct from charity, according to the more common opinion, or is it essentially identical with that virtue, as was taught not only by the followers of Scotus, but also by Lessius, Bellarmine, and many others? These and many similar questions remain still unsolved in the theology of sanctifying grace.

(d) *Predestination and Reprobation.*— These two points were and still are discussed chiefly between the Molinists and Thomists, the question being whether God predestines *post* or *ante praevisa merita.* The Molinists contend for the former view, and the Thomists for the latter.

According to the Molinists, the order of divine decrees in regard to predestination is as follows: (a) Antecedently, even presupposing the existence of original sin, God truly and sincerely wills the salvation of all men, and in accordance with this will prepares for them means of salvation that are at least remotely sufficient. (b) By reason of a special predilection, for some He destines graces which He foreknows by the *scientia media* will prove efficacious. (c) By the knowledge of vision He foresees that these same persons will perform meritorious actions and die in the state of grace; and thus, after foreseeing their merits, He predestines them to eternal glory. In a similar way He foresees that others will die in the state of mortal sin; and these, in view of their demerits, He condemns to the punishment of hell.

In the Thomists' view the divine decrees are arranged in this order: (a) Antecedently, even presupposing original sin, God truly and sincerely intends eternal blessedness for all rational creatures, and with this intention He prepares for them sufficient graces. (b) When He foresees in His decrees of sufficient grace that no one makes a good use of the grace thus offered, He chooses some from amongst them whom He decrees absolutely and efficaciously to save. (c) For these He prepares efficacious graces, through which they will infallibly work out their salvation. (d) Foreseeing in these same decrees that the elect will perform good works, He decrees furthermore in the order of execution to confer eternal life upon them as a reward. (e) As He foresees that all others, not belonging to the elect, will die in mortal sin, He condemns them to eternal punishment.— The Congruists arrange the divine decrees in a similar order, but they derive God's foreknowledge from the *scientia media*.

Comparing the two systems, one cannot help noticing that in regard to reprobation the Molinists have a decided advantage over the Thomists. For in their system of grace reprobation follows from the free choice of the reprobate themselves, whereas in the system of the Thomists it is ultimately due to the absence of a *praemotio physica* without which the free will of man cannot act. Hence the advocates of this system are forced to hold negative reprobation, in the sense that the reprobate had really no chance of saving their souls. The inference is, of course, denied; but it appears too obvious to admit of denial.

(e) *Sacramental Theology.*— The chief theological differences in regard to the sacraments bear upon sacramental causality, the composition of the sacramental sign, the immediate institution by Christ, and the nature of the sacramental character. The following few remarks will suffice to indicate the differences in question.

Sacramental causality is explained in many different ways, but all these ways may be classified in four systems. The first of these is usually called the system of dispositive causality, which holds that the sacraments are the instrumental causes, not directly of grace, but of a disposition thereto. In baptism, confirmation, and orders, this disposition is identified with the sacramental character, while in the remaining sacraments it is said to be a corresponding ornament of the soul — *ornatus animae.* This view was defended by St. Thomas in his commentary of the *Sentences,* and by the Thomists generally up to the time of Cajetan (+ 1510). Since his day most Thomists are in favor of the second system, which is that of perfective physical causality. It differs from the foregoing in this, that the sacraments are said to be the direct instrumental causes of grace. According to its modern advocates, the system is in accord with the teaching of St. Thomas as contained in the *Summa Theologica*. However, Cardinal Billot and others still contend for dispositive causality, but under a different name. They call it intentional causality. The system of perfective physical causality is also defended by many Jesuit theologians, as Suarez, Bellarmine, Gregory de Valentia, and Sylvester Maurus.

The third system advocates what is usually termed occasional causality. The name is taken from the fact that the sacraments are regarded as occasional conditions on which the bestowal of grace has been made dependent by the divine will. The power of God is said to operate in the sacramental rite, but in such a way that the rite itself does not instrumentally contribute to the conferring of grace. Hence the sacraments are not really causes of the grace bestowed. This view of sacramental causality is usually attributed to St. Bonaventure, Scotus, and many of their early followers. Modern Scotists for the most part subscribe, though with some reservations, to the fourth system, which is known in the schools by the name of moral causality. In this system the sacraments are considered to be only mediate causes of grace. Their causality is conceived to consist in the fact that they are morally the actions of Christ, and as such have the inherent power of infallibly moving God to bestow grace upon the worthy recipient. The system is defended by the greater number of Jesuit theologians, and also by some of the older Thomists. The term, moral causality, as here used seems to have been introduced by Melchoir Cano.

In regard to the second point mentioned above, the composition of the sacramental sign, it need only be stated that there is a difference of opinion among theologians as to whether all the sacraments are intrinsically and essentially made up of things and words, or matter and form. Many agree with Scotus that penance does not include matter as an essential part, and also that the Eucharist as a sacrament does not include words by way of form. In regard to the sacrament of orders there is quite a variety of opinions as to what parts of the rite of ordination constitute the sacramental sign. Not only is it a disputed question whether the *traditio instrumentorum* forms an essential part, but also what particular imposition of hands is to be regarded as essential. At least four different views are held by theologians of note.

The immediate institution of the sacraments by Christ seems to be implied in several statements made by the Council of Trent, and hence it is commonly admitted by theologians. But when there is question of the exact meaning of the term, opinions begin to differ. Some hold that Christ designated all the sacramental rites *in specie,* as He did that of baptism and the Eucharist; while others contend that in regard to five sacraments He indicated only in a general way what external signs should be used. This latter view is rapidly gaining ground, as it lends itself more readily to the solution of historical difficulties. If not pushed too far, it seems to be perfectly safe.

On the nature of the sacramental character there are two different views, each one of which is defended by a large number of theologians. Most Thomists consider the character to be a physical potency, which has regard to the due administration or reception of the sacraments. This view was also taken by St. Thomas. Outside the Thomistic school of theology the sacramental character is quite generally held to be a *habitus,* a spiritual quality which consecrates the soul and assimilates it to Jesus Christ. It must be noted, however, that the fundamental ideas contained in these two views are accepted by individual theologians with various modifications, so that there is quite a variety of opinions on the matter. Besides, during the seventeenth and eighteenth centuries the view of Durandus, that the character is nothing but a relation, came again into vogue. This, however, is generally regarded as out of harmony with the teaching of the Council of Trent.

(f) *The Eucharistic Sacrifice.*— That the Mass is in the strict sense of the term a sacrificial rite, and that both victim and priest are the same as in the sacrifice of the cross, is a matter of faith and taught as such by all theologians. But in what particular part of the Mass the sacrifice consists, and what is the formal reason of the Eucharistic sacrifice, are questions in regard to which theological opinions are very much at variance. Some answer the first question by saying that the essence of the sacrifice consists in the oblation that follows the consecration, others contend that it is found in the communion of the celebrating priest, others hold that both consecration and communion are essential parts, while very many maintain that the consecration alone constitutes the essence of the sacrifice. At the present time this last view is the more common, and is usually regarded as certain.

There is a similar variety of opinions as regards the formal reason of the sacrifice. What is it that makes the Eucharistic rite a true sacrifice? Suarez and others answer that it is the destruction of the bread and wine and the positing in place thereof of the body and blood of Christ as peculiarly pleasing to God. Others hold with Lessius that the Mass is a sacrifice because the words of consecration tend to bring about the actual separation of Christ's body and blood, and the realization of this tendency is impeded only by the present impassible state of the Savior. De Lugo, whose view is accepted by many modern theologians, sees the specific reason of the Eucharistic sacrifice in the fact that Christ is placed illocally under the species of bread and wine, and is thus deprived of the connatural functions of His humanity, becoming present in the condition of food and drink. Again, very many hold with Cardinal Billot, that by reason of the separate consecration of bread and wine Christ is mystically immolated *in specie sacramenti* as He was once really immolated in His natural body. Beside these views there are many others, but they contribute little towards clearing up the mystery.

Some of the remaining theological differences, which are almost innumerable, will be briefly touched upon in the following chapter. Enough has been said to make the reader keenly conscious of two facts: First, that since the Council of Trent there has been displayed an intense activity in the theological world; secondly, that without the guidance of an infallible Church, religious belief can find no security anywhere.

CHAPTER XXIX

HERETICAL TENDENCIES

Although the Council of Trent, besides defining many points of doctrine, also afforded much help to theological inquirers by embodying in the chapters of its various sessions timely expositions of truths still open for discussion, yet it only partially succeeded in suppressing such heretical tendencies as were not directly affected by its condemnation of Protestant errors. Men's minds were restless, and not a few of those who still remained faithful to the Church allowed the critical attitude of the sixteenth-century innovators to influence their views and judgments. Hence the repeated appearance of theological opinions that called for censure on the part of the Church; hence, too, the tenacity with which writers clung to their views after judgment had been given against them by the teaching authority which they themselves acknowledged as competent to decide matters of faith. The following few points will suffice to illustrate the tendencies in question.

1. *Baius and Baianism.*— Michael Baius and his friend John Hessels were both connected with the University of Louvain, and they first broached their untenable views during the absence of Chancellor Tapper, who had been sent as theologian to the Council of Trent. On his return, in 1552, he took immediate steps to counteract the evil influence of the two innovators. Through the intervention of Cardinal Granvelle, archbishop of Mechlin, Baius and Hessels were induced to discontinue the spreading of opinions that could apparently not be sustained. They remained quiet till Tapper's death, in 1559, but after that they began the discussion anew. Though ably opposed by the Jesuits and Franciscans, they carried on an active propaganda and gained many adherents. Then the

Franciscans brought the matter before the Sarbonne of Paris, with the result that eighteen propositions taken from the writings of Baius and Hessels were severely censured. As this did not end the dispute, Pope Pius IV imposed silence on both parties. A few years later, Baius and his friend were sent to the Council of Trent as theologians of the king of Spain.

It was in 1566, two years after the closing of the Council, and the very year of Hessel's death, that Baius gathered together the various tracts he and his friend had issued from time to time, and published them under the title *Opuscula Omnia*. Shortly after their appearance, complaint was lodged with the Pope that they contained many unsound doctrines. In consequence of this, Pius V, on October 1, 1567, issued the Bull *Ex omnibus afflictionibus,* which condemned seventy-nine propositions defended by Baius, but did not mention the author's name. The Bull closes with the sentence: *Quas quidem sententias . . . quamquam nonnullae aliquo pacto sustineri possent* * *in rigore et proprio verborum sensu ab assertoribus intento* ** *haereticas erroneas suspectas . . . damnamus.* As the document was without punctuation, a controversy immediately arose about the *comma Pianum,* that is, whether a comma should be placed at * or at **, the meaning of the sentence being obviously quite different according as the one or the other position were chosen. The discussion dragged on for a number of years, and it was not until Gregory XIII, in 1579, by the Bull *Provisionis nostrae,* confirmed the preceding condemnation that Baius finally submitted.

The errors of Baius have a bearing upon the threefold state of man: The state of innocence, of fallen nature, and of redeemed nature. The following is a brief outline of them as contained in his writings.

(a) The state of innocence, in which our first parents were placed, was not supernatural in the strict sense of the term. For the various gifts from which that state resulted were due to human nature, at least in the sense that without them man could not be saved. Destination to heaven, the inherent power of meriting, freedom from concupiscence, immunity from ignorance, preservation from suffering and death, are all normal requirements of human nature, and therefore they cannot strictly be called gratuitous gifts of grace.

(b) Fallen nature was not only deprived of sanctifying grace and the various gifts connected with the state of innocence, but was vitiated by a positive evil quality, which consists in concupiscence; and this concupiscence, as transmitted by the laws of heredity, constitutes original sin. Concupiscence is a sin irrespective of its relation to the will; hence, aside from the redemption, human nature is incapable of doing good; its actions are necessarily sinful. Furthermore, moral responsibility does not require that the agent enjoy freedom from internal determinism, but only from external coercion. Hence, in the state of fallen nature, man's will is not really free.

(c) In the state of redeemed nature, the gifts of primitive innocence are restored; and as they are no longer due to man because of the fall, they must now be regarded as gifts of grace. However, they are supernatural only in a relative sense, that is, as referred to man's present unworthiness. Grace does not elevate human nature to a strictly supernatural state; its office and purpose is to keep concupiscence under control, and thus enable man to fulfill the law and perform moral actions. Hence in justification there is no interior renovation, but only a canceling of liability to punishment.[1]

These views of Baius are evidently irreconcilable with the teaching of the Church as formulated by the Council of Trent. For in its decree on original sin, the Council quite clearly assumes that the gift of primitive justice was supernatural, and that original sin consists, not in a positive deterioration of human nature, but in the forfeiture of purely gratuitous privileges. Then, in the decree on justification, it describes the process by which man is transferred from the state of sin to that of justice as an interior renovation of the soul by means of inherent grace.[2] Consequently, the condemnation of Baianism by Pius V, though an *ex cathedra* pronouncement, does little more than apply the principles laid down at Trent.

---

[1] Cfr. Schwane, VI, 239 sqq.; DB.   [2] Cfr. DB. 787 sqq.; 793 sqq.
1001 sqq.

2. *Jansenius and Jansenism.*— Cornelius Jansen was born in 1585, near Leerdam, Holland. He received his early education at Utrecht, and then studied philosophy and theology at Louvain. During his theological studies he came under the influence of Jacques Janson, who was deeply imbued with the errors of Baius. It was most likely owing to this influence that Jansenius later on revived Baianism in a somewhat modified form. Whilst studying at Louvain, he formed a close friendship with Jean du Verger de Hauranne, through whose recommendation he was afterwards appointed director of the episcopal college at Bayonne, in France. There the two friends devoted about twelve years to a close study of the Fathers, especially of St. Augustine. Then Jansenius returned to Louvain, where he was appointed president of the new college de Sainte-Pulchérie. He received the degree of Doctor of Theology in 1619, and then taught exegesis with great renown. In 1636 he was consecrated bishop of Ypres, where he died two years later in sentiments of great piety.

He is the author of many works, mostly on Holy Scripture, all of which were published after his death. With the exception of one, they are all perfectly orthodox in doctrine. This one exception is a work in three volumes, usually cited under the title *Augustinus*. It purports to be a faithful exposition of the teaching of St. Augustine against the Pelagians and Semi-Pelagians. Hence the full title is: *Cornelii Jansenii, Episcopi Yprensis, Augustinus, seu doctrina S. Augustini de humanae naturae sanitate, aegritudine, medicina, adversus Pelagianos et Massilienses.* In making provisions for its publication, the author is said to have declared: ".' If the Holy See wishes any change, I am an obedient son, and I submit to that Church in which I have lived to my dying hour. This is my last wish." Hence, although the work contains grave errors against the faith, it would not be fair to accuse Jansenius of formal heresy.

The errors of Jansenius are fundamentally the same as those of Baius. He, too, looks upon the primitive state of our first parents as devoid of strictly supernatural gifts, in as much as the beatific vision is the necessary end of human nature. Consequently, when man by his fall into sin forfeited the spiritual endowments that fitted him for the attainment of his end, he was deprived of what belonged to his natural integrity. The result of this privation is the utter corruption of our nature, which shows itself chiefly in the powerlessness of our will. In fact, our will is purely passive, and is irresistibly moved to good or evil according as the attraction of grace or concupiscence is stronger. Thus the will always acts under the pressure of internal necessity; but this necessity is conceived to be compatible with freedom, and therefore we are morally responsible for our actions.

This, according to Jansenius, represents the genuine teaching of St. Augustine, whose writings against the Pelagians he claimed to have read thirty times. The book was received with great applause in the Netherlands, and also found many admirers in France, where the ground had been prepared by the author's friend, Verger de Hauranne. At the same time it was severely attacked by Jesuit theologians, with the result that Urban VIII forbade its circulation. It found an ardent defender in the person of the Sarbonnist Antoine Arnauld, whose hatred of the Jesuits injected a great deal of unnecessary bitterness into the discussion. In 1649, at the instance of the Syndic Cornet, the Sarbonne took up the matter, and the result was that eighty-eight bishops demanded the condemnation of five theses taken from the *Augustinus*. They wrote in this sense to the Sovereign Pontiff, Innocent X, but as eleven other bishops asked for further investigation, a commission of five cardinals and thirteen consultors was appointed for that purpose. The examination lasted two years, and although some members of the commission were in favor of Jansenius, the five propositions were solemnly condemned in the Bull *Cum occasione,* May 31, 1653.

The condemned propositions read as follows: —

(a) Some of God's commandments are impossible to just men who wish and strive to keep them, considering the powers they actually have; the grace by which these precepts may become possible is also wanting to them.

(b) In the state of fallen nature no one ever resists interior grace.

(c) In order to merit or demerit, in the state of fallen nature, we must be free from all external constraint, but not from interior necessity.

(d) The Semi-Pelagians admitted the necessity of interior preventing grace for all acts, even for the beginning of faith; but they fell into heresy in pretending that this grace is such that man may either follow or resist it.

(f) It is Semi-Pelagian to say that Christ died or shed His blood for all men.[3]

The first four of these propositions are absolutely condemned as heretical; while the fifth is condemned as heretical when taken in the sense that Christ died only for the predestined.

The condemnation was accepted by the Jansenists in so far as the doctrine contained in the five propositions came in question, but they denied that these propositions represented the genuine teaching of Jansenius. Innocent X, in 1656, rejected the distinction thus made between the question of right and fact, and so did Alexander VII a year later. In the Bull *Ad sanctam Beati Petri sedem,* of October 16, he confirmed the condemnation pronounced by his predecessor in these terms: "We declare and define that the five propositions have been drawn from the book of Jansenius entitled *Augustinus,* and that they have been condemned in the sense of the same Jansenius, and we once more condemn them as such." However, in spite of this clear condemnation, the conflict continued. Not only Arnauld, Pascal, and the religious of Port Royal, but several bishops also refused to subscribe the formula enjoined by the Constitution *Regiminis Apostolici,* of February 15, 1664. The more moderate of the French Jansenists then took the position that a respectful silence was all that could be required by the Holy See. This view was finally condemned by Clement XI, who on July 16, 1705, issued the Bull *Vineam Domini Sabaoth.* After that the opposition in France broke down, and Port Royal, the center of the rebellion, was destroyed.[4]

Meanwhile the followers of Jansenius in the Netherlands

[3] Cfr. DB. 1092 sqq.
[4] Cfr. Schwane, VI, 383 sqq.; Paquier, Jansenisme, etude doctrinal d'apres les sources, Paris, 1909.

prepared the way for a schism.   In 1702, the Vicar Apostolic
Peter Kodde had been suspended on suspicion of Jansenistic
leanings, and when a successor was nominated, the States-
General and a number of the clergy protested.   The conflict
lasted till 1723, when the Jansenist chapter of Utrecht elected
Cornelius Steenoven archbishop of that see.   Some years later
two suffragan bishoprics were established, one at Haarlem and
the other at Deventer.   As Rome refused to recognize these
appointments, the schism became permanent.   However, even
to-day, the Jansenist party in Holland counts only a few thousand adherents.[5]

3. *Paschase Quesnel.*— Quesnel was at first a member of
the French Oratory, but was expelled from that congregation
for his Jansenistic opinions in 1684.   He published several
editions of the New Testament, with comments and moral reflections.   The last edition, in four large volumes, appeared
in 1693, under the title: *The New Testament in French with
Moral Reflections on Each Verse.*   It had the approbation of
Noailles, bishop of Chalons, and was very favorably received.
However, as the " reflexions " reproduced the teaching of
Jansenius and Baius on grace and the salvific will of God, several bishops forbade the reading of the book.   Noailles, who
had meanwhile been created cardinal and made archbishop of
Paris, found himself under the necessity of withdrawing his
approbation, but for a time hesitated· to do so.   Then appeal
was made to Clement XI, who, after a·careful examination of
the book, issued the Bull *Unigenitus,* in which 101 propositions
were condemned.[6]

As several of the condemned propositions, when taken apart
from the context, seemed to have an orthodox sense, Noailles
and eight other bishops applied to Rome for explanations before accepting the Bull.   Thereupon a lengthy discussion ensued, in course of which a number of bishops, and hundreds
of clerics and religious appealed from the Pope to a general
council.   However, the Pope remained firm, and in the Bull
Pastoralis officii, of 1718, excommunicated the appellants.

---

[5] Cfr. Hergenrother, VI, 359 sqq.   [6] Cfr. DB. 1351 sqq.

But they refused to submit, and it was not until Cardinal Noailles, in 1728, finally accepted the Bull *Unigenitus,* that the conflict gradually came to an end.

4. *Gallicanism.*—The essence of Gallicanism may be said to consist in a tendency to restrain and limit the Pope's authority in the Church in favor of the rights of bishops and of the temporal ruler. This tendency manifested itself in France for the first time at the beginning of the fourteenth century, during the conflict between Philip the Fair and Boniface VIII. In virtue of certain privileges, which he claimed had been granted to Charlemagne and his successors, the king maintained that he had the right to dispose of vacant ecclesiastical benefices. When Boniface refused to allow this claim, he, with the consent of the nobility and a large number of the clergy, appealed from the Pope to a future general council, implying thereby the superiority of the council to the Pope. Similar ideas were introduced into the schools by William Ockam, John of Jandun, and Marsilius of Padua, professors in the University of Paris. Although condemned by John XXII, and also by the University authorities, they persisted and found many defenders. At the time when the Council of Constance opened, Gallicanism had already struck deep root in the minds of the French people and clergy, and the action of the Council in a manner legitimatized the principles involved. It must be noted, however, that the proceedings of the Council in this matter were irregular and without proper authority.

Gallicanism is of two kinds: Parliamentary and Episcopal. The former involves the tendency to augment the right of the State to the prejudice of those of the Church. The latter involves a similar tendency to augment the ecclesiastical authority of the bishops to the prejudice of those of the Pope. Both claim to be a defense of the so-called Liberties of the Gallican Church.

The most important of the Liberties defended by Parliamentary Gallicanism are the following: The kings of France have the right to assemble councils in their dominions, and to make laws and regulations touching ecclesiastical matters.

The Pope's legates cannot be sent into France, or exercise their powers within that kingdom, except at the king's request or with his consent. Bishops, even when commanded by the Pope, cannot go out of the kingdom without the consent of the king. The royal officers cannot be excommunicated for any act performed in the discharge of their official duties. The Pope cannot authorize the alienation of any ecclesiastical landed estate, or the diminishing of any foundations. The Pope's Bulls and Letters may not be executed without the *Pareatis* of the king or his officers. He cannot issue dispensations to the prejudice of the laudable customs and statutes of cathedral churches. It is lawful to appeal from him to a future council, or to have recourse to the " appeal as from an abuse " against acts of the ecclesiastical power.— Altogether, as drawn up by the Jurisconsults Guy Coquille and Pierre Pithou, there were eighty-three of these " Liberties," and they practically did away with the Pope's authority in France.

Episcopal Gallicanism, which had found expression at Constance and Basle, grew constantly in force till the beginning of the sixteenth century, when through the exertions of the League against the Huguenots there was a brief reaction. It was revived after the assassination of Henry IV in 1610, and through the activity of Edmond Richer, syndic of the Sarbonne, again rapidly gained in strength. In 1663, the Sarbonne openly declared that it did not recognize the Pope's superiority to a general council, nor his infallibility apart from the consent of the Church. Matters came to a crisis some twenty years later, when Pope Innocent XI resisted the pretensions of Louis XIV in reference to the *regalia*. In the General Assembly of 1682, at which were present thirty-six prelates and thirty-four deputies of the second order, four articles were adopted in which Episcopal Gallicanism found its official expression. The first, however, deals only with temporal matters. They were drafted by Bossuet, bishop of Meaux. In substance they read as follows: —

(a) St. Peter and the Popes, his successors, and the Church itself have received dominion from God only over things spiritual and such as concern salvation, and not over things temporal and civil. Hence kings and sovereigns are not by God's command subject to any ecclesiastical dominion in things temporal; they cannot be deposed, whether directly or indirectly, by the authority of the rulers of the Church; their subjects cannot be dispensed from that submission and obedience which they owe to their sovereign, nor can they be absolved from the oath of allegiance.

(b) The plenitude of authority in things spiritual, which belongs to the Holy See and the successors of St. Peter, in no wise affects the permanence and immovable strength of the decrees of the Council of Constance drawn up in the fourth and fifth sessions, approved by the Holy See, confirmed by the practice of the whole Church and the Roman Pontiff, and observed in all ages by the Gallican Church. That Church does not countenance the opinion of those who cast a slur on those decrees, or who lessen their force by saying that their authority is not well established, that they are not approved, or that they apply only to the period of the schism.

(c) The exercise of the Apostolic authority must also be regulated in accordance with the canons drawn up under the guidance of the Spirit of God, and consecrated by the respect of the whole world. The rules, customs, and constitutions received within the kingdom and the Gallican Church must have their force and their effect, and the usages of our fathers must remain inviolable, since the dignity of the Apostolic See itself demands that the laws and customs established with the consent of that august see and of the Churches be constantly maintained.

(d) Although the Pope has the chief authority in questions of faith, and his decrees apply to all the Churches, and to each Church in particular, yet his judgment is not irreformable, at least pending the consent of the Church.[7]

A few days later, Louis ordered the registration of the articles in all the schools and faculties of theology, and no one could be admitted to a degree without having defended the articles in one of his theses. Furthermore, it was strictly for-

[7] Cfr. DB. 1322 sqq.

bidden to attack them in writing. Pope Innocent XI took a firm stand against the action of the General Assembly, and so did his successor Alexander VIII. The latter, in the Constitution *Inter multiplices,* of August 4, 1690, issued a strong condemnation of the four articles, and refused to confirm any bishop elected in accordance with the provisions contained therein. Under his successor, Innocent XII, some kind of an understanding was reached, and thereafter Gallicanism began to decline. It was, however, not entirely eradicated until after the Vatican Council.[8]

5. *Febronianism.*— In concept and purpose, Febronianism is a politico-ecclesiastical system founded on a denial of the monarchical constitution of the Church. Its author was Johann Nikolaus von Hontheim, auxiliary bishop of Trier, who wrote under the pseudonym Justinus Febronius. He had studied at Louvain under the canonist van Espen, through whose influence he became deeply imbued with Gallican principles. However, in the development of these principles, he went far beyond the traditional Gallicanism which his master had introduced into the Low Countries. In working out his system, he seems to have been guided by the thought of facilitating the reconciliation of Protestant bodies with the Church. At least to this thought he gives expression in the title under which he published his work, which reads: *Justini Febronii Juris consulti de Statu Ecclesiae et legitima potestate Romani Pontificis singularis ad reuniendos dissidentes in religione christianos compositus.* The work appeared first in 1763, and in a short time ran through several editions. Its contents may be briefly summarized as follows: —

The power of the keys was entrusted by Christ to the Church as a body, but in such a way that it should be exercised through her prelates. Hence the power is possessed by the Church, and the prelates have only the use of it in so far as she communicates it to them for her own purposes. The first place among her prelates is held by the Pope, but even he is subordinated to the Church as a whole. The Roman Primacy does not

[8] Ibid. 1326.

rest on the authority of Christ, but on that of Peter and the Church, and therefore the Church has power to attach the primatial dignity to any other church, as may be expedient under given circumstances. As head of the Church, it is incumbent on the Pope to watch over her welfare, to promulgate laws in her name, and to enforce the observance of the canons; yet he has no real power of jurisdiction. He merely uses the jurisdiction that belongs to the Church as a whole.

Now, in course of time, especially through the influence of the False Decretals of Pseudo-Isidore, the See of Rome has acquired a far-reaching authority, to which it has no right; of this it must be deprived, so as to bring back the condition of things that obtained during the first eight centuries. Accordingly, such questions as were in olden times left to the decision of provincial synods and of metropolitans, but are now reserved to the Holy See, must no longer be submitted to the judgment of the Pope. Hence the election and confirmation of bishops, their transfer and removal, the establishment of new sees, the condemnation of heresies, and similar matters of local interest, lie outside the scope of the primatial power. So, too, does the granting of benefices, and the exemption of religious orders.

Furthermore, as the Pope is not infallible, he cannot, on his own authority, give any decisions on matters of faith that are of universal obligation. Nor can he in matters of discipline legislate for the whole Church, and laws once properly promulgated he cannot alter. He is subordinate to a general council, and hence the right of appeal from his authority to a future general council must be admitted. He has neither the exclusive right to summon a general council nor to preside at its sessions. Moreover, the decrees of general councils do not need the ratification of the Pope. On the other hand, such decrees are not binding until they have been accepted by the whole Church.

Lastly, although the Pope is to a certain extent entrusted with the care of the whole Church, yet in the exercise of his power in that regard he is not wholly independent of the State. Catholic sovereigns ought to take a reasonable interest in the welfare of the Church in their dominions, and for this purpose, according to the need there may be of it, they should avail themselves of the *Regium Placet* as regards the publication of papal decrees. In like manner they should refuse obedience to the Pope, if the interests of the national Church require it. Subjects, moreover, must have the right to appeal to the secular authority by way of the *Apellatio ab abusu.*[9]

As is quite evident from this brief summary, the real object aimed at by Febronius was nothing less than the establishment of national Churches that were to be practically independent of the Pope, and more or less subject to the State. His system is a combination of Gallicanism and Cæsarism, and as such it is the very antithesis of the Church Catholic. It was reduced to practice by Joseph II of Austria, with the result that in his dominions the Church was almost ruined. The book was formally condemned by Clement XIII, in 1764, but it continued to be widely read and was translated into German, French, Spanish, and Portuguese. Pius VI, in 1778, induced the author to retract his views; but it is very doubtful whether the retractation was sincere, as he continued to write in defense of his position. At all events, the pernicious effects of his work were not checked, and many Catholic sovereigns eagerly accepted his ideas in order to promote their own interests at the expense of the Church.

6. *The Synod of Pistoia.*— The politico-ecclesiastical system of Febronius, tried on a grand scale in Austria by Emperor Joseph II, was also introduced into Italy by Joseph's brother, Grand Duke Leopold of Tuscany. The reform measures to be enacted were outlined in two instructions sent to the bishops in Leopold's dominion, and it was made incumbent upon the prelates to convene synods at which doctrinal, disciplinary, and liturgical matters were to be discussed and regulated. The bishops, however, proved intractable, the only one who entirely fell in with Leopold's designs being Scipio de' Ricci, bishop of Pistoia and Prato. He convoked a synod on July 31, 1786, having invited thereto many canonists and

---

[9] Cfr. Schwane, VI, 529 sqq.; DB. 1500 sqq.

theologians who were noted for their Gallican and Jansenistic tendencies. The synod was attended by 246 members, who for the most part were strongly in sympathy with de' Ricci's designs. Many of them had been irregularly intruded from other dioceses, while those of Ricci's priests who were known for their orthodoxy had not been invited.

As might have been expected under the circumstances, Leopold's ideas were fully carried out. The four Gallican articles were adopted, the Pope was declared to be merely the ministerial head of the Church, episcopal powers and rights were said to be derived immediately from Christ, and parish priests, when acting in conjunction with the bishop, were held to be judges of the faith. Regarding questions of strictly doctrinal import, such as the primitive condition of man, the nature and action of grace, the administration of the sacraments, the sacrifice of the Mass, indulgences, the veneration of images, and the practice of the Sacred Heart devotion, strongly Jansenistic views prevailed. The Synod closed on September 28, and in February of the following year its proceedings were published with the royal *imprimatur*. After a careful examination of the Pistoian enactments by a commission of cardinals and bishops, Pius VI condemned eighty-five propositions, in the Bull *Auctorem fidei* of August 28, 1794. Meanwhile, on the accession of Leopold to the imperial throne, de' Ricci had been compelled to resign his see. With his retirement and the papal condemnation of the Synod, Jansenistic influence in Italy came to an end.[10]

7. *Rationalism.*— From the middle of the eighteenth centurn forward there was a decided turning away of men's minds from the supernatural, with the result that many, especially among the upper classes of society, gave up all belief in revealed religion. Naturalism, deism, and rationalism were substituted for the teaching of Christianity, and intellectual Europe seemed to be drifting back into paganism. This condition of things obtained mostly among non-Catholics, but traces of it were found also in Catholic circles. And in not

10 Cfr. DB. 1501 sqq.

a few instances, well intentioned men only aggravated the evil by their misdirected efforts to counteract it. The most distinguished of these men were Hermes, Guenther, Bonnety, and Bautain. Both philosophical and theological learning were at a low ebb, Scholasticism had again fallen into disrepute, and in their endeavor to strike out into new directions they went considerably astray.

Hermes, for ten years professor of dogmatic theology at Bonn, was strongly influenced by the teaching of Kant and Fichte, although he professedly opposed their systems of thought. At the same time he followed Descartes in making "methodical doubt" the starting point of all certitude. In fact, he goes even a step farther and asserts that one must *positively* doubt everything until reason finds something that admits of no doubt. And this holds true in theology as well as in philosophy. Hence faith no less than science rests upon the demonstrations of reason. In this, however, he distinguishes between practical and theoretical reason. The former accepts revelation because it is compelled to do so by man's moral needs; while the latter yields only to the evidence of a demonstrated truth.

The author developed his system in two works, entitled respectively, *Introduction to Philosophy,* and, *Introduction to Theology,* and then applied it in his *Dogmatik.* He had many followers, and, protected by the Prussian government and his own archbishop, he was left unmolested during his life time; but some years after his death a commission was appointed by the Pope to investigate the charge of unorthodoxy lodged against him at Rome. The commission found the charge only too true, and in consequence Gregory XVI, in a Brief of September 26, 1835, condemned the theological teaching of Hermes as "false, rash, captious, leading to skepticism and indifferentism, erroneous, scandalous, harmful to Catholic schools, subversive of divine faith, savoring of heresy and already condemned by the Church." The chief errors of Hermes designated by the papal Brief bear on the nature and rule of faith; on Holy Scripture and tradition, revelation, and the teaching office of the Church; the motives of credibility, the proofs of the existence of God, and the doctrines concerning the nature of the holiness, justice, and freedom of God, and His ultimate purpose in His works *ad extra;* on the necessity of grace and its bestowal; on the reward and punishment of men; on the primitive state of our first parents; on original sin and on the powers of man in the fallen state.[11]

Similar lines of thought were followed by Anton Guenther, a private ecclesiastic residing at Vienna, who from 1818 until the condemnation of his works in 1857, displayed a ceaseless literary activity. His constant aim was to refute the pantheism of modern philosophy, and to demonstrate from the standpoint of natural reason the truth of positive Christianity. The better to accomplish this, he departed from the beaten path of Scholasticism and endeavored to construct an entirely new system of Christian philosophy. Unfortunately, he allowed himself to be unduly influenced by the methods of Hegel and Schelling, whose philosophy he tried to refute. His views, however, were widely adopted by Catholic scholars in Germany, although their unsoundness was clearly pointed out by men of recognized ability and learning.

In 1852, the Congregation of the Index began an official investigation of Guenther's writings, and five years later placed them on the list of forbidden books. This condemnation was approved by Pius IX, who, on June 15, 1857, addressed a Brief to Cardinal von Geissel, archbishop of Cologne, in which he pointed out some of the more serious of Guenther's errors. Aside from the fundamental rationalism which vitiates the author's philosophy, these errors bear especially on the Trinity, the person of Christ, the nature of man, creation, and particularly on the relation of faith to knowledge. Guenther himself submitted to the judgment passed on his works, and discontinued writing; but some of his followers kept up an active propaganda for his views until after the Vatican Council.[12]

An altogether opposite tendency, by way of reaction against rationalism, manifested itself in France, where Bautain and

[11] Cfr. DB. 1618 sqq.　　　　[12] Cfr. DB. 1655 sqq.

Bonnety labored for the establishment of traditionalism. They built on the philosophical concepts of Bonald and F. de Lamennais, according to which human reason is of itself radically unable to know with certainty the fundamental truths of the metaphysical, moral, and religious order. Hence all knowledge must ultimately be traced back to revelation, and only by the transmission of revealed truths is the human mind put into the possession of such first principles as it needs for its proper operation. The system was condemned by Rome in so far as the authors were required to subscribe a number of theses in which the priority of reason to faith, the demonstrability of the existence of God, of the spirituality of the soul, of human liberty, and the harmony between faith and reason were asserted.[13]

Besides the tendencies thus briefly outlined, there were many others, in all the various fields of intellectual activity, that ran more or less counter to received views and approved teaching. Some of them, like the quietistic vagaries of Michael de Molinos,[14] were almost entirely confined to the order of Christian morality; others, like the ontological speculations of Gioberti and Rosmini,[15] bore primarily upon philosophical questions. Indirectly, indeed, they also touched Christian dogma, but they never exerted a far-reaching influence in that direction.

[13] Cfr. DB. 1622 sqq.; 1649 sqq.   [15] Cfr. DB. 1659 sqq.
[14] Cfr. DB. 1221 sqq.

CHAPTER XXX

SOME PAPAL DECISIONS: THE VATICAN COUNCIL: MODERNISM

Although the infallibility of the Pope had not yet been defined, in practice it was accepted by the whole Church. It is true, the Gallicans made it dependent on the assent of the episcopate, but they were only a small faction and had little influence outside of France. Hence papal decisions in matters of faith were generally regarded as final, provided it was sufficiently clear that the Pope intended to speak in his capacity of chief shepherd of the faithful. In the lapse of centuries, many such decisions issued from the Holy See, as is quite evident from what has been said in the preceding chapter. Most of them have been referred to in the course of the book, but a few deserve special notice in this place.

A — Some Papal Decisions [1]

1. *The Immaculate Conception.*— The most important of these decisions regard the doctrine of the Immaculate Conception of the Blessed Virgin Mary. The question had been in dispute for centuries, although after the Council of Trent there were but few theologians who did not consider it rash to impugn the doctrine. The very fact that the Council took occasion to declare that it was in no wise its intention to include the Blessed Virgin among those who had incurred the guilt of original sin, and that it renewed " the constitutions of Pope Sixtus IV," [2] was generally considered as a clear indication that the Church regarded the question to be no longer open for discussion. The constitutions of Sixtus IV referred to by the Council are two in number. One was issued on February 28, 1476, and in it the Pope adopted the feast for the entire

[1] Cfr. Bachelet. Immac. Concept.;   [2] Cfr. DB. 792.
Reiner, Der Syllabus.

Latin Church, at the same time granting an indulgence to all who would assist at the divine offices of the solemnity.[3]   The other appeared on September 4, 1483, and was intended to end the dispute between the opponents of the doctrine and those who were in favor of it.   Therein also excommunication was pronounced against either of the disputants who charged their adversaries with heresy.[4]

After the Council of Trent, the doctrine was denied, among others, by Baius, who explicitly asserted that "no one but Christ was without original sin, and that therefore the Blessed Virgin had died because of the sin contracted in Adam, and had endured afflictions in this life, like the rest of the just, as a punishment of actual and original sin."[5]   This proposition was condemned by Pius V, as already noted in the preceding chapter.   The same Pontiff, moreover, issued a Constitution in which he forbade all public discussion of the subject, and also inserted a new office of the Immaculate Conception in the liturgical books.[6]   On December 8, 1661, Alexander VII promulgated the Constitution *Solicitudo omnium Ecclesiarum,* in which he defined the true sense of the term *conceptio,* and forbade all further discussion in any way opposed to the common and pious sentiment of the Church.   He declared it to be the object of the feast that Mary was preserved immune from original sin in the first moment of the creation of her soul and its infusion into the body.[7]

From that time forward the definition of the doctrine was only a question of time.   Hence when Pius IX, soon after his elevation to the pontifical chair, directed the bishops of the whole world to send in a report both as to their own views and the belief of the faithful, there was not a dissentient voice as regarded the truth of the doctrine.   Furthermore, only four bishops considered the definition inopportune.   In consequence, on December 8, 1854, the Pope issued the Bull *Ineffabilis,* in which the truth of Mary's Immaculate Conception was defined as having been revealed by God.[8]

---

[3] Cfr. Ibid. 734, 735.
[4] Ibid. 735.
[5] Ibid. 1073.

[6] Cfr. Bullar. Mar. 72 sqq.
[7] Cfr. DB. 1100.
[8] Cfr. DB. 1641.

2. *The Syllabus of Pius IX.*— On December 8, 1864, a document was sent to all Catholic bishops under the title: " A Syllabus containing the most important errors of our time, which have been condemned by our Holy Father Pius IX in Allocutions, at Consistories, in Encyclicals, and other Apostolic Letters." The document was accompanied by a letter of Cardinal Antonelli, Secretary of State, explaining the purpose of the Syllabus. As there was danger, the letter stated, that the various papal documents, in which modern errors had been condemned, might not reach each and every bishop of the Catholic world, a syllabus of these same errors had been drawn up for the proper instruction of all ordinaries, so that thereby they might be enabled to apply necessary remedies. At the same time, the Bull *Quanta cura,* which contains an exposition and explicit condemnation of the more fundamental modern errors, was also published.

The Syllabus had been in preparation for about twelve years, and three different commissions had successively labored at its composition. Its contents are divided into eighty theses, the wording of which is taken from the official declarations of the Pope. To each thesis a reference is attached, indicating the particular papal document from which it was taken. It is only by referring to the documents in question that the full meaning and theological value of the subjects treated can be determined. The eighty theses are grouped in ten paragraphs, the respective headings of which are: Pantheism, Naturalism, Absolute Rationalism (1–7); Moderate Rationalism (8–14); Indifferentism and false Religious Tolerance (15–18); Socialism, Communism, Secret Societies, Bible Societies, Liberal Clerical Associations, Errors regarding the Church and its Rights (19–38); Errors on the State and its Relation to the Church (39–55); Errors on Natural and Christian Ethics (56–64); Errors on Christian Marriage (65–74); Errors on the Temporal Power of the Pope (75, 76); Errors in Connection with Modern Liberalism (77–80).[9]

[9] Cfr. Ibid. 1700–1780.

The publication of the Syllabus caused a most violent outcry among non-Catholics, who regarded it as a formal rejection of modern culture and an open declaration of war against the rights of the State. On the other hand, Catholics viewed it with great satisfaction, as it clearly defined the position of the Church in regard to matters of the gravest practical importance. Its binding force was universally and gladly admitted, although lively discussions ensued in regard to its exact theological value. In fact the discussion is still going on, nor is it likely to be ever set completely at rest. While many theologians contend that the Syllabus is an ex-cathedra pronouncement, and therefore final and irreformable, others seriously question this, although they admit that it commands not only exterior submission but also interior assent. Furthermore, all are agreed that many propositions contained in the Syllabus have been condemned by final and irreformable decisions in the various documents from which they were taken. It is, therefore, to these documents that one must have recourse in order to determine the theological censure attached to any given proposition.

B — The Vatican Council [10]

On December 6, 1864, therefore two days before the publication of the Syllabus, Pope Pius IX, at a meeting of the Congregation of Rites, announced his intention of convening a general council. He then requested the cardinals to express their opinion in writing, both as to the opportuneness of carrying out his intention and the subjects that were to be discussed. As, with one exception, the reports of the cardinals favored the holding of a council, a commission was appointed to discuss preliminary questions and make all necessary preparations. At its suggestion, a number of bishops of both rites were also requested to send in their views under pledge of silence. Then many of the ablest theologians and canonists

[10] Cfr. Granderath und Kirch, Geschichte des vaticanischen Konzils; Granderath, Constitutiones dogmaticae; Vacant, Etudes theologiques sur les constitutions du concile Vatican; Gibbons, A Retrospect of Fifty Years, vol. I.

were summoned from the various countries to coöperate in the work of preparing the subjects to be debated in the Council.

The first public announcement of the contemplated Council was made at a Consistory held on June 26, 1867. As it was the centennial celebration of the Apostles SS. Peter and Paul, there were nearly five hundred bishops present in Rome, and in an address, dated July 1, they communicated their joyous agreement to the Sovereign Pontiff. The Bull of Convocation was issued on June 29, 1868, and it appointed December 8, 1869, as the date on which the Council was to open. A special Brief, *Arcano divinae providentiae,* was issued on September 8, 1868, to invite the non-Uniate Orientals; while another Brief, *Jam vos omnes,* of September 13, notified the various Protestant sects of the approaching Council, and exhorted them to reflect on the possibility of returning to the true faith.

By way of preparation, five special committees, each presided over by a cardinal, had been appointed to prepare the *schemata* that were to be laid before the Council. Their respective work bore on dogma, Church discipline, religious orders, Oriental Churches and missions, and ecclesiastico-political questions. When the Council opened, the following drafts were ready for discussion: (a) three drafts on dogmatic subjects, namely, on Catholic doctrine in opposition to the errors of rationalism, on the Church of Christ, and on Christian marriage. (b) twenty-eight drafts treating of Church discipline, in respect to bishops, episcopal sees, the different grades of the lower clergy, seminaries, the arrangement of philosophical and theological studies, marriage, Christian morals, etc. (c) eighteen drafts of decrees on religious orders. (d) two drafts in reference to Oriental Rites and missions. Besides the matter thus officially prepared, many petitions had been received from various bishops, asking for the discussion of certain subjects in which they were specially interested. Among these were nine petitions, signed by nearly two hundred bishops, that requested the definition of the bodily assumption of the Blessed Virgin.

On December 2, 1869, a preliminary session was held in the Sistine Chapel, at which the officials of the Council were announced and the conciliar procedure was outlined. The formal opening took place six days later, December 8, in the northern right transept of St. Peter's. Between that date and September 1, when the Council was prorogued, four public sessions and eighty-nine general congregations were held. The voting in the congregations was by *placet, placet juxta modum, non placet*. In the public sessions it was by *placet* or *non placet*, according as the vote cast was affirmative or negative. The decrees promulgated by the Pope were to bear the title: *Pius Episcopus, servus servorum Dei: sacro approbante Concilio ad perpetuam rei memoriam*. Altogether 774 prelates took part in the Council, out of a total of 1050 who were entitled to attend.

Owing to the outbreak of the Franco-Prussian war, and the subsequent occupation of Rome by the Piedmontese, only a small part of the contemplated work was accomplished by the Council. Two Constitutions were promulgated, both rather brief, but of great importance. The first is the dogmatic Constitution on the Catholic faith, which defends the fundamental principles of Christianity against the errors of modern rationalism, materialism, and atheism. The second is the dogmatic Constitution on the Church of Christ, or, as it is more frequently styled, on the Roman Pontiff. This latter contains the definition of papal infallibility, for which petitions had been sent in by a large number of bishops. Both Constitutions are divided into preambles, chapters, and canons.

The contents of the first Constitution may be thus summarized: In the first chapter is set forth the doctrine of the existence of a personal God, who for the manifestation of His perfections freely created all things out of nothing, foresees all things, even the future free actions of rational creatures, and through His providence leads all things to their appointed end. In the second chapter the knowability of God is maintained, both in regard to natural reason and supernatural revelation. The necessity and existence of revelation is pointed out, and the two sources of revealed knowledge, Holy Scripture and tradition, are defended. The doctrine here set forth is a restatement of the teaching of Trent The third chapter treats of supernatural faith, its reasonableness, supernatural character, and necessity; the possibility and actuality of miracles as a confirmation of divine revelation, and the founding of the Catholic Church by Jesus Christ as the guardian and herald of revealed truth.

The fourth chapter is of special importance in these modern times, pointing out as it does the connection between faith and reason. The mysteries of faith are indeed above reason, but not contrary to it. On the other hand, any assertion that contradicts the teaching of faith is by that very fact to be regarded as false. Faith and true learning are never in opposition to one another, but each supports the other in many ways. However, faith is not like a philosophical system subject to intrinsic development; it is a sacred deposit entrusted to the Church for safeguarding and infallible interpretation. Hence the interpretation of dogmas given by the Church holds good for all times, and no deviation from it under pretense of more profound investigation can ever be lawful.— The Constitution closes with eighteen canons, in which heresies opposed to its teaching are condemned.

The second Constitution has the following contents: In the preamble it is pointed out how the Roman Primacy, so essential to the unity, strength, and stability of the Church, has always been an object of fierce attacks by the enemies of the Church of Christ. It is for this reason that the doctrine of its origin, permanency, and nature must be clearly set forth. Hence the first chapter establishes the fact that the primacy was given to Peter, not merely of honor but of jurisdiction. This is followed by a canon, in which anathema is pronounced upon those who teach the contrary doctrine. The second chapter, pointing out that Peter established his see at Rome, declares that his successors in that see hold the primacy in virtue of its institution by Christ. To this, again, a canon is attached in which the contrary doctrine is condemned.

The third and fourth chapters deal more directly with the nature of the primacy, and the powers involved therein.

After restating and confirming the definition of the Council of
Florence, the third chapter explains that the primacy of the
Roman Pontiff implies not merely precedence of honor, but a
regularly constituted authority over all other Churches, and a
true, direct, episcopal power of jurisdiction, which the clergy
and faithful of every rite and rank are bound to obey. However, the jurisdiction of the Pope does not interfere with the
jurisdiction of individual bishops in their own dioceses, but
rather strengthens and defends the same. In virtue of his primatial power, the Pope has the right of direct and free relations with the clergy and laity of the entire Church, and his
decrees are in no wise subject to the *placet* of the secular
power. The Pope is the supreme judge of all the faithful,
and may be appealed to in all matters that come up for adju-
dication. And from his decisions there is no appeal, even to
a general council. Then follows the condemnation of all contrary teaching, appended in form of a canon.

In the fourth chapter is contained the definition of papal infallibility. First the historical proofs of the doctrine are
briefly summarized, both as derived from the Sixth, Fourteenth, and Seventeenth General Councils, and as contained in
the undisputed use of the prerogative by the Roman Pontiffs,
and the constant appeal made to them in matters of faith.
Thereupon the definition is given in the following terms:
" Faithfully adhering, therefore, to the tradition inherited
from the beginning of the Christian faith, we, with the approbation of the sacred Council, for the glory of God our Saviour,
for the exaltation of the Catholic religion, and the salvation of
Christian peoples, teach and define, as a divinely revealed
dogma, that the Roman Pontiff, when he speaks *ex cathedra,*
that is, when he, in the exercise of his office as shepherd and
teacher of all Christians, by virtue of his supreme Apostolic
authority, decides that a doctrine concerning faith and morals
is to be held by the entire Church, possesses, in consequence of
the divine aid promised him in St. Peter, that infallibility with
which the Divine Saviour wished to have His Church endowed
for the definition of doctrines concerning faith and morals;
and that such definitions of the Roman Pontiff are of them-

selves, and not in consequence of the Church's consent, irreformable." In the canon that follows, anathema is pronounced upon such as presume to contradict the definition thus given.[11]

Although the Council accomplished only part of the work it had set out to do, nevertheless in these two Constitutions most important results were achieved. This is especially true of the second, which finally settled a question that had from time to time disturbed men's minds for nearly four hundred years. After the definition of the Pope's primacy of jurisdiction and infallible teaching authority, as contained in the Constitution on the Church of Christ, anything like Gallicanism and Febronianism is simply impossible. Furthermore, a most effective means has thereby been provided to meet the peculiar difficulties of modern times, which often necessitate the intervention of a teaching authority whose supremacy is universally acknowledged as contained in the sacred deposit of faith. Hence, although a small minority of the assembled bishops regarded the definition of papal infallibility as inopportune, subsequent events have made it quite clear that nothing more opportune could have been attempted.

Much of the work that had been prepared for the Council, and which had to be left undone on account of the political disturbances that arose, was subsequently more or less fully accomplished by the prudent zeal of the Sovereign Pontiffs. The great encyclicals of Leo XIII and the many reform measures of Pius X may be regarded as carrying out what the Vatican Council had been expected to do. Hence, even if there should never be an opportunity of reassembling the Council, its object may still be fully attained with the passing of years. On the other hand, the evil results which some apprehended and predicted, by way of schism and increased hostility of the sects, proved to be negligible quantities. A few secessions from the Church there were, which gave rise to the Old Catholic party in Germany and Switzerland, but they were mostly of men whose Catholicity amounted to little

[11] Cfr. DB. 1781-1840.

more than the name.   Nor did the increased hostility of Protestants interfere seriously with the various activities of the Church.   For some years Catholicity was fiercely assailed from the pulpit, on the platform, and in the press; but most of that hostility has disappeared with the passing of time.

C — Modernism [12]

Pius X, in his Encyclical *Pascendi,* of September 8, 1907, designates Modernism as a synthesis of all heresies.   And this designation is perfectly just, in as much as the tendencies usually indicated by the term are subversive of the very foundation upon which Christianity is built.   Hence Loisv, its high priest and apostle, states quite frankly: " All Catholic theology, even in its fundamental principles, the general philosophy of religion, divine law, and the laws that govern our knowledge of God, come up for judgment before this new court of assize." [13]   As an intellectual tendency, Modernism is traceable to the agnostic philosophy of the eighteenth century, first manifesting itself in a false liberalism, then in crude rationalism, and finally in theological anarchism.   This last phase became prominent at the beginning of the present century.

As a theological movement, Modernism made its first inroads into France and Italy.   In the latter country it spread so rapidly that as early as 1905 it was recognized as an imminent danger to religion.   Hence several bishops uttered grave warnings against it in their pastoral letters.   About the same time it attracted attention in France, where Abbé Loisy, for many years professor at the Catholic Institute of Paris, had done much to inoculate the younger generations of the clergy with its virus.   It had also distinguished representatives in other countries, but in none of them did it find so many and such devoted followers as in Italy and France.

The first thorough synthesis of Modernism was given in

[12] Cfr. Pesch, Theologische Zeitfragen, 4th series; Rickaby, The Modernist; Vermeersch. De Modernismo; Heiner, Der neue Syllabus Pius X.

[13] Simples réflexions, p. 24.

the Encyclical *Pascendi,* and although some Modernistic writers found in it matter for criticism, it was generally admitted that the statements contained in that papal document were substantially correct. The doctrinal decisions touching the tenets of Modernism had already appeared in the Decree *Lamentabili sane exitu,* which was issued by the Holy Office on July 3, 1907. This Decree was ratified by Pius X on the following day, and ordered to be published. On November 18, of the same year, the Pope published a *Motu Proprio,* in which he prohibited the defense of the condemned propositions under the penalty of excommunication, reserved to himself.

The Decree *Lamentabili* is usually called the Syllabus of Pius X, on account of its similarity to the Syllabus of Pius IX, issued in 1864. Its contents are mainly taken from the writings of Loisy, and the condemned propositions are substantially as follows.[14]

(a) The Church's interpretation of Holy Scripture, and also her dogmatic decisions, are subject to the judgment of scientific scrutiny and do not demand interior assent; nor has the law of the Index any binding force (1–8).

(b) " Excessive simplicity or ignorance is shown by those who believe that God is really the author of Holy Scripture " (9).

(c) Taking the term in the Catholic sense, God neither inspired the sacred writers nor guarded them from all error; the Gospels in particular are not books worthy of historic belief, as their authors have consciously, though piously, falsified facts (10–19).

(d) Revelation is nothing else than the consciousness acquired by man of his relation to God, and did not close with the Apostles (20, 21).

(e) " The dogmas, which the Church proposes as revealed, are not truths fallen from heaven, but an interpretation of religious facts, acquired by the human mind through the laborious process of thought " (22).

(f) One and the same fact can be historically false and

[14] Cfr. DB. 2001–2065.

dogmatically true; faith is based upon a number of probabilities; dogmatic definitions have only a passing practical value; they are not norms of belief but of conduct (23–26).

(g) The divinity of Christ is a dogma which Christian consciousness deduced from its idea of the Messiah; the real historical Christ is inferior to the Christ idealized by faith; Christ's knowledge was circumscribed, and He even fell into error; His resurrection is not an historical event; his vicarious death is a Pauline invention (27–38).

(h) The sacraments were not instituted by Christ, but they originated with the Apostles and their successors, who, influenced by the circumstances of their time, interpreted Christ's mind in that sense (39–51).

(i) The thought of founding a Church was never entertained by Christ; the Church is a purely human society, subject to all the changes of time; Peter was unaware of any primatial rights vested in himself; the Church is inimical to scientific progress (52–57).

(k) "Truth is as changeable as man himself, because it is evolved with him, in him, and by him" (58).

(l) There are no immutable Christian dogmas, because they have developed and must develop with the progress of the centuries (59–63).

(m) "Scientific progress demands a reform of the Christian dogmatic conception of God, creation, revelation, the person of the Word Incarnate, and the redemption" (64).

(n) "The Catholicism of to-day is irreconcilable with genuine scientific knowledge, unless it be transformed into a Christianity without dogmas, that is, into a broad and liberal Protestantism" (65).

The sixty-five propositions of the Syllabus, summing up the teaching of Modernism, are all condemned, but without a definite censure attached to each. That many of them are openly heretical is admitted by all theologians, while with regard to some others the matter is not clear. Nor have theologians thus far been able to pronounce definitely what precise dogmatic value should be attached to the Syllabus. Not a few contend that the Decree of the Holy Office is infallible and irreformable on account of its confirmation by the Pope, as the sanction of excommunication seems to evidence; others, however, maintain that this inference is not valid, since, in spite of the papal confirmation and sanction, it remains simply the doctrinal decision of a Roman Congregation, and as such it need not be absolutely immune from error. But all are agreed that it binds in conscience, and that no Catholic is at liberty to defend any of the condemned propositions.

It may be added that this authoritative condemnation sounded the death-knell of Modernism within the ranks of Catholics. Those who had been deceived by the specious arguments advanced by the propagators of the system, without being aware of its real nature, turned away from it in horror; while others, who had suffered shipwreck in their faith, severed their connection with the Church. Furthermore, as all candidates for higher orders, newly appointed confessors, preachers, parish priests, canons, the beneficed clergy, the officials of the Roman congregations or tribunals, superiors and professors in religious institutions, are obliged to take an oath which binds them to reject and oppose Modernism, a remedy has been applied to the evil that appears to make its revival impossible.

CONCLUSION

By the end of the ninth century, as was stated at the close of the first volume of the present work, the Church's teaching on God, the Trinity, the Incarnation, original sin, grace, some of the sacraments, the veneration of saints, and eschatology, was more or less fully developed. Yet that there was still room for further development, and partly even with regard to these doctrines, is sufficiently clear from the contents of this second volume. The following points may be noted by way of general summary.

In reference to God, the Fourth Lateran Council found it expedient to bring out more definitely the Church's teaching on the divine attributes, and also on the mystery of the Blessed Trinity — the unity of the divine nature, the distinction of persons, and the principles of the immanent processions in the Godhead.

The same Council defined that the three divine persons act as one principle in their operations *ad extra,* and that there is only one Creator, from whom all finite beings, material, spiritual, and composite, have their origin. This had been the common belief of Christians from primitive times, but it had never been defined by the Church. The same doctrine was restated by the Vatican Council, which also defined that God created the world freely and for His own greater glory.

No particular aspect of either Christology or soteriology was made the object of a special definition; yet there was progress along both lines of theological inquiry, occasioned chiefly by the aberrations of Abelard and the sixteenth-century innovators. The condemnation of Christological Nihilism by Alexander III directed the attention of theologians to the real nature of the hypostatic union; while the Church's opposition to Protestantism, Baianism, and Jansenism brought out more clearly the meaning and extent of the redemption.

Man's primitive state, his fall, the existence and transmission of original sin, and to some extent its nature also, were discussed and defined by the Council of Trent. In connection with these truths, the same Council defined the nature of justification, man's freedom under the action of grace, the necessity of grace for salutary works, and the uncertainty of final perseverance. These definitions were restated and in some measure amplified by the papal decisions against Baius and Jansenius.

The most striking development took place in the doctrine on the sacraments, which was almost entirely due to the work of the thirteenth-century Scholastics. Nearly all of their conclusions were sustained by the Council of Trent, which also defined the number of the sacraments, their institution by Christ, their objective connection with grace, certain conditions for their valid administration, and the existence of a sacramental character. The same Council also restated previous definitions regarding the Real Presence and the nature of the Holy Sacrifice.

In the teaching on the Church it was particularly the authoritative position of the Roman Pontiff that was brought out more clearly with the lapse of time. His universal jurisdiction was definitely stated by the Second Council of Lyons, reaffirmed by that of Florence, and, together with his official infallibility, formally defined by the Council of the Vatican. In this latter Council the visibility of the Church, her position in the economy of salvation, and the four notes by which she may be recognized as the Church of Christ, were also set forth and affirmed.

The teaching of the Church on indulgences came into prominence only since the beginning of the tenth century, and then developed steadily till it was defined by the Council of Trent. On the other hand, the Council's definition of the doctrine on purgatory was merely a restatement of what had been for centuries a matter of faith. The same is true of its teaching on the veneration of saints and of images. Mariology was considerably developed during the Middle Ages, but, aside from the Immaculate Conception, no point of doctrine in regard to Mary's prerogatives has been defined since the Council of Ephesus.

Eschatology did not advance beyond the development it had received by the end of the Patristic age, although the Fourth Lateran found it necessary to define Catholic teaching on the resurrection and eternal retribution. The nature of the beatific vision was definitely stated by Benedict XII in the Constitution *Benedictus Dei,* in which he also defined the Church's teaching on the resurrection, the general judgment, and the immediate bestowal of reward or infliction of punishment according to each one's deserts.

The sources of faith, Holy Scripture and tradition, were made the object of a formal definition by the Council of Trent, and the same definition was restated by the Council of the Vatican. The same two Councils reaffirmed the traditional teaching on the canon of Holy Scripture, declared the Church to be the sole authorized interpreter of the Sacred Writings, and explained the meaning of inspiration in the sense that God Himself is to be accepted as the author of the Bible. Finally, as the truths of both reason and revelation have their source in the same God, the Vatican Council declared that there can be no real opposition between natural and supernatural truths.

Thus, as there had been considerable development of doctrine in the Patristic age, so was there in later centuries; and so will there be in the centuries to come. Very much is still to be accomplished — especially in the teaching on God's knowledge, on predestination, on the nature of grace, on the causality of the sacraments, and on many other subjects — before dogmatic development is complete. But in the very nature of things, complete dogmatic development is not to be looked for here on earth, where we see only " through a glass in a dark manner." That perfection of knowledge shall not be ours until we see " face to face," and " know even as we are known "; and then faith will have merged into vision.

INDEX

Ábelard: position in the schools, 7; compared to St. Anselm, 7, 8; his teaching on divine omnipotence, 61; the Blessed Trinity, 85–87; condemned by the Council of Soissons, 88; his error on creation, 104; on the freedom of the creative act, 109; his Adoptionism, 172, 173; soteriological errors, 197; Christ's descent into hell, 212; definition of a sacrament, 273; number of the sacraments, 293.

Adoptionism: Spanish, 171; Ábelard's, 172, 173; of Durandus, 175.

Alanus of Lille: works of, 11; his teaching on the simplicity of God, 40; on the spirituality of God, 46.

Albertus Magnus: his works, 16, 17; his teaching on the existence of God, 34; on divine knowledge, 59; predestination, 77, 78; principles of divine processions, 90; on the perfection of the world, 104; eternal creation, 110; conservation, 112; elevation of the angels, 115; their spirituality, 118; the composition of the human soul, 134, 135; its simplicity, 134, 137; original justice, 146, 147; original sin, 160; human personality, 188; merit of Christ, 208; supremacy of the Pope, 222, 223; actual and sanctifying grace, 240, 241; subject of faith, 259; material object of faith, 260; virtue of charity, 267; sacramental character, 288; institution of the sacraments, 296; baptismal rite, 302; institution of baptism, 304; Holy Eucharist, 333; virtue of penance, 345; indulgences, 376; form of extreme unction, 389; extinction of the *fomes peccati*

in Mary, 400; the Immaculate Conception, 407; the punishment of hell, 428.

Albigenses: heretics, 442; their teaching, 442, 443.

Alcuin: his teaching on penance, 340, 341.

Alexander II, Pope: grants a plenary indulgence, 368.

Alexander III, Pope: condemns Christological Nihilism, 174; intention in the administration of the sacraments, 290; number of the sacraments, 294.

Alexander VII, Pope: defends the Immaculate Conception, 522.

Alexander VIII, Pope: condemns Gallicanism, 514.

Alexander of Hales: his works, 14; position in the schools, 14, 15; contents of the *Summa*, 15; his teaching on the existence of God, 29; on divine knowledge, 56, 59; on predestination, 74, 75; definition of person, 88; principles of divine processions, 91; the perfection of the world, 104; instrumental cause of creation, 107; eternal creation, 110; conservation, 112; spirituality of the angels, 117; original justice, 143–145; nature of original sin, 158; transmission, 165, 166; final cause of the Incarnation, 181; human personality, 185, 186; the grace of union, 189, 190; ecclesiology, 216; jurisdiction of bishops, 228; actual and sanctifying grace, 238, 239; justification, 247, 248; infused virtues, 253–255; classification of virtues, 256; subject of faith, 259; material object, 260; charity, 268; causality of the sacraments, 279, 280; sacramental character, 287; necessity of inten-

537

Dionysius the Carthusian: his teaching on the simplicity of God, 44; the elevation of the angels, 115; their spirituality, 118.

Duns Scotus: his position in the schools, 21; his writings, 21, 22; his teaching on the existence of God, 33; God's infinite perfection, 36; essence, 39; simplicity, 44; the *distinctio formalis*, 44, 45; unicity of God, 47; infinity, 48; immutability, 51; knowledge, 57, 59, 60; omnipotence, 62; freedom of the divine will, 63, 64; predestination, 81, 82; definition of person, 89; principles of divine processions, 91, 92, 93; relations, 95; divine persons, 97; the creative act, 103; efficient cause of creation, 107; instrumental cause, 107; eternal creation, 110; conservation, 112; elevation of the angels, 115; their spirituality, 117, 118; relation to place, 121; knowledge, 123; volition, 125; locution, 127; man the image of God, 130; composition of the human soul, 134, 136; orignal justice, 152, 153; nature of original sin, 163, 164; transmission, 168, 169; final cause of the Incarnation, 182; human personality, 185, 186; impeccability of Christ, 193, 194; adequacy of the satisfaction, 202; the moral value of the Savior's death, 206; Christ's merit, 208; infallibility of the Pope, 228; actual and sanctifying grace, 245, 246; justification, 249; subject of infused virtues, 254, 271; material object of faith, 260; formal, 262; material object of hope, 265; subject of hope, 266; virtue of charity, 267; matter and form of the sacraments, 275, 276; causality, sacramental, 279; character, 287, 290; institution of the sacraments, 296; of baptism, 305; baptism of desire, 303, 304; effects of confirmation, 308; transubstantiation, 319, 320; Eucharistic acci-

dents, 325; form of consecration, 328; the Eucharist as a sacrament, 333; as a sacrifice, 336; effects of penance, 348, 349; penance as a sacrament, 349, 350; contrition, 356, 357; satisfaction, 359; indulgences, 378; holy orders, 382; effects of extreme unction, 392; sacrament of matrimony, 394; Immaculate Conception, 410, 411; resurrection of the dead, 420; punishment of hell, 428, 429, 430; essence of the beatific vision, 437.

Dupasquier: Sarbonne professor, 484.

Durandus of Saint-Pourçain: his relation to Nominalism, 22, 23; his teaching on the principles of divine processions, 90; the instrumental cause of creation, 107; final cause, 109; eternal creation, 110; conservation, 112; elevation of the angels, 115; their spirituality, 118; human personality, 188; adequacy of the satisfaction, 202; Christ's descent into hell, 212; the moral virtues, 256; material object of faith, 260; material object of hope, 264; virtue of charity, 267; sacramental character, 287; Eucharistic accidents, 324; holy orders, 383; rite of ordination, 385; effects of extreme unction, 392; extinction of the *fomes peccati* in Mary, 400.

Eadmer: defends the Immaculate Conception, 409.

Ecclesiology: general subject, 214–219; in the writings of the Fathers, 214; of the Scholastics, 214–219; Church and State, 215, 216; constitution of the Church, 216, 217.

Eighth General Council: on the oneness of the rational soul, 131; the primacy of Rome, 220, 221.

Eon de Stella: mediæval heretic, 440, 441.

Eschatology: resurrection of the dead, 418–422; general judgment,